CEDU(쎄듀)는 **A C**omprehensive **E**nglish e**DU**cation(종합적 영어교육)의 약자입니다.

펴낸이   김기훈 김진희

펴낸곳   ㈜쎄듀/서울시 강남구 논현로 305 (역삼동)

발행일   2023년 3월 2일 제1개정판 1쇄

내용 문의   www.cedubook.com

구입 문의   콘텐츠 마케팅 사업본부

        Tel. 02-6241-2007

        Fax. 02-2058-0209

등록번호   제22-2472호

ISBN   978-89-6806-278-0

수능영어
절대유형

저자

김기훈   現 ㈜ 쎄듀 대표이사

現 메가스터디 영어영역 대표강사

前 서울특별시 교육청 외국어 교육정책자문위원회 위원

   저서   천일문 / 천일문 Training Book / 천일문 GRAMMAR

첫단추 BASIC / 어법끝 / 문법의 골든룰 101 / Grammar Q

어휘끝 / 쎄듀 본영어 / 절대평가 PLAN A / 독해가 된다

The 리딩플레이어 / 빈칸백서 / 오답백서 / 거침없이 Writing

첫단추 / 파워업 / ALL쏨 서술형 / 수능영어 절대유형 / 수능실감 등

쎄듀 영어교육연구센터

쎄듀 영어교육센터는 영어 콘텐츠에 대한 전문지식과 경험을 바탕으로

최고의 교육 콘텐츠를 만들고자 최선의 노력을 다하는 전문가 집단입니다.

오혜정 수석연구원 · **장정문** 선임연구원

마케팅	콘텐츠 마케팅 사업본부
제작	정승호
영업	문병구
인디자인 편집	올댓에디팅
디자인	윤혜영 · 이승연
표지 일러스트	이승연
영문교열	Stephen Daniel White

Preface

2018학년도부터 수능 영어영역이 절대평가로 바뀌고 EBS 연계율은 축소됨에 따라 시험이 더욱 어려워지면서 1등급을 받기가 쉽지는 않다는 것이 중론입니다. 절대평가 시행 이래 1등급 비율은 낮게는 5.3%, 높게는 12.66%가 배출되며 난이도 조절에도 어려움을 겪고 있는 것으로 보입니다.

수시 전형에서는 영어를 전략 과목으로 삼아 최대한 좋은 등급을 받으면 수능 최저등급 충족에 매우 유리할 수 있습니다. 정시는 대학에 따라 더 다양하게 반영이 되는데, 크게 '등급별 가산점, 감점 반영'과 '등급별 환산점수 + 반영 비율 적용' 대학으로 나눌 수 있습니다. 대부분의 대학이 적용하는 '등급별 환산점수 + 반영 비율 적용' 방식은 등급별 점수 차가 커서 영어의 비중이 상대적으로 높습니다. 그러므로 영어 영역은 확실한 1등급 실력을 갖추어야 하고, 주요 대학의 최저학력 기준인 2등급은 반드시 충족하도록 해야 할 것입니다.

특히 모의고사에서 2, 3개씩 틀리는 수험생이나, 2등급을 넘나드는 수험생, 3등급이지만 조금만 더 노력하면 2등급이 될 수험생 등은 전략적으로 영어를 학습해야 할 필요성이 있습니다. 이 모든 경우에 가장 중요한 문제 유형은 바로 3점 문항과 비연계 문제가 집중 등장하는 31번~42번입니다. 이 유형에서 독해 3점 문항 총 7개 중 4~5개가 출제되고, 원점수 28~29점을 차지하기 때문입니다. 과거에는 EBS 연계교재를 학습함으로써 비교적 단기간에 점수 향상을 꾀할 수 있었으나, 지금은 EBS 교재에 나온 지문이 그대로 출제되는 직접 연계가 없어져서 3점 문항과 비연계 문항을 EBS 교재만으로 대비하기에는 충분치 못합니다.

본 교재는 바로 이러한 문제 유형(31번~42번)을 집중적으로 공략하도록 기획되었습니다.

1. 3점 문항 유형별 전략
유형별 최신 전략을 제시합니다. 수능 및 모의 기출 문제를 철저히 분석하여 도식화를 통해 3점 문항 유형에 보다 전략적으로 접근할 수 있습니다.

2. 고품질 3142 모의고사
앞서 살펴본 전략을 적용하여 확실한 실력을 갖출 수 있게 하는 실전 모의고사입니다. 높은 오답률의 원인이 되는 요소들(생소한 소재, 내용의 추상성, 구문 및 어휘 난이도, 비유적 표현)을 완벽하게 반영한 고품질 문제만을 수록하였습니다.

3. 대의 파악 PLUS 변형 문제
글의 내용을 제대로 이해했는지 확인할 수 있는 대의 파악 변형 문제를 수록하여 실질적인 역량 강화에 도움이 될 수 있도록 하였습니다.

상대평가인 다른 과목과 달리, 영어는 학습하면 반드시 성적 향상으로 이어지는 영역입니다. 전략적 학습을 겨냥한 본 교재로, 반드시 여러분의 목표를 달성하시기 바랍니다.

저자

Preview

www.cedubook.com에서 무료 부가서비스(어휘리스트·어휘테스트)를 다운로드하세요.

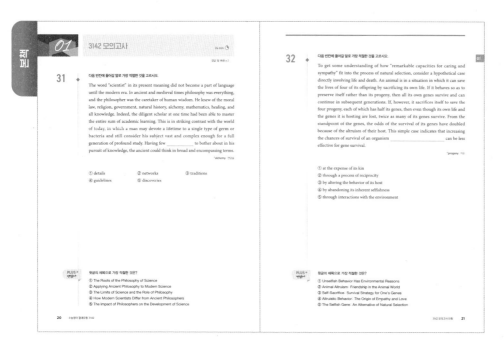

◆ 고품질 **3124 모의고사 12회분**으로 3점 문항 완벽 대비

◆ 대의 파악을 위한 **PLUS 변형문제**로 실력 UP!

◆ **해석 및 해설, 오답 Check, PLUS 변형문제 해설**까지 수록된 친절한 해설

◆ **상세한 지문 분석**(주제문, 추론 근거, 끊어 읽기 등)

◆ 복잡한 문장의 이해를 돕는 **구문 해설** 및 배경 지식이 필요한 어휘는 **어휘**로 자세한 설명 제공

Contents

Orientation

31-42 유형별 전략

Summary

31-34번 문항
: 빈칸추론

1. 빈칸 문장(+ 선택지)부터 읽어라
2. 주제문의 빈칸 어구 = 개괄적(General)/재진술
3. 빈칸 문장의 위치에 주목하라
   └→ 초반, 중반, 후반, 마지막
4. 비유 표현 가능성을 염두에 두라
5. 논리적으로 추론하라
   └→ 원인-결과 / 비교-대조
6. 오답의 성격을 이해하라
   └→ 상식-통념(×) / 언급 없음 / 정반대

35번 문항
: 무관 문장

1. 주어진 도입부로 글의 핵심 소재부터 파악하라
2. 함정에 주의하라
   └→ 앞에서 언급된 어구나 핵심어, 지시어, 연결어 등

36-37번 문항
: 글의 순서

38-39번 문항
: 주어진 문장 넣기

1. 대명사, 지시어, 연결어 등에 주목하라
2. 글의 논리적 흐름에 집중하라
   └→ 개괄 → 구체 / 순차적 시간 흐름 / 질문 → 답변
3. 함정에 주의하라
   └→ 동일 어구 반복

40번 문항
: 요약문 완성

1. 요약문과 선택지부터 읽어라
2. 말바꿈 표현에 주의하라

41-42번 문항
: 2문항 장문

1. 글의 제목은 단락 모두를 포괄하라
2. 밑줄 어휘 문제는 반의어를 떠올려보라

1 빈칸 문장(+ 선택지)부터 읽어라

이는 곧 '목적'을 가지고 읽으라는 의미이다. 지문을 두 번 세 번 반복해서 읽게 되는 비율이 줄어들고 근거가 되는 부분에 집중할 수 있어 효율적이다.

---

1. ... The _____ social sharing of the bad news contributes to realism. ... [수능]

① biased　　② illegal　　③ repetitive
④ temporary　　⑤ rational

빈칸 문장에 남아 있는 어구를 통해 지문 속에서 어떤 내용을 찾아야 할지 파악한다. 선택지가 짧을 경우는 같이 파악을 하는 것도 좋다.

빈칸 문장 나쁜 소식의 어떠한 사회적 공유가 현실주의[현실성, 사실성]에 기여하는가?

▶ 현실주의, 즉 현실성, 사실성을 높이는 사회적 공유의 특성을 찾는다.

---

2. ... [단서] A chair could keep its basic, accepted characteristics while still being closely shaped in detail to the physique and proportions of a specific person. **This basic principle** of _____ allowed a constant stream of incremental modifications to be introduced, ... [모의]

① dedication　　② customization
③ cooperation　　④ generalization
⑤ preservation

빈칸 문장의 남아 있는 어구를 통해 단서가 되는 부분을 바로 알 수 있는 경우도 있다.

빈칸 문장 이러한 _____의 기본 원리로 인해 계속해서 일련의 증가하는 변형이 도입되었고 ~

▶ 단서 위치 = 빈칸 직전 문장(의자는 여전히 특정 개인의 체격과 (신체) 비율에 맞게 세부적으로 면밀히 모양이 만들어지면서도 그것의 일반적이고 용인되는 특성을 유지할 수 있었다.)을 요약하면 ② '주문 제작'이 된다.

---

3. ... Writing, arithmetic, science — all are recent inventions. Our brains did not have enough time to evolve for **them**, but I reason that **they** were made possible because _____. ... [수능]

빈칸 문장에 지시어 등이 있을 경우는 지시하는 바를 정확히 판단해야 한다.

빈칸 문장 그것들(= 글, 셈, 과학)은 어떤 이유로 가능했는가?

▶ 우리의 두뇌가 진화해서 글, 셈, 과학이 가능했던 것이 아닌, 다른 이유로 그것들이 가능했음을 설명하는 것을 찾는다.

---

4. ... How, then, do minorities ever have any influence over the majority? The social psychologist Serge Moscovici claims that **the answer** lies in their *behavioural style*, i.e. the *way* _____. ... [수능응용]

지시어가 아니더라도 앞 내용을 통해 파악해야하는 것이 있을 수 있다.

빈칸 문장 그 대답(= 소수자들이 다수자들에게 어떻게 영향을 미치는가라는 질문에 대한)은 소수자들의 행동 양식, 즉 어떤 방식에 달려있는가?

---

2 주제문의 빈칸 어구 = 개괄적(General) / 재진술

주제문에 빈칸이 있을 경우, 주제문은 개괄적(General)으로 표현되므로 세부 사항의 구체적(Specific) 어구를 개괄적으로 표현한 것을 찾아야 한다. 양괄식이거나 주제문을 재진술한 문장이 있는 경우, 이를 이용하여 빈칸을 추론하면 된다.

---

1. One unspoken truth about creativity — it isn't about wild talent so much as it is about _____.
[단서] To find a few ideas that work, you need to try a lot that don't. ... Geniuses don't necessarily have a higher success rate than other creators; they simply do more — and they do a range of different things. They have more successes *and* more failures. [모의]

① sensitivity　　　② superiority
③ imagination　　 ④ productivity
⑤ achievement

빈칸 문장 창의성에 대한 무언의 진리는 그것이 타고난 재능이라기보다는 _____에 관한 것이라는 점이다.

단서 쓸모 있는 아이디어 몇 개를 발견하기 위해 그렇지 않은 많은 것들을 시도해야 한다. 천재들이 반드시 다른 창작자들보다 더 높은 성공률을 가지고 있는 것은 아니다. 그들은 그저 더 많이 할 뿐이고 여러 다양한 것을 하는 것이다. 그들은 더 많은 성공과 더 많은 실패를 한다.

▶ 이는 곧 창의성이 ④ '생산성'에 관한 것이라고 개괄적으로 표현할 수 있다.

---

2. Although most people, including Europe's Muslims, have numerous identities, few of these are politically salient at any moment. It is only when a political issue affects the welfare of those in a particular group that _____. [단서] For instance, when issues arise that touch on women's rights, women start to think of gender as their principal identity. Whether such women are American or Iranian or whether they are Catholic or Protestant matters less than the fact that they are women. Similarly, ... [모의]

*salient: 두드러진

① identity assumes importance
② religion precedes identity
③ society loses stability
④ society supports diversity
⑤ nationality bears significance

빈칸 문장 _____인 것은 바로 정치적 이슈가 어떤 특정 그룹에 속한 사람들의 행복에 영향을 주는 때뿐이다.

단서 여성의 권리에 대한 이슈(= 정치적 이슈)가 일어나면 여성들은 '성'을 자신들의 주요 '정체성'으로 생각하기 시작한다. 국적이나 종교는 그들이 '여성'이라는 사실보다 덜 중요하다 (matters less).

▶ 이를 달리 표현하면 ① '정체성이 중요성을 띤다'이다.

1. 첫 한두 문장에 빈칸이 있을 경우

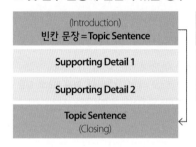 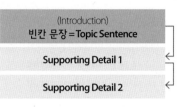

빈칸 문장이 주제문일 가능성이 크다. 양괄식 구성을 고려하여 마지막 문장을 우선 살펴보고, 단서가 없다면 빈칸 다음 문장부터 읽어 내려가며 근거를 포착한다.

2. 글의 중반에 빈칸 문장이 있을 경우

빈칸 문장 앞부분은 주제문을 말하기 위한 도입 또는 세부 사항 중 일부이고 빈칸 문장 뒷부분에 단서가 있을 가능성이 높다.

3. 글의 후반에 빈칸 문장이 있을 경우

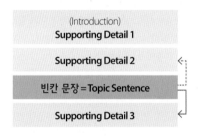

빈칸 문장 뒤 이어지는 마지막 문장 혹은 바로 앞 문장이 명백한 추론 근거가 되는 경우가 많다.

4. 마지막 문장에 빈칸이 있을 경우

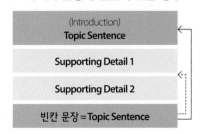

빈칸 문장이 주제문일 가능성이 크다. 또 다른 주제문일 가능성이 있는 첫 한두 문장을 살펴봐서 근거가 나오지 않으면 빈칸 직전 문장을 본다.

4 비유 표현 가능성을 염두에 두라

최근 들어 빈칸에 들어가는 어구가 개괄적, 재진술 성격을 넘어 이를 비유적으로 표현한 것들이 보이고 있다.

1. ... [단서] The fact that you can't recall what you ate for last week's lunch doesn't mean your memory of last week's lunch has disappeared; **if provided with the right cue, like where you ate it**, you would likely recall what had been on your plate. ... The memory of last Wednesday's lunch isn't necessarily gone; it's that you lack   . ...

[수능응용]

① the channel to let it flow into the pool of ordinary memories
② the right hook to pull it out of a sea of lunchtime memories
③ the glue to attach it to just another lunch memory
④ the memory capacity to keep a box of sleeping memories
⑤ the sufficient number of competitors in a battle for attention

빈칸 문장 지난 수요일 점심에 대한 기억이 반드시 사라진 것이 아니라 당신에게 _____ 이 없어서이다.

단서 지난주에 먹은 점심을 기억해내지 못하는 것은 기억이 사라졌음을 의미하지 않는다. **먹은 장소와 같은 적절한 신호가 주어지면** 접시에 무엇이 있었는지 기억해낼 가능성이 크다.

▶ '기억을 되살려주는 적절한 신호'를 비유적으로 표현한 것은 ② '점심에 대한 기억의 바다에서 그것을 끌어낼 적절한 고리'이다.

2. ... [단서] Moreover, genes would undoubtedly have changed during the human revolution after 200,000 years ago, but **more in response to new habits than as causes of them**. ....   .
The appeal to a genetic change driving evolution gets gene-culture co-evolution backwards: it is a top-down explanation for a bottom-up process. [수능]

① Genetic evolution is the mother of new habits
② Every gene is the architect of its own mutation
③ The cultural horse comes before the genetic cart
④ The linguistic shovel paves the way for a cultural road
⑤ When the cultural cat is away, the genetic mice will play

빈칸이 문장 전체이다. 선택지를 통틀어 많이 반복되는 어휘는 genetic, gene, cultural이고, 이와 함께 비유적 표현들(mother, architect, horse, cart, shovel, road, cat, mice)이 같이 쓰였다.

▶ 빈칸 이전의 문장에서 유전자는 새로운 습관의 원인이라기보다는 이에 반응하여 변한다고 하였고(= 습관 → 유전자 변화), 뒤의 문장에서는 유전자 변화로 일어나는 진화는 유전자와 문화(= 글 전체 문맥상 '습관'을 뜻함)의 공동 진화를 거스르는 것이라고 했다. 이 역시 습관[문화]이 유전자 변화를 이끈다는 것이므로 이를 비유적으로 표현하면 ③ '문화적인 말은 유전자의 수레보다 먼저 온다'이다.

빈칸은 반드시 주제문에만 주어지는 것이 아니고 세부 내용에 주어지기도 한다. 이때는 내용들 간의 논리적 관계에 의거하여 판단해야 한다.

1. 원인 vs. 결과

[원인] However, private capital started to flow into seed production and took it over as a sector of the economy, creating an artificial split between the two aspects of the seed's nature: **its role as means of production and its role as product**. ... Today most maize seed cultivated are hybrids. The companies that sell them are able to keep the distinct parent lines from farmers, and **the grain that they produce is not suited for seed saving and replanting**. [결과] The combination guarantees that farmers will have to _____. [수능]

*maize: 옥수수

① buy more seed from the company each season
② use more chemical fertilizer than before

'원인-결과' 중 어느 하나에 빈칸이 있으면 다른 하나에 의해 논리적으로 그 내용을 추론할 수 있다.

원인 종자는 생산의 수단으로서의 역할과 생산물로서의 역할로 나뉘게 됨 + 회사에서 판매하는 종자로 수확한 곡물은 보관 후 다시 심기 적절하지 못함. (생산의 수단으로서의 역할을 제대로 하지 못함.)

↓

결과 ① 농부는 종자를 시즌마다 회사로부터 더 많이 구입해야 할 것임.

2. 비교-대조

The audience receives a sound signal entirely through the vibrations generated in the air, whereas in a singer some of the auditory stimulus is conducted to the ear through the singer's own bones. Since these two ways of transferring sound have quite different relative efficiencies at various frequencies, the overall quality of the sound will be quite different. ... The major effect comes from the fact that you hear yourself differently from the way others hear you. This is one of the main reasons why even the most accomplished singers have to listen to the opinion of coaches and voice teachers as to 'how they sound,' whereas no concert violinist would have to do such a thing. To the violinist _____ to someone else standing nearby. [모의]

① sounds spread a lot more widely than they do
② playing sounds almost exactly the same as it does

두 가지 이상의 것들을 비교 또는 대조하는 글에서 어느 한 대상에 빈칸을 두는 문제가 출제되고 있다. 각 대상에 해당하는 A, B를 구분하기 위해 서로 다른 표시(A=동그라미, B=밑줄 등)로 마킹하면서 읽어 내려가는 것이 좋다.

A (연주 소리를 들음) ≠ B (자신이 내는 소리를 들음)

A 바이올린 연주자	B 노래하는 사람
② 본인이 듣는 소리와 다른 사람이 듣는 소리가 같으므로 다른 사람의 의견을 들을 필요가 없음	어떻게 들리는지 다른 사람들에게 의견을 물어야 함

각 선택지의 정답률을 조사하다 보면 정답보다 오답의 선택률이 더 높은 경우를 보게 된다. 출제자들이 구성하는 오답의 성격을 이해함으로써 정답의 선택률을 높일 수 있다.

---

1. ... Further, heritage is more concerned with meanings than material artefacts. It is the former that give value, either cultural or financial, to the latter and explain why they have been selected from the near infinity of the past. In turn, they may later be discarded as the demands of present societies change, or even, as is presently occurring in the former Eastern Europe, when pasts have to be reinvented to reflect new presents. **Thus heritage is** _____. [수능]

① a collection of memories and traditions of a society
② as much about forgetting as remembering the past
③ neither concerned with the present nor the future
④ a mirror reflecting the artefacts of the past
⑤ about preserving universal cultural values

상식이나 통념에 의존하지 마라.

상식이나 통념에 반하는 내용을 출제하는 비율이 높다는 점을 명심하자. 빈칸은 항상 지문 내용에 의거해서 추론해야 한다.

▶ 'heritage(유산)'를 상식적으로 생각하면 ①도 맞으나, 지문에서 말하고 있는 유산은 '수많은 과거의 것들 중에서 선택되는 것이고 또 현재 사회의 요구에 맞지 않으면 버려지는 것'이라고 했으므로 정답은 ②이다.

---

2. ... Psychological studies indicate that it is knowledge possessed by the individual that determines which stimuli become the focus of that individual's attention, ... This subjective world, interpreted in a particular way, is for us the "objective" world; we cannot know any world other than _____. [모의]

① the reality placed upon us through social conventions
② the one we know as a result of our own interpretations
③ the world of images not filtered by our perceptual frame
④ the external world independent of our own interpretations
⑤ the physical universe our own interpretations fail to explain

대개, 오답 선택지는 지문에 나온 어구를 포함하지만
1. 전체적인 내용은 지문에 언급이 없었거나
2. 언급이 있긴 하지만 정반대 내용으로 구성된다. 즉, 지문에 나온 어구가 보인다고 해서 정답으로 판단해서는 안 된다.

▶ 우리가 자극을 처리할 때 우리 자신이 가지고 있는 지식을 통해서 처리한다는 것은 우리가 주관적으로 정보를 해석함을 의미한다. 따라서 정답은 ②이다.
① 사회적 관습을 통해 우리에게 주어지는 현실
→ 언급 없음
③ 우리의 지각적 틀에 의해 걸러지지 않는 이미지의 세계
→ 주관적인 정보 해석과 정반대
④ 우리의 해석과는 별개인 외부 세계
→ 주관적인 정보 해석과 정반대
⑤ 우리 해석이 설명하지 못하는 물리적 우주
→ 언급 없음

1 주어진 도입부로 글의 핵심 소재부터 파악하라

선택지 번호가 없는 도입부는 주제문 또는 지문에서 말하려는 핵심 소재를 담고 있다. 그러므로 이를 통해 대충의
내용을 먼저 파악한 뒤 읽어 내려가면서 흐름이 어색한 선택지를 찾는다.

[도입] When photography came along in the nineteenth century, painting was put in crisis. The photograph, it seemed, did the work of imitating nature better than the painter ever could.

19세기 사진술이 도입되자 그림이 위기에 처하게 되었다. 사진은 화가보다 자연을 더 잘 모방했다.

▶ 글의 핵심 소재는 '**사진의 사실성, 그림의 위기**'이다.

① Some painters made practical use of the invention.

① 어떤 화가들은 사진을 실용적으로 이용함.

② There were Impressionist painters who used a photograph in place of the model or landscape they were painting.

② 모델이나 경치 대신 사진을 이용함.
(①에 대한 부연설명)

③ But by and large, the photograph was a challenge to painting and was one cause of painting's moving away from direct representation and reproduction to the abstract painting of the twentieth century.

③ 20세기에 추상적 그림이 등장함.

④ Therefore, the painters of that century put more focus on expressing nature, people, and cities as they were in reality.

④ 20세기 화가들은 자연, 사람, 도시를 현실적으로 표현하는 데 집중함.
▶ 위의 ③과 정반대되는 내용이므로 정답이 된다.

⑤ Since photographs did such a good job of representing things as they existed in the world, painters were freed to look inward and represent things as they were in their imagination, rendering emotion in the color, volume, line, and spatial configurations native to the painter's art. [수능]

*render: 표현하다 **configuration: 배치

⑤ 사진이 사물을 있는 그대로 표현하므로, 화가들은 상상 속의 사물을 표현함. (③에 대한 부연설명)

19세기 사진술 도입
↓
① 사진을 실용적으로 이용 ② 사진을 보고 그림을 그림
↓
③ 20세기에 추상적 그림 등장 ⑤ 상상 속의 사물 표현

2 함정에 주의하라

무관 문장에 이미 언급된 어구나 핵심어, 지시어, 연결어 등이 있으면 흐름이 자연스러운 것으로 착각할 수 있다. 반대로 이미 언급된 어구나 핵심어 등이 없어도 자연스러운 흐름에 해당하는 문장이 될 수 있다. 그러므로 일부 어구로 판단하기보다는 단락 전체의 논리 흐름에 따라 판단해야 한다.

[도입] While the **transportation** infrastructure may shape *where* we travel today, in the early eras of **travel**, it determined whether people could travel at all.

교통 기반 시설은 오늘날에는 우리가 여행하는 장소를 결정하고 과거에는 여행이 가능한지 자체를 결정했음.

▶ **핵심 소재:** 교통과 여행[관광]

---

① The development and improvement of transportation was one of the most important factors in allowing modern tourism to develop on a large scale and become a regular part of the lives of billions of people around the world.

교통 개발과 향상은 현대 **관광**이 발전하는 데 가장 중요 요인 중 하나임.

---

② Another important factor was the industrialization that led to more efficient transportation of factory products to consumers than ever before.

또 다른 중요 요인은 **산업화**가 공장 제품을 소비자에게 **더 효율적으로 운송 가능**하게 한다는 것임.

▶ 산업화와 공장 제품 운송에 관한 내용이므로 정답이 된다. 핵심 소재에 해당하는 transportation이 포함되어 있고, 윗 문장에 one of the most important factors가 있어 Another important factor로 시작하는 것이 자연스럽게 느껴진다.

---

③ Technological advances provided the basis for the explosive expansion of local, regional, and global transportation networks and made travel faster, easier, and cheaper.

교통망 발전으로 **관광**이 여러모로 편리해짐.

---

④ This not only created new tourist-generating and tourist-receiving regions but also prompted a host of other changes in the tourism infrastructure, such as accommodations.

이는(= 윗 문장) 새로운 **관광**지뿐만 아니라 **관광** 기반 시설의 다른 요소인 숙박에도 변화를 촉발함.

▶ 글의 핵심어인 transportation이 없지만 흐름과 무관하지 않다.

---

⑤ As a result, the availability of transportation infrastructure and services has been considered a fundamental precondition for tourism. [모의]

*infrastructure: 산업 기반 시설

그 결과, **교통** 기반 시설과 서비스의 이용 가능성은 **관광**의 전제 조건으로 여겨져 왔음.

---

1 대명사, 지시어, 연결어 등에 주목하라

대명사나 지시어가 가리키는 명사, 연결어에 따른 논리 관계를 정확히 판단해야 한다.

1. 글의 순서

> Most Americans are at best poorly informed about politics.

정치에 대한 국민들의 부족한 정보

(C) **However**, **there is something worse than an inadequately informed public, and that's a misinformed public.** ....

연결어 However

▶ 부족한 정보보다 잘못된 정보가 더 나쁨

(B) **It**'s **the difference between ignorance and irrationality.** .... Our misinformation owes partly to **psychological factors**, ...

대명사 It = (C)의 전체 내용

▶ 잘못된 정보는 부분적으로는 심리적 요인 때문임 (우리가 바라는 대로 세상을 봄)

(A) **Such factors**, **however**, can explain only the misinformation that has always been with us. The sharp rise in misinformation in recent years has a different source: our media. .... [모의응용]

지시어 such factors = (B)의 psychological factors
연결어 however: 잘못된 정보는 미디어 때문임.

---

2. 주어진 문장 넣기

> **For example**, the first step in servicing or installing equipment is talking with the clients to understand how they used the equipment.

The customer service representatives in an electronics firm were told they had to begin selling service contracts for their equipment in addition to installing and repairing them. This generated a great deal of resistance. (①) To the service representatives, learning to sell was a very different game from what they had been playing. (②) But it turned out they already knew a lot more about sales than they thought. (③) The same is true in selling. (④) The salesperson first has to learn about the customer's needs.... [모의]

주어진 문장이 For example로 시작하므로 어떤 것의 예가 되는지 찾는다.

▶ 고객 서비스 직원들은 장치 설치와 수리 외에 판매를 시작하라는 지시에 반발함. (①) 그들에게 판매는 매우 다른 업무이기 때문. (②) **그러나 그들은 이미 판매에 대해 생각보다 많은 것을 알고 있음이 드러남.** (③) 장치를 서비스하고 설치하는 첫 단계는 고객들이 그 장치를 어떻게 사용했는지 이해하기 위해 고객과 이야기하는 것임.) 판매도 마찬가지임. (④) 판매원은 고객의 니즈부터 알아야 함.

2 글의 논리적 흐름에 집중하라

앞에서 살펴본 단서들이 보이지 않을 경우 다음과 같은 논리적이고도 자연스러운 흐름에 의거하여 파악한다.

1. 개괄적 표현 → 구체적인 내용 (이와 반대되는 순서를 유도하는 연결사 등이 없는 경우)
2. 순차적인 시간 흐름에 의거 (당연히 아침-점심-저녁 순서가 자연스럽다.)
3. 질문 → 답변

주어진 글 다음에 이어질 내용으로 가장 적절한 것은?
Researchers in psychology follow the scientific method to perform studies that help explain and may predict human behavior. This is a much more challenging task than studying snails or sound waves.

심리학 연구자들은 인간의 행동에 대한 설명과 그것을 예측할 수 있는 연구를 수행하는 데 과학적 방법을 따름. **이는 매우 도전적인 과제임.**

(A) Simply knowing they are being observed may cause people to behave differently (such as more politely!). ...
(B) It often requires compromises, ... It often requires great cleverness to conceive of measures that tap into what people are thinking without altering their thinking, called reactivity. [수능응용]

① (A)   ② (B)

(A) 사람들은 관찰되고 있다는 것을 알고 있는 것만으로도 행동을 다르게 함.
(B) 타협이 요구되고, 사람들이 진짜 생각하고 있는 것을 알아내기 위한 영리함이 요구됨.

▶ 주어진 내용의 마지막 문장(개괄적)을 좀 더 구체적으로 밝히고 있는 것은 (B)이다. 즉 개괄적 내용 뒤에 구체적 내용이 나오는 것이 자연스럽다.

---

3 함정에 주의하라

일부 어구가 동일하게 반복된 것만 보고 순서를 판단하지 않도록 해야 한다.

주어진 글 다음에 이어질 내용으로 가장 적절한 것은?
... However, there is more to attention than just moving the eyes to look at objects.

눈의 움직임만으로 주의를 집중하고 있는 것을 알 수는 없음.

(A) Even though you were *looking at* the words, you apparently were not *paying attention*. There is a mental aspect of attention that involves processing that can occur independently of eye movements.
(B) We can pay attention to things that are not directly in our line of vision, ... We can also look directly at something without paying attention to it. [모의]

① (A)   ② (B)

(A) 단어를 보고 있어도 집중하지 않을 수 있음.
(B) 우리는 직접 보지 않고도 집중할 수 있고 집중하지 않고 무언가를 볼 수도 있음.

▶ (B)는 주어진 글의 마지막 문장에 이어지고 (A)는 (B)의 마지막 문장에 대한 구체적인 예로 시작하므로 '주어진 문장-(B)-(A)'의 순서가 맞다. 주어진 문장과 (A)에 look at이 있다고 해서 순서를 착각하면 안 된다.

1 요약문과 선택지부터 읽어라

요약문은 주제나 제목보다 글의 핵심을 더 자세히 담고 있어, 먼저 읽으면 글의 내용을 어느 정도 짐작할 수 있고 어느 부분에 초점을 두어 읽어야 할지도 미리 알 수 있다.

… **Our ancestors regularly made choices designed to produce** not the best opportunity for obtaining a hyperabundant supply of food but, instead, **the least danger of ending up with an insufficient supply**. … If our ancestors hadn't felt anxious over losses in food and instead had taken too many chances in going after the big gains, **they'd have been more likely to lose out and never become anyone's ancestor**. [모의응용]

↓

Our ancestors gave priority to ___(A)___ minimum resources rather than pursuing maximum gains, and that was the rational choice for human ___(B)___ from an evolutionary perspective.

(A)	(B)
① sharing	…… interaction
② securing	…… survival

요약문 우리 조상들이 최대치의 이득을 추구하기보다 최소한의 자원을 '무엇'하는 것에 우선순위를 두었고, 그것이 인간의 '무엇'을 위해 합리적인 선택이었는지를 찾아야 한다.

본문 우리 조상들은 음식의 과도한 공급이 아니라 부족한 공급이 되지 않도록 선택했다. 음식 부족에 두려움을 느끼지 않고 큰 이득을 추구했다면 살아남지 못했을 것이다.

▶ 본문 내용으로 보아, 우리 조상들은 최소한의 음식을 (A) '확보하려' 했으며 이는 (B) '살아남기' 위한 합리적 선택이었음을 알 수 있다. 따라서 정답은 ②이다.

2 말바꿈 표현에 주의하라

… A prosecuting attorney constructs an argument to persuade the judge or a jury that the accused is guilty; a defense attorney in the same trial constructs an argument to persuade the same judge or jury toward the opposite conclusion …. [모의응용]

↓

Lawyers tend to utilize information _____ to support their arguments.

① objectively   ② selectively

요약문 변호사들은 자신들의 주장을 뒷받침하는 정보를 _____하게 이용한다.

본문 검사는 피고가 유죄임을, 피고인측 변호사는 피고가 무죄임을 설득하기 위해 주장을 구성한다.

▶ 이는 곧 정보를 ② '선별적으로' 활용하는 것이다. 말바꿈이 심하게 되어있어 적절한 답을 찾지 못하고, 상식에 의거하여 변호사들이 '객관적으로' 정보를 사용할 것이라 잘못 판단할 수 있다.

1 글의 제목은 단락 모두를 포괄하라

2문항 장문은 두 단락 이상인 경우가 대부분인데, 제목은 모든 단락을 포괄하는 것이다.

Industrial capitalism not only created work, it also created 'leisure' in the modern sense of the term. This might seem surprising, for the early cotton masters wanted to keep their machinery running as long as possible and forced their employees to work very long hours. However, by requiring continuous work during work hours and ruling out non-work activity, employers had (a) separated out leisure from work. ...

산업 자본주의에서 현대적 의미의 여가가 탄생함.

▶ 여가의 탄생

Leisure was also the creation of capitalism in another sense, through the commercialization of leisure. This no longer meant participation in traditional sports and pastimes. Workers began to (d) pay for leisure activities organized by capitalist enterprises. ... The importance of this can hardly be exaggerated, for whole new industries were emerging to exploit and (e) develop the leisure market, which was to become a huge source of consumer demand, employment, and profit. [수능]

*discipline: 통제하다 **enterprise: 기업(체) ***exaggerate: 과장하다

여가가 상업화되고 완전히 새로운 산업이 출현해서 레저 시장이 발달함. 이는 소비자 수요, 고용, 이익의 거대한 원천이 되었음.

▶ 여가의 진화

---

① What It Takes to Satisfy Workers
② Why Workers Have Struggled for More Leisure
③ The Birth and Evolution of Leisure in Capitalism
④ How to Strike a Balance Between Work and Leisure
⑤ The Light and Dark Sides of the Modern Leisure Industry

① 근로자를 만족시키기 위해 필요한 것
② 근로자들이 더 많은 여가를 위해 분투해 온 이유
③ 자본주의에서 여가의 탄생과 진화
④ 일과 여가의 균형을 맞추는 방법
⑤ 현대 여가 산업의 명암

▶ 정답인 ③ 외의 다른 오답들은 모두 본문에 언급되지 않았다.

② 밑줄 어휘 문제는 반의어를 떠올려보라

보통 글의 초반부에 소재나 주제 등 무엇에 관한 글인지가 소개되고 이후 내용에 밑줄이 그어지는데, 어휘의 쓰임이 적절한지 확신할 수 없을 때는 반의어를 떠올리고 바꿔 읽어보자. 대부분의 경우, 반의어로 바꿔서 정답을 출제하기 때문이다.

밑줄 친 (a), (b) 중에서 문맥상 낱말의 쓰임이 적절하지 <u>않은</u> 것은?

… by requiring continuous work during work hours and ruling out non-work activity, employers had (a) <u>separated</u> out leisure from work. Some did this quite explicitly by creating distinct holiday periods, when factories were shut down, because it was better to do this than have work (b) <u>promoted</u> by the casual taking of days off. … [수능응용]

① (a)　　　　　② (b)

▶ 근무시간 동안 지속적인 일을 요구하고 비업무 활동을 배제함으로써 고용주들은 여가를 업무와 (a) **분리했다**(○).

▶ 공장이 문을 닫는 별도의 휴가 기간을 가지는 것이 그때그때 휴가를 내어 일이 (b) **진척**(✕) → **중단**(○)되는 것보다 더 나았다.

31

다음 빈칸에 들어갈 말로 가장 적절한 것을 고르시오.

The word "scientist" in its present meaning did not become a part of language until the modern era. In ancient and medieval times philosophy was everything, and the philosopher was the caretaker of human wisdom. He knew of the moral law, religion, government, natural history, alchemy, mathematics, healing, and all knowledge. Indeed, the diligent scholar at one time had been able to master the entire sum of academic learning. This is in striking contrast with the world of today, in which a man may devote a lifetime to a single type of germ or bacteria and still consider his subject vast and complex enough for a full generation of profound study. Having few _____ to bother about in his pursuit of knowledge, the ancient could think in broad and encompassing terms.

*alchemy: 연금술

① details　　　　② networks　　　　③ traditions
④ guidelines　　　⑤ discoveries

PLUS⁺
변형문제

윗글의 제목으로 가장 적절한 것은?

① The Roots of the Philosophy of Science
② Applying Ancient Philosophy to Modern Science
③ The Limits of Science and the Role of Philosophy
④ How Modern Scientists Differ from Ancient Philosophers
⑤ The Impact of Philosophers on the Development of Science

32 ◆

To get some understanding of how "remarkable capacities for caring and sympathy" fit into the process of natural selection, consider a hypothetical case directly involving life and death. An animal is in a situation in which it can save the lives of four of its offspring by sacrificing its own life. If it behaves so as to preserve itself rather than its progeny, then all its own genes survive and can continue in subsequent generations. If, however, it sacrifices itself to save the four progeny, each of which has half its genes, then even though its own life and the genes it is hosting are lost, twice as many of its genes survive. From the standpoint of the genes, the odds of the survival of its genes have doubled because of the altruism of their host. This simple case indicates that increasing the chances of survival of an organism _____ can be less effective for gene survival.

*progeny: 자손

① at the expense of its kin
② through a process of reciprocity
③ by altering the behavior of its host
④ by abandoning its inherent selfishness
⑤ through interactions with the environment

PLUS +
변형문제

윗글의 제목으로 가장 적절한 것은?

① Unselfish Behavior Has Environmental Reasons
② Animal Altruism: Friendship in the Animal World
③ Self-Sacrifice: Survival Strategy for One's Genes
④ Altruistic Behavior: The Origin of Empathy and Love
⑤ The Selfish Gene: An Alternative of Natural Selection

다음 빈칸에 들어갈 말로 가장 적절한 것을 고르시오.

We have already known how our emotions often take someone else's experiences as their object. It also seems that we take into account their evaluations and interpretations when making our own appraisals of other emotional objects. For example, we may enjoy a comedy film less when our companions are evidently offended by its content, or become more anxious partly because those sharing our fate seem to find the situation worrying. In effect, we tune perceptions of emotional meaning against the apparent perspective of key others. Because these processes of social appraisal work in both directions, others are also affected by our own apparent evaluations. Indeed, sometimes we may only arrive at emotional conclusions as a consequence of discussion with each other, or by otherwise registering mutual reactions (in smiles, frowns, or diverted gazes). In either of these cases, the appraisals shaping emotions are _____

_____.

① determined by the way you talk to yourself
② stimulated in us by all sorts of things and events
③ conceptualized as a highly influential mechanism
④ influenced by a fundamentally interpersonal process
⑤ revealed through mainly physical postures and gestures

PLUS +
변형문제

윗글의 제목으로 가장 적절한 것은?

① Emotions Are Contagious: Choose Your Company Wisely
② Role of the Self-Concept in the Perception of Others
③ Cognitive Bias in Human Perception and Judgment
④ Emotional Responses to Environmental Stimulation
⑤ The Social Nature of Emotional Appraisals

34 ◆ 다음 빈칸에 들어갈 말로 가장 적절한 것을 고르시오.

Genetic commands tell the neurons in the brain to start growing more and more connections. This creates an initial over-production of connectivity between the neurons. Then, this bout of over-production is followed by a period of pruning, where connections are lost between neurons. Around four out of every ten connections are lost with about 100,000 lost every second during the peak rate. This loss of connectivity is particularly interesting and at first surprising. Why would nature put in all the effort to build bridges between neurons only to knock them down almost equally as fast at a later date? It turns out that the over-production and subsequent destruction of connections may be a cunning strategy to shape the brain to deal with the specific situation. Many connections mean that the brain is prepared for every potential experience that it may encounter. However, only the neurons that repeatedly work together can maintain these connections. When neurons are not reciprocally activated, nature prunes their connections through inactivity. To put it in terms of a metaphor of a neighborhood, '_____.'

① If your neighbor smiles at you, you tend to turn away
② If you don't love yourself, you can't love your neighbor
③ If your neighbor's house is on fire, you too are not safe
④ If you need urgent help, knock on your neighbor's door
⑤ If you don't return my call, I'll not bother contacting you

PLUS+
변형문제

윗글의 제목으로 가장 적절한 것은?

① The More Connections, the Less Detachment
② Why More Experiences Help Your Brain Grow
③ How Independent Neurons Activate Individually
④ Critical Factors Leading to Loss of Neurons' Connections
⑤ Startling Tactic of Your Brain: Pruning After Overabundance

35 ◆

다음 글에서 전체 흐름과 관계 <u>없는</u> 문장은?

One of the biggest challenges of green marketing is the need to address environmental issues while at the same time satisfying core customer needs. ① This is one of the challenges "green" ad campaigns have to face — convincing consumers that environmental products do not perform lower than regular products. ② Rather, they often — with regard to specific features — perform better. ③ The environmental benefits of green products are that their environmental impacts are less than those of similar products. ④ For example, energy-saving light bulbs last longer, offer better convenience (they do not have to be replaced as often as regular bulbs), and reduce energy expenses. ⑤ Convenience and fulfillment of basic human needs are two of the most significant reasons why consumers buy green products — not necessarily for environmental reasons but for better value (safety, money).

PLUS +
변형문제

윗글의 제목으로 가장 적절한 것은?

① Green Marketing: Challenges and Costs
② Why Are Eco-friendly Products More Expensive?
③ Reasons That Green Marketing Is Going Nowhere
④ Green Products: More Than Just Environmentally Friendly
⑤ Going Green: Enhancing Sustainability of the Environment

36 ◆

주어진 글 다음에 이어질 글의 순서로 가장 적절한 것을 고르시오.

> Einstein held that the speed of light is constant and that events in one place cannot influence events in another place simultaneously. In relativity theory, the speed of light has to be taken into account for information to travel from one particle to another.

(A) All of this implies that Einstein's concept of spacetime, neatly divided into separate regions by light velocity, is indefensible. Instead, the events we observe exist in a space that is not limited by an external spacetime.

(B) However, experiment after experiment has shown that this is not the case. In 1965, Irish physicist John Bell created an experiment that showed that separate particles can influence each other instantaneously over great distances.

(C) This has since been performed numerous times and confirms that the properties of polarized light are correlated, or linked, no matter how far apart the particles are. There is some kind of instantaneous — faster than light — communication between them.

① (A) – (C) – (B)　　　　　② (B) – (A) – (C)

③ (B) – (C) – (A)　　　　　④ (C) – (A) – (B)

⑤ (C) – (B) – (A)

PLUS +
변형문제

윗글의 주제로 가장 적절한 것은?

① influence of speed of light on events
② limitations of particles in Einstein's theory
③ ways of testing Einstein's relativity theory
④ modern physics challenging Einstein's concept
⑤ reasons for light velocity divisions in spacetime

주어진 글 다음에 이어질 글의 순서로 가장 적절한 것을 고르시오.

> One reason that some apparent sunk cost ventures may not be irrational is that the decision makers are choosing actions to project and preserve their reputations for being decisive or for not being wasteful.

(A) Such future reputational costs are perfectly reasonable factors to consider in determining whether or not to abandon a particular course of action. So long as other people believe in honoring sunk costs, the person who does not may be regarded as weird.

(B) If, indeed, abandonment of a sunk cost negatively affects future reputation, then it may be wise not to do it. The auto maker who abandons an unpopular model may be ridiculed for making a "gutless" decision and lose future authority and actual power within his or her organization.

(C) Just as the person who orders too much food might be labeled a poor judge of his or her own appetite and wasteful, these decision makers might be trying to protect their *future* reputations as morally consistent individuals or good decision makers.

*sunk cost: 매몰비용 ((이미 지불하여 회수할 수 없는 비용)) **gutless: 배짱 없는

① (A) – (C) – (B)　　　　② (B) – (A) – (C)

③ (B) – (C) – (A)　　　　④ (C) – (A) – (B)

⑤ (C) – (B) – (A)

PLUS +
변형문제

윗글의 제목으로 가장 적절한 것은?

① The Sunk Cost Bias Distorts Moral Judgment
② Business Success Means Letting Go of Sunk Costs
③ Why Decision Makers Continue with Sunk Cost Ventures
④ How Abandoning Sunk Costs Can Maintain Your Reputation
⑤ Overcoming the Sunk Cost Fallacy: Get Better at Decision Making

38

글의 흐름으로 보아, 주어진 문장이 들어가기에 가장 적절한 곳을 고르시오.

> Because they lack the ability to flee or to hide behind strong walls, the plants' only defensive option is to soak their bodies in chemicals that play havoc with the guts, nerves, and hormones of their enemies.

Ginseng, yam, and mayapple are all small plants that overwinter as nutritious underground stems or roots. (①) This shared way of living explains why they are all so rich in medicinal chemicals. (②) Unlike fast-moving animals or thick-barked trees, these stationary, thin-skinned plants are highly vulnerable to attack from mammals and insects. (③) Their underground stores of food are particularly attractive to would-be predators. (④) Because natural selection has designed the defensive chemicals specifically to attack the physiology of animals, these poisons can, in careful human hands, be turned into medicines. (⑤) By finding just the right dose, herbalists can turn the plants' defensive arsenal into an impressive collection of stimulants, blood thinners, hormones, and other medicines.

*arsenal: 무기고; 축적

PLUS +
변형문제

윗글의 요지로 가장 적절한 것은?

① 몸에 좋은 약이라도 과하면 독이 될 수 있다.
② 약초의 효과는 뛰어나지만 부작용의 문제가 있다.
③ 자연에서 유래한 성분의 치료제는 인체에 안전하다.
④ 독성이 있는 식물을 다루는 데에는 특별한 주의가 요구된다.
⑤ 뿌리 식물의 독은 의약 성분이 많아 약으로도 활용 가능하다.

글의 흐름으로 보아, 주어진 문장이 들어가기에 가장 적절한 곳을 고르시오.

> Yet, although there have been phenoms who went on to great success later in their careers, this perception is as much fantasy as reality.

If you're a young athlete, you, your parents, and your coaches want you to experience success now because you and they believe that early success is highly predictive of later success in your sport. (①) Our athletic culture is obsessed with the "phenom" and the "can't-miss kid," who show earlier dominance in a sport. (②) For example, out of the thousands of young baseball players who have competed in the Little League World Series throughout the years, fewer than 50 went on to major-league careers. (③) In fact, phenoms are a statistical rarity, and those can't-miss kids often do miss later in their athletic careers. (④) More often than not, it is the athletes who keep at it through setbacks, plateaus, and failures who ultimately "make it." (⑤) Your efforts early on as you strive for your sports goals should be devoted to preparing yourself for success in the future, when it matters most, not achieving quick and immediate success.

*phenom: 천재 **plateau: 정체기

PLUS +
변형문제 윗글의 제목으로 가장 적절한 것은?

① How to Measure A Young Athlete's Success
② Do's and Don'ts for Parents of Young Athletes
③ Helping Young Athletes Deal with a Fear of Failure
④ Things Youth Athletes Can Learn from Pro Athletes
⑤ What Should Young Athletes Pursue to Achieve Success?

40 ◆

We live in a world where leaders frequently disappoint us. Meticulous biographers sometimes diminish the image of great leaders, such as Martin Luther King, Jr., and George Washington, by carefully examining their moral shortcomings. It's difficult to have heroes in a world where every wart and wrinkle of a person's life is public. Ironically, the increase in information that we have about leaders has increased the confusion surrounding the ethics of leadership. The more flawed our leaders are, the greater our desire for highly ethical leaders. The ethical issues of leadership are found not only in public debates but lie simmering below the surface of the existing leadership literature.

*wart: (피부의) 사마귀

> Greater access to information about leaders has _____(A)_____ them, and this has left people desiring leaders with _____(B)_____ character.

	(A)		(B)
①	glorified	⋯⋯	solid
②	inspired	⋯⋯	moral
③	unmasked	⋯⋯	outgoing
④	demystified	⋯⋯	flawless
⑤	distinguished	⋯⋯	exceptional

다음 글을 읽고, 물음에 답하시오.

Philosophers have debated the relationship of the mind to the brain and the rest of the body for centuries. Materialists believe that the mind emerges from the brain and that the mind is an artifact of the brain. This has been the (a) prevailing paradigm in the western scientific world since Charles Darwin's Theory of Evolution became the dominant scientific dogma. Recently, however, there has been growing (b) dissent in the area of neuroscience and psychology. Psychologists argue that every mental event involves a brain event. In one study, people suffering from spider phobias were treated with cognitive behavior therapy. After therapy, they could actually touch spiders (although they might not have been ready to appear on *Fear Factor*). Their brain images revealed (c) enhanced activity in the brain areas involved in the phobia. Not only did they change their minds about spiders, they literally changed their brains.

Another study focused on patients with language difficulties caused by damage to the left sides of their brains. To aid their recovery, the patients were given training in language comprehension. Not only did the training help improve their ability to understand language, but brain images revealed that the right sides of their brains had become more active to (d) compensate for their left-brain damage. Again, a learning experience served as an adaptive mechanism and changed their brains. Every time you learn something, you are (e) reshaping your living brain. Just think: as you study this psychology article you are changing your mind, and your brain, about psychology.

41 ◆ 윗글의 제목으로 가장 적절한 것은?

① Is Brain Therapy Effective?
② How Does Your Mind Work?
③ Learning Can Change Your Brain
④ Your Brain Determines Your Thoughts
⑤ Can Brain Research Explain Everything?

42 ◆ 밑줄 친 (a) ~ (e) 중에서 문맥상 낱말의 쓰임이 적절하지 <u>않은</u> 것은?

① (a)　　② (b)　　③ (c)　　④ (d)　　⑤ (e)

31

다음 빈칸에 들어갈 말로 가장 적절한 것을 고르시오.

Studies have indicated that a great many species have some capacity to track the _____ properties of objects in their environment. In one experiment, the psychologists Russell Church and Warren Meck exposed rats to both tones and flashes of light. The rats were initially trained to press the left lever when they heard two tones and the right lever when they heard four tones. The rats were also taught to press the left lever in response to two flashes of light and the right lever in response to four flashes of light. What would the rats do when presented with one tone and one flash of light? They immediately pressed the left lever, indicating that they had coded the stimulus as 'two events', and they immediately pressed the right lever in response to two tones and two flashes of light, indicating that they had coded that stimulus as 'four events'.

① optical　　　　② common　　　　③ invariable

④ functional　　　⑤ mathematical

PLUS +
변형문제

윗글의 제목으로 가장 적절한 것은?

① Repetition: The Key to Successful Training

② Calculation: What Even Small Animals Can Do

③ The Possibility of Rats Finding Common Features

④ Vision vs. Hearing: Which One Stimulates Us More?

⑤ Even Numbers Are Easier to Teach than Odd Numbers

32 ◆

다음 빈칸에 들어갈 말로 가장 적절한 것을 고르시오.

The concept of a rational action can be seen to be quite complex: it is a hybrid concept. A rational action is one that is not irrational. Any action that is not irrational counts as rational; that is, any action that does not have (is not believed to have) harmful consequences for you or those for whom you care is rational. So rationality does involve, if only indirectly, the egocentric character of an irrational action. However, the concept of a rational action also incorporates the concept of a reason, and reasons need not be egocentric. The fact (belief) that anyone will benefit from your actions is a reason. Reasons are not limited to facts (beliefs) about benefits to you or those for whom you care. Thus an action that has (is believed to have) harmful consequences for you can be rational if (you believe) _____, even if you do not care about them.

① there are compensating benefits for others
② it is goal-oriented and consistent all along
③ they also deal a death-blow to your enemies
④ there is no other option left for all concerned
⑤ it eventually maximizes your own self-interest

PLUS +
변형문제

윗글의 제목으로 가장 적절한 것은?

① Ways to Distinguish Rational and Irrational Behavior
② When There Is Benefit to Anyone, There Is Rationality
③ Self-centered Behavior Can Also Serve the Public Good
④ The Impossibility of Reasonable Judgment On Social Impact
⑤ Intervention by Others: An Essential Element of Rational Judgment

33

다음 빈칸에 들어갈 말로 가장 적절한 것을 고르시오.

Arbitrage is a term which refers to the buying and selling of the same commodities in different markets to profit from unequal prices and information. The successful arbitrageur is a trader who knows to buy something for $1 in Chicago and sell it for $1.50 in New York. The key to being a successful arbitrageur is having a wide net of informants and information and then knowing how to synthesize it in a way that will produce a profit. If one can do arbitrage in markets, one can do it in other fields. Today, more than ever, the traditional boundaries between politics, culture, technology and finance are disappearing. You often cannot explain one without referring to the others. Therefore, to be an effective foreign affairs analyst or reporter, you have to learn how to arbitrage information from these disparate perspectives and then weave it all together to produce a picture of the world that you would never have if you looked at it from only one perspective. That is the essence of information arbitrage. In a world where we are all so much more interconnected, the ability _____ is the real value added provided by a journalist.

*arbitrage: 차익 거래 **arbitrageur: 차익 거래자

① to collect information from their readers

② to provide more information than anyone else

③ to learn in-depth details about their connections

④ to read the connections, and to connect the dots

⑤ to obtain facts, and to immediately disperse them

PLUS⁺
변형문제

윗글의 제목으로 가장 적절한 것은?

① How to Draw Connections in Information Arbitrage

② Pass through Boundaries with Ease Using Arbitrage

③ Importance of a Wide Net of Informants in Arbitrage

④ Necessary Quality For Journalists: Information Arbitrage

⑤ Separate Disparate Perspectives in an Interconnected World

34

다음 빈칸에 들어갈 말로 가장 적절한 것을 고르시오.

We have seen only cases in which human intelligence is equal to or greater than animal intelligence. Perhaps the wild mind is altogether inferior to the human mind. Clearly, humans are vastly superior to all earthly animals in their ability to learn and use language. However, if we accept this view we have jumped to the wrong conclusion. Animals do have unique abilities not shared by humans. Perhaps the most convincing case is dolphins' talent for acquiring and processing acoustic information. This skill is highly adaptive and is a type of intelligence according to any reasonable general definition. Furthermore, not only can unaided humans not match dolphins' ability, but also the best human-designed transducers, computers, and software cannot match their ability. Only by _____ could we deny that this ability is a type of intelligence.

*transducer: 변환기

① defining reasonably the intellectual abilities of all species
② adopting radically human-centered notions of intelligence
③ examining thoroughly the mental processes of other species
④ viewing animal behaviors as being conscious and considerate
⑤ emphasizing the capabilities of animals rather than those of humans

PLUS⁺
변형문제

윗글의 주제로 가장 적절한 것은?

① indisputable existence of animal intelligence
② benefits of animal training for animal welfare
③ different types of intelligence and learning styles
④ demerits of believing superiority of human intelligence
⑤ discovery of animal intelligence and their learning ability

다음 글에서 전체 흐름과 관계 없는 문장은?

The modern symphony orchestra can be understood as a logical extension of human expressive capacities. It has been suggested, for example, that musical instruments have their precursors in the natural ways in which human beings produce sound. ① That is, string instruments correspond to voice production; wind instruments, to vocalization and whistling; and percussion, to clapping and foot tapping. ② If this supposition is valid, then the vast number of instruments that have been devised in various cultures since prehistory have merely been means of imitating and extending the musical qualities of the innate modes of human expression. ③ Especially songs that are made by the human voice are, therefore, the most universal and important music both from a historical and cultural standpoint. ④ While the development of the modern orchestra has greatly diversified the sound palette available to the composer, the overall range of tonal frequency has remained within that of the human voice, although the human auditory range is much broader. ⑤ Moreover, the string instruments, which are most closely analogous to the voice, form the core of the orchestra.

*precursor: 전신(前身), 선도자 격인 사람이나 사물 **percussion: 타악기

PLUS +
변형문제

윗글의 제목으로 가장 적절한 것은?

① Orchestra: A History of Cumulative Cultural Evolution
② How Modern Orchestras Mirror Various Human Expressions
③ Instrument Sound vs. Human Voice: Which One Is More Varied?
④ All the Sounds of Instruments Come from the Sounds of Nature
⑤ The Discovery of Various Sounds through the Efforts of Mankind

36

주어진 글 다음에 이어질 글의 순서로 가장 적절한 것을 고르시오.

> For animals without skeletons, like worms or jellyfish, fossilization is a very rare event. For a soft-bodied animal to be fossilized, its body must be protected from decomposition. The body is usually exposed to air and water with a lot of oxygen, so it decomposes rapidly.

(A) Sometimes, however, the soft-bodied animal is buried rapidly by fine mud. Water creeps through mud much more slowly than through sand, so the body does not decompose as fast.

(B) The animal is likely to be fossilized only if it is buried soon after it dies, or when it is buried alive. Even then, it is likely to decompose, because water that seeps through the sediment around it is usually rich in oxygen.

(C) The very soft wet earth often contains a lot of other organic matter as well, and that uses up oxygen faster. Some of these animals then escape decomposition. Under just the right conditions, a delicate impression of the animal might be preserved.

① (A) – (C) – (B)　　　　　　② (B) – (A) – (C)

③ (B) – (C) – (A)　　　　　　④ (C) – (A) – (B)

⑤ (C) – (B) – (A)

PLUS +
변형문제

윗글의 주제로 가장 적절한 것은?

① difficulties of fossilizing animal skeletons
② roles of oxygen in the process of fossilization
③ types of animals that are difficult to be fossilized
④ conditions for soft-bodied animals to be fossilized
⑤ reasons sea creatures are more decomposed than fossilized

주어진 글 다음에 이어질 글의 순서로 가장 적절한 것을 고르시오.

> Many genetic and biological mechanisms control hunger and satiety, ensuring that people will eat enough to meet their energy needs. Throughout most of human history, getting enough food was the primary challenge.

(A) In such an environment, people who are not devoting substantial conscious effort to managing body weight are probably gaining weight. This means that nutrition education has an important role.

(B) Today's environment, however, is one in which food is widely available, inexpensive, and often high in energy density, while minimal physical activity is required for daily living. Researchers have proposed that the modern environment has taken body weight control from an instinctual (unconscious) process to one that requires substantial cognitive effort.

(C) The human body developed to function in an environment where food was scarce and high levels of physical activity were mandatory for survival. This situation resulted in the development of various physiological mechanisms that encourage the body to deposit energy (i.e., fat) and defend against energy loss.

*satiety: 포만감

① (A) – (C) – (B)　　　　　② (B) – (A) – (C)

③ (B) – (C) – (A)　　　　　④ (C) – (A) – (B)

⑤ (C) – (B) – (A)

PLUS +
변형문제

윗글의 요지로 가장 적절한 것은?

① 식량의 풍족함과 인간의 신체 활동량은 비례한다.
② 현대 환경에서 체중 조절은 저절로 이루어지기 어렵다.
③ 영양 교육보다 개인의 노력이 비만 예방에 더 중요하다.
④ 오늘날 인간은 생존뿐만 아니라 즐거움을 위해 음식을 먹는다.
⑤ 서구화된 식습관과 편리해진 생활 환경으로 비만 인구가 증가하고 있다.

38

글의 흐름으로 보아, 주어진 문장이 들어가기에 가장 적절한 곳을 고르시오.

> But they may instead decide to reduce their effort to match what they perceive as a low level of current pay.

Although individual incentives may increase the effort of the individual group members, and thus enhance group performance, they also have some potential disadvantages for group process. One potential problem is that the group members will compare their own rewards with those of others. (①) It might be hoped that individuals would use their coworkers as models (upward comparison), which would inspire them to work harder. (②) For instance, when corporations set up "employee of the week" programs, they are attempting to develop this type of positive comparison. (③) On the other hand, if group members believe that others are being rewarded more than they are for what they perceive as the same work (downward comparison), they may change their behavior to attempt to restore equity. (④) Perhaps they will attempt to work harder in order to receive greater rewards for themselves. (⑤) It has been found, for instance, that job absenteeism is increased when employees make unfavorable comparisons between their own rewards and those of others.

*absenteeism: 잦은 결근

PLUS+
변형문제

윗글의 제목으로 가장 적절한 것은?

① Upward and Downward Comparisons Influence Our Self-esteem
② Differences in Equity between Relative and Absolute Evaluations
③ Importance of Differential Compensation Based on Competence
④ How Does Providing Individual Rewards Affect Group Members?
⑤ The More Rewards One Gets, The More One's Behavior Changes

글의 흐름으로 보아, 주어진 문장이 들어가기에 가장 적절한 곳을 고르시오.

> You wouldn't buy an extended warranty on your smartphone if you were only going to keep it for a week.

One theory suggests that there is a direct connection between shorter life expectancy and greater external threats. Essentially, animals with a greater risk of being eaten evolve to live shorter lives — even if they aren't eaten. (①) Here's how — if a species faces significant environmental threats and predators, it's under greater evolutionary pressure to reproduce at an early age, so it evolves to reach adulthood faster. (②) A shorter lifespan also means a shorter length of time between generations, which allows a species to evolve faster — which is important for species that face a lot of environmental threats. (③) At the same time, there's never any real evolutionary pressure to evolve mechanisms to repair DNA errors that occur over time, because most individuals in the species don't live long enough to experience those errors. (④) On the flip side, a species that is more dominant in its environment, and that can continue to reproduce for most of its life, will gain an advantage in repairing accumulated DNA errors. (⑤) If it lives longer, it can reproduce more.

PLUS +
변형문제

윗글의 제목으로 가장 적절한 것은?

① The Value of an Animal's Dominance in Nature
② What Determines Creatures to Develop Evolution?
③ Evolutionary Pressure: Reproduction's Greatest Friend
④ Evolutionary Pressure of Creatures Scarcely Facing Death
⑤ The Correlation between Danger, Lifespan, and Evolution

40 ◆ 다음 글의 내용을 한 문장으로 요약하고자 한다. 빈칸 (A), (B)에 들어갈 말로 가장 적절한 것은?

Mills suggests imagining extreme cases as a way to stimulate thinking: If something is small, imagine it to be enormous and ask "How would that change things?" An example of this heuristic can be seen in the research on globalization in the fields of geography, anthropology, political science, and economics. Theorists in these disciplines consider how processes operating at the global level might be mirrored at the local level, as well as how processes operating at the local level might be generalized or altered if they are moved to the global level. For example, if we think about the effects and challenges of unionizing workers at the local level, what would happen if we focused on unionizing workers at the global level? How might thinking in such terms alter our theories and understanding of unionization at the local level?

⬇

> To stimulate thinking, try to ___(A)___ the problem by changing the ___(B)___ of its application.

	(A)		(B)
①	reframe	······	scale
②	share	······	consequence
③	solve	······	order
④	visualize	······	purpose
⑤	reassess	······	moment

다음 글을 읽고, 물음에 답하시오.

Information is transferred when the thought of a single mind is shared with another. In hunter-gather societies, information may have been very limited, but it was (a) self-correcting — misinformation was minimized. A hunter who routinely led his kin away from the best hunting grounds was soon either excluded from his group or simply ignored, and anyone who gathered poisonous berries instead of nutritious ones was quickly eliminated.

In his recent book *The Social Conquest of Earth*, E. Wilson described in evolutionary terms how this sharing of valid information was rewarded. Wilson's view is that (b) collaboration among humans has become an essential part of our wiring through natural selection. Throughout most of human prehistory, then, validating information and sharing it was both valued and rewarded. Information may have been quite limited, but its quality was high.

We now occupy the (c) opposite state. How did this happen? When one doesn't know, has never met, and, furthermore, shares no common interest with the individual with whom information is being shared, there is little incentive to assure the reliability of that information. Indeed, if there is an personal (d) loss to be had by providing misinformation to one's unknown targets, there is an incentive to misinform. In a target market of seventy million consumers — or seven billion — there is no incentive for altruism. If more profit — in dollars, in power, in fame — is to be gained from misinformation, why not go for it? And when dollars, power, and fame are combined (as they often are in politics), the incentive is all the (e) stronger.

41

윗글의 제목으로 가장 적절한 것은?

① What's So Bad about Misinformation?
② Why Is Misinformation So Prevalent Today?
③ A Survival Guide to the Misinformation Age
④ Incentive Structures Maximizing Individual Gain
⑤ Since the Ancient Times, Misinformation Predominates

42

밑줄 친 (a) ~ (e) 중에서 문맥상 낱말의 쓰임이 적절하지 않은 것은?

① (a)   ② (b)   ③ (c)   ④ (d)   ⑤ (e)

31 ◆   다음 빈칸에 들어갈 말로 가장 적절한 것을 고르시오.

An anthropologist named Nina G. Jablonski and a geographic computer specialist named George Chaplin have produced an equation to express the relationship between a given population's skin color and its annual exposure to ultraviolet rays. Interestingly, their research proposes that we carry sufficient genes within our gene pool to ensure that, within 1,000 years of a population's migration from one climate to another, its descendants would have skin color light enough to maximize the use of available sunlight to create sufficient vitamin D production. There is one notable _____ to Jablonski and Chaplin's equation — and it is the case that demonstrates the existence of the rule. The Inuit — the indigenous people of the subarctic — are dark-skinned, despite the limited sunlight of their home. But the reason they don't need to evolve the lighter skin necessary to ensure sufficient vitamin D production is refreshingly simple. Their diet is full of fatty fish — which just happens to be one of the only foods in nature that is chock-full of vitamin D.

① omission   ② intention   ③ exception
④ inclination   ⑤ commonality

PLUS+
변형문제

윗글의 제목으로 가장 적절한 것은?

① Two Sources of Vitamin D Production
② Why Should We Block Ultraviolet Rays?
③ Essential Food for Vitamin D Production
④ The Key to Vitamin D Absorbance: Dark Skin
⑤ The Relationship between Skin Color and Vitamin D

32 ◆

다음 빈칸에 들어갈 말로 가장 적절한 것을 고르시오.

For ages, yoga teachers have been saying, "Calm your body, calm your mind." They argue that action and feeling go together, and by regulating the action, which is under the more direct control of the will, we can indirectly regulate the feeling. Social neuroscience now provides evidence to support that prescription. In fact, some studies go further and suggest that actively taking on the physical state of a happy person by, say, forcing a smile can cause you to actually feel happier. My young son Nicolai seemed to understand this intuitively: after breaking his hand in a freak accident while playing basketball, he suddenly stopped crying and started to laugh — and then explained that when he has pain laughing seems to make it feel better. The old "＿＿＿＿＿＿＿＿＿＿" idea, which Nicolai had rediscovered, is now also the subject of serious scientific research.

① add fuel to the fire
② fake it till you make it
③ let go of all preconceptions
④ healthy mind in a healthy body
⑤ break a plan into smaller pieces

PLUS +
변형문제

윗글의 요지로 가장 적절한 것은?

① 웃음은 인간의 고유한 본성이다.
② 감정은 신체적 반응을 이끌어 낸다.
③ 다른 사람의 감정은 쉽게 전염이 된다.
④ 속임수 행동이라도 감정에 영향을 준다.
⑤ 인간의 행동은 감정에 의거하여 표출된다.

다음 빈칸에 들어갈 말로 가장 적절한 것을 고르시오.

The writer very quickly loses the ability to see his prose as a reader. He knows exactly what he's trying to say, but that's because he's the one saying it. For writers, knowledge can be a subtle curse. When we learn about the world, we also learn all the reasons why the world cannot be changed. We become numb to the possibilities of something new. In fact, the only way to remain creative over time — not to be undone by our expertise — is _____ . This is the lesson of Samuel Taylor Coleridge, the nineteenth-century Romantic poet. One of his favorite pastimes was attending public chemistry lectures in London, watching eminent scientists set elements on fire. When Coleridge was asked why he spent so much time watching these pyrotechnic demonstrations, he had a ready reply. "I attend the lectures," Coleridge said, "so that I can renew my stock of metaphors." He knew that we see the most when we are on the outside looking in.

*pyrotechnic: 불꽃

① to pursue a deeper ignorance
② to ask "why not" instead of "why"
③ to share our knowledge with others
④ to borrow old ideas and combine them
⑤ to make connections with creative people

PLUS +
변형문제

윗글의 제목으로 가장 적절한 것은?

① Gain Meaning in Life through Education
② How to Best Comprehend Prose as a Reader
③ A Poet's Peculiar Inquiry into Science Lectures
④ Renew Your Creativity by Trying Something New
⑤ Knowledge Leads to Our Extended Understanding

34 ◆

다음 빈칸에 들어갈 말로 가장 적절한 것을 고르시오.

Charlotte Linde noticed in her study of police helicopter crews that when the immediate demands of work subside, the crew may engage in social chat, which will stop if work requirements intrude. And she found that the switch from work talk to social talk was more often initiated by the pilot, who functioned as a superior in command. For example, if it was quiet, the pilot might begin free conversation by noticing the view, returning to a previous topic or commenting on the mission just completed. This is exactly the pattern that sociolinguist Janice Hornyak noticed in a study of talk in an all-female office at an accounting firm. As the women in the office shifted between work and personal talk, the shift was always initiated by the highest-ranking person in the room, the office manager. If she was busy, nobody else began telling personal stories or chatting. But if the office manager was ready to take a break and chat, the others followed suit. In this way, _____, in even the most automatic and casual conversation.

① taking a break is very important

② no one takes any initiative to follow orders

③ everyone waits for superiors to stop talking

④ workers avoid chatting as much as possible

⑤ hierarchies are reflected throughout a workday

PLUS +
변형문제

윗글의 주제로 가장 적절한 것은?

① importance of keeping a work-life balance

② benefits of small talk with colleagues at work

③ the way social interaction is triggered at the workplace

④ impacts of superior-subordinate relationships on job satisfaction

⑤ conversation topics to build a good relationship with employees

35 ◆

다음 글에서 전체 흐름과 관계 없는 문장은?

How does a major-league baseball player manage to hit a fastball? The answer is that the brain begins collecting information about the pitch long before the ball is ever thrown. As soon as the pitcher begins his wind-up, the batter automatically starts to pick up on "anticipatory clues" that narrow down the list of possibilities. ① A twisted wrist suggests a curveball, while an elbow fixed at a right angle means that a fastball is coming, straight over the plate. ② Two fingers on the seam might indicate a slider, which is thrown fast and curves slightly as it approaches the batter. ③ A ball gripped with the knuckles is a sure sign that a wavering knuckleball is on its way. ④ The forkball, which is thrown with the same speed of a fastball, is known to be a cause of significant and increasingly common damage to the shoulder and elbow. ⑤ The batters, of course, aren't consciously studying these signs; they can't explain what made them swing at certain pitches.

*knuckle: 손가락 마디

PLUS +
변형문제

윗글의 제목으로 가장 적절한 것은?

① Ways to Become a Good Pitcher
② Various Types of Pitches in Baseball
③ How Batters Predict the Type of Pitch
④ What Pitch is the Hardest for Batters to Hit
⑤ Who Has More Chances: Pitchers vs. Batters

36

주어진 글 다음에 이어질 글의 순서로 가장 적절한 것을 고르시오.

> The Greek roots of the word 'homeostasis' mean "like standing still." In a living organism, this means that the environment inside an organism stays the same no matter what happens outside.

(A) Yet at a certain point there's just not enough oxygen outside and your body can't cope. Similarly, an organism whose internal environment changes along with the external environment still needs to maintain its internal chemistry.

(B) That is, there has to be something that defines a living creature as different from what's outside — and that has to be able to stay the same, at least within a certain range of external environments. So every organism has some level of homeostasis, but there is a huge variation in scope.

(C) But homeostasis is not perfect. On a mountaintop, for example, your body produces more red blood cells to keep the level of oxygen in your body the same even though it's lower outside.

① (A) – (C) – (B)   ② (B) – (A) – (C)

③ (B) – (C) – (A)   ④ (C) – (A) – (B)

⑤ (C) – (B) – (A)

PLUS +
변형문제

윗글의 요지로 가장 적절한 것은?

① 우리 신체는 외부 환경 변화에 저항성이 있다.
② 모든 유기체는 항상성이 있으나 한계를 가진다.
③ 고산 지대에서 더 많은 산소 공급은 필수적이다.
④ 항상성은 자율신경계와 내분비계에 의해 조절된다.
⑤ 적절한 산소 수준은 우리 몸의 화학 작용을 조절한다.

주어진 글 다음에 이어질 글의 순서로 가장 적절한 것을 고르시오.

> We tend to think of imitation as a solo action. However, in many contexts — and normally in mother-infant interactions — achieving successful imitation is more of a cooperative undertaking.

(A) So the model's "you are successfully imitating me" display will typically be met by the imitator's "I am successfully imitating you" display, and this makes the success display mutual.

(B) The person being imitated (the model) becomes the "demonstrator," and, by smiling and encouraging, facilitates the imitator's efforts. Even in contexts where no such assistance is necessary, where the imitation is effortless, the model will usually be aware of being (successfully) imitated and will display this back to the imitator.

(C) This "acknowledgment of success" display might consist of a smile and/or a meeting of gazes, and performance of the action might become more enthusiastic. Furthermore, the imitator will be aware of when his imitation is successful and may produce a similar success display.

① (A) – (C) – (B)   ② (B) – (A) – (C)

③ (B) – (C) – (A)   ④ (C) – (A) – (B)

⑤ (C) – (B) – (A)

PLUS⁺
변형문제

윗글의 제목으로 가장 적절한 것은?

① What Can Imitation Do for Cooperation?

② Anticipation and Imitation in Social Interaction

③ The Desire for Recognition Facilitates Success

④ Imitation: Joint Activity between Model and Imitator

⑤ Mimicry in Social Interaction and Its Effect on Learning

38 ◆

글의 흐름으로 보아, 주어진 문장이 들어가기에 가장 적절한 곳을 고르시오.

> As a result, children come to a strange setting that has been designed for the convenience of the adults who work there.

It is probably true that most teachers' decisions about classroom arrangement are based on aesthetics — that is, their subjective judgments about an attractive room order. (①) Classrooms are often set up or arranged before the first child sets foot in the room. (②) The adults neither consider the needs of individual children, nor do they seek any direct input from the children about space arrangement. (③) They probably do not feel any sense of ownership of it, which influences their interest in and care of that space. (④) In a similar, but slightly different way, consider how many people are careless of others' property while they are fussy and particular in the care of their own things. (⑤) Children react in similar ways, being more likely to act in destructive ways toward an environment that they don't feel they own.

PLUS +
변형문제

윗글의 제목으로 가장 적절한 것은?

① Ownership: Integral Attitude in Buying Properties to Live
② Lack of Ownership Leads to Indifference to the Property
③ Is Children's Direct Input Necessary in Choosing a Home?
④ Classrooms: The Clearer, the Better Learning Environment
⑤ What Makes It Difficult to Reflect Students' View in Classrooms

글의 흐름으로 보아, 주어진 문장이 들어가기에 가장 적절한 곳을 고르시오.

> American advantages in robotics and unmanned drones will eventually be available to opponents in later ones.

Technology is a double-edged sword. It eventually spreads and becomes available to adversaries that may have more primitive capabilities but also are less vulnerable to dependence on advanced technologies. (①) American military theorists used to argue that other nations would eventually buy some high technology commercially "off the shelf." (②) Meanwhile, the United States would be progressing to the next generation and integrating technologies into a system of systems. (③) But that was round one in the chess game. (④) For example, in 2009 the American military discovered that insurgents were hacking into the downlinks of data from a Predator unmanned aircraft, using software that cost less than $30. (⑤) Simultaneously, growing reliance on elaborate satellite and computer network–controlled systems makes the United States more vulnerable than some of its adversaries.

*insurgent: 폭도, 반란자

PLUS+
변형문제

윗글의 제목으로 가장 적절한 것은?

① The Theft of New Technologies from America
② The Better the Technology, the Safer We Become
③ Is Playing a Leading Role in Technology Always Good?
④ The Key to American Security: Modernized Technology
⑤ The Most Difficult Game of Chess: Technology Development

다음 글의 내용을 한 문장으로 요약하고자 한다. 빈칸 (A), (B)에 들어갈 말로 가장 적절한 것은?

A group of college women, of roughly the same age and life experiences, were asked to participate in a study. Half of the group (the first group) was told that they would be given a harmless, yet painful, electric shock. The other half of the group (the second group) was told that they would be given an electric shock that would be entirely painless. Thus, the researchers created two groups: the first believing they would be exposed to pain, and the second believing they had nothing to fear. The researchers then told the women they had ten minutes until the test would begin, and watched to see how they interacted. During the waiting time, the women in the first group started to mingle together. They talked about their concerns, gave each other support, and debated the test. In fact, 63% of the women ended up in a group with other subjects, while 37% preferred to be alone. In the other room, a different situation was occurring. The second-group women preferred to spend their time without associating with the other participants. Here, only 33% wanted to spend that time with another participant.

↓

> For the high-anxiety subjects, anxiety was a strong motivating factor in _____(A)_____; the low-anxiety subjects preferred to remain _____(B)_____.

	(A)		(B)
①	evasion	⋯⋯	inattentive
②	affiliation	⋯⋯	solitary
③	concentration	⋯⋯	active
④	confidence	⋯⋯	indifferent
⑤	empathy	⋯⋯	insecure

다음 글을 읽고, 물음에 답하시오.

A new study suggests that Chimpanzees specifically refer to favorite foods with distinct grunts, but the calls differ between populations. The chimps could then learn the "foreign" grunts, making communication (a) easier when two groups merge into one. The findings show that, like human words, chimp food calls are not (b) fixed in their structure. When exposed to a new group, chimps can change their calls to sound more like their group mates. A big topic of conversation is food. Chimpanzees produce acoustically distinct grunts in response to foods of low, medium, or high quality, and in captivity they give distinct grunts for certain foods, including bananas, bread, and mangoes. It has been shown that listeners are able to distinguish between these different grunts and extract information that helps guide their own search for food appropriately. The researchers studied what happened after two separate groups of adult chimps moved in together at the Edinburgh Zoo. Before the merger, the groups produced their (c) particular food grunts. After the merger, the "newcomer" group significantly changed their calls to (d) differentiate those of the long-term residents. "If one were to make an analogy with human beings, it could be the process of (e) dialect change. Just as people moving between groups of speakers of the same language subtly modify their accents to sound like the group into which they are moving, the chimps modify their grunts to ensure that the other chimps understand them correctly," says Simon Townsend of the University of Zürich.

41 ◆ 윗글의 제목으로 가장 적절한 것은?

① Chimps Can Learn Local Accents
② Controversy over Chimps' Language
③ Chimps' Grunts Are Not a Language
④ Chimps' Well-developed Food Language
⑤ Different Languages Leading to Conflict

42 ◆ 밑줄 친 (a) ~ (e) 중에서 문맥상 낱말의 쓰임이 적절하지 <u>않은</u> 것은?

① (a) ② (b) ③ (c) ④ (d) ⑤ (e)

31

다음 빈칸에 들어갈 말로 가장 적절한 것을 고르시오.

Scientists who study the history of life on Earth are sure that the fossil record is _____. The potential for fossil preservation varies dramatically from environment to environment. Preservation is enhanced under conditions that limit destructive physical and biological processes. Thus marine and fresh water environments with low oxygen levels, high salinities, or relatively high rates of sediment deposition favor preservation. Similarly, in some environments biochemical conditions can favor the early mineralization of skeletons and even soft tissues by a variety of compounds. In addition to these preservational problems, the erosion, deformation and metamorphism of originally fossiliferous sedimentary rock have eliminated significant portions of the fossil record over geologic time. Furthermore, much of the fossil-bearing sedimentary record is located in poorly accessible or little studied geographic areas. For these reasons, of those once-living species actually preserved in the fossil record, only a small portion have been discovered and described by science.

*metamorphism: ((지질)) 변성(變成) (작용)

① biased　　　　② transient　　　　③ duplicated
④ stereotyped　　⑤ detail-oriented

PLUS+
변형문제

윗글의 제목으로 가장 적절한 것은?

① Is the Fossil Record Really Credible?
② Fossil Record: A Glimpse into the Past
③ An Unsolved Problem in Preserving Fossils
④ Skeletons: Foundation of Our Prehistoric History
⑤ The Many Environments Where Fossils Are Found

32

다음 빈칸에 들어갈 말로 가장 적절한 것을 고르시오.

We set up a tasting venue at a local supermarket and invited passerby shoppers to sample two different varieties of jam and tea, and to decide which alternative in each pair they preferred the most. Immediately after the participants had made their choice, we asked them to again sample the chosen alternative, and to verbally explain why they adopted it. The cunning aspect of the study was that we secretly switched the contents of the sample containers, so that we intended participants to describe a choice they hadn't made. The majority of them were unaware that their choice was not their choice and explained why. In total, no more than a third of the manipulated trials were detected. Even for remarkably different tastes like Cinnamon-Apple and bitter Grapefruit, or the smell of Mango and strong flavored wine, no more than half of all trials were detected, thus demonstrating considerable levels of choice blindness for the taste and smell of two different consumer goods. It would seem that, once we have made a preference, we _____.

① try to avoid adding new preferences
② are committed to justifying our decision
③ consistently explore other possible choices
④ fear loss greater than the potential for gains
⑤ prefer it more and more to the other options

PLUS +
변형문제

윗글의 요지로 가장 적절한 것은?
① 결정이 빠를수록 추후에 뒤집힐 가능성이 크다.
② 사람들은 자신의 선호도를 좀처럼 바꾸지 않는다.
③ 선택에 영향을 주는 요소들은 지속적으로 변화한다.
④ 다른 사람의 결정에 따라 자신의 선택도 바뀔 수 있다.
⑤ 사람들은 자신의 선택이나 선호에 대해 무지할 수 있다.

다음 빈칸에 들어갈 말로 가장 적절한 것을 고르시오.

Peter Norvig, an artificial intelligence expert, likes to think about big data with an analogy to images. First, he asks us to consider the iconic horse from the cave paintings in Lascaux, France, which date to the Old Stone Age some 17,000 years ago. Then think of a photograph of a horse — or better, the dabs of Pablo Picasso, which do not look much dissimilar to the cave paintings. In fact, when Picasso was shown the Lascaux images he remarked that, since then, "We have invented nothing." Picasso's words were true on one level but not on another. Recall that photograph of the horse. Where it took a long time to draw a picture of a horse, now a representation of one could be made much faster with photography. That is a change, but it may not be the most essential, since it is still fundamentally the same: an image of a horse. Yet now, Norvig asks, consider capturing the image of a horse and speeding it up to 24 frames per second. Now, the quantitative change has produced a qualitative change. A movie is fundamentally different from a frozen photograph. It's the same with big data: _____.

*dab: 붓으로 쓱 그린 그림

① paradigm shift in data analysis promises change
② by changing the amount, we change the essence
③ new technologies have brought quantitative data
④ the more data you have, the less use you make of it
⑤ as quality precedes relation, quality precedes quantity

PLUS⁺
변형문제

윗글의 제목으로 가장 적절한 것은?

① Big Data: Quality Wins Every Time!
② How to Make Photos Look Like Film
③ Artistic Style Isn't Static, It's Dynamic
④ The More Big Data We Have, the Worse
⑤ Understanding Big Data: How It Makes a Difference

34

다음 빈칸에 들어갈 말로 가장 적절한 것을 고르시오.

The word "pitch" refers to the mental representation an organism has of the fundamental frequency of a sound. That is, pitch is a purely psychological phenomenon related to the frequency of vibrating air molecules. Sound waves do not themselves have pitch. Their motion and oscillations can be measured, but it takes a human or animal brain to connect them to that internal quality we call pitch. We perceive color in a similar way. Isaac Newton, who first realized this, pointed out that light is colorless, and that consequently color has to occur inside our brains. He wrote, "The waves themselves are not colored." Since his time, we have learned that light waves are characterized by different frequencies of oscillation, and when they affect the retina of an observer, they set off a chain of neurochemical events, the end product of which is an internal mental image that we call color. The essential point here is: _____

_____.

*frequency: 주파수 **oscillation: 진동

① what we perceive is not just the way the objects are
② these vary depending on the person perceiving them
③ the nature of light and sound indicates a lack of waves
④ it is color that occurs solely in our brains, not vibrations
⑤ how we see and how we hear share very little in common

PLUS +
변형문제

윗글의 제목으로 가장 적절한 것은?

① The Waves in the Air: Pitch and Color
② Our Brains Are Affected by Waves of Light
③ Pitch and Color Are Merely Internalized Products
④ Roles of Frequency in Perceiving Pitch and Color
⑤ Our Perception: Absolute Representation of Reality

다음 글에서 전체 흐름과 관계 <u>없는</u> 문장은?

Edward Sapir, a pioneer in the field of Native American linguistics, grouped more than 1,500 Native American languages into six "families" more than three-quarters of a century ago. Ever since that time, the classification of Native American languages has been a source of controversy. ① A small group of linguists has recently argued that all Native American languages fit into three linguistic families. ② These scholars believe that similarities and differences among words and sounds leave no doubt about the validity of their classification-scheme. ③ The vast majority of linguists, however, reject both the methods and conclusions of these scholars, arguing that linguistic science has not yet advanced far enough to be able to group Native American languages into a few families. ④ Furthermore, the absence of grammars handed down from the past, owing to either the dearth of writing or the destruction of written texts, has given weight to the theory of this minority group. ⑤ According to these scholars, Native American languages have diverged to such an extent over the centuries that it may never be possible to group them in distinct language families.

PLUS +
변형문제

윗글의 제목으로 가장 적절한 것은?

① What Best Advances the Science of Linguistics
② What Conditions Can Prove Your Assertions True?
③ Issues with Categorizing Native American Languages
④ Difficulties of Translating Native American Languages
⑤ Limitations of Grammar Research in Native American Languages

36 ◆ 주어진 글 다음에 이어질 글의 순서로 가장 적절한 것을 고르시오.

In the past few decades nitrogen has asphyxiated many miners in caves and it always happens under the same horror-movie circumstances. The first person to walk in collapses within seconds for no apparent reason. A second dashes in and succumbs as well. The scariest part is that no one struggles before dying.

(A) It is nitrogen that impedes that system. It's odorless and colorless and causes no acid buildup in our veins. We breathe it in and out easily, so our lungs feel relaxed. It "kills with kindness."

(B) They judge only two things: whether gas is inhaled and whether carbon dioxide is exhaled. Carbon dioxide dissolves in blood to form carbonic acid, so as long as we remove CO_2 with each breath and reduce the acid, our brains will relax.

(C) Panic never kicks in. If you've ever been trapped underwater, the instinct not to suffocate will take you to the surface. But our hearts, lungs, and brains actually have no gauge for detecting oxygen.

*asphyxiate: 질식시키다

① (A) – (C) – (B)　　　　② (B) – (A) – (C)

③ (B) – (C) – (A)　　　　④ (C) – (A) – (B)

⑤ (C) – (B) – (A)

PLUS +
변형문제

윗글의 제목으로 가장 적절한 것은?

① Our Organs' Inability to Detect Gas
② How Dangerous Working in Caves Is
③ Ways to Survive When Trapped Underwater
④ Human's Weakness: Insensitivity to Nitrogen
⑤ Nitrogen's Smart Strategy to Dissolve in Blood

주어진 글 다음에 이어질 글의 순서로 가장 적절한 것을 고르시오.

> The savanna theory holds that our apelike ancestors abandoned the dark African forests and moved into the great grassy plains, perhaps because of climate changes that led to massive environmental change. One of the effects of the changes was food scarcity.

(A) Some combination of these new circumstances — the need to scan the horizon for food or predators, the need to cover long distances between food and water — led the savanna hominid to begin walking upright. It could help this species survive in the grasslands.

(B) Other advancements were similarly related to the new environment — hunting required tools and cooperation; smarter prehumans made better tools and better teammates, so they survived longer and attracted more mates, and the process selected for bigger brains.

(C) Out in the savanna, life was tougher, so the theory goes, and our ancestors had to find new ways to get food. Males began to hunt bravely for meat among the herds of grazing animals.

*hominid: 인류의 조상

① (A) – (C) – (B)　　　　② (B) – (A) – (C)
③ (B) – (C) – (A)　　　　④ (C) – (A) – (B)
⑤ (C) – (B) – (A)

PLUS⁺
변형문제

윗글의 제목으로 가장 적절한 것은?

① Survival Skills Obtained from Walking Upright
② Why Did We Start to Have a Carnivorous Diet?
③ What Is Considered to Be Authoritative Theory?
④ Human's Desire for a World beyond His Territory
⑤ What Our Ancestors Achieved in a New Environment

38 ◆

글의 흐름으로 보아, 주어진 문장이 들어가기에 가장 적절한 곳을 고르시오.

> Thus born were the violence and rivalries that characterize today's culture of honor.

Several factors explain why the culture of honor, willingness to protect reputation by resorting to violence, arose in some but not all regions of the United States. Northern states were settled by farmers benefited by stronger legal systems from early settlement. (①) On the other hand, the south and west were inhabited by ranchers, and their livelihood could be threatened by thieves. (②) Crimes were difficult to punish in the expansive south and west, so herders were forced to act themselves. (③) Meanwhile, warmer weather and poverty only encouraged violence. (④) Although some experts dispute this causal chain, there's no doubt that these settlers embraced combat and military law far more deeply than did their northern counterparts. (⑤) As they were passed from generation to generation, the culture of honor gained a foothold in the south and west, which distinguishes their violent responses from tamer responses in the north.

PLUS +
변형문제

윗글의 제목으로 가장 적절한 것은?

① The Rise of Violence in the United States
② The Culture of Honor's Impact on Violence
③ Why Farmers Adopted the Culture of Honor
④ The Military's Influence on the South and West
⑤ Why Violence Was Embraced in the South and West

39

글의 흐름으로 보아, 주어진 문장이 들어가기에 가장 적절한 곳을 고르시오.

> But many other processes are also at play, and many of these reflect changes in how the person comes to terms with their situation.

Factual errors in autobiographical recollection increase substantially as the temporal distance from the to-be-remembered event increases. (①) For example, research indicates that accuracy in recollections of how people heard the news of the September 11, 2001 terrorist attacks in New York City decreased substantially over an 8-month period. (②) Research on personal recollections of dramatic historical events suggests that despite people's beliefs to the contrary, accuracy for memories of the John F. Kennedy assassination or the 9/11 attacks may be no greater than for memories of any other events in life. (③) The temporal instability of autobiographical memory, therefore, contributes to change in the life story over time. (④) The most obvious one is people accumulate new experiences over time, some of which may prove to be so important as to make their way into narrative identity. (⑤) In addition to that, as people's motivations, goals, personal concerns, and social positions change, their memories of important events in their lives and the meanings they attribute to those events may also change.

PLUS +
변형문제

윗글의 제목으로 가장 적절한 것은?

① Oblivion: A Blessed State for a Contented Life
② The Vulnerability of Human's Memory Capacity
③ Ways to Remember Important Memories Clearly
④ Retentive Memory: An Essential Skill for Identity
⑤ How Experiences Attribute Meaning to an Event

40

다음 글의 내용을 한 문장으로 요약하고자 한다. 빈칸 (A)와 (B)에 들어갈 말로 가장 적절한 것은?

Uri Gneezy and Aldo Rustichini conducted an experiment where subjects were given fifty questions from an IQ test. One group was instructed to do the best they could. Another was given 3¢ per correct answer. A third group was rewarded with 30¢ per correct answer and a fourth was paid 90¢ per correct answer. As you may have guessed, the two groups receiving 30¢ and 90¢ both outperformed the ones with no bonus — on average, they got 34 questions right compared to 28. The surprise was that the group receiving the 3¢ payment did the worst of all, getting only 23 right on average. Once money enters the equation, it becomes the main motivation, and 3¢ was just too little. It may also have conveyed that the task wasn't very important. Thus Gneezy and Rustichini conclude that you should offer significant financial rewards or none at all.

⬇

Money as a motivation doesn't necessarily play a ____(A)____ role in yielding results; paying a little can be ____(B)____ than paying nothing at all.

	(A)		(B)
①	trivial	⋯⋯	easier
②	limited	⋯⋯	poorer
③	significant	⋯⋯	cheaper
④	decisive	⋯⋯	better
⑤	proportional	⋯⋯	worse

다음 글을 읽고, 물음에 답하시오.

In a recent study, Professor Deborah Tannen of Georgetown University asked students in her class to tape-record conversations between women friends and men friends. It was easy to get recordings of women friends talking, partly because most of the students were women, but also because the request to "record a conversation with your friend" met with easy (a) compliance from the students' female friends and family members. But asking men to record conversations with their friends had mixed results. One woman's mother agreed readily, but her father insisted that he didn't have conversations with his friends. "Don't you ever call Fred on the phone?" she asked, naming a man she knew to be his good friend. "Not often," he said. "But if I do, it's because I have something to ask, and when I get the answer, I hang up."

Another woman's husband delivered a tape to her with great satisfaction and pride. "This is a good conversation," he announced, "because it's not just him and me making small talk, like 'Hi, how are you? I saw a good movie the other day,' and stuff. It's a problem-solving task. Each line is (b) meaningful." When the woman listened to the tape, she heard her husband and his friend trying to solve a computer problem. Everything they said was technical and (c) factual. Not only did she not consider it "a good conversation," but she didn't really regard it as a conversation at all. His idea of a good conversation was one with task-focused content. Hers was one with (d) impersonal content. These differences also showed up in relations between parents and children. Deborah Tannen's students told her that when they talked to "their parents" on the phone, they spent most of the time talking to their mothers. Their fathers typically joined the conversation only when they had a business matter to discuss or report. This happened since they believed talk is designed to convey (e) information.

41 ◆ 윗글의 제목으로 가장 적절한 것은?

① How to Improve Communication Between Men and Women

② Women, Men, and Type of Talk: What Makes the Difference?

③ Gender Communication Differences: Rapport-Talk vs. Report-Talk

④ Gender Differences in Language: Who Talks More, Women or Men?

⑤ Differences in Gesture Use by Men and Women in Verbal Interaction

42 ◆ 밑줄 친 (a) ~ (e) 중에서 문맥상 낱말의 쓰임이 적절하지 <u>않은</u> 것은?

① (a)　　　② (b)　　　③ (c)　　　④ (d)　　　⑤ (e)

31

다음 빈칸에 들어갈 말로 가장 적절한 것을 고르시오.

People have always noticed that works of art affect them, and have variously explained, classified, evaluated, justified, regulated, and enjoyed this phenomenon. Whereas Plato banned poets from his republic in order to restrict influences upon the citizenry, Aristotle formulated his theory of catharsis to legitimate the effects of art upon persons. Noting that drama consistently produces in audiences certain effects — fear, pity, admiration, awe, superiority, affinity, belief, skepticism, compassion, and relief — Aristotle identified these responses as official aims of art. Since the late seventeenth century, when mass print culture provided greater numbers of persons with the regular affective experience of literature, the novel became another focal point in the ongoing debate and discourse about the effects of representation. Even more than drama and poetry, the novel seemed to demand the reader's _____.

① patience   ② attention   ③ sentiments
④ engagement   ⑤ expectations

PLUS+
변형문제

윗글의 제목으로 가장 적절한 것은?

① The Most Effective Motivation to Read
② Aristotle's Theory of How Catharsis Works
③ The Impact of Literature: Emotion Triggers
④ The Functions of Literature in the Historical View
⑤ Lack of Representing Reality in Traditional Literature

32 ◆

다음 빈칸에 들어갈 말로 가장 적절한 것을 고르시오.

Natural selection, a process in which an organism adapts to its environment by means of selectively reproducing changes in its genotype, _____ _____. Our current adaptations are "designed" to work well in past environments: Those who had more offspring in past environments tended to pass their traits on to current generations. If the environment stays relatively constant, then those traits will function well in the current environment. However, if the environment has changed recently, then traits which were once adaptive may no longer be adaptive. This idea is known as "evolutionary lag" or "mismatch," because the changes in genes lag slightly behind the changes in environments. The classic example of evolutionary lag is our preferences for sweets, salts, and fats: it was adaptive to crave these when they were rare, because they were valuable sources of energy and nutrients. People still crave them even though they are overabundant in modern environments and lead to obesity and other health problems.

*genotype: 유전자형

① leads to complexity
② does not plan ahead
③ directs genetic changes
④ works for all organisms
⑤ controls evolutionary mechanisms

PLUS +
변형문제

윗글의 주제로 가장 적절한 것은?

① factors that affect the rates of adaptation
② role of natural selection in human evolution
③ reasons why humans become non-adaptive
④ importance of keeping up with environmental change
⑤ misconceptions about natural selection and adaptation

33

◆ 다음 빈칸에 들어갈 말로 가장 적절한 것을 고르시오.

You might first come up with advanced technology in the classroom when asked, "What is the most influential factor in teaching and learning?" However, there is no greater influence in the teaching and learning process than _____ _____. We live in an era shaped not by the rising and setting of the sun and moon, as in eons ago, but in an era when technology and a sense of urgency speed up everything we do. This cultural reality slips into early care and education programs with policies and mandates that fragment our time into little boxes on a schedule. Teachers move children through the day as if they are cars on an assembly line. Neither the teachers nor the children are afforded time to ponder, wonder, and make meaning out of the day's activities. Some early childhood commercial curricula even market themselves proclaiming, "This lesson will only take five minutes of your day." You should question why that might be a good thing. If it's worth learning and adding to your program, doesn't it deserve more time? What about the learning that comes from really slowing down and paying attention to what you are undertaking?

① how time is viewed and used

② content structure of the course

③ personal motivation for the subject

④ classrooms with appropriate facilities

⑤ how the teachers interact with students

PLUS +
변형문제

윗글의 제목으로 가장 적절한 것은?

① How to Adapt to Fast-Changing Education

② Grow the Ability to Discern Good Curricula

③ Don't Be Too Fast in Teaching and Learning

④ Time-Consuming Learning Is Worthless to Do

⑤ The Faster the Learner, the Better Understanding

34 ◆

다음 빈칸에 들어갈 말로 가장 적절한 것을 고르시오.

Among the monkeys and apes there is some evidence of abstract thinking. But it is only with man that artifacts and abstraction have run free. With his weak body, he has dramatically externalized his behavior, scattering the surface of the globe with his artifacts — his implements, machines, weapons, vehicles, roads, works of art, buildings, villages and cities. He has become a thinking, building animal, surrounded by everything he built. One might almost suppose that simple animal action would be beneath him, surviving only as a remnant from the past. But this is not so. Throughout it all, he has remained a creature of action, a gesturing, posturing, moving, expressive primate. He is as far today from becoming a creation of science fiction as he was in prehistoric times. Philosophy and engineering have not replaced animal activity, but they have added to it. We have developed a concept of happiness and words to express it, but we also still perform the action-pattern of stretching our lips into a smile.

_____ .

*remnant: 잔존물, 유물

① You don't have to swing hard to hit a home run
② The water does not flow until the faucet is turned on
③ While one door seems to be closing, another is opening
④ We do not have to reinvent the wheel with each generation
⑤ The fact that we have boats doesn't stop us from swimming

PLUS⁺
변형문제

윗글의 제목으로 가장 적절한 것은?

① We Are Still Creatures of Action
② How to Externalize Human Behavior
③ Smiling: Distinct Action-Pattern of Man
④ Artifacts: The Result of Human's Activity
⑤ What Makes Humans Far Beyond Animals

다음 글에서 전체 흐름과 관계 <u>없는</u> 문장은?

It's tempting to believe that we can trust the media with our kids, that we don't need to pay close attention to what movies or TV shows our kids are watching, what computer games they're playing, or where they're surfing on the Internet. It's much easier to believe that we can trust the media. ① After all, we're only adding more work and more worry to our lives if we admit that we now need to be as wary of the media as we are of strangers approaching our children on the street. ② As a result, many parents are in a state of "media denial," while others feel overwhelmed and helpless. ③ This means that social media is sometimes like a wild animal, and that the range of influences on children's cognitive and social learning has broadened. ④ But the fact is, we need to take as much responsibility for our children's media consumption as we do for their performance in school and their physical well-being. ⑤ If we're worried about what our kids eat, then we should certainly be worried about what our kids are watching.

*wary of: ~을 조심하는

PLUS +
변형문제

윗글에서 필자의 주장으로 가장 적절한 것은?

① 부모는 자녀와 신뢰 관계를 구축해야 한다.
② 부모는 자녀의 미디어 사용에 관여해야 한다.
③ 부모는 자녀의 미디어 노출 시간을 줄여야 한다.
④ 부모는 자녀 앞에서 미디어 이용을 자제해야 한다.
⑤ 부모는 자녀의 소셜 미디어 활동에 간섭하지 말아야 한다.

36 ◆ 주어진 글 다음에 이어질 글의 순서로 가장 적절한 것을 고르시오.

> Beech trees and oak trees register pain as soon as some creature starts nibbling on them. When a caterpillar takes a hearty bite out of a leaf, the tissue around the site of the damage changes.

(A) If the roots find themselves in trouble, this information is broadcast throughout the tree, which can trigger the leaves to release scent compounds. And those are not just any old scent compounds, but ones that are specifically formulated for the task at hand.

(B) Accordingly, it takes an hour or so before defensive compounds reach the leaves to spoil the pest's meal. Trees live their lives in the really slow lane, even when they are in danger. But this slow tempo doesn't mean that a tree is not on top of what is happening in different parts of its structure.

(C) In addition, it sends out electrical signals, just as human tissue does when it is hurt. However, the signal is not transmitted in milliseconds, as human signals are; instead, the plant signal travels at the slow speed of a third of an inch per minute.

① (A) – (C) – (B)　　　　　② (B) – (A) – (C)

③ (B) – (C) – (A)　　　　　④ (C) – (A) – (B)

⑤ (C) – (B) – (A)

PLUS +
변형문제

윗글의 요지로 가장 적절한 것은?

① 나무의 방어 속도는 느리지만 효과가 있다.
② 어떤 나무는 특히 느린 방어 속도를 갖는다.
③ 나무의 방어 속도는 고통이 클수록 빨라진다.
④ 나무는 향기 화합물을 방출하여 적을 물리친다.
⑤ 나무의 전기 신호는 인간의 신호만큼 강하지 않다.

주어진 글 다음에 이어질 글의 순서로 가장 적절한 것을 고르시오.

As Charles Darwin points out, species diversity can increase the productivity of ecosystems due to the division of labour among species, because each species is unique in how it exploits its environment.

(A) A large number of species may imply a certain level of functional redundancy: the loss of one species has a smaller effect in a diverse system than in a species-poor one. Diversity within one population of the same species may also improve resistance to environmental change.

(B) It thus follows that species-rich systems can exploit resources more efficiently than species-poor systems. Diversity is also thought to make ecosystems, species and populations more resilient to environmental stresses.

(C) For example, it is well documented that the diversity of a population can increase its resistance to epidemics. Diversity could also favor the emergence of complex collective behaviors, as demonstrated by the cooperative behavior in army ants, which self-assemble to form bridges and even nests out of their own bodies.

① (A) – (C) – (B)　　　　　② (B) – (A) – (C)
③ (B) – (C) – (A)　　　　　④ (C) – (A) – (B)
⑤ (C) – (B) – (A)

PLUS +
변형문제

윗글의 요지로 가장 적절한 것은?

① 같은 종 내에서의 다양성은 생존력을 높여준다.
② 노동의 분업이 종 다양성을 촉진시키는 주요 원인이다.
③ 환경 변화에 대한 대비책으로 종 다양화를 이뤄야 한다.
④ 종 다양성은 생태계의 생산성 향상을 포함한 여러 이점이 있다.
⑤ 종 다양성을 가진 생태계에서 한 종의 멸종의 영향은 치명적이다.

38 ◆

글의 흐름으로 보아, 주어진 문장이 들어가기에 가장 적절한 곳을 고르시오.

> But in recent decades, China, India, and Russia have joined the global workforce and now sell the sorts of advanced products Americans long thought were invulnerable to such competition.

To economists, the benefits of both exports and imports are so obvious that it's one of the few things this notoriously fractious profession agrees on. (①) Yet, in recent years, trade has changed radically, rattling even normally faithful supporters. (②) Traditionally, Americans bought toys, clothing, and other things from poor countries that required more manual and less intellectual labor. (③) They bought more advanced products like aircraft, software, and microprocessor chips from other rich countries. (④) The decrease in the cost of using huge quantities of data across undersea cables in other countries makes it possible for foreigners to read Americans' X-rays, take their hotel reservations, or report on town council meetings. (⑤) Alan Blinder, a former vice-chairman of the Federal Reserve Board, has estimated that perhaps a quarter of U.S. jobs can now be done abroad.

PLUS+
변형문제

윗글의 제목으로 가장 적절한 것은?

① Trends in Global Trade and Prospects for the Near Future
② How Shifts in International Trade Have Hurt the US Economy
③ The Spread of Advanced Technology: An International Trend
④ Breakthroughs in Competition: Removing Traditional Thought
⑤ The Monopoly of Developed Countries' Intellectual Commodities

39

> A painting of a rose, by a name other than the one it has, might very well smell different, aesthetically speaking.

"What's in a name? That which we call a rose, by any other name would smell as sweet." This thought of Shakespeare's points up a difference between roses and, say, paintings. Natural objects, such as roses, are not interpreted. (①) They are not taken as vehicles of meanings and messages. (②) They belong to no tradition, strictly speaking have no style, and are not understood within a framework of culture and convention. (③) Rather, they are sensed and savored relatively directly, without intellectual mediation, and so what they are called, either individually or collectively, has little bearing on our experience of them. (④) What a work of art is titled, on the other hand, has a significant effect on the aesthetic face it presents and on the qualities we correctly perceive in it. (⑤) The painting titled *Rose of Summer* and an indiscernible painting titled *Vermillion Womanhood* are physically, but also semantically and aesthetically, distinct objects of art.

*savor: 음미하다 **semantically: 의미적으로

PLUS +
변형문제

윗글의 주제로 가장 적절한 것은?

① ways to intuitively appreciate a work of art
② the importance of grasping the essence of things
③ reasons why paintings can't keep up with natural objects
④ common misunderstandings of interpretations and intentions
⑤ impacts of names in understanding artworks and natural objects

40 ◆ 다음 글의 내용을 한 문장으로 요약하고자 한다. 빈칸 (A), (B)에 들어갈 말로 가장 적절한 것은?

What a woman might see as a simple request — no big deal — is seen by a man an attempt to manipulate him into a "one-down" position. These traits can lead women and men to starkly different views of the same situation. Here is an example. When John's old high school friend called him at work to say he'd be in town, John invited him to stay for the weekend. That evening he told Linda they were having a house guest. Linda was upset. How could John make these plans without discussing them with her beforehand? She would never do that to him. "Why don't you tell your friend you have to check with your wife?" she asked. John replied, "I can't tell my friend, 'I have to ask my wife for permission'!" To John, checking with his wife would mean he was not free to act on his own. It would make him feel like a child or an underling. But Linda actually enjoys telling someone, "I have to check with John." It makes her feel good to show that her life is intertwined with her husband's.

Since women often think in terms of consensus, they struggle to preserve _____(A)_____, when men, concerned with status, focus on _____(B)_____.

	(A)		(B)
①	rights	⋯⋯	dignity
②	closeness	⋯⋯	confirmation
③	intimacy	⋯⋯	independence
④	courtesy	⋯⋯	control
⑤	mutuality	⋯⋯	competition

다음 글을 읽고, 물음에 답하시오.

Faces are an unusual class of patterns because they all share the same basic structure of two eyes, a nose and a mouth. Yet despite the (a) <u>similarity</u>, the average human can recognize thousands of separate faces. Our love of faces begins very early. Infants have built-in brain circuitry for following faces. Even though their vision is bad enough to qualify them as legally blind, faces are like (b) <u>magnets</u> to young babies. They can hardly take their eyes off a human face even if it is just a rudimentary pattern made up of two dots for eyes and a third for a mouth. This initial preference for face-like patterns is quickly replaced by a system that learns to recognize specific faces. By six months, if you show infants a face they have never seen before, they easily remember it much later. They are learning who's who.

Early face experience also (c) <u>shapes</u> human brains. For example, children born with cataracts never see faces clearly as infants. When their vision is surgically corrected later in life, they still have problems with recognizing faces even though they can then see clearly. No matter how much training and practice you have later in life, some early exposures are important for affecting brain development. The same goes for telling the difference between individuals from another race. Unlike most adults who think members of other ethnic groups look very similar, babies initially have no problem. They can tell everyone apart. It is only after exposure to lots of faces from the same race that our (d) <u>discrimination</u> kicks in. However, you can train babies not to become tuned into their own race if you keep exposing them to faces from other races. So the next time you think that other races all look alike, don't worry, it isn't racism — it's your (e) <u>excess</u> of brain flexibility.

*cataract: 백내장

41 ◆ 윗글의 제목으로 가장 적절한 것은?

① How Infants Learn from Facial Expressions
② Effects of Early Experiences on Personalities
③ Roles of Early Experiences on Face Recognition
④ Individual Differences in Infants' Face Processing
⑤ Brain Development and Facial Patterns in Infants

42 ◆ 밑줄 친 (a) ~ (e) 중에서 문맥상 낱말의 쓰임이 적절하지 <u>않은</u> 것은?

① (a)　　　② (b)　　　③ (c)　　　④ (d)　　　⑤ (e)

31 ◆

다음 빈칸에 들어갈 말로 가장 적절한 것을 고르시오.

Since birds consume up to 65 percent of a year's seed production and squirrels and mice take care of a good part of the rest, it is not surprising that fewer than one-tenth of 1 percent of Douglas-fir seeds survive where they fall to become new trees. Seed production is one way trees attempt to compensate for such huge losses. Douglas-fir seed production is trifling compared with that of some flowering plants — a single capsule of some orchids, for example, can contain up to 4 million seeds and has a much lower rate of success than a Douglas-fir. Medieval philosophers such as Saint Thomas Aquinas, attempting to make a synthesis of reason and faith, saw in this seed production evidence of the Creator's grand design. Nature was "God's work" and _____ was seen both as a sign of God's will and as the result of a natural cause.

*Douglas-fir: ((나무 이름)) 미송(美松)

① conformity   ② asymmetry   ③ predictability
④ underestimation   ⑤ overabundance

PLUS +
변형문제

윗글의 제목으로 가장 적절한 것은?

① The Philosophical Doctrine about Nature
② How to Increase Plants' Seed Production
③ Nature's Failure at Successful Proliferation
④ Natural Causes Leading to Overproduction
⑤ Balanced Production of Plants and Their Predators

32 ◆

다음 빈칸에 들어갈 말로 가장 적절한 것을 고르시오.

In marketing, the term strategic thinking is thrown around with abandon. It's a very general term that really only takes on meaning when applied to a specific situation. As a general proposition, the term is quite vague. As a specific application, it can be indispensable. Much the same is true of practice. Practicing to become faster has benefits, no doubt, but those benefits may not apply to every situation. Being fast in football is not necessarily the same as being fast at a track meet. In football, the application of "fast" likely includes knowing how to make sharp cuts while running, following routes, or avoiding being tackled. For a track runner, those skills are meaningless. He should take the best of his generally applicable skills and apply them to his training; in other words, _____. Without the application, his preparation isn't even halfway complete.

*cut: (미식축구에서) 공을 가진 선수가 순간적으로 방향을 전환하여 수비를 따돌리는 기술

① practice for the purpose
② attempt for the first time
③ set a realistic time frame
④ maximize personal strengths
⑤ integrate varied perspectives

PLUS +
변형문제

윗글의 요지로 가장 적절한 것은?

① 목적에 맞는 최적의 전략을 선택해야 한다.
② 성공을 위해 전략적 사고는 필수 불가결하다.
③ 지나친 전문화는 전략적 사고에 오히려 해가 된다.
④ 모든 운동 종목에는 빠르게 달리는 연습이 필수적이다.
⑤ 전략적 사고는 여러 방면에 걸쳐 일반적인 의미를 지닌다.

33 ◆

다음 빈칸에 들어갈 말로 가장 적절한 것을 고르시오.

Philosophers of science have repeatedly demonstrated that more than one theoretical construction can always be placed upon a given collection of data. History of science indicates that, particularly in the early developmental stages of a new paradigm, it is not even very difficult to invent such alternates. But that invention of alternates is just what scientists seldom undertake except during the pre-paradigm stage of their science's development and at very special occasions during its subsequent evolution. So long as the tools a paradigm supplies continue to prove capable of solving the problems it defines, science moves fastest and penetrates most deeply through confident employment of those tools. The reason is clear. As in manufacture so in science — retooling is an extravagance to be reserved for the occasion that demands it. The significance of crises is the indication they provide that _____.

① a given paradigm must be settled

② retooling is unnecessary in science

③ an occasion for retooling has arrived

④ a new method of discovery is avoidable

⑤ paradigms are inevitable aspects of science

PLUS+
변형문제

윗글의 주제로 가장 적절한 것은?

① reasons alternates are seldom made in science

② constant efforts to prove capability of retooling

③ various ways to demonstrate a paradigm's validity

④ necessity of regularly retooling scientific paradigms

⑤ differences between manufacture and science in crises

34 ◆

다음 빈칸에 들어갈 말로 가장 적절한 것을 고르시오.

People prefer to believe that the world is a just and fair place and that everyone gets what he or she deserves. And since people tend to think they themselves are deserving, they come to think that if they just do a good job and behave appropriately, things will take care of themselves. Moreover, when they observe others doing things they consider to be inappropriate, most people do not see anything to be learned, believing that even if those people are successful at the moment, in the end they will be brought down. This belief has a big negative effect on the ability to acquire power. It hinders people's ability to learn from all situations and all people, even those whom they don't like or respect. If you are in a position of modest power and want to attain a position of great power, you need to pay particular attention to those holding the positions you aspire to. As soon as you recognize the influence of this belief on your perceptions and _____, you will be able to learn more in every situation.

① discover that fairness is tied directly to your experiences
② abandon all power confining you to unrealistic expectations
③ try to combat the tendency to see the world as inherently fair
④ put effort into behaving appropriately to be in a higher position
⑤ acquire as much power as possible in as short a time as you can

PLUS +
변형문제

윗글의 요지로 가장 적절한 것은?

① Things help those who behave appropriately.
② Respect people in a higher position than you.
③ Try to be humble as you get a higher position.
④ Everyone has some quality you can learn from.
⑤ There is much power you can get without learning.

다음 글에서 전체 흐름과 관계 없는 문장은?

Most of us are limited in our linguistic fluency. While we may have some acquaintance with languages other than our native tongue, few would claim mastery of more than a handful of the world's languages. ① But, through art, we have before us an avenue for understanding and appreciating the extraordinary diversity of thoughts, feelings, and cultures in the world. ② Taken together, the visual arts and music of a culture, which are not tied as directly to narrative and, therefore, to language as literature and theater, comprise an integrated cultural style that is accessible to the outsider. ③ Another basis for claiming that there are universal dimensions of aesthetic appreciation is 'to treat a cultural production as art.' ④ There is a potential for cross-cultural understanding and appreciation inherent in each culture's artistic expression. ⑤ While the key elements of a culture can be understood intuitively through its arts, a more structured understanding of the major themes of artistic expression can help add depth and order to this understanding.

PLUS+
변형문제

윗글의 주제로 가장 적절한 것은?

① importance of nurturing art appreciation in youth
② benefits of exploring visual arts from different cultures
③ ways to understand and interpret art in various cultures
④ necessity of unified perspectives in art appreciation
⑤ functions of art in muticultural understanding

36 ◆ 주어진 글 다음에 이어질 글의 순서로 가장 적절한 것을 고르시오.

Wolves disappeared from Yellowstone, the world's first national park, in the 1920s. When they left, the entire ecosystem changed. Elks, a type of large deer, in the park increased their numbers and began to make quite a meal of the aspens, willows, and cottonwoods that lined the streams.

(A) This, in turn, created space for semiaquatic animals such as beavers to return, and these industrious builders could now find the materials they needed to construct their lodges and raise their families.

(B) This space allowed animals that depended on the meadows near streams to come back, as well. The wolves turned out to be better stewards of the land than people, creating conditions that allowed the trees to grow and exert their influence on the landscape.

(C) Vegetation declined and animals that depended on the trees left. When the wolves returned, the elks' languorous browsing days were over, and the roots of cottonwoods and willows once again stabilized stream banks and slowed the flow of water.

*languorous: 나른한

① (A) – (C) – (B)
② (B) – (A) – (C)
③ (B) – (C) – (A)
④ (C) – (A) – (B)
⑤ (C) – (B) – (A)

PLUS+
변형문제

윗글의 제목으로 가장 적절한 것은?

① Nature's Splendor is Coming Back One by One
② Nature's Brilliant Ability to Recover from Disasters
③ A Variety of Trees for Species Diversity nearby Streams
④ Who Should Be Considered the Best Guardian of the Meadow?
⑤ Role of Vegetation in Making an Agreeable Living Environment

주어진 글 다음에 이어질 글의 순서로 가장 적절한 것을 고르시오.

> The measure of velocity, and subsequent acceleration, is one of the most important measures in sport because this variable is very useful for determining whether an athlete's current performance is better than a previous performance, or if it is better or worse than the opposition's.

(A) By measuring the speed of the smaller intervals within this length, coaches can identify "where" an athlete is running fast and where she is slowing down. Once the velocity has been calculated, the acceleration can be determined; and often in sport, acceleration, the rate of change in velocity, is what separates an athlete from an elite athlete.

(B) To calculate the direction and the speed at which someone is traveling, we need to accurately measure the distance and the time. Tests to measure this, such as 30m sprint drills, are often used in sport as part of an athlete's training.

(C) From this new information, the coach can devise specific training for each individual athlete. For example, if it is known that an athlete has a velocity over 30m, technique and strength training can be developed that appropriately match it.

① (A) – (C) – (B)　　　　② (B) – (A) – (C)
③ (B) – (C) – (A)　　　　④ (C) – (A) – (B)
⑤ (C) – (B) – (A)

PLUS⁺
변형문제

윗글의 요지로 가장 적절한 것은?

① 엘리트 선수에게 가속보다 정교한 기술이 요구된다.
② 측정 장비의 발달로 속도 측정의 정확성은 향상되었다.
③ 속도와 가속도는 선수별 맞춤 훈련 개발에 중요한 요소이다.
④ 선수의 실력 향상은 이전과 현재의 속도를 비교하여 이뤄진다.
⑤ 속도를 정확히 측정하기 위해 거리와 시간이 제공되어야 한다.

38

글의 흐름으로 보아, 주어진 문장이 들어가기에 가장 적절한 곳을 고르시오.

> It does this without accounting for the effects of refraction, so the object's appearance is distorted.

When an underwater object is seen from outside the water, its appearance becomes distorted. This is because refraction changes the direction of the light rays that come from the object. (①) When these rays enter the eyes of an observer, nerves in the eyes send signals to the observer's brain. (②) The brain then constructs a picture based on where the rays appear to have come from. (③) When one looks at a straw in a glass of water, light rays from the part of the straw that is underwater refract at the surfaces between the water and the glass and between the glass and the air. (④) The rays appear to come from closer to the surface than they are, and the straw looks bent. (⑤) If the straw were viewed from underwater, the part above water would be distorted.

*refraction: 굴절

PLUS +
변형문제

윗글의 제목으로 가장 적절한 것은?

① How Light Rays Leave the Water and Enter the Air
② How Accurately The Optic Nerves Transmit Information
③ An Explanation of Why Things Seem to Bend in Water
④ A Smart Human Brain Considers the Effects of Refraction
⑤ Distortion: The Dangers of Not Seeing Things as They Are

39 ◆

글의 흐름으로 보아, 주어진 문장이 들어가기에 가장 적절한 곳을 고르시오.

> These changes in energy expenditure are great and help to explain why it is so difficult for an obese person to maintain weight losses.

One popular theory of why people can maintain their body weight at a relatively stable level is the set-point theory. (①) The set-point theory proposes that body weight, like body temperature, is physiologically regulated. (②) Researchers have noted that many people who lose weight on reducing diets quickly regain all their lost weight. (③) This suggests that somehow the body chooses a weight that it wants to be and defends that weight by regulating eating behaviors and hormonal actions. (④) Research confirms that the body adjusts its metabolism whenever it gains or loses weight — in the direction that returns to the initial body weight: the body burns more calories with weight gain and burns fewer calories with weight loss. (⑤) An individual's set point for body weight may be adjustable, shifting over the life span in response to physiological changes and to genetic, dietary, and other factors.

PLUS⁺
변형문제

다음 글의 요지로 가장 적절한 것은?

① 체중 감량의 가능성은 신진대사에 달려 있다.
② 체중은 식단을 개선함으로써 가장 크게 줄어든다.
③ 신체는 체중 증가 시 더 많은 칼로리를 소모한다.
④ 몸무게는 원래의 몸무게로 돌아가려는 성질이 있다.
⑤ 신체가 유지하려고 하는 몸무게를 파악하는 것이 중요하다.

40 ◆ 다음 글의 내용을 한 문장으로 요약하고자 한다. 빈칸 (A), (B)에 들어갈 말로 가장 적절한 것은?

Suppose that a school administrator argues, "Let's cut out the pledge of allegiance each morning. We'll be able to save two minutes a day. That's ten minutes a week. That'll be nearly an entire extra day by the end of the year." Such computation is true on paper only. The extra two minutes a day are, in fact, less effective in achieving your goal than one single day, and even potentially harmful to your morale. A variation of this fallacy also occurs when people try to redistribute something, claiming that "as long as it all comes out the same in the end, everything will be fine." An administrator says to a football coach, "You will not be able to have ninety minutes a day, Monday through Thursday, for football practice. However, don't worry: You won't lose anything. You can have from noon until six P.M. on Fridays." The problem here is that a football team needs time each day; its improvement is cumulative. The administrator has fallaciously presumed that six hours is six hours, no matter how it is distributed, that a team can get the same results from one six-hour session as from four ninety-minute sessions. The administrator has ignored the fact that after a while the long practice will become unproductive.

⬇

The assumption that a small amount over time is _____(A)_____ in value compared to the full amount of time is a fallacy, because it does not consider the effect of _____(B)_____ returns.

	(A)		(B)
①	larger	‥‥‥	expected
②	equivalent	‥‥‥	diminishing
③	differentiated	‥‥‥	indirect
④	similar	‥‥‥	flexible
⑤	lower	‥‥‥	increasing

다음 글을 읽고, 물음에 답하시오.

We can't choose our families, but we can certainly choose whom we spend our free time with. We should be (a) selective in the people we associate with. It becomes clear that we must choose our friends wisely. This allows us to reinforce the same dynamic — the influence that those close to us have on our decisions — in a positive direction. Our brains, it seems, see others the same way they see ourselves. This provides a clear explanation for why behavior can be so (b) contagious. When others do something, we literally feel ourselves engaging in it, and manifest the urge to do it, too.

In many cases, social pressure drives behavior. We know of the examples of teens doing dumb things because of peer pressure. But it can be a positive influence as well. As adults, we like to think that we are no longer as easily (c) swayed by peer behaviors, but we are still undoubtedly influenced in one way or another by the people surrounding us. Social pressure is commonly utilized by organizations such as sports teams and the military. People feel a sense of loyalty to their teammates and don't want to hold them back, so they give (d) minimum effort. A deeply felt sense of loyalty can be a powerful source of self-discipline. Armed with this insight, what can we do to improve our lives? We need to fill our networks with people that we admire and whom we look up to. The benefits this will provide for us go beyond improving our own self-discipline; it will ultimately (e) enhance our emotional health and quality of life.

41 ◆ 윗글의 제목으로 가장 적절한 것은?

① Reasons to Expand Your Network

② Social Network: A Driving Force of Life

③ How Do Friends Influence Your Decisions?

④ Who's in Your Circle? Invest in Your Network!

⑤ Circle of Influence, How Can You Make Friends?

42 ◆ 밑줄 친 (a) ~ (e) 중에서 문맥상 낱말의 쓰임이 적절하지 <u>않은</u> 것은?

① (a)   ② (b)   ③ (c)   ④ (d)   ⑤ (e)

31

다음 빈칸에 들어갈 말로 가장 적절한 것을 고르시오.

Traditional logic and metaphysics are themselves in no better position to understand and solve the riddle of man. Rational, logical and metaphysical thought can comprehend only those objects which have a consistent nature and truth. It is, however, just this homogeneity which we never find in man. The philosopher is not permitted to construct an artificial man; he must describe a real one. All the so-called definitions of man are nothing but airy speculation so long as they are not based upon and confirmed by our experience of man. There is no other way to know man than to understand his life and conduct. But what we find here defies every attempt at inclusion within a single and simple formula. _____ is the very element of human existence. Man has no "nature" — no simple or homogeneous being. He is a strange mixture of being and nonbeing. His place is between these two opposite poles.

*homogeneity: 동질성

① Unity　　　　　② Fragility　　　　　③ Continuity
④ Adaptability　　⑤ Inconsistency

PLUS+
변형문제

윗글의 제목으로 가장 적절한 것은?

① What Philosophers Seek to Explain Man
② Humans Stand between Life and Conduct
③ The Key to Understanding Human Nature
④ Inevitable Fate of a Real Man: Consistency
⑤ Making an Artificial Man Through Philosophy

32 ◆

Draw a circle on a piece of paper, but leave a small gap such that the circle is not all the way closed. Now stare at it for a couple minutes and notice what happens. For some people the urge to close it is so strong that they'll eventually pick up the pencil and draw it closed. The same dynamic can be applied to stop procrastination from ruining your life. The trick is simply to start whatever project is front of you — just start anywhere. Psychologists call this the Zeigarnik effect, named for the Russian psychologist who first documented the finding that when someone is faced with an overwhelming goal and is procrastinating as a result, getting started anywhere will _____.

When you start a project — even if you begin with the smallest, simplest part — you begin drawing the circle. Then you'll move on to another part (draw more of the circle), and another (more circle), and so forth. The Zeigarnik effect reveals that incompleteness represents instability to our brain.

① limit the desire of completing urgent tasks

② generate a new goal that sparks inspiration

③ launch motivation to finish what was started

④ lead to a heightened sense of procrastination

⑤ intensify the need to start from the beginning

PLUS⁺
변형문제

윗글의 주제로 가장 적절한 것은?

① separating yourself from a tedious project

② defeating procrastination by beginning a task

③ coping with a difficult project by putting it off

④ role of procrastination in completing your work

⑤ increasing motivation by choosing the easiest duty

33

다음 빈칸에 들어갈 말로 가장 적절한 것을 고르시오.

In the old days, when aircraft routinely fell out of the sky because large and obvious components failed — the fuel pumps gave out or the engines exploded — it felt sensible to cast aside the claims of organized religions in favor of a trust in science. Rather than praying, the urgent task was to study the root causes of malfunctions and root out error through reason. But as aviation has become ever more subject to scrutiny, as every part has been equipped with backup systems, so, too, have the reasons for becoming superstitious paradoxically increased. The sheer remoteness of a catastrophic event occurring invites us to forgo scientific assurances in favor of a more humble stance towards the dangers which our feeble minds struggle to contain. While never going so far as to ignore maintenance schedules, we may nevertheless _____ to take a few moments before a journey to fall to our knees and pray to the mysterious forces of fate to which all aircraft remain subject and which we might as well call God.

① judge it far from unreasonable
② consider it thoroughly unacceptable
③ not think it necessary for us believers
④ regard it as a result of the forces of fate
⑤ take it from the inevitable power of God

PLUS +
변형문제

윗글의 제목으로 가장 적절한 것은?

① The Failure of Science Leads to Faith
② Is God Really the Existing Mysterious Force?
③ Science Is Not Enough to Fully Set Us at Ease
④ Scientific Assurance: A Long Distance to Go
⑤ How People Gain Religion After Disaster

34 ◆

07

다음 빈칸에 들어갈 말로 가장 적절한 것을 고르시오.

A good way to understand the story invention process is to observe it firsthand. Unfortunately, when people create a new story, we have difficulty knowing exactly how they found the various pieces of the story they are telling. We cannot easily know what has been invented out of thin air and what has been adapted from prior experiences or other stories. We can reasonably assume, however, that true creation can hardly exist with respect to stories. Every story we tell has to have _____. Of course, the better we are at telling stories, the better we are at giving them the appearance of being complete fiction. This can mean that even we as tellers see the story as fictional, not realizing the adaptation process that we ourselves have used. Even stories that are pure fantasy are adaptations of more realistic stories where certain constraints of the real world are relaxed.

① a purpose to make people believe what we're saying
② its basis in something that we have already experienced
③ a sequence of events that are not difficult for us to follow
④ a cluster of other stories, which echo across different contexts
⑤ some fictions that can facilitate listeners' interest and imagination

PLUS +
변형문제

윗글의 제목으로 가장 적절한 것은?

① Can Science Fiction Become Reality?
② Tips to Refuel Your Writing Inspiration
③ How We Tell Apart Fiction from Reality
④ Experience: The Roots of Story Invention
⑤ Adaptation: Make True Stories More Realistic

35 ◆

다음 글에서 전체 흐름과 관계 <u>없는</u> 문장은?

In a popular sense, "insect" usually refers to familiar pests or disease carriers, such as bedbugs, houseflies, clothes moths, Japanese beetles, mosquitoes and fleas, or to conspicuous groups, such as butterflies, moths, and beetles. ① Many insects, however, are beneficial from a human viewpoint; they pollinate plants, produce useful substances, control pest insects, act as scavengers, and serve as food for other animals. ② Furthermore, insects are valuable objects of study in elucidating many aspects of biology and ecology. ③ Much of the scientific knowledge of genetics has been gained from fruit fly experiments and of population biology from flour beetle studies. ④ Scientists familiar with insects realize the difficulty in attempting to estimate individual numbers of insects beyond areas of a few acres or a few square miles in extent. ⑤ Insects are also used as environmental quality indicators to assess water quality and soil contamination and are the basis of many studies of biodiversity.

*scavenger: (썩은 고기를 먹는) 동물

PLUS +
변형문제

윗글의 주제로 가장 적절한 것은?

① possibilities of utilizing pest insects in our everyday life
② roles of insects for humans as well as the environment
③ increasing awareness of the falling population of insects
④ coping with scientific puzzles by analyzing insects' traits
⑤ reasons for complex categorizations of particular insects

36

주어진 글 다음에 이어질 글의 순서로 가장 적절한 것을 고르시오.

Climate change is throwing up some tricky dilemmas for liberal-minded-people. The big problem is that climate change is a global problem that individuals don't seem to be able to solve.

(A) And yet, if they are taking such action to control it, then they are, inevitably, restricting someone's freedom to use it. This is why climate control measures are proving so slow to make progress and are so stuck in controversy.

(B) Since individuals and a free market have singularly failed, it's very clear that consensus and concerted official action are needed to make any headway. In other words, if we are to avoid potential disaster on a global scale, we have to accept that governments need to take control of measures to limit carbon emissions.

(C) Economists would say this inability is caused because people act in their own self-interest. Scientists are in no doubt about the vital and urgent need to cut emissions of greenhouse gases, which implies the necessity of institutional law enforcement.

① (A) – (C) – (B)   ② (B) – (A) – (C)
③ (B) – (C) – (A)   ④ (C) – (A) – (B)
⑤ (C) – (B) – (A)

PLUS +
변형문제

윗글의 주제로 가장 적절한 것은?

① the role of the market in limiting global carbon production
② the success scientists have had at controlling carbon emissions
③ why controlling climate change is a challenging issue worldwide
④ ways people and the market have negatively impacted the climate
⑤ potential methods of restricting the production of carbon emissions

> The flu can kill tens of millions of people, and unrelenting strains of tuberculosis and cholera continue to cause premature death among populations throughout the world. This means humans have little or no immunity to it, and everyone is at risk.

(A) Specifically, for people in good health and whose immune systems are functioning properly, the organisms are usually harmless. But in sick people or people with weakened immune systems, these normally harmless potentially disease-causing organisms can cause serious health problems.

(B) In spite of our best efforts to eradicate them, these health problems are a continuing menace to all of us. Just like there are only a few things which do not have both positives and negatives, however, the news isn't all bad.

(C) Even though we are bombarded by potentially disease-causing threats, our immune systems are remarkably adept at protecting us. However, this is not always the case. Microorganisms originating in the body live in peaceful coexistence with their human host most of the time.

*tuberculosis: (폐)결핵

① (A) – (C) – (B)　　　　② (B) – (A) – (C)

③ (B) – (C) – (A)　　　　④ (C) – (A) – (B)

⑤ (C) – (B) – (A)

PLUS +
변형문제

윗글의 주제로 가장 적절한 것은?

① symbiotic relationship of many diseases and microorganisms
② advantage of microorganisms in the body in affecting humans
③ unremarkable capability of our immune system to face diseases
④ ways to remove harmful organisms without weakening ourselves
⑤ role of a healthy immune system in preventing a health problem

38 ◆

글의 흐름으로 보아, 주어진 문장이 들어가기에 가장 적절한 곳을 고르시오.

> And yet, in practice, it's virtually impossible to calculate the shape from the sequence.

The shape of a protein is important. Many proteins do their jobs by binding to other proteins — sticking to them, usually temporarily, but in a controllable way. When the protein haemoglobin picks up or releases a molecule of oxygen, it changes shape. (①) A protein is a long chain of amino acids, and it gets its shape by folding up into a compact tangle. (②) The shape of this is principally determined by the sequence of amino acids. (③) The same sequence can fold up in a gigantic number of ways, and it is generally thought that the actual shape it chooses is the one with the least energy. (④) Finding this minimal energy shape, among the truly gigantic list of possibilities, is a bit like trying to rearrange some list of thousands of letters of the alphabet in the hope of getting a paragraph from Shakespeare. (⑤) Running through all the possibilities in turn is totally impractical: the lifetime of the universe is too short.

PLUS+
변형문제

윗글의 제목으로 가장 적절한 것은?

① How the Protein Gets Its Compact Shape
② Influence of Oxygen Molecules on Proteins
③ Discovery of the Century: The Form of the Protein
④ Can Amino Acid Sequences Indicate Protein Shape?
⑤ Calculate the Number of Proteins Before It's Too Late!

글의 흐름으로 보아, 주어진 문장이 들어가기에 가장 적절한 곳을 고르시오.

> All sorts of cultural and social factors are involved, and the issue has become so highly politicized, for both the left and right, that voters will embrace the positions of politicians with whom they are ideologically aligned.

Labour migration is an important facet of the development of markets. When countries industrialize, workers move from rural to urban areas, attracted by the higher wages offered by industrial enterprises. (①) A similar phenomenon happens internationally: huge numbers of migrants flowed to the New World during the 19th century and international migration has remained important ever since. (②) As with internal migration, economists stress the role of wage gaps between different countries in generating international migration: migrants flow from low-wage to high-wage countries. (③) Eventually one might see a levelling off, if wages begin to equalize across countries. (④) In practice, what is suggested by simple economic models implies that migration is an intricate phenomenon. (⑤) Nevertheless, basic knowledge of economics helps to remind us that labour migration is as much a part of the logic of globalization as the expansion of international markets for goods and finance.

PLUS +
변형문제

윗글의 주제로 가장 적절한 것은?

① major labour market forces that result in globalization
② effective labour migration management in a global context
③ the global balance of wages generated from migration abroad
④ the economic importance of labour migration on a global scale
⑤ the benefits of immigration overseas in the economy of a country

40

다음 글의 내용을 한 문장으로 요약하고자 한다. 빈칸 (A)와 (B)에 들어갈 말로 가장 적절한 것은?

Apparently, the restricted linguistic environment of one's native language does not inactivate unused perceptual mechanisms completely. Of course, we learn to listen primarily for the acoustic distinctions that correspond to phonemic contrasts in our own language. Given the right task or instructions, however, we can detect unfamiliar acoustic distinctions even though we do not perceive them as marking phonemic contrasts. Furthermore, with enough experience, the perception of non-native distinctions begins to operate at the phonemic level: after considerable experience with spoken English, native speakers of Japanese can distinguish the phonemes /r/ and /l/ categorically and almost as accurately as native English speakers. The fact that perceptual mechanisms available to us as infants can still operate after long disuse causes trouble for hypotheses that early experience with language permanently alters some of the mechanisms of speech perception.

↓

Although lack of _____(A)_____ to certain phonemes at an early age makes their recognition more difficult later, the ability to learn to identify them _____(B)_____ with age.

	(A)		(B)
①	accuracy	......	lasts
②	access	......	increases
③	connection	......	collapses
④	contact	......	endures
⑤	insight	......	changes

다음 글을 읽고, 물음에 답하시오.

For some people, there's so much sensory cross talk in the brain that using one sense can (a) simultaneously activate another. This is best seen in the phenomenon of synesthesia, a syndrome of overly connected sensory pathways. For example, some people have an auditory-visual connection in which hearing certain pitches causes them to see colors. And those associations are (b) consistent: one color associated with one sound. Others have reported having an olfactory-visual connection in which the scent of fresh lemons makes them picture angular shapes, while the smell of raspberry or vanilla brings to mind rounded shapes. There are many varieties of synesthesia, because there are many combinations of senses, but they all demonstrate the same insight: our sensory pathways are linked.

Our sensory systems are designed for (c) survival. Initially processed through parallel pathways, sensory signals are eventually integrated with each other, interpreted, and organized into a conceptual network. Our senses merge to create a singular, streamlined perception of the world. This (d) collaboration doesn't just enhance our conscious experience; it also creates a backup system in case one of our senses fails. When a person goes blind, the other sensory systems kick into gear, attempting to (e) widen the gap in perception. The brain does its utmost to rebuild our picture of the world, even by recreating one sense by combining others.

*synesthesia: 공감각 **olfactory: 후각의

41 ◆ 윗글의 제목으로 가장 적절한 것은?

① We Sense More Than We Can Perceive

② Open Up the Potential of the Five Senses

③ Senses: Interconnected to Overcome Barriers

④ There Are No Junctions in Sensory Pathways

⑤ Sense of Smell Triggers Emotional Memories

42 ◆ 밑줄 친 (a) ~ (e) 중에서 문맥상 낱말의 쓰임이 적절하지 <u>않은</u> 것은?

① (a)   ② (b)   ③ (c)   ④ (d)   ⑤ (e)

31 ◆

다음 빈칸에 들어갈 말로 가장 적절한 것을 고르시오.

An American naturalist suggested that the pink color of the flamingo was an adaptation so they would be less visible to predators against the setting sun. But in fact the pink color depends on their diet. If they eat a lot of shrimp they go brighter pink, if they don't eat a shrimp diet they go a paler pink. It would be very hard to argue that the pink color was a Darwinian adaptation to protect against predators rather than a consequence of the diet. That's one of the things that is actually an extremely important issue within biology: what's adaptive, what's not adaptive, what's accidental in some sort of ways. Some scientists would probably answer there has to be an evolutionarily adaptive explanation for it — something arose during evolution for other reasons or by accident and then got converted for current purposes. The point is that we need to be much more _____ to there being multiple explanations of what happens in nature. They cannot simply be reduced to the working out of the imperative of the selfish genes.

① defiant   ② discerning   ③ authentic
④ receptive   ⑤ aggressive

PLUS +
변형문제

윗글의 제목으로 가장 적절한 것은?

① Ways to Tell What Features Are Adaptive
② Why Nature Evolved to Have Selfish Genes
③ The High Reliability of Darwinian Adaptation
④ Open Your Mind to All Explanations in Nature
⑤ What Decides between Accidental and Adaptive in Nature

32 ◆

다음 빈칸에 들어갈 말로 가장 적절한 것을 고르시오.

In 2013, Forbes magazine explored exactly how Warren Buffett attempts to avoid succumbing to confirmation bias, which causes people to interpret and recall information in a way that confirms their preexisting beliefs, and what this means to financial investors. It warned: "For investors, confirmation bias is particularly dangerous. Once an investor starts to like a company, for example, he may dismiss negative information as irrelevant or inaccurate." The same can be said for entrepreneurs or any businessperson. Explaining what it labeled the 'Buffett Approach,' Forbes described the 2013 annual general meeting for Berkshire Hathaway, a multinational conglomerate for which Buffett is the chief executive officer. Instead of inviting professional applauders, who would applaud at whatever Buffett said, he invited Doug Kass, a fund manager and constant critic of Buffett and Berkshire Hathaway, as a guest speaker. Forbes described this as "largely unprecedented" and applauded Buffett's simple act. Indeed, _____ _____ was one of the suggestions for fighting confirmation bias.

① creating a culture of challenge
② asking for a detailed refutation
③ admitting that you have a problem
④ identifying the flaws in the strategy
⑤ criticizing a fellow director's strategy

PLUS⁺
변형문제

윗글의 요지로 가장 적절한 것은?

① Everybody's business is nobody's business.
② A fish always stinks from the head downwards.
③ Keep your friends close, but your enemies closer.
④ The grass is greener on the other side of the fence.
⑤ Don't count your chickens before they are hatched.

◆ 다음 빈칸에 들어갈 말로 가장 적절한 것을 고르시오.

The term 'straw man' refers to a form of informal fallacy used in arguments and debates. A type of rhetorical device, straw man is based on ＿＿＿＿＿＿＿＿ ＿＿＿＿＿＿＿＿＿＿＿＿＿. The straw man argument is usually more absurd than the actual argument, making it an easier target to attack. For example, maybe you're arguing with a friend about global warming. You think the government should raise fuel efficiency standards to cut down the amount of CO_2 we release over the next 20 years. Your friend thinks cars have nothing to do with it, and as you argue, he says something like, "Our cities are built so that we have to drive cars. Your solution will kill the economy. How would people get to work without cars? It'll never work." He's responding to an extreme version of your proposal that's easier to shoot down than your real proposal. He's arguing against the extreme idea that we need to get rid of all cars because it's easier than arguing against the moderate idea that we need to raise fuel efficiency.

① appealing to authoritative figures in the field
② refuting an opponent's argument with evidence
③ exaggerating some portion of an opponent's stance
④ attacking the opponent rather than the argument itself
⑤ pointing out illogical aspects of an opponent's argument

PLUS+ 변형문제

윗글의 제목으로 가장 적절한 것은?

① How to Prevent Exaggeration in Arguments
② Successful Guides to Convincing Opponents
③ Be Careful, Your Opponent Is Saying a Fallacy!
④ Ways Not to Become the Straw Man in Arguments
⑤ Straw Man Argument: The Best Method in Debates

34

In one study, six-month-olds watched as a "climber," which was nothing more than a disk of wood with large eyes glued onto its circular "face," started at the bottom of a hill and repeatedly tried but failed to make its way to the top. After a while, a "helper," a triangle with similar eyes glued on, would sometimes approach from farther downhill and help the climber with an upward push. On other attempts, a square "hinderer" would approach from uphill and shove the circular disk back down. The experimenters wanted to know if the infants, uninvolved bystanders, would cop an attitude toward the hinderer square. When the experimenters gave the infants a chance to reach out and touch the figures, the infants showed a definite reluctance to reach for the hinderer square, as compared to the helper triangle. Moreover, when the experiment was repeated with either a helper and a neutral bystander block or a hinderer and a neutral block, the infants preferred the friendly triangle to the neutral block, and the neutral block to the nasty square. This study showed that infants as young as 6 months of age _____.

*cop an attitude: 부정적 태도를 보이다

① reveal an aversion or attraction to the specific shape
② recognize neutral attitudes impeding the goals of others
③ distinguish positive facial expressions from negative ones
④ are able to notice others' feeling through their expressions
⑤ evaluate others based on their social behavior toward third parties

PLUS+
변형문제

윗글의 제목으로 가장 적절한 것은?

① Infants' Acquired Preference for Round Figures
② The Effect of Shapes on Children's Thinking Skills
③ Neutrality: Why It Is Difficult for Infants to Understand
④ Infants Become Negative When Observing Certain Behaviors
⑤ How a Person Treats Others Affects Attitudes Towards That Person

다음 글에서 전체 흐름과 관계 없는 문장은?

In ancient Egypt a woman enjoyed the same rights as a man. What her rightful entitlement rights depended upon was her social class, not her sex. ① All property descended in the female line, on the assumption that maternity is a matter of fact; paternity a matter of opinion. ② When a man married an heiress, he enjoyed her property only so long as she lived, but on her death it passed to her daughter and daughter's husband. ③ Marriage in ancient Egypt was a totally private affair in which the state took no interest and of which the state kept no record. ④ A woman was entitled to administer her own property and dispose of it as she wished: She could buy, sell, be executor in wills and witness to legal documents, bring an action at court, and adopt children. ⑤ In comparison, an ancient Greek woman was supervised by a male guardian, and many Greek women living in Egypt during the Ptolemaic Period, observing Egyptian women acting without a male guardian, were encouraged to do so themselves.

PLUS +
변형문제

윗글의 주제로 가장 적절한 것은?

① gender discrimination in ancient Egyptian society
② aspects of power obtained by women in ancient Egypt
③ roles of women as a property owner in ancient Greece
④ beneficial effects of women playing a major role in society
⑤ differences in women's role in ancient and modern society

36

주어진 글 다음에 이어질 글의 순서로 가장 적절한 것을 고르시오.

Mathematics has been, is, and ever will be a current running almost unseen beneath the surface of our affairs. We should, however, be careful not to get carried away with the flow by attempting to extend its application beyond its remit.

(A) No code or equation will ever imitate the true complexities of the human condition. Nevertheless, a little mathematical knowledge in our increasingly quantitative society can help us to harness the power of numbers for ourselves.

(B) Simple rules allow us to make the best choices and avoid the worst mistakes. Small alterations in the way we think about our rapidly evolving environments help us to 'keep calm' in the face of rapidly accelerating change, or adapt to our increasingly automated realities.

(C) There are places where mathematics is completely the wrong tool for the job: activities in which human supervision is unquestionably necessary. Even if some of the most complex mental tasks can be farmed out to an algorithm, matters of the heart can never be broken down into a simple set of rules.

*remit: 소관

① (A) – (C) – (B)
② (B) – (A) – (C)
③ (B) – (C) – (A)
④ (C) – (A) – (B)
⑤ (C) – (B) – (A)

PLUS+
변형문제

윗글의 요지로 가장 적절한 것은?

① 일상생활 속에는 숨겨져 있는 수학적 원리가 많이 있다.
② 정보의 수량화는 오히려 합리적인 선택을 방해할 수 있다.
③ 수학으로 삶의 다양한 문제들을 쉽고 빠르게 해결할 수 있다.
④ 복잡한 인간의 정신은 알고리즘을 활용한 분석을 필요로 한다.
⑤ 수학을 아는 것은 도움이 되지만 모든 문제에 적용할 수는 없다.

주어진 글 다음에 이어질 글의 순서로 가장 적절한 것을 고르시오.

> Bad deflation occurs when spending collapses and companies have to cut their prices to prop up sales, just as hotels cut their rates when tourist traffic dries up. If people expect falling prices, they may delay purchases since their money will buy more later.

(A) If prices and wages are falling at the same rate, then, is anyone the worse for it? Paychecks have shrunk but because prices have as well, purchasing power remains the same.

(B) Employers must lay some workers off to cope with falling prices. Workers initially resist pay cuts, but eventually, fear of unemployment persuades them to accept lower pay.

(C) The problem is that debt is fixed as incomes and prices fall, so the burden of debt rises. Homeowners slash spending to keep up with their mortgage payments. Or worse, the home can't be sold for enough to repay the loan.

① (A) – (C) – (B)   ② (B) – (A) – (C)
③ (B) – (C) – (A)   ④ (C) – (A) – (B)
⑤ (C) – (B) – (A)

PLUS +
변형문제

윗글의 제목으로 가장 적절한 것은?

① Why Deflation Occurs and Price Levels Fluctuate
② Ways to Deal With Household Debt during Deflation
③ Deflation vs. Inflation, Which Is Worse to Employers?
④ What Consumers' Purchasing Behavior Drives Pricing
⑤ Causes and Effects of a Decrease in General Price Level

38 ◆

글의 흐름으로 보아, 주어진 문장이 들어가기에 가장 적절한 곳을 고르시오.

> Its companion is the green alga, a tiny unicellular plant, which lives within its tissues.

A coral reef is one of the most biologically diverse ecosystems on earth, rivaled only by tropical rain forests. (①) The environment of the coral reef is formed over thousands of years by the life cycle of vast numbers of coral animals. (②) The main architect of the reef is the stony coral, a relative of the sea anemone that lives in tropical climates and secretes a skeleton of almost pure calcium carbonate. (③) The organisms coexist in a mutually beneficial relationship, with the algae consuming carbon dioxide given off by the corals and the corals thriving in the abundant oxygen produced photosynthetically by the algae. (④) When the coral dies, its skeleton is left, and other organisms grow on top of it. (⑤) Over the years, the sheer mass of coral skeletons, together with those of associated organisms, combine to form the underwater forest that divers find so fascinating.

*sea anemone: 말미잘

PLUS +
변형문제

윗글의 제목으로 가장 적절한 것은?

① How Tropical Climates Help Coral Reefs Be Built
② Difficulties of Coexistence of Organisms in the Ocean
③ The Effective Role of Coral in Global Warming Reduction
④ Establishment of a Diverse Ecosystem in Ocean's Kingdom
⑤ Ocean's Complex Food Chain: From a Tiny Unicellular Plant

39 ◆ 글의 흐름으로 보아, 주어진 문장이 들어가기에 가장 적절한 곳을 고르시오.

> Furthermore, one must aggressively attack society to help liberate others, and purposefully lay oneself open to ridicule and abuse in order to retain this emotional detachment.

According to the Greek philosopher Diogenes, mastery of the self, or "self-sufficiency," leads to both happiness and freedom but requires constant practice and training in the face of adversity. (①) His uncompromising philosophy requires that one should abandon all property, possessions, family ties, and social values in order to minimize the distraction of "illusory" emotional and psychological attachments. (②) Though more radical and uncompromising, Diogenes' philosophy has its counterpart in the teachings of the oriental schools of Buddhism and Taoism. (③) However, critics complain that Diogenes' lifestyle is self-indulgent, relying on the generosity and productivity of others to support his drifting lifestyle. (④) There is a philosophical point here, not just a pragmatic one, concerning the universalizability of ethical rules for life. (⑤) If everyone were to follow Diogenes' example, society would collapse, making it economically impossible for anyone — including Diogenes — to concentrate on the mastery of the self.

*Taoism: 도교

PLUS+ 변형문제
윗글의 제목으로 가장 적절한 것은?

① How a Radical Philosophy Affects Oriental Religions
② Leaving Society Behind Reduces Social Connections
③ The Key to Self-Sufficiency in Diogenes's Philosophy
④ Diogenes's Philosophy Brings about Societal Destruction
⑤ Why Everyone Should Embrace Diogenes's Self-Indulgence

40 ◆ 다음 글의 내용을 한 문장으로 요약하고자 한다. 빈칸 (A)와 (B)에 들어갈 말로 가장 적절한 것은?

A few years ago, three Harvard researchers gave dozens of Asian American women at Harvard a difficult math test. But before getting them started, the researchers asked them to fill out a questionnaire about themselves. These Asian American women were members of two in-groups with conflicting norms: they were Asians, a group recognized as being good at math, and they were women, a group recognized as being poor at it. One set of participants received a questionnaire asking about what languages they, their parents, and grandparents spoke and how many generations of their family had lived in America. These questions were designed to trigger the women's connection to Asian Americans. Other subjects answered inquiries about coed dormitory policy, designed to trigger their connection to women. A third group, the control group, was quizzed about their phone and cable TV service. After the test, the researchers found that the women who had been manipulated to think of themselves as Asian Americans had done better on the test than did the control group, who, in turn, had done better than the women reminded of their female in-group.

*coed dormitory: (대학의) 남녀 공용 기숙사

⬇

According to the experiment, cueing a(n) _____(A)_____ that is stereotyped actually influenced the _____(B)_____ of members of the group to follow the stereotype.

	(A)		(B)
①	community	⋯⋯	behavior
②	personality	⋯⋯	evaluation
③	identity	⋯⋯	performance
④	psychology	⋯⋯	preference
⑤	status	⋯⋯	self-image

다음 글을 읽고, 물음에 답하시오.

The reason travels are mentally useful involves a unique characteristic of cognition, in which problems that feel 'close' — and the closeness can be physical, temporal or even emotional — get contemplated in a more concrete manner. As a result, when we think about things that are nearby, our thoughts are constricted, bound by a more (a) limited set of ideas. While this habit can be helpful — it allows us to focus on the facts at hand — it also (b) inhibits our imagination. Consider a field of corn. When you're standing in the middle of a farm, the air smelling faintly of fertilizer and popcorn, your mind is automatically drawn to thoughts related to the primary definition of corn, which is that it's a plant, a cereal, a staple of Midwestern farming. But imagine that same field of corn from a different perspective. Instead of standing on a farm, you're now in a crowded city street dense with taxis and pedestrians. The plant will no longer be just a plant; instead, your vast neural network will pump out all sorts of (c) associations. You'll think about unhealthy corn syrup, obesity, and the Farm Bill: you'll contemplate those corn mazes for kids at state fairs and the deliciousness of succotash made with bacon and beans. The noun is now a vast web of connections. And this is why travel is so open to (d) clarity: When you escape from the place you spend most of your time, the mind is suddenly made aware of all those unusual ideas previously suppressed. You start thinking about obscure possibilities — corn can fuel cars! — that never would have occurred to you if you'd stayed back on the farm. Furthermore, this (e) expansive kind of cognition comes with practical advantages, since you can suddenly draw on a whole new set of possible solutions.

*succotash: 옥수수 콩 요리

41 ◆ 윗글의 제목으로 가장 적절한 것은?

① Travel Can Help Squeeze Your Creative Juice
② Why Do We Travel? We're a Migratory Species
③ Solo Travel Leads to More Creative Problem Solving
④ Travel Changes Your View and Helps You Be Yourself
⑤ Want to Travel? It's About Taking Control of Your Life

08

42 ◆ 밑줄 친 (a) ~ (e) 중에서 문맥상 낱말의 쓰임이 적절하지 <u>않은</u> 것은?

① (a) ② (b) ③ (c) ④ (d) ⑤ (e)

31 ◆ 다음 빈칸에 들어갈 말로 가장 적절한 것을 고르시오.

Although resources and houses are both built over time, resource construction isn't like building construction — starting with one brick, putting another one on top of that one, and another one on top of that one. Building resources is more like being a currency broker, trading one resource for another depending on what you need and what the market demands, striving to come out ahead at the end of the day. Resources are, in large part, very _____. Much of what we do every day is to convert some resource — especially time or energy — into some other resource. Money can buy a bigger house, knowledge can translate into a better job, and time spent with friends builds "capital" in those friendships. Even social roles, such as that of child, can be converted into resources, such as money. Depending on what our needs and goals are, we organize our resources toward meeting those needs and reaching those goals, using resources in one area to build resources in another or using momentum in one area to overcome a roadblock in another.

① fluid   ② limited   ③ minute
④ feasible   ⑤ cumulative

PLUS +
변형문제

윗글의 제목으로 가장 적절한 것은?

① The Ultimate Goal of a Currency Broker
② Utilize Resources Flexibly to Reach Your Goal
③ Save Your Time, and Your Resources Increase
④ Is the Sum of Resources Bigger Than Its Parts?
⑤ The Quality of Resources: Ease of Organization

32

09

다음 빈칸에 들어갈 말로 가장 적절한 것을 고르시오.

Although convenient, _____ can lead to costly and catastrophic results. There is an example in *Alice's Adventures in Wonderland,* where Alice infers that, since she is floating in a body of water, a railway station, and thus help, must be close by: "Alice had been to the seaside once in her life, and had come to the conclusion, that wherever you go to on the English coast you find a number of bathing machines in the sea, some children digging in the sand with wooden spades, then a row of lodging houses, and behind them a railway station." In another example, it may be argued that an engineering assumption led to the explosion of the Ariane 5 rocket during its first test flight: The control software had been extensively tested with the previous model, Ariane 4 — but unfortunately these tests did not cover all the possible scenarios of the Ariane 5, so it was wrong to assume that the data would carry over. Signing off on such decisions typically comes down to engineers' and managers' ability to argue.

① selective attention
② irrelevant premises
③ accidental examples
④ hasty generalization
⑤ ambiguous definition

PLUS+
변형문제

윗글의 제목으로 가장 적절한 것은?

① A First Try Brings about a Series of Results
② Connect One Event to Another with Intuition
③ An Accidental Discovery Leads to Smart Solutions
④ Quick Logical Reasoning Can Spoil Desired Results
⑤ Equivocal Standards of Performance Tests in Engineering

33 ◆

다음 빈칸에 들어갈 말로 가장 적절한 것을 고르시오.

Research psychologists have rejected much of Freudian theory, but one idea Freudian therapists and experimental psychologists agree on today is that our ego fights fiercely to defend its honor. This agreement is a relatively recent development. For many decades, research psychologists thought of people as detached observers who assess events and then apply reason to discover truth and decipher the nature of the social world. We were said to gather data on ourselves and to build our self-images based on generally good and accurate inferences. In that traditional view, a well-adjusted person was thought to be like a scientist of the self, whereas an individual whose self-image was clouded by illusion was regarded as vulnerable to, if not already a victim of, mental illness. Today, we know that _____. Normal and healthy individuals — students, professors, engineers, doctors, business executives — tend to think of themselves as not just competent but proficient, even if they aren't.

① the opposite is closer to the truth
② it only works the other way around
③ no one can deny the traditional view
④ the point of view is highly ambiguous
⑤ these individuals shouldn't be concerned

PLUS +
변형문제

윗글의 제목으로 가장 적절한 것은?

① Our Pursuit to Exaggerate Our Self-Image
② Be Free from All Prejudices as an Objective Observer
③ How to Be Unaffected by Individual Positive Imagination
④ People's Vulnerability to Becoming Victims of Mental Illness
⑤ Our Ego toward Objective Analyzation in Creating Self-Image

34

다음 빈칸에 들어갈 말로 가장 적절한 것을 고르시오.

Imagine that a large number of observers are shown a glass jar containing coins and are challenged to estimate the number of coins in the jar. This is the kind of task in which individuals do very poorly, but pools of individual judgments hit the mark. The mechanism is straightforward: the average of many individual errors tends toward zero. However, this works well only when _____ _____. If the observers lean in the same direction, the collection of judgments will not help. For this reason, when there are multiple witnesses to an event, they are not allowed to discuss their testimony beforehand. The goal is not only to prevent the cheating of hostile witnesses, it is also to prevent unbiased witnesses from affecting each other. When this practice is not enforced, witnesses will tend to make similar errors in their testimony, which reduces the total value of the information they provide.

① the participants have a diversity of reliable opinions
② the observers think about the situation scientifically
③ the conclusion is based on many people's assumptions
④ the observers are completely independent from one another
⑤ the participants are those who respect both sides of an issue

PLUS+
변형문제

윗글의 제목으로 가장 적절한 것은?

① Independent Thinking and Responsibility
② Eyewitness Testimony and Memory Biases
③ How Preventing Social Influence Improves Accuracy
④ The Pitfalls of Groupthink: Degrading Critical Thinking
⑤ Wisdom of Crowds: Why the Many Are Smarter Than the Few

35 ◆ 다음 글에서 전체 흐름과 관계 <u>없는</u> 문장은?

The growth characteristics of weeds and the colour of their leaves and flowers may be as important as their presence in revealing information about the soil. ① The observant farmer and gardener will notice subtle changes in the weed populations on his land in response to his agricultural practices. ② As his soil improves he may find that chickweed, chicory, common groundsel, common horehound, and lambsquarter become the dominant weeds. ③ However, if he finds that the daisy, wild carrot, and wild radish become dominant, he should review his practices as these weeds thrive on soils of low fertility. ④ As all weeds are considered bad for crop growth, removing them all is thought the best way to deal with them, although this method can be both time-consuming and tough work. ⑤ The addition of well-balanced compost, organic manures, and other fertilizers together with certain cultivation and drainage practices may be required to bring the soil back into production.

*manure: 거름

PLUS +
변형문제

윗글의 주제로 가장 적절한 것은?

① role of weeds to indicate soil productivity
② formation of fields for preventing weed damage
③ various types of soil for more profitable produce
④ importance of fertilizer to keep the soil nutritious
⑤ ways to determine plant health through technology

36

주어진 글 다음에 이어질 글의 순서로 가장 적절한 것을 고르시오.

> Most people think of sneezes as symptoms — but that's really only half the story. A normal sneeze occurs when the body's self-defense system senses a foreign invader trying to get in through your nasal passages and acts to repel the invasion by expelling it with a sneeze. But sneezing when you've got a cold?

(A) So yeah, sneezes are symptoms, but they've evolved a simple and efficient method of host manipulation. When they're caused by a cold, they're symptoms with a purpose, and the purpose isn't yours.

(B) There's obviously no way to expel the cold virus when it's already lodged in your upper respiratory tract. That sneeze is a whole different animal — the cold virus has learned to trigger the sneezing so it can find new places to live by infecting your family, your colleagues, and your friends.

(C) That's true for many of the things we think of as symptoms of infectious disease. They're actually the product of host manipulation as whatever bacteria or virus has infected us works to engage our unconscious assistance in making the jump to its next host.

① (A) – (C) – (B)   ② (B) – (A) – (C)
③ (B) – (C) – (A)   ④ (C) – (A) – (B)
⑤ (C) – (B) – (A)

PLUS +
변형문제

윗글의 제목으로 가장 적절한 것은?

① The Process of Getting the Cold Virus
② Ways to Effectively Expel the Cold Virus
③ Facts about Sneezing Caused by Cold Viruses
④ Manipulation: Our Body's Self-Defense System
⑤ Sneezing Reflex: Fight Against Foreign Invaders

주어진 글 다음에 이어질 글의 순서로 가장 적절한 것을 고르시오.

> Historically, ethics is not concerned with the natural environment. Instead, it is an attempt to answer either of two questions: "How ought I to treat others?" and "What actions that affect others are morally right?"

(A) In response to these value-laden questions, a new form of applied ethics, environmental ethics, has evolved to address issues on human interactions with nonhuman nature. It helps people develop an ethical attitude towards nature.

(B) Nature is not included in these, except as some part of nature that "belongs" to some human being. That is, polluting a stream is morally wrong only if this action diminishes someone's enjoyment of the stream or its utility. The stream has no value and no ethical standing.

(C) However, we realize that we owe responsibility to nature for its own sake. But how? Scientists and engineers look at the world objectively with technical tools, which are often inappropriate for solving value problems. We are ill-equipped to make decisions where the value of nature is concerned.

① (A) – (C) – (B)　　　　② (B) – (A) – (C)

③ (B) – (C) – (A)　　　　④ (C) – (A) – (B)

⑤ (C) – (B) – (A)

PLUS +
변형문제

윗글의 주제로 가장 적절한 것은?

① limitations of value problems

② difficulties of answering ethics

③ emergence of environmental ethics

④ appropriate tools in decision-making

⑤ making decisions about nature's value

38 ◆ 글의 흐름으로 보아, 주어진 문장이 들어가기에 가장 적절한 곳을 고르시오.

> As a precaution, the plants took certain steps to protect their seeds from the eagerness of their partners.

Anthropologists have found that cultures vary enormously in their liking for bitter, sour, and salty flavors, but a taste for sweetness appears to be universal. (①) This goes for many animals, too, which shouldn't be surprising, since sugar is the form in which nature stores food energy. (②) By encasing their seeds in sugary and nutritious flesh, fruiting plants such as the apple hit on an ingenious way of exploiting the mammalian sweet tooth. (③) In exchange for fructose, the animals provide the seeds with transportation, allowing the plant to expand its range. (④) As parties to this grand coevolutionary bargain, animals with the strongest preference for sweetness and plants offering the biggest, sweetest fruits have prospered together and multiplied. (⑤) They had held off on developing sweetness and color until the seeds matured completely — before then fruits tend to be inconspicuously green — and in some cases, the plants developed poisons in their seeds to ensure that only the sweet flesh is consumed.

*fructose: 과당

PLUS +
변형문제

윗글의 주제로 가장 적절한 것은?

① the way plants use animals for their transportation
② preconditions for plants to produce the sweetest fruits
③ ways to get the green fruits to mature for a short time
④ the relationship between animals and seeds in maturing
⑤ reciprocal deal between plants and animals regarding fruits

39

글의 흐름으로 보아, 주어진 문장이 들어가기에 가장 적절한 곳을 고르시오.

> In attempting to explain this finding, researchers suggest one reason may be that watching violence raises one's physiological arousal by making people angry and putting them in a bad mood.

One of the most common types of entertainment programming on television involves high levels of violence. Violence also finds its way into advertising. (①) It may surprise you, however, that violent TV programming actually reduces memory for the commercials in those shows and reduces the chance that people will intend to buy those products. (②) An angry mood can prime aggressive thoughts, which in turn may interfere with recall of the ad content. (③) Negative moods are known to interfere with the brain's encoding of information. (④) Also, the effort taken to try to repair the bad mood may distract one from attending to and processing the ad. (⑤) Thus, it may be that advertisers are not getting as much "bang for their buck" with violent content as with nonviolent content.

*bang for one's buck: 본전을 뽑을 만한 가치

PLUS+
변형문제

윗글의 주제로 가장 적절한 것은?

① reasons why audiences are drawn to violent programs
② bad influence of violent programs on advertising effectiveness
③ efforts not to provoke negative emotions in advertising viewers
④ ways to overcome negative emotions created by bad commercials
⑤ necessity of distinguishing between violent and nonviolent content

40 ◆ 다음 글의 내용을 한 문장으로 요약하고자 한다. 빈칸 (A)와 (B)에 들어갈 말로 가장 적절한 것은?

The psychologists at the University of British Columbia were interested in looking at how the color of interior walls influence the imagination. Six hundred subjects, most of them undergraduates, were recruited, and they were made to perform a variety of basic cognitive tests displayed against red-, blue- or neutral-colored backgrounds. The differences were striking. People who took tests in the red condition — surrounded by walls the color of a stop sign — were much better at such skills as catching spelling mistakes or keeping random numbers in short-term memory. According to the scientists, this is because people automatically associate red with danger. However, a completely different set of psychological benefits were indicated by the color blue. While people belonging to the blue group performed worse on short-term memory tasks, they did far better on those requiring some imagination, such as designing a children's toy out of simple geometric shapes. In fact, subjects in the blue condition generated twice as many outputs as subjects in the red condition.

Red-colored backgrounds are advantageous in the performance of measuring
___(A)___ , while the blue-colored ones are advantageous in increasing
___(B)___ .

	(A)		(B)
①	flexibility	······	inspiration
②	swiftness	······	solidarity
③	alertness	······	originality
④	concentration	······	awareness
⑤	accuracy	······	adaptability

다음 글을 읽고, 물음에 답하시오.

Ideas can be patented, or copyrighted. Patents and copyrights can affect the spread of ideas and society. A lot (a) <u>fewer</u> books would have been written if the estate of Johannes Gutenberg, which included typography, had collected a fee on every one. It's not just companies that thrive by imitating their competitors. Entire countries can (b) <u>accelerate</u> their development by strategically copying the ideas and technologies that other countries already use. Eckhard Höffner, an economic historian, attributes Germany's rapid industrial development in the nineteenth century to weak copyright laws, which encouraged publishers to flood the country with cheap and often plagiarized copies of essential technical manuals. Japan's computer makers benefited from a government order that IBM make its patents (c) <u>available</u> as a condition of doing business there. More recently, China's adaptation of existing ideas from other countries has resulted in significant economic growth. Since 1978, it has moved workers from unproductive farms and state-owned companies to more productive privately-owned factories that used machinery and technology bought, borrowed, and sometimes stolen — which means it is obtained unethically — from foreigners. Foreign companies are routinely required to (d) <u>share</u> their expertise with local partners as a condition of doing business in China. Still, once a country has copied all the ideas it can, future growth depends on waiting for new ideas or developing its own. Inevitably, a country at the technological frontier grows more (e) <u>sharply</u> than one catching up to the frontier. That's just what happened to Japan, and it could also happen to China.

41 ◆ 윗글의 제목으로 가장 적절한 것은?

① Necessity of Strengthening Copyright Law
② Patents and Copyrights: Double-Edged Sword
③ Unethical Sides of Copying Ideas and Technologies
④ Patents and Copyrights: Differences and Similarities
⑤ Ideas and Technology: Major Factors of Economic Growth

42 ◆ 밑줄 친 (a) ~ (e) 중에서 문맥상 낱말의 쓰임이 적절하지 <u>않은</u> 것은?

① (a)　　　② (b)　　　③ (c)　　　④ (d)　　　⑤ (e)

31

다음 빈칸에 들어갈 말로 가장 적절한 것을 고르시오.

For scientific problems where the solution is likely buried in our creativity, the answer arrives only if we _____ . Ben Jones, a professor at the Kellogg Business School of Management, has demonstrated this by analyzing trends in "scientific production." By analyzing 19.9 million peer-reviewed papers and 2.1 million patents from the last fifty years, he was able to show that more than 99 percent of scientific subfields have experienced increased levels of alliance, with the size of the average team increasing by about 20 percent per decade. While the most cited studies in a field used to be the product of lone geniuses, he has demonstrated that the best research now emerges from groups. It doesn't matter what the researchers are studying: science papers produced by multiple authors are cited more than twice as often as those authored by individuals. This trend was even more apparent when it came to highly successful papers, which were more than six times as likely to come from a team of scientists.

① persevere   ② investigate   ③ contradict

④ collaborate   ⑤ contemplate

PLUS+
변형문제

윗글의 제목으로 가장 적절한 것은?

① Too Many Cooks Spoil the Broth
② Are Scientific Analyses Really Accurate?
③ Scientific Production: A Lonely Journey
④ The Credibility of Peer-Reviewed Papers
⑤ The Collective Achieves the Best Results

다음 빈칸에 들어갈 말로 가장 적절한 것을 고르시오.

Most people think of redundancy as repetition, and, usually, redundancy in this sense has a negative connotation. In the psycholinguistic sense, redundancy is quite different: it is a necessary and naturally occurring characteristic of language that makes sure of _____. An example of this type of redundancy is found in a sentence such as "The teachers were grading their papers," in which the plurality of the subject is conveyed by the -s ending, by the plural verb form *were*, and by the plural pronoun *their*. In case the reader or listener misses the plural marker on the subject, either the verb or the pronoun will convey the same information about the subject's plurality. In acquiring language, whether spoken or written, learners must grasp the redundancy of the language if they wish to guarantee an information exchange. In this sense, redundancy is a positive and necessary feature of the communication capacity of language.

① consistent and correct expression

② accurate information transmission

③ efficient phrasing of complex ideas

④ sufficient capacity in spoken language

⑤ interpretation of the speaker's psychological state

PLUS +
변형문제

윗글의 주제로 가장 적절한 것은?

① transition of linguistics markers in human language

② attempts to convey information by adding redundancy

③ side effects of eliminating redundancy in communication

④ importance of understanding redundancy for communication

⑤ ways to increase communication efficiency by avoiding redundancy

33 ◆ 다음 빈칸에 들어갈 말로 가장 적절한 것을 고르시오.

Could it be that we are drawn instinctively to flowers? Some evolutionary psychologists have proposed an interesting answer. Their hypothesis goes like this: our brains developed under the pressure of natural selection to make us good at searching for provisions, which is how humans have spent 99 percent of their time on earth. The presence of flowers is _____.
People who were drawn to flowers, and who further could distinguish among them and then remember where in the landscape they'd seen them, would be much more successful at seeking provisions than people who were blind to their significance. According to the neuroscientist Steven Pinker, who outlines this theory in *How the Mind Works*, natural selection was bound to favor those among our ancestors who noticed flowers and had a gift for botanizing — for recognizing plants, classifying them, and then remembering where they grow. In time the moment of recognition would become pleasurable, and the signifying thing a thing of beauty.

① a reliable predictor of future food
② the accurate means to avoid poison
③ a notable aspect of evolution in nature
④ an aspect of nature's desire to reproduce
⑤ an imprecise method of seeking resources

PLUS +
변형문제

윗글의 제목으로 가장 적절한 것은?

① What Made Us Successful Hunters?
② Without Flowers, We Would Not Be
③ Natural Selection Led Us to Prosper
④ What Do Flowers Evoke in Our Mind?
⑤ Biological Benefits of Natural Selection

34 ◆

To look at a novel or a sculpture or to listen to a piece of music as if it were simply an object — a "what" to be analyzed — is to perceive only the illusion. Reality can be experienced only when we understand how the art emerges from and relates to life itself. More than sixty years ago the educational philosopher John Dewey argued in his classic *Art as Experience* that conventional art education fails in exactly the same way science education fails — by concealing rather than revealing the links between theory and practice. For Dewey, the more we consider artistic objects _____,
the more we cut art off into a separate realm and remove its significance. The "refined and intensified forms of experience that are works of art" are thus disconnected from "the everyday events, doings, and sufferings that are universally recognized to constitute experience."

① exclusive due to the process of their production
② limited by their complexity in the audience's eyes
③ distinct from the original experience that formed them
④ related directly to the context surrounding their creation
⑤ significant in their position as a timeless aesthetic object

PLUS +
변형문제

윗글의 제목으로 가장 적절한 것은?

① Understand Art Better: Isolation from Education
② How to Appreciate Artistic Objects Independently
③ A Connection to Experience: Way to Reality of Art
④ The Creation of Art from Separation to Combination
⑤ Where Original Artworks Come From: Outside Objects

다음 글에서 전체 흐름과 관계 <u>없는</u> 문장은?

Edward Muybridge was very influential in the late 1800s, after he began taking multiple photographs of running horses. ① Cinematography, the rapid viewing of a succession of images, was a direct development of his photographic invention, which takes advantage of our mind's inability to process separate images that appear in rapid succession. ② Cinematography has led to time-lapse photography, in which very slow events, such as a flower opening or the rise and fall of the tides, are photographed not thirty times per minute like most movies, but once an hour or once a week. ③ They are then viewed at a fast enough speed that we cannot separate the individual movements. ④ Similarly, the first attempts in film processing were possible due to research which brought about continuous progress in many aspects of still photography. ⑤ The result is a representation of long periods of time onto short ones — a sort of time distortion similar to physically viewing the letters in "SHORT" at an angle.

*cinematography: 영화 촬영 기법

PLUS +
변형문제

윗글의 제목으로 가장 적절한 것은?

① The Birth of Muybridge's Photography
② Cinematography: A Distortion of Visual Perception
③ The Slower Photographed, the Clearer the Images
④ Time-Lapse Photography Upgraded the Film Industry
⑤ Advancement of Photographing Techniques in Capturing Motion

36 ◆

주어진 글 다음에 이어질 글의 순서로 가장 적절한 것을 고르시오.

> Engagement and exploration are enhanced when the process includes some uncertainty and surprise. Scientists who study animal behavior have known this for many years.

(A) This psychological principle is used all over Las Vegas, where gamblers play on the slot machines for hours, waiting for random payouts. This principle can be used to enhance creativity by giving intermittent recognition for creative work.

(B) The famous psychologist B. F. Skinner found that intermittent, or random, rewards lead to more robust behavior. For example, if a monkey discovers that sometimes pressing a bar produces a piece of fruit and other times it doesn't, the monkey will press the bar more consistently, knowing that sometimes the effort will pay off.

(C) Consider using surprise rewards for creative contributions, or randomly giving special bonuses for particularly innovative ideas. Knowing that at any time there could be a wonderful surprise as a reward leads to enhanced creative work.

① (A) – (C) – (B)　　　② (B) – (A) – (C)

③ (B) – (C) – (A)　　　④ (C) – (A) – (B)

⑤ (C) – (B) – (A)

PLUS+
변형문제

윗글의 제목으로 가장 적절한 것은?

① Boosting Innovation with Unpredictable Rewards
② Why Random Bonuses Are Detrimental to Innovation
③ Is It True That Praise Can Even Make Animals Behave?
④ Without a Guaranteed Bonus, There Is No Creative Work
⑤ An Unchanging Truth: Patience Is Bitter, But Its Fruit Is Sweet

37 ◆

주어진 글 다음에 이어질 글의 순서로 가장 적절한 것을 고르시오.

> At the center of Niccolò Machiavelli's political philosophy is the Renaissance idea of viewing human society in human terms. To achieve this, he analyzed human nature based on his observations of human behavior, which leads to the conclusion that the majority of people are by nature selfish, short-sighted, and easily deceived.

(A) Other negative human traits can also be turned to the common good, such as the tendency to imitate rather than think as individuals. This, Machiavelli notes, leads people to follow a leader's example and act cooperatively.

(B) Man's innate self-centeredness, for example, is shown in his instinct for self-preservation. However, when threatened by aggression or a hostile environment, he reacts with acts of courage, hard work, and cooperation.

(C) While they might appear to be an obstacle to creating an efficient, stable society, Machiavelli argues that some of these human failings can in fact be useful in establishing a successful society, though this requires the correct leadership.

① (A) – (C) – (B)　　　　② (B) – (A) – (C)
③ (B) – (C) – (A)　　　　④ (C) – (A) – (B)
⑤ (C) – (B) – (A)

PLUS +
변형문제

윗글의 요지로 가장 적절한 것은?

① 인간은 선천적으로 자기중심적인 동물이다.
② 안정적인 사회의 건설에는 지도자가 필요하다.
③ 인간의 자기중심성은 자기 보호 본능에서 비롯된다.
④ 인간의 부정적인 특성들도 공익에 이바지할 수 있다.
⑤ 공격이나 적대적 위협이 인간의 부정적 반응을 자극한다.

38 ◆ 글의 흐름으로 보아, 주어진 문장이 들어가기에 가장 적절한 곳을 고르시오.

> Similarly, solitary subjects responded much more strongly to unpleasant images of people than to pleasant images of objects.

Social neuroscientist John Cacioppo conducted a 2009 brain imaging study to identify differences in the neural mechanism of lonely and nonlonely people. (①) In this study, a key ingredient in loneliness has nothing to do with being physically alone, and everything to do with feeling alone. (②) While in an MRI machine, subjects viewed a series of images, some with positive connotations, such as happy people doing fun things, and others with negative associations, such as quarrels in the workplace. (③) As the two groups watched pleasant imagery, the area of the brain that recognizes rewards showed a significantly greater response in nonlonely people than in lonely people. (④) Their counterparts showed no such difference. (⑤) In short, people with an acute sense of loneliness appear to have a reduced response to things that make most people happy, and a heightened response to the bad emotions of others.

 PLUS⁺ 변형문제

윗글의 제목으로 가장 적절한 것은?

① Sympathy Caused by Negative Associations
② Effects of Positive Attitude at the Workplace
③ Loneliness Arouses Different Levels of Response
④ Does Being Physically Alone Make People Lonely?
⑤ Recognizing Rewards: Brain's Strategy to Be Happy

글의 흐름으로 보아, 주어진 문장이 들어가기에 가장 적절한 곳을 고르시오.

Gravity doesn't say I will fall to the ground tomorrow, but that I shall fall downward if for some reason I fall at all; biology doesn't predict that I will die at 74, my life expectancy, but only that I am likely to, and more likely if I smoke too much in the meantime.

A rudimentary variety of determinism is the view that events occurred in the past simply for the purpose of creating the present situation. (①) This is the belief that it is the ultimate end that brings about the chain of events, rather than the causes operating beforehand. (②) This underlies the popular notion of so-called progress, with the suggestion that events in the past worked together towards success. (③) However, deterministic theories actually go beyond the scope of a scientific law. (④) In the same way, most scientific laws only state probabilities, with plenty of scope allowed for human choices. (⑤) It is more fruitful to look at history this way, to seek lesser but more meaningful laws, "if ... then" conditions.

*determinism: 결정론

PLUS +
변형문제

윗글에서 필자가 주장하는 바로 가장 적절한 것은?

① 역사는 결정론의 관점에서 바라볼 필요가 있다.
② 역사에 과학 법칙을 적용하는 것은 삼가야 한다.
③ 과학 교육에 있어서 역사 교육이 선행되어야 한다.
④ 선택의 여지를 감안하여 역사를 보는 것이 필요하다.
⑤ 객관적으로 역사를 보기 위해 국가주의를 버려야 한다.

40 ◆ 다음 글의 내용을 한 문장으로 요약하고자 한다. 빈칸 (A), (B)에 들어갈 말로 가장 적절한 것은?

Suppose you drop lumps of sugar in two adjacent areas. If you are a student of statistics, you may expect the ants to divide themselves between the two food areas. This is because there is no reason why ants should prefer one food area to the other. But you may be surprised to find that the train of ants moves toward only one food area. Why? The behavior of individual ants influences the group. The first ant may randomly choose one location. The choice of the first ant resulted in a train of ants following suit, which magnifies the primary action. Economists study such behavior as part of the interacting agent models. A businessman may have randomly selected a street to establish his shop, but other businessmen wanting to do the same business follow his or her action. That's why Bangalore first housed all software companies in India, as did the Silicon Valley in the US. Or why a particular street has all shops selling paper products.

⬇

As ants do, humans tend to follow a(n) _____(A)_____ action as an agent model, and this tendency is applied to the business field in which the same business competitors _____(B)_____ together.

	(A)		(B)
①	group	⋯⋯	analyze
②	initial	⋯⋯	cluster
③	unwise	⋯⋯	merge
④	adventurous	⋯⋯	grow
⑤	random	⋯⋯	cooperate

다음 글을 읽고, 물음에 답하시오.

Salicylic acid is found in copious amounts in the bark of willow trees. In fact, the ancient Greek physician Hippocrates described a bitter substance — salicylic acid — drawn from willow bark that could (a) ease aches and reduce fevers. Other cultures in ancient times also used willow bark as a medicine, and salicylic acid itself is a key ingredient in many modern anti-acne face washes. Although willow is a well-known producer of salicylic acid, this chemical is (b) manufactured in various amounts by all plants. But why would a plant produce a pain reliever and fever reducer? Salicylic acid is not made for our benefit. For plants, it is salicylic acid that is a defence hormone that (c) increases the plant's immune system. Plants produce it when they've been attacked by bacteria or viruses. Salicylic acid is soluble and released at the exact spot of infection to signal through the veins to the rest of the plant that bacteria are on the loose. The healthy parts of the plant respond by initiating a number of steps that either kill the bacteria or stop the plague's spread. One includes blocking the movement of the bacteria to other parts of the plant. Areas of white spots appearing on leaves are proof of these barriers. These are where cells have killed themselves so that the bacteria can't (d) block farther.

At a broad level, salicylic acid serves (e) similar functions in both plants and people. Salicylic acid is what plants use to help ward off infection. We've used salicylic acid since ancient days, and we use the modern derivative of aspirin when we have an infection that causes aches and pains.

41 ◆ 윗글의 제목으로 가장 적절한 것은?

① The Scientific Functions of Salicylic Acid

② Salicylic Acid: The Original Form of Aspirin

③ The Intrinsic Value of Trees: Pain Reduction

④ The Well-Known Ancient History of Medicine

⑤ Benefits of Salicylic Acid for Plants and Humans

42 ◆ 밑줄 친 (a) ~ (e) 중에서 문맥상 낱말의 쓰임이 적절하지 <u>않은</u> 것은?

① (a)   ② (b)   ③ (c)   ④ (d)   ⑤ (e)

3142 모의고사

24 min. ⏱

정답 및 해설 p.118

31 ◆

다음 빈칸에 들어갈 말로 가장 적절한 것을 고르시오.

Early experiences in the arts are important because they produce _____ as well as aesthetic gains. In the best-researched example, participation in music seems to do mysterious but wonderful things. Music educators have recently become so concerned about parents sending kids off to computer camps instead of music lessons that they have begun funding some expert studies. Researchers at the University of California, Irvine, studied how regular piano practice and computer training affect children's spatial-temporal skills. Such skills are key to understanding proportion, geometry, and other mathematical and scientific concepts. After six months, the piano-taught children in the study had dramatically improved their scores on a spatial-temporal task, whereas the computer training had shown little effect. "If I were a parent, I'd want to take these findings into consideration," reported one of the experiment's designers.

① intuitional   ② emotional   ③ practical
④ intellectual   ⑤ functional

 PLUS +
변형문제

윗글의 제목으로 가장 적절한 것은?

① Does Arts Education Boost Young Brains?
② Good at Math Means Good at Playing Piano
③ Advantages of Teaching Piano and Computer
④ The Biggest Worry for Today's Music Educators
⑤ How Regular Practice Affects Spatial-Temporal Skills

32 ◆

다음 빈칸에 들어갈 말로 가장 적절한 것을 고르시오.

People often think that a proposition is true because it has not yet been proven false or a proposition is false because it has not yet been proven true. Carl Sagan gives this example: "There is no compelling evidence that UFOs are not visiting the Earth; therefore UFOs exist, and there is intelligent life elsewhere in the universe." Similarly, before we knew how the pyramids were built, some concluded that, unless proven otherwise, they must have been built by a supernatural power. But in fact, the "burden of proof" always lies with the person making a claim. More logically, and as several others have put it, one should ask what is likely based on _____.
Which is more likely: That an object flying through space is a man-made artifact or natural phenomenon, or that it is aliens visiting from another planet? Since we have frequently observed the former and never the latter, it is more reasonable to conclude that UFOs are probably not aliens visiting from outer space.

① evidence from past observation
② truth that doesn't need evidence
③ an inference from various sources
④ current expectations and assumptions
⑤ a proposition that has not been disproved

PLUS +
변형문제

윗글의 제목으로 가장 적절한 것은?

① How to Deal With Historical Mysteries
② Where There Is Evidence, There Is Faith
③ We Are Living in a Sea of New Evidence
④ UFOs: Man-Made Artifact vs. Proof of Aliens
⑤ You Can't Justify a Belief without Information

다음 빈칸에 들어갈 말로 가장 적절한 것을 고르시오.

Most recent works of Western theatre dance have been created by choreographers, who have been regarded as the authors and owners of their works in a way comparable to writers, composers, and painters. New York choreographer Merce Cunningham has crossed artistic barriers and stretched the parameters of dance. He always looks for _____ _____. He begins by outlining the movement, timing, spacing, number of dancers. He then assigns each a different variable and generates their combinations, such as the flip of a coin. As Carolyn Brown, one of Cunningham's dancers, has said, "The dances are treated more as puzzles than works of art; the pieces are space and time, shape and rhythm." Cunningham's choreography is considered to avoid traditional preconceptions and explore all possible arrangements inherent in the art of dance, in the same way new gene combinations are generated with every throw of the reproductive dice. As Cunningham says, "You can see what it is like to break these actions up in different ways" and then see what surprises new combinations may hold.

*choreographer: 안무가 **choregraphy: 안무법

① advantages of the qualities of natural dance movements

② a strong technique which extends across all areas of dance

③ the conventional patterns inherent in different dance forms

④ pattern-forming inspiration, randomly mixing dance elements

⑤ the transformation of disorderly movements into systematic ones

PLUS+
변형문제

윗글의 주제로 가장 적절한 것은?

① necessity of new choreography in Western theatre

② ways to avoid traditional preconceptions in dancing

③ factors contributing to making combinations of dancing

④ unique method of developing dances of a choreographer

⑤ critics' negative view of generating movements by abstraction

34

다음 빈칸에 들어갈 말로 가장 적절한 것을 고르시오.

Grasshoppers behave as solitary insects immediately after hatching or when isolated, but if they are forcibly crowded for as little as 6 hours they subsequently tend to group together, or exhibit gregarious behavior. For a long time scientists thought the grasshopper "migrants" that appeared so suddenly were a unique species arriving from and departing for unknown locations. Now we know that the migrants are a "phase" of a common grasshopper species that changes its color, form, and behavior in response to crowding. Proof comes from experiments: to create these "migrants" from isolated individuals, one takes a nymph, which is the immature stage of a grasshopper, puts it in a jar, and has a motor-driven brush tickle it continuously. The constant tickling mimics the crowding, which triggers the nervous system to alter the hormones that result in development into the restless migratory phase with a different color, wing length, and behavior. It is a good example that shows " _____ _____ ."

*gregarious: 군거하는

① mutual cooperation is key to the survival of a species
② the fittest members of a species always manage to survive
③ changes in gene expression can be triggered by the environment
④ migrating ability is an inherent instinct in some species of animals
⑤ migration isn't a one-directional process but instead multidirectional

PLUS +
변형문제

윗글의 주제로 가장 적절한 것은?

① the reason grasshoppers tend to be solitary creatures
② the discovery that "migrant" grasshoppers are a new species
③ why genetics causes grasshoppers to enter a migratory stage
④ how grasshoppers change their behavior and become gregarious
⑤ hormone changes leading grasshoppers to pursue isolation from others

다음 글에서 전체 흐름과 관계 <u>없는</u> 문장은?

Closely observing the color of the ocean surface provides a powerful means of determining ocean productivity. ① The ocean reflects the color of the sky, but even on cloudless days the color of the ocean is not a consistent blue. ② Variations in ocean color are determined primarily by variations in the concentrations of algae and phytoplankton, which are the basis of the marine food chain. ③ Because these microscopic plants absorb blue and red light more readily than green light, regions of high phytoplankton concentrations appear greener than those with low concentration. ④ Sunlight, water, and nutrients are essential for phytoplankton to survive, so any of these ingredients over time for a given region will affect the phytoplankton variations. ⑤ Because fish feed on the phytoplankton, regions of greener sea indicate the possibility of greater fish population.

PLUS +
변형문제

윗글의 제목으로 가장 적절한 것은?

① What the Color of the Ocean Surface Signifies
② How to Attempt to Increase the Fisheries' Yield
③ Microscopic Plants' Preference for Blue and Red
④ The Low Concentration Rate of Microscopic Plants
⑤ How Many Variations Determine the Fish Population

> Evolutionary psychologists hypothesize that the human mind is equipped with many (some say very many) different evolved psychological mechanisms.

(A) Rather, it possesses different mechanisms to confront different problems: a liver to filter out toxins, lungs to take in oxygen, antibodies to fight off bacteria and viruses, and so on. It's true that each mechanism is profoundly limited in what it can do.

(B) However, this cost is made up for by the benefits. With only one task to complete, each system should be efficient. And even if some systems break down (you lose your eyesight, for example), most other systems should remain operational. Evolutionary psychologists contend that this is the way we should understand the human mind.

(C) Instead of viewing the mind as a single all-purpose "problem-solver," evolutionary psychologists consider it in roughly the way we consider the body. We understand that the body does not contain a *single* physical mechanism.

① (A) – (C) – (B)
② (B) – (A) – (C)
③ (B) – (C) – (A)
④ (C) – (A) – (B)
⑤ (C) – (B) – (A)

PLUS +
변형문제

윗글의 주제로 가장 적절한 것은?

① role of human mind in problem solving
② evolution of humans' psychological mechanism
③ effects of mental functions on the human body
④ experimental comparison of the human mind and body
⑤ human mind being comprised of multiple mechanisms

The instruments used in a modern orchestra have changed tremendously since even the late-nineteenth century. Yet Beethoven, Mozart, and Haydn seemed able to come up with awfully good pieces in spite of the technical deficiencies of their technology (poorly tuned woodwinds, brass with limited agility, etc.).

(A) There is no question that new games offer a greater palette of graphical and interface possibilities, but that doesn't mean that they will be more fun or engaging. The success of a work depends on how it uses its medium, not on the absolute sophistication of that medium.

(B) This is not different from other domains, even technological ones. A major movement in video games in the last few years has been retro.

(C) A major trend of the last couple of decades has even been to use these less-developed instruments to play more "historically accurate" versions of the pieces. These recordings are often more popular and more critically admired than recordings that are more technically perfect (more in tune, better balanced, greater range of instrumental timbre, etc.).

*agility: 경쾌(함) **timbre: 음색

① (A) – (C) – (B) 　　　　② (B) – (A) – (C)

③ (B) – (C) – (A) 　　　　④ (C) – (A) – (B)

⑤ (C) – (B) – (A)

PLUS +
변형문제

윗글의 요지로 가장 적절한 것은?

① Every cloud has a silver lining.

② The early bird catches the worm.

③ Actions speak louder than words.

④ Necessity is the mother of invention.

⑤ A good craftsman never blames his tools.

글의 흐름으로 보아, 주어진 문장이 들어가기에 가장 적절한 곳을 고르시오.

> Although the placebo effect is generally harmless, it does account for the expenditure of millions of dollars on health products and services every year, and they are responsible for the figure.

The placebo effect is an apparent cure or improved state of health brought about by a substance, product, or procedure that has no generally recognized therapeutic value. (①) It is not uncommon for patients to report improvements based on what they expect, desire, or were told would happen after taking simple sugar pills that they believed were powerful drugs. (②) The placebo effect is related to the brain's reward system, and it's not a big leap to say that much of marketing is trying to achieve a non-medical placebo effect in the minds of customers. (③) About 10 percent of the population is believed to be exceptionally susceptible to the power of suggestion and may be easy targets for aggressive marketing. (④) For instance, megadoses of vitamin C have never been proven to treat cancer but expenditures on them add up to over 30 billion dollars a year. (⑤) People who mistakenly use placebos when medical treatment is urgently needed increase their risk for health problems.

PLUS⁺
변형문제

윗글의 제목으로 가장 적절한 것은?

① Methods Attracting More Expenditures on Products
② How to Avoid Aggressive Marketing and Shop Smart
③ The Power of Suggestion Influences Medical Treatment
④ The Placebo Effect Is Targeting Your Wallet and Health
⑤ Why Is the Application of the Placebo Effect So Popular?

글의 흐름으로 보아, 주어진 문장이 들어가기에 가장 적절한 곳을 고르시오.

> These were not information in our genes but rather knowledge obtained from others: Our ancestors had thousands of years of knowledge passed down from each generation.

Approximately 250,000 years ago, a few thousand Homo sapiens migrated out of Africa aided by a brain that was not only sophisticated enough to adapt to new environments, but also one that had evolved the capacity for the transmission of knowledge from one generation to the next. (①) Humans were born to learn: Long before writing and the Internet were invented, humans had the capacity to communicate with each other in ways that no other animal could. (②) With communication came an explosion in technology and skills, which led to our overall growth as a species. (③) That's why every newborn baby does not have to start from scratch. (④) This is such an obvious fact about human civilization that we often forget that we are the only animals on this planet that retain skills and knowledge that we pass on to our offspring. (⑤) Other animals can learn about their environments but no other animal has the human capacity for acquiring thousands of years of experience within a lifetime.

PLUS +
변형문제

윗글의 요지로 가장 적절한 것은?
① 인간의 의사소통 능력은 동물보다 훨씬 뛰어나다.
② 인간의 두뇌는 의사소통으로 인해 정교하게 발달하였다.
③ 인간의 의사소통은 현 과학기술의 발전에 크게 이바지한다.
④ 인간은 지구상에서 언어로 의사소통을 하는 유일한 동물이다.
⑤ 인류의 발전은 의사소통 능력과 조상에게 물려받은 지식 덕분이다.

40 ◆

An elite-level gymnast took a semester off from his university study in order to dedicate maximum time and attention to his training before the upcoming competitive season. The coach agreed to work with the gymnast in his off time alone in an empty gym. It seemed like an ideal situation, a coach's undivided attention, no distractions — perfect. However, in about a week, the gymnast's interest in the training process declined, his emotional state worsened, and the stability of the learned skills worsened as well. Workouts became mechanical actions without emotional color. It was quite obvious that the cause of the recession in the gymnast's performance was due to the absence of the social environment. After some discussion and reasoning, the coach decided to resume the gymnast's training in his "old time." It was the right decision. The next day, the gymnast entered the gym smiling, happy to see all his teammates and the usual working atmosphere. It could be said that he was at his best at his training session that day. The situation having changed dramatically, within a week he restored and improved his skills.

⬇

| If a talented individual is far removed from their ____(A)____ and asked to perform, the results may prove ____(B)____. |

	(A)		(B)
①	community	......	encouraging
②	duties	......	valuable
③	surroundings	......	unsatisfactory
④	schoolwork	......	counterproductive
⑤	families	......	stable

다음 글을 읽고, 물음에 답하시오.

Today, many landscape architects like the word 'natural.' They talk about 'natural surveillance', for instance, 'natural access control.' The idea is that instead of conventional methods of military-level surveillance, you exploit thoughtful design so that neighborhoods become naturally self-policing. Crime is much (a) <u>less</u> likely in settings where people are more involved in each other's lives and care about their shared spaces. This means housing must be 'human'-scale. In a large development, housing should be divided into small enclaves with a (b) <u>common</u> space where neighbours are likely to meet casually all the time — something which can be enhanced by landscaping gardens. But each enclave needs to be at least subtly different to (c) <u>personalize</u> it, and given features such as signs and ornaments in styles that may have special meaning for the residences. The mutual space needs to be attractive, too, with places for sitting, and the boundaries between common and private space need to be soft and appealing to encourage a sense of pride and common ownership. This common space, and the arrangement of doors and windows to face it, may help, too, to reduce social (d) <u>isolation</u>, another factor behind crime.

Natural access control means using architectural design to discourage intruders. For instance, it's worth creating space for planting and plant barriers rather than building a lot of walls, bars and concrete. Planting not only gives a place a more attractive, cared-for look; burglars are actually more (e) <u>encouraged</u> by flower beds and bushes than they are by walls. It's surprisingly hard to climb over a bush! Architectural devices like these are being used more and more, and police and social workers are now often brought in as consultants on architectural schemes.

*enclave: 고립된 장소

41 ◆ 윗글의 제목으로 가장 적절한 것은?

① Increased Visibility Means Increased Security

② How Can Technology Help in Reducing Crime?

③ Crime Prevention through the Design of Nature

④ Crime and the Environment: Types and Solutions

⑤ Environmental Crime and Its Victims: Now and Then

42 ◆ 밑줄 친 (a) ~ (e) 중에서 문맥상 낱말의 쓰임이 적절하지 <u>않은</u> 것은?

① (a)　　　② (b)　　　③ (c)　　　④ (d)　　　⑤ (e)

31

다음 빈칸에 들어갈 말로 가장 적절한 것을 고르시오.

Any tree's life is _____. A tree doesn't move; yet it must cast its pollen as far from its own territory as possible and then disperse its seeds into its own sphere of influence. It has evolved amazing mechanisms to achieve this, from exploiting animals as agents of dispersal to attaching propellers. Anyone who has seen the mist of pollen above an evergreen forest knows the extravagant profligacy of trees to ensure survival of a very few. Wherever a seed lands, its fate is sealed, and for most that means lying exposed to insects, birds, or mammals, withering on rocks, or drowning in water. Even when a seed lands on soil, its future is in doubt. That tiny seed contains its entire inheritance from its parent, a store of food to get it through its first growth, and a genetic blueprint informing the growing plant to send its root down and its stem up and telling it how to capture the energy, water, and materials it needs to live. Its life is programmed; yet it must also be flexible enough to handle unexpected storms, drought, fire, and predators.

*profligacy: 낭비, 방탕

① elaborate
② uncertain
③ integrative
④ irreversible
⑤ paradoxical

PLUS+
변형문제

윗글의 제목으로 가장 적절한 것은?

① Why Are Some Trees in Serious Danger?
② Efforts to Discover the Secrets of Nature
③ Essential Conditions for the Life of Trees
④ A Tree's Vulnerability and Efforts to Survive
⑤ A Tree's Ability to Transmit Traits to Offspring

32

다음 빈칸에 들어갈 말로 가장 적절한 것을 고르시오.

Humans generally act to avoid episodes of treacherous personal trouble, and many of today's "hostile forces of nature" that would have put our ancestors in jeopardy have been harnessed or controlled. We have laws to deter robbery, assault, and murder. We have police to perform many of the functions previously performed by one's friends. We have medical knowledge that has eliminated or reduced many sources of disease and illness. We live in an environment that is in many ways safer and more stable than that inhabited by our ancestors. Paradoxically, therefore, we suffer from a relative scarcity of serious events that would allow us to accurately assess those who are deeply engaged in our welfare and discriminate them from our fair-weather friends. It is possible that the loneliness and sense of alienation that many feel in modern living — a lack of a feeling of deep social connectedness despite the presence of many warm and friendly interactions — might stem from _____ that tell us who is deeply engaged in our welfare.

*treacherous: 위험한, 믿을 수 없는

① the fragility of human relationships

② the lack of critical assessment events

③ unstoppable competition for survival

④ the effects of social network diversity

⑤ the lack of society's tolerance and humanity

PLUS⁺
변형문제

윗글의 제목으로 가장 적절한 것은?

① The Decline in Moral Values in Modern Times

② Ways to Be Safely Connected with Members of Society

③ Modern Society: Too Competitive to Make Real Friends

④ The Safer We Are, The Harder It Is to Discern True Friends

⑤ The Negative Emotions Resulting from Superficial Relationships

33

다음 빈칸에 들어갈 말로 가장 적절한 것을 고르시오.

We often choose to use equivocal language when we're in _____. Suppose, for example, that you're asked to provide a reference for your friend Dylan, who is applying for a job on the police force in your town. One of the questions you're asked is how well Dylan handles pressure. Even though Dylan's your friend, you can immediately think of several occasions when he hasn't handled pressure well. Now you're caught in a bind. On the one hand, you want Dylan to get the job because he's your friend. On the other hand, you don't want to lie to the police lieutenant who's phoning you for the reference. Several studies have shown that when we're faced with two unappealing choices such as these, we often use ambiguous language to get ourselves out of that bind. In response to the lieutenant's question about how well Dylan handles pressure, for instance, you might say something like this: "Well, that depends; there are lots of different kinds of pressure."

① incidents which lead to a single positive decision

② a situation when none of our options is a good one

③ a position that provides us with many reasonable choices

④ circumstances beyond our control despite our best efforts

⑤ a state of indifference where we don't need to do anything

PLUS +
번뜩문제

윗글의 제목으로 가장 적절한 것은?

① Why Do Your Friends Tend to Speak Directly?

② How to Deal with Dilemma: Ambiguous Words

③ Judging Whether an Acquaintance Speaks Truly

④ How We Handle Problems Using Specific Words

⑤ Helping Your Friends Get a Job By Speaking for Them

34 ◆

12

다음 빈칸에 들어갈 말로 가장 적절한 것을 고르시오.

There is obviously a wide gap between the promises of the 1948 Declaration and the real world of human-rights violations. In so far as we sympathize with the victims, we may criticize the UN and its member governments for failing to keep their promises. However, we cannot understand the gap between human-rights ideals and the real world of human-rights violations by sympathy or by legal analysis. Rather, it requires investigation by the various social sciences of the causes of social conflict and political oppression, and of the interaction between national and international politics. The UN introduced the concept of human rights into international law and politics. The field of international politics is, however, dominated by states and other powerful actors (such as multinational corporations) that have priorities other than human rights. It is a leading feature of the human-rights field that the governments of the world proclaim human rights but _____. We must understand why this is so.

① try to strengthen their substantive authority
② lead easily to conflicts in the political context
③ deal with the issues based on ethnic identities
④ hold onto responsibilities to fight for the issues
⑤ have a highly variable record of implementing them

PLUS⁺
변형문제

윗글의 제목으로 가장 적절한 것은?

① Universal Implementation of Human Rights
② Human Rights: The Priority of International Politics
③ The UN's Efforts to Eradicate Human Rights Violations
④ Close the Divide: How to Ensure Human Rights for All
⑤ Human Rights: The Gap between Principle and Practice

35

다음 글에서 전체 흐름과 관계 <u>없는</u> 문장은?

Future land use and food security will be determined largely by the dynamics and interactions of agricultural markets, climatic suitability, and direct interventions along the supply chain. ① More than any other major economic sector, agriculture is highly dependent on local climatic conditions and is expected to be highly responsive to changes in climate that are expected in coming decades. ② This sensitivity toward the climate is compounded by pressure on the global agricultural system to meet food security objectives. ③ While climate change effects will be felt everywhere, some regions will be more negatively affected than others — up to a point. ④ Additionally, rapid increases in global demand for agricultural commodities for food, animal feed and fuel are driving dramatic changes in the way we think about crops and land use. ⑤ Along with recent supply side shocks driven by extreme weather events and other disasters, these conditions have led to wild swings in agricultural commodity markets.

PLUS +
변형문제

윗글의 제목으로 가장 적절한 것은?

① Climate Change: A Potential Catastrophe
② How to Prevent Global Agricultural Changes
③ Causes of Rapidly Increasing Demand for Produce
④ Growing Pressure on the Global Agricultural System
⑤ What Affects Our Potential Land Use and Food Security

36 ◆ 주어진 글 다음에 이어질 글의 순서로 가장 적절한 것을 고르시오.

> One evening in the late 1920s, Richard Hollingshead Jr. tested a creative idea: watching a movie from the front seat of a car parked in his driveway. He set up a movie screen in front of the car and put the movie projector on top of his car.

(A) But he realized he needed some assurance that light rain wouldn't interfere with viewing the movie, so he set up a lawn sprinkler to simulate rain on his car window. He also tested the feasibility of eating snacks in the car while watching the movie.

(B) The arrangement worked fine. Then Hollingshead began to wonder about the practicality of building a large outdoor movie theater where people could conveniently watch a movie from their cars.

(C) So it was wise that Hollingshead didn't immediately assume that his idea would be feasible. He first tested his "automobile movie theater" idea on a small scale, before he invested the large amounts of money, time, and effort required to build a full-scale drive-in movie theater.

① (A) – (C) – (B)
② (B) – (A) – (C)
③ (B) – (C) – (A)
④ (C) – (A) – (B)
⑤ (C) – (B) – (A)

PLUS +
변형문제

윗글의 제목으로 가장 적절한 것은?

① Outdoor Activity: Not So Outdoor Anymore
② A Man's Failure at Implementing His Curiosity
③ What Might Have Been First Automobile Movie Theater
④ How to Increase the Practicality of Outdoor Movie Theaters
⑤ Accidental Discovery Became Popular Form of Entertainment

주어진 글 다음에 이어질 글의 순서로 가장 적절한 것을 고르시오.

> Cold ocean currents are large masses of cold water that move towards the equator, from a level of high altitude to lower levels. They absorb the heat they receive in the tropics, thereby cooling the air above them.

(A) It is these that bring cold water to the surface of the earth from the depths, and in the process they force away the original surface water. This happens in a clockwise direction above the equator, and counterclockwise below it. So the ocean is often cooler to the eastern coastal side than the western.

(B) They form when salty cold water becomes heavy and sinks, in the process forcing warm and lighter water to move in the opposite direction. The influence of the flow of currents usually depends on the level of saltiness of the water, the rotation of the earth, the topography of the land and the orientation of the wind.

(C) The cold currents often form when the air on the subtropical high blows over a cold mass of water, then the cold air is dragged to the equator. Warm currents, on the other hand, are large masses of warm water moving further away from the equator, at higher temperatures.

① (A) – (C) – (B)   ② (B) – (A) – (C)
③ (B) – (C) – (A)   ④ (C) – (A) – (B)
⑤ (C) – (B) – (A)

PLUS +
변형문제

윗글의 제목으로 가장 적절한 것은?

① Why Warm Currents Form in the Ocean
② The More Salty the Ocean Is, The Cooler
③ What Makes the Sea's Temperature Stable
④ The Unsolved Secret of the Sea's Temperature
⑤ How the Ocean's Hot and Cold Currents Form

38 ◆

글의 흐름으로 보아, 주어진 문장이 들어가기에 가장 적절한 곳을 고르시오.

> They would further be expected to name all the stars of each cycle in order of their appearance.

The education of a traditional navigator was the work of a lifetime, and learning the sidereal compass, a special compass used in Polynesia, was but a small part of it. (①) The star positions were usually taught to junior sailors by master seamen using classroom techniques ashore as well as on-the-job training at sea. (②) A typical classroom session might present the students with a model canoe surrounded by a circle of thirty-two stones representing the direction-finding star cycles. (③) These cycles are what they would be required to name when pointed to at random. (④) And as a more advanced exercise, they had to name the reciprocal of each star — that is, the star that lies on the exact opposite compass point. (⑤) Those corresponding are important because they represent the directions of return voyages.

*sidereal: 항성[별]의

12

PLUS +
변형문제

윗글의 주제로 가장 적절한 것은?

① the difficulty of learning the traditional names of stars
② the importance of navigational education in Polynesia
③ the way traditional navigators were gradually educated
④ the method of designing the traditional sidereal compass
⑤ the necessity of navigators memorizing the star positions

> We might be cautious about a food at first, then eat it frequently and with joy, but few people would enjoy eating the same main course for a thousand meals in a row.

People spend much of their waking lives passively listening to music. You might expect, as a very simple hypothesis, that we tend to enjoy the music we hear the most — the same version of the "mere exposure" effect regarding food. (①) The problem, though, is that too familiar becomes unpleasant. (②) A rule of pleasure is that it is an inverted U (a ∩) — when you first experience something, it's hard to process and not enjoyable; upon repeated exposure, it's easy to process and gives pleasure; then it gets too easy, and therefore boring or even annoying. (③) For music, the middle peak of the inverted U can last a little longer than that, but any song will become unbearable if you hear it often enough. (④) The shape of the curve is stretched and squeezed by the complexity of the music. (⑤) A complex piece might take a long while to like and then a long time to get sick of; usually a simple children's song will go through the curve a lot quicker.

PLUS +
변형문제

윗글의 요지로 가장 적절한 것은?

① 청중은 단조로운 음악에 더 쉽게 빠져든다.
② 우리의 취향은 우리가 처한 환경에 좌우된다.
③ 즐거움의 법칙은 노출 빈도와 상관관계가 있다.
④ 음식에 관해서 거꾸로 된 U자는 적용되지 않는다.
⑤ 지루함을 예방하기 위해 환경을 자주 바꿔야 한다.

40 ♦

Researchers who study all kinds of animals — from mammals to reptiles to insects — have long noted the ability of some organisms to produce offspring suited to their environment. The vole is a furry little rodent that looks something like a fat mouse. Depending upon the time of year its mother is due to give birth, baby voles are born with either a thick coat or a thin coat. The gene for a thick coat is always there — it's just turned on or off depending on the level of light the mother senses in her environment around the time of pregnancy. The mother of the tiny freshwater flea *Daphnia* will produce offspring with a larger helmet and spines if it's going to give birth in an environment crowded with predators. One species of lizard is born with a long tail and large body or a small tail and small body depending on one thing only — whether their mother smelled a lizard-eating snake while pregnant. When her babies are entering a snake-filled world, they are born with a long tail and big body, making them less likely to be snake food.

↓

Some animals have the ability to ___(A)___ the characteristics of their offspring on the basis of the mother's ___(B)___ during pregnancy.

	(A)		(B)
①	combine	······	nutrition
②	change	······	stress
③	uncover	······	migration
④	determine	······	experiences
⑤	divide	······	preferences

다음 글을 읽고, 물음에 답하시오.

In recent years, the word 'natural' has acquired a positive aura. Every GM food has been labelled 'unnatural' by its opponents, as if that is enough to damn it forever, while advertisers can put a (a) positive spin on just about anything by describing it as 'natural.' In one of those ironies, an orange tart labelled as full of 'natural orange flavor' has almost certainly never been near an orange, natural or unnatural. Food retailers can legally label food as 'naturally flavored' if the cocktail of chemicals it contains creates a taste that just vaguely resembles the real thing. Yet just why is natural so easily seen as good and unnatural bad? After all, diseases such as malaria and cholera are natural. In fact, death is quite natural, too. It is in part a hangover from the ancient belief that things in their proper, natural form were, in their way, (b) perfect, and, in Christian times, reflections of God's creation. (c) Unnatural things were distortions of these flawless forms created by the devil. When people talked about 'unnatural acts' they were talking about something a lot nastier than making 'natural strawberry flavor' drinks from chemicals. That ancient prejudice has been (d) removed in the modern world by big manufacturing companies and agribusinesses, scientists and food technologists. 'Natural' seems to be wholesome, tried-and-tested over millions of years. It's free from dangerous artifice. In this sense, nature is always (e) natural.

*GM: 유전자 변형의

41

윗글의 제목으로 가장 적절한 것은?

① Mother Nature: Friend and Foe of Humans
② Artifact Is Man's Nature; Nature Is God's Art
③ Human Activities Alter Natural Environment
④ Why Do People Turn Away From the Unnatural?
⑤ How Much of the Environment is Actually Natural?

42

밑줄 친 (a) ~ (e) 중에서 문맥상 낱말의 쓰임이 적절하지 <u>않은</u> 것은?

① (a)　　② (b)　　③ (c)　　④ (d)　　⑤ (e)

'나'에게 딱! 맞는 암기&문제모드만 골라서 학습!

5가지 암기모드

8가지 문제모드

 암기모드를 선택하면, 최적의 문제 모드를 자동 추천!

2 **미암기 단어는 단어장에! 외워질 때까지 반복 학습 GO!**

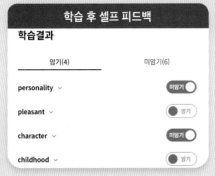

수능
영어

절대
유형

Go deeper and deeper!

3
1
2
4

삼일~사이

쎄듀

수능영어
절대유형

정답 및 해설

31 ① + ④	32 ① + ③	33 ④ + ⑤	34 ⑤ + ⑤	35 ③ + ④	36 ③ + ④
37 ⑤ + ③	38 ④ + ⑤	39 ② + ⑤	40 ④	41 ③	42 ③

31 ① PLUS + ④

¹The word "scientist" (in its present meaning) did not become a part of language / until the modern era. In ancient and medieval times / philosophy was everything, // and the philosopher was the caretaker (of human wisdom). He knew of the moral law, religion, government, natural history, alchemy, mathematics, healing, and all knowledge. Indeed, the diligent scholar at one time had been able to master the entire sum (of academic learning). ²This is in striking contrast with the world of today, // in which a man may devote a lifetime to a single type of germ or bacteria / and still consider his subject vast and complex enough / for a full generation of profound study. ³Having few <u>details</u> (to bother about) in his pursuit of knowledge, / the ancient could think in broad and encompassing terms.

해석 현재 의미의 '과학자'라는 단어는 현대에 이르러서야 언어의 일부분이 되었다. 고대와 중세 시대에는 철학이 모든 것이었고, 철학자가 인간의 지혜의 관리인이었다. 그는 도덕률, 종교, 통치 체제, 자연사, 연금술, 수학, 치료, 그리고 모든 지식을 알고 있었다. 정말로, 끊임없이 노력하는 학자는 한때 학문적 지식의 총합에 정통할 수 있었다. 추론근거 이것은 오늘날의 세계와는 현저한 대조를 이루는데, 그곳(오늘날의 세계)에서는 한 사람이 단일 유형의 미생물이나 세균에 평생을 바치고도 여전히 자신의 (학문) 주제를 온전히 한 세대가 심오한 연구를 할 만큼 충분히 방대하고 복잡하다고 생각할지도 모른다. 자신의 지식을 추구하는 데 신경을 써야 할 세부 사항이 거의 없었기에, 고대인들은 폭넓고 많은 것을 아우르는 측면에서 사고할 수 있었다.

어휘 era 시대 medieval 중세의 caretaker 관리인, 돌보는 사람 moral law 도덕률 striking 현저한, 눈에 띄는, 두드러진 contrast 대조; 차이 devote A to B A를 B에 바치다[쏟다] germ 미생물, 세균 vast 방대한, 막대한 profound 심오한, 깊은 pursuit 추구; 추적; 연구 encompass (많은 것을) 아우르다[포함하다]; 에워[둘러]싸다

해설 고대 철학자와 현대 과학자가 지식을 추구하는 방식에서 어떤 차이가 있는지를 대조하는 글이다. 예전에는 철학자가 모든 학문적 지식에 정통한 존재였지만 현대의 과학자는 한 주제에 평생을 바치고도 여전히 그 주제가 방대하고 복잡하다고 여긴다고 했다. 따라서 고대인들에게 광범위한 지식 추구가 가능했던 것은 현대 과학자와 달리 폭넓고 많은 것을 아우르는 측면에서 사고하면서 신경 써야 할 ① '세부 사항'이 거의 없었기 때문임을 추론할 수 있다.

오답 Check
② 네트워크 ③ 전통 ④ 지침 ⑤ 발견
→ ② ~ ⑤ 모두 고대 철학자와 관련 없는 사항이므로 오답.

PLUS + 변형문제

해설 고대 철학자와 현대 과학자의 지식 추구 방식에서의 차이를 대조하는 글이므로 제목으로 가장 적절한 것은 ④ '현대 과학자는 고대 철학자와 어떻게 다른가'이다.
① 과학 철학의 기원 → 과학 철학에 관한 내용이 아님
② 고대 철학을 현대 과학에 적용하기
③ 과학의 한계와 철학의 역할
⑤ 과학 발전에 있어 철학자의 영향
→ ②, ③, ⑤ 철학과 과학의 연계에 관한 내용이 아님.

 ¹*The word "scientist"* (in its present meaning) did **not** become a part of language / **until** the modern era.
• ( )는 형용사적 역할을 하는 전명구로 앞에 있는 명사 The word "scientist"를 수식한다.
• 「not A until B」는 'B할 때까지 A하지 않다, B하고 나서야 비로소 A하다'의 의미이다.

²This is in striking contrast with *the world of today*, // <u>in which</u> a man may <u>devote</u> a lifetime to a single type of germ or bacteria / and still **consider** *his subject* **vast and complex** enough / for a full generation of profound study.
• in which 이하는 the world of today를 보충 설명하는 계속적 용법의 관계사절이다. 관계사절 내에서 밑줄 친 두 부분이 병렬 구조를 이룬다.
• 두 번째 밑줄 친 부분에서 his subject는 consider의 목적어, vast and complex는 목적격보어이다.

³Having *few details* (to bother about) in his pursuit of knowledge, / the ancient could think in broad and encompassing terms.
• Having ~ knowledge는 이유를 나타내는 분사구문으로 Because they had few details ~ knowledge의 절로 바꿔 쓸 수 있다.

¹To get some understanding (of how "remarkable capacities for caring and sympathy" / fit into the process of natural selection), / consider a hypothetical case (directly involving life and death). An animal is in a situation [in which it can save the lives of four of its offspring / by sacrificing its own life]. If it behaves so as to preserve itself rather than its progeny, // then all its own genes survive and can continue in subsequent generations. 추론 근거 ²If, however, it sacrifices itself to save the four progeny, / each of which has half its genes, // then even though its own life and the genes [it is hosting] are lost, / twice as many of its genes survive. From the standpoint of the genes, / the odds of the survival (of its genes) have doubled / because of the altruism (of their host). 주제문 This simple case indicates // that increasing the chances of survival (of an organism) at the expense of its kin / can be less effective for gene survival.

어휘 remarkable 놀라운, 주목할 만한　capacity 능력; 수용력　sympathy 동정(심); 공감　●natural selection 자연 선택　hypothetical 가상의; 가설(가정)의　offspring (동물의) 새끼; 자식, 자손　sacrifice 희생(하다); 제물　so as to-v v하기 위해서　preserve 지키다; 보호[보존]하다　A rather than B B라기보다는 A　subsequent 그다음의, 차후의　generation 세대, 대(代); 발생　host 숙주; 주인; 주최하다　standpoint 관점, 견지　odds 가능성　altruism 이타주의, 이타심　indicate 보여주다, 나타내다　kin 동족; 친족, 친척　**[선택지 어휘]** reciprocity 호혜(서로 특별한 혜택을 주고받는 일)　alter 바꾸다, 변경하다　abandon 버리다; 그만두다　inherent 타고난, 내재하는

어휘● 자연 선택: 다윈이 도입한 개념으로 환경에 적응한 개체는 생존하고 그러지 못한 개체는 사라지는 일

해설 빈칸 문장으로 보아 한 유기체의 생존 가능성을 '어떻게' 증가시키는 것이 유전자의 생존에는 덜 효과적인지를 찾아야 한다. 동물의 예에서 새끼들을 위해 자신의 목숨을 희생하는 것이 결과적으로 더 많은 유전자를 남기는 것임을 알 수 있다. 따라서 빈칸에는 그와 반대로 유전자의 생존에 덜 효과적인 상황, 즉 ① '동족을 희생해서'가 들어가는 것이 가장 적절하다.

해석 '보살핌과 동정심에 대한 놀라운 능력'이 어떻게 자연 선택의 과정에 잘 들어맞는지에 대한 이해를 하기 위해, 삶과 죽음에 직접적으로 관련된 한 가상의 사례를 생각해보라. 한 동물이 자신의 목숨을 희생함으로써 새끼 네 마리의 목숨을 구할 수 있는 상황에 있다. 만약 자손이 아닌 자기 자신을 지키기 위해 행동한다면, 그 자신의 모든 유전자는 살아남아서 후대에서도 지속될 수 있다. 추론 근거 하지만 만약 그 동물이 자손 넷을 구하기 위해 자신을 희생하면, 자식들 각자가 그것의 유전자의 반을 갖고 있어서 비록 그 동물 자신의 목숨과 가지고 있는 유전자들은 사라질지라도, 그 동물의 유전자의 두 배가 살아남는 것이다. 유전자의 관점에서 유전자의 생존 가능성은 유전자 숙주의 이타주의 때문에 두 배가 된다. 주제문 이 단순한 사례는 동족을 희생해서 한 유기체의 생존 가능성을 증가시키는 것이 유전자의 생존에는 덜 효과적일 수 있다는 것을 보여준다.

오답 Check
② 호혜의 과정을 통해 → 호혜의 과정은 언급되지 않음.
③ 숙주의 행동을 바꿈으로써 → 숙주의 행동을 바꾼다는 내용은 없음.
④ 타고난 이기심을 버림으로써 → 이기심을 타고났다는 내용은 없고, 오히려 이기심을 버리고 자신을 희생하는 것이 유전자의 생존에 더 효과적이라는 내용과 반대됨.
⑤ 환경과의 상호 작용을 통해 → 환경과의 상호 작용은 언급되지 않음.

PLUS+ 변형문제
어휘 empathy 공감, 감정 이입
해설 동물이 자기를 희생해 새끼를 구함으로써 더 많은 유전자를 남겨 생존 가능성을 높인다고 했으므로 글의 제목으로 가장 적절한 것은 ③ '자기희생: 자신의 유전자를 위한 생존 전략'이다.
① 이기적이지 않은 행동은 환경의 이유 때문이다
→ 이타적 행동이 환경 때문이라는 언급은 없음.
② 동물의 이타주의: 동물 세계의 우정
④ 이타적 행동: 공감과 사랑의 기원
→ ②, ④ 이타주의는 맞으나 우정, 공감, 사랑은 언급되지 않음.
⑤ 이기적 유전자: 자연 선택의 대안
→ 이기적인 것과 반대인 자기희생에 관한 내용임.

구문 ¹To get *some understanding* (of how "remarkable capacities for caring and sympathy" fit into the process of natural selection), / consider *a hypothetical case* (directly involving life and death).
• 첫 번째 ( )는 전명구로 앞의 some understanding을 수식한다.
• how ~ selection은 전치사 of의 목적어로 쓰인 간접의문문이며, 「의문사(how)+주어("remarkable capacities for caring and sympathy")+동사 (fit into)」의 어순을 따른다.
• 두 번째 ( )는 a hypothetical case를 수식하는 현재분사구이다.

²If, however, it sacrifices itself to save *the four progeny*, / **each of which has half its genes**, // then even though its own life and *the genes* [(which[that]) it is hosting] are lost, / twice as many of its genes survive.
• 「대명사+of+관계대명사」 형태의 each of which가 이끄는 관계사절이 선행사 the four progeny를 부연 설명한다.
• [ ]는 목적격 관계대명사 which 또는 that이 생략된 관계사절로 the genes를 수식한다.

We have already known // how our emotions often take someone else's experiences / as their object. ¹It also seems // that we take into account their evaluations and interpretations / when making our own appraisals (of other emotional objects). ²For example, / we may enjoy a comedy film less // when our companions are evidently offended by its content, / or become more anxious // partly because those (sharing our fate) seem to find the situation worrying. In effect, / we tune perceptions (of emotional meaning) / against the apparent perspective of key others. Because these processes (of social appraisal) work in both directions, // others are also affected by our own apparent evaluations. ³Indeed, / sometimes we may only arrive at emotional conclusions / as a consequence of discussion with each other, / or by otherwise registering mutual reactions (in smiles, frowns, or diverted gazes). In either of these cases, / the appraisals (shaping emotions) are influenced / by a fundamentally interpersonal process.

해석 우리는 우리의 감정이 어떻게 다른 사람의 경험들을 그것(우리의 감정)들의 대상으로 종종 받아들이는지를 이미 알고 있다. 주제문 또한 우리는 다른 감정적 대상들에 대해 우리 자신이 평가를 내릴 때 그것(우리의 감정)들의 평가와 해석을 고려하는 것 같다. 예를 들어, 우리는 우리의 동행들이 코미디 영화의 내용에 명백히 기분 나빠할 때 그것을 덜 즐기거나, 부분적으로는 우리의 운명을 공유하는 사람들이 상황을 걱정스럽다고 생각하기 때문에 더 걱정할지도 모른다. 추론 근거 사실상 우리는 감정적 의미의 인식을 가장 중요한 타인들의 관점인 것처럼 보이는 것에 맞서 조정한다. 이러한 사회적 평가 과정은 양방향으로 작동하기 때문에, 다른 사람들 또한 우리 자신의 평가인 것처럼 보이는 것에 의해 영향받는다. 과연 때때로 우리는 오직 서로 간의 토의의 결과로, 혹은 상호 간의 반응을 다르게 나타냄으로써 (미소로, 찌푸림으로, 혹은 곁눈질로) 감정적 결론에 도달할 뿐일지도 모른다. 주제문 이 중 어느 경우에서도, 감정을 형성하는 평가는 근본적으로 대인적 과정의 영향을 받는다.

어휘 object 대상; 물체; 목적 take into account 고려하다 interpretation 해석, 이해 appraisal 평가; 감정, 견적 companion 동행, 친구 evidently 명백히 offend 기분 상하게 하다 fate 운명 in effect 사실상 tune 조정하다; 음을 맞추다, 조율하다 perception 인식, 인지 apparent (주로 명사 앞에 씀) ~인 것처럼 보이는; 명백한 perspective 관점 key 가장 중요한 as a consequence of ~의 결과로 otherwise 다르게, 달리; (만약) 그렇지 않으면 register (감정을) 나타내다; 등록하다 mutual 상호 간의 frown 찌푸림 divert 방향을 바꾸게 하다 gaze 응시 interpersonal 대인 관계의

[선택지 어휘] conceptualize 개념화하다 mechanism 메커니즘, 방법; 기계 장치, 기구; 구조, 기제 posture 자세, 태도

해설 우리는 어떤 대상을 평가할 때 다른 사람들이 그 대상에 대해 느끼는 감정에 따라 자신의 평가를 조정하며, 다른 사람들도 우리가 그 대상에 대해 어떻게 느끼는지에 따라 자신들의 평가를 조정한다는 내용이므로, 빈칸 문장을 완성하면 감정을 형성하는 평가는 ④ '근본적으로 대인적 과정의 영향을 받는다'가 된다.

오답 Check
① 당신이 자기 자신에게 말하는 방식에 의해 결정된다
→ 자신이 아닌 타인의 영향을 받는다는 내용임.
② 온갖 종류의 것들과 사건들에 의해 우리 속에서 자극받는다
→ 사물이나 사건 자체가 감정을 형성하는 평가에 영향을 준다는 내용은 없음.
③ 매우 영향력 있는 메커니즘으로 개념화된다
→ 지문에서 유추할 수 없는 내용.
⑤ 주로 신체적 자세와 제스처를 통해 드러난다
→ 지문의 smiles, frowns 등을 활용한 오답.

PLUS⁺ 변형응용문제

어휘 contagious 전염성의 cognitive bias 인지 편향
해설 개인이 어떤 대상에 대한 감정적 평가를 내리는 데 다른 사람들의 평가가 영향을 미친다는 내용이므로 제목으로 가장 적절한 것은 ⑤ '감정적 평가의 사회적 특징'이다.
① 감정은 전염적이니 친구를 현명하게 선택하라
② 타인의 인지에 있어 자아 개념의 역할
③ 인간 인지와 판단에서 인지 편향
④ 환경 자극에 대한 감정적 반응
→ ① ~ ④ 모두 지문에 언급된 단어를 활용한 오답.

구문 ¹It also seems // that we take into account their evaluations and interpretations / **when** making *our own appraisals* (of other emotional objects).
• It seems that ~은 '~인 것 같다'의 뜻이다. 여기서 It은 '막연한 상황'을 나타낸다.
• when 이하는 의미를 분명히 하기 위해 접속사를 생략하지 않은 분사구문이다.
• ( )는 전명구로 our own appraisals를 수식한다.

²For example, / we **may** enjoy a comedy film less // when our companions are evidently offended by its content, / [or] become more anxious // partly because *those* (sharing our fate) seem to find the situation worrying.
• may 뒤의 두 밑줄 친 부분이 or로 연결되어 병렬 구조를 이룬다.
• ( )는 those를 수식하는 현재분사구이다.

³Indeed, / sometimes we may only arrive at emotional conclusions / as a consequence of discussion with each other, [or] by otherwise registering mutual reactions ~.
• 밑줄 친 두 전치사구가 or로 연결되어 병렬 구조를 이룬다.

Genetic commands tell the neurons (in the brain) to start growing more and more connections. This creates an initial over-production (of connectivity between the neurons). Then, this bout of over-production is followed / by a period of pruning, // where connections are lost between neurons. Around four out of every ten connections are lost / with about 100,000 lost every second / during the peak rate. This loss of connectivity is particularly interesting and at first surprising. Why would nature put in all the effort / to build bridges between neurons / only to knock them down almost equally as fast / at a later date? ^{주제문} ¹It turns out // that the over-production and subsequent destruction of connections / may be a cunning strategy (to shape the brain to deal with the specific situation). ^{추론 근거} ²Many connections mean // that the brain is prepared / for every potential experience [that it may encounter]. However, only the neurons [that repeatedly work together] can maintain these connections. When neurons are not reciprocally activated, // nature prunes their connections / through inactivity. To put it in terms of a metaphor of neighborhood, 'If you don't return my call, // I'll not bother contacting you.'

[해석] 유전적 명령은 뇌의 뉴런들에게 점점 더 많은 연결을 산출하기 시작하라고 말한다. 이것은 뉴런 사이의 연결에 있어 초기 과잉 생산을 일으킨다. 그리고 이 한 차례의 과잉 생산 다음에는 가지치기의 기간이 뒤따르는데, 거기서 뉴런 사이의 연결이 끊어진다. 최고 속도를 내는 동안에는 매초 약 10만 개가 상실되면서 10개의 연결마다 약 4개가 상실된다. 이러한 연결의 상실은 특히 흥미롭고 처음에는 놀랍다. 왜 자연은 뉴런 사이에 다리를 놓으려고 그 모든 노력을 들이고는 결국 나중에 거의 동일하게 빠른 속도로 그것들을 때려 부술까? ^{주제문} 과잉 생산과 뒤이어 일어나는 연결의 도태는 뇌를 특정한 상황에 대처하도록 만든 교묘한 전략일 수 있음이 밝혀진다. ^{추론 근거} 많은 연결은 뇌가 맞닥뜨릴 수도 있는 모든 가능성 있는 경험에 대비한다는 것을 의미한다. 하지만 함께 반복적으로 작동하는 뉴런들만이 이런 연결을 유지할 수 있다. 뉴런이 서로 활성화되지 않으면, 자연은 비활성을 통해 그들의 연결을 잘라낸다. 이웃에 대한 은유의 관점에서 말하자면 '당신이 내 전화에 답하지 않으면 나는 당신과 연락하려고 애쓰지 않을 것이다.'

[어휘] command 명령(하다); 지휘(하다) bout 한 차례; 한 시합 prune 가지치기하다; 잘라내다 knock down 부수다; 해체하다 turn out ~인 것으로 밝혀지다[드러나다] subsequent 뒤이어 일어나는 destruction 파괴, 파멸; (문서의) 파기 cunning 교묘한; 교활한 deal with ~에 대처하다; ~을 다루다 potential 가능성이 있는, 잠재적인 encounter 맞닥뜨리다; 접하다; 만남 reciprocally 서로; 호혜적으로 in terms of ~의 관점에서, ~면에서 bother 애를 쓰다, 신경 쓰다 metaphor 은유

[해설] 뉴런의 많은 연결은 모든 가능성 있는 경험에 대비를 위한 것인데, 서로 활성화되지 않는 뉴런은 연결이 끊긴다고 했으므로 빈칸에 들어갈 말로는 ⑤ '당신이 내 전화에 답하지 않으면 나는 당신과 연락하려고 애쓰지 않을 것이다'가 적절하다.

[오답 Check]
① 이웃이 당신에게 미소 지으면 당신은 외면하는 경향이 있다
→ 상대방의 신호를 거부하는 것으로 적절하지 않음.
② 자신을 사랑하지 않으면 이웃을 사랑할 수 없다
→ 지문 내용을 크게 벗어남.
③ 이웃의 집이 불타고 있으면 당신 역시 안전하지 않다
→ 이웃이 당신에게 신호를 보내고, 당신도 함께 신호를 보내는 상황이 아님.
④ 긴급한 도움이 필요하면 이웃의 문을 두드려라
→ 지문 내용을 크게 벗어남.

PLUS + 변형문제

[어휘] detachment 분리, 이탈 individually 개별적으로, 각각 따로 lead to ~을 야기하다; ~로 이어지다 startling 놀라운, 깜짝 놀랄 tactic 전략, 전술 overabundance 과잉; 과다

[해설] 뉴런 사이의 연결을 과잉 생산한 후에 함께 신호를 보내지 않는 연결이 끊기는 방식으로 뇌가 특정 상황에 대처한다고 했으므로 제목으로는 ⑤ '여러분의 뇌의 놀라운 전략: 과잉 후 가지치기'가 알맞다.
① 더 많은 연결이 있을수록, 더 적은 분리가 있다
→ 연결과 분리의 반비례 관계에 대한 언급은 없음.
② 더 많은 경험이 여러분의 뇌가 자라도록 돕는 이유
→ 경험이 뇌 성장에 도움이 된다는 언급은 없음.
③ 어떻게 독립적인 뉴런이 개별적으로 활성화하는가
→ 뉴런은 서로 활성화되어야 하므로 반대 내용임.
④ 뉴런 연결의 상실을 야기하는 결정적인 요소들
→ 연결의 상실을 일으키는 요소에 대해서는 언급하지 않음.

[구문] ¹**It** turns out // **that** the over-production and subsequent destruction of connections / may be *a cunning strategy* (to shape the brain to deal with the specific situation).
• It이 가주어, 접속사 that이 이끄는 명사절(that ~ the specific situation)이 진주어이다.
• ( )는 형용사적 용법으로 쓰인 to부정사구로 앞에 있는 명사구 a cunning strategy를 수식한다.

²Many connections **mean** // that the brain is prepared / for *every potential experience* [**that** it may encounter].
• 밑줄 친 that은 접속사로 동사 mean의 목적어 역할을 하는 명사절(that ~ may encounter)을 이끈다.
• [ ]는 목적격 관계대명사 that이 이끄는 관계사절로 선행사 every potential experience를 수식한다.

One of the biggest challenges (of green marketing) / is the need (to address environmental issues / while at the same time satisfying core customer needs). ① This is one of the challenges "green" ad campaigns have to face — convincing consumers // that environmental products do not perform lower than regular products. ② Rather, they often — with regard to specific features — perform better. ③ The environmental benefits (of green products) are // that their environmental impacts are less than those of similar products. ④ ¹For example, / energy-saving light bulbs last longer, / offer better convenience (they do not have to be replaced as often as regular bulbs), / and reduce energy expenses. ⑤ ²Convenience and fulfillment (of basic human needs) / are two of the most significant reasons [why consumers buy green products] — / not necessarily for environmental reasons / but for better value (safety, money).

해석 그린 마케팅의 최대의 난제 중 하나는 소비자의 핵심 욕구를 충족시키는 동시에 환경 사안들을 다룰 필요성이 있다는 것이다. ① 이것이 '친환경적인' 광고 캠페인이 직면해야 하는 난제 중 하나인데, 즉 소비자들에게 친환경 제품이 일반 제품보다 성능이 더 낮지 않다는 것을 납득시키는 것이다. ② 주제문 오히려, 그것들은 종종, 특정한 성능에 관해서는 성능이 더 좋다. ③ 친환경 제품의 환경적 이점들은 그것들의 환경적 영향이 비슷한 제품들의 영향보다 더 적다는 것이다. ④ 예를 들어, 에너지를 절약하는 백열전구는 더 오래가고, 더 나은 편의를 제공하고 (그것들은 일반 전구만큼이나 자주 갈지 않아도 된다), 그리고 에너지 비용을 줄인다. ⑤ 편의와 인간의 기본적인 욕구 충족이 소비자가 친환경 제품을 구매하는 가장 중요한 두 가지 이유인데, 즉 반드시 환경적인 이유 때문이 아니라 더 나은 가치(안전, 돈)를 위해서이다.

어휘 ○green marketing 그린 마케팅 need 필요(성); 욕구; 요구 address (문제·상황을) 다루다; 연설하다 environmental 환경의, 환경과 관련된 issue 사안, 쟁점; 문제 satisfy 충족시키다, 만족시키다 core 핵심; 중심부 convince 납득시키다, 확신시키다 with regard to A A에 관해서는 specific 특정한; 구체적인, 명확한 feature 성능, 특징 energy-saving 에너지를 절약하는 light bulb 백열전구 convenience 편의, 편리 replace 갈다, 교체하다; 대신[대체]하다 expense 비용, 돈 fulfillment 충족, 성취; 실행, 이행 significant 중요한, 의미 있는, 커다란 necessarily 반드시; 물론; 불가피하게

어휘 ○ 그린 마케팅: 자연환경 보전, 생태계 균형 등을 중시하는 기업 판매 전략으로 공해 요인을 제거한 상품을 제조, 판매해야 한다는 소비자 보호 운동에 입각해 인간 삶의 질을 높이려는 기업 활동을 일컫는다.

해설 무관한 문장은 주제와 관련 있는 어구를 넣어 만든다는 것에 유의한다. 이 글은 그린 마케팅의 최대의 난제 중 하나가 친환경 제품이 일반 제품보다 성능이 떨어지지 않고 오히려 특정 성능은 더 좋다는 것을 소비자에게 납득시키는 것이라는 내용인데, ③은 친환경 제품이 비슷한 제품보다 환경에 미치는 영향이 적다는 환경적 이점에 관한 내용으로 글의 전체 흐름과 관계가 없다.

오답 Check

⑤는 소비자가 환경적인 이유 때문만이 아닌 더 나은 가치 때문에 친환경 제품을 구입한다는 내용으로 친환경 제품의 특정 성능이 더 좋을 수 있다는 글의 주제와 밀접하게 연결된다.

PLUS⁺ 변형문제

어휘 go nowhere 실패하다, 아무 성과를 못보다 sustainability 지속 가능성

해설 친환경 제품은 환경에만 도움이 되는 것이 아니라 편의, 내구성, 비용 절감과 같은 성능 면에서도 일반 제품과 비교해 떨어지지 않는다는 내용이므로 글의 제목으로 가장 적절한 것은 ④ '친환경 제품은 그저 환경친화적인 것 이상이다'이다.

① 그린 마케팅의 난제와 비용
→ 그린 마케팅의 비용은 언급되지 않음.

② 왜 환경친화적인 제품이 더 비싼가?
→ 친환경 제품의 가격은 언급되지 않음.

③ 그린 마케팅이 성공하지 못하는 이유
→ 그린 마케팅이 실패했다는 내용은 언급되지 않음.

⑤ 친환경적이 되는 것은 환경 지속가능성을 높이는 것
→ 상식적인 내용을 이용한 오답.

구문 ¹For example, / energy-saving light bulbs last longer, / offer better convenience (they do not have to be replaced **as** *often* **as** regular bulbs), / and reduce energy expenses.

• 동사 last, offer, reduce가 콤마(,)와 and로 연결되어 병렬 구조를 이루고 있다.

• better convenience를 보충 설명하는 ( )가 문장 중간에 삽입된 형태이다. 여기서 「as 원급 as ~ (~만큼 …하다)」 구문이 쓰여 they(= energy-saving light bulbs)와 regular bulbs를 비교하고 있다.

²Convenience and *fulfillment* (of basic human needs) / are two of *the most significant reasons* [why consumers buy green products] — / not necessarily for environmental reasons / but for better value (safety, money).

• ( )는 전명구로 앞의 fulfillment를 수식하고, [ ]는 관계부사절로 선행사 the most significant reasons를 수식한다.

• 대시(—) 뒤의 내용은 앞 어구에 대한 부연 설명을 이끈다. 여기에 「not A but B (A가 아니라 B)」가 쓰였으며 A와 B 자리에 전명구가 병렬 구조를 이루고 있다.

Einstein held // that the speed of light is constant // and that events (in one place) cannot influence events (in another place) simultaneously. ¹In relativity theory, / the speed of light has to be taken into account / for information (to travel from one particle to another).

(B) However, / experiment after experiment has shown // that this is not the case. In 1965, Irish physicist John Bell created an experiment [that showed // that separate particles can influence each other instantaneously / over great distances].

(C) ²This has since been performed numerous times / and confirms // that the properties of polarized light are correlated, or linked, // no matter how far apart the particles are. There is some kind of instantaneous — faster than light — communication (between them).

주제문
(A) All of this implies // that Einstein's concept of spacetime, (neatly divided into separate regions by light velocity), is indefensible. ³Instead, the events [we observe] exist in a space [that is not limited by an external spacetime].

어휘 constant 일정한, 불변의; 지속적인 simultaneously 동시에, 일제히 take A into account A를 고려[참작]하다 particle 입자, 조각 instantaneously 동시에; 즉각, 당장에 property (사물의) 속성, 특성; 재산; 부동산 ◑polarized light 편광 velocity 속도, 속력 indefensible 옹호할 수 없는, 변호의 여지 없는
어휘◑ 편광: 빛의 진동면, 즉 전기장과 자기장의 방향이 항상 일정한 평면에 한정되어 있는 빛.

해설 주어진 글은 아인슈타인의 이론에 대한 설명이고, (B)와 (C)를 통해 그 이론을 흔드는 다른 실험이 있다는 것을 알 수 있다. 그중 계속되는 실험에서 아인슈타인의 이론(this)이 그렇지 않다는 것을 역접의 접속사 However와 함께 나타내는 (B)가 주어진 글 다음에 와야 한다. (B)에 나온 존 벨의 실험이 반복해서 행해졌다는 내용의 (C)가 오고 결론적으로 아인슈타인의 시공간의 개념을 옹호할 수 없다는 내용인 (A)가 오는 게 적절하다.

오답 Check
(B)와 (C)의 내용이 아인슈타인의 이론과 반대된다는 점에서 유사한데, 주어진 글의 이론을 반박하므로 역접의 접속사 However가 들어간 (B)가 먼저 와야 한다. (C)의 This는 (B)에 나온 an experiment를 가리킨다.

해석 아인슈타인은 빛의 속도는 일정하고, 한 장소에서 일어난 사건들이 다른 장소에서 일어난 사건들에 동시에 영향을 줄 수 없다고 생각했다. 상대성 이론에서 빛의 속도는 한 입자에서 다른 입자로 이동할 정보를 위해 고려되어야 한다.
(B) 그러나 계속되는 실험에서 이것이 그렇지 않다는 것을 보여주었다. 1965년 아일랜드의 물리학자인 존 벨은 따로 떨어진 입자들이 먼 거리에서 동시에 서로 영향을 줄 수 있다는 것을 보여주는 실험을 창안했다.
(C) 이것은 그 후 수없이 여러 번 행해졌고, 아무리 입자가 멀리 떨어져 있더라도 편광의 성질이 상호 연관되어 있거나 연결되어 있음이 확인되었다. 그들 사이에는 빛보다 더 빠른 일종의 즉각적인 의사소통이 있다.
(A) 주제문 이 모든 것은 아인슈타인의 광속에 의해 분리된 영역으로 깔끔하게 나누어진 시공간의 개념을 옹호할 수 없다는 것을 의미한다. 대신에, 우리가 관찰하는 사건은 외부의 시공간에 제한되지 않는 공간에 존재한다.

PLUS + 변형문제
해설 이 글은 아인슈타인의 시공간 이론이 현대의 반복된 존 벨의 실험에서 잘못된 것으로 밝혀졌다는 내용이므로 정답으로는 ④ '아인슈타인의 개념에 도전하는 현대 물리학'이 적절하다.
① 사건에 미치는 광속의 영향
→ 언급된 단어를 활용한 오답임.
② 아인슈타인의 이론에서 입자의 한계
→ 입자가 아닌 이론 자체의 한계에 가까움.
③ 아인슈타인의 상대성 이론을 시험하는 방법
→ 시험하는 방법이 아닌 상대성 이론에 반하는 결과를 언급함.
⑤ 시공간에서 광속 분리에 대한 이유
→ 광속에 의해 분리된 영역에서 연상되는 내용임.

구문 ¹In relativity theory, / the speed of light has to be taken into account / *for information* (to travel from one particle to another).
• ( )는 형용사적 용법으로 쓰인 to부정사구로 information을 수식하고, for information은 to부정사구의 의미상 주어이다.

²This has since been performed numerous times / and confirms // **that** the properties of polarized light are correlated, or linked, // **no matter how far apart the particles are**.
• 접속사 that이 이끄는 명사절은 동사 confirms의 목적어절 역할을 한다.
• 밑줄 친 두 개의 분사가 콤마(,)와 or로 연결되었다.
• no matter how ~ are는 양보의 부사절로 however the particles are far apart로 바꿔 쓸 수 있다.

³Instead, *the event*s [(which[that]) we observe] exist in *a space* [that is not limited by an external spacetime].
• 첫 번째 [ ]는 목적격 관계대명사 which 또는 that이 생략된 관계사절로 선행사 the events를 수식한다.
• 두 번째 [ ]는 주격 관계대명사 that이 이끄는 관계사절로 선행사 a space를 수식한다.

주제문
One reason // that some apparent sunk cost ventures may not be irrational / is that the decision makers are choosing actions / to project and preserve their reputations / for being decisive or for not being wasteful.

(C) ¹Just as the person [who orders too much food] might be labeled a poor judge (of his or her own appetite) and wasteful, // these decision makers might be trying to protect their *future* reputations / as morally consistent individuals or good decision makers.

(B) ²If, indeed, abandonment (of a sunk cost) negatively affects future reputation, // then it may be wise not to do it. The auto maker [who abandons an unpopular model] may be ridiculed for making a "gutless" decision / and lose future authority and actual power within his or her organization.

(A) Such future reputational costs are perfectly reasonable factors (to consider in determining whether or not to abandon a particular course of action). So long as other people believe in honoring sunk costs, // the person [who does not] may be regarded as weird.

[해석] 주제문 매몰 비용 모험인 것처럼 보이는 것들이 비합리적이지 않을지도 모르는 한 가지 이유는 의사 결정자들이 결단력이 있다는 혹은 낭비하지 않는다는 명성을 보여주고 유지하려는 행동을 선택하고 있기 때문이다.
(C) 너무 많은 음식을 주문하는 사람이 자신의 식욕을 잘 판단하지 못하며 낭비적이라는 꼬리표가 붙을 수 있는 것과 꼭 마찬가지로, 이러한 의사 결정자들은 도덕적으로 일관된 개인으로 혹은 훌륭한 의사 결정자로 자신의 '미래' 평판을 보호하려고 노력하고 있는 것일지도 모른다.
(B) 매몰 비용을 포기하는 것이 미래의 평판에 정말로 부정적으로 영향을 미친다면, 그러지 않는 것이 현명할지도 모른다. 인기가 없는 모델을 포기한 자동차 제조자는 '배짱이 없는' 결정을 내렸다고 조롱받으며 자기 조직 내에서 미래의 권위와 실제 권력을 상실할지도 모른다.
(A) 그러한 미래의 평판 손실은 특정한 행동 방침을 포기할지 말지를 결정하는 데 있어서 고려해야 할 완벽하게 합리적인 요인이다. 다른 사람들이 매몰 비용을 받아들이는 것을 옳다고 믿는 한, 그러지 않는 사람은 이상하다고 간주될지도 모른다.

[어휘] venture 모험[적 시도]; 모험하다 irrational 비합리[비이성]적인 project 보여주다, 나타내다 preserve 유지[보존]하다, 지키다 reputation 명성, 평판 *cf.* reputational 평판의; 명성 있는 decisive 결단력이 있는; 확고한 label 꼬리표[딱지]를 붙이다 appetite 식욕 wasteful 낭비하는, 사치스러운 consistent 일관된, 한결같은 abandonment 포기 *cf.* abandon 포기하다, 버리다 ridicule 조롱하다, 비웃다 authority 권위, 권력 so long as ~하는 한 honor 받아들이다; 존경하다; 명예 weird 이상한, 기이한

[해설] 매몰 비용에서 발을 빼지 못하는 이유가 미래의 평판을 보호하기 위함이라는 주어진 문장 다음에는 같은 맥락으로 이러한 판단을 내리는 사람들은 미래의 좋은 평판을 지키려는 것일 수 있다는 (C)가 나온다. (C)의 these decision makers는 주어진 문장에 있는 '미래 평판을 보호하고자 매몰 비용을 유지하는 의사 결정자들'을 가리킨다. 그 뒤로는 (C)의 반대 상황을 가정하여 매몰 비용을 포기할 경우 미래의 평판이 손상되는 피해를 볼 수 있다는 내용의 (B)가 이어진다. (A)의 Such future reputational costs는 (B)의 마지막에 나온 인기 없는 모델을 단종해서 평판이 깎이고 권위와 권력을 잃게 되는 자동차 제조자가 감수하게 될 손실을 지칭하므로 (B) 다음에 오는 것이 자연스럽다.

PLUS+ 변형문제

[어휘] distort 왜곡하다 let A go A를 버리다[포기하다]; 놓다 fallacy 오류, 틀린 생각
[해설] 의사 결정자들이 미래 평판을 보호하기 위해 매몰 비용을 버리지 못하고 손실을 감수한다는 내용의 글이므로 제목으로 가장 적절한 것은 ③ '왜 의사 결정자들은 매몰 비용 모험을 계속하는가'이다.
① 매몰 비용 편향이 도덕적 판단을 왜곡한다
→ 글에 언급된 어구를 활용한 오답.
② 사업 성공은 매몰 비용을 포기하는 것을 의미한다
→ 사업 성공과 매몰 비용 포기와의 인과관계는 언급되지 않음.
④ 매몰 비용을 포기하는 것이 어떻게 당신의 명성을 유지할 수 있는가 → 오히려 매몰 비용을 포기하지 않아야 명성을 유지할 수 있다고 했으므로 글의 내용과 반대됨.
⑤ 매몰 비용 오류를 극복하면 의사 결정을 더 잘하게 된다
→ 매몰 비용 오류는 언급되지 않은 내용임.

[구문] ¹**Just as** *the person* [who orders too much food] might be labeled a poor judge (of his or her own appetite) and wasteful, // these decision makers might be trying to protect their *future* reputations / **as** morally consistent individuals or good decision makers.
• Just as는 부사절 접속사로 '~한 것과 꼭 마찬가지로'의 뜻이다.
• [ ]는 주격 관계대명사 who가 이끄는 관계사절로 the person을 수식한다.
• 전치사 as의 목적어로 밑줄 친 두 부분이 or로 병렬 연결된다.

²If, indeed, *abandonment* (of a sunk cost) negatively affects future reputation, // then **it** may be wise **not to do it**.
• 주절에서 it은 가주어 not to do it이 진주어이다.
• do의 목적어로 쓰인 it은 문맥상 abandonment of a sunk cost를 의미한다.

Ginseng, yam, and mayapple are all small plants [that overwinter as nutritious underground stems or roots]. (①) ¹This shared way (of living) explains // why they are all so rich in medicinal chemicals. (②) Unlike fast-moving animals or thick-barked trees, / these stationary, thin-skinned plants are highly vulnerable to attack from mammals and insects. (③) Their underground stores (of food) are particularly attractive to would-be predators. (④ ²Because they lack the ability (to flee or to hide behind strong walls), // the plants' only defensive option is / to soak their bodies in chemicals [that play havoc with the guts, nerves, and hormones of their enemies].) Because natural selection has designed the defensive chemicals specifically to attack the physiology of animals, // these poisons can, in careful human hands, be turned into medicines. (⑤) By finding just the right dose, / herbalists can turn the plants' defensive arsenal / into an impressive collection (of stimulants, blood thinners, hormones, and other medicines).

해석 인삼과 참마와 포도필름은 모두 영양분이 많은 땅속줄기나 뿌리로 겨울을 나는 작은 식물들이다. 주제문 이러한 공유된 삶의 방식은 왜 그들이 모두 그토록 의약적 화학물질이 풍부한지를 설명해준다. 빠르게 이동하는 동물이나 껍질이 두꺼운 나무와는 달리, 이 움직이지 않는 껍질이 얇은 식물들은 포유류와 곤충의 공격에 대단히 취약하다. 그들의 지하 식량 저장고는 장차 포식자가 될 수 있는 존재들에게 특히 매력적이다. 그들에게는 도망치거나 튼튼한 벽 뒤에 숨는 능력이 없기 때문에 그 식물들의 유일한 방어적 선택은 자신의 천적의 내장, 신경, 그리고 호르몬을 엉망으로 만드는 화학물질로 자신의 몸을 흠뻑 적시는 것이다. 자연 선택은 동물들의 생리 기능을 특별히 공격하기 위한 방어적 화학 물질을 고안해왔으므로, 이러한 독들은 주의 깊은 인간의 손에서 약으로 변할 수 있다. 그저 올바른 복용량을 찾아냄으로써, 약초 재배자들은 식물의 방어적 무기고를 각성제, 혈액 희석제, 호르몬, 그리고 다른 약의 인상적인 모음으로 바꿀 수 있다.

어휘 ginseng 인삼 yam 참마 mayapple 포도필름(속(屬)의 식물) overwinter 겨울을 나다[나게 하다] nutritious 영양분이 많은; 영양의 medicinal 의약의; 약효가[치유력이] 있는 bark 나무껍질 stationary 움직이지 않는; 고정된 vulnerable 취약한, 받기 쉬운 would-be 장래의; (장차) ~이 되려고 하는 predator 포식자 lack ~이 없다, 부족하다 flee 도망치다, 달아나다 defensive 방어적인, 방어[수비]의 soak 흠뻑 적시다; 담그다[담기다] play havoc with ~을 엉망으로 만들다[혼란시키다] gut 내장, 소화관 specifically 특별히; 명확하게 physiology 생리 기능[현상]; 생리학 dose (1회) 복용량; 약 herbalist 약초 재배자; 약초상 stimulant 각성제, 자극제 blood thinner 혈액 희석제

해설 ④ 앞 문장은 일부 뿌리 식물들이 양분이 풍부하여 포식자에게 매력적이라는 내용인데 ④ 뒤에는 식물이 방어적 화학물질, 즉 독을 고안해왔다는 내용이 나오므로 두 문장이 논리적으로 연결되지 않는다. 주어진 문장은 특별한 방어 능력이 없는 식물이 자신을 지키기 위해 포식 동물들에게 독이 될 수 있는 물질을 몸속에 생성한다는 내용이므로 이를 ④에 위치시키면, '그 독은 인간의 손에 의해 약으로 바뀔 수 있다'는 뒤의 내용과 자연스럽게 연결된다.

오답 Check
③ 뒤의 문장은 뿌리 식물이 포식자들에게 매력적이라는 내용인데, 주어진 문장의 식물은 자신을 방어하기 위해 그러한 포식자들에게 독이 될 수 있는 물질을 만들게 되었다는 내용은 앞 문장(원인)에 대한 결과에 해당하므로 그 뒤에 오는 것은 자연스럽다.

PLUS⁺ 변형문제
해설 식물이 포식자로부터 자신을 지키기 위해 만들어낸 독성 물질이 인간의 약으로 사용될 수 있다는 내용의 글이므로 요지로 가장 적절한 것은 ⑤이다.
① → 그럴듯하지만 글에 언급되지 않은 상식에 의거한 오답.
② → 글의 마지막에 식물 물질로 만든 약이 언급되긴 했지만 부작용에 대한 내용은 없음.
③ → 글에 언급되지 않은 내용.
④ → 인간의 손에서 주의 깊게 쓰여야 한다고 했지만 글의 요지는 아님.

구문 ¹This shared way (of living) **explains** // why they are all so rich in medicinal chemicals.
• 동사 explains의 목적어로 의문사 why가 이끄는 절이 간접의문문(의문사+주어+동사)의 어순으로 쓰였다.

²Because they lack the ability (to flee or to hide behind strong walls), // the plants' only defensive option is / **to soak** their bodies in chemicals [that play havoc with the guts, nerves, and hormones of their enemies].
• ( )는 the ability와 동격 관계이다.
• to soak 이하는 to부정사의 명사적 용법으로 문장의 보어 역할을 한다.
• [ ]는 관계대명사 that이 이끄는 관계사절로 선행사 chemicals를 수식한다.

If you're a young athlete, // you, your parents, and your coaches want you to experience success now // because you and they believe // that early success is highly predictive of later success in your sport. (①) Our athletic culture is obsessed with the "phenom" and the "can't-miss kid," // who show earlier dominance in a sport. (② <u>Yet, although there have been phenoms [who went on to great success later in their careers], // this perception is as much fantasy as reality.</u>) For example, / out of the thousands (of young baseball players [who have competed in the Little League World Series throughout the years]), / fewer than 50 went on to major-league careers. (③) In fact, / phenoms are a statistical rarity, // and those can't-miss kids often do miss later in their athletic careers. (④) [1]More often than not, / it is the athletes [who keep at it through setbacks, plateaus, and failures] who ultimately "make it." (⑤) ^{주제문} [2]<u>Your efforts early on as you strive for your sports goals / should be devoted to preparing yourself for success in the future, // when it matters most, / not achieving quick and immediate success.</u>

[해석] 여러분이 어린 운동선수라면, 여러분과 부모님, 그리고 코치들은 여러분이 지금 성공을 경험하기를 원하는데, 왜냐하면 여러분과 그들은 이른 성공이 여러분이 하는 스포츠에서 이후의 성공의 강력한 전조가 된다고 믿기 때문이다. 우리의 운동 문화는 '천재'와 '성공할 것이 틀림없는 아이'에 사로잡혀 있는데, 그들은 스포츠에서 일찍 우위를 보인다. 그러나 비록 선수 생활 후반까지 계속해서 큰 성공을 거둔 천재들이 있기는 했지만, 이러한 인식은 현실인 만큼이나 환상이기도 하다. 예를 들어 수년 동안 내내 리틀 리그 월드 시리즈에서 겨룬 수천 명의 어린 야구 선수 중에서, 50명도 안 되는 수가 메이저 리그 선수 생활로 넘어갔다. 사실 천재는 통계적으로 희귀하며, 성공할 것이 틀림없다는 그 아이들은 운동 경력 후반에 종종 실패한다. 대개 궁극적으로 '성공하는' 사람은 바로 좌절, 정체기, 그리고 실패를 겪으며 견디는 선수들이다. ^{주제문} 자신의 스포츠 목표를 위해 애쓰는 초기부터의 여러분의 노력은 빠르고 즉각적인 성공을 달성하는 데가 아니라, 그것이 가장 중요할 때인 미래에 성공할 수 있도록 준비하는 데 바쳐져야 한다.

[어휘] athlete 운동선수 predictive of ~의 전조가 되는 be obsessed with ~에 사로잡혀 있다 dominance 우위, 우세 perception 인식, 지각 compete (시합에서) 겨루다, 경쟁하다 statistical 통계적인 rarity 희귀 more often than not 자주, 대개 keep at it 견디어 내다 setback 차질, 좌절 strive for ~을 얻으려 노력하다 be devoted to ~에 헌신하다[바쳐지다] immediate 즉각적인

[해설] 주어진 문장이 '그러나(Yet)'로 시작되며, 경력 후반까지 성공을 이어 나갈 수 있다는 '이러한 인식'이 환상에 가깝다고 진술했으므로, 주어진 문장 앞에는 '경력 초반의 성공이 나중의 성공을 보증해준다'는 내용이 나와야 한다. 이른 성공이 나중의 성공을 보증한다고 생각하며 어린 천재 선수에게 과도한 의미를 부여하는 상황이 ② 전까지 기술되고 ② 다음에서는 어린 천재 선수가 성공을 성인기까지 이어 나갈 확률이 매우 낮다는 예시를 제시하고 있어서 앞 문장과 맥락이 이어지지 않는다. 따라서 주어진 문장은 ②에 위치해야 한다.

PLUS+ 변형문제

[해설] 어린 운동선수가 성인기까지 성공하기 위해서는 즉각적인 성공보다 실패를 극복하며 장기적인 목표를 위해 노력해야 한다고 조언하는 글이므로 제목으로 가장 적절한 것은 ⑤ '어린 운동선수들은 성공하기 위해 무엇을 추구해야 하는가?'이다.
① 어린 운동선수의 성공을 판단하는 방법
② 어린 운동선수들의 부모가 해야 할 것과 하지 말아야 할 것
③ 어린 운동선수들이 실패의 두려움을 다루도록 돕기
④ 프로 선수들에게서 어린 선수들이 배울 수 있는 것
→ ① ~ ④ 모두 글에 언급되지 않은 내용.

[구문] [1]More often than not, / **it is** *the athletes* [who keep at it through setbacks, plateaus, and failures] **who** ultimately "make it."
• 「It is ~ who[that] ...」 강조 구문은 '…한 것은 바로 ~이다'의 의미로 It is와 who[that] 사이의 말이 강조된다. 이 문장에서는 the athletes ~ and failures가 강조되고 있다.
• [ ]는 the athletes를 수식하는 관계사절로 첫 번째 who를 강조 구문의 who로 착각하지 않도록 한다.

[2]Your efforts early on as you strive for your sports goals / **should be devoted to** preparing yourself for success in *the future*, // when it matters most, / not (to) achieving quick and immediate success.
• Your ~ goals 부분이 주어이며 should be devoted가 동사이다.
• 「be devoted to v-ing」는 'v하는 데 바쳐지다'의 뜻이다. 밑줄 친 두 부분이 콤마(,)로 연결되며, achieving 앞에는 to가 생략되었다.
• when it matters most는 the future를 보충 설명하는 관계사절로 it은 success를 지칭한다.

40 ④

We live in a world [where leaders frequently disappoint us]. Meticulous biographers sometimes diminish the image (of great leaders), / such as Martin Luther King, Jr., and George Washington, / by carefully examining their moral shortcomings. ¹It's difficult to have heroes in a world [where every wart and wrinkle of a person's life is public]. Ironically, the increase in information [that we have about leaders] has increased the confusion / surrounding the ethics of leadership. ²The more flawed our leaders are, // the greater our desire for highly ethical leaders. The ethical issues (of leadership) are found not only in public debates / but lie simmering below the surface (of the existing leadership literature).

↓

Greater access to information (about leaders) has (A) demystified them, // and this has left people desiring leaders / with (B) flawless character.

해석 우리는 지도자들이 우리를 자주 실망시키는 세상에서 산다. 추론 근거 꼼꼼한 전기 작가들은 때때로 마틴 루터 킹 주니어와 조지 워싱턴 같은 지도자의 이미지를 그들의 도덕적 결점을 주의 깊게 검토함으로써 깎아내린다. 어떤 사람의 인생의 모든 사마귀와 주름이 공개되는 세상에서 영웅을 갖기란 어려운 일이다. 주제문 아이러니하게도, 우리가 지도자들에 대하여 알게 되는 정보의 증가는 리더십의 윤리를 둘러싼 혼란을 증가시켰다. 추론 근거 우리의 지도자들에게 결함이 많으면 많을수록, 대단히 윤리적인 지도자에 대한 우리의 갈망은 더 커진다. 리더십의 윤리적 문제는 공적 토론에서 나타날 뿐만 아니라 현존하는 리더십 문헌의 표면 아래에서 심화되고 있는 상태에 있다.

↓

지도자들에 대한 정보에 더 많이 접근할 수 있게 된 것이 그들의 (A) 신비성을 없앴고, 이로 인해 사람들은 (B) 결함 없는 인성을 갖춘 지도자를 갈망하는 상태가 되었다.

어휘 meticulous 꼼꼼한, 세심한 biographer 전기 작가 diminish (중요성을) 깎아내리다, 폄하하다; 줄이다 shortcoming 결점 public 공개되는; 공공의, 공적인 ethics 윤리; 윤리학 cf. ethical 윤리적인; 도덕적으로 옳은 flawed 결함[결점]이 있는 simmer 부글부글 끓다 surface 표면, 표층 literature 문헌; 인쇄물; 문학

해설 지도자에 대한 정보가 낱낱이 밝혀지는 현대 사회에서 지도자들은 신비성이 없어졌고(demystified), 이에 대한 반작용으로 윤리적이고 결함 없는(flawless) 지도자에 대한 대중들의 갈망은 더 커지게 되었다고 설명하는 글이다.

오답 Check
　　　　(A)　　　(B)
① 미화하다 – 건실한 → (A)는 틀리고 (B)는 맞음.
② 고무하다 – 도덕의 → (A)는 틀리고 (B)는 맞음.
③ 드러내다 – 외향적인 → (A)는 맞지만, (B)는 틀림.
⑤ 구별하다 – 특출한 → (A), (B) 모두 오답.

구문 ¹**It's** difficult **to have** heroes in a world [where every wart and wrinkle (of a person's life) is public].
• It은 가주어이고 to have 이하가 진주어이다.
• [ ]는 a world를 수식하는 관계부사절이다.

²**The more** flawed our leaders are, // **the greater** our desire for highly ethical leaders.
• 「The 비교급 ~, the 비교급 …」 구문은 '~하면 할수록 더 …하다'의 뜻이다.

41 ③　42 ③

Philosophers have debated the relationship (of the mind to the brain and the rest of the body) for centuries. ¹Materialists believe // that the mind emerges from the brain / and that the mind is an artifact of the brain. This has been the (a) prevailing paradigm in the western scientific world // since Charles Darwin's Theory of Evolution became the dominant scientific dogma. Recently, however, / there has been growing (b) dissent in the area (of neuroscience and psychology). Psychologists argue // that every mental event involves a brain event. In one study, / people

어휘 debate 토론하다, 논쟁하다 materialist 유물론자 emerge 나오다 artifact 인공물, 가공품 prevail 우세하다, 유력하다 paradigm 패러다임, 이론적 틀 dominant 지배적인 dogma 교리, 신조 dissent 반대 (의견) neuroscience 신경과학 psychology 심리학 phobia (병적) 공포 cognitive 인지의, 인식의 therapy 치료(법) literally 문자(말) 그대로, 실제로 difficulty 장애 comprehension 이해(력) active 활동적인, 활동하는 compensate for ~을 보상[보충]하다 adaptive 적합한, 적응하는 reshape 고쳐 만들다

(suffering from spider phobias) / were treated with cognitive behavior therapy. After therapy, / they could actually touch spiders (although they might not have been ready to appear on *Fear Factor*). Their brain images revealed (c) <u>enhanced</u> activity / in the brain areas (involved in the phobia). Not only did they change their minds about spiders, // they literally changed their brains.

Another study focused on patients (with language difficulties (caused by damage to the left sides of their brains)). To aid their recovery, / the patients were given training in language comprehension. ²Not only did the training help improve their ability (to understand language), // but brain images revealed / that the right sides (of their brains) had become more active / to (d) <u>compensate</u> for their left-brain damage. Again, a learning experience served as an adaptive mechanism / and changed their brains. ^{주제문} Every time you learn something, / you are (e) <u>reshaping</u> your living brain. Just think: as you study this psychology article // you are changing your mind, and your brain, about psychology.

해석 철학자들은 마음과, 뇌와 몸의 나머지와의 관계를 여러 세기 동안 논쟁해왔다. 유물론자들은 마음이 뇌에서 나오고, 마음은 뇌의 가공품이라고 믿는다. 이것은 찰스 다윈의 진화론이 지배적인 과학적인 신조가 된 이후로 서구 과학계에서 (a) 우세적인 패러다임이었다. 그러나 최근에 신경과학과 심리학 분야에서 (b) 반대가 커지고 있다. 심리학자들은 모든 정신적 사건이 뇌의 사건을 포함하고 있다고 주장한다. 한 연구에서는 거미 공포로 고통당하는 사람들이 인지 행동 치료법으로 치료받고 있었다. (그들은 비록 '공포 요인'에 보일 준비가 되어있지 않을 수 있지만.) 치료받은 후에 실제로 거미에 손을 댈 수가 있었다. 그들의 뇌 영상은 공포와 관련된 뇌 영역에서의 (c) 강화된(→ 감소된) 활동을 보여주었다. 그들은 거미에 대한 그들의 마음을 바꾸었을 뿐 아니라 문자 그대로 그들의 뇌를 바꾸었다.

또 다른 연구는 뇌의 좌측면에 입은 손상 때문에 생긴 언어 장애를 가진 환자에 집중이 되었다. 그들의 회복을 돕기 위해서 환자들은 언어 이해에 관한 훈련을 받았다. 그 훈련은 언어를 이해하는 그들의 능력을 향상시키는 것을 도왔을 뿐만이 아니라. 뇌 영상은 그들 뇌의 우측면이 좌뇌의 손상을 (d) 보충하기 위해 더욱 활동적이 되었다는 것을 보여주었다. 또 학습 경험이 적응을 돕는 기제(機制)의 역할을 해서 그들의 뇌를 변화시켰다. ^{주제문} 여러분이 어떤 것을 배울 때마다, 여러분은 여러분의 현재 쓰이고 있는 뇌를 (e) 고쳐 만들고 있는 것이다. 한번 생각해보라. 여러분이 이 심리학 글을 읽을 때 여러분은 심리학에 관한 자신의 마음, 그리고 자신의 뇌를 바꾸고 있는 것이다.

해설 **41** 마음이 두뇌에서 나온다는 기존의 통념과 다르게 거미 공포를 가진 사람이나, 좌뇌가 손상당한 사람의 예에서 보듯이 치료와 훈련을 통한 새로운 학습이 뇌를 변화시켰다는 것이 글의 요지이므로 ③ '학습이 뇌를 바꿀 수 있다'가 제목으로 가장 적절하다.

42 거미 공포증을 가진 사람이 인지 행동 치료 후 거미를 만질 수 있게 된 것에 관해 거미에 대한 마음뿐만 아니라 뇌도 바뀐 것이라는 내용에서 공포와 관련된 뇌의 부분에서 강화된 활동이 아닌 감소된 활동을 보였을 것이라고 추론할 수 있다. 그러므로 (c)의 enhanced는 reduced 등으로 고치는 것이 적절하다.

오답 Check

41 ① 뇌 치료법이 효과적인가?

→ 뇌가 아닌 인지 치료로 뇌를 바꾸는 것에 관한 내용임.

② 여러분의 마음은 어떻게 작용하는가?

→ 글에 언급되지 않은 내용.

④ 여러분의 뇌가 여러분의 생각을 결정한다

→ 생각이 뇌를 변화시킨다고 했으므로 글의 내용과 반대됨.

⑤ 뇌 연구가 모든 것을 설명할 수 있는가?

→ 글에 언급되지 않은 내용.

42 언어 훈련에서 우뇌가 더 활동적이었던 이유는 손상된 좌뇌의 역할을 보충하기 위함이므로 (e)의 compensate는 적절하다.

구문 ¹Materialists believe // that the mind emerges from the brain / [and] that the mind is an artifact of the brain.

• 동사 believe의 목적어로 밑줄 친 두 개의 that절이 and로 병렬 연결되었다.

²[Not only] *did* the training *help* improve their ability (to understand language), // [but] brain images revealed / that the right sides

(of their brains) had become more active / **to compensate** for their left-brain damage.

• 「not only A but also B」 구문이 사용되었으며 A와 B에 각각 절이 병렬 연결되었다.

• 부정어구 Not only가 문두에 나와 「조동사(did)+주어(the training)+동사(help)」의 어순으로 도치되었다.

• their ability와 to understand language는 동격 관계이다.

• to compensate는 목적을 의미하는 부사적 용법의 to부정사이다.

| 31 ⑤ + ② | 32 ① + ② | 33 ④ + ④ | 34 ② + ① | 35 ③ + ② | 36 ② + ④ |
| 37 ⑤ + ② | 38 ⑤ + ④ | 39 ④ + ⑤ | 40 ① | 41 ② | 42 ④ |

31 ⑤ PLUS+ ②

주제문
Studies have indicated // that a great many species have some capacity (to track the <u>mathematical</u> properties (of objects in their environment)). In one experiment, / the psychologists Russell Church and Warren Meck / exposed rats to both tones and flashes of light. The rats were initially trained to press the left lever // when they heard two tones / and the right lever // when they heard four tones. The rats were also taught to press the left lever / in response to two flashes of light / and the right lever / in response to four flashes of light. ¹What would the rats do / when presented with one tone and one flash of light? ²They immediately pressed the left lever, / indicating that they had coded the stimulus as 'two events', // and they immediately pressed the right lever / in response to two tones and two flashes of light, / indicating that they had coded that stimulus as 'four events'.

해석 **주제문** 연구들은 대단히 많은 종이 그들의 환경에 있는 물체들의 <u>수학적</u> 속성을 추적할 수 있는 어느 정도의 능력이 있다는 것을 보여주었다. 한 실험에서, 심리학자 Russell Church와 Warren Meck는 쥐들을 신호음과 섬광 두 가지 모두에 노출시켰다. 그 쥐들은 처음에는 두 번의 신호음을 들으면 왼쪽 레버를 누르고 네 번의 신호음을 들으면 오른쪽 레버를 누르도록 훈련받았다. 그 쥐들은 또한 두 번의 섬광에 대한 반응으로 왼쪽 레버를 누르고 네 번의 섬광에 대한 반응으로 오른쪽 레버를 누르도록 훈련을 받았다. 한 번의 신호음과 한 번의 섬광을 받았을 때 쥐들은 무엇을 할 것인가? **추론 근거** 그 쥐들은 즉시 왼쪽 레버를 눌렀는데, 그것은 그들이 그 자극을 '두 개의 사건'으로 부호화했다는 것을 나타내고, 그 쥐들은 두 번의 신호음과 두 번의 섬광에 대한 반응으로 즉시 오른쪽 레버를 눌렀는데, 그것은 그들이 그 자극을 '네 개의 사건'으로 부호화했음을 나타낸다.

어휘 indicate 보여주다, 나타내다 species (분류상의) 종(種) capacity 능력; 수용력; 용량 mathematical 수학적인 property 속성, 특성; 재산, 소유물 expose 노출시키다; 드러내다; 폭로하다 tone 신호음; 어조, 말투; 음조 initially 처음에는 in response to A A에 반응하여 be presented with ~을 받다 code 부호로 처리하다; 암호 stimulus (pl. stimuli) 자극
[선택지 어휘] optical 시각적인 invariable 변하지 않는, 변함 없는 functional 기능적인, 기능상의; 실용적인

해설 빈칸 문장으로 보아 많은 종이 물체들의 '어떠한' 속성을 추적할 수 있는 능력이 있는지를 찾아야 한다. 각 한 번씩의 신호음과 섬광을 합하여 두 개의 사건으로 처리하고, 각 두 번씩의 신호음과 섬광을 합하여 네 개의 사건으로 처리했다는 실험의 내용을 통해서 쥐들이 덧셈을 할 수 있다는 것을 알 수 있으므로, 빈칸에는 ⑤ '수학적인'이 들어가는 것이 가장 적절하다.

오답 Check
① 시각적인 → '섬광'에만 국한된 선택지임.
② 공통된 → 물체들의 공통된 속성이 언급되진 않음.
③ 변하지 않는 → 변하지 않는 속성에 관한 내용은 없음.
④ 기능적인 → 기능적인 속성은 언급된 바 없음.

PLUS+ 변형문제

어휘 repetition 반복, 되풀이 calculation 계산, 산출 even number 짝수(↔ odd number 홀수)
해설 많은 종이 물체들의 수학적 속성을 추적할 수 있다는 것을 쥐 실험을 통해 보여주었으므로, 글의 제목으로는 ② '계산: 작은 동물들조차도 할 수 있는 것'이 가장 적절하다.
① 반복: 성공적인 훈련의 핵심 → 쥐 훈련 실험 내용을 활용한 오답.
③ 쥐들이 공통점을 찾을 확률 → 공통점을 찾는 내용은 없음.
④ 시각 대 청각: 어느 것이 우리를 더 자극하는가?
→ 둘 중 뭐가 더 자극적인지에 대한 언급은 없음.
⑤ 짝수가 홀수보다 가르치기 더 쉽다
→ 짝수가 더 가르치기 쉽다는 내용은 없음.

구문 ¹What would the rats do / when (they were) presented with one tone and one flash of light?
• 부사절 when ~ light에서 주어(they)와 be동사(were)가 생략된 형태이다.

²They immediately pressed the left lever, / **indicating** that they had coded the stimulus as 'two events', // [and] they immediately pressed the right lever / in response to two tones and two flashes of light, / **indicating** that they had coded that stimulus as 'four events'.
• indicating ~ 'two events'와 indicating ~ 'four events'는 부대상황을 나타내는 분사구문이다.
• 밑줄 친 두 개의 절이 and로 병렬 연결되었다.

주제문

The concept (of a rational action) can be seen to be quite complex: // it is a hybrid concept. A rational action is one [that is not irrational]. [1]Any action [that is not irrational] counts as rational; // that is, any action [that does not have (is not believed to have) harmful consequences for you or those [for whom you care]] / is rational. So rationality does involve, / if only indirectly, / the egocentric character (of an irrational action). However, the concept (of a rational action) also incorporates the concept (of a reason), // and reasons need not be egocentric. The fact (belief) // that anyone will benefit from your actions / is a reason. Reasons are not limited to facts (beliefs) (about benefits to you or those [for whom you care]). Thus an action [that has (is believed to have) harmful consequences for you] can be rational // if (you believe) there are compensating benefits for others, // even if you do not care about them.

해석 주제문 합리적인 행동이라는 개념은 꽤 복잡해 보일 수 있다. 그것은 혼합된 개념이다. 합리적인 행동은 비합리적이지 않은 행동이다. 비합리적이지 않은 어떤 행동도 합리적이라고 간주되는데, 즉, 당신이나 당신이 좋아하는 사람들에게 해로운 결과를 가져오지 않는(가져온다고 믿어지지 않는) 그 어떤 행동도 합리적인 것이다. 그래서 합리성은 단지 간접적이기는 하지만, 비합리적 행동의 자기중심적인 특징을 포함한다. 하지만, 합리적 행동이라는 개념은 이성이라는 개념을 또한 포함하고 있으며, 이성은 자기중심적일 필요가 없다. 추론 근거 누구라도 당신의 행동으로 이익을 얻을 것이라는 사실(믿음)이 이성이다. 이성은 당신이나 당신이 좋아하는 사람들의 이익에 관한 사실(믿음)에 제한되어 있지 않다. 따라서 당신에게 해로운 결과를 가져오는 (가져온다고 믿어지는) 행동이 비록 당신이 그들을 좋아하지 않는다고 할지라도, 만약 (그) 다른 이들에게 보상이 되는 이익이 있다면(그렇게 당신이 믿는다면) 합리적일 수 있다.

어휘 concept 개념; 구상 rational 합리적인, 이성적인 (↔ irrational 비합리적인, 비이성적인) cf. rationality 합리성 hybrid 혼합[혼성]의; 잡종, 혼합물 count as ~이라 간주되다[간주하다] consequence 결과; 중요성 care (for) (~을) 좋아하다; 보살피다 involve 포함하다, 수반하다 if only ~이지만, ~라도; ~이면 좋을 텐데 indirectly 간접적으로 egocentric 자기중심적인, 이기적인 incorporate 포함하다; 통합하다 reason 이성; 이유, 근거; 추론하다 compensating 보상하는, 상쇄하는

[선택지 어휘] goal-oriented 목표 지향[중심]적인 consistent 일관된, 지속되는, 한결 같은 deal a death-blow 치명적인 타격을 가하다 concerned 관련된; 우려하는 self-interest 사리사욕; 이기심

해설 빈칸 문장으로 보아 당신에게 해로운 결과를 가져오는 행동이 만약 '무엇' 한다면 합리적일 수 있는지를 찾아야 한다. 자신이나 자신이 좋아하는 사람들에게 해로운 결과를 가져다주지 않는 행위를 합리적이라고 여기는데, 여기에 자기중심성을 탈피한 '이성'이 수반되면 자신에게 해로운 결과를 가져다주더라도 자신이 좋아하지 않는 사람을 포함한 다른 이들에게 혜택을 가져다주는 행위도 합리적일 수 있다는 내용이다. 그러므로 빈칸에 들어가기에 가장 적절한 것은 ① '(그) 다른 이들에게 보상이 되는 이익이 있다'이다.

오답 Check

② 그것이 계속 목표 지향적이고 일관성이 있다
→ 목표 지향성과 일관성에 대한 내용은 없음.

③ 그것들이 또한 당신의 적에게 치명적인 타격을 가한다
→ 어느 누구라도 당신의 행동으로 이익을 얻을 것이라는 사실(믿음)이 이성이라고 했으므로 해를 가한다는 내용은 오답.

④ 관련된 모든 사람들을 위해 남겨진 다른 선택이 없다
→ 불가피한 선택에 관한 내용이 아님.

⑤ 그것이 결국에 당신 자신의 사리 추구를 극대화한다
→ 이성은 자기중심적일 필요가 없다고 했으므로 반대되는 내용임.

PLUS+ 변형문제

어휘 self-centered 자기중심의 intervention 개입, 간섭

해설 합리적 행동은 자기중심적일 필요가 없는 '이성'을 포함하고 따라서 좋아하는 사람이든 싫어하는 사람이든 그들에게 보상이 되는 이익이 있다면 그 행동은 합리적일 수 있다고 했으므로 글의 제목으로는 ② '누구에게든 이익이 있다면 합리성이 있다'가 적절하다.

① 합리적인 행동과 비합리적인 행동을 구분하는 방법들
→ 둘을 구분하는 방법이 아닌 합리적 행동의 복합적인 개념을 설명하는 내용임.

③ 자기중심적 행동도 공익에 이바지할 수 있다
→ 공익에 대한 언급은 없음.

④ 사회적 영향에 대한 합리적인 판단의 불가능성
→ 합리적인 판단의 가능 여부에 대한 내용이 아님.

⑤ 타인의 개입: 합리적 판단의 필수 요소
→ 합리성을 판단하는 데 타인의 개입이 필요하다는 내용은 없음.

구문 [1]*Any action* [**that** is not irrational] counts as rational; // that is, *any action* [**that** does not have (is not believed to have) harmful consequences for you [or] *those* [**for whom** you care]] / is rational.

• 첫 번째, 두 번째 [ ]는 모두 주격 관계대명사 that이 이끄는 관계사절로 앞에 나온 any action을 각각 수식한다.

• 세 번째 [ ]는 '전치사+관계대명사' 형태의 for whom이 이끄는 관계사절로 those를 수식한다. 관계대명사가 관계사절 내에서 전치사의 목적어로 쓰여 whom 앞에 for가 왔으며 whom you care for로도 쓸 수 있다.

33 ④ PLUS+ ④

Arbitrage is a term [which refers to the buying and selling of the same commodities / in different markets / to profit from unequal prices and information]. The successful arbitrageur is a trader [who knows to buy something for $1 in Chicago / and sell it for $1.50 in New York]. ¹The key (to being a successful arbitrageur) is having a wide net of informants and information / and then knowing how to synthesize it / in a way [that will produce a profit]. If one can do arbitrage in markets, // one can do it in other fields. Today, more than ever, the traditional boundaries (between politics, culture, technology and finance) are disappearing. You often cannot explain one / without referring to the others. ²Therefore, to be an effective foreign affairs analyst or reporter, / you have to learn how to arbitrage information (from these disparate perspectives) / and then weave it all together / to produce a picture of the world [that you would never have // if you looked at it from only one perspective]. That is the essence of information arbitrage. In a world [where we are all so much more interconnected], / the ability (to read the connections, and to connect the dots) is the real value added (provided by a journalist).

[해석] 차익 거래는 같지 않은 가격과 정보로부터 이익을 얻기 위해 같은 상품을 다른 시장에서 사고파는 것을 나타내는 용어이다. 성공적인 차익 거래자는 어떤 것을 시카고에서 1달러에 사서 그것을 뉴욕에서 1.5달러에 파는 거래자이다. 성공적인 차익 거래자가 되기 위한 비결은 광범위한 정보망과 정보를 확보하고 나서 이를 이익을 창출할 방식으로 종합하는 방법을 아는 것이다. 만약 한 사람이 시장에서 차익 거래를 할 수 있다면, 다른 분야에서도 그것을 할 수 있다. 오늘날에는 정치와 문화, 기술, 그리고 금융 사이의 전통적인 경계가 그 어느 때보다 많이 사라지고 있다. 다른 분야를 알아보지 않고서는 어떤 분야를 설명할 수 없다. 주제문/추론 근거 그러므로 유능한 외교 문제 분석가나 기자가 되려면 서로 전혀 다른 관점에서 나오는 정보를 차익 거래하는 방법을 배운 다음 어느 한 관점에서만 보면 결코 그려낼 수 없는 세계를 그려내기 위해 이 모든 것을 함께 엮어야 한다. 그것이 정보 차익 거래의 핵심이다. 주제문 재진술 우리 모두가 더욱 밀접하게 연결된 세계에서는 그 상호 연관성을 읽고, 그 점들을 연결하는 능력이 저널리스트에 의해 제공되는 진정한 부가가치이다.

[어휘] refer to ~을 나타내다; 알아보다; 참조하다; 언급하다 commodity 상품; 필수품 informant 정보 제공자 synthesize 종합[통합]하다; 합성하다 disparate 서로 전혀 다른, 이질적인 perspective 관점; 원근법 weave 엮다, 짜다; (이야기를) 꾸미다 interconnected 상호 연결된 value added ((경제)) 부가가치 [선택지 어휘] in-depth 철저한; 면밀한 disperse 퍼뜨리다; 흩어지다

[해설] 이 글은 모든 분야가 상호 연관된 세계에서 서로 다른 분야의 정보를 차익 거래한 후 그 모든 것을 함께 엮어 한 관점에서는 결코 보지 못하는 세계를 그려내는 것이 정보 차익 거래의 핵심이자 저널리스트에게 필요한 역량이라고 말하고 있으므로, 빈칸에 들어갈 능력으로는 ④ '그 상호 연관성을 읽고, 그 점들을 연결하는' 능력이 적절하다.

[오답 Check]
① 그들의 독자로부터 정보를 수집하는
→ 정보를 수집하는 대상이 독자에 국한되는 것은 아님.
② 다른 어떤 사람보다 더 많은 정보를 제공하는
③ 그들의 관계에 관한 철저한 세부 사항을 배우는
→ ②, ③ 모두 글에 언급된 어구를 활용한 오답.
⑤ 사실을 손에 넣고, 곧바로 그것들을 퍼뜨리는
→ 상식적으로 유추할 수 있는 내용이지만, 글의 내용과는 거리가 먼 오답.

PLUS+ 변형문제

[어휘] boundary 경계[한계](선) with ease 쉽게; 용이하게
[해설] 글의 주제문을 제목으로 잘 표현한 것으로는 ④ '저널리스트의 필수 자질: 정보 차익 거래'가 가장 적절하다.
① 정보 차익 거래에서 관련성을 이끌어내는 방법
→ 그 방식은 글에 언급되지 않음.
② 차익 거래를 이용하여 쉽게 경계를 통과하라
→ 전통적인 경계가 사라지고 있다고 언급했고, 차익 거래를 이용하여 그 경계를 쉽게 통과하는 것은 아님.
③ 차익 거래에서 광범위한 정보망의 중요성
→ 글의 일부 내용으로 정보망의 중요성을 설명하는 글은 아님.
⑤ 상호 연결된 세계에서 서로 다른 관점을 분리하라
→ 서로 다른 관점을 함께 엮어야 한다고 했으므로 글의 내용과 반대됨.

[구문] ¹The key (to being a successful arbitrageur) is having a wide net of informants and information / and then knowing how to synthesize it / in a way [that will produce a profit].
• ( )는 전명구로 앞에 있는 The key를 수식한다.
• 밑줄 친 두 개의 동명사구가 and로 연결되어 동사 is의 보어로 병렬 구조를 이룬다.
• [ ]는 주격 관계대명사 that이 이끄는 관계사절로 선행사 a way를 수식한다.

²Therefore, to be an effective foreign affairs analyst or reporter, / you have to learn how to arbitrage information (from these disparate perspectives) / and then weave it all together / to produce a picture of the world [that you would never have // if you looked at it from only one perspective].
• ( )는 형용사적 역할을 하는 전명구로 information을 수식한다.
• 밑줄 친 두 개의 동사구가 and로 연결되어 병렬 구조를 이룬다.
• [ ]는 목적격 관계대명사 that이 이끄는 관계사절로 선행사 the world를 수식하고, [ ] 내에는 「S+would+동사원형 ...., if+S'+과거동사 ~」 구조의 가정법 과거가 쓰여 '만약 ~라면, …할 텐데'를 의미한다.

We have seen only cases [in which human intelligence is equal to or greater than animal intelligence]. Perhaps the wild mind is altogether inferior to the human mind. 추론 근거 Clearly, humans are vastly superior to all earthly animals / in their ability (to learn and use language). 주제문 However, if we accept this view // we have jumped to the wrong conclusion. Animals do have unique abilities (not shared by humans). Perhaps the most convincing case is dolphins' talent / for acquiring and processing acoustic information. This skill is highly adaptive / and is a type of intelligence / according to any reasonable general definition. ¹Furthermore, / not only can unaided humans not match dolphins' ability, // but also the best human-designed transducers, computers, and software / cannot match their ability. ²Only by adopting radically human-centered notions of intelligence could we deny // that this ability is a type of intelligence.

해석 우리는 인간의 지능이 동물의 지능과 같거나 더 뛰어난 사례만을 보아왔다. 아마도 야생 동물의 두뇌는 인간의 두뇌보다 전적으로 열등한 듯하다. 추론 근거 분명히, 인간은 언어를 배우고 사용하는 능력에서 모든 지구상의 동물들보다 굉장히 우수하다. 주제문 그렇지만, 이러한 견해를 받아들인다면 우리는 성급하게 잘못된 결론을 내린 것이다. 동물들은 인간과 공유하지 않는 독특한 능력을 정말로 가지고 있다. 아마도 가장 납득이 가는 사례는 음향 정보를 포착하고 처리하는 돌고래의 재능일 것이다. 이 기능은 고도로 적응성이 있고 어떤 합리적이고 일반적인 정의를 따르더라도 지능의 한 유형이다. 뿐만 아니라 도움을 받지 않은 인간이 돌고래의 능력에 필적할 수 없을 뿐만 아니라 인간이 만든 최고의 변환기, 컴퓨터, 소프트웨어도 돌고래들의 능력에 필적할 수 없다. 오직 지능에 대해 철저하게 인간 중심적인 개념을 채택함에 의해서만 우리는 이 능력이 지능의 유형이라는 것을 부인할 수 있을 것이다.

어휘 **case** 경우; 사례; (조사 중인) 사건 **intelligence** 지능 **wild** 야생의 **mind** 두뇌, 지력; 마음, 정신 **altogether** 전적으로, 완전히 **inferior to** ~보다 열등한(↔ **superior to** ~보다 우수한) **vastly** 굉장히, 대단히 **earthly** 지상의 **jump to the conclusion** 성급한 결론[판단]을 내리다, 속단하다 **convincing** 설득력 있는, 확실한 (a) **talent for** ~에 대한 재능 **acquire** (목표물을 레이더로) 포착하다, 잡다; 획득하다 **acoustic** 음향의, 청각의 **adaptive** 적응성이 있는, 적응할 수 있는 **reasonable** 합리적인, 이성적인 **unaided** 도움을 받지 않는 **match** 맞먹다, 필적하다; 어울리다; 일치하다 **adopt** 채택하다; 입양하다 **radically** 철저하게, 극단적으로 **notion** 개념, 생각 **deny** 부인[부정]하다 **[선택지 어휘] conscious** 의식하는; 의식적인; 의식이 있는 **considerate** 사려 깊은, 배려하는

해설 However 뒤에서, 언어능력 때문에 인간이 모든 동물보다 월등하다고 생각하는 것은 성급하다고 하였고, 동물도 인간에게 없는 월등한 능력을 가지고 있는 사례로 돌고래의 음향 정보를 포착하고 처리하는 능력을 설명하고 있다. 따라서 이러한 능력이 지능의 한 유형이라는 것을 부인하는 것은 오로지 ② '지능에 대해 철저하게 인간 중심적인 개념을 채택함'으로써만 가능할 것이다.

오답 Check
① 모든 종의 지적 능력을 합리적으로 정의함
③ 다른 종의 정신 작용을 철저히 검토함
④ 동물 행동을 의식적이고 사려 깊은 것으로 간주함
⑤ 동물의 능력을 인간의 능력보다 더 강조함
→ ①, ③, ④, ⑤ 모두 다른 종의 능력을 인정한다는 의미이므로 정답이 될 수 없음.

PLUS + 변형문제

어휘 **indisputable** 반론의 여지가 없는 **existence** 실재, 존재 **demerit** 단점, 약점
해설 인간에게는 없는 동물의 독특한 능력을 지능의 한 유형으로 볼 수 있다고 설명하는 내용이므로 글의 주제로 가장 적절한 것은 ① '반박할 수 없는 동물 지능의 실재'이다.
② 동물 복지를 위한 동물 조련의 이점
→ 동물 조련에 관한 내용은 없음.
③ 지능의 다양한 종류와 학습 방식들
→ 지능의 범위를 동물의 지능까지 넓히고 있지만, 학습 방식에 관한 내용은 없음.
④ 인간 지능의 우월성을 믿는 것의 단점들
→ 도입을 활용해 만든 오답. 단점에 대해 언급된 내용은 없음.
⑤ 동물 지능과 학습 능력의 발견
→ 동물의 학습 능력에 대한 언급은 없음.

구문 ¹Furthermore, not only *can* **unaided humans** *not match* dolphins' ability, // but also the best human-designed transducers, computers, and software / cannot match their ability.
• 「not only A but also B」는 'A뿐만 아니라 B도'의 뜻이다.
• not only가 문두로 나오게 되어 「not only+조동사(can)+주어(unaided humans)+동사(not match)」 어순으로 도치되었다.

²**Only** by adopting radically human-centered notions of intelligence *could* **we** *deny* // that this ability is a type of intelligence.
• only가 이끄는 부사구가 문두로 나오게 되면서 「only ~+조동사(could)+주어(we)+동사(deny)」 어순으로 도치가 일어났다.
• 밑줄 친 부분은 동사 deny의 목적어로 쓰인 접속사 that이 이끄는 명사절이다.

주제문
The modern symphony orchestra can be understood / as a logical extension (of human expressive capacities). ¹It has been suggested, for example, // that musical instruments have their precursors in the natural ways [in which human beings produce sound]. ① That is, string instruments correspond to voice production; wind instruments, to vocalization and whistling; and percussion, to clapping and foot tapping. ② If this supposition is valid, // then the vast number of instruments [that have been devised in various cultures since prehistory] / have merely been means (of imitating and extending the musical qualities (of the innate modes of human expression)). ③ Especially songs [that are made by the human voice] are, therefore, / the most universal and important music / both from a historical and cultural standpoint. ④ ²While the development (of the modern orchestra) has greatly diversified the sound palette (available to the composer), // the overall range (of tonal frequency) has remained / within that (of the human voice), // although the human auditory range is much broader. ⑤ Moreover, the string instruments, / which are most closely analogous to the voice, / form the core of the orchestra.

해석 **주제문** 현대 교향악단은 인간의 표현 능력의 논리적 확장으로서 이해될 수 있다. 예를 들어, 악기는 각기 인간이 소리를 만들어 내는 자연스러운 방식에 그것들의 전신(前身)을 두고 있다는 말이 있다. ① 즉, 현악기는 성대가 만들어 내는 소리, 관악기는 발성과 휘파람, 그리고 타악기는 손뼉치기, 발 두드리기에 상응한다. ② 만약 이러한 추정이 타당하다면, 선사 시대 이래로 다양한 문화에서 고안된 수많은 악기들은 단지 인간의 타고난 표현 방식의 음악적 특성을 모방하고 확장하는 수단에 불과하다. ③ 그러므로 특히 인간의 목소리에 의해서 만들어지는 노래들은 역사적이고 문화적인 관점 둘 다에서 가장 보편이고 가장 중요한 음악이다. ④ 비록 인간의 전체 청각 범위가 훨씬 더 넓지만, 현대 오케스트라의 발전은 작곡가가 이용 가능한 소리의 색깔들을 크게 다양화한 반면, 전반적인 음조의 주파수 범위는 인간의 목소리의 범위 안에 남아 있다. ⑤ 게다가, 목소리와 가장 밀접하게 유사한 현악기가 오케스트라의 핵심을 형성한다.

어휘 symphony orchestra 교향악단 extension 확장, 연장 cf. extend 확장하다 capacity 능력; 수용력 string instrument 현악기 correspond to ~에 상응하다 wind instrument 관악기 vocalization 발성 whistling 휘파람 clapping 손뼉 치기 supposition 추정, 가정 valid 타당한, 유효한 devise 고안하다 innate 선천적인 standpoint 관점, 견지 diversify 다양화하다 palette 색깔들 composer 작곡가 tonal 음의 frequency 주파수; 빈도 auditory 청각[귀]의 analogous 유사한 core 핵심

해설 인간이 만든 악기는 선천적으로 인간이 낼 수 있는 소리와 그 원리가 같고, 목소리에서 발전된 것이라는 게 글의 요지이다. ① 이후로 그러한 인간의 음악적 특성이 악기에 어떻게 발현되어 있는지에 관한 내용이 이어지는데, ③은 인간의 목소리로 만드는 노래가 가장 보편적인 음악이라는 내용으로 글의 흐름과 무관하다.

오답 Check
④ 현대 오케스트라의 소리 범위가 다양해졌지만, 그것의 음조 주파수가 인간의 목소리 범주 안에 있다는 내용은 악기가 인간이 내는 소리에 근간을 두고 있다는 중심 내용에 자연스럽게 연결된다.

PLUS+ 변형문제

어휘 cumulative 누적되는; 누계의 mirror 반영하다; 비추다; 거울 mankind 인류

해설 첫 문장에서 현대 교향악단은 인간 표현 능력의 논리적 확장이라고 하고 이후에는 악기가 인간의 표현을 모방했다는 구체적인 예시를 나열하므로 글의 제목으로는 ② '현대 오케스트라는 인간의 다양한 표현을 어떻게 반영하는가'가 가장 적절하다.

① 오케스트라는 누적된 문화 진화의 역사
→ 문화 진화의 역사에 대한 내용은 없음.
③ 악기 소리 대 인간 목소리: 뭐가 더 다양한가?
→ 소리의 다양성을 비교하는 내용은 아님.
④ 모든 악기의 소리는 자연의 소리로부터 왔다
→ 자연의 소리보다는 인간의 소리라고 해야 정확함.
⑤ 인류의 노력을 통한 다양한 소리의 발견
→ 인류가 노력해서 다양한 소리를 찾았다는 내용은 없음.

구문 ¹**It** has been suggested, for example, // **that** musical instruments have their precursors / in *the natural ways* [**in which** human beings produce sound].
• It은 가주어, that이 이끄는 절이 진주어이다.
• [ ]는 '전치사+관계대명사' 형태의 in which가 이끄는 관계사절로 the natural ways를 수식한다.

²While *the development* (of the modern orchestra) has greatly diversified *the sound palette* (available to the composer), // the overall *range* (of tonal frequency) has remained / within **that** (of the human voice), // although the human auditory range is ***much broader***.
• available to the composer는 형용사구로 the sound palette를 수식한다.
• 굵게 표시된 that은 range를 받는 대명사이다.
• although가 이끄는 부사절에서 much가 비교급 broader를 강조한다.

For animals without skeletons, like worms or jellyfish / fossilization is a very rare event. 주제문 For a soft-bodied animal to be fossilized, / its body must be protected / from decomposition. The body is usually exposed to air and water (with a lot of oxygen), // so it decomposes rapidly.

(B) The animal is likely to be fossilized // only if it is buried // soon after it dies, // or when it is buried alive. ¹Even then, it is likely to decompose, // because water [that seeps through the sediment around it] is usually rich in oxygen.

(A) Sometimes, however, the soft-bodied animal is buried rapidly by fine mud. ²Water creeps through mud much more slowly / than through sand, // so the body does not decompose as fast.

(C) The very soft wet earth often contains a lot of other organic matter as well, and that uses up oxygen faster. Some of these animals then escape decomposition. Under just the right conditions, a delicate impression (of the animal) might be preserved.

해석 벌레나 해파리처럼, 뼈대가 없는 동물에게 화석화는 매우 드문 일이다. 주제문 연체동물이 화석화되기 위해서는, 그것의 사체가 부패로부터 보호되어야 한다. 사체는 보통 산소가 많은 공기와 물에 노출되기에, 빠르게 부패한다.
(B) 동물은 죽은 후 곧바로 매장되어야만 아니면 산 채로 매장되었을 때 화석이 될 가능성이 있다. 그렇다 하더라도, 그것은 부패할 가능성이 있는데, 왜냐하면 그것(사체) 주변의 침전물을 통해 스며드는 물은 보통 산소가 풍부하기 때문이다.
(A) 그러나 때로 연체동물은 고운 진흙으로 빠르게 묻힌다. 물이 모래를 통하는 것보다 훨씬 더 천천히 진흙을 통해 퍼지므로, 그 사체는 그렇게 빨리 부패하지 않는다.
(C) 그 아주 부드럽고 축축한 토양에는 종종 많은 다른 유기물 또한 포함되어 있고, 그것은 산소를 더 빨리 소모한다. 따라서 이러한 동물 중 일부는 부패를 면한다. 아주 적절한 조건하에서는, 동물의 섬세한 흔적이 보존될 수도 있다.

어휘 skeleton 뼈대, 골격; 해골   fossilization 화석화 (작용) cf. fossilize 화석화하다   rare 드문, 보기 힘든   decomposition 부패; 분해 (작용) cf. decompose 부패하다; 분해하다   seep (물기 등이) 스며들다, 배다   sediment 침전물; 퇴적물   fine (알갱이가) 고운; 미세한; 좋은   creep 퍼지다; 살금살금 움직이다; 기다   use up 소모하다, 다 써버리다   delicate 섬세한; 예민한   impression 흔적, 자국; 인상; 감명   preserve 보존하다; 지키다; 보호하다

해설 연체동물의 화석화와 부패에 대한 내용으로 사체가 공기와 물에 노출되어 빠르게 부패한다는 주어진 내용 다음에는 바로 매장되면 화석이 될 수 있다는 (B)가 와야 적절하다. (B)의 묻히더라도 부패하기 쉽다는 내용 이후 역접의 접속사와 함께 부패를 늦출 수 있는 조건(고운 진흙)을 처음 언급하는 (A)가 와야 하고 (A)에 이어 부패를 막는 진흙의 특징을 한 가지 더 언급하는 (C)가 와야 자연스럽다.

오답 Check
(C)에 나오는 The very soft wet earth가 '진흙'을 지칭하므로 (A) 다음에 (C)가 나와야 하는 것에 유의한다. 또한 (C)의 as well은 앞서 나온 특징에 이어 덧붙일 때 사용하기도 한다.

PLUS + 변형문제

해설 연체동물이 화석화되기 위해서는 사체가 부패하지 않아야 하는데, 진흙에 묻힐 경우 부패 과정을 늦추거나 부패를 막을 수 있다는 내용이므로 주제로는 ④ '연체동물이 화석화되기 위한 조건'이 가장 적절하다.
① 동물의 뼈대를 화석화하는 것의 어려움
→ 뼈대가 없는 연체동물에 관한 내용이므로 적절하지 않음.
② 화석화 과정에서 산소의 역할
→ 산소가 부패시키는 원인임을 언급하지만 전반적인 주제는 아님.
③ 화석화되기 어려운 동물의 종류
→ 연체동물의 화석화가 드문 일이라고 설명하지만 그 종류를 상세히 다룬 글은 아님.
⑤ 바다 생명체가 화석화되기 보다 더 부패되는 이유
→ 바다 생명체가 화석화보다 부패할 가능성이 더 높은 이유는 언급되지 않음.

구문 ¹Even then, it is likely to decompose, // because water [that seeps through the sediment around it] is usually rich in oxygen.
• 밑줄 친 두 개의 it은 문맥상 모두 동물의 사체(the dead animal)를 의미한다.
• [ ]는 주격 관계대명사 that이 이끄는 관계사절로 선행사 water를 수식한다.

²Water creeps through mud **much more slowly** / than (water creeps) through sand, // so the body does not decompose as fast.
• much가 비교급 more를 강조한다.
• through sand 앞에는 반복되는 water creeps가 생략되었다.

Many genetic and biological mechanisms control hunger and satiety, / ensuring that people will eat enough / to meet their energy needs. Throughout most of human history, / getting enough food was the primary challenge.

(C) The human body developed / to function in an environment [where food was scarce and high levels of physical activity were mandatory for survival]. ¹This situation resulted in the development of various physiological mechanisms [that encourage the body to deposit energy (i.e., fat) and defend against energy loss].

(B) ²Today's environment, however, is one [in which food is widely available, inexpensive, and often high in energy density, // while minimal physical activity is required for daily living]. 주제문 Researchers have proposed // that the modern environment has taken body weight control / from an instinctual (unconscious) process / to one [that requires substantial cognitive effort].

(A) In such an environment, / people [who are not devoting substantial conscious effort to managing body weight] are probably gaining weight. This means // that nutrition education has an important role.

해석 많은 유전적 그리고 생물학적 기제가 배고픔과 포만감을 조절하여 사람들이 그들의 에너지 요구를 충족시키기에 충분히 먹는 것을 확실히 한다. 인류 역사의 대부분의 시기 내내 충분한 음식을 얻는 것은 주요한 과제였다.
(C) 인간의 신체는 식량이 부족하고 높은 수준의 신체 활동이 생존에 필수적이었던 환경에서 기능하도록 발달했다. 이러한 상황은 신체가 에너지(즉 지방)를 축적하고 에너지 손실에 맞서 방어하도록 장려하는 다양한 생리적 기제의 발달을 일으켰다.
(B) 그러나 오늘날의 환경은, 식량을 폭넓게 구할 수 있고 비싸지 않으며 대개 에너지 밀도가 높은 반면 일상생활에는 최소한의 신체적 활동만이 요구되는 곳이다. 주제문 연구자들은 현대의 환경이 체중 조절을 본능에 따른 (무의식적인) 과정에서 상당한 인지적 노력을 요구하는 과정으로 옮겼다고 말했다.
(A) 그러한 환경에서 체중 관리에 상당한 의식적인 노력을 쏟지 않는 사람들은 아마 체중이 증가하고 있을 것이다. 이는 영양 교육이 중요한 역할을 한다는 것을 의미한다.

어휘 genetic 유전적인 mechanism (생물체 내에서 특정한 기능을 수행하는) 기제; 구조 primary 주요한; 초기의 function 기능하다, 작용하다 scarce 부족한, 모자라는 mandatory 필수의, 의무적인 result in ~을 야기하다 physiological 생리적인 deposit 비축하다; 쌓이게 하다 density 밀도; 농도 instinctual 본능에 따른 unconscious 무의식적인(↔ conscious 의식적인, 의식하는) substantial 상당한; 실재의 cognitive 인지적인 devote A to B A를 B에 쏟다[바치다] nutrition 영양

해설 인류는 대부분의 시기 동안 식량 부족 상태로 살았다는 주어진 글 다음에는 이와 유사한 상황(식량이 부족하고 신체 활동 요구량은 많은 환경)이 제시된 (C)가 나온다. however로 연결되는 (B)에서는 이와 대조적으로 식량은 풍요롭지만 신체 활동 요구량은 최소화가 된 현대 환경이 제시되며, (A)의 체중 유지에 의식적 노력이 요구되는 '그러한 환경(such an environment)'은 (B)에 언급된 현대의 환경(modern environment)을 지칭하므로 (A)가 마지막으로 오는 것이 적절하다.

오답 Check
주어진 글에서 충분한 음식을 얻는 것이 주요한 과제(primary challenge)였다고 했는데, 이러한 상황에서 체중 관리에 의식적인 노력이 필요하다는 현대인의 상황을 설명한 (A)가 바로 이어지는 것은 적절하지 않다.

PLUS+ 변형문제
해설 식량이 부족하여 에너지 축적이 필수적이었던 과거와는 달리 오늘날에는 식량이 풍족하고 신체 활동도 최소만 요구되기 때문에 체중 조절에 의식적인 노력이 필요하다는 내용의 글이므로 요지로 가장 적절한 것은 ②이다.
① → 식량이 풍족한 오늘날 오히려 신체 활동량은 최소만 요구됨.
③ → 영양 교육보다 개인의 노력이 더 중요하다는 내용은 없음.
④ → 인간이 즐거움을 위해 먹는다는 내용은 언급되지 않음.
⑤ → 서구화된 식습관과 비만 인구가 증가한다는 내용은 언급되지 않음.

구문 ¹This situation resulted in the development of *various physiological mechanisms* [that **encourage** *the body* to deposit energy (i.e., fat) |and| (to) defend against energy loss].
• [ ]는 관계대명사 that이 이끄는 관계사절로 various physiological mechanisms를 수식한다.
• [ ] 내에 「encourage+O+C」 구조가 쓰였고, 목적격보어로 쓰인 밑줄 친 두 개의 to부정사구가 and로 병렬 연결된다. 이때, 뒤에 반복되는 to는 생략되었다.

²Today's environment, however, is *one* [**in which** food is widely available, inexpensive, and often high in energy density, // **while** minimal physical activity is required for daily living].
• one은 an environment를 대신하며 [ ]는 '전치사+관계대명사'가 이끄는 관계사절로 선행사 one을 수식한다.
• 관계사절 내의 while은 대조의 의미를 나타내는 부사절 접속사이다.

38 ⑤ PLUS+ ④

주제문
Although individual incentives may increase the effort (of the individual group members), / and thus enhance group performance, // they also have some potential disadvantages for group process. One potential problem is // that the group members will compare their own rewards with those of others. (①) It might be hoped // that individuals would use their coworkers as models (upward comparison), // which would inspire them to work harder. (②) For instance, when corporations set up "employee of the week" programs, // they are attempting / to develop this type of positive comparison. (③) ¹On the other hand, if group members believe // that others are being rewarded more than they are / for what they perceive as the same work (downward comparison), // they may change their behavior to attempt to restore equity. (④) Perhaps they will attempt to work harder / in order to receive greater rewards for themselves. (⑤ But they may instead decide to reduce their effort / to match what they perceive as a low level of current pay.) ²It has been found, for instance, // that job absenteeism is increased // when employees make unfavorable comparisons (between their own rewards and those of others).

해석 주제문 개인적인 유인책이 개별적인 집단 구성원들의 노력을 증대시켜서 집단의 성과를 향상시킬 수 있겠지만, 그것은 또한 집단 과정에 어떤 잠재적인 불리함을 지닐 수도 있다. 한 가지 잠재적 문제점은 집단 구성원들이 자기 자신의 보상을 다른 사람들의 그것(보상)과 비교할 것이라는 점이다. 개인들이 자신의 동료들을 모범(상향 비교)으로 사용하여 그들이 더욱 열심히 일하도록 장려할 것이라고 기대될지 모른다. 예를 들어 기업들이 '금주의 직원' 프로그램을 마련할 때, 그들은 이러한 유형의 긍정적인 비교를 발전시키려고 시도하고 있는 것이다. 반면에 집단 구성원들이 같은 일이라고 인식하는 것에 다른 사람들이 자기들보다 더 많이 보상받고 있다고 믿는다면(하향 비교), 그들은 형평을 복구하려는 시도로 자신의 행동을 바꿀지도 모른다. 아마 그들은 혼자 힘으로 더 큰 보상을 받기 위해 더 열심히 일하려고 시도할지도 모른다. 그러나 대신에 그들은 자기들이 현재 보수의 낮은 수준으로 인식하는 것과 맞추기 위해 자신의 노력을 감소시키기로 결심할지도 모른다. 예를 들어 직원들이 자신의 보상과 다른 사람들의 보상 간에 비판적인 비교를 할 때 직장에서의 잦은 결근이 증가한다는 것이 발견되었다.

어휘 incentive 유인[장려]책; 동기 enhance 향상시키다; 강화하다 potential 잠재적인; 가능성 reward 보상(하다), 보수 comparison 비교, 대조 inspire 고무[격려]하다 corporation 기업; 법인 attempt 시도하다 perceive 인식[감지]하다 restore 복구하다, 회복시키다 equity 형평, 공평 unfavorable 비판적인, 호의적이지 않은; 불길한

해설 ⑤ 앞 문장은 직원들이 열심히 일하려 시도한다는 내용이고, for instance가 있는 ⑤ 다음 문장은 직원들의 결근이 증가한다는 내용으로 연결이 자연스럽지 않다. 따라서 직원들이 자신의 노력을 감소시키기로 결심한다는 내용의 주어진 문장은 ⑤에 위치해야 한다. ⑤ 앞 문장에서처럼 하향 비교가 긍정적인 결과(직원들의 노력 증대)를 이끌어낼 수도 있지만, But으로 시작하는 주어진 문장이 하향 비교의 부정적인 결과를 나타내면서 그 뒤에 결근 증가를 초래할 수 있다는 예가 이어지는 흐름이 자연스럽다.

오답 Check
② 앞의 상향 비교 내용과 But으로 연결되어 그들의 노력을 감소시킨다는 상반된 내용의 주어진 문장이 이어지는 것은 얼핏 보기에 자연스러울 수 있다. 그러나 이 부분이 역접으로 연결되는 경우, 이후 예시에서 this type of positive comparison이 가리키는 바를 찾을 수 없으므로 주어진 문장은 ②에 위치할 수 없음에 유의한다.

PLUS+ 변형문제

어휘 self-esteem 자존감, 자부심 relative 상대적인 differential 차등을 두는, 차별하는 compensation 보상(금)
해설 개인적 유인책의 잠재적 문제점 중 한 가지로 집단 구성원이 자신과 타인의 보상을 비교해서 다른 사람들이 자신보다 더 많이 보상받고 있다고 믿는다면 노력을 감소시킨다고 했으므로 글의 제목으로 가장 적절한 것은 ④ '개인적 포상을 제공하는 것이 집단 구성원에게 어떻게 영향을 미치는가?'이다.
① 상향, 하향 비교가 우리 자존감에 영향을 미친다
→ 상향, 하향 비교와 자존감의 연관성은 언급되지 않음.
② 상대 평가와 절대 평가의 형평성 차이
→ 일부 어휘(equity)를 활용한 오답.
③ 능력에 따른 차등 보상의 중요성
→ 개인적 유인책의 단점에 관한 내용임.
⑤ 보상을 많이 받을수록 행동 수정이 증가한다
→ 타인보다 낮은 보상을 받았을 때 형평을 복구하려고 행동 수정을 일으킴.

구문 ¹On the other hand, if group members believe // that others are being rewarded more than they are / for what they perceive as the same work (downward comparison), // they may change their behavior to attempt to restore equity.
• believe의 목적어로 접속사 that이 이끄는 명사절이 쓰였다.
• 밑줄 친 what they ~ same work는 선행사를 포함한 관계대명사 what이 이끄는 명사절로 전치사 for의 목적어 역할을 한다.

²It has been found, for instance, // that job absenteeism is increased // when employees make unfavorable comparisons (between their own rewards and those of others).
• It은 가주어이고, that이 이끄는 명사절이 진주어이다.
• ( )는 전명구로 unfavorable comparisons를 수식하며 ( ) 안의 those는 the rewards를 대신하는 대명사이다.

주제문
One theory suggests // that there is a direct connection / between shorter life expectancy and greater external threats. Essentially, animals (with a greater risk of being eaten) evolve to live shorter lives — even if they aren't eaten. (①) Here's how — if a species faces significant environmental threats and predators, // it's under greater evolutionary pressure (to reproduce at an early age), // so it evolves to reach adulthood faster. (②) ¹A shorter lifespan also means a shorter length of time (between generations), // which allows a species to evolve faster — which is important / for species [that face a lot of environmental threats]. (③) ²At the same time, there's never any real evolutionary pressure (to evolve mechanisms / to repair DNA errors [that occur over time]), // because most individuals (in the species) don't live long enough to experience those errors. (④ You wouldn't buy an extended warranty on your smartphone // if you were only going to keep it for a week.) On the flip side, a species [that is more dominant in its environment, // and that can continue to reproduce for most of its life], will gain an advantage / in repairing accumulated DNA errors. (⑤) If it lives longer, // it can reproduce more.

해석 주제문 한 이론에서는 더 짧은 수명과 더 큰 외적 위협 간에 직접적 연관이 있음을 암시한다. 본질적으로 잡아먹힐 위험이 더 큰 동물들은 설령 잡아먹히지 않더라도 더 짧은 삶을 살도록 진화한다. 여기에 그 방식이 있다. 어떤 종이 상당한 환경상의 위협과 포식자에 직면한다면, 그것은 이른 연령에 번식을 해야 할 더 큰 진화적 압박을 받게 되어, 성인기에 더 빨리 도달하도록 진화한다. 보다 짧은 수명은 또한 세대 간의 시간 길이가 더 짧아짐을 의미하는데, 이는 종이 더 빨리 진화하는 것을 허용하고, 그것은 많은 환경적 위협에 직면하는 종에게 중요하다. 동시에 종의 대부분의 개체들이 DNA 오류를 경험할 정도로 충분히 오래 살지 못하기 때문에, 시간이 흐르며 발생하는 그러한 오류를 복구할 방법을 진화시켜야 한다는 어떠한 실질적인 진화적 압박도 결코 존재하지 않는다. 당신이 스마트폰을 오직 일주일 동안만 가지고 있을 예정이라면 그것을 위해 연장된 품질 보증서를 구매하지 않을 것이다. 다른 한편으로는, 자신의 환경에서 더 지배적이며 자신의 생애 대부분 동안 계속하여 번식할 수 있는 종은 축적된 DNA 오류를 복구하는 데 이점을 얻을 것이다. 더 오래 살면, 번식도 더 많이 할 수 있다.

어휘 life expectancy 수명 external 외부의(↔ internal 내부의) evolutionary 진화의; 진화(론)적인 reproduce 번식하다; 재생[재현]하다 cf. reproduction 번식; 재생, 재현 lifespan 수명 extend (기간을) 연장하다, 늘이다; 확대[확장]하다 warranty 보증(서) on the flip side 다른 한편으로는; 반면에 dominant 지배적인; 우세한 cf. dominance 지배; 우세 accumulate 축적하다, 모으다

해설 주어진 문장에서 일주일만 갖고 있을 당신의 스마트폰은 짧은 수명을 의미하며, 연장된 기간의 품질 보증서가 불필요함은 DNA 오류를 복구할 진화적 필요가 없음을 암시한다. 짧은 수명으로 인한 DNA 오류 복구의 불필요성을 충분히 설명한 후에 주어진 문장이 비유적 표현으로 등장해야 하므로 정답은 ④이며, ④ 이후는 On the flip side로 시작되어 수명이 긴 종에 대한 진술이 이어진다.

PLUS⁺ 변형문제

어휘 correlation 상관관계, 연관성

해설 이 글은 외적 위협이 많을수록 수명이 짧아진다는 내용이므로 이를 가장 잘 나타낸 제목은 ⑤ '위험, 수명 그리고 진화 사이의 상관관계'이다.

① 자연에서 동물의 지배의 가치
→ 지문에 언급된 dominant를 활용한 오답.

② 무엇이 생물이 진화를 발현시키도록 결정하는가?
→ 글에 언급된 진화적 압박은 일부 진화에만 해당되는 내용으로, 모든 진화를 발현시키는 원인은 아님.

③ 진화적 압박: 번식의 최고의 친구
→ 진화적 압박으로 더 이른 연령에 번식한다고 언급되었으나 글의 일부 내용에 해당함.

④ 죽음을 거의 직면하지 않는 생물의 진화적 압박
→ 죽음을 거의 직면하지 않는 생물의 진화적 압박이 언급되었으나 글의 일부 내용일 뿐임.

구문 ¹A shorter life span also means *a shorter length of time (between generations)*, // **which** allows a species to evolve faster — **which** is important / for *species* [**that** face a lot of environmental threats].
- 첫 번째 밑줄 친 which는 계속적 용법의 관계대명사로 앞에 있는 명사 a shorter ~ between generations를 보충 설명하는 절을 이끈다.
- 두 번째 밑줄 친 which는 앞 문장 전체(A shorter ~ to evolve faster)를 선행사로 하며 보충 설명한다.
- [   ]는 관계대명사 that이 이끄는 관계사절로 선행사 species를 수식한다.

²At the same time, there's never *any real evolutionary pressure* (to evolve mechanisms / to repair *DNA errors* [that occur over time]), // because most individuals (in the species) don't live long enough to experience those errors.
- (   )로 표시된 to evolve ~ over time은 앞에 있는 any real evolutionary pressure를 수식한다.
- [   ]는 관계대명사 that이 이끄는 관계사절로 선행사 DNA errors를 수식한다.

주제문
Mills suggests imagining extreme cases / as a way (to stimulate thinking): If something is small, // imagine it to be enormous / and ask "How would that change things?" An example of this heuristic can be seen / in the research (on globalization in the fields of geography, anthropology, political science, and economics). Theorists in these disciplines consider // how processes (operating at the global level) might be mirrored at the local level, // as well as how processes (operating at the local level) might be generalized or altered // if they are moved to the global level. ¹For example, if we think about the effects and challenges of unionizing workers at the local level, // what would happen // if we focused on unionizing workers at the global level? How might thinking in such terms alter our theories and understanding (of unionization at the local level)?

↓

To stimulate thinking, / try to (A) reframe the problem / by changing the (B) scale (of its application).

해석 주제문 Mills는 사고를 자극하는 방법으로서 극단적인 경우를 상상할 것을 제안한다. 만약 어떤 것이 작으면, 그것을 거대하다고 상상하고 "그것이 어떻게 바뀔까?"라고 질문하라. 이런 발견법의 한 가지 예는 지리학, 인류학, 정치학, 경제학 분야에서의 세계화에 대한 연구에서 볼 수 있다. 추론 근거 이러한 학문 분야의 이론가들은 지역 수준에서 작용하는 과정들이 세계적 수준으로 옮겨진다면 어떻게 일반화되거나 바뀔 수 있을까 뿐만 아니라, 세계적 수준에서 작용하는 과정들이 지역 수준에서 어떻게 반영될 수 있을까에 대해서도 고려한다. 가령, 지역 수준에서 노동조합을 결성한 노동자들의 영향들과 문제들에 대해 고려해 볼 때, 세계적 수준에서 노동조합을 결성한 노동자들로 초점을 맞추면 어떤 일이 일어날 것인가? 그러한 관점에서의 생각은 지역 수준에서 노동조합을 결성하는 것에 대한 우리의 이론과 이해를 어떻게 변화시킬 수 있을까?

↓

사고를 자극하기 위해서 문제 적용의 (B) 규모를 바꿈으로써 문제를 (A) 재구성하도록 시도하라.

어휘 **extreme** 극단적인　**stimulate** 자극하다, 격려하다　**heuristic** 발견법, 발견적 학습법; 체험적인　**globalization** 세계화　**geography** 지리학　**anthropology** 인류학　**discipline** (학문의) 분야; 규율, 훈육; (대학의) 학과; 훈육하다　**operate** 작용하다; 작동하다; 수술하다　**mirror** 잘 보여주다, 반영하다; 거울; 비추다　**generalize** 일반화하다　**alter** 바꾸다, 변경하다　**unionize** 노동조합을 결성하다; 노동조합에 가입하다　*cf.* **unionization** 노동조합 결성; 노조 가입

해설 사고를 자극하는 방법으로 극단적인 경우, 즉 어떤 것이 작으면 거대한 것으로 상상하고 질문하라고 하였다. 이어지는 예시도 이를 뒷받침하는데, 지역 수준의 과정들(즉 작은 규모)이 세계적 수준(큰 규모)으로 옮겨진다면 어떻게 바뀔지를 고려한다는 내용이다. 그러므로 빈칸에는 ① '(A) 재구성하다 – (B) 규모'가 적절하다.

오답 Check
　　(A)　　　(B)
② 공유하다 － 결과
→ (A), (B) 모두 오답.
③ 해결하다 － 순서
→ 규모의 변경을 통해 문제가 어떻게 바뀔까에 대한 고려를 한다는 내용일 뿐 그 문제를 해결한다는 내용이 아니고, '순서'에 관한 언급은 없음.
④ 시각화하다 － 목적
→ (A), (B) 모두 오답.
⑤ 재평가하다 － 순간
→ (A)는 맞지만 (B)는 오답.

구문 ¹For example, **if** we think about the effects and challenges of unionizing workers at the local level, // what would happen // **if** we focused on unionizing workers at the global level?
• 한 개의 주절 what would happen과 두 개의 if절 if we think ~ at the local level과 if we focused ~ at the global level로 구성된 문장이다. 앞의 if절은 직설법으로 when의 의미와 같고, 뒤에 if는 가정법 과거로 현재나 미래에 대한 불확실한 가정을 나타낸다.

Information is transferred // when the thought of a single mind is shared with another. In hunter-gather societies, information may have been very limited, // but it was (a) self-correcting — misinformation was minimized. ¹A hunter [who routinely led his kin away from the best hunting grounds] was soon either excluded from his group or simply

어휘 **transfer** 옮기다　**self-correcting** 자기 수정적인　**kin** 친족　**valid** 타당한, 유효한　**collaboration** 협업　**prehistory** 선사 시대　**validate** (타당성을) 확인하다; 승인하다　**occupy** 점유하다, 차지하다　**incentive** 유인[장려]책; 동기　**assure** 보장하다, 확언하다　**altruism** 이타주의

ignored, // and anyone [who gathered poisonous berries instead of nutritious ones] was quickly eliminated.

In his recent book *The Social Conquest of Earth*, E. Wilson described in evolutionary terms // how this sharing of valid information was rewarded. Wilson's view is // that (b) collaboration among humans has become an essential part of our wiring through natural selection. Throughout most of human prehistory, / then, validating information and sharing it / was both valued and rewarded. Information may have been quite limited, // but its quality was high.

We now occupy the (c) opposite state. How did this happen? ²When one doesn't know, / has never met, / and, furthermore, shares no common interest with the individual [with whom information is being shared], // there is little incentive (to assure the reliability of that information).

주제문
Indeed, if there is an personal (d) loss (to be had by providing misinformation to one's unknown targets), // there is an incentive (to misinform). In a target market of seventy million consumers — or seven billion — / there is no incentive for altruism. If more profit — in dollars, in power, in fame — is to be gained from misinformation, // why not go for it? And when dollars, power, and fame are combined (as they often are in politics), // the incentive is all the (e) stronger.

해석 정보는 한 사람의 생각이 다른 사람과 공유될 때 옮겨진다. 수렵 채집 사회에서 정보는 매우 제한되었을지 모르지만 (a) 자기 수정적이었다. 즉 잘못된 정보는 최소화되었다. 일상적으로 자신의 친족을 최고의 사냥터에서 멀리 떨어진 곳으로 이끄는 수렵인은 곧 집단에서 제외되거나 그저 무시되었으며, 영양분이 풍부한 열매 대신 독성 열매를 채집한 사람은 누구든지 빠르게 제거되었다.

자신의 최근에 나온 책 〈지구의 사회적 정복〉에서 E. Wilson은 이러한 타당한 정보의 공유가 어떻게 보상받았는지를 진화론적 관점에서 기술했다. Wilson의 견해는 인간 간의 (b) 협업이 자연 선택을 통하여 우리의 회로망의 필수 부분이 되었다는 것이다. 그러면 인간의 선사 시대 대부분의 기간 내내 정보를 확인하고 공유하는 것은 가치 있는 일로 여겨지고 보상받았다. 정보는 꽤 제한되었을지도 모르지만 질은 높았다.

우리는 지금 (c) 반대 상태를 점유하고 있다. 어떻게 이런 일이 일어났는가? 정보를 공유하고 있는 사람을 알지 못하고, 만난 적도 없고, 더욱이 아무런 공통의 관심도 공유하지 않는 때에 그 정보의 신뢰성을 보장할 유인책은 거의 없다. 주제문 실은, 미지의 대상에게 잘못된 정보를 제공하여 갖게 될 개인적 (d) 손실(→ 이득)이 존재한다면, 잘못된 정보를 전달할 동기가 존재한다. 7천만, 혹은 70억의 소비자가 있는 표적 시장에는 이타주의를 위한 동기는 없다. 잘못된 정보로부터 더 많은 수익을 (돈으로, 권력으로, 명성으로) 얻게 된다면 왜 덤벼들지 않겠는가? 그리고 돈과 권력과 명성이 (정치에서 종종 그러하듯이) 결합될 때, 동기는 더욱 (e) 더 강력하다.

02

해설 41 옛날의 인류는 잘못된 정보를 퍼뜨릴 시 도태되었지만, 현대에는 정보를 공유할 때 정보의 신뢰성을 보장할 유인책이 없고, 잘못된 정보를 제공하는 것이 개인의 이득이 된다면 그러지 않을 이유가 없으므로 잘못된 정보의 확산이 만연하게 되었다는 내용의 글이므로 제목으로 가장 적절한 것은 ② '왜 오늘날 잘못된 정보가 그토록 만연한가?'이다.

42 잘못된 정보를 제공해서 개인에게 손실(loss)이 된다면 잘못된 정보를 전달할 이유가 없을 것이다. 따라서 (d)의 loss를 gain 등으로 바꿔 써야 한다.

오답 Check
41 ① 잘못된 정보에 대해 그토록 나쁜 점은 무엇인가?
→ 잘못된 정보의 나쁜 점을 언급하는 내용은 아님.
③ 잘못된 정보의 시대에 대한 생존 안내
→ 잘못된 정보의 시대는 맞으나 생존을 안내하는 내용은 아님.
④ 개인의 이득을 극대화하는 유인책 구조 → 잘못된 정보 공유로 얻는 이득이 유인책이 될 수는 있으나 그 구조에 대해 설명하는 글은 아님.
⑤ 고대부터 잘못된 정보는 우세하다
→ 고대에는 잘못된 정보를 퍼트릴 시 도태되었음.

42 '잘못된 정보로부터 더 많은 수익을 얻게 된다면 왜 덤벼들지 않겠는가?'라는 말은 곧 본인이 얻을 여러 이득이 결합될 때 잘못된 정보를 전달할 동기가 더욱 커진다는 말이므로 (e)의 stronger는 적절하다.

구문 ¹*A hunter* [who routinely led his kin away from the best hunting grounds] **was** soon either excluded from his group or simply ignored, ~.

• [ ]는 주어 A hunter를 수식하는 관계사절이며 동사는 was이다.
• 「either A or B」는 'A나 B 둘 중 하나'의 뜻이며 A와 B에는 과거분사로 이루어진 구가 병렬 구조를 이룬다.

²When one doesn't know, / has never met, / and, furthermore, shares no common interest with *the individual* [with whom information is being shared], // there is *little incentive* (to assure the reliability of that information).

• the individual ~ shared는 밑줄 친 doesn't know, has never met, shares no common interest with의 공통 목적어이다.
• [ ]는 '전치사+관계대명사'로 시작되는 관계사절로 앞의 the individual을 수식한다.
• ( )는 to부정사의 형용사적 용법으로 little incentive를 수식한다.

| 31 ③ ⁺ ⑤ | 32 ② ⁺ ④ | 33 ① ⁺ ④ | 34 ⑤ ⁺ ③ | 35 ④ ⁺ ③ | 36 ④ ⁺ ② |
| 37 ③ ⁺ ④ | 38 ③ ⁺ ② | 39 ④ ⁺ ③ | 40 ② | 41 ① | 42 ④ |

31 ③ PLUS⁺ ⑤

[1]An anthropologist (named Nina G. Jablonski) and a geographic computer specialist (named George Chaplin) / have produced an equation (to express the relationship (between a given population's skin color and its annual exposure to ultraviolet rays)). Interestingly, their research proposes // that we carry sufficient genes within our gene pool to ensure that, // (within 1,000 years of a population's migration from one climate to another), its descendants would have skin color light enough to maximize the use of available sunlight / to create sufficient vitamin D production. 주제문 [2]There is one notable exception to Jablonski and Chaplin's equation — // and it is the case [that demonstrates the existence of the rule]. 추론 근거 The Inuit — the indigenous people of the subarctic — are dark-skinned, / despite the limited sunlight of their home. But the reason [they don't need to evolve the lighter skin necessary to ensure sufficient vitamin D production] is refreshingly simple. Their diet is full of fatty fish — which just happens to be one of the only foods in nature [that is chock-full of vitamin D].

어휘 anthropologist 인류학자 equation 방정식; 균등화; 평형 상태 given 특정한; 정해진 ultraviolet rays 자외선 sufficient 충분한 ○gene pool 유전자 풀 migration 이동; 이주 descendant 후손, 자손 notable 주목할 만한; 유명한 indigenous 토착의; 타고난 subarctic 아(亞)북극의, 북극에 가까운 chock-full 꽉 들어찬 **[선택지 어휘]** omission 생략(된 것); 탈락 inclination 경향; 기울기 commonality 공통성; 보통
어휘○ 유전자 풀: 어떤 생물 종 집단을 구성하는 모든 개체가 지닌 유전 정보의 총량

해설 Jablonski와 Chaplin의 방정식을 통해 햇빛을 최대로 받기 위해서는 충분히 밝은 피부색을 가져야 함을 추론할 수 있는데, 이누이트족은 햇빛이 제한되어 있음에도 피부색이 검다고 했으므로 이는 그 방정식의 ③ '예외'로 보아야 한다.

오답 Check
① 생략된 것 ② 의도 ④ 경향 ⑤ 공통성
→ 모두 이누이트족의 예시를 설명할 수 없는 오답.

PLUS ⁺ 변형문제

어휘 absorbance 흡수
해설 비타민 D를 생산하기 위해서는 햇빛이 필요한데, 햇빛을 충분히 흡수하기 위해 인간이 밝은 피부색을 가지는 유전자를 지니게 되었다는 내용으로 이를 제목으로 잘 표현한 것은 ⑤ '피부색과 비타민 D의 관계'가 적절하다.
① 비타민 D 생산의 두 가지 근원
→ 근원으로 햇빛과 생선이 언급되긴 했지만, 글의 제목으로 볼 수는 없음.
② 왜 우리는 자외선을 차단해야 하는가?
③ 비타민 D 생산을 위한 필수 식품
→ 이누이트의 식단이 언급되긴 했지만 주제문을 아우르지 못함.
④ 비타민 D 흡수의 열쇠: 어두운 피부
→ 글의 내용과 반대됨.

해석 Nina G. Jablonski라는 인류학자와 George Chaplin이라는 지리 컴퓨터 전문가는 특정한 인구의 피부색과 그것의 연간 자외선 노출 사이의 관계를 나타내는 방정식을 만들어 냈다. 흥미롭게도, 그들의 연구는 우리가 한 기후에서 다른 기후로 인구가 이동한 지 1,000년 이내에 그 후손들이 충분한 비타민 D를 생산하기 위해 이용할 수 있는 햇빛의 사용을 최대화할 수 있을 만큼 충분히 밝은 피부색을 가지는 것을 보장하기 위해 우리의 유전자 풀 안에 충분한 유전자를 지니고 있다고 시사한다. 주제문 Jablonski와 Chaplin의 방정식에는 한 가지 주목할 만한 예외가 있는데, 그것은 그 규칙이 존재함을 증명하는 경우이다. 추론 근거 아(亞)북극의 토착 민족인 이누이트족은 그들 본거지의 제한된 햇빛에도 불구하고 피부가 검다. 그러나 그들이 충분한 비타민 D 생산을 보장하기 위해 필요한 더 밝은 피부로 진화할 필요가 없는 이유는 참신하게도 단순하다. 그들의 식단은 지방이 많은 생선으로 가득한데, 그것이 마침 비타민 D가 꽉 들어찬 자연에서의 유일한 음식들 중 하나인 것이다.

구문 [1]*An anthropologist* (**named** Nina G. Jablonski) and *a geographic computer specialist* (**named** George Chaplin) / have produced *an equation* (**to express** the relationship (between a given population's skin color and its annual exposure to ultraviolet rays)).
• named가 이끄는 두 개의 분사구가 각각 앞에 나온 명사(구)를 수식한다.
• to express가 이끄는 ( )는 형용사적 용법으로 사용된 to부정사구로 앞에 나온 an equation을 수식한다.

[2]There is one notable **exception to** Jablonski and Chaplin's equation — and it is *the case* [**that** demonstrates the existence of the rule].
• exception to에서 to는 전치사이고, [ ]는 주격 관계대명사 that이 이끄는 관계사절로 the case를 수식한다.

추론 근거

For ages, yoga teachers have been saying, // "Calm your body, calm your mind." ¹They argue // that action and feeling go together, // and by regulating the action, which is under the more direct control of the will, / we can indirectly regulate the feeling. Social neuroscience now provides evidence (to support that prescription). ²In fact, / some studies go further and suggest // that actively taking on the physical state of a happy person by, say, / forcing a smile can cause you to actually feel happier. My young son Nicolai seemed to understand this intuitively: // ³after breaking his hand in a freak accident / while playing basketball, // he suddenly stopped crying and started to laugh — and then explained // that when he has pain // laughing seems to make it feel better. The old "fake it till you make it" idea, which Nicolai had rediscovered, is now also the subject of serious scientific research.

해석 추론 근거 요가를 가르치는 사람들은 오랜 세월 동안 "몸을 차분하게 진정시키고, 마음을 진정시키세요."라고 말해 왔다. 그들은 행동과 감정은 함께 가고, 의지의 더 직접적인 통제 아래에 있는 행동을 조절해서 우리는 간접적으로 감정을 조절할 수 있다고 주장한다. 오늘날 사회 신경 과학은 그 처방을 지지하는 증거를 제공한다. 추론 근거 사실 몇몇 연구는 그보다 더 나아가 가령, 억지로 미소를 지음으로써 행복한 사람의 육체적 상태를 적극적으로 취하는 것이 여러분을 실제로 더 행복하게 느끼게 할 수 있다는 것을 보여준다. 추론 근거 나의 어린 아들 Nicolai는 이것을 직관적으로 이해하는 것 같았다. 농구를 하다가 별난 사고로 손이 부러진 후에, 아들은 갑자기 울음을 멈추더니 웃기 시작했다. 그러고는 통증이 올 때 크게 웃는 것이 통증을 더 낫게 하는 것 같다고 설명했다. 주제문 Nicolai가 재발견한 지혜, '실제로 이루어질 때까지 그런 척하라'는 격언은 오늘날 진지한 과학 연구의 주제이기도 하다.

어휘 calm 진정시키다; 침착한; 평온 regulate 조절[조정]하다; 규제하다 will 의지(력); 유언장 social neuroscience 사회 신경 과학 prescription 처방(전); 규정; 법규 state 상태; 국가; 말하다 intuitively 직관적으로 freak 별난, 희한한 fake ~인 척하다; 위조하다; 가짜의; 모조[위조]품 **[선택지 어휘]** let go of ~을 버리다[놓다] preconception 선입견; 예상

해설 빈칸이 글의 마지막 문장에 있을 때, 빈칸 문장이 주제문일 가능성이 크다. 행동이 감정을 조절할 수 있다고 말해온 요가 강사들, 그 명제를 지지하는 연구 결과와 크게 웃는 것이 통증을 더 낫게 하는 것 같다는 필자의 아들의 예시를 통해 빈칸에는 모두를 포함한 개괄적인 개념인 ② '실제로 이루어질 때까지 그런 척하라'는 말이 가장 적절하다.

오답 Check
① 불에 연료를 덧보태라(불난 집에 부채질하다)
③ 모든 선입견을 버려라
④ 건강한 신체에 건강한 마음
⑤ 계획을 조각으로 나누어라
→ ①, ③, ⑤는 지문의 내용과 전혀 관계가 없고, ④는 추론 근거에서 연상되는 그럴듯한 오답으로 행동이 감정을 조절한다는 내용과는 관련 없음.

PLUS⁺ 변형문제

해설 인간의 행동이 거짓일지라도 감정을 조절할 수 있다는 내용이므로 글의 요지로는 ④가 가장 적절하다.
→ ①, ②, ③, ⑤ 모두 글에 언급된 어구를 활용했지만, 글의 요지와는 거리가 먼 오답.

구문 ¹They argue // **that** action and feeling go together, // |and| by regulating *the action*, **which** is under the more direct control of the will, / we can indirectly regulate the feeling.
- 밑줄 친 두 개의 절은 동사 argue의 목적어로 쓰였으며 and로 병렬 연결된다.
- 두 번째 절에서 which는 계속적 용법의 관계대명사로 선행사 the action을 보충 설명한다.

²In fact, / some studies go further and **suggest** // that actively taking on the physical state of a happy person **by**, (say), **forcing** a smile / can **cause** *you* **to actually feel happier**.
- 밑줄 친 that절은 suggest의 목적어절 역할을 하며, that절 내에서 주어는 actively ~ a smile이다.
- that절은 SVOC의 구조로 동사 cause는 목적격보어로 to부정사를 취한다.
- 전치사 by와 by의 목적어인 forcing 사이에 say가 삽입된 구조로, 이때 say는 '가령, 이를테면'의 의미이다.

³after breaking his hand in a freak accident / **while playing basketball**, // he suddenly stopped crying and started to laugh — and then explained // that when he has *pain* // laughing seems to make *it* feel better.
- while playing basketball은 접속사가 생략되지 않은 분사구문이다.
- 밑줄 친 부분은 「make+목적어(it)+원형부정사(feel)」의 구조로 이때 it은 앞에 나온 명사 pain을 의미한다.

The writer very quickly loses / the ability (to see his prose as a reader). He knows exactly // what he's trying to say, // but that's because he's the one (saying it). For writers, / knowledge can be a subtle curse. When we learn about the world, // we also learn all the reasons [why the world cannot be changed]. We become numb / to the possibilities of something new. In fact, the only way (to remain creative over time — not to be undone by our expertise —) is / to pursue a deeper ignorance. This is the lesson (of Samuel Taylor Coleridge, the nineteenth-century Romantic poet). One of his favorite pastimes / was attending public chemistry lectures in London, / watching eminent scientists set elements on fire. ¹When Coleridge was asked // why he spent so much time watching these pyrotechnic demonstrations, // he had a ready reply. "I attend the lectures," Coleridge said, "so that I can renew my stock of metaphors." He knew // that we see the most // when we are on the outside looking in.

해석 작가는 독자로서 자신의 산문을 보는 능력을 매우 빠르게 상실한다. 그는 자신이 하고자 하는 말을 정확히 알고 있지만, 이는 그가 그것을 말하는 사람이기 때문이다. 추론 근거 작가들에게, 지식은 미묘한 저주일 수 있다. 세상에 대해 배울 때 우리는 또한 세상이 변화될 수 없는 온갖 이유들을 배운다. 우리는 새로운 것의 가능성에 무감각해진다. 주제문 사실, 시간이 흘러도 창의성을 유지할 수 있는, 즉 우리의 전문 지식에 의해 실패하지 않는 유일한 방법은 더 깊은 무지를 추구하는 것이다. 이것이 19세기 낭만주의 시인인 Samuel Taylor Coleridge의 교훈이다. 추론 근거 그가 가장 좋아했던 취미 중 하나는 런던의 대중 화학 강연에 참석하여, 저명한 과학자들이 원소들에 불을 지피는 것을 보는 것이었다. 왜 이러한 불꽃 시연을 보는 데 그토록 많은 시간을 쓰는지 질문을 받았을 때, Coleridge에게는 준비된 답변이 있었다. "저는 강연에 참석합니다." Coleridge가 말했다. "제 은유를 비축한 것을 새로이 할 수 있도록 말이죠." 그는 우리가 외부에서 안을 들여다볼 때(의역: 우리가 (지식으로부터) 멀어질 때) 가장 많은 것을 본다는 점을 알고 있었다.

어휘 prose 산문 subtle 미묘한; 교묘한 curse 저주; 악담 numb 무딘, 감각이 없는 undone 완전히 실패한; 끝나지 않은 expertise 전문 지식 ignorance 무지, 무식 pastime 취미, 기분 전환 eminent 저명한; 탁월한 element 원소; 요소 demonstration 시연; 증명 stock 비축; 저장 on the outside looking in (과정, 그룹 등에서) 멀어진[소외된]

해설 빈칸 문장이 중반부에 있는 경우 빈칸 문장의 앞부분은 주제문을 말하기 위한 도입 또는 세부 사항 중 일부이고 빈칸 문장 뒷부분에 단서가 있는 경우가 많다. 도입에서 우리는 무언가를 앎으로써 새로운 것에 무뎌진다고 했고, 빈칸 문장 뒤에 나오는 예시를 보면 비축한 은유를 새로이 하기 위해 그 분야에 지식이 없을 것 같은 화학 강연에 참여하는 것을 즐겼다고 하므로 시간이 흘러도 창의성을 유지할 수 있는 방법으로는 ① '더 깊은 무지를 추구하는 것'이 가장 적절하다.

오답 Check
② '왜' 대신에 '왜 안 돼'를 묻는 것
→ 이유에 대해서 질문하라는 언급은 없음.
③ 다른 사람들과 우리의 지식을 공유하는 것
→ 글에서는 지식을 부정적으로 여기므로 틀림.
④ 오래된 생각을 차용해서 그것을 결합하는 것
→ 창의적 생각에 대한 것이지 오래된 생각은 언급되지 않음.
⑤ 창의적인 사람들과 인맥을 만드는 것 → 창의적인 사람을 통해서가 아닌 알지 못하는 것을 통해 창의성을 유지할 수 있음.

PLUS⁺ 변형문제

어휘 comprehend 이해하다; 깨닫다 peculiar 특이한; 고유의 inquiry 연구; 조사; 질문
해설 창의성을 유지하기 위해 잘 모르는 분야에 도전해야 하므로, 제목으로는 ④ '새로운 것을 시도함으로써 당신의 창의력을 새로이 하라'가 가장 적절하다.
① 교육을 통해 삶에서 의미를 얻어라
→ 화학 강연을 활용한 오답으로 삶의 의미를 얻는 방법이 주제는 아님.
② 독자로서 산문을 가장 잘 이해하는 방법
→ 지문의 내용과 관계없음.
③ 과학 강연에 관한 시인의 특이한 연구
→ 화학 강연에 참여한 시인의 예를 활용한 오답으로 일부 내용임.
⑤ 지식은 우리의 확장된 이해로 이끈다
→ 지식의 긍정적인 내용은 언급되지 않음.

구문 ¹When Coleridge **was asked** // why he *spent* so much time *watching* these pyrotechnic demonstrations, // he had a ready reply. "I attend the lectures," Coleridge said, "**so that** I can renew my stock of metaphors."
• 부사절의 동사 was asked는 「ask+IO+DO」 구조를 수동태로 전환한 것이다.
• 「spend+시간+v-ing」는 'v하는 데 시간을 쓰다'라는 의미이고, 밑줄 친 so that은 '~하기 위해서'라는 의미의 목적을 나타내는 접속사이다.

Charlotte Linde noticed in her study (of police helicopter crews) // that when the immediate demands (of work) subside, / the crew may engage in social chat, // which will stop if work requirements intrude. And she found // that the switch from work talk to social talk / was more often initiated by the pilot, // who functioned as a superior in command. ¹For example, if it was quiet, // the pilot might begin free conversation / by noticing the view, returning to a previous topic or commenting on the mission (just completed). ²This is exactly the pattern [that sociolinguist Janice Hornyak noticed / in a study of talk in an all-female office at an accounting firm]. As the women in the office shifted between work and personal talk, // the shift was always initiated by the highest-ranking person in the room, the office manager. If she was busy, // nobody else began telling personal stories or chatting. But if the office manager was ready to take a break and chat, // the others followed suit. In this way, hierarchies are reflected throughout a workday, / in even the most automatic and casual conversation.

해석 Charlotte Linde는 경찰 헬기 대원 연구에서, 즉각적인 업무 요구가 잦아들면 대원들이 사교적 대화에 참여할 것이고 업무적 요구가 방해하면 멈출 것임에 주목했다. 추론 근거 그리고 그녀는 업무 대화에서 사교적 대화로의 전환이 조종사에 의하여 더 빈번히 주도되었음을 발견했고, 그 조종사는 지휘하는 상관으로서 기능을 했다. 예를 들어, 조용하면 그 조종사는 풍경에 주목하거나, 이전의 주제로 돌아가거나 방금 완수한 임무에 대해 논평함으로써 자유로운 대화를 시작할지도 모른다. 이것은 사회언어학자인 Janice Hornyak이 한 회계 회사에서 전부 여성으로 구성된 사무실에서의 대화에 대한 연구에서 주목했던 바로 그 패턴이었다. 추론 근거 사무실의 여성들이 업무 대화와 개인적 대화 사이를 오갈 때, 이러한 전환은 항상 사무실에서 가장 지위가 높은 사람인 사무장에 의해 개시되었다. 그녀가 바쁘면, 다른 누구도 개인적 이야기나 잡담을 시작하지 않았다. 그러나 사무장이 휴식을 취하고 잡담할 준비가 되면, 다른 사람들도 이를 따랐다. 주제문 이러한 방식으로, 가장 자동적이고 평상적인 대화에서조차 계급이 근무일 내내 반영된다.

어휘 immediate 즉각적인 demand 요구(하다) subside 가라앉다 engage in ~에 참여하다 intrude 침범하다; 방해하다 initiate 개시되게 하다 superior 상급자, 상관 command 지휘, 명령; 지시하다 comment 논평하다 sociolinguist 사회언어학자 accounting 회계 follow suit 남이 한 대로 따라 하다 hierarchy 계급[계층] reflect 반영하다; 비추다; 반사하다 throughout ~동안, 내내; 도처에 automatic 자동의; 무의식적인, 반사적인 [선택지 어휘] initiative 솔선, 시작; 계획; 주도(권)

해설 빈칸 앞 내용에서, 업무 중 사교적 대화의 시작은 집단 내의 상급자에 의해 이루어진다는 두 가지 예가 제시되었으므로 평상적인 대화조차 ⑤ '계급이 근무일 내내 반영된다'고 할 수 있다.

오답 Check
① 휴식을 취하는 것은 매우 중요하다
→ 글에 언급되지 않은 내용.
② 누구도 명령을 따르는 솔선을 하지 않는다
→ 명령을 따르지 않는다는 내용은 없음.
③ 모든 사람들이 상사가 말을 멈추기를 기다린다
→ 상관과 잡담을 나눌 때 말이 끝날 때까지 기다려야 한다는 내용은 없음.
④ 직원들은 잡담을 가능한 한 많이 피한다
→ 부하직원들이 상관을 따라 함께 잡담을 나눈다고 했으므로 오답.

PLUS+ 변형문제
어휘 colleague 동료 trigger 유발하다. 촉발시키다; (총의) 방아쇠 subordinate 부하, 하급자; 부차적인
해설 직장에서 사교적 대화가 주로 상급자에 의해 이루어진다는 내용이므로 글의 주제로 가장 적절한 것은 ③ '직장에서 사회적 상호작용이 유발되는 방법'이다.
① 일과 삶의 균형을 유지하는 것의 중요성
② 직장에서 동료들과의 잡담하는 것의 이점
④ 직업 만족도에 미치는 상사-부하 관계의 영향
⑤ 직원들과 좋은 관계를 쌓아 줄 대화 주제들
→ ①, ②, ④, ⑤ 모두 글과 관련 없는 내용.

구문 ¹For example, **if it was** quiet, // the pilot **might begin** free conversation / **by** noticing the view, / returning to a previous topic or commenting on the mission (just completed).
• 「if+S'+과거동사 ~, S+조동사 과거형+동사원형 …」은 가정법 과거로 '만약 ~라면, …할 텐데'의 의미이다.
• 전치사 by 다음의 동명사 noticing, returning, commenting이 콤마(,)와 or로 연결되었다.
• ( )는 수동의 의미로 the mission을 수식한다.

²This is exactly *the pattern* [**that** sociolinguist Janice Hornyak noticed / in a study of talk in an all-female office at an accounting firm].
• [ ]는 목적격 관계대명사 that이 이끄는 관계사절로 선행사 the pattern을 수식한다.

How does a major-league baseball player manage to hit a fastball? ^{주제문} The answer is // that the brain begins collecting information (about the pitch) // long before the ball is ever thrown. ¹As soon as the pitcher begins his wind-up, // the batter automatically starts to pick up on "anticipatory clues" [that narrow down the list of possibilities]. ① A twisted wrist suggests a curveball, // while an elbow (fixed at a right angle) means / that a fastball is coming, straight over the plate. ② Two fingers (on the seam) might indicate a slider, // which is thrown fast and curves slightly // as it approaches the batter. ③ ²A ball (gripped with the knuckles) is a sure sign // that a wavering knuckleball is on its way. ④ The forkball, / which is thrown with the same speed of a fastball, / is known to be a cause of significant and increasingly common damage (to the shoulder and elbow). ⑤ The batters, of course, aren't consciously studying these signs; they can't explain // what made them swing at certain pitches.

[해석] 메이저리그 야구선수가 어떻게 속구를 쳐낼 수 있을까? ^{주제문} 해답은 공을 던지기도 훨씬 전에 뇌가 투구에 관한 정보를 수집하기 시작한다는 것이다. 투수가 와인드업을 시작하자마자, 타자는 가능한 것들의 목록을 줄여 주는 '예측 단서들'을 반사적으로 알아차리기 시작한다. ① 비틀어진 손목은 커브볼을 암시하는 반면, 직각으로 고정된 팔꿈치는 플레이트를 일직선으로 넘어 패스트볼이 다가오는 것을 의미한다. ② 실땀에 얹은 두 개의 손가락은 슬라이더의 징후일 수 있는데, 그것은 빠르게 던져지고 공이 타자에게 다가가면서 약간 곡선을 그린다. ③ 손가락 마디로 쥔 공은 너울거리는 너클볼이 오고 있다는 확실한 신호이다. ④ 포크볼은, 패스트볼과 같은 속도로 던져지는데, 어깨와 팔꿈치에 상당하고 갈수록 더 흔한 손상의 원인으로 알려져 있다. ⑤ 타자는 물론 의식적으로 이 신호들을 유심히 보고 있는 것은 아니다. 그들은 무엇이 그들을 특정한 투구에 (배트를) 휘두르게 했는지 설명할 수 없다.

[어휘] pitch (공의) 투구; 내던지다 cf. pitcher 투수; 던지는 사람 wind-up 와인드업 ((투수의 투구 예비 동작)) batter ((야구)) 타자 automatically 반사적으로; 자동적으로 pick up 알아차리다; 집어 올리다 anticipatory 예측의; 선행하는 narrow down 줄이다; 좁히다 wrist 손목; 손목을 써서 움직이다 at a right angle 직각으로 seam 솔기의 바늘땀[실땀] indicate 나타내다; 보여 주다 slider 슬라이더 ((타자 가까이에서 외각으로 빠지는 공)) waver 너울거리다; 흔들리다; 약해지다 on one's way 오는[가는] 중인 consciously 의식적으로

[해설] 야구에서 구종을 예측할 수 있는 단서들이 있고, 타자들은 이 단서들을 이용해 속구를 쳐낸다는 것을 설명하는 글로, 구종 중 하나인 포크볼이 신체에 손상을 미치는 것에 관한 ④는 전체적인 흐름과 무관하다.

PLUS+ 변형문제

[해설] 야구에서 타자가 예측 가능한 단서들을 바탕으로 구종을 파악하여 공을 쳐 낸다는 내용이므로 글의 제목으로는 ③ '어떻게 타자는 구종을 예측하는가'가 가장 적절하다.

① 좋은 투수가 되는 방법들
→ 글에 언급되지 않음.

② 야구에서 다양한 구종
→ 여러 구종이 언급되었지만, 단순히 구종을 설명하는 글은 아님.

④ 어떤 투구가 타자가 치기 가장 어려운가
→ 어떤 투구가 가장 치기 어려운지는 언급되지 않음.

⑤ 누구에게 더 많은 기회가 있는가: 투수 대 타자
→ 투수와 타자 중 누구에게 더 많은 기회가 있는지는 글에서 언급되지 않음.

[구문] ¹As soon as the pitcher begins his wind-up, // the batter automatically starts to pick up on "anticipatory clues" [that narrow down the list of possibilities].
• as soon as는 '~하자마자'라는 뜻의 부사절을 이끄는 접속사이다.
• [ ]는 주격 관계대명사 that이 이끄는 관계사절로 선행사 "anticipatory clues"를 수식한다.

²A ball (gripped with the knuckles) is a sure sign // that a wavering knuckleball is on its way.
• ( )는 주어 A ball을 수식하는 분사구이다.
• 밑줄 친 a sure sign과 that절(that ~ on its way)은 동격 관계이다.

The Greek roots of the word 'homeostasis' / mean "like standing still." In a living organism, / this means // that the environment (inside an organism) stays the same // no matter what happens outside.
(C) But homeostasis is not perfect. ¹On a mountaintop, / for example, your body produces more red blood cells / to keep the level of oxygen (in your body) the same // even though it's lower outside.
(A) Yet at a certain point / there's just not enough oxygen outside // and your body can't cope. ²Similarly, an organism [whose internal environment changes / along with the external environment] still needs to maintain its internal chemistry.
(B) ³That is, there has to be something [that defines a living creature / as different from what's outside] — and [that has to be able to stay the same, / at least within a certain range of external environments]. So every organism has some level of homeostasis, // but there is a huge variation in scope.

해석 '항상성'이라는 단어의 그리스 어원은 '현상을 유지하는 것 같은'을 의미한다. 살아 있는 유기체에서, 이것은 외부에서 무슨 일이 일어나더라도 유기체 내부 환경이 동일하게 유지됨을 의미한다.
(C) 그러나 항상성은 완벽하지 않다. 예를 들어, 산꼭대기에서 여러분의 신체는 비록 외부가 (산소 수준이) 더 낮더라도 체내의 산소 수준을 동일하게 유지하기 위해 더 많은 적혈구를 생산한다.
(A) 하지만 어떤 지점에서는 외부의 산소가 정말 충분치 않아서 여러분의 신체가 대처할 수 없다. 마찬가지로 체내의 환경이 외부 환경과 함께 변화하는 어떤 유기체는 여전히 내부 화학 작용을 유지해야 한다.
(B) 즉, 살아 있는 생명체를 외부에 있는 것과는 다른 것으로 규정짓고, 적어도 일정 범위의 외부 환경 안에서 동일하게 유지할 수 있어야 하는 무언가가 있어야 한다. 주제문 그래서 모든 유기체는 어느 정도의 항상성을 가지고 있지만, 그 범위에는 엄청난 차이가 있다.

어휘 root 어원, 기원; 뿌리 ⊕homeostasis 항상성(恒常性) organism 유기체; 생물; 유기적 조직체 cope 대처하다, 대응하다 internal 체내의; 내부의; 국내의(↔ external 외부의) chemistry 화학(적 작용) define A as B A를 B로 규정하다 creature 생물, 생명이 있는 존재 variation 차이; 변화(의 정도), 변형 scope 범위; 한계; 여지

어휘⊕ 항상성: 자동 정상화 장치라고도 하며 외부 환경과 생물체 내의 변화에 대응하여 생물체 내의 환경을 일정하게 유지하려는 현상을 말하며 자율 신경계와 내분비계(호르몬)의 상호 협조로 이루어진다.

해설 주어진 글은 생체 내의 균형을 유지하려는 경향인 항상성을 설명하는 것으로 유기체 내부 환경이 외부에 상관없이 동일하게 유지된다는 내용이다. But으로 시작하여 항상성이 완벽하지 않다고 설명하는 (C)가 주어진 글에 이어지고, (C)의 예시의 내용이 연결되는 (A)가 이어진다. 이 모든 내용을 요약하며 항상성의 특징을 주제문으로 정리하는 (B)가 마지막에 오는 것이 자연스럽다.

오답 Check
(A)와 (C) 모두 역접을 의미하는 접속사가 쓰였지만, 앞 내용에 어떤 반대 상황이 나와야 하는지 추론하는 것이 중요하다.

PLUS⁺ 변형문제
해설 (B)의 마지막 문장인 주제문으로 보아 글의 요지로는 ②가 적절하다.
① → 항상성에 대한 내용으로 저항성은 언급되지 않음.
③ → 예시로 언급된 내용으로 글 전체의 요지라고 볼 수 없음.
④ → 항상성이 무엇에 의해 조절되는지 언급되지 않음.
⑤ → 우리 몸의 화학 작용을 조절하는 주체에 대한 언급 없음.

구문 ¹On a mountaintop, / for example, your body produces more red blood cells / to **keep** *the level of oxygen* (in your body) **the same** // even though it's lower outside.
• 「keep+O+C」의 구조로 목적어는 the level of oxygen in your body, 목적격보어는 the same이다. 목적어구 내에서 전명구 in your body가 the level of oxygen을 수식한다.

²Similarly, *an organism* [**whose** internal environment changes / along with the external environment] still needs to maintain its internal chemistry.
• 소유격 관계대명사 whose가 이끄는 [ ]는 선행사 an organism을 수식한다. 선행사인 an organism과 관계대명사 뒤에 오는 명사 internal environment가 소유 관계이므로 소유격 관계대명사가 쓰였다.
• 문장의 주어는 an organism ~ environment이고 동사는 needs이다.

³That is, there has to be *something* [**that** defines a living creature / as different from what's outside] — and [**that** has to be able to stay the same, / at least within a certain range of external environments].
• 두 개의 [ ] 내에 있는 각각의 that은 모두 주격 관계대명사로, 선행사 something을 수식하는 관계사절을 이끈다.

We tend to think of imitation / as a solo action. ^{주제문}However, in many contexts — and normally in mother-infant interactions — / achieving successful imitation is more of a cooperative undertaking.

(B) ¹The person (being imitated) (the model) becomes the "demonstrator," / and, by smiling and encouraging, / facilitates the imitator's efforts. ²Even in contexts [where no such assistance is necessary], (where the imitation is effortless), / the model will usually be aware of being (successfully) imitated / and will display this back to the imitator.

(C) This "acknowledgment of success" display might consist of a smile and/or a meeting of gazes, // and performance (of the action) might become more enthusiastic. Furthermore, the imitator will be aware of when his imitation is successful / and may produce a similar success display.

(A) So the model's "you are successfully imitating me" display will typically be met by the imitator's "I am successfully imitating you" display, // and this makes the success display mutual.

해석 우리는 모방을 단독 행동으로 여기는 경향이 있다. ^{주제문}하지만 많은 상황에서, 그리고 보통 엄마와 아기의 교류에서, 성공적인 모방을 이루는 것은 오히려 협동적인 일에 가깝다. (B) 모방의 대상이 되는 자(모델)가 '실연자(實演者)'가 되어, 미소를 건네고 격려함으로써 모방자의 노력을 촉진한다. 심지어 그런 도움이 필요치 않은 상황에서도, 즉 모방이 쉽게 이루어질 때에도, 모델은 보통 (상대방이) 자신을 (성공적으로) 모방하였다는 사실을 인식하고 이것을 다시 모방자에게 표현할 것이다. (C) '성공을 인정해주는' 이러한 표시는 미소나 눈이 마주치는 것으로 이루어질 수도 있을 것이고, 그 동작의 수행은 더욱 열정적이게 될 수도 있을 것이다. 뿐만 아니라, 모방자는 자신의 모방이 성공적일 때를 알게 될 것이고, 비슷한 성공의 표시를 하게 될지 모른다. (A) 그래서 모델(엄마)의 '네가 나를 성공적으로 모방하고 있구나.'라는 표시는 보통 모방자(아기)의 '저는 당신을 성공적으로 모방하고 있어요.'라는 표시와 만나게 되어, 성공의 표시가 상호적인 것이 되게 한다.

어휘 think of A as B A를 B로 여기다[생각하다] normally 보통(은); 정상적으로 infant 유아 cooperative 협력하는, 협조하는 undertaking (중요한·힘든) 일; 약속, 동의 demonstrator (무엇의 작동 과정이나 사용법을) 시범 설명하는 사람; 시위[데모] 참가자 facilitate 촉진하다; 가능하게[용이하게]하다 imitator 모방[모조, 위조]하는 사람 assistance 도움, 원조 effortless 노력이 필요 없는, 쉽게 되는 acknowledgement 인정; 감사(의 표시) gaze 응시, 시선; 뚫어지게 보다 enthusiastic 열렬한, 열광적인 typically 보통, 일반적으로; 전형적으로 mutual 상호의, 서로의

해설 주어진 글은 모방이 단독 행동이라기보다 상호 협동이라는 내용으로 그 뒤에는 상호 협동의 예시가 시작되는 (B)가 이어지는 것이 적절하다. (B)에서 모방의 대상이 되는 모델은 모방 행위가 성공하면 그것을 모방자에게 표현한다고 했으므로, 바로 이 성공을 인정하는 표시, 즉 미소나 눈 마주침 등을 부연 설명하는 (C)가 뒤에 이어진다. 마지막으로 이 표시를 모방자와 모델이 서로에게 보냄으로써 모방을 상호적인 것으로 만든다고 마무리하는 내용의 (A)가 오는 것이 자연스럽다.

PLUS + 변형문제

어휘 anticipation 기대, 예상 recognition 인정; 알아봄, 인식 joint 공동의, 합동의; 관절 mimicry 흉내, 모방
해설 모방은 모델과 모방자의 상호 협동에 의해 이루어진다는 내용이므로 글의 제목으로 가장 적절한 것은 ④ '모방: 모델과 모방자 사이의 합동 활동'이 가장 적절하다.
① 모방이 협력을 위해 무엇을 할 수 있는가?
→ 글에 언급된 어구를 활용한 오답.
② 사회적 상호작용에서 기대와 모방
→ 글에 언급된 어구를 활용한 오답.
③ 인정에 대한 갈망이 성공을 촉진한다
→ 모방에서 성공은 성공을 인정하는 표시로 촉진됨.
⑤ 사회적 상호작용에서의 모방과 그것이 학습에 미치는 영향
→ 모방이 학습에 미치는 영향은 언급되지 않음.

구문 ¹The person (being imitated) (the model) becomes the "demonstrator," and, / by smiling and encouraging, / facilitates the imitator's efforts.
• 첫 번째 ( )는 주어인 The person을 수식하는 분사구이다.
• 동사 becomes와 facilitates가 and로 병렬 연결되었다.

²Even in contexts [where no such assistance is necessary], (where the imitation is effortless), the model will usually be aware of being (successfully) imitated ~.
• [ ]는 contexts를 수식하는 관계부사절이다.
• ( )는 where ~ necessary를 부연 설명하는 삽입된 동격절이다.

It is probably true // that most teachers' decisions (about classroom arrangement) are based on aesthetics — that is, their subjective judgments (about an attractive room order). (①) Classrooms are often set up or arranged // before the first child sets foot in the room. (②) ¹The adults neither consider the needs of individual children, // nor do they seek any direct input (from the children about space arrangement). (③ ²As a result, / children come to a strange setting [that has been designed for the convenience of the adults [who work there]].) They probably do not feel any sense of ownership of it, // which influences their interest in and care of that space. (④) In a similar, but slightly different way, / consider how many people are careless of others' property // while they are fussy and particular in the care of their own things. (⑤) ³Children react in similar ways, / being more likely to act in destructive ways toward an environment [that (they don't feel) they own].

주제문

해석 교실 배치에 대한 대부분의 교사들의 결정이 미적 가치관, 즉 매력적인 방 정렬에 대한 그들의 주관적인 판단에 기초하고 있다는 것은 아마도 사실일 것이다. 교실은 종종 첫 번째 아동이 교실에 발을 들여놓기 전에 준비되거나 배치된다. 어른들은 개별 아동의 요구를 고려하지도 않고, 공간 배치에 대한 아동들의 어떤 직접적인 의견 제공을 구하지도 않는다. 주제문 **그 결과 아이들은 그곳에서 일하는 어른들의 편의를 위해 설계된 낯선 환경에 놓인다.** 그들은 아마 그곳에 대한 어떤 주인 의식도 느끼지 못할 것인데, 그것은 그 장소에 대한 그들의 흥미와 관심에 영향을 미친다. 비슷하지만, 약간 다른 방식으로, 얼마나 많은 사람들이 자신의 것을 관리하는 데에는 까다롭고 각별한 반면 다른 사람의 소유물에 대해서는 무관심한지 생각해 보라. 아동들도 비슷한 방식으로 반응하여 자신이 소유하고 있다고 느끼지 않는 환경을 향해 파괴적인 방법으로 행동할 가능성이 더 많다.

어휘 arrangement 배치 cf. arrange 배치[배열]하다; 준비하다 aesthetics 미학 subjective 주관적인(↔ objective 객관적인) neither A nor B A도 B도 아닌 input (의견 등의) 제공; 투입 convenience 편의, 편리 ownership 주인 의식, 소유(권) property 소유(물); 부동산; 재산, 자산 fussy 까다로운; 신경질적인 particular 까다로운; 특정한 destructive 파괴적인

해설 주어진 문장은 '결과적으로(As a result) 아이들은 낯선 환경에 놓인다'는 내용이므로, 그 원인이 되는 문장 뒤에 위치해야 하는데, ③ 앞 문장에서 어른들이 교실을 배치할 때 아동의 요구를 고려하지 않고, 그들의 의견을 구하지도 않는다고 했다. 그 결과로서 주어진 문장이 이어져야 하므로 주어진 문장은 ③에 위치하는 것이 가장 적절하다.

오답 Check
주어진 문장이 ②에 들어갈 경우, ③ 뒤의 '그들(they)'은 바로 앞 문장의 주어인 '어른들'을 의미하게 되는데, 문맥상 '그들(they)'은 어른들을 위해 설계된 환경에 놓인 아이들을 의미한다.

PLUS⁺ 변형문제

어휘 integral 필수적인 indifference 무관심
해설 이 글은 어떤 것에 대한 주인 의식이 그에 대한 흥미와 관심에 영향을 미친다는 내용이므로 제목으로는 ② '주인 의식의 부족이 소유물에 대한 무관심으로 이어진다'가 적절하다.
① 주인 의식: 거주할 부동산을 구입하는 데 있어서 필수적인 태도
→ 부동산 구입에 관한 내용은 없음.
③ 집을 선택하는 데 아이들의 직접적인 의견 제공이 필요한가?
→ 주인 의식을 느끼는 데 의견 제공이 필요한 것은 맞지만, 집을 선택하는 데 국한된 상황은 아님.
④ 교실: 더 깨끗할수록, 더 나은 학습 환경
→ 교실의 청결에 관련된 내용은 없음.
⑤ 학생들의 의견을 교실에 반영하는 것을 어렵게 만드는 것
→ 학생들의 의견을 반영하지 않는다는 내용은 있지만, 그것을 어렵게 만드는 것은 언급하지 않음.

구문 ¹The adults neither consider the needs of individual children, // nor do they seek any direct input (from the children about space arrangement).
• 상관접속사 「neither A nor B(A도 B도 아닌)」가 사용되었으며, nor 뒤에는 「조동사(do)+주어(they)+동사(seek)」 어순으로 도치가 일어났다.

²As a result, / children come to a strange setting [that has been designed for the convenience of the adults [who work there]].
• 관계사절 내에 또 다른 관계사절이 있는 구조이다. that has been ~ work there는 주격 관계대명사 that이 이끄는 관계사절로 a strange setting을 수식하고, who work there는 주격 관계대명사 who가 이끄는 관계사절로 the adults를 수식한다.

³Children react in similar ways, / being more likely to act in destructive ways toward an environment [that (they don't feel) they own].
• being 이하는 '결과'를 나타내는 분사구문이다.
• [ ]는 목적격 관계대명사 that이 이끄는 관계사절로 선행사 an environment를 수식하며, 관계사절 내에 they don't feel이 삽입되었다.

주제문
Technology is a double-edged sword. ¹It eventually spreads / and becomes available to adversaries [that may have more primitive capabilities / but also are less vulnerable to dependence on advanced technologies]. (①) American military theorists used to argue // that other nations would eventually buy / some high technology commercially "off the shelf." (②) Meanwhile, the United States would be progressing to the next generation / and integrating technologies / into a system of systems. (③) But that was round one / in the chess game. (④ American advantages (in robotics and unmanned drones) will eventually be available / to opponents in later ones.) ²For example, in 2009 the American military discovered // that insurgents were hacking into the downlinks of data (from a Predator unmanned aircraft), / using software [that cost less than $30]. (⑤) Simultaneously, growing reliance on elaborate satellite and computer network–controlled systems / makes the United States more vulnerable / than some of its adversaries.

해석 **주제문 과학기술은 양날의 검이다.** 그것은 결국에는 더 발달되지 않은 역량을 갖고 있을지 모르지만 고급 과학기술 의존에 덜 취약하기도 한 적들에게 퍼져 이용 가능하게 될 것이다. 미국의 군사 이론가들은 다른 국가들이 결국에는 첨단 과학기술을 상용화된 '기성품으로' 구입하게 될 것이라고 주장했었다. 그동안에 미국은 다음 세대로 발전하여 과학기술들을 시스템들 중 한 시스템으로 통합하고 있을 것이다. 하지만 그것은 체스 게임의 1라운드였다. 로봇 공학과 무인 드론에서의 미국의 우위는 이후의 라운드들에서 결국에는 적들이 이용할 수 있게 될 것이다. 예를 들어 2009년에 미군은 폭도들이 30달러어치도 안 되는 소프트웨어를 사용해 무인 항공기인 Predator에서 전해 오는 데이터의 다운링크들을 해킹하고 있는 것을 발견했다. 동시에 정교한 위성과 컴퓨터 통신망에 의해 제어되는 시스템들에 점점 더 의존하는 것이 미국을 그것의 일부 적들보다 더 취약하게 만들고 있다.

어휘 double-edged 양날의; 두 가지로 해석될 수 있는　adversary 적수; 상대방(= opponent)　primitive 발달되지 않은; 원시의　vulnerable 취약한; 연약한　dependence 의존, 의지(= reliance)　advanced 고급[상급]의; 선진의　eventually 결국, 언젠가는　off the shelf 기성품인; 재고의　integrate 통합하다　advantage 우위; 강점; 유리　unmanned 무인의, 사람이 타지 않은　downlink 다운링크 《우주나 항공기에서 지상으로 보내는 데이터》　simultaneously 동시에　elaborate 정교한; 복잡한　satellite 위성

해설 주어진 문장은 특정 분야에서의 미국의 우위는 결국 '나중의 것들'에서 적들이 이용할 것이라는 내용으로 ones가 무엇을 지칭하는지 파악해야 한다. ③의 앞부분은 다른 국가가 과학기술을 기성품으로 구입하는 반면에 미국은 다음 세대로 발전하고 있을 것이라는 내용이다. ③의 뒤 문장은 But으로 시작하여 이것은 1라운드였다는 내용이 나오고 ④ 뒤 문장에서 미국이 무인기의 자료를 해킹당하는 대조적인 예시가 언급되므로 주어진 문장은 ③ 이후에 나와야 하는데 문맥상 '나중의 것들'은 1라운드에 이어지고 ④ 뒤의 대조적 예시는 주어진 문장의 예로 볼 수 있으므로 주어진 문장은 ④에 들어가야 한다.

PLUS + 변형문제

해설 이 글은 미국이 첨단 과학기술을 발전시키는 것에 반하여 다른 국가들은 이것을 값싼 가격에 이용한다는 내용이므로 가장 잘 나타낸 제목은 ③ '과학기술에서 주도적 역할을 하는 것이 항상 좋은 것인가?'이다.
① 미국에서 새로운 기술을 훔침
→ 글의 일부 내용으로 과학기술의 양날의 검의 특징을 나타내지 못함.
② 기술이 더 좋아질수록, 우리는 더 안전해진다
→ 기술의 발전과 우리의 안전성의 상관관계는 언급되지 않음.
④ 미국 안보의 핵심: 현대화된 기술 → 고급 기술에 의존성이 높은 미국이 오히려 적들에 의한 해킹으로 취약해짐을 언급함.
⑤ 가장 어려운 체스 게임: 기술 개발
→ 글의 일부 어구를 활용한 오답임.

구문 ¹It eventually spreads / and becomes available to *adversaries* [**that** <u>may have more primitive capabilities</u> / [but] also <u>are less vulnerable to dependence on advanced technologies</u>].
• [ ]는 주격 관계대명사 that이 이끄는 관계사절로 adversaries를 수식한다.
• [ ] 내에서 밑줄 친 두 개의 동사구를 but이 병렬 연결한다.

²For example, in 2009 the American military **discovered** // **that** insurgents were hacking into *the downlinks of data* (from a Predator unmanned aircraft), / **using** *software* [**that** cost less than $30].
• 동사 discovered의 목적어로 that이 이끄는 명사절이 쓰였다.
• ( )는 전명구로 앞에 있는 the downlinks of data를 수식한다.
• using 이하는 부대상황을 나타내는 분사구문이다.
• [ ]는 주격 관계대명사 that이 이끄는 관계사절로 앞에 있는 software를 수식한다.

40 ②

A group of college women, of roughly the same age and life experiences, / were asked to participate in a study. Half of the group (the first group) was told // that they would be given a harmless, yet painful, electric shock. The other half of the group (the second group) was told // that they would be given an electric shock [that would be entirely painless]. Thus, the researchers created two groups: the first (believing they would be exposed to pain), / and the second (believing they had nothing to fear). ¹The researchers then told the women // they had ten minutes until the test would begin, / and watched to see // how they interacted. During the waiting time, / the women (in the first group) started to mingle together. They talked about their concerns, gave each other support, and debated the test. In fact, / 63% of the women ended up in a group with other subjects, // while 37% preferred to be alone. In the other room, a different situation was occurring. The second-group women preferred to spend their time / without associating with the other participants. Here, only 33% wanted to spend that time with another participant.

↓

For the high-anxiety subjects, / anxiety was a strong motivating factor in (A) affiliation; // the low-anxiety subjects preferred / to remain (B) solitary.

해석 대략 같은 연령이고 같은 인생 경험을 가진 한 무리의 여대생이 한 연구에 참여하도록 요청을 받았다. 집단의 절반(첫 번째 집단)은 무해하지만 고통스러운 전기 충격을 받을 거라고 들었다. 집단의 나머지 절반(두 번째 집단)은 그들이 전혀 고통이 없을 전기 충격을 받을 거라고 들었다. 이렇게 연구원들은 두 집단을 만들었는데, 첫 번째는 그들이 고통에 노출될 것이라고 믿고, 두 번째는 두려워할 것이 전혀 없다고 믿었다. 그리고 나서 연구원들은 여성들에게 실험이 시작될 때까지 10분이 남았다고 말하고, 그들이 어떻게 상호작용하는지 보려고 주시했다. 대기 시간 동안, 첫 번째 집단의 여성들은 함께 어울리기 시작했다. 그들은 그들의 우려에 대해 이야기하고, 서로 도움을 주며, 실험에 대해 토의했다. 실제로 여성의 63%는 결국 다른 피실험자들과 함께 한 집단을 이룬 반면에 37%는 혼자 있는 것을 선호했다. 다른 방에서는 다른 상황이 벌어지고 있었다. 두 번째 집단의 여성들은 다른 참가자들과 어울리지 않고 자신들의 시간을 보내는 것을 더 좋아했다. 여기서는 단지 33%만이 다른 참가자와 함께 시간을 보내고 싶어 했다.

↓

불안이 높은 피실험자들에게 있어서 불안은 (A) 합동의 강한 동기부여 요인이었지만, 불안이 낮은 피실험자들은 여전히 (B) 홀로 있기를 선호했다.

어휘 roughly 대략 mingle 어울리다; 혼합하다 concern 우려, 걱정; 관심사 end up (결국) ~이 되다 subject 피험자, 실험 대상; 주제; 학과, 과목 associate with ~와 어울리다 affiliation 합동, 합병 solitary 홀로 있는, 혼자의
[선택지 어휘] evasion 회피; 탈출 inattentive 주의를 기울이지 않는 indifferent 무관심한 empathy 공감, 감정이입 insecure 자신이 없는; 불안정한

해설 요약문을 통해 불안이 '무엇'의 강한 동기부여 요인이었고, 불안이 낮은 실험자들은 '무엇'을 선호했는지를 파악한다. 고통이 있는 전기 충격을 받을 것이라는 이야기를 들은 집단(불안이 높음)은 상당수가 함께 어울렸지만, 고통이 없을 것이라는 말을 들은 집단(불안이 낮음)은 대다수가 혼자서 자기 시간을 보냈다고 했으므로 빈칸에는 ② '(A) 합동 – (B) 홀로 있는'이 적절하다.

오답 Check
	(A)	(B)
①	회피	주의를 기울이지 않는
③	집중	적극적인
④	자신감	무관심한
⑤	공감	자신이 없는

→ 모두 글에서 추론할 수 없는 오답.

구문 ¹The researchers then **told** the women // (that) they had ten minutes until the test would begin, / and **watched** to see // how they interacted.
• 문장의 동사 told와 watched가 접속사 and로 연결되어 병렬 구조를 이룬다.
• 여기에서 told는 간접목적어(IO)와 직접목적어(DO)를 취하는 4문형 동사로 쓰였다.

A new study suggests // that Chimpanzees specifically refer to favorite foods with distinct grunts, / but the calls differ between populations. The chimps could then learn the "foreign" grunts, / making communication (a) easier / when two groups merge into one. The findings show // that, like human words, chimp food calls are not (b) fixed in their structure. When exposed to a new group, // chimps can change their calls to sound more like their group mates. A big topic of conversation is food. Chimpanzees produce acoustically distinct grunts / in response to foods of low, medium, or high quality, // and in captivity they give distinct grunts for certain foods, / including bananas, bread, and mangoes. It has been shown // that listeners are able to distinguish / between these different grunts and extract information [that helps guide their own search for food appropriately].

The researchers studied // what happened after two separate groups of adult chimps moved in together at the Edinburgh Zoo. Before the merger, the groups produced their (c) particular food grunts. After the merger, the "newcomer" group significantly changed their calls / to (d) differentiate those of the long-term residents. [1]"If one were to make an analogy with human beings, // it could be the process of (e) dialect change. [2]Just as people (moving between groups of speakers of the same language) subtly modify their accents / to sound like the group [into which they are moving], // the chimps modify their grunts / to ensure that the other chimps understand them correctly," / says Simon Townsend of the University of Zürich.

어휘 specifically 구체적으로, 특정하게 refer to A A를 언급하다 distinct 구별되는, 뚜렷한 grunt 꿍꿍거리는 소리; 꿍꿍거리다 population 집단; 인구; 개체수 merge 합치다, 합병하다; (도로 등이) 합류하다 cf. merger 합병 fixed 고정된 structure 구조(물); 구조화하다, 조직하다 expose 노출시키다; 드러내다; 폭로하다 mate 동료, 친구; 짝 acoustically 음향적으로 medium 중간 정도의; 매체, 수단 in captivity 사육되고 있는 distinguish 구별[구분]하다 extract 끌어내다; 추출하다, 뽑아내다; 추출물; 발췌 appropriately 적절하게, 알맞게 particular 개별적인; 특정한; 특별한 significantly 상당히, 크게; 중요하게 resident 거주자, 주민 analogy 비유; 유사점 dialect 방언, 지방 사투리 subtly 미묘하게; 교활하게 modify 바꾸다, 수정[변경]하다 accent 억양

해설 41 침팬지는 집단마다 먹이를 표현하는 소리가 다르며, 다른 집단으로 옮겨간 경우 그 집단의 침팬지가 내는 소리를 배워서 낸다는 내용의 글이므로, 글의 제목으로는 ① '침팬지는 지역 억양을 배울 수 있다'가 가장 적절하다.

42 이주민들이 이주한 곳의 집단과 비슷하게 들리도록 억양을 바꾸듯이, 새로 이사 온 침팬지들도 자신들의 말이 정확하게 이해되도록 먹이를 표현하는 소리를 원래 있던 침팬지들의 것과 일치하게 바꾼다는 내용이 되어야 하므로 (d)의 differentiate는 match 등으로 고치는 것이 적절하다.

오답 Check
41 ② 침팬지 언어에 대한 논쟁
→ 침팬지의 언어에 관한 내용은 맞지만, 논쟁이 있는 것은 아님.
③ 침팬지의 꿍꿍거리는 소리는 언어가 아니다
→ 침팬지의 꿍꿍거리는 소리는 언급되었지만, 이것이 언어가 아니라는 것은 언급하지 않음.
④ 침팬지의 잘 발달된 먹이 언어
→ 침팬지의 먹이 언어의 발달 정도에 대한 언급은 없으며, 글의 요지에서 벗어남.
⑤ 갈등으로 이어지는 다른 언어
→ 다른 언어 사용이 갈등으로 이어진다는 내용은 언급되지 않음.
42 침팬지 연구 내용을 인간에 적용한다면 같은 언어를 쓰는 다른 집단으로 이주했을 때, 그곳의 말투를 배우는 것을 (e) '방언'의 변화 과정으로 보는 것은 적절하다.

해석 새로운 연구는 침팬지가 구별되는 꿍꿍거리는 소리로 좋아하는 음식을 구체적으로 언급하며, 그 소리는 무리마다 다르다는 것을 나타낸다. 주제문 침팬지는 '낯선' 소리를 배워서, 두 집단이 하나로 합쳐질 때 의사소통을 (a) 더 쉽게 할 수 있었다. 이 발견은 인간의 말처럼 침팬지의 먹이를 부르는 말이 구조적으로 (b) 고정되어 있지 않다는 것을 보여준다. 새로운 집단에 노출될 때, 침팬지는 집단의 동료들과 비슷하게 들리도록 소리를 바꿀 수 있다. 대화의 큰 주제는 음식이다. 침팬지는 음식에 반응해서 낮거나 중간 정도이거나 높은 특성으로 음향적으로 구별되는 소리를 만들어내며, 사육되는 상태일 때 침팬지들은 바나나, 빵, 망고를 포함해서 특정한 음식에 대해 구별되는 소리를 낸다. 소리를 듣는 침팬지는 이런 다른 소리를 구별할 수 있으며 스스로 음식을 적절히 찾는 것을 도와주는 정보를 끌어낼 수 있다는 것이 밝혀졌다.
연구가들은 두 개의 독립된 어른 침팬지 집단이 에든버러 동물원에 함께 살게 되었을 때 무슨 일이 일어나는지를 연구했다. 합쳐서 살기 전에는, 그 집단들은 음식을 말하는 (c) 개별적인 소리를 내었다. 합쳐서 살게 된 뒤에는 '새로 이사를 온' 집단은 오랜 기간 살고 있는 집단의 소리와 (d) 차이 나도록(→ 일치하도록) 자기들의 소리를 상당히 바꾸었다. "만약 인간에 비유한다면, 그것은 (e) 방언의 변화 과정일 수 있습니다. 같은 언어를 말하는 집단들 사이에서 이주하는 사람들이 이주하게 된 곳의 집단과 비슷하게 들리도록 억양을 미묘하게 바꾸듯이, 침팬지는 다른 침팬지들이 자기들의 말을 정확하게 이해하도록 하기 위해서 소리를 바꿉니다."라고 취리히 대학의 Simon Townsend가 말한다.

구문 [1]**If** one **were to make** an analogy with human beings, // it **could be** the process of dialect change.

• 「If+S´+were+to-v ~, S+조동사 과거형+동사원형 ....」 구조인 가정법으로, 어떤 일이 일어날 가능성이 더 희박하다는 느낌을 준다.

[2]**Just as** *people* (moving between groups of speakers of the same language) subtly modify their accents / to sound like *the group* [**into which** they are moving], // the chimps modify their grunts / **to ensure** that the other chimps understand them correctly," / says Simon Townsend of the University of Zürich.

• Just as는 '꼭 ~인 것처럼 …하다'를 의미하는 부사절 접속사이다.

• ( )는 people을 수식하는 분사구이다.

• [ ]에서 which는 the group을 선행사로 한다. 관계대명사가 자신이 이끄는 절 속에서 전치사의 목적어로 쓰일 때, 그 전치사는 관계대명사 바로 앞에 위치할 수 있다. 이 문장에서 전치사 into는 그 목적어인 관계대명사 바로 앞에 왔다.

• to ensure는 '목적'을 나타내는 부사적 용법의 to부정사로 '~하기 위해서'라는 의미이다.

| 31 ① + ① | 32 ② + ⑤ | 33 ② + ⑤ | 34 ① + ③ | 35 ④ + ③ | 36 ⑤ + ④ |
| 37 ④ + ⑤ | 38 ④ + ⑤ | 39 ④ + ② | 40 ⑤ | 41 ③ | 42 ④ |

---

31 ① PLUS+ ①

주제문
Scientists [who study the history of life on Earth] are sure // that the fossil record is biased. The potential (for fossil preservation) varies dramatically / from environment to environment. Preservation is enhanced under conditions [that limit destructive physical and biological processes]. ¹Thus marine and fresh water environments (with low oxygen levels, high salinities, or relatively high rates of sediment deposition) favor preservation. Similarly, in some environments / biochemical conditions can favor the early mineralization (of skeletons and even soft tissues) / by a variety of compounds. In addition to these preservational problems, / the erosion, deformation and metamorphism (of originally fossiliferous sedimentary rock) have eliminated / significant portions of the fossil record / over geologic time. Furthermore, much of the fossil-bearing sedimentary record is located / in poorly accessible or little studied geographic areas. ²For these reasons, / of those once-living species (actually preserved in the fossil record), / only a small portion / have been discovered and described by science.

해석 **주제문** 지구상의 생명체의 역사를 연구하는 과학자들은 화석 기록이 편향되어 있다고 확신한다. 화석 보존의 가능성은 환경에 따라 상당히 다르다. 보존은 파괴적인 물리적, 생물학적 과정을 제한하는 조건하에서 강화된다. 따라서 산소 농도가 낮거나 염도가 높거나 침전물이 퇴적되는 비율이 상대적으로 높은 해양 및 담수 환경은 보존에 유리하다. 마찬가지로, 어떤 환경에서는 생화학적 조건이 다양한 화합물에 의해 골격과 심지어 연조직의 이른 무기화 작용을 쉽게 할 수 있다. 이러한 보존 문제 외에도, 원래 화석을 함유한 퇴적암의 침식, 변형, 변성 작용은 지질 연대에 걸쳐 화석 기록의 상당한 부분들을 제거해왔다. 더군다나 화석을 가지고 있는 퇴적 기록의 많은 부분이 접근하기 나쁘거나 거의 연구가 되고 있지 않은 지리적 지역에 위치하고 있다. 이러한 이유로 실제로 화석 기록으로 보존된 한때 살았던 그 종들 중에서 단지 일부분만이 과학에 의해 발견되고 설명되어 왔다.

어휘 vary 서로[각기] 다르다 destructive 파괴적인 salinity 염도, 염분 sediment 침전물; 퇴적물 *cf.* sedimentary 퇴적성의; 침전물의 deposition 퇴적; 면직; 폐위 favor ~에 유리하다, 쉽게 하다; 찬성하다 ◎mineralization 무기화 작용; 광화 작용 tissue 조직; 얇은 직물 deformation 변형; 기형 fossiliferous 화석을 함유한, 화석이 나오는 geologic 지질학(상)의
[선택지 어휘] transient 일시적인; 단기 체류의
어휘◎ 무기화 작용: 유기물이 미생물의 공격을 받아 분해되는 과정에서 유기물에 포함된 원소가 식물이나 미생물이 이용할 수 있는 무기태로 변화하는 과정

해설 빈칸 문장이 주제문으로 화석 기록에 대한 설명에 주목하여 이를 개괄적으로 표현한 단어를 찾는다. 화석의 보존은 환경에 따라 매우 다르고, 가능성은 화석이 있는 퇴적암 또한 침식, 변형 등에 의해 사라져버리며 그나마 남은 화석도 접근하기 어려운 지역에 있어 극히 일부만이 발견되고 있다고 했으므로 빈칸에는 ① '편향된'이 적절하다.

오답 Check
② 일시적인 ③ 복제한 ④ 진부한 → ②, ③, ④ 언급되지 않음.
⑤ 세밀한 → 화석 기록이 세밀한 것은 아님.

PLUS+ 변형문제

어휘 credible 믿을 만한, 믿을 수 있는 glimpse 흘긋 봄; 잠깐[언뜻] 보다
해설 화석 기록이 편향되어 있다는 근거로 화석 보존의 어려움과 화석 기록의 한정적인 발견과 연구를 들고 있으므로 글의 제목으로 적절한 것은 ① '화석 기록은 정말로 믿을 만한가?'이다.
② 화석 기록: 과거를 엿보기
→ 화석과 연상되는 내용이나 언급되지 않음.
③ 화석을 보존하는 데 풀리지 않는 문제점
→ 화석을 이용한 선택지이지만 지문에 언급되지 않음.
④ 해골: 우리 선사시대 역사의 기반
→ skeleton은 언급되었으나 글의 내용과 관련 없음.
⑤ 화석이 발견되는 많은 환경들
→ 글의 내용과 반대임.

구문 ¹Thus *marine and fresh water environments* (with low oxygen levels, high salinities, or relatively high rates of sediment deposition) favor preservation.
• ( )는 형용사적 역할을 하는 전명구로 주어 marine ~ environments를 수식한다.
• 밑줄 친 세 개의 명사구는 전치사 with의 목적어로 콤마(,)와 접속사 or로 연결되어 병렬 구조를 이룬다.

²For these reasons, / of *those once-living species* (actually preserved in the fossil record), / only a small portion / have been discovered and described by science.
• ( )는 과거분사구로 앞에 있는 명사구 those ~ species를 수식한다.

¹We set up a tasting venue at a local supermarket / and invited passerby shoppers to sample two different varieties (of jam and tea), / and to decide which alternative (in each pair) they preferred the most. Immediately after the participants had made their choice, // we asked them to again sample the chosen alternative, / and to verbally explain why they adopted it. The cunning aspect of the study was // that we secretly switched the contents (of the sample containers), // so that we intended participants to describe a choice [they hadn't made]. The majority of them were unaware // that their choice was not their choice and explained why. In total, no more than a third of the manipulated trials were detected. ²Even for remarkably different tastes (like Cinnamon-Apple and bitter Grapefruit), or the smell (of Mango and strong flavored wine), // no more than half of all trials / were detected, / thus demonstrating considerable levels of choice blindness (for the taste and smell (of two different consumer goods)). 주제문 It would seem that, once we have made a preference, // we are committed to justifying our decision.

해석 우리는 동네 슈퍼마켓에 시식장을 차려놓고 지나가는 쇼핑객으로 하여금 두 가지 다른 종류의 잼과 차를 시식하고 각각의 쌍에서 어떤 하나를 가장 좋아하는지 결정하도록 부탁했다. 참가자들이 선택을 한 직후, 우리는 그들에게 선택된 하나를 다시 시식하고 왜 그것을 선택했는지 말로 설명해줄 것을 요청했다. 그 연구의 교묘한 측면은 우리가 시식 용기의 내용물을 몰래 바꿔서 참가자들로 하여금 자신들이 택하지 않았던 선택을 설명하도록 의도한 것이다. 그들 중 대다수는 그들의 선택이 자신들이 선택했던 것이 아님을 눈치채지 못하고는 이유를 설명했다. 통틀어서, 조작된 실험의 3분의 1 이하만이 간파되었다. 계피-사과와 쓴 자몽 같은 현저하게 다른 맛, 혹은 망고와 향미가 강한 와인의 냄새에서조차, 모든 실험의 절반 이하가 간파되었기에 두 가지 다른 소비재의 맛과 냄새에 대해 상당한 수준의 선택맹을 입증했다. 주제문 우리는 일단 선택을 하게 되면 우리의 결정을 정당화하는 데 전념하는 것 같다.

어휘 venue 장소 invite 부탁[요청]하다, 초대하다 passerby 지나가는 사람 sample 시식을 하다; 견본, 시료 variety 종류 alternative 선택 가능한 것, 둘 중에서의 선택(물) verbally 말로, 구두로 adopt 선택하다, 채택하다; 입양하다 cunning 교묘한 aspect 측면, 양상 switch 바꾸다 content 내용(물); 함유량 intend 의도하다, (~하려고) 생각하다 majority 대다수, 대부분 manipulate 조작하다 trial 실험; 재판 detect 간파하다, 발견하다 remarkably 현저하게, 뚜렷하게, 눈에 띄게 ○choice blindness 선택맹 be committed to ~에 전념[헌신]하다
[선택지 어휘] consistently 시종일관하여, 지속적으로 potential 가능성, 잠재력
어휘○ 선택맹: 사람들의 인지 능력이 혼동을 겪으며 자신의 선택을 합리화하는 현상

해설 우리가 일단 선택을 하면 '어떻게' 되는지 찾아야 한다. 시식으로 선택한 제품을 다른 제품으로 몰래 바꾼 후, 다시 시식을 하고 선택한 이유를 설명하도록 했을 때 대다수가 현저히 다른 맛과 냄새에도 불구하고 나중에 시식한 제품이 자신의 선택이 아님을 간파하지 못하고 이유를 설명했다는 실험 결과로 보아 빈칸에는 ② '우리의 결정을 정당화하는 데 전념하는'이 적절하다.

오답 Check
① 새로운 선호를 추가하는 것을 피하려고 노력하는
→ 빈칸이 포함된 문장의 단어 preference를 활용한 오답임.
③ 다른 가능성 있는 선택을 지속적으로 탐색하는
→ 다른 선택을 탐색한다는 것은 언급되지 않음.
④ 이익의 가능성보다 손실을 더 두려워하는
⑤ 다른 선택들보다 점점 더 그것을 선호하는
→ ④, ⑤ 모두 언급되지 않음.

PLUS⁺ 변형문제
해설 실험 결과에 따라 지문의 요지로는 ⑤가 적절하며, ①, ②, ③, ④ 모두 지문의 어휘(preference, choice 등)를 활용하여 만들어낸 오답으로 글의 요지와는 무관하다.

구문 ¹We **set up** a tasting venue at a local supermarket / and **invited** *passerby shoppers* to sample *two different varieties* (of jam and tea), / and to decide **which alternative (in each pair) they preferred the most**.
• 문장의 동사 set up과 invited가 첫 번째 접속사 and로 연결되어 병렬 구조를 이룬다.
• 동사 invited의 목적격보어로서 to sample과 to decide가 두 번째 접속사 and로 연결되어 병렬 구조를 이룬다.
• which alternative ~ the most는 decide의 목적어로 쓰인 명사절이다.

²Even **for** remarkably different tastes (like Cinnamon-Apple and bitter Grapefruit), or the smell (of Mango and strong flavored wine), // no more than half of all trials / were detected, / **thus demonstrating** considerable levels of choice blindness (for the taste and smell (of two different consumer goods)).
• 전치사 for의 목적어로 두 개의 밑줄 친 명사구가 접속사 or로 연결되어 병렬 구조를 이룬다.
• thus demonstrating 이하는 결과를 나타내는 분사구이다.

Peter Norvig, an artificial intelligence expert, / likes to think about big data / with an analogy to images. ¹First, he asks us to consider the iconic horse / from the cave paintings in Lascaux, France, // which date to the Old Stone Age some 17,000 years ago. ²Then think of a photograph (of a horse) — / or better, the dabs of Pablo Picasso, // which do not look much dissimilar to the cave paintings. In fact, when Picasso was shown the Lascaux images // he remarked / that, since then, "We have invented nothing." Picasso's words were true on one level / but not on another. Recall that photograph of the horse. Where it took a long time to draw a picture (of a horse), // now a representation (of one) could be made much faster with photography. That is a change, // but it may not be the most essential, // since it is still fundamentally the same: an image (of a horse). Yet now, Norvig asks, // consider capturing the image (of a horse) and speeding it up to 24 frames per second. Now, the quantitative change has produced a qualitative change. A movie is fundamentally different from a frozen photograph. It's the same with big data: by changing the amount, / we change the essence.

추론 근거

주제문

[어휘] artificial 인공의 analogy 비유; 유사, 유추 iconic 잘 알려진; 상징이 되는 date 거슬러 올라가다 dissimilar 다른, 닮지 않은 remark 말하다, 언급하다 recall 상기하다; 회상하다 representation 묘사, 표현 fundamentally 근본적으로 frame (필름의) 프레임, 한 토막 quantitative 양적인, 분량의 qualitative 질적인 frozen 고정된; 냉담한 essence 본질
[선택지 어휘] paradigm 패러다임 ((어느 시대나 분야에 특징적인, 과학적 인식 방법의 체계·시스템)) precede ~에 앞서다, ~보다 먼저 일어나다

[해설] Lascaux의 동굴벽화에 새겨진 말이나, 피카소의 말이나, 말의 사진으로 똑같은 말 한 마리의 이미지이다. 하지만 그것을 촬영하여 초당 24프레임까지 매우 빠르게 넘기면, 즉 양적인 변화를 가하면 그것은 영상이 되어 이미지는 질적으로 변화한다. 그러므로 빈칸에는 ② '양을 변화시킴으로써 우리는 본질을 바꾼다'가 들어가는 것이 가장 적절하다.

[오답 Check]
① 데이터 분석의 패러다임 전환이 변화를 약속한다
→ 데이터 분석에 관한 내용은 아님.
③ 새로운 기술이 양적인 데이터를 가져왔다
→ 일부 어휘(quantitative)를 활용한 오답.
④ 당신이 더 많은 데이터를 가질수록, 더 적게 데이터를 이용한다
→ 글에 언급되지 않은 내용.
⑤ 품질이 관계를 앞서는 것처럼, 품질은 수량을 앞선다
→ 양적 변화가 질적 변화를 만든다고 했으므로 글의 내용과 반대됨.

PLUS + 변형문제
[어휘] static 고정적인
[해설] 빅데이터가 만들어 내는 변화를 이미지에 빗대어 양적 변화가 질적 변화를 이끈다고 설명하는 내용이므로 글의 제목으로 가장 적절한 것은 ⑤ '빅데이터 이해하기: 그것이 어떻게 변화를 만들어 내는가'이다.
① 빅데이터: 품질이 항상 이긴다!
→ 양과 품질 중 더 중요한 것을 가리는 내용이 아님.
② 사진을 영화처럼 보이게 만드는 방법
→ 글에 언급된 어휘를 활용한 오답.
③ 미술 양식은 고정적이지 않다, 그것은 역동적이다
→ 말 그림은 빅데이터가 만드는 변화를 설명하기 위한 비유로 쓰였으며 미술이 글의 중심 내용은 아님.
④ 우리가 빅데이터를 더 많이 가질수록 더 나쁘다
→ 양이 많으면 질적 변화를 만들어 낼 수 있다고 했으므로 글의 내용과 반대됨.

[해석] 인공지능 전문가인 Peter Norvig는 이미지에 비유하여 빅데이터를 생각하는 것을 좋아한다. 우선, 그는 우리에게 프랑스 Lascaux의 동굴벽화에 나오는 잘 알려진 말을 생각해보라고 하는데, 그것은 약 17,000년 전 구석기 시대로 거슬러 올라간다. 그러고 나서 말의 사진 혹은 더 나은 방법으로는 그 동굴 벽화와 크게 다르지 않아 보이는 파블로 피카소의 붓으로 그린 그림을 생각하라. 사실, 피카소가 Lascaux의 이미지를 보았을 때 그는, 그때 이후로 "우리는 아무것도 창조하지 못했다."라고 말했다. 피카소가 한 말은 어느 면에서는 사실이지만 다른 면에서는 사실이 아니다. 그 말의 사진을 떠올려보라. 말의 그림을 그리는 데 오랜 시간이 걸렸던 것에 반해, 이제 말 한 마리에 대한 묘사는 사진으로 훨씬 더 빨리 만들어질 수 있다. 그것은 변화지만, 그것이 가장 본질적인 것은 아닐 수도 있는데, 왜냐하면 그것은 여전히 근본적으로 같은 것, 즉 말 한 마리의 이미지이기 때문이다. 추론 근거 그러나 이제 Norvig은 말의 이미지를 포착하여 초당 24프레임까지 속도를 내는 것을 고려해보라고 요청한다. 이제 양적 변화는 질적 변화를 만들어내고 있다. 영화는 움직일 수 없는 사진과는 근본적으로 다르다. 주제문 이는 빅데이터의 경우와 마찬가지인데, 양을 변화시킴으로써 우리는 본질을 바꾼다.

[구문] ¹First, he **asks** us **to consider** the iconic horse / from *the cave paintings in Lascaux, France,* // **which** date to the Old Stone Age some 17,000 years ago.
• 「ask+O+C(to-v)」의 구조로 목적격보어에 to부정사가 쓰였다.
• which는 계속적 용법의 관계대명사로 선행사 the cave paintings in Lascaux, France를 보충 설명한다.

²Then **think of** a photograph (of a horse) — ⌐or⌐ better, *the dabs of Pablo Picasso,* // **which** do not look much dissimilar to the cave paintings.
• or은 think of의 목적어로 쓰인 두 개의 밑줄 친 명사구를 병렬 연결한다.
• 계속적 용법의 which가 이끄는 관계사절은 the dabs of Pablo Picasso를 보충 설명한다.

추론 근거
¹The word "pitch" refers to the mental representation [an organism has / of the fundamental frequency of a sound]. That is, pitch is / a purely psychological phenomenon (related to the frequency of vibrating air molecules). Sound waves do not themselves have pitch. Their motion and oscillations can be measured, // but it takes a human or animal brain / to connect them to that internal quality [we call pitch]. We perceive color in a similar way. Isaac Newton, // who first realized this, / pointed out that light is colorless, // and that consequently color has to occur / inside our brains. He wrote, "The waves themselves are not colored." ²Since his time, we have learned // that light waves are characterized / by different frequencies of oscillation, // and when they affect the retina (of an observer), / they set off a chain of neurochemical events, // the end product of which is an internal mental image [that we call color]. The essential point here is: // what we perceive is not just the way [the objects are].

해석 추론 근거 '음높이'라는 말은 어떤 소리의 근본 주파수에 대해 유기체가 갖는 정신적 표상을 말한다. 즉, 음높이는 진동하는 공기 분자의 주파수와 관련된 순전히 심리적 현상이다. 음파 자체에는 음높이가 없다. 음파의 움직임과 진동은 측정될 수 있지만, 그것들을 우리가 음높이라고 부르는 내적 속성에 연결하기 위해서는 인간 혹은 동물의 뇌가 필요하다. 추론 근거 우리는 비슷한 방식으로 색채를 지각한다. 이 사실을 가장 먼저 깨달은 아이작 뉴턴은 빛에는 색채가 없고 따라서 색채는 우리의 뇌 안에서 일어나야 하는 것임을 지적했다. 그는 "(빛의) 파동 자체에는 색채가 없다"고 썼다. 그 이후 우리는 빛의 파동이 다양한 진동의 주파수로 특징지어지며, 그것들이 관찰자의 망막에 영향을 미칠 때 일련의 신경 화학적 사건들을 일으키고, 그것의 최종 결과물이 우리가 색채라고 부르는 내적 심상이라는 것을 알게 되었다. 주제문 여기서 요점은 우리가 지각하는 것이 꼭 대상이 있는 방식은 아니라는 것이다.

어휘 pitch 음높이; 내던지다   representation 표상; 표현; 설명   fundamental 근본적인; 기초적인   vibrate 진동하다; 반향하다 cf. vibration 진동; 감정적 반응   molecule 분자; 미립자   measure 측정하다, 재다   retina (눈의) 망막   set off 일으키다; 시작하게 하다   a chain of 일련의   neurochemical 신경 화학의; 신경 화학 물질   perceive 지각하다, 인지하다   object 대상; 물체; 목적, 목표   [선택지 어휘] vary 서로 다르다   a lack of ~의 결핍[부족]   solely 오로지, 단지

해설 빈칸 문장이 마지막 문장일 경우 주제문일 가능성이 크다. 우리가 인지하는 음높이(pitch)와 색채(color)는 뇌 또는 신경에서 일어나는 정신적 표상의 결과물로 실제로는 그것들이 존재하지 않는다는 내용을 통해 글의 요점은 ① '우리가 지각하는 것이 꼭 대상이 있는 방식은 아니라는' 것임을 추론할 수 있다.

오답 Check
② 그것들을(음높이, 색채) 지각하는 사람에 따라 다르다는
③ 빛과 소리의 본질이 파동의 결핍을 나타낸다는
④ 우리 뇌에서만 발생하는 것은 진동이 아닌 바로 색채라는
⑤ 우리가 보는 방식과 듣는 방식이 공통으로 공유하는 것이 거의 없다는
→ ② ~ ⑤ 모두 글에서 언급된 단어를 활용했지만 근거를 찾을 수 없는 오답.

PLUS＋ 변형문제

어휘 merely 그저, 단지   internalize 내재[내면]화하다
해설 우리가 인지하는 음높이와 색채는 심리적이고 내적인 표상이라는 내용이므로 글의 제목으로는 ③ '음높이와 색채는 단지 내재화된 산물이다'가 가장 적절하다.
① 대기 안의 파동: 음높이와 색채
→ 파동 자체에는 색채가 없다고 언급함.
② 우리의 뇌는 빛의 파동에 영향을 받는다
→ 일부 내용으로 글 전체를 나타내지 못함.
④ 음높이와 색채를 인식하는 데 있어서 주파수의 역할
→ 주파수는 음높이와 관련된 것으로 그 역할은 언급되지 않음.
⑤ 우리의 지각: 실체를 완벽히 나타낸 것
→ 주제와 반대되는 오답.

구문 ¹The word "pitch" refers to *the mental representation* [(which[that]) an organism has / of the fundamental frequency of a sound].
• [ ]는 목적격 관계대명사 which 또는 that이 생략된 관계사절로 앞에 있는 the mental representation을 수식한다.
• 관계사절은 '~ and an organism has it(= the mental representation) of the fundamental ~ a sound'로 바꿔 쓸 수 있다.

²Since his time, we *have learned* // **that** light waves are characterized / by different frequencies of oscillation, // **and** (that) **when** they affect the retina (of an observer), / they set off *a chain of neurochemical events*, // **the end product of which** is *an internal mental image* [**that** we call color].
• 문장의 동사 have learned의 목적어로 that이 이끄는 명사절과 앞에 that이 생략된 명사절 when ~ we call color가 and로 연결되어 병렬 구조를 이루고 있다.
• 「명사＋전치사＋관계대명사」 형태인 the end product of which가 이끄는 관계사절이 선행사 a chain of neurochemical events를 부연 설명한다. 이때, the end product of which는 whose end product로 바꿔 쓸 수 있다.
• [ ]는 목적격 관계대명사 that이 이끄는 관계사절로 앞에 있는 an internal mental image를 수식한다.

Edward Sapir, a pioneer in the field of Native American linguistics, / grouped more than 1,500 Native American languages into six "families" / more than three-quarters of a century ago. **Ever since that time, / the classification of Native American languages / has been a source of controversy.** ① A small group of linguists has recently argued // that all Native American languages fit into three linguistic families. ② These scholars believe // that similarities and differences (among words and sounds) leave no doubt / about the validity of their classification-scheme. ③ [1]The vast majority of linguists, however, reject both the methods and conclusions (of these scholars), / arguing that linguistic science has not yet advanced far enough / to be able to group Native American languages into a few families. ④ Furthermore, the absence of grammars (handed down from the past), / owing to either the dearth of writing / or the destruction of written texts, / has given weight to the theory (of this minority group). ⑤ [2]According to these scholars, / Native American languages have diverged to such an extent over the centuries // that it may never be possible / to group them in distinct language families.

해석 아메리카 원주민 언어학 분야의 선구자인 Edward Sapir는 약 75년도 더 전에 1,500개가 넘는 아메리카 원주민 언어들을 6개의 '어족'으로 분류했다. **주제문** 그 이후 아메리카 원주민 언어의 분류는 논란의 근원이 되었다. ① 소수의 언어학자들은 최근에 모든 아메리카 원주민 언어가 세 개의 어족에 들어맞는다고 주장했다. ② 이 학자들은 단어와 소리 사이의 유사점과 차이점들이 자신들의 분류 체계의 타당성에 대해 의심의 여지를 남기지 않는다고 믿는다. ③ 그러나 대다수의 언어학자는 언어학이 아직 아메리카 원주민 언어를 몇 개의 어족으로 분류할 수 있을 만큼 충분히 발전하지 않았다고 주장하며 이 학자들의 방법론과 결론 모두를 거부한다. ④ 더구나, 저술의 부족이나 저술된 문서의 파괴로 인해 과거로부터 전해진 문법의 부재가 이 소수 단체의 이론을 강화했다. ⑤ 이 학자들에 따르면, 아메리카 원주민 언어들은 그것들을 별개의 어족으로 분류하는 것이 전혀 불가능할지도 모를 정도로 수 세기에 걸쳐 갈라져 나왔다.

어휘 pioneer 선구자, 개척자 linguistics 언어학 *cf.* linguist 언어학자 classification 분류 controversy 논란, 논쟁 ○linguistic family 어족 validity 타당(성); 유효(성) scheme 체계; 계획 owing to ~때문에 dearth 부족; 결핍 give weight to (주장·가능성 따위를) 강화하다; ~을 중요시하다 diverge 갈라져 나오다; 빗나가다 extent 정도, 규모 distinct 별개의; 뚜렷한

어휘○ 어족: 언어학에서 하나의 공통된 조어에서 갈라나왔다고 추정되는 여러 언어들을 통틀어 일컫는 말.

해설 아메리카 원주민 언어의 어족 분류에 대한 논란을 다룬 내용으로 소수의 언어학자들은 어족을 세 개로 분류 가능하다고 했고, 대다수의 언어학자들은 아직은 언어학이 그만큼 충분히 발전되지 않았으므로 그들의 주장을 거부했다. ④에서 나온 저술의 부족이나 문서의 파괴로 인한 문법의 부재는 소수의 언어학자가 아닌, 대다수의 언어학자의 의견을 뒷받침하므로, 그것이 소수 단체의 이론을 강화했다는 ④는 글의 흐름과 무관하다.

오답 Check

⑤의 these scholars는 뒤에 이어지는 내용으로 보아 ④의 소수 단체가 아닌 ③의 The vast majority of linguists를 가리킴에 유의한다.

PLUS+ 변형문제

어휘 science -학; 학문 assertion 주장 categorize 분류하다

해설 아메리카 원주민 언어의 분류는 계속 논란이 되고 있다는 지문의 내용을 가장 잘 나타낸 제목으로는 ③ '아메리카 원주민 언어를 분류하는 것의 문제'가 가장 적절하다.

① 언어학을 가장 발전시킨 것
→ 언어학의 발전이 이뤄졌다고 언급하지 않음.
② 어떤 조건들이 여러분의 주장을 진실로 입증할 수 있는가?
→ 주장을 진실로 입증하기 위한 조건은 언급하지 않음.
④ 아메리카 원주민 언어를 번역하는 것의 어려움
→ 해당 언어를 번역하는 것이 어렵다는 내용은 없음.
⑤ 아메리카 원주민 언어의 문법 연구에 대한 한계점
→ 문법 연구에만 국한된 내용은 아님.

구문 [1]The vast majority of linguists, however, reject both the methods and conclusions (of these scholars), / **arguing** that linguistic science has not yet advanced **far** *enough* / **to be** able to group Native American languages into a few families.
• arguing은 부대상황을 나타내는 분사구문을 이끈다.
• 밑줄 친 부분은 「부사+enough +to부정사」의 구조로 '…할 만큼 충분히 ~하게'의 의미이다.

[2]According to these scholars, / Native American languages have diverged to **such an extent** over the centuries // **that** it may never be possible / to group them in distinct language families.
• to such an extent that ~은 '~할 정도로 …한'의 의미로 어떤 상황이 얼마나 어렵거나 위험하거나 놀라운지 등을 강조할 때 사용한다.
• that절 내에서 밑줄 친 it은 가주어, to group 이하는 진주어를 나타낸다.

In the past few decades / nitrogen has asphyxiated many miners in caves // and it always happens under the same horror-movie circumstances. The first person (to walk in) collapses within seconds / for no apparent reason. A second dashes in and succumbs as well. The scariest part is // that no one struggles before dying.

(C) Panic never kicks in. If you've ever been trapped underwater, // the instinct (not to suffocate) will take you to the surface. But our hearts, lungs, and brains actually have no gauge (for detecting oxygen).

(B) They judge only two things: whether gas is inhaled // and whether carbon dioxide is exhaled. ¹Carbon dioxide dissolves in blood to form carbonic acid, // so as long as we remove CO_2 with each breath and reduce the acid, // our brains will relax.

(A) ²It is nitrogen that impedes that system. It's odorless and colorless and causes no acid buildup in our veins. We breathe it in and out easily, // so our lungs feel relaxed. It "kills with kindness."

어휘 nitrogen 질소　miner 광부　collapse 쓰러지다; 붕괴되다　apparent 명백한, 분명한　succumb 쓰러지다; 굴복하다　struggle 몸부림치다; 싸우다　instinct 본능; 직감　suffocate 질식시키다; 숨이 막히다　surface 표면, 수면　gauge 측정기; 판단[측정]하다　inhale 들이마시다(↔ exhale 내쉬다)　carbon dioxide 이산화탄소　dissolve 녹다, 용해시키다; 사라지다　acid 산; 산성의; (맛이) 신　impede 방해하다, 지연시키다　odorless 냄새가 없는　buildup 축적; 증강　vein 혈관; 정맥

해석 지난 수십 년 동안 질소는 동굴 속의 많은 광부들을 질식시켰고, 그것은 마치 공포 영화와 같은 상황에서 발생한다. 맨 처음 들어간 사람이 아무런 명백한 이유도 없이 몇 초 안에 픽 쓰러진다. 두 번째 사람이 황급히 달려가지만, 역시 쓰러지고 만다. 무엇보다 섬뜩한 부분은 어느 누구도 죽기 전에 몸부림치지 않는다는 것이다.
(C) 공포는 결코 나타나지 않는다. 만약 당신이 물속에서 빠진 경험이 있다면, 질식사하지 않으려는 본능이 당신을 수면 위로 데려갈 것이다. 그러나 우리의 심장과 폐와 뇌는 사실 산소를 감지하는 측정기가 없다.
(B) 그것들은 오직 두 가지만 판단할 뿐인데, 우리가 기체를 들이마시고 있는지와 이산화탄소를 내쉬고 있는지이다. 이산화탄소는 혈액 속에서 녹아 탄산을 만드는데, 우리가 숨을 쉴 때마다 이산화탄소를 내보내 산을 줄이는 한, 뇌는 안심할 것이다.
(A) 그러한 시스템을 방해하는 것이 바로 질소이다. 그것은 냄새도 색깔도 없으며, 우리의 혈관 속에서 어떤 산의 축적을 유발하지도 않는다. 우리는 그것(질소)을 쉽게 들이마시고 내보내는데, 폐도 편안함을 느낀다. 그것은 우리를 '자비롭게 죽인다.'

해설 질소가 사람을 질식시키는 상황을 나타내는 주어진 글에 이어, 대조적으로 물속에 빠졌을 때 질식사를 피하기 위해 애쓰는 우리의 본능을 설명하는 (C)가 이어진다. 우리의 심장, 폐, 뇌는 산소를 감지하는 측정기가 없다는 (C)의 마지막 문장 이후로 그것들(심장, 폐, 뇌)이 대신 이산화탄소를 감지하여 숨을 쉴 때마다 이산화탄소를 내보내 뇌가 안심한다는 내용의 (B)가 오고, 마지막으로 질소는 그러한 시스템을 방해하여 우리가 아무것도 느끼지 못한 채로 죽게 한다는 (A)가 오는 것이 적절하다.

오답 Check
접속사 없이도 주어진 상황과 대명사로 적절한 답을 찾는 것이 중요하다. (A)의 that system은 (B)에 언급된 '우리가 숨을 쉴 때마다 이산화탄소를 내보내 산을 줄이는' 것을 말한다.

PLUS⁺ 변형문제

어휘 organ (신체의) 장기, 기관　inability 무능(력); ~할 수 없음　insensitivity 무감각, 둔감

해설 질소는 인간을 소리 없이 죽이는데, 이는 질소가 색깔도 냄새도 없어 우리가 그것을 인식하지 못하기 때문이라는 내용의 글이므로 제목으로는 ④ '인간의 약점: 질소에 대한 무감각'이 가장 적절하다.
① 우리 기관의 기체를 감지하는 것에 대한 무능
→ 산소를 감지하는 측정기가 없다고 언급했지만, 기체를 들이마시는 것은 감지할 수 있음.
② 동굴에서 일하는 것이 얼마나 위험한가
③ 물속에 빠졌을 때 살아남는 방법들
⑤ 혈액 속에 녹기 위한 질소의 현명한 전략
→ ②, ③, ⑤ 글에 언급된 어구를 활용한 오답.

구문 ¹Carbon dioxide dissolves in blood **to form** carbonic acid, // so **as long as** we remove CO_2 with each breath and reduce the acid, // our brains will relax.
• to form은 앞 내용의 결과를 나타내며, as long as는 '~하는 한'을 의미하는 부사절 접속사이다.

²**It is** *nitrogen* **that** impedes that system.
• 「It is ~ that ...」의 강조 구문이 쓰여 nitrogen을 강조한다.

[1]The savanna theory holds // that our apelike ancestors abandoned the dark African forests / and moved into the great grassy plains, / perhaps because of climate changes [that led to massive environmental change]. One of the effects of the changes / was food scarcity.

(C) Out in the savanna, life was tougher, // so the theory goes, // and our ancestors had to find new ways (to get food). Males began to hunt bravely for meat / among the herds of grazing animals.

(A) [2]Some combination of these new circumstances — the need (to scan the horizon / for food or predators), the need (to cover long distances / between food and water) — led the savanna hominid / to begin walking upright. It could help this species survive / in the grasslands.

(B) Other advancements / were similarly related to the new environment — hunting required tools and cooperation; // smarter prehumans made better tools and better teammates, // so they survived longer and attracted more mates, // and the process selected for bigger brains.

해석 사바나 이론에서는 우리의 유인원과 비슷한 조상들이 아마도 거대한 환경 변화를 초래한 기후 변화 때문에 어두운 아프리카 숲을 버리고 광대한 초지 평야로 이동했다고 여긴다. 변화의 영향 중 하나는 식량 부족이었다.
(C) 이론에 따르면, 사바나로 나오니 삶이 더 힘들어졌고 우리 조상들은 식량을 얻기 위한 새로운 방법들을 찾아야 했다. 남성들은 풀을 먹는 동물 떼 사이에서 고기를 얻기 위해 용감하게 사냥하기 시작했다.
(A) 이러한 새로운 상황(식량이나 포식자를 찾기 위해 지평선을 자세히 살펴볼 필요성, 식량과 물 사이의 먼 거리를 이동할 필요성)의 어떤 조합은 사바나의 인류 조상이 직립하여 걷기 시작하도록 이끌었다. 그것은 이 종이 초원 지대에서 생존하는 것을 도울 수 있었다.
(B) 다른 진보는 마찬가지로 새로운 환경과 관련이 있었다. 사냥은 도구와 협동을 요구했다. 더 똑똑해진 선행 인류들은 더 나은 도구와 더 나은 팀 동료들을 형성하여, 더 오래 살아남았고 더 많은 짝을 유인했으며, 이 과정은 더 큰 두뇌를 선택했다.

어휘 hold ~라고 여기다; 유지하다 plain 평야, 평지; 명백한; 소박한 massive 거대한 scarcity 부족; 결핍 graze 풀을 뜯어먹다 scan 자세히 살펴보다; 훑어보다 cover 이동하다; 가리다; 보도하다 upright 직립하여; 수직으로 prehuman 선행 인류(의); 인류 이전의 (동물)

해설 조상 인류가 초원으로 이동한 이후 식량 부족을 겪게 되었다는 주어진 글 다음에는 이러한 식량 부족 문제를 타개하기 위해 사냥을 시작했다는 (C)가 나와야 한다. 그다음 사냥을 하게 되면서 새로운 환경에 놓이게 되고 지평선을 자세히 보고, 먼 거리를 갈 필요성으로 인해 직립하게 됐다는 인류의 첫 번째 진보에 대한 내용인 (A)가 나와야 한다. (A)의 these new circumstances는 (C)에서 사바나의 삶이 더 어려워져서 식량을 얻을 새로운 방법을 찾아야 하는 상황과 이어진다. 마지막으로 새로운 환경과 관련된 인류의 또 다른 진보들(Other advancements)을 설명한 (B)가 이어지는 것이 적절하다.

PLUS+ 변형문제

어휘 carnivorous 육식(성)의 authoritative 권위 있는, 믿을 만한 territory 영역; 영토
해설 기후 변화로 조상들이 사바나에 가게 되고 새로운 상황에 적응하기 위해 이룩 온 진보를 설명하므로 제목으로는 ⑤ '우리의 조상들은 새로운 환경에서 무엇을 이루었는가'가 가장 적절하다.
① 직립보행으로부터 얻은 생존 기술
→ 언급된 진보 중 일부에만 해당되는 내용.
② 왜 우리는 육식을 하기 시작했는가?
→ 고기를 얻기 위해 사냥을 했다고 언급하지만 그 이유가 중심 내용은 아님.
③ 무엇이 권위 있는 이론으로 여겨지는가?
→ '이론'이라는 단어를 활용한 오답임.
④ 자신의 영역 너머의 세상에 대한 인간의 갈망
→ 기후 변화로 인해 자신의 영역을 떠나게 된 것이므로 지문의 내용과 다름.

구문 [1]The savanna theory holds // **that** our apelike ancestors abandoned the dark African forests / and moved into the great grassy plains, / perhaps because of *climate changes* [**that** led to massive environmental change].
• 접속사 that이 이끄는 명사절은 문장의 동사 holds의 목적어절 역할을 한다.
• [ ]는 주격 관계대명사 that이 이끄는 관계사절로 climate changes를 수식한다.

[2]Some combination of these new circumstances — *the need* (to scan the horizon / for food or predators), *the need* (to cover long distances / between food and water) — **led** *the savanna hominid* / **to begin walking upright.**
• 두 개의 ( )는 모두 형용사적 용법으로 쓰인 to부정사구로 각각 바로 앞에 있는 the need를 수식한다. 또한, 대시(—) 사이에 있는 밑줄 친 the need to scan ~ and water는 앞에 있는 어구 these new circumstances를 보충 설명한다.
• 문장의 동사 led 이하는 「lead+O+C」의 구조로 목적격보어로 to begin walking upright가 쓰였다.

38 ④ PLUS+ ⑤

Several factors explain // why the culture of honor, willingness to protect reputation by resorting to violence, arose / in some but not all regions of the United States. [1]Northern states were settled / by farmers (benefited by stronger legal systems / from early settlement). (①) On the other hand, the south and west were inhabited / by ranchers, // and their livelihood could be threatened / by thieves. (②) Crimes were difficult to punish / in the expansive south and west, // so herders were forced to act themselves. (③) Meanwhile, warmer weather and poverty / only encouraged violence. (④ [2]Thus born were / the violence and rivalries [that characterize today's culture of honor].) Although some experts dispute this causal chain, // there's no doubt // that these settlers embraced combat and military law / far more deeply than did their northern counterparts. (⑤) [3]As they were passed from generation to generation, // the culture of honor gained a foothold in the south and west, // which distinguishes their violent responses from tamer responses (in the north).

해석 주제문 폭력에 의존함으로써 명예를 기꺼이 보호하고자 하는 마음인 명예의 문화가 왜 미국 전역이 아니라 일부 지역에서만 생겼는지를 몇 가지 요인으로 설명한다. 북부의 주들에는 정착 초기부터 보다 강력한 법률 제도의 혜택을 받은 농민들이 정착했다. 반면 남부와 서부에는 목장주들이 많이 살았는데, 그들의 생계는 도둑에 의해 위협받을 수 있었다. 광활한 남부와 서부에서 범죄를 처벌하기란 어려웠기에, 목동들은 직접 해결할 수밖에 없었다. 한편, 더 따뜻한 날씨와 빈곤도 폭력을 촉진할 뿐이었다. 이렇게 해서 오늘날의 명예의 문화를 특징짓는 폭력과 대립 관계가 탄생했다. 이런 인과관계를 반박하는 전문가들도 있지만, 이 정착민들(남부와 서부에 정착했던 사람들)이 결투와 군법을 북부의 상대(정착민들)보다 훨씬 더 가슴속 깊이 받아들였다는 것에는 의심의 여지가 없다. 이런 관습들이 여러 세대를 거쳐 내려오면서 명예의 문화가 남부와 서부에서 기반을 구축했는데, 이것은 그들의 폭력적 반응과 북부의 비교적 유순한 반응과의 차이를 나타낸다.

어휘 willingness 기꺼이 하는 마음 resort to ~에 의존하다 rancher 목장주; 목장 감독 livelihood 생계 (수단) expansive 광활한; 포괄적인 herder 목동; 양치기 rivalry 대립 (관계); 경쟁 dispute 반박하다; 이의를 제기하다; 논란 causal chain 인과 관계 embrace 받아들이다, 수용하다; 껴안다 combat 결투; 싸움 counterpart 상대; 대응 관계에 있는 것[사람] foothold 기반; 거점; 발 디딜 곳 tame 유순한; 길들여진

해설 주어진 문장을 읽은 후, 연결어나 지시어 등을 활용해야 한다. 주어진 문장은 Thus로 시작하여 어떤 결론을 나타내는데, 명예의 문화를 특징짓는 폭력과 대립 관계가 탄생했다는 내용이다. 따라서 그 앞 문장에는 폭력과 대립 관계가 탄생한 원인이 나와야 한다. ④의 앞 문장까지 북부와 남부, 서부를 대조시키면서 남부와 서부에서 폭력을 촉진한 원인들을 설명한다. ④의 뒤 문장의 '인과 관계(this casual chain)'를 보아 결과도 그 앞에 나와야 하므로 주어진 문장은 ④에 들어가야 한다.

오답 Check
⑤ 뒤 문장의 they는 문맥상 ④에 들어가는 주어진 문장의 the violence and rivalries that ~ culture of honor를 나타낸다.

PLUS+ 변형문제

해설 이 글은 미국의 남부와 서부에서 폭력에 의존한 명예의 문화가 어떻게 생겨났는지 원인을 밝히는 내용이므로 이를 가장 잘 나타낸 제목은 ⑤ '폭력이 남부와 서부에서 수용된 이유'이다.
① 미국에서 폭력의 증가
→ 지문에 언급된 내용을 활용한 오답.
② 폭력에 영향을 미치는 명예의 문화
→ 폭력은 명예의 문화의 속성이므로 영향을 받는 관계가 아님.
③ 왜 농부들은 명예의 문화를 채택했는가
→ 농부는 북부에 정착한 사람들로 법률 제도의 혜택을 받았으므로 명예의 문화를 채택하지 않음.
④ 남부와 서부에 미치는 군대의 영향력
→ 지문에 언급된 내용을 활용한 오답.

구문 [1]Northern states were settled / by *farmers* (benefited by stronger legal systems / from early settlement).
• ( )는 과거분사구이며 앞에 있는 명사 farmers를 수식한다.

[2]Thus born were / *the violence and rivalries* [**that** characterize today's culture of honor].
　　　 C 　 V 　　　　　　　　　　　　　　　　S
• 보어를 문두에 두어 강조하는 경우 「보어+be동사+긴 주어」의 어순으로 도치가 일어난다.
• [ ]는 주격 관계대명사 that이 이끄는 관계사절로 앞에 있는 the violence and rivalries를 수식한다.

[3]As they were passed from generation to generation, // *the culture of honor gained a foothold in the south and west*, // **which** distinguishes their violent responses.
• 계속적 용법의 관계대명사 which가 이끄는 관계사절은 앞 문장 전체에 대한 부연 설명을 한다.

39 ④ PLUS⁺ ②

주제문

Factual errors (in autobiographical recollection) increase substantially // as the temporal distance (from the to-be-remembered event) increases. (①) ¹For example, research indicates // that accuracy (in recollections of how people heard the news of the September 11, 2001 terrorist attacks in New York City) decreased substantially over an 8-month period. (②) Research (on personal recollections of dramatic historical events) suggests // that despite people's beliefs to the contrary, accuracy (for memories of the John F. Kennedy assassination or the 9/11 attacks) may be no greater / than for memories of any other events in life. (③) The temporal instability of autobiographical memory, therefore, / contributes to change in the life story over time. (④ <u>But many other processes are also at play, // and many of these reflect changes / in how the person comes to terms with their situation.</u>) ²The most obvious one is // people accumulate new experiences over time, // some of which may prove to be so important as to make their way into narrative identity. (⑤) ³In addition to that, / as people's motivations, goals, personal concerns, and social positions change, // their memories (of important events in their lives) and the meanings [they attribute to those events] may also change.

해석 주제문 자전적 기억의 실제적 오류는 기억될 사건으로부터의 시간적 거리가 증가함에 따라 크게 증가한다. 예를 들어, 2001년 9월 11일 뉴욕시의 테러 공격 소식을 사람들이 어떻게 들었는지에 대한 기억의 정확도가 8개월의 기간 동안 현저히 감소했다는 연구가 나왔다. 극적인 역사적 사건들의 개인적인 기억들에 대한 연구는 그 반대에 대한 사람들의 믿음에도 불구하고, 존 F. 케네디의 암살이나 9/11 공격에 대한 기억의 정확성이 인생의 다른 어떤 사건들에 대한 기억의 정확성보다 더 크지 않을 수 있다는 것을 보여준다. 그러므로 자전적 기억의 시간적 불안정성은 시간이 지남에 따라 인생 이야기에 변화를 일으키는 원인이 된다. 그러나 다른 많은 과정들 또한 작용하고, 그것들 중 다수가 그 사람이 어떻게 그들의 상황을 받아들이는 법을 배우는지에 대한 변화를 반영한다. 가장 명백한 하나는 사람들은 시간이 지남에 따라 새로운 경험을 축적하는데, 그중 일부는 서사적 정체성으로 나아가는 데 매우 중요한 것으로 판명될 수도 있다. 그것 외에도 사람들의 동기, 목표, 개인적 우려와 사회적 지위가 변화함에 따라, 그들의 삶에서 중요한 사건들에 대한 기억과 그들이 그 사건들에 있다고 생각하는 의미 또한 바뀔 수 있다.

어휘 factual 실제[사실]의, 사실에 입각한 autobiographical 자전적인, 자서전의 recollection 기억(력); 회상 substantially 크게, 상당히 temporal 시간의; 일시적인; 현세[속세]의 substantially 크게, 상당히 accuracy 정확도 assassination 암살 instability 불안정(성) come to terms with (좋지 않은 일을) 받아들이는 법을 배우다; ~와 타협하다 accumulate 축적하다 make one's way 나아가다, 가다 ●narrative identity 서사적 정체성 attribute A to B A(성질 등)가 B에게 있다고 생각하다; A(결과 등)를 B의 덕[탓]으로 보다

어휘○ 서사적 정체성: 개인이 자신들의 인생 경험을 내재화하고 전개 중인 자신의 이야기에 통합함으로써 정체성을 형성한다는 이론

해설 주어진 문장을 읽은 후, 연결어나 지시어 등을 활용하거나 글의 흐름이 끊기는 곳을 찾는다. But으로 시작하는 주어진 문장은 인생 이야기에 변화를 주는 다른 과정(other processes)에 대한 언급이므로 자전적 기억의 시간적 불안정성이 인생 이야기에 변화를 일으킨다는 첫 번째 원인 언급과 경험 축적이라는 다른 과정의 구체적 예시가 언급된 문장 사이(④)에 오는 것이 적절하다.

PLUS⁺ 변형문제

어휘 oblivion 망각; 무의식 상태 contented 만족[자족]스러운 vulnerability 취약성 retentive 기억력이 좋은; 보유하는

해설 주제문을 통해 시간이 지남에 따라 인간의 기억에 오류가 발생할 확률이 높아진다는 것을 알 수 있다. 이를 제목으로 가장 잘 나타낸 것은 ② '인간 기억 능력의 취약성'이다.

① 망각: 만족스러운 삶을 위한 축복받은 상태
→ 망각과 만족스러운 삶의 관계는 언급되지 않음.
③ 중요한 추억들을 분명히 기억하는 방법들
→ 글에 언급되지 않음.
④ 좋은 기억력: 정체성을 위한 필수적인 기술
→ 정체성에 관한 언급은 있지만, 기억력이 정체성에 필수적이라는 언급은 없음.
⑤ 어떻게 경험이 사건에 의미를 부여하는가
→ 글의 일부 내용에 해당하는 오답임.

구문 ¹For example, research indicates // that *accuracy* (in recollections *of* how people heard the news of the September 11, 2001 terrorist attacks in New York City) **decreased** substantially over an 8-month period.
• ( )는 that절 내의 주어인 accuracy를 수식하는 전명구이고 that절 내의 동사는 decreased이다.
• 의문사 how가 이끄는 명사절(how ~ New York City)이 전치사 of의 목적어로 쓰였다.

²The most obvious one is // people accumulate *new experiences* over time, // **some of which** may prove to be so important as to make their way into narrative identity.
• 「부정대명사+of+목적격 관계대명사」 형태의 some of which는 and some of them으로 바꿔 쓸 수 있고, 여기에서 which는 앞에 나온 new experiences를 선행사로 한다.

³In addition to that, / **as** people's motivations, goals, personal concerns, and social positions change, // *their memories* (of important events in their lives) and *the meanings* [(which[that]) they attribute to those events] may also change.
• as는 부사절 접속사로 '~함에 따라'의 의미이다.
• of ~ their lives는 전명구로서 their memories를 수식하고, [ ]는 선행사 the meanings를 수식하는 관계사절로 목적격 관계대명사 which[that]가 생략되었다.

Uri Gneezy and Aldo Rustichini conducted an experiment [where subjects were given fifty questions from an IQ test]. One group was instructed to do the best [they could]. Another was given 3¢ per correct answer. A third group was rewarded with 30¢ per correct answer // and a fourth was paid 90¢ per correct answer. ¹As you may have guessed, // the two groups (receiving 30¢ and 90¢) both outperformed the ones (with no bonus) — / on average, they got 34 questions right (compared to 28). The surprise was // that the group (receiving the 3¢ payment) did the worst of all, / getting only 23 right on average. Once money enters the equation, // it becomes the main motivation, and 3¢ was just too little. It may also have conveyed // that the task wasn't very important. Thus Gneezy and Rustichini conclude // that you should offer significant financial rewards or none at all.

↓

Money as a motivation doesn't necessarily play a (A) proportional role / in yielding results; paying a little can be (B) worse / than paying nothing at all.

해석 Uri Gneezy와 Aldo Rustichini는 피실험자들에게 아이큐 검사에서 나온 50문제가 주어지는 실험을 시행하였다. 한 집단은 최선을 다하라는 지시를 받았다. 또 다른 집단은 정답 한 개마다 3센트를 받았다. 세 번째 집단은 정답 한 개에 30센트를, 네 번째는 정답 한 개에 90센트를 받았다. 여러분이 짐작했을지 모르겠지만, 30센트와 90센트를 받는 두 집단 둘 다 보너스가 없는 집단들을 능가하였는데, 평균적으로 그들은 28개와 비교해 34개의 정답을 맞혔다. 추론 근거 놀라운 것은 3센트를 받은 집단이 전체 중 가장 못했고, 평균적으로 겨우 23개만 맞혔다는 것이다. 일단 돈이 상황에 개입하면, 그것이 주된 동기 부여가 되고, 3센트는 단지 너무 적었던 것이다. 그것은 또한 그 일이 매우 중요하지는 않았다는 것을 시사했을지도 모른다. 따라서 Gneezy와 Rustichini는 상당한 금전적 보상을 제공하거나 아무것도 주지 말아야 한다고 결론 내린다.

↓

동기 부여로서의 돈은 결과 산출에 있어서 반드시 (A) 비례적인 역할을 하는 것은 아니다. 적게 지급하는 것은 아무것도 지급하지 않는 것보다 (B) 더 안 좋을 수 있다.

어휘 subject 주제; 문제; 과목; 피실험자   outperform 능가하다, 우수하다   equation 방정식; 상황; 문제   convey 전달하다; 사하다   yield (수익·결과를) 내다; 항복하다; 양보하다; 산출, 수익
[선택지 어휘] trivial 사소한, 하찮은   significant 중요한, 소중한; 상당한   proportional (~에) 비례하는

해설 실험에서 정답에 30센트와 90센트를 받는 두 집단 둘 다 보너스가 없는 집단들을 능가하였지만 오히려 3센트를 받은 집단은 보상 없는 집단보다 잘하지 못했다. 이는 동기 부여로 돈이 사용될 때 이것이 결과 산출에 반드시 정비례하는 것은 아니며, 돈을 적게 지급하는 것은 아예 지급하지 않는 것보다 더 안 좋을 수 있다고 요약할 수 있으므로 빈칸에는 ⑤ '(A) 비례적인 – (B) 더 나쁜'이 적절하다.

오답 Check

	(A)	(B)
①	사소한	– 더 쉬운

→ (A)와 (B) 모두 틀림.

②	제한된	– 더 가난한

→ (A)와 (B) 모두 틀림.

③	중요한	– 더 저렴한

→ (A)는 정답이 될 수 있지만, (B)는 틀림.

④	결정적인	– 더 나은

→ (A)는 정답이 될 수 있고, (B)는 지문의 내용과 반대됨.

구문 ¹**As** you **may have guessed**, // *the two groups* (receiving 30¢ and 90¢) both outperformed *the ones* (with no bonus) ~.
• 접속사 As는 '~하는 것처럼', '~하는 대로'의 뜻으로 쓰였다.
• may have p.p.는 '~했을지도 모른다'는 의미로 과거의 일에 대해 추측하는 표현이다.
• 주어는 the two groups이고 receiving 30¢와 90¢는 주어를 수식하는 분사구이다.

In a recent study, Professor Deborah Tannen of Georgetown University / asked students (in her class) to tape-record conversations (between women friends and men friends). It was easy / to get recordings of women friends talking, // partly because most of the students were women, // but also because the request (to "record a conversation with your friend") / met with easy (a) compliance (from the students' female friends and family members). But asking men to record conversations with their friends had mixed results. One woman's mother agreed readily, // but her father insisted / that he didn't have conversations (with his friends). [1]"Don't you ever call Fred on the phone?" she asked, / naming a man [she knew to be his good friend]. "Not often," he said. "But if I do, // it's because I have something to ask, and // when I get the answer, I hang up."

Another woman's husband delivered a tape to her / with great satisfaction and pride. "This is a good conversation," he announced, / "because it's not just him and me making small talk, / like 'Hi, how are you? I saw a good movie the other day,' and stuff. It's a problem-solving task. Each line is (b) meaningful." [2]When the woman listened to the tape, // she heard her husband and his friend / trying to solve a computer problem. Everything [they said] was technical and (c) factual. [3]Not only did she not consider it "a good conversation," // but she didn't really regard it as a conversation at all. His idea of a good conversation / was one (with task-focused content). Hers was one with (d) impersonal content). These differences also showed up / in relations (between parents and children). Deborah Tannen's students told her // that when they talked to "their parents" on the phone, // they spent most of the time talking to their mothers. Their fathers typically joined the conversation // only when they had a business matter (to discuss or report). This happened // since they believed talk is designed to convey (e) information.

해석 최근의 한 연구에서 조지타운 대학의 Deborah Tannen 교수는 자신의 반 학생들에게 여자 친구들과 남자 친구들 사이의 대화를 녹음해 달라고 요청했다. 여자 친구들의 대화 녹음 기록을 얻는 것은 쉬웠는데, 대부분의 학생들이 여성이었기 때문이기도 하지만, '친구와의 대화를 녹음하라'는 요구가 학생들의 여성 친구들과 가족들로부터 쉽게 (a) 응낙을 얻었기 때문이었다. 하지만 남자들에게 친구들과의 대화를 녹음해 달라고 부탁하는 것은 엇갈린 결과를 낳았다. 한 여성의 어머니는 흔쾌히 동의했지만, 그녀의 아버지는 자신이 친구들과 대화를 나누지 않는다고 우겼다. 그녀가 아버지의 친한 친구라고 알고 있는 이름을 대며 "아버지는 Fred 아저씨랑 전화하지 않나요?"라고 물었다. 그는 "자주는 아니지. 하지만 내가 전화를 한다면 물어볼 게 있기 때문이고, 답을 얻으면 전화를 끊는단다."라고 말했다.
또 다른 여성의 남편은 그녀에게 큰 만족과 자부심을 가지고 테이프를 전달했다. 그는 "이것은 좋은 대화예요. '안녕, 잘 지내니? 며칠 전에 좋은 영화를 봤어.' 등과 같이 그와 내가 잡담을 나누는 것이 아니고 문제 해결의 작업이었기 때문이죠. 모든 말이 (b) 의미가 있어요."라고 말했다. **주제문** 그 여성이 그 테이프를 들었을 때, 그녀는 그녀의 남편과 그의 친구가 컴퓨터 문제를 해결하려고 노력하고 있는 것을 들었다. 그들이 말한 모든 것은 전문적이고 (c) 사실적인 것이었다. 그녀는 그것을 '좋은 대화'로 여기지 않았을 뿐만 아니라, 사실 전혀 대화로 여기지도 않았다. 남편의 좋은 대화에 대한 생각은 과업에 초점을 맞춘 내용이었다. 그녀의 생각은 (d) 비개인적인(→ 개인적인) 내용을 가진 대화였다. 이러한 차이점들은 부모와 자식 간의 관계에서도

어휘 compliance 응낙, 승낙, 수락 mixed (의견 등이) 엇갈리는, 뒤섞인 readily 흔쾌히; 손쉽게 small talk 잡담 technical 전문적인; 기술적인 factual 사실적인, 사실에 입각한 regard A as B A를 B로 여기다[간주하다] impersonal 비개인적인; 비인격적인 convey 전달하다, 나르다 **[선택지 어휘]** rapport (친밀한) 관계 verbal 언어의[말의]

해설 41 주제문을 먼저 찾아 이를 가장 잘 반영한 선택지를 고른다. 제목 유형은 글의 핵심을 나타내면서도 압축적이고 상징적인 다양한 형태로 표현될 수 있음에 유의한다. 이 글은 의사소통에서 여자는 개인적인 관계를 중시하는 반면 남자는 보고하는 것을 중시한다는 것에 관한 내용이다. 그러므로 ③ '성별에 따른 의사소통 차이: 관계-대화 대 보고-대화'가 적절하다.
42 남자에게 의미 있는 대화는 문제 해결에 도움이 되고, 전문적이고, 사실 중심인 것이지만, 여자는 개인적인 내용 중심이므로 (d)의 impersonal(비개인적인)은 '개인적인'이라는 뜻의 personal로 고쳐야 적절하다.

오답 Check
41 ① 남녀 사이의 의사소통을 향상시키는 법
② 여자, 남자, 그리고 대화의 유형: 무엇이 차이를 만드는가?
→ ①, ② 핵심어인 것처럼 생각될 수 있는 단어들을 조합했으나 언급되지 않음.
④ 언어의 성별 차이: 누가 더 많은 말을 하는가, 여자인가 남자인가? → 누가 더 말을 많이 하는지에 관한 것은 아님.
⑤ 언어의 상호작용에서 남성과 여성의 제스처 사용의 차이점
→ 제스처 사용은 언급되지 않음.
42 밑줄 친 (b)는 남성의 입장으로 문제 해결의 작업을 의미 있는 것으로 보는 것은 자연스럽다.

나타났다. Deborah Tannen의 학생들은 '자신의 부모들'과 통화할 때, 대부분의 시간을 어머니와 대화하는 데 쓴다고 그녀에게 말했다. 그들의 아버지는 일반적으로 그들이 논의하거나 보고할 일이 있을 때만 대화에 참여했다. 이것은 그들이 대화가 (e) 정보를 전달하기 위한 것이라고 믿기 때문에 일어났다.

구문 [1]"Don't you ever call Fred on the phone?" she asked, / **naming** *a man* [(who(m)[that]) she knew to be his good friend].
- naming 이하(naming ~ his good friend)는 동시동작을 나타내는 분사구문이다.
- [ ]는 목적격 관계대명사 who(m)[that]가 생략된 관계사절로 앞에 있는 선행사 a man을 수식한다.

[2]When the woman listened to the tape, // she **heard** *her husband and his friend* / **trying to solve a computer problem**.
- 주절에서 지각동사 heard의 목적어는 her husband and his friend이고, trying ~ problem이 목적격보어로 쓰였다.

[3]**Not only** *did she not consider* it "a good conversation," // but she didn't really regard it as a conversation at all.
- 부정어구 Not only가 문두에 나와 「조동사(did)+주어(she)+동사(not consider)」의 어순으로 도치되었다.

| 31 ③ + ③ | 32 ② + ③ | 33 ① + ③ | 34 ⑤ + ① | 35 ③ + ② | 36 ⑤ + ① |
| 37 ② + ④ | 38 ④ + ② | 39 ⑤ + ⑤ | 40 ③ | 41 ③ | 42 ⑤ |

31 ③ PLUS+ ③

¹People have always noticed // that works of art affect them, / and have variously explained, classified, evaluated, justified, regulated, and enjoyed this phenomenon. Whereas Plato banned poets from his republic / in order to restrict influences upon the citizenry, Aristotle formulated his theory of catharsis / to legitimate the effects of art upon persons. ^{주제문/추론 근거} ²Noting // that drama consistently produces in audiences certain effects — fear, pity, admiration, awe, superiority, affinity, belief, skepticism, compassion, and relief — // Aristotle identified these ^{추론 근거} responses as official aims of art. Since the late seventeenth century, // when mass print culture provided greater numbers of persons / with the regular affective experience of literature, // the novel became another focal point / in the ongoing debate and discourse / about the effects of representation. Even more than drama and poetry, / the novel seemed to demand the reader's sentiments.

해석 사람들은 예술 작품이 자신들에게 영향을 미치는 것을 항상 인지해 왔고, 이 현상을 다양하게 설명하고, 분류하고, 평가하고, 정당화하고, 관리하고, 즐겨 왔다. 플라톤은 시민에게 미치는 영향력을 제한하기 위해 자신의 국가에 시인을 금지한 반면에, 아리스토텔레스는 사람들에게 미치는 예술의 효과를 정당화하기 위해 카타르시스(감정 정화)에 대한 자신의 이론을 만들어 냈다. ^{주제문/추론 근거} 연극이 관중들에게서 두려움, 동정, 감탄, 경외, 우월, 친밀감, 믿음, 회의, 동정, 위안과 같은 특정한 영향을 끊임없이 준다는 것에 주목하며, 아리스토텔레스는 이런 반응들을 예술의 공식적인 목적으로 확인했다. ^{추론 근거} 17세기 말 이래로, 그때에는 대량 인쇄 문화가 더 많은 사람들에게 문학의 정기적인 정서적 경험을 제공했는데, 소설은 표현의 영향에 관한 계속되는 논쟁과 담론에 있어서 또 다른 초점이 되었다. 연극과 시보다 훨씬 더, 소설은 독자의 감정을 요구하는 듯했다.

어휘 citizenry 시민 formulate (세심히) 만들어 내다; 공식화하다 catharsis 카타르시스 《(비극 등에 의한 감정의 정화)》 legitimate 정당화하다; 합법화하다; 합법의 admiration 감탄, 존경 awe 경외; 두려움 affinity 친밀감; 관련성 skepticism 회의(론); 무신론 compassion 동정; 불쌍히 여김 affective 정서적인, 감정적인 focal point (관심 등의) 초점[중심] discourse 담론; 강연 **[선택지 어휘]** sentiment 감정; 감상

해설 예술 작품들(시, 드라마, 소설)이 사람들에게 영향, 특히 감정적인 영향을 끼친다는 내용이므로 빈칸 문장은 소설이 독자의 ③ '감정'을 요구하는 듯했다는 내용이 되어야 한다.

오답 Check
① 인내 ② 관심 ④ 참여 ⑤ 예상
→ 소설을 비롯한 예술 작품이 독자들의 감정을 일으키므로 오답.

PLUS+ 변형문제
어휘 trigger (반응을 유발하는) 자극; 방아쇠
해설 주제문을 가장 잘 표현한 제목은 ③ '문학의 효과: 감정 자극'이다.
① 독서에 가장 효과적인 동기부여
→ 독서에 동기부여가 되는 것에 대한 언급은 없음.
② 어떻게 카타르시스가 작용하는지에 대한 아리스토텔레스의 이론
→ 아리스토텔레스가 카타르시스에 대한 이론을 만들었지만 그것의 작동 방식에 대한 설명은 없음.
④ 역사적인 관점에서 문학 작품의 기능
→ 문학 작품의 기능은 맞지만, 역사적인 관점에서 본 것은 아님.
⑤ 전통 문학에서 현실을 표현하는 것의 부족함
→ 전통 문학이 현실을 표현하는 것에 대한 언급은 없음.

구문 ¹People **have always noticed** // that works of art affect them, / and have variously **explained**, classified, evaluated, justified, regulated, and enjoyed *this phenomenon*.
• 두 개의 동사구 have always noticed와 have variously explained가 접속사 and로 연결되어 병렬 구조를 이룬다.
• 밑줄 친 여섯 개의 분사는 콤마(,)와 and로 병렬 연결되어 모두 this phenomenon을 목적어로 취한다.

²**Noting** // that drama consistently produces in audiences certain effects — fear, pity, admiration, awe, superiority, affinity, belief, skepticism, compassion, and relief — // Aristotle **identified** these responses **as** official aims of art.
• Noting ~ and relief는 부대상황을 나타내는 분사구문이다.
• 문장의 동사는 「identify A as B」의 구조를 취하며 'A를 B라고 확인하다'를 의미한다.

주제문

¹Natural selection, / a process [in which an organism adapts to its environment by means of selectively reproducing changes in its genotype], / does not plan ahead. Our current adaptations are "designed" to work well in past environments: Those [who had more offspring in past environments] / tended to pass their traits on to current generations. If the environment stays relatively constant, // then those traits will function well in the current environment. 추론 근거 ²However, if the environment has changed recently, // then traits [which were once adaptive] may no longer be adaptive. This idea is known as "evolutionary lag" or "mismatch," // because the changes in genes lag slightly behind the changes in environments. The classic example (of evolutionary lag) is our preferences for sweets, salts, and fats: it was adaptive to crave these // when they were rare, // because they were valuable sources (of energy and nutrients). People still crave them // even though they are overabundant in modern environments / and lead to obesity and other health problems.

해석 주제문 유전자형의 변화를 선택적으로 재생하는 방법으로 유기체가 환경에 적응하는 과정인 자연 선택은 미리 계획하지 않는다. 우리의 현재 적응은 과거 환경에서 잘 작용하도록 '설계되어' 있는데, 과거 환경에서 더 많은 자식을 가진 사람들은 자신들의 형질을 현세대에게 전해주는 경향이 있었다. 환경이 비교적 변함이 없다면, 그러한 형질들은 현재의 환경에서 잘 기능할 것이다. 추론 근거 하지만 최근에 환경이 변화했다면, 한때 적응성이 있던 형질은 더는 적응성이 없을지도 모른다. 이 개념은 '진화적 지체' 또는 '부조화'로 알려져 있는데, 그 이유는 유전자의 변화가 환경의 변화보다 약간 뒤처지기 때문이다. 진화적 지체의 대표적인 예는 당, 염분, 그리고 지방에 대한 우리의 선호이다. 그것들이 귀할 때 그것들을 갈망하는 것은 적응성이 있는 것이었는데, 왜냐하면 그것들이 에너지와 영양분의 귀중한 근원이었기 때문이다. 그것들은 현대 환경에서 과잉이고 비만과 다른 건강 문제를 가져오는데도 불구하고, 사람들은 여전히 그것들을 갈망한다.

어휘 natural selection 자연 선택 adapt to ~에 적응하다 *cf.* adaptation 적응 adaptive 적응성이 있는; 적응하는 by means of ~을 써서[~의 도움으로] selectively 선택적으로 reproduce 재생[재현]하다 offspring 자식; 새끼 trait 형질, 특성 relatively 비교적 constant 변함없는 lag 지체, 지연; 경과 *cf.* lag behind ~보다 뒤처지다 mismatch 부조화 crave 갈망[열망]하다 rare 희귀한, 드문 overabundant 과잉의, 남아도는 obesity 비만

해설 유전자의 변화가 환경의 변화보다 약간 뒤처지기 때문에 환경이 최근에 변화했다면, 한때 적응성이 있던 형질은 더는 적응성이 없고 환경 변화에 도태된 것이 되어 진화적 지체나 부조화는 자연 선택의 특성이라고 했다. 즉, 자연 선택은 환경 변화에 뒤이어 발생하여 미리 계획된 것이 아닌 특성이 있다고 볼 수 있으므로 빈칸에는 ② '미리 계획하지 않는다'가 가장 적절하다.

오답 Check
① 복합성을 초래한다
→ 자연 선택이 복합성을 초래한다는 내용은 없음.
③ 유전적 변화를 지시한다
→ 자연 선택에 관한 상식을 활용한 오답.
④ 모든 유기체를 위해 작용한다
→ 상식적으로 맞지만 글에 언급되지 않은 내용.
⑤ 진화적 기제를 통제한다
→ 자연 선택이 진화를 통제한다는 내용은 언급되지 않음.

PLUS⁺ 변형문제

어휘 rate 속도; 비율; 요금 keep up with ~을 따라가다, ~에 뒤지지 않다 misconception 오해

해설 환경 변화보다 유전적 변화가 뒤처지는 진화의 지체 현상이 일어나는 것을 설명하는 글이므로 글의 주제로는 ③ '인간이 비적응하게 되는 이유'가 적절하다.
① 적응의 속도에 영향을 주는 요인들
→ 적응의 속도에 영향을 주는 요인들은 언급되지 않음.
② 인간 진화에서 자연 선택의 역할
④ 환경적 변화를 따라가는 것의 중요성
⑤ 자연 선택과 적응에 관한 오해들
→ ②, ④, ⑤ 모두 글에 언급된 어구를 활용한 오답.

구문 ¹Natural selection, / *a process* [**in which** an organism adapts to its environment / **by means of** selectively reproducing changes in its genotype], / does not plan ahead.
• 밑줄 친 두 부분은 콤마(,)로 연결된 동격 관계이다. 문장의 주어는 Natural selection이고 동사는 does not plan이다.
• in which가 이끄는 [ ]는 선행사 a process를 수식한다.
• by means of는 '수단'을 나타내는 전치사구이다.

²However, if the environment has changed recently, // then *traits* [**which** were once adaptive] may no longer be adaptive.
• [ ]는 관계대명사 which가 이끄는 관계사절로 traits를 수식한다.

You might first come up with advanced technology (in the classroom) / when asked, "What is the most influential factor in teaching and learning?" 주제문 However, there is no greater influence / in the teaching and learning process / than how time is viewed and used. ¹We live in an era (shaped not by the rising and setting of the sun and moon, / as in eons ago), / but in an era [when technology and a sense of urgency speed up everything [we do]]. This cultural reality slips into early care and education programs (with policies and mandates [that fragment our time into little boxes on a schedule]). Teachers move children through the day // as if they are cars on an assembly line. ²Neither the teachers nor the children are afforded time (to ponder, wonder, and make meaning out of the day's activities). Some early childhood commercial curricula even market themselves / proclaiming, "This lesson will only take five minutes of your day." You should question // why that might be a good thing. 추론 근거 If it's worth learning and adding to your program, // doesn't it deserve more time? What about the learning [that comes from really slowing down and paying attention to // what you are undertaking]?

해석 "교수와 학습에서 가장 영향력이 큰 요인은 무엇인가?"라는 질문을 받으면 여러분은 맨 먼저 교실 안의 선진 기술을 떠올릴지도 모른다. 주제문 그러나 교수와 학습 과정에서 시간이 여겨지고 사용되는 방식보다 더 큰 영향은 없다. 우리는 까마득한 옛날처럼 해와 달이 뜨고 지는 것에 의해 형성되는 시대가 아니라, 과학기술과 긴박감이 우리가 하는 모든 일의 속도를 높이는 시대에 살고 있다. 이런 문화적 현실이 우리의 시간을 일정표상의 작은 네모 칸들로 세분화하는 정책과 지령이 딸린 유아 보육 및 교육 프로그램들로 슬그머니 들어간다. 교사들은 마치 조립 라인에 있는 자동차들처럼 낮 시간 내내 아이들을 움직이게 한다. 교사도 아이들도 깊이 생각하고, 궁금해하고, 그날의 활동에서 의미를 만들 시간이 주어지지 않는다. 일부 유아기의 상업적인 교육 과정은 심지어 "이 수업은 여러분의 하루 중 단지 5분밖에 걸리지 않을 것입니다."라고 선언하며 스스로를 광고한다. 여러분은 왜 그것이 좋은 것일지 질문을 해야 한다. 추론 근거 만약 그것이 배우고 여러분의 프로그램에 더할 가치가 있다면, 그것에 더 많은 시간을 들일 만하지 않을까? 실제로 속도를 늦추고 여러분이 착수하고 있는 것에 집중하는 것으로부터 배우는 것은 어떠한가?

어휘 come up with 떠올리다 advanced 선진[고급]의 era 시대, 시기; 연대 eon 영겁, 무궁한 시간 urgency 긴박함, 긴급한 일 slip into ~로 슬그머니 들어가다 mandate 지령, 명령(하다) fragment 세분화하다; 분해하다; 조각, 파편 assembly line (대량 생산의) 조립 라인 afford 제공하다; 여유가 되다 ponder 깊이 생각하다, 숙고하다 commercial 상업적인 curriculum (pl. curricula) 교육 과정 market (상품을) 광고하다[내놓다] proclaim 선언[선포]하다; 증명하다 deserve ~할[받을] 만하다 undertake 착수하다

해설 모든 일에 속도를 높이는 시대이지만, 배울 가치가 있는 일이라면 시간을 오래 들일 만하며, 속도를 늦추고 하고 있는 일에 집중하는 것에서 배울 것을 상기시키고 있으므로 교수와 학습 과정에서 가장 큰 영향으로는 ① '시간이 여겨지고 사용되는 방식'이 가장 적절하다.

오답 Check
② 과정의 내용 구성
→ 일부 어휘(curricula)를 활용한 오답.
③ 주제에 대한 개인적인 동기
→ 글에 언급되지 않음.
④ 적절한 시설을 갖춘 교실
→ 첫 문장의 내용을 활용한 오답.
⑤ 교사가 학생들과 상호 작용하는 방식
→ 언급되지 않은 내용.

PLUS⁺ 변형문제

어휘 discern 알아보다, 식별하다; 이해하다
해설 모든 일에 속도를 높이는 시대에서 배울 가치가 있는 것에는 속도를 늦추고 집중하는 것을 권하는 내용이므로 제목으로는 ③ '교수와 학습에 있어서 너무 서두르지 마라'가 가장 적절하다.
① 빠르게 변화하는 교육에 적응하는 방법
→ 빠르게 변화하는 교육에 적응하는 방법은 언급되지 않음.
② 좋은 교육 과정을 알아보는 능력을 키워라
→ 일부 어휘(curricula)를 활용한 오답.
④ 시간이 걸리는 배움은 할 가치가 없다
⑤ 학습자가 더 빠를수록, 더 잘 이해한다
→ ④, ⑤ 글의 요지와 반대되는 오답.

구문 ¹We live in an era (shaped not by the rising and setting of the sun and moon, / as in eons ago), / but in an era [when technology and a sense of urgency speed up everything [(that) we do]].
• ( )는 바로 앞의 an era를 수식하는 분사구이다.
• 관계부사 when이 이끄는 [ ]는 바로 앞의 an era를 수식하는 관계사절이고, 그 안의 [we do]는 목적격 관계대명사 that이 생략된 관계사절로 선행사는 everything이다.

²Neither the teachers nor the children are afforded time (to ponder, wonder, and make meaning out of the day's activities).
• 「neither A nor B」 구문은 'A도 B도 아닌'의 의미이다.
• ( )는 형용사적 용법의 to부정사구로 time을 수식한다.

Among the monkeys and apes / there is some evidence of abstract thinking. ¹But it is only with man // that artifacts and abstraction have run free. With his weak body, / he has dramatically externalized his behavior, / scattering the surface of the globe with his artifacts — his implements, machines, weapons, vehicles, roads, works of art, buildings, villages and cities. He has become a thinking, building animal, / surrounded by everything [he built]. One might almost suppose // that simple animal action would be beneath him, / surviving only as a remnant (from the past). But this is not so. Throughout it all, / he has remained a creature of action, / a gesturing, posturing, moving, expressive primate. ²He is as far today / from becoming a creation of science fiction // as he was in prehistoric times. Philosophy and engineering have not replaced animal activity, // but they have added to it. ³We have developed a concept of happiness and words (to express it), // but we also still perform the action-pattern (of stretching our lips into a smile). The fact // that we have boats / doesn't stop us from swimming.

해석 원숭이와 유인원 사이에 추상적 사고의 몇몇 증거는 존재한다. 그러나 인공물과 추상적 개념이 마음껏 펼쳐나가는 것은 바로 오직 인간에게서만이다. 허약한 육체를 가지고 그는 지구 표면에 자신의 인공물 즉 자신의 도구, 기계, 무기, 교통수단, 도로, 예술 작품, 건물, 마을과 도시를 퍼뜨려 자신의 행동을 극적으로 외면화했다. 그는 생각하는, 건설하는 동물이 되어, 자신이 만들어 낸 모든 것에 둘러싸이게 되었다. 누군가는 어떤 단순한 동물적 행동이 오직 과거의 잔존물로서만 살아남았기에 자신보다 밑에 있을 거라고 거의 생각할지도 모른다. 그러나 이는 그렇지 않다. **주제문** 역사를 통틀어, 그는 여전히 행동의 동물, 즉 몸짓을 하고, 자세를 잡고, 움직이고, 표현하는 영장류이다. 이전의 선사 시대에서만큼이나 그는 오늘날 공상 과학 소설의 창조물이 되는 것과 거리가 멀다. **추론 근거** 철학과 공학은 동물적 행동을 대체한 것이 아니라 그것에 첨가를 했을 뿐이다. 우리는 행복의 개념과 그것을 표현하는 단어들을 발달시켰지만, 또한 우리는 여전히 우리의 입술을 당겨 미소를 짓는 행동 패턴을 수행한다. 배가 있다는 사실이 우리를 헤엄치지 못하게 막는 것은 아니다.

어휘 ape 유인원 abstract thinking 추상적 사고 artifact 인공물; 가공품 abstraction 추상 개념 run free 마음대로 돌아다니다; 매여[갇혀]있지 않다 externalize 외면화[구체화]하다 scatter (흩)뿌리다; 쫓아버리다 implement 도구, 기구; 시행하다 primate 영장류 prehistoric times 선사 시대
[선택지 어휘] faucet 수도꼭지 reinvent the wheel (이미 있는 것을 다시 만드느라) 쓸데없이 시간을 낭비하다

해설 인간은 추상 능력이 뛰어나고 인공물을 제작하는 데도 능하여 동물적 행동의 영역을 벗어난 것처럼 보일 수 있으나, 어떠한 철학이나 공학도 인간의 동물적 행동을 대체하지 못했고 인간은 여전히 행동의 동물이라는 내용의 글로, ⑤ '배가 있다는 사실이 우리를 헤엄치지 못하게 막는 것은 아니다'라는 말이 글의 주제를 가장 잘 나타낸다. 배는 인간의 추상적 사고와 공학적 능력을, 헤엄치기는 인간의 동물적 행동을 상징한다.

오답 Check
① 홈런을 치기 위해 스윙을 세게 할 필요는 없다
② 수도꼭지를 틀 때까지 물은 흐르지 않는다 (일단 시작하라는 의미)
③ 문 하나가 닫히고 있는 것처럼 보이는 반면에 다른 문이 열리고 있다
④ 세대마다 바퀴를 다시 발명할 필요는 없다 (쓸데없이 시간을 낭비할 필요는 없다는 의미)
→ ① ~ ④ 모두 지문의 내용으로 추론할 수 없는 오답임.

PLUS⁺ 변형문제
어휘 distinct 뚜렷이 다른, 독특한 beyond ~을 넘어서, ~ 이상으로; ~을 지나서
해설 이 글은 인간이 추상 능력과 인공물을 만드는 능력을 발전시켰지만, 인간은 여전히 행동을 하는 영장류임을 말하고 있다. 따라서 제목으로는 ① '우리는 여전히 행동의 동물이다'가 가장 적절하다.
② 인간의 행동을 외면화하는 방법 → 인간이 자신의 인공물을 퍼뜨려 행동을 외면화했다는 내용은 있지만 그 방법이 주제는 아님.
③ 미소: 인간의 독특한 행동 패턴
④ 인공물: 인간 행동의 결과
⑤ 인간이 동물을 훨씬 넘어서도록 만드는 것
→ ③, ④, ⑤ 모두 지문에 언급된 어구를 활용한 오답.

구문 ¹But **it is** *only with man* // **that** artifacts and abstraction have run free.
• 「it is ~ that ...」 강조 구문이 사용되어 only with man이 강조되고 있다.

²He is **as far** today / from becoming a creation of science fiction // **as** he was in prehistoric times.
• 원급 비교 형태인 「as ... as ~ (~만큼 …하다)」 구문으로 '오늘날의 그'와 '선사 시대의 그'를 비교하고 있다.

³We **have developed** <u>a concept of happiness</u> and <u>words</u> (to express it), // but we also still perform *the action-pattern* (of stretching our lips into a smile).
• have developed의 목적어로 밑줄 친 두 부분이 병렬 구조를 이루며, to express it은 words를 수식한다.
• 두 번째 ( )는 전명구로 the action-pattern과 동격 관계이다.

It's tempting to believe // that we can trust the media with our kids, // that we don't need to pay close attention to what movies or TV shows [our kids are watching], / what computer games [they're playing], / or where they're surfing on the Internet. It's much easier to believe // that we can trust the media. ① ¹After all, / we're only adding more work and more worry to our lives // if we admit that we now need to be as wary of the media / as we are of strangers (approaching our children on the street). ② As a result, / many parents are in a state of "media denial," // while others feel overwhelmed and helpless. ③ This means // that social media is sometimes like a wild animal, / and that the range of influences on children's cognitive and social learning has broadened. ④ ²But the fact is, // we need to take as much responsibility for our children's media consumption / as we do for their performance in school and their physical well-being. ⑤ If we're worried about what our kids eat, // then we should certainly be worried about what our kids are watching.

해석 우리가 미디어에 우리 아이들을 믿고 맡길 수 있다고, 우리 아이들이 어떤 영화나 TV 프로그램을 보고 있는지, 어떤 컴퓨터 게임을 하고 있는지, 또는 인터넷상에서 어디를 검색하고 있는지 주의 깊게 관심을 가질 필요가 없다고 믿는 것은 매력적이다. 미디어를 믿을 수 있다고 생각하는 것이 훨씬 더 편하다. ① 결국, 우리가 거리에서 우리 아이들에게 접근하는 낯선 사람들을 조심하는 것만큼이나 이제는 미디어도 조심해야 할 필요가 있다는 사실을 인정하면 우리 삶에 더 많은 부담과 더 많은 걱정을 더하고 있는 것일 뿐이다. ② 그 결과 많은 부모가 '미디어 부정' 상태에 있는 한편, 다른 부모들은 어찌할 줄 몰라 무력감을 느낀다. ③ 이것은 소셜 미디어가 때로는 야생 동물과 같으며, 어린이들의 인지적, 사회적 학습에 미치는 영향의 범위가 넓어졌음을 의미한다. ④ ^{주제문} 하지만 사실은, 우리가 우리 아이들의 학교 성적과 신체적 건강에 대해 책임을 지는 것만큼 우리는 우리 아이들의 미디어 소비에 대해서도 책임감을 가질 필요가 있다. ⑤ 우리가 우리 아이들이 무엇을 먹는지에 대해 걱정한다면, 그렇다면 우리는 우리 아이들이 무엇을 보고 있는지에 대해 당연히 걱정해야 한다.

어휘 tempting 매력적인, 솔깃한; 유혹하는 trust A with B A에게 B를 맡기다 admit 인정하다 state 상태; 국가; 말하다, 진술하다; 명시하다 denial 부정, 부인 overwhelm 어찌할 줄 모르게 하다; 압도하다 helpless 무력한 cognitive 인지의 broaden 넓어지다; 확장하다 take responsibility for ~에 책임을 지다

해설 미디어를 믿고 어린이의 미디어 소비에 대해 간섭하지 않는 것이 편하겠지만, 우리가 어린이들이 누려야 할 건강한 환경에 대해 염려하는 것과 동일한 자세로 어린이의 미디어 소비 문제를 진지하게 다루어야 한다는 내용의 글인데, ③은 앞에서 언급된 바가 없는 소셜 미디어를 논하고 있고, 아동 학습에 대한 소셜 미디어의 영향력이 확장되고 있다는 내용으로 어린이의 미디어 소비를 주의 깊게 지켜봐야 한다는 글의 논지에서 벗어난다.

PLUS+ 변형문제

해설 부모는 아이들이 무엇을 보는지 자녀가 접하는 미디어에 책임을 져야 한다고 했으므로 필자의 주장으로 가장 적절한 것은 ②이다.
① → 신뢰 관계 구축에 관한 내용은 없음.
③ → 자녀의 미디어 노출 시간이 아닌 미디어에서 보는 내용에 관한 내용임.
④ → 글에 언급되지 않은 내용.
⑤ → 소셜 미디어 이용에 관한 내용이 아님.

구문 ¹After all, / we're only **adding** more work and more worry **to** our lives // if we admit that we now need to *be* **as** wary of the media / **as** we <u>are</u> of *strangers* (approaching our children on the street).
• 「add A to B」는 'A를 B에 더하다, 첨가하다'의 뜻이다.
• 「as ... as ~」의 원급 비교 표현은 '~만큼 …하다'를 의미한다. as we are에서 밑줄 친 are는 앞의 동사 be에 대응되는 대동사이고, are 다음에 wary가 생략된 것으로 볼 수 있다.
• ( )는 strangers를 수식하는 분사구이다.

²But the fact is, // we need to take **as** much responsibility for our children's media consumption / **as** we <u>do</u> for their performance in school and their physical well-being.
• 원급 비교 형태인 「as ... as ~ (~만큼 …하다)」 구문이 쓰였으며, as we do에서 밑줄 친 do는 take responsibility를 지칭하는 대동사이다.

Beech trees and oak trees register pain // as soon as some creature starts nibbling on them. ¹When a caterpillar takes a hearty bite out of a leaf, // the tissue (around the site of the damage) changes.

(C) In addition, / it sends out electrical signals, // just as human tissue does // when it is hurt. ²However, the signal is not transmitted in milliseconds, // as human signals are; // instead, the plant signal travels / at the slow speed of a third of an inch per minute.

(B) Accordingly, it takes an hour or so // before defensive compounds reach the leaves to spoil the pest's meal. Trees live their lives in the really slow lane, // even when they are in danger. But this slow tempo doesn't mean // that a tree is not on top of // what is happening in different parts (of its structure).

(A) ³If the roots find themselves in trouble, // this information is broadcast throughout the tree, // which can trigger the leaves to release scent compounds. ⁴And those are not just any old scent compounds, / but ones [that are specifically formulated for the task at hand].

[해석] 너도밤나무와 떡갈나무는 어떤 생물이 그것을 조금씩 갉아먹기 시작하자마자 고통을 나타낸다. 애벌레가 잎사귀를 식욕 왕성하게 한 입 베어 물면, 손상된 부위 주변의 조직이 변한다.
(C) 게다가, 인체 조직이 다칠 때 꼭 그러하듯이 그것은 전기 신호를 보낸다. 그러나 그 신호는 인간의 신호가 그러한 것처럼 1,000분의 1초로 전송되지 않는다. 대신에 식물 신호는 분당 3분의 1인치의 느린 속도로 이동한다.
(B) 따라서, 방어용 화합물이 잎에 도착해서 해충의 식사를 망치기까지 한 시간 정도가 걸린다. 나무들이 위험에 처했을 때조차도 나무들은 정말로 서행 차선에서 일생을 보낸다. 주제문 그러나 이 느린 속도가 그 조직의 다른 부분에서 일어나고 있는 일을 잘 처리하지 않는다는 뜻은 아니다.
(A) 뿌리가 곤경에 빠지면, 이 정보가 나무 전체에 퍼지고, 그것은 잎이 향기 화합물을 방출하도록 자극할 수 있다. 그리고 그것들은 단지 어떤 오래된 향기 화합물이 아니라, 당면한 과제를 위해 특별히 처방된 것이다.

[어휘] register (감정을) 나타내다; 등록하다; 기록하다   nibble 조금씩 갉아먹다   take a bite 한 입 베어 물다   hearty (식사나 식욕이) 왕성한; (마음이) 따뜻한   tissue 조직   transmit 전송[전도]하다   millisecond 1,000분의 1초   compound 화합물, 혼합물   spoil 망치다; 상하게 하다   tempo 속도; 리듬   on top of ~을 잘 처리하여   broadcast (소문 등을) 퍼뜨리다; 방송하다   scent 향기; 냄새를 맡다; 감지하다   specifically 특별히; 명확하게   formulate 처방하다; 공식화하다

[해설] 주어진 글을 먼저 읽고, 각 단락에서 글의 흐름을 알려주는 근거가 되는 표현을 찾는다. 연결어나 지시어가 중요한 단서가 된다. 나무가 고통을 느낄 때, 조직이 변한다는 주어진 글 다음에는 연결어 In addition으로 이어지는 인체 조직과 같이 전기 신호를 보낸다는 (C)가 와야 하고, (C)의 마지막 부분에 언급된 나무 전기 신호의 느린 속도에 계속 이어지는 내용인 (B)가 온다. 마지막으로 (B)의 나무가 처리 속도가 느리다고 해서 일을 잘 처리하지 않는 것이 아니라는 내용 다음에는 그 예시를 언급한 (A)가 오는 것이 자연스럽다.

[오답 Check]
(A)에는 어떠한 연결사나 지시어가 등장하진 않지만, 뿌리가 곤경에 빠졌을 때 나무가 잘 처리하는 내용을 설명하므로 (B)의 마지막 문장(나무가 일을 잘 처리한다는 내용)의 예시가 됨을 파악해야 한다.

PLUS+ 변형문제
[해설] 글의 주제문으로 보아, 요지로는 ①이 가장 적절하다.
② → 너도밤나무와 떡갈나무가 예시로 언급되었지만, 그 나무들에만 국한된 설명은 아님.
③ → 고통의 정도와 방어 속도의 연관성은 언급되지 않음.
④ → 향기 화합물을 방출한다는 언급은 있지만, 전체 내용을 포괄하는 요지는 아님.
⑤ → 인간의 신호보다 느린 속도는 언급되었지만, 신호의 강도에 관한 언급은 없음.

[구문] ¹When a caterpillar takes a hearty bite out of a leaf, // the tissue (around the site of the damage) changes.
 S   V
• ( )는 형용사 역할을 하는 전명구로 주절의 주어 the tissue를 수식하고, 동사는 changes이다.

²However, the signal is not *transmitted in milliseconds*, // **as** human signals are (transmitted in milliseconds); ~.
• as는 양태를 나타내는 부사절 접속사로 '~인 것처럼'의 의미이며 부사절 내 동사 are 다음에는 반복되는 transmitted in milliseconds가 생략되었다.

³If the roots find themselves in trouble, // *this information is broadcast throughout the tree*, // **which** can trigger the leaves to release scent compounds.
• 계속적 관계대명사 which는 앞 문장을 보충 설명하는 관계사절을 이끈다.

⁴And those are **not** just any old scent compounds, **but** *ones* [that are specifically formulated for the task at hand].
• 「not A but B」는 'A가 아니고 B'를 의미한다.
• [ ]는 주격 관계대명사 that이 이끄는 관계사절로 선행사 ones를 수식하며, 여기서 ones는 scent compounds를 의미한다.

As Charles Darwin points out, // species diversity can increase the productivity of ecosystems due to the division of labour among species, // because each species is unique in how it exploits its environment.

(B) It thus follows // that species-rich systems can exploit resources more efficiently than species-poor systems. [1]Diversity is also thought / to make ecosystems, species and populations more resilient to environmental stresses.

(A) A large number of species may imply a certain level of functional redundancy: // the loss of one species has a smaller effect in a diverse system / than in a species-poor one. Diversity (within one population of the same species) may also improve resistance to environmental change.

(C) [2]For example, it is well documented // that the diversity (of a population) can increase its resistance to epidemics. [3]Diversity could also favor the emergence of complex collective behaviors, / as demonstrated by the cooperative behavior in army ants, // which self-assemble to form bridges and even nests / out of their own bodies.

해석 찰스 다윈이 지적하듯이 종의 다양성은, 각각의 종들이 그 환경을 이용하는 방식에서 독특하기 때문에 종 간의 노동 분업으로 인해 생태계의 생산성을 높일 수 있다.
(B) 따라서 종이 풍부한 계통은 종이 빈약한 계통보다 더 효과적으로 자원을 이용할 수 있다. 다양성은 또한 생태계, 종, 그리고 개체군을 환경적 스트레스에 더 회복력 있게 만드는 것으로 여겨진다.
(A) 많은 수의 종들은 일정한 수준의 기능적 중복을 포함할 수도 있는데, 한 종의 손실은 종이 빈약한 계통에서보다 다양한 계통에서 더 적은 영향을 미친다. 같은 종의 한 개체군 내의 다양성 역시 환경적 변화에 대한 저항력을 향상시킬 수도 있다.
(C) 예를 들어, 한 개체군의 다양성이 전염병에 대한 저항력을 증진시킬 수 있다는 것은 관련 증거가 많다. 또한 다양성은 병정개미의 협동적인 행동에 의해 입증된 것처럼 복잡한 집단행동의 출현을 뒷받침할 수 있는데, 그것들은 그것들 자신의 몸으로 다리나 심지어는 보금자리를 만들어 내기 위해 스스로 모인다.

어휘 diversity 다양성 cf. diverse 다양한 productivity 생산성 ecosystem 생태계 division 분업 labo(u)r 노동(을 하다); 애를 쓰다 exploit 이용[활용]하다; 개발하다 resilient 회복력 있는, 탄력적인 imply 포함[수반]하다; 의미하다 redundancy (불필요한) 중복[반복] resistance 저항(력) well documented (문서로 된) 관련 증거가 많은 epidemic 전염병; 유행(성) favor 지지하다, 돕다; 호의를 보이다, 찬성하다 emergence 출현, 발생 collective 집단의, 단체의 demonstrate 입증하다; 설명하다, 보여주다 assemble 모이다; 조립하다

해설 종의 다양성의 장점에 대해 소개하는 글로 종의 다양성이 생산성을 높일 수 있다는 주어진 글 다음에는 그러므로 종이 풍부한 계통이 더 효과적으로 자원을 이용할 수 있다는 (B)가 오는 것이 자연스럽다. 또한 다양성이 환경적 스트레스 회복력에 도움을 준다는 (B) 다음에는 그 내용을 상술하는 (A)가 와야 하고, 이어서 전염병에 대한 저항력 증진에 대한 예로 이어지는 (C)가 오는 것이 적절하다.

오답 Check
(C)에 나오는 예는 (A) 마지막에 언급된 '한 개체군 내의 다양성이 환경적 변화에 대한 저항력을 향상시키는' 내용에 해당하는 예임에 유의한다.

PLUS + 변형문제
해설 종의 다양성의 여러 이점을 소개하는 글이므로 요지로는 ④가 적절하다.
① → 글의 일부 내용에만 해당하는 내용임.
② → 반대로 종 다양성이 노동의 분업을 촉진함.
③ → 글의 일부 내용에만 해당하는 내용임.
⑤ → 글의 내용과 반대되는 내용임.

구문 [1]Diversity is also thought / **to make** *ecosystems, species and populations* **more resilient to environmental stresses**.
• to make의 목적어로 ecosystems, species and populations가, 목적격보어로 more resilient to environmental stresses가 쓰인 구조이다.

[2]For example, **it** is well documented // **that** the diversity (of a population) can increase its resistance to epidemics.
• it은 가주어, that 이하가 진주어이다.

[3]Diversity could also favor the emergence of *complex collective behaviors*, / **as (they are) demonstrated by the cooperative behavior in *army ants***, // **which** self-assemble to form bridges and even nests / out of their own bodies.
• as 뒤에 'they(= complex collective behaviors) are'가 생략되어 있으며, 여기서 as는 '~처럼'의 의미이다.
• which는 계속적 용법의 관계대명사로 which가 이끄는 절이 army ants를 보충 설명한다.

주제문
To economists, the benefits of both exports and imports are so obvious // that it's one of the few things [this notoriously fractious profession agrees on]. (①) Yet, in recent years, trade has changed radically, / rattling even normally faithful supporters. (②) ¹Traditionally, Americans bought toys, clothing, and other things / from poor countries [that required more manual and less intellectual labor]. (③) They bought more advanced products (like aircraft, software, and microprocessor chips) / from other rich countries. (④ ²But in recent decades, / China, India, and Russia have joined the global workforce / and now sell the sorts of advanced products [(Americans long thought) were invulnerable to such competition].) ³The decrease (in the cost of using huge quantities of data across undersea cables (in other countries)) makes it possible / for foreigners to read Americans' X-rays, take their hotel reservations, or report on town council meetings. (⑤) Alan Blinder, a former vice-chairman of the Federal Reserve Board, has estimated // that perhaps a quarter of U.S. jobs can now be done abroad.

해석 주제문 경제학자들에게. 수출과 수입의 이익은 이 악명 높게 까다로운 직업이 동의하는 몇 안 되는 것의 하나일 정도로 너무나 명백하다. 그러나 최근 몇 년간, 무역이 급격하게 변화해서, 평소에는 충실한 지지자들조차도 당황시키고 있다. 전통적으로 미국인들은 가난한 나라로부터 수작업을 더 많이 필요로 하고 지적 노동력은 덜 필요로 하는 장난감과 의류, 그리고 다른 것들을 구입했다. 그들은 항공기, 소프트웨어, 마이크로프로세서 칩 같은 더 선진 제품은 다른 부유한 나라에서 구입했다. 그러나 최근 수십 년간, 중국, 인도와 러시아가 세계 노동 인구에 합류했고 이제 미국인들이 오랫동안 그런 경쟁에서 난공불락이라고 생각했던 종류의 선진 제품들을 판매한다. 다른 나라들에서 해저 케이블을 통해 거대한 양의 데이터를 사용하는 비용의 감소는 외국인들로 하여금 미국인들의 엑스레이를 판독하거나 그들의 호텔 예약을 받거나 시의회의 회의에 대해 보도하는 것을 가능하게 한다. 전 연방 준비 제도 이사회의 부의장인 Alan Blinder는 아마도 미국 일자리의 4분의 1이 이제 외국에서 있을 수 있다고 추정했다.

어휘 notoriously 악명 높게 fractious 까다로운; 다루기 힘든 profession 직업 radically 급격하게; 근본적으로 rattle 당황하게 하다; 덜걱[대그락]거리게 하다 faithful 충실한; 신뢰할 만한 manual 수공의; 설명서 workforce 노동 인구; 전 종업원 invulnerable 난공불락의; 물리칠 수 없는 vice-chairman 부의장 ◦Federal Reserve Board 연방 준비 제도 이사회
어휘◦ 연방 준비 제도 이사회: 미국의 중앙은행인 연방 준비 제도(Fed)의 핵심 기관으로 신용상태의 규제와 연방 준비 은행에 대한 감독이 주요 임무임.

해설 주어진 글은 중국, 인도 등에서 이제 선진 제품을 판다는 내용이다. 도입에서 무역의 급격한 변화에 대해 언급한 후 ②와 ③ 뒤의 문장에서 이전에는 수작업 제품은 가난한 나라에서, 선진 제품은 부유한 나라에서 구입했다고 했으므로 최근의 변화에 대해 설명한 주어진 문장은 ④에 들어가는 것이 적절하다.

오답 Check
④ 다음에 나오는 문장은 변화에 대한 보충 설명이므로 주어진 문장 뒤에 나와야 한다. ⑤ 다음에 나오는 문장 역시 그 결과로 선진 제품을 만들던 미국의 일자리도 영향을 받는다는 것이다.

PLUS + 변형문제

어휘 breakthrough 획기적인 발전; 돌파 monopoly 독점; 전유물 commodity 상품
해설 최근 무역의 결과로 중국, 인도, 러시아가 세계 노동 인구에 합류했고 선진 제품들을 판매하기 시작했으며 다른 나라에서 해저 케이블을 통해 데이터를 사용하는 비용도 감소했다. 이로 인해 미국 일자리도 좋지 않은 영향을 받는다는 내용이므로 글의 제목으로는 ② '국제 무역에서의 변화가 어떻게 미국 경제에 피해를 주는가'가 가장 적절하다.
① 세계 무역의 경향과 가까운 미래에 대한 전망
→ 세계 무역이 최근에 어떻게 변화했는지 그 경향은 언급하지만 앞으로의 전망은 언급하지 않음.
③ 선진 기술의 전파: 국제적인 유행 → 선진 기술의 비용이 감소해 그것의 이용이 가능한 건 맞지만, 글의 일부 내용일 뿐임.
④ 경쟁에서 획기적인 발전: 전통적 사고 없애기 → 과거와 최근의 무역 경향을 대조시키지만, 전통적 사고를 없애라는 언급은 없음.
⑤ 선진국의 지성을 필요로 하는 상품의 독점
→ 과거에는 지성을 필요로 하는 선진 제품을 부유한 나라로부터 구입했지만, 최근에는 그렇지 않다고 언급함.

05

구문 ¹Traditionally, Americans bought *toys, clothing, and other things* / *from poor countries* [**that** required more manual and less intellectual labor].
• [ ]는 주격 관계대명사 that이 이끄는 관계사절로 앞에 나온 명사 toys, ~ poor countries를 수식한다.

²But in recent decades, / China, India, and Russia have joined the global workforce / and now sell *the sorts of advanced products* [(which[that]) (Americans long thought) were invulnerable to such competition].
• [ ]는 the sorts of advanced products를 수식하는 관계사절로 주격 관계대명사 which 또는 that이 생략된 형태이다. 주격 관계대명사는 바로 뒤에 「S+V」 형태의 삽입절(Americans long thought)이 나올 때 흔히 생략된다.

³The decrease (in the cost of using huge quantities of data across undersea cables (in other countries)) **makes** *it* **possible** / *for foreigners* **to read** Americans' X-rays, (to) **take** their hotel reservations, **or** (to) **report** on town council meetings.
• 「make+O+C」의 구조로 가목적어 it이 목적어로, possible은 목적격보어로 쓰였다.
• for foreigners는 진목적어인 to부정사의 의미상 주어이며, 세 개의 밑줄 친 진목적어가 콤마(,)와 or로 병렬 연결되는데, take와 report 앞에 반복되는 to는 생략되었다.

"What's in a name? That [which we call a rose], by any other name would smell as sweet." This thought (of Shakespeare's) points up a difference (between roses and, say, paintings). Natural objects, such as roses, / are not interpreted. (①) They are not taken as vehicles of meanings and messages. (②) [1]They belong to no tradition, strictly speaking have no style, / and are not understood within a framework (of culture and convention). (③) Rather, they are sensed and savored relatively directly, / without intellectual mediation, // and so what they are called, either individually or collectively, / has little bearing on our experience of them. (④) [2]What a work of art is titled, on the other hand, / has a significant effect on the aesthetic face [it presents] and on the qualities [we correctly perceive in it]. (⑤ A painting of a rose, by a name other than the one [it has], / might very well smell different, aesthetically speaking.) The painting (titled *Rose of Summer*) and an indiscernible painting (titled *Vermillion Womanhood*) are physically, but also semantically and aesthetically, distinct objects of art.

해석 "이름에는 무엇이 있는가? 우리가 장미라고 부르는 것은 다른 어떤 이름으로 부른다 해도 똑같이 달콤한 향기가 날 것이다." 셰익스피어의 이 생각은 장미와 이를테면 그림의 차이를 강조한다. 장미와 같은 자연물은 해석되지 않는다. 그것들은 의미와 메시지의 매개체로 받아들여지지 않는다. 그것들은 어떤 전통에도 속하지 않고, 엄밀히 말하면 양식이 없으며, 문화와 관습의 틀 안에서 이해되지 않는다. 오히려 그것들은 지적인 매개 없이 비교적 직접적으로 감지되고 음미되며, 따라서 그것들이 개별적으로나 집합적으로나 뭐라고 불리는지는 그것들에 대한 우리의 경험에 영향을 거의 미치지 않는다. 반면에 미술 작품에 무슨 제목이 붙는지는 그것이 제시하는 미적 측면과 그 속에서 우리가 올바르게 인지하는 특징에 상당한 영향을 미친다. 장미 한 송이의 그림은, 그것이 가지고 있는 이름과 다른 이름으로 불리면, 미학적으로 말해서 너무나 당연히도 다른 향이 날 것이다. '여름의 장미'라는 제목의 그림과 'Vermillion의 여자들'이라는 제목의 분간하기 어려운 그림은 물리적으로, 또한 의미적으로도 미적으로도 별개의 미술품이다.

어휘 interpret 해석하다; 이해하다; 통역하다 vehicle 수단, 매개체 convention 관습, 관례 intellectual 지적인 mediation 중재, 매개 bearing 영향, 관련 aesthetic 미(학)적인 *cf.* aesthetically 미학적으로 other than ~ 외에 might well ~하는 것도 당연한 일이다 indiscernible 분간하기 어려운 distinct 별개의; 독특한

해설 자연물과 예술품을 대조하는 글로, 장미와 같은 자연물에는 어떤 이름이 붙든 그 꽃을 대하는 인간의 경험에 영향을 미치는 바가 거의 없다는 내용이 ④ 이전까지 전개된다. on the other hand를 포함한 ④ 이후 문장부터는 예술품의 제목이 인지에 미치는 영향을 논하고 있는데, 주어진 문장은 장미 그림의 제목에 따라 그것을 감상하는 인간의 경험도 달라진다는 내용이므로 반드시 ④ 이후에 위치해야 하기 때문에 정답은 ⑤이다.

오답 Check ①, ②, ③ 뒤의 문장은 모두 they로 시작하는데 주어진 문장에는 이를 나타내는 복수명사가 없으므로 ④ 또는 ⑤에 위치해야 함을 알 수 있다. ④ 뒤의 역접 연결어 on the other hand를 포함한 문장에서 미술 작품의 제목이 그것이 제시하는 미적 측면과 우리가 인지하는 특징에 상당한 영향을 미친다고 했으므로, 그에 대한 구체적인 예를 제시하는 주어진 문장은 그 이후에 들어가는 것이 적절하다.

PLUS + 변형문제

해설 자연물은 그 어떤 다른 이름으로 부른다고 해도 본질적으로 똑같을 테지만, 미술 작품은 제목이 다르면 그에 따라 인식도 달라진다는 내용이므로, 글의 주제로는 ⑤ '예술품과 자연물을 이해하는 데 이름의 영향'이 적절하다.

① 예술 작품을 직관적으로 감상하는 방법들
→ 예술 작품을 감상하는 방법에 관한 내용은 없음.

② 사물의 본질을 파악하는 것의 중요성
→ 본질을 파악하라는 내용은 없음.

③ 그림이 자연물을 따라가지 못하는 이유들
→ 그림이 자연물보다 뒤처진다는 내용은 언급되지 않음.

④ 해석과 의도에 대한 일반적인 오해
→ 일부 어휘(interpret)를 활용한 오답.

구문 [1]They belong to no tradition, strictly speaking have no style, and are not understood within a framework (of culture and convention).
• 밑줄 친 세 개의 동사구가 콤마(,)와 and로 연결되어 병렬 구조를 이룬다.

[2]**What a work of art is titled**, on the other hand, / **has a significant effect** on *the aesthetic face* [(which[that]) it presents] and on *the qualities* [(which[that]) we correctly perceive in it].
• What a work of art is titled는 의문대명사 what이 이끄는 명사절로 문장에서 주어 역할을 한다.
• has a significant effect 다음에 on으로 시작하는 두 밑줄 부분이 병렬 구조를 이룬다. 두 개의 [ ] 앞에는 모두 목적격 관계대명사 which[that]가 생략되어 각각 the aesthetic face와 the qualities를 수식한다.

[1]What a woman might see as a simple request — no big deal — / is seen by a man an attempt (to manipulate him into a "one-down" position). These traits can lead women and men / to starkly different views (of the same situation). Here is an example. When John's old high school friend called him at work / to say he'd be in town, // John invited him to stay for the weekend. That evening / he told Linda they were having a house guest. Linda was upset. How could John make these plans / without discussing them with her beforehand? She would never do that to him. "Why don't you tell your friend // you have to check with your wife?" she asked. John replied, "I can't tell my friend, 'I have to ask my wife for permission'!" To John, checking with his wife would mean // he was not free to act on his own. It would make him feel like a child or an underling. But Linda actually enjoys telling someone, // "I have to check with John." [2]It makes her feel good / to show // that her life is intertwined with her husband's.

↓

Since women often think in terms of consensus, they struggle to preserve (A) intimacy, when men, concerned with status, focus on (B) independence.

해석 한 여자가 대수롭지 않은 단순한 요청이라고 볼 수 있는 것이 한 남자에게는 그를 '한 단계 낮은' 위치로 조종하려는 시도로 보인다. 이러한 특징들은 여성과 남성들로 하여금 같은 상황에 대해 전혀 다른 견해를 가져오게 할 수 있다. 여기 한 예시가 있다. John의 오랜 고등 학교 친구가 자기가 시내에 있을 것이라고 말하려고 직장에 있는 그에게 전화를 걸자, John은 주말 동안 머물라고 그를 초대했다. 그날 저녁 그는 Linda에게 집에 묵고 갈 손님이 있다고 말했다. Linda는 화가 났다. 어떻게 John은 그녀와 미리 상의하지 않고 이런 계획들을 세울 수 있었을까? 그녀는 그에게 절대 그렇게 하지 않았을 것이다. "당신 친구에게 아내에게 물어봐야 한다고 말하는 게 어때요?"라고 그녀가 물었다. John은 "나는 내 친구에게 '아내에게 허락을 구해야 해.'라고 말할 수 없어요!"라고 대답했다. John에게 있어서, 아내에게 물어본다는 것은 그가 단독으로 행동할 자유가 없다는 것을 의미했을 것이다. 그것은 그를 어린아이나 아랫사람 같이 느끼게 할 것이었다. 하지만 Linda는 사실 누군가에게 "John한테 물어봐야 해요."라고 말하는 것을 즐긴다. 그녀의 삶이 남편의 삶과 밀접하게 관련되어있다는 것을 보여주는 것이 그녀의 기분을 좋게 한다.

↓

여성은 종종 합의의 관점에서 생각하기 때문에 (A) 친밀[밀접]함을 유지하기 위해 열심히 노력하고, 남성은 지위에 신경을 써서 (B) 독립에 초점을 맞춘다.

어휘 request 요청(하다) attempt 시도(하다) manipulate 조종[조작]하다 starkly 전혀, 완전히 house guest 묵을[자고 갈] 손님 permission 허락, 허가 underling 아랫사람, 부하 intertwine 밀접하게 관련되다 consensus 합의, 의견 일치 intimacy 친밀감 status 지위; 상태 [선택지 어휘] dignity 품위; 존엄(성) confirmation 확인; 확증; 확정 courtesy 예의 (바름); 공손함 mutuality 상호 관계; 상호 의존

해설 요약문을 통해, 여성이 '무엇'을 유지하려고 하고, 남성은 '무엇'에 더 초점을 맞추는지 찾아야 한다. 본문의 예에서 볼 수 있듯이 여성은 자신과 남편의 삶이 밀접하게 관련되어 있음을 보여주는 것을 즐기고 남성은 단독으로 행동할 자유를 중요하게 생각한다. 그러므로 빈칸에는 ③ '(A) 친밀[밀접]함 – (B) 독립'이 적절하다.

오답 Check

	(A)	(B)
①	권리	– 품위

→ (B)는 맞지만, (A)는 틀림.

② 친근함 – 확인

→ (A)는 맞지만, (B)는 틀림.

④ 예의 – 통제

→ (A), (B) 모두 틀림.

⑤ 상호 관계 – 경쟁

→ (A)는 답이 될 수 있지만 (B)는 틀림.

구문 [1]What a woman might see as a simple request — no big deal — / is seen by a man *an attempt* (to manipulate him into a "one-down" position).
• 밑줄 친 부분은 선행사를 포함하는 관계대명사 what이 이끄는 명사절로 문장의 주어 역할을 한다.
• ( )는 형용사 역할을 하는 to부정사구로 앞의 명사 an attempt를 수식한다.

[2]**It** makes her *feel* good / **to show** // that her life is intertwined with her husband's.
• it은 가주어이고, to show 이하가 진주어이다.
• 밑줄 친 부분은 「make+O+C」 구조로 동사 makes의 목적격보어로 원형부정사(feel)가 쓰였다.

Faces are an unusual class of patterns // because they all share the same basic structure of two eyes, a nose and a mouth. Yet despite the (a) similarity, / the average human can recognize thousands of separate faces. Our love of faces begins very early. Infants have built-in brain circuitry for following faces. Even though their vision is bad enough to qualify them as legally blind, // faces are like (b) magnets to young babies. They can hardly take their eyes off a human face // even if it is just a rudimentary pattern (made up of two dots for eyes and a third for a mouth). This initial preference for face-like patterns / is quickly replaced by a system [that learns to recognize specific faces]. By six months, if you show infants a face [they have never seen before], // they easily remember it much later. They are learning who's who.

Early face experience also (c) shapes human brains. For example, children (born with cataracts) never see faces clearly as infants. When their vision is surgically corrected later in life, // they still have problems (with recognizing faces) // even though they can then see clearly. No matter how much training and practice you have later in life, // some early exposures are important / for affecting brain development. The same goes for telling the difference (between individuals from another race). Unlike most adults [who think members of other ethnic groups look very similar], babies initially have no problem. They can tell everyone apart. ¹It is only after exposure to lots of faces (from the same race) // that our (d) discrimination kicks in. ²However, you can train babies / not to become tuned into their own race // if you keep exposing them to faces (from other races). So the next time you think that other races all look alike, // don't worry, it isn't racism — it's your (e) excess of brain flexibility.

해석 얼굴은 모두 두 개의 눈과 하나의 코, 그리고 하나의 입이라는 동일한 기본 구조를 공유하기 때문에 특이한 종류의 형태이다. 그러나 (a) 유사함에도 불구하고, 보통의 인간은 수천 개의 개별적인 얼굴을 알아볼 수 있다. 우리의 얼굴 사랑은 아주 어릴 적에 시작된다. 유아는 얼굴을 따라가기 위한 내장된 뇌 회로를 가지고 있다. 그들의 시력이 법률적으로 시각 장애인으로 간주할 만큼 나쁘지만, 얼굴은 어린 아기들에게 (b) 자석과도 같다. 비록 그것이 단지 눈을 나타내는 두 개의 점과 입을 나타내는 세 번째 점으로 이루어진 기본적인 형태일지라도 그들은 사람의 얼굴에서 거의 눈을 뗄 수가 없다. 얼굴과 같은 형태에 대한 이런 초기의 선호는 곧 특정한 얼굴을 인식하도록 배우는 체계로 빠르게 대체된다. 여러분이 6개월까지 유아에게 그들이 전에 본 적이 없는 얼굴을 보여준다면, 그들은 훨씬 뒤에 그것을 쉽게 기억한다. 그들은 누가 누구인지를 배우고 있다.

초기의 얼굴 경험은 또한 인간의 뇌를 (c) 형성한다. 예를 들어, 백내장을 가지고 태어난 아이들은 유아일 때 얼굴을 명확하게 보지 못한다. 그들의 시력이 후년에 수술로 교정될 때, 그들이 그때에는 명확하게 볼 수 있음에도 불구하고 그들은 여전히 얼굴을 알아보는 데 문제가 있다. 후년에 아무리 많은 훈련과 연습을 하더라도, 어느 정도의 초기 노출은 뇌 발달에 영향을 주는 데 중요하다. 다른 인종의 개인들 사이의 차이를 구분하는 것도 마찬가지이다. 다른 인종 집단의 구성원들이 아주 비슷하게 보인다고 생각하는 대부분의 성인들과 달리, 아기들은 처음에 아무런 문제가 없다. 그들은 모두를 구별할 수 있다. 같은 인종의 많은 얼굴들에 노출된 후에야 비로소 (d) 차별이 시작된다. 그러나, 여러분이 아기들을 다른 인종의 얼굴에 계속 노출시킨다면 여러분은 아기들을 그들 자신의 인종으로 동화되지 않도록 훈련시킬 수 있다. 그러므로 다음번에

어휘 brain circuitry 뇌 회로 qualify A as B A를 B로 간주하다[칭하다] rudimentary 기본적인; 초보의 initial 초기의 infant 유아 surgically 외과 수술에 의해; 외과적으로 ethnic 인종의; 민족의 tell apart 분간하다 discrimination 편견; 차별 racism 인종 차별(주의); 민족 우월 의식 flexibility 유연성; 탄력성

해설 41 주제문이 여러 보충 설명에 의해 구체적으로 설명되고 있는 가장 포괄적 내용인 경우다. 제목 유형은 글의 핵심을 나타내면서도 압축적이고 상징적인 다양한 형태로 표현될 수 있음에 유의한다. 유아가 초기에 얼굴을 보는 것이 인간 뇌를 형성해서 후년에 얼굴을 알아보는 데 영향을 준다는 내용이므로 제목으로는 ③ '얼굴 인식에 대한 초기 경험의 역할'이 적절하다.

42 다른 인종의 얼굴을 구분하지 못하는 것은 같은 인종의 많은 얼굴에 노출된 후에 다른 인종의 얼굴에는 많이 노출되지 않았기 때문이므로 뇌 유연성의 excess(과다)가 아니라 lack(결핍)이 되어야 한다.

오답 Check

41 ① 어떻게 유아들은 얼굴 표정에서 배우는가
→ 얼굴 표정에 관해 언급하지 않음.

② 초기 경험이 성격에 미치는 영향
→ 초기 경험과 성격의 관계는 언급되지 않음.

④ 유아의 얼굴 처리(과정)에서 개인별 차이
→ 개인별 차이에 대해서는 다루지 않음.

⑤ 유아의 뇌 발달과 얼굴의 패턴
→ 뇌 발달은 맞지만, 얼굴의 패턴은 일부 내용일 뿐임.

42 (d)의 앞 내용은 아이들이 처음에는 다른 인종들의 구성원을 구별하는 데 문제가 없었다는 것으로, 문맥상 같은 인종의 많은 얼굴에 노출된 후에는 다른 인종의 구성원들을 똑같이 생겼다고 생각하게 되므로 이를 '차별'로 표현한 것은 적절하다. 또한 (e) 앞에서 '차별'을 'racism(인종 차별)'이 아니라고 다시 언급한다.

다른 인종이 모두 비슷하게 보인다고 생각할 때에 걱정하지 마라. 그것은 인종 차별이 아니라 여러분의 뇌 유연성의 (e) 과다(→ 결핍)이다.

구문 [1]**It is** *only after exposure to lots of faces (from the same race)* // **that** our discrimination kicks in.
- 「It is ~ that ...」 강조 구문으로 only after ~ same race를 강조한다.

[2]However, you can **train** *babies* / **not to become tuned into their own race** // if you keep **exposing** them **to** *faces* (from other races).
- 「train+O+C」의 구조로 train은 to부정사를 목적격보어로 취하며, to부정사의 부정형인 not to로 쓴 것에 유의한다.
- 'A를 B에 노출시키다'라는 의미의 「expose A to B」는 keep의 목적어인 동명사 형태로 쓰였고, (   )는 faces를 수식한다.

05

| 31 ⑤ + ④ | 32 ① + ① | 33 ③ + ① | 34 ③ + ④ | 35 ③ + ⑤ | 36 ④ + ④ |
| 37 ② + ③ | 38 ③ + ③ | 39 ⑤ + ④ | 40 ② | 41 ④ | 42 ④ |

31 ⑤ PLUS + ④

Since birds consume up to 65 percent of a year's seed production // and squirrels and mice take care of a good part of the rest, // [1]it is not surprising // that fewer than one-tenth of 1 percent of Douglas-fir seeds survive // where they fall to become new trees. [2]Seed production is one way [trees attempt to compensate for such huge losses]. Douglas-fir seed production is trifling / compared with that of some flowering plants — / a single capsule of some orchids, / for example, / can contain up to 4 million seeds / and has a much lower rate of success than a Douglas-fir. Medieval philosophers such as Saint Thomas Aquinas, / attempting to make a synthesis of reason and faith, / saw in this seed production evidence of the Creator's grand design. Nature was "God's work" / and overabundance was seen / both as a sign of God's will and as the result of a natural cause.

해석 새들이 한 해의 씨앗 생산의 65퍼센트까지 섭취하고 다람쥐와 생쥐가 그 나머지의 상당 부분을 처리하기 때문에, 미송 씨앗의 1퍼센트의 10분의 1도 안 되는 수가 새로운 나무가 되기 위해 떨어진 곳에서 살아남는다는 것은 놀라운 일이 아니다. **주제문** 씨앗 생산은 나무들이 그렇게 큰 손실을 보상하기 위해 시도하는 한 가지 방법이다. 미송의 씨앗 생산은 일부 꽃이 피는 식물의 그것(생산)과 비교해 사소한 양이다. 예를 들어, 어떤 난초의 단 하나의 씨주머니는 4백만 개까지의 씨앗을 포함할 수 있는데 미송보다 훨씬 낮은 성공률을 가진다. 이성과 신앙을 통합하려고 시도한 성 토마스 아퀴나스 같은 중세 철학자들은 이런 씨앗 생산에서 창조주의 원대한 설계의 증거를 보았다. 자연은 '신의 일'이고 과잉은 신의 뜻이자 자연적 원인의 결과로 여겨졌다.

어휘 compensate 보상하다; 상쇄하다 trifling 사소한, 하찮은 orchid 난초 rate −율, 비율; 속도; 가격 synthesis 통합; 합성 will 의사; 의지 [선택지 어휘] conformity 순응 asymmetry 불균형, 비대칭 underestimation 과소평가

해설 무엇이 신의 뜻이자 자연적 원인의 결과로 여겨졌는지 찾아야 한다. 큰 손실을 보상하기 위해 식물이 엄청난 양의 씨앗을 생산하는 자연의 현상을 설명하고, 중세 철학자들은 이를 신의 일이자 뜻으로 보았다는 내용이 이어지므로 빈칸에는 엄청난 씨앗 생산을 나타내는 ⑤ '과잉'이 적절하다.

오답 Check
① 순응 ② 불균형 ③ 예측 가능성 ④ 과소평가
→ ①, ②, ③, ④ 모두 본문에 언급되지 않음

PLUS + 변형문제

어휘 doctrine 교리 proliferation 증식
해설 식물은 큰 손실을 보상하기 위해 씨앗을 과잉 생산하는데, 중세 철학자들은 이를 창조주의 원대한 설계 증거로 보았다는 내용이고, 글의 중반부에 있는 주제문으로 보아 제목으로는 ④ '과잉 생산을 이끄는 자연적 원인'이 가장 적절하다.
① 자연에 관한 철학적 교리
→ 중세 철학자들의 견해를 활용한 오답.
② 식물의 씨앗 생산을 증가시키는 방법
→ 식물의 씨앗 생산을 증가시키는 방법에 대한 내용은 아님.
③ 성공적인 증식에 대한 자연의 실패
→ 오히려 성공적으로 증식했다는 내용임.
⑤ 식물들과 그 포식자들의 균형 잡힌 생산
→ 포식자의 균형 잡힌 생산은 언급되지 않음.

구문 [1]it is not surprising // that fewer than one-tenth of 1 percent of Douglas-fir seeds survive // where they fall to become new trees.
• it은 가주어이며 that 이하(that ~ new trees)가 진주어이다.
• where는 부사절(where ~ new trees)을 이끄는 접속사로 '~하는 곳에(서)'라는 의미이다.

[2]Seed production is *one way* [(which[that]) trees attempt **to compensate** for such huge losses].
• [ ]는 목적격 관계대명사 which[that]가 생략된 관계사절로, 선행사 one way를 수식한다.
• to compensate는 '목적'을 나타내는 부사적 용법으로 '보상하기 위해'라고 해석된다.

In marketing, / the term strategic thinking is thrown around / with abandon. ¹It's a very general term [that really only takes on meaning / when applied to a specific situation]. As a general proposition, / the term is quite vague. As a specific application, / it can be indispensable. Much the same is true of practice. Practicing to become faster has benefits, no doubt, // but those benefits may not apply to every situation. Being fast (in football) / is not necessarily the same as being fast (at a track meet). ²In football, / the application (of "fast") likely includes / knowing how to make sharp cuts (while running), following routes, or avoiding being tackled. For a track runner, / those skills are meaningless. He should take the best of his generally applicable skills / and apply them to his training; // in other words, practice for the purpose. Without the application, / his preparation isn't even halfway complete.

해석 마케팅에서는, 전략적 사고라는 용어가 아무렇게나 언급되고 있다. 그것은 특정 상황에 적용될 때만이 정말로 의미를 지니게 되는 아주 일반적인 용어이다. 일반적인 명제로서 그 용어는 아주 모호하다. 특정한 적용으로서, 그것은 필수 불가결한 것일 수 있다. 연습도 거의 마찬가지다. 추론 근거 더 빨라지기 위해 연습하는 것은 틀림없이 이점이 있지만, 그러한 이점이 모든 상황에 적용되지 않을 수도 있다. 미식축구에서 빠른 것이 반드시 육상 경기에서 빠른 것과 같은 것은 아니다. 축구에서, '빠른'의 적용은 아마 달리는 동안 날카롭게 방향을 바꾸는 방법을 알거나, 루트를 따르거나, 태클 당하는 것을 피하는 것을 포함할 것이다. 육상 선수에게는 그러한 기술들은 무의미하다. 주제문 그는 일반적으로 적용 가능한 자신의 기술 중 알짜를 골라내고 그것들을 자신의 훈련에 적용해야 한다. 즉, 목적에 맞추어 연습해야 한다. 적용이 없이, 그의 준비는 심지어 절반도 끝낸 게 아니다.

어휘 term 용어, 말; 학기; 기간 **○**strategic thinking 전략적 사고 throw around 말하다, 논의하다 with abandon 아무렇게나, 되는대로 proposition 명제; 제안 vague 모호한, 애매한 application 적용, 응용; 지원(서) *cf.* applicable 적용할 수 있는, 해당되는 indispensable 필수의, 없어선 안 될 track meet 육상 경기 대회 take the best of 알짜를 골라내다
[선택지 어휘] integrate 통합하다 perspective 관점, 시각
어휘○ 전략적 사고: 의도하는 최고의 목적을 달성하기 위해서 자사, 경쟁사, 고객, 시장 등의 전략적 요소를 분석하여 최적의 대안을 모색하는 사고 능력

해설 빈칸 문장이 후반부에 위치한 경우 그다음에 이어지는 문장이 부연 설명으로 명백한 추론 근거가 되는 경우가 많다. 만일 근거가 충분하지 않다면 앞부분의 예시를 통해 해결책을 추론해야 한다. 전략적인 사고의 이점이 모든 상황에 적용되지 않는다는 말과, 축구에서 빠른 것이 반드시 육상 경기에서 빠른 것과 같은 것은 아니라는 예시로 보아 빈칸에는 ① '목적에 맞추어 연습해야'가 들어가는 것이 가장 적절하다.

오답 Check
예시를 통해 문제 상황을 명확히 파악해서 해결책을 도출하는 것이 중요하다. 추론한 해결책이 빈칸 문장 뒤의 보충 설명과 잘 이어지는지 확인하면 정답을 더 명확히 할 수 있다.
② 처음으로 시도해야
→ 시도 횟수에 대한 언급은 없음.
③ 현실적인 기간을 설정해야
④ 개인적 강점을 최대화해야
→ ③, ④ 상식적인 내용이나 언급되지 않음.
⑤ 다양한 관점을 통합해야
→ 주제문과 반대되는 성격임.

PLUS + 변형문제
해설 이 글은 적용 가능한 기술 중 알짜를 골라내고 그것을 자신의 훈련에 적용하는, 즉 목적에 맞추어 연습해야 한다는 주제를 담고 있으므로 이를 요지로 가장 잘 표현한 것은 ①이다.
→ ②, ③, ④는 글에 언급된 단어를 활용했지만 주제로 볼 수 없고, ⑤는 주제와 반대되는 내용임.

구문 ¹It's *a very general term* [that really only takes on meaning / when (being) applied to a specific situation].
• 주어 It은 앞 문장의 the term strategic thinking을 가리키는 대명사이다.
• [ ]는 주격 관계대명사 that이 이끄는 관계사절로 선행사 a very general term을 수식한다.
• when ~ situation은 접속사를 포함한 분사구문으로 과거분사(applied) 앞에 being이 생략되었다.

²In football, / the application (of "fast") likely **includes** / knowing *how to make sharp cuts while running*, following routes, or avoiding being tackled.
• 밑줄 친 세 부분은 동사 includes의 목적어로 콤마(,)와 or로 연결되어 병렬 구조를 이룬다.
• how to ~ while running은 knowing의 목적어로 쓰인 명사구이다.

Philosophers of science have repeatedly demonstrated // that more than one theoretical construction can always be placed / upon a given collection of data. History of science indicates // that, particularly in the early developmental stages of a new paradigm, / it is not even very difficult / to invent such alternates. But that invention of alternates is just what scientists seldom undertake / except during the pre-paradigm stage of their science's development / and at very special occasions during its subsequent evolution. ¹So long as the tools [a paradigm supplies] continue to prove capable of solving the problems [it defines], // science moves fastest and penetrates most deeply / through confident employment of those tools. The reason is clear. As in manufacture so in science — retooling is an extravagance (to be reserved) for the occasion [that demands it]. ²The significance of crises is the indication [they provide] // that an occasion for retooling has arrived.

해석 과학 이론가들은 주어진 데이터의 수집에 언제나 한 가지 이상의 이론적 구성이 있을 수 있다고 거듭해서 증명해 왔다. 과학의 역사는, 특히 새로운 패러다임의 초기 발전 단계에서는 그러한 대안들을 고안하는 일이 심지어 별로 어렵지도 않다는 것을 보여 준다. 추론 근거 그러나 그런 대안들의 고안은 그들의 과학 발전의 전(前) 패러다임 단계 동안과 뒤이은 발달 기간의 매우 특수한 경우를 제외하고는 과학자들이 좀처럼 착수하지 않는 바로 그런 일이다. 하나의 패러다임이 제공하는 도구들이 그것이 정의하는 문제들을 풀 수 있다고 계속 증명되는 한, 과학은 가장 빠르게 나아가며 그 도구들을 자신 있게 이용하여 가장 깊이 침투한다. 그 이유는 분명하다. 제조업에서처럼 과학에서도 그러하다. 주제문/추론 근거 기계를 교체하는 일은 그것을 요구하는 경우를 위해 비축되는 사치인 것이다. 위기의 중대성은 도구를 교체할 때가 왔다는 것을 위기가 알리는 표시이다.

어휘 demonstrate 증명하다; 설명하다 theoretical 이론적인, 이론(상)의 construction 구성; 건설 alternate 대안; 번갈아 하는 undertake 착수하다; 책임을 지다 occasion 경우, 때; 행사, 의식 subsequent 뒤이은, 그다음의 tool 도구, 수단 supply 제공[공급]하다 define 정의하다; 규정하다, 분명히 밝히다 penetrate 침투하다, 꿰뚫어 보다 manufacture 제조[생산](하다) retool 도구[기계]를 바꾸다; (조직을) 개편하다 extravagance 사치(품), 낭비(벽); 터무니없는 생각 reserve 비축하다, 남겨 두다; 예약하다 significance 중요성, 중대성; 의미 crisis (*pl.* crises) 위기 **[선택지 어휘]** inevitable 불가피한

해설 과학에서 하나의 패러다임의 유효성이 증명되는 한 위기의 상황이 아니라면 과학자들은 좀처럼 그것의 대안을 만들지 않는다는 내용이다. 과학에서 대안을 만드는 일을 제조업에서 도구를 교체하는 일에 비유한다면, 위기의 중대성은 곧 ③ '도구를 교체할 때(대안을 고안할 때)가 왔다'는 것을 알리는 표시로 보는 것이 적절하다.

오답 Check
① 주어진 패러다임이 정착되어야 한다
② 도구를 교체하는 것이 과학에서는 불필요하다
→ 패러다임이 유효하지 않을 때에는 교체가 필요함.
④ 새로운 발견의 방법을 피할 수 있다
⑤ 패러다임은 과학의 불가피한 측면이다
→ ①, ④, ⑤ 모두 지문에 나온 어구를 활용했으나, 빈칸에 올 근거가 없는 오답.

PLUS + 변형문제

어휘 validity 유효성; 타당성; 정당성
해설 이 글은 과학에서는 대안이 거의 필요하지 않으며, 중대한 위기가 닥쳤을 때만 대안을 마련한다는 내용이므로 주제로는 ① '과학에서 대안이 거의 만들어지지 않는 이유들'이 가장 적절하다.
② 도구 교체의 능력을 입증하는 지속적인 노력
→ 글에 언급되지 않음.
③ 패러다임의 유효성을 증명하는 많은 방법들
→ 패러다임의 유효성을 증명하는 방법은 언급되지 않음.
④ 과학적 패러다임을 주기적으로 개편하는 것의 필요성
→ 패러다임 개편은 잘 일어나지 않으므로 반대되는 내용.
⑤ 위기 속에서 제조업과 과학의 차이
→ 제조업과 과학 모두 위기 상황에서는 도구를 교체한다고 함.

구문 ¹**So long as** *the tools* [(which[that]) a paradigm supplies] continue to prove capable of solving *the problems* [(which[that]) it defines], // science moves fastest and penetrates most deeply / through confident employment of those tools.
• so long as는 '~하는 한'을 의미하는 부사절 접속사이다.
• 두 개의 [ ]는 모두 목적격 관계대명사 which 또는 that이 생략된 관계사절로 각각 앞에 있는 선행사 the tools와 the problems를 수식한다.

²The significance of crises is *the indication* [(which[that]) they provide] // that an occasion for retooling has arrived.
• 목적격 관계대명사 which 또는 that이 생략된 [ ]는 the indication을 수식한다.
• 밑줄 친 두 부분은 동격 관계이다.

People prefer to believe // that the world is a just and fair place // and that everyone gets what he or she deserves. And since people tend to think / they themselves are deserving, // they come to think / that if they just do a good job and behave appropriately, / things will take care of themselves. ¹Moreover, when they observe others doing things [they consider to be inappropriate], // most people do not see anything (to be learned), / believing that even if those people are successful at the moment, // in the end they will be brought down. This belief has a big negative effect on the ability (to acquire power). It hinders people's ability (to learn from all situations and all people, even those [whom they don't like or respect]). ²If you are in a position (of modest power) / and want to attain a position (of great power), // you need to pay particular attention to those (holding the positions [you aspire to]). As soon as you recognize the influence of this belief on your perceptions / and try to combat the tendency (to see the world as inherently fair), // you will be able to learn more in every situation.

해석 사람들은 세상은 공정하고 공평한 장소이며 모든 사람이 받을 만한 것을 받는다고 믿고 싶어 한다. 그리고 사람들은 그들 자신이 받을 만하다고 생각하는 경향이 있기 때문에, 그들이 단지 좋은 일을 하고 적절하게 행동한다면, 상황이 스스로를 돌볼 것이라(의역: 모든 것이 잘될 것이라) 생각하게 된다. 게다가 그들이 자신이 부적절하다고 여기는 일들을 다른 사람들이 하고 있는 것을 보면, 대부분의 사람들은 비록 그 사람들이 그 순간에는 성공적일지라도, 결국엔 패배할 것이라고 믿으며 배울 것이 없다고 본다. 추론 근거 이 믿음은 권력을 얻는 능력에 큰 부정적인 영향을 끼친다. 그것은 그들이 모든 상황과 모든 사람들, 심지어 그들이 싫어하고 존경하지 않는 사람들로부터 배우는 사람들의 능력을 방해한다. 만약 당신이 그다지 대단하지 않은 권력의 위치에 있고, 큰 권력의 자리에 이르기를 원한다면, 당신은 당신이 갈망하는 자리를 차지한 사람들에게 특히 주의를 기울일 필요가 있다. 주제문 당신이 이 믿음이 당신의 인식에 주는 영향을 깨닫고 세상을 본질적으로 공평하다고 여기는 경향에 강력히 반항하기 위해 노력하자마자, 당신은 모든 상황에서 더 많은 것을 배울 수 있게 될 것이다.

어휘 just 공정한; 적정한 deserve 받을 만하다; ~할 가치가 있다 cf. deserving 받을 만한, 자격이 있는 appropriately 적절하게 inappropriate 부적절한 bring down ~을 패배시키다; ~을 줄이다[낮추다] hinder 방해[저해]하다 modest 그다지 대단하지 않은, 보통의; 겸손한 attain 이르다, 도달하다; 달성하다 aspire to ~을 갈망하다 combat 강력히 반항하다; 싸우다 inherently 본질적으로; 선천적으로 [선택지 어휘] tied to ~와 연관[관련]된 confine 국한시키다; 가두다

해설 사람들은 세상이 공평하다고 생각해서 자신이 보기에 부적절한 행동을 하는 사람은 결국 패배할 것이라 믿으며 그에게서는 배울 것이 없다고 보지만, 사실 모든 상황과 사람에게서(싫어하는 사람일지라도) 배울 점이 있다는 내용의 글이다. 모든 상황에서 더 많은 것을 배울 수 있게 되기 위해서는 앞서 언급된 믿음을 버려야 하므로 ③ '세상을 본질적으로 공평하다고 여기는 경향에 강력히 반항하기 위해 노력한다'가 빈칸에 가장 적절하다.

오답 Check
① 공평함은 당신의 경험에 직접적으로 연관되어 있다는 것을 발견한다 → 오히려 세상을 공평하다고 보는 경향은 버려야 한다고 함.
② 당신을 비현실적인 기대에 국한시키는 모든 권력을 버린다 → 비현실적인 기대는 언급되지 않음.
④ 더 높은 자리에 있기 위해 적절하게 행동하는 것에 힘쓴다 → 적절하게 행동하는 것이 모든 상황에서 더 많은 것을 배우기 위해 가져야 할 자세는 아님.
⑤ 당신이 할 수 있는 한 짧은 시간에 가능한 한 많은 권력을 획득한다 → 글에서 유추할 수 없는 내용.

PLUS⁺ 변형문제
어휘 humble 겸손한; 초라한
해설 이 글은 모든 상황과 사람에게 배울 점이 있다는 내용이므로 요지로 가장 적절한 것은 ④ '모든 사람에게는 당신이 배울 수 있는 특성이 있다.'이다.
① 상황은 적절하게 행동하는 사람들을 돕는다.
② 당신보다 더 높은 자리에 있는 사람들을 존경하라.
③ 더 높은 자리를 얻을수록 겸손해지려 노력하라.
⑤ 배우지 않고도 얻을 수 있는 많은 권력이 있다.
→ ①, ②, ③, ⑤ 모두 글에 언급된 어구를 활용했지만, 요지와는 거리가 먼 오답.

구문 ¹Moreover, when they observe others doing *things* [(which[that]) they consider to be inappropriate], // most people do not see *anything* (to be learned), / **believing** that even if those people are successful at the moment, // in the end they will be brought down.
• [ ]는 목적격 관계대명사 which 또는 that이 생략된 관계사절로 선행사는 things이다.
• ( )는 형용사적 용법으로 쓰인 to부정사구로 anything을 후치 수식한다.
• believing 이하는 부대상황을 나타내는 분사구문이다.

²If you are in a position (of modest power) / and want to attain a position (of great power), // you need to pay particular attention to *those* (holding *the positions* [(which[that]) you aspire to]).
• holding ~ aspire to는 holding이 이끄는 분사구로 those를 수식한다.
• [ ]는 선행사 the positions를 수식하는 관계사절로, 목적격 관계대명사 which 또는 that이 생략되었다.

Most of us are limited in our linguistic fluency. While we may have some acquaintance with languages other than our native tongue, // few would claim mastery of more than a handful of the world's languages. ① ¹But, through art, / we have before us an avenue for understanding and appreciating the extraordinary diversity (of thoughts, feelings, and cultures in the world). ② ²Taken together, / the visual arts and music of a culture, // which are not tied as directly to narrative and, therefore, to language as literature and theater, / comprise an integrated cultural style [that is accessible to the outsider]. ③ Another basis (for claiming // that there are universal dimensions (of aesthetic appreciation)) / is 'to treat a cultural production as art.' ④ There is a potential for cross-cultural understanding and appreciation (inherent in each culture's artistic expression). ⑤ While the key elements (of a culture) can be understood intuitively through its arts, // a more structured understanding of the major themes of artistic expression / can help add depth and order to this understanding.

해석 우리들 대부분은 언어적 유창성에서 제한되어 있다. 모국어 이외의 언어를 어느 정도 알지라도, 세계의 언어 중 몇 개 이상을 마스터했다고 주장할 사람은 거의 없을 것이다. ① 주제문 그러나 예술을 통하면 우리 앞에 세상의 비범한 여러 사상, 감정과 문화를 이해하고 감상하기 위한 방안이 펼쳐진다. ② 종합해 보면, 한 문화의 시각 예술과 음악은 외부인이 접할 수 있는 통합된 문화적 양식을 구성하는데, 그것들은 문학과 연극만큼 직접적으로 이야기에, 따라서 언어에 연결되지 않는다. ③ 미적 감상에 보편적인 관점이 있다는 주장의 또 다른 근거는 '문화적 생산을 예술로 대하기'이다. ④ 각 문화의 예술적 표현에는 다른 문화에 대한 이해와 인정의 가능성이 내재되어 있다. ⑤ 한 문화의 핵심 요소는 그 예술을 통해 직관적으로 이해될 수 있지만, 미적 표현의 주된 주제에 대한 보다 구조화된 이해는 이러한 이해에 깊이와 질서를 더하는 데 도움이 될 수 있다.

어휘 fluency 유창성 have acquaintance with ~을 알고 있다, ~에 대한 지식이 있다 other than ~외에 native tongue 모국어 mastery 숙달, 통달 avenue 길, 방안 appreciate 감상하다; 진가를 알아보다, (제대로) 인식하다 extraordinary 비범한, 대단한 comprise 구성하다 integrate 통합하다 universal 보편적인 dimension 관점, 차원 aesthetic 미적인 cross-cultural 비교 문화적인; 여러 문화가 섞인 inherent 내재하는 intuitively 직관적으로

해설 세상을 더 잘 이해하게 해주는 예술의 기능에 관한 글이다. 즉, 예술은 직관적으로 이해할 수 있으며, 언어에 얽매이지 않기 때문에 세상의 여러 사상, 감정과 문화를 이해하는 수단이라는 내용인데, ③은 '미적 감상에 보편적이고 단일화된 관점이 존재한다'는 내용이므로 글의 흐름과 관련 없다.

오답 Check
⑤는 예술을 통해 문화를 더 깊게 이해할 수 있다는 내용으로 앞 문장의 예술이 다른 문화에 대한 이해를 내재하고 있다는 설명에 자연스럽게 연결된다.

PLUS+ 변형문제
어휘 nurture 양성하다, 교육하다; 양육하다 unified 통일된, 통합된
해설 예술이 다양한 세상을 이해하는 데 도움이 된다는 내용의 글이므로 글의 주제로 가장 적절한 것은 ⑤ '다문화적 이해에서의 예술의 기능'이다.
① 어릴 때 예술 감상을 교육하는 것의 중요성
→ 예술 감상 교육에 관한 내용은 언급되지 않음.
② 다양한 문화의 시각 예술을 탐구하는 것의 이점
→ 시각 예술에 한정된 내용이 아님.
③ 다양한 문화의 예술을 이해하고 해석하는 방법들
→ 예술을 이해하고 해석하는 구체적인 방법들에 대한 언급은 없음.
④ 예술 감상에 있어 통합된 관점의 필요성
→ 예술 감상이 아닌 예술을 통해 세상을 이해하는 것에 관한 내용임.

구문 ¹But, through art, / we **have** before us an avenue *for* understanding [and] appreciating *the extraordinary diversity* (of thoughts, feelings, and cultures in the world).
• 동사 have의 목적어는 밑줄 친 an avenue ~ the world이다.
• 전치사 for의 목적어인 understanding과 appreciating은 and로 연결되어 병렬 구조를 이룬다.
• the extraordinary ~ the world는 understanding과 appreciating의 공통 목적어이다.

²**Taken together**, / *the visual arts and music of a culture*, // which **are** not **tied** *as* directly **to narrative** [and], therefore, **to language** *as* literature and theater, / comprise *an integrated cultural style* [that is accessible to the outsider].
• Taken together는 수동의 의미의 분사구문이며, 의미상 주어는 주절의 주어인 the visual arts and music of a culture이다.
• which 절에서 「be tied to」는 '~에 연결되다'의 뜻이며 to narrative와 to language는 병렬 구조를 이룬다. 원급 비교 표현으로 「A as directly as B」가 쓰였다.
• 문장의 동사는 comprise이며 [ ]는 an integrated cultural style을 수식하는 관계사절이다.

Wolves disappeared from Yellowstone, the world's first national park, in the 1920s. When they left, // the entire ecosystem changed. Elks, a type of large deer, in the park increased their numbers / and began to make quite a meal of the aspens, willows, and cottonwoods [that lined the streams].

(C) Vegetation declined and animals [that depended on the trees] left. When the wolves returned, // the elks' languorous browsing days were over, and the roots of cottonwoods and willows / once again stabilized stream banks / and slowed the flow of water.

(A) ¹This, in turn, created space for semiaquatic animals (such as beavers) to return, // and these industrious builders could now find the materials [they needed / to construct their lodges] and raise their families.

(B) This space allowed animals [that depended on the meadows near streams] to come back, as well. 주제문 ²The wolves turned out to be better stewards (of the land) than people, / creating conditions [that allowed the trees to grow and exert their influence on the landscape].

해석 1920년대에 세계 최초의 국립공원인 옐로우스톤에서 늑대가 사라졌다. 그것들이 떠나자, 생태계 전체가 바뀌었다. 공원에 있는 큰 사슴의 일종인 엘크는 수를 늘렸고, 개울가에 늘어선 사시나무, 버드나무, 미루나무를 꽤 먹기 시작했다.
(C) 초목이 줄었고 나무에 의지하던 동물들은 떠나갔다. 늑대가 돌아왔을 때, 엘크의 나른하게 풀을 뜯던 시대는 끝났고 미루나무와 버드나무의 뿌리는 다시 한번 개울둑을 견고하게 했고 물의 흐름을 늦췄다.
(A) 이것은, 결과적으로, 비버와 같은 물 근처에서 생활하는 동물들이 돌아올 공간을 만들었고, 이 근면한 건설자들은 이제 그들의 집을 짓는 데 필요한 재료를 찾을 수 있었고, 그들의 가족을 부양할 수 있었다.
(B) 이 공간은 또한 강가 주변의 초원에 의존하던 동물들도 다시 돌아오게 했다. 주제문 늑대들은 나무들이 자라서 그것들의 영향력을 풍경에 미치도록 하는 환경을 만들면서 사람들보다 이 땅의 더 나은 관리인임이 밝혀졌다.

어휘 make a meal of ~을 먹다 aspen 사시나무 willow 버드나무 cottonwood 미루나무 browse 풀을 뜯어 먹다; 대강 훑어보다 stabilize 견고하게 하다; 안정시키다 stream bank 개울둑 semiaquatic 물 근처에서 생활하는 industrious 근면한; 열심인 lodge (짐승의) 잠 굴 meadow 초원; 목초지 steward 관리인; 승무원 condition 환경; 상태; 조건 exert (영향 등을) 미치다; 발휘하다

해설 주어진 문장은 늑대가 사라진 후 엘크가 나무를 많이 먹기 시작한 상황이고, 이후 풀이 줄어들고 나무에 의지해 살던 동물이 떠나갔다는 내용의 (C)가 와야 한다. 늑대가 돌아와 엘크들이 편하게 초목을 먹어치우던 시절이 끝나면서 개울의 둑이 안정되고 물의 흐름이 느려져 비버가 돌아올 공간이 생겼다는 (A)가 이어지고, 그 공간의 또 다른 역할과 늑대의 영향력을 요약하는 (B)가 마지막으로 와야 적절하다.

오답 Check
(A)의 This는 (C)의 the elks' languorous ~ of water를 나타낸다. (B)의 This space는 (A)의 space for animals를 지칭하며, 그 다음에 나오는 as well은 (A)의 space가 비버뿐만이 아니라 다른 동물들도 돌아오게 했다는 것을 나타내므로 (B)는 (A) 다음에 오는 것이 적절하다.

PLUS+ 변형문제
어휘 splendor 장관; 웅장함 guardian 수호자; 관리인; 보호자 agreeable 적당한, 알맞은; 쾌적한
해설 늑대가 떠났다가 돌아옴에 따라 자연이 회복되었다는 글의 내용을 잘 보여주는 제목은 ④ '누가 목초지의 최고의 수호자로 여겨져야 하는가?'이다.
① 차례대로 자연의 장관이 돌아오고 있다
→ 아름다움과 관련된 자연의 장관이 돌아오는 것이 아님.
② 천재지변에서 회복하는 자연의 뛰어난 능력
→ 늑대가 사라진 것을 천재지변이라고 볼 수 없음.
③ 개울가의 종 다양성을 위한 다양한 나무들
→ 개울가에 늘어선 나무들이 언급되었지만, 종 다양성은 언급되지 않음.
⑤ 적당한 생활환경을 만드는 데 있어서 초목의 역할
→ 초목은 글의 일부 내용으로 전체를 나타낼 수 없음.

구문 ¹This, in turn, created *space* (for semiaquatic animals (such as beavers) to return), // and these industrious builders could now **find** *the materials* [(which[that]) they needed / to construct their lodges] and **raise** their families.
• to return은 형용사적 용법으로 앞에 있는 space를 수식하며, 밑줄 친 for ~ beavers는 to부정사의 의미상 주어이다.
• [ ]는 목적격 관계대명사가 생략된 관계사절로 선행사 the materials를 수식한다.
• 두 번째 절에서, 동사 find와 raise가 접속사 and로 연결되어 병렬 구조를 이룬다.

²The wolves turned out to be better stewards (of the land) than people, / **creating** *conditions* [that **allowed** *the trees* to grow and (to) exert their influence on the landscape].
• creating 이하는 부대상황을 나타내는 분사구문이다.
• [ ]는 주격 관계대명사 that이 이끄는 관계사절로 앞에 있는 conditions를 수식한다.
• [ ]에는 「allow+O+C」 구문이 쓰여 두 개의 목적격보어 to grow와 (to) exert가 and로 병렬 연결된다. 이때 exert 앞에 반복되는 to는 생략되었다.

주제문

The measure of velocity, and subsequent acceleration, / is one of the most important measures in sport // because this variable is very useful / for determining // whether an athlete's current performance is better than a previous performance, // or if it is better or worse than the opposition's.

(B) ¹To calculate the direction and the speed [at which someone is traveling], / we need to accurately measure the distance and the time. Tests (to measure this), such as 30m sprint drills, / are often used in sport / as part of an athlete's training.

(A) By measuring the speed of the smaller intervals (within this length), / coaches can identify // "where" an athlete is running fast // and where she is slowing down. Once the velocity has been calculated, // the acceleration can be determined; ²and often in sport, / acceleration, the rate of change in velocity, is // what separates an athlete from an elite athlete.

(C) From this new information, the coach can devise specific training (for each individual athlete). ³For example, if it is known // that an athlete has a velocity over 30m, // technique and strength training / can be developed [that appropriately match it].

해석 주제문 속도, 그리고 이어지는 가속도의 측정은 스포츠에서 가장 중요한 측정 중 하나이다. 왜냐하면 이 변수가 선수의 현재 수행이 이전 수행보다 더 나은지, 아니면 그것이 상대방의 것(수행)보다 더 나은지 더 못한지를 결정하는 데 매우 유용하기 때문이다.
(B) 어떤 사람이 이동하는 방향과 속도를 계산하기 위해서는, 거리와 시간을 정확히 측정할 필요가 있다. 30m 단거리 연습과 같이 이를 측정하기 위한 테스트가 스포츠에서 운동선수의 훈련의 일환으로 흔히 사용된다.
(A) 이 거리 내의 더 작은 간격의 속도를 측정함으로써, 코치는 '어디에서' 선수가 빠르게 달리고 어디에서 속도를 늦추는지를 확인할 수 있다. 일단 속도가 계산되면, 가속도가 결정될 수 있다. 그리고 스포츠에서는 흔히 속도의 변화 비율인 가속도가 선수와 엘리트 선수를 가르는 것이다.
(C) 이러한 새로운 정보로부터 코치는 각 개개인 선수들을 위한 특정한 훈련을 고안할 수 있다. 예를 들어 선수가 30m 내내 어떤 속도를 갖고 있다는 것을 알게 되면, 이 속도에 적절히 걸맞은 기술과 근력 훈련이 개발될 수 있다.

어휘 measure 측정(하다), 재다; 조치, 대책 velocity 속도, 속력 subsequent 뒤이어 일어나는; 다음의 variable 변수; 변하기 쉬운 calculate 계산하다; 결정하다 sprint 단거리 경주 drill (반복) 연습; 훈련 interval 간격; 거리 devise 고안하다

해설 속도와 가속도가 스포츠에서 중요한 척도라는 주어진 문장 다음에는 속도 측정을 위한 30m 단거리 훈련 테스트가 제시된 (B)가 나오며, 그 거리 내에서 세분화된 간격의 속도를 계산하면 가속도도 알아낼 수 있다는 (A)가 그 뒤에 나온다. 이러한 정보를 취합하여 선수 개개인에게 적합한 훈련 기법을 개발할 수 있다는 (C)가 그다음에 온다. (C)의 첫 부분에 나오는 From this new information은 (B)와 (A)에 나온 선수의 테스트 결과 취득된 속도와 가속도에 관한 정보를 지칭한다.

오답 Check
(A)의 첫째 줄의 this length는 30m를 나타낸다. (A)는 코치가 작은 간격에서 속도를 측정해 가속도를 알아내는 방법을 설명하므로 (B)의 30m 단거리 연습의 방식을 자세히 설명한 부분이다.

PLUS+ 변형문제

해설 이 글은 스포츠에서 중요한 척도인 속도와 가속도를 활용해 개개인의 선수들을 위한 훈련을 고안할 수 있다고 설명하므로 요지로는 ③이 가장 적절하다.
① → 정교한 기술은 언급되지 않음.
② → 상식적인 내용을 활용한 오답임.
④, ⑤ → 주어진 문장에서 언급되었으나 글 전체의 요지는 아님.

구문 ¹To calculate *the direction and the speed* [**at which** someone is traveling], / we need to accurately measure the distance and the time.
• [ ]는 '전치사+관계대명사'가 이끄는 관계사절로 앞에 있는 the direction and the speed를 수식한다.

²and often in sport, / acceleration, the rate of change in velocity, is // **what separates an athlete from an elite athlete**.
• the rate ~ in velocity는 앞에 있는 명사 acceleration을 부연 설명하는 동격 명사구이다.
• is의 보어로 관계대명사 what이 이끄는 절이 나왔다.

³For example, if **it** is known // **that** an athlete has a velocity over 30m, // *technique and strength training* / can be developed [**that** appropriately match it].
• 밑줄 친 it은 가주어, that이 이끄는 명사절은 진주어이다.
• [ ]는 관계대명사 that이 이끄는 관계사절로 선행사 technique and strength training을 수식한다.

주제문
When an underwater object is seen from outside the water, // its appearance becomes distorted. This is // because refraction changes the direction (of the light rays [that come from the object]). (①) When these rays enter the eyes (of an observer), // nerves (in the eyes) send signals to the observer's brain. (②) ¹The brain then constructs a picture / based on where the rays appear to have come from. (③ It does this / without accounting for the effects of refraction, // so the object's appearance is distorted.) ²When one looks at a straw in a glass of water, // light rays (from the part of the straw [that is underwater]) refract at the surfaces (between the water and the glass and between the glass and the air). (④) The rays appear to come from closer to the surface than they are, // and the straw looks bent. (⑤) ³If the straw were viewed from underwater, // the part above water would be distorted.

해석 주제문 물속에 있는 물체가 물 밖에서 관찰될 때, 그것의 모습이 왜곡된다. 이것은 굴절이 그 물체로부터 나오는 광선의 방향을 바꾸기 때문이다. 이런 빛이 관찰자의 눈에 들어올 때, 눈 속의 신경은 관찰자의 뇌로 신호를 보낸다. 그다음에 뇌는 빛이 나온 것으로 보이는 곳에 근거하여 그림을 구축한다. 그것(뇌)은 굴절의 효과에 대한 고려 없이 이렇게 하고, 그래서 그 물체의 겉모습은 일그러진다. 물이 담긴 잔 속에 있는 빨대를 볼 때, 물속에 있는 빨대의 부분에서 나오는 빛은 물과 유리잔 사이와 유리잔과 공기 사이의 표면에서 굴절이 된다. 그 빛은 실제보다 표면에 더 가까운 곳에서 나오는 것처럼 보이고, 빨대는 구부러져 보인다. 만약 빨대가 물속으로부터 관찰되면, 물 위쪽 부분이 일그러질 것이다.

어휘 appearance (겉)모습; 나타남, 출현 distorted 왜곡된; 비뚤어진 light ray 광선 observer 관찰자 nerve 신경 construct 그리다; 구성하다 account for ~을 고려하다, 설명하다; 차지하다 bent 구부러진, 휜

해설 주어진 문장 속의 It does this는 ③ 앞에 있는 The brain then constructs a picture ~ come from을 가리키며, 주어진 문장은 첫 번째 문장부터 설명되고 있는 '굴절로 인해 물체가 왜곡되어 보이는 과정'의 마지막 부분이다. 따라서 주어진 문장이 ③에 들어가면 뒤에 물잔 속의 빨대가 구부러져 보이는 현상의 구체적인 예가 자연스럽게 전개될 수 있다.

06

PLUS + 변형문제

어휘 optic 눈[시력]의 transmit 전달[전송]하다
해설 물속에 있는 물체가 왜곡되어 보이게 하는 굴절 현상에 대해 설명하는 글이므로 제목으로 가장 적절한 것은 ③ '왜 물속에서 사물이 구부러져 보이는지에 대한 설명'이다.
① 어떻게 광선이 물속에서 나와 공기 중으로 들어가는가
→ 광선이 물속에서 물 밖으로 나올 때 굴절된다는 내용은 있으나 그 방법이나 과정에 대한 설명은 없음.
② 시신경은 얼마나 정확하게 정보를 전달하는가
→ 시신경의 정확성에 대한 언급은 없음.
④ 똑똑한 인간 뇌는 굴절의 효과를 고려한다
→ 오히려 뇌가 굴절의 효과에 대해 고려하지 않아서 왜곡이 일어남.
⑤ 왜곡: 사물을 있는 그대로 보지 않는 것의 위험성
→ 사물을 있는 그대로 보지 않는 것이 위험하다는 내용은 아님.

구문 ¹The brain then constructs a picture / *based on* where the rays appear **to have come from**.
• based on의 목적어로 의문사 where가 이끄는 명사절이 왔다.
• to부정사의 완료형인 「to have p.p.」는 문장의 동사(appear)가 가리키는 때보다 이전의 일임을 나타낸다.

²When one looks at a straw in a glass of water, // *light rays* (from *the part of the straw* [**that** is underwater]) refract at *the surfaces*
S ─── V
(between the water and the glass [and] between the glass and the air).
• 첫 번째 ( )는 주어인 light rays를 수식하는 전명구이고, 동사는 refract이다.
• [ ]는 주격 관계대명사 that이 이끄는 관계사절로 the part of the straw를 수식한다.

³**If** the straw **were** viewed from underwater, // the part above water **would be** distorted.
• 「If+S'+동사의 과거형 ~, S+조동사의 과거형(would)+동사원형 ....」의 가정법 과거 표현으로, 현재 사실에 대한 반대 상황을 가정한다.

One popular theory (of why people can maintain their body weight / at a relatively stable level) is the set-point theory. (①) The set-point theory proposes // that body weight, like body temperature, is physiologically regulated. (②) Researchers have noted // that many people [who lose weight on reducing diets] quickly regain all their lost weight. (③) ¹This suggests // that somehow the body chooses a weight [that it wants to be] and defends that weight / by regulating eating behaviors and hormonal actions. (④) Research confirms // that the body adjusts its metabolism // whenever it gains or loses weight — in the direction [that returns to the initial body weight]: // the body burns more calories with weight gain / and burns fewer calories with weight loss. (⑤ ²These changes (in energy expenditure) are great / and help to explain // why it is so difficult for an obese person to maintain weight losses.) ³An individual's set point (for body weight) may be adjustable, / shifting over the life span / in response to physiological changes / and to genetic, dietary, and other factors.

해석 왜 사람들이 비교적 안정적인 수준으로 그들의 체중을 유지할 수 있는지에 대한 한 가지 인기 있는 이론은 고정점 이론이다. 고정점 이론은 체온과 마찬가지로 체중도 생리적으로 조절된다고 말한다. 연구원들은 식사를 줄여서 감량한 수많은 사람들이 빠르게 그들이 감량한 체중을 모두 되찾는다는 데 주목했다. **주제문** 이것은 어떻게든 신체가 되길 원하는 체중을 선택하고, 식습관과 호르몬 작용을 조절함으로써 그 체중을 지킨다는 것을 시사한다. 연구는 신체가 체중이 증가하거나 감소할 때마다 처음의 체중으로 돌아가려는 방향으로, 즉 체중이 증가하면 신체가 더 많은 칼로리를 소모하고 체중이 감소하면 더 적은 칼로리를 소모하면서 그 신진대사를 조절한다는 것을 확인해 준다. 에너지 소비의 이러한 변화는 크고, 비만인 사람이 체중 감소를 유지하는 것이 왜 그렇게 어려운지를 설명하는 데 도움이 된다. 체중에서 개인의 고정점은 생리적 변화와 유전적, 식이 요법의 그리고 다른 요소에 대응하여 일생을 통해 바뀌면서 조정될 수도 있다.

어휘 maintain 유지하다; 주장하다 stable 안정적인 ○set-point theory 고정점 이론 physiologically 생리적으로 regulate 조절[조정]하다; 규제하다 somehow 어떻게든, 그럭저럭 metabolism 신진대사 expenditure 소비, 소모; 지출 obese 비만의 shift 변화하; 이동하다 life span 수명

어휘 ○ 고정점 이론: 우리 몸이 일정한 체중, 체온, 전해질 농도 등을 유지하기 위해 노력한다는 이론으로 항상성이라고도 불린다. 이 이론에 따르면 체중이 원래의 설정치에서 벗어났을 때 원래대로 돌아가기 위해 에너지 섭취와 소비가 적절하게 조절된다.

해설 주어진 문장을 읽은 후, 연결어나 지시어 등을 활용하거나 글의 흐름이 끊기는 곳을 찾아야 한다. 주어진 문장은 '어떤' 변화가 왜 비만인 사람이 체중 감소를 유지하기 힘든지를 설명해준다는 내용이다. 따라서 앞 내용으로 왜 감량한 체중을 되찾게 되는지에 대한 설명이 나와야 하고, 주어진 문장의 These changes는 체중 증감에 따라 신체가 칼로리 소모의 양을 조절하면서 신진대사를 조절하는 것을 나타내므로 ⑤에 들어가는 것이 가장 적절하다.

오답 Check

주어진 문장의 왜 비만인 사람이 체중 감소를 유지하는 것이 어려운지를 설명해준다는 내용을 ③ 이후에 나오는 문장의 defends that weight와 연결하지 않도록 유의한다. 해당 문장에서는 주어진 문장의 These changes가 가리키는 어구를 찾을 수 없다.

PLUS + 변형문제

해설 처음의 체중에서 벗어나면 원래대로 돌아가려고 하는 고정점 이론에 관한 설명이므로 이를 잘 드러내는 요지는 ④이다.

①, ② → 신진대사와 식단은 체중을 조절하는 요소 중 하나일 뿐임.

③ → 신진대사를 조절하는 방법의 일부일 뿐, 글 전체의 요지가 될 수는 없음.

⑤ → 언급되지 않음.

구문 ¹This **suggests** // that somehow the body <u>chooses</u> *a weight* [that it wants to be] and <u>defends</u> that weight / by regulating eating behaviors and hormonal actions.
- suggest가 '제안하다'의 의미가 아니라 '시사하다, 암시하다'의 의미일 경우, that절이 '당위성'을 나타내지 않으므로 that절에 「(should +)동사원형」을 쓰지 않고 동사를 주어의 인칭과 수, 그리고 시제에 맞게 써야 한다.
- that절의 밑줄 친 동사 chooses와 defends가 and로 병렬 연결되었다.
- [ ]는 관계사절 내에서 보어 역할을 하는 관계대명사 that이 이끄는 절로 선행사 a weight를 수식한다.

²*These changes* (in energy expenditure) are great / and help to explain // <u>why **it** is so difficult *for an obese person* **to maintain weight losses**</u>.
- ( )는 전명구로 주어인 These changes를 수식한다.
- 밑줄 친 명사절에서 가주어 it과 진주어 to maintain weight losses가 쓰였고, for an obese person은 to부정사의 의미상의 주어이다.

³An individual's set point (for body weight) may be adjustable, / **shifting** over the life span / in response to <u>physiological changes</u> / and to <u>genetic, dietary, and other factors</u>.
- shifting ~ other factors는 부대상황(~하면서)을 나타내는 분사구문이다.
- in response to로 이어지는 밑줄 친 전치사구는 and로 병렬 연결되었다.

Suppose that a school administrator argues, // "Let's cut out the pledge of allegiance each morning. We'll be able to save two minutes a day. That's ten minutes a week. That'll be nearly an entire extra day by the end of the year." Such computation is true on paper only. The extra two minutes a day are, in fact, less effective / in achieving your goal than one single day, / and even potentially harmful to your morale. [1]A variation of this fallacy also occurs // when people try to redistribute something, / claiming that "as long as it all comes out the same in the end, // everything will be fine." An administrator says to a football coach, // "You will not be able to have ninety minutes a day, Monday through Thursday, for football practice. However, don't worry: You won't lose anything. You can have from noon until six P.M. on Fridays." The problem here is // that a football team needs time each day; // its improvement is cumulative. The administrator has fallaciously presumed that six hours is six hours, // no matter how it is distributed, // that a team can get the same results from one six-hour session / as from four ninety-minute sessions. [2]The administrator has ignored the fact // that after a while the long practice will become unproductive.

↓

The assumption / that a small amount over time is (A) equivalent in value compared to the full amount of time / is a fallacy, // because it does not consider the effect of (B) diminishing returns.

해석 한 학교 관리자가 다음과 같이 주장한다고 가정해 보자. "매일 아침 국기에 대한 맹세를 뺍시다. 우리는 하루에 2분을 절약할 수 있을 겁니다. 일주일이면 10분이고요, 연말 무렵에는 거의 추가적인 하루 전체가 될 것이죠." 그러한 계산은 오직 이론상으로만 맞는 말이다. 사실 하루의 추가적인 2분은 목표를 달성함에 있어 하루보다 덜 효과적이고 심지어 여러분의 사기에 잠재적으로 해가 된다. 이러한 잘못된 생각의 변형은 사람들이 "마지막에 전부 똑같이 끝나는 한, 모든 게 괜찮을 거예요."라고 주장하면서 무언가를 재분배하려고 노력할 때에도 발생한다. 한 관리자가 축구 코치에게 말한다. "당신은 월요일부터 목요일까지 축구 연습을 위해 하루에 90분을 쓸 수 없을 겁니다. 하지만 걱정 마세요. 잃는 건 아무것도 없을 겁니다. 금요일 정오부터 오후 6시까지 쓰실 수 있으니까요." 여기서 문제는 축구팀은 매일 시간을 필요로 한다는 것이다. 그것의 향상은 누적적이다. 관리자는 여섯 시간이 어떻게 배분되더라도 여섯 시간은 여섯 시간이고, 팀은 한 번의 6시간의 (연습) 시간에서 네 번의 90분의 (연습) 시간들과 같은 결과를 얻을 수 있다고 잘못 추정했다. 관리자는 얼마 후에 긴 연습은 생산적이지 못하게 될 거라는 사실을 무시했다.

↓

시간의 흐름에 따르는 적은 양(의 시간)이 완전한 양의 시간과 견주어볼 때 가치상 (A) 동등하다는 가정은 오류인데, 왜냐하면 그것은 (B) 줄어드는 성과의 영향을 고려하지 않기 때문이다.

어휘 administrator 관리자   cut out ~을 빼다; 그만두다 pledge of allegiance 국기에 대한 맹세 computation 계산 on paper 이론[서류]상; 기획[계획] 중인   morale 사기, 의욕 variation 변형; 변화 fallacy 잘못된 생각; 오류 cf. fallaciously 잘못되게; 오류에 빠져 redistribute 재분배하다 improvement 향상 cumulative 누적적인, 쌓이는 presume 추정하다, 생각하다; 간주하다 session 시간, 기간 equivalent 동등한; ~에 상당하는 (것) **[선택지 어휘]** differentiate 차별화하다, 구별 짓다

해설 하루 2분씩을 1년에 걸쳐 투입한 결과는 1년에 하루를 온전히 쓴 결과보다 못하다. 마찬가지로 일주일에 4일간 90분 동안 축구 연습을 하는 것이 일주일에 한 번 6시간 축구 연습을 하는 것보다 성과가 좋다. 이렇듯 장기간에 걸친 작은 시간의 합과, 죽 이어서 한 번에 긴 시간을 갖는 것은 이론상으로는 같은 값을 가질지라도 가치상으로는 (A) 동등하지(equivalent) 않은데, 이는 성과가 투입된 자원의 양에 정비례하여 증가하지 않고 이상적인 투입 빈도의 영역을 벗어나면 오히려 (B) 줄어들기(diminishing) 때문이다.

오답 Check

(A)	(B)
① 더 큰 | – 기대되는 |
→ (A), (B) 모두 오답.
③ 차별화된 | – 간접적인 |
→ (B)는 틀리고, (A)는 지문의 내용과 반대됨.
④ 비슷한 | – 탄력적인 |
→ (A)는 맞지만 (B)는 오답.
⑤ 더 낮은 | – 증가하는 |
→ (A), (B) 모두 지문의 내용과 다르거나 반대됨.

구문 [1]A variation of this fallacy also occurs // when people try to redistribute something, / **claiming** that "as long as it all comes out the same in the end, // everything will be fine."
• claiming 이하는 부대상황을 나타내는 분사구문이다.

[2]The administrator has ignored the fact // that after a while the long practice will become unproductive.
• 밑줄 친 the fact와 that절은 동격 관계로 that절이 the fact를 부연 설명한다.

We can't choose our families, // but we can certainly choose [whom we spend our free time with]. We should be (a) selective in the people [we associate with]. It becomes clear // that we must choose our friends wisely. This allows us to reinforce the same dynamic — the influence [that those close to us have on our decisions] — in a positive direction. [1]Our brains, (it seems), see others the same way [they see ourselves]. This provides a clear explanation (for why behavior can be so (b) contagious). When others do something, // we literally feel ourselves engaging in it, / and manifest the urge (to do it), too.

In many cases, social pressure drives behavior. We know of the examples of teens (doing dumb things because of peer pressure). But it can be a positive influence as well. As adults, we like to think // that we are no longer as easily (c) swayed by peer behaviors, // but we are still undoubtedly influenced / in one way or another / by the people (surrounding us). Social pressure is commonly utilized by organizations (such as sports teams and the military). People feel a sense of loyalty to their teammates / and don't want to hold them back, // so they give (d) minimum effort. A deeply felt sense of loyalty can be a powerful source of self-discipline. Armed with this insight, / what can we do to improve our lives? [2]We need to fill our networks with people [that we admire] and [whom we look up to]. The benefits [this will provide for us] go beyond improving our own self-discipline; // it will ultimately (e) enhance our emotional health and quality of life.

어휘 reinforce 강화하다 dynamic (서로 관계되는 세력 사이의) 역학; 역동적인 contagious 전염성의; 옮기 쉬운 literally 문자[말] 그대로 engage in ~에 참여하다; 종사하다 manifest 나타내다, 드러내 보이다 urge 충동 dumb 멍청한, 어리석은 sway 흔들다 undoubtedly 의심할 여지 없이 utilize 활용하다 loyalty 충성[심] hold A back A를 저지[억제]하다 self-discipline 자기 훈련, 수양 armed with ~을 갖춘, ~을 준비한 insight 통찰력 look up to ~을 우러러보다, 존경하다 enhance 높이다, 향상시키다

해설 41 친구를 잘 골라 사귀어야 하는 이유는 친구들이 자신의 행동에 영향을 미치기 때문이며 이는 사회적 압력에 기인하는 것인데, 삶을 향상시키기 위해서는 자신의 네트워크를 존경할만한 사람들로 채워 넣어야 한다는 내용의 글이므로 제목으로 가장 적절한 것은 ④ '당신의 서클에 누가 있는가? 당신의 네트워크에 투자하라!'이다.

42 팀 동료들에게 충성심을 느끼는 팀원은 동료들의 발목을 잡고 싶지 않을 것이므로 가능한 최소한의 노력이 아닌 최대한의 노력을 제공하고자 할 것이다. 따라서 (d)의 minimum을 maximum으로 바꿔 써야 한다.

오답 Check
41 ① 당신의 네트워크를 확장할 이유들
→ 네트워크를 넓혀야 하는 이유는 언급되지 않음.

② 소셜 네트워크: 삶의 추진력
→ 우리의 네트워크를 존경할만한 사람들로 채우는 것이 삶의 추진력이 될 수는 있겠으나 단순히 소셜 네트워크 자체가 추진력이라고 볼 수는 없음.

③ 친구들이 당신의 결정에 어떻게 영향을 미치는가?
→ 친구들이 결정에 영향을 미치기는 하나, 영향을 미치는 방식이 글의 주제는 아님.

⑤ 영향의 순환, 어떻게 친구를 사귈 수 있는가?
→ 친구 사귀는 방법에 대한 언급은 없음.

42 (c)가 있는 문장은 중간에 역접 접속사로 이어지는데 but 뒤에서 우리를 둘러싼 사람들에 의해 이리저리 영향받는다고 하였으므로 앞에는 그와 반대되는 내용인 '흔들리지' 않는다고 생각한다는 내용이 들어가는 것이 자연스럽다.

해석 우리는 가족을 고를 수는 없지만, 누구와 함께 자유 시간을 보내는지는 확실히 선택할 수 있다. 주제문 우리는 관련을 맺는 사람들에 대해 (a) 선별적이어야 한다. 친구를 현명하게 선택해야 한다는 점은 분명해진다. 이것은 우리가 동일한 역학, 즉 우리와 가까운 사람들이 우리의 결정에 미치는 영향을 긍정적인 방향으로 강화하게 해준다. 우리의 두뇌는 다른 사람들이 우리 자신을 보는 것과 동일한 방식으로 그들을 보는 것 같다. 이것은 행동이 왜 그토록 (b) 전염적인지에 대한 분명한 설명을 제공한다. 다른 사람들이 무언가를 할 때 우리는 문자 그대로 우리 자신이 그 일에 참여하고 있음을 느끼며, 또한 그것을 하고자 하는 충동을 나타내 보인다. 많은 경우에 사회적 압력이 행동을 추진시킨다. 우리는 또래 집단의 압력 때문에 어리석은 행동을 하는 십 대들의 사례에 대해 알고 있다. 그러나 그것은 또한 긍정적인 영향이 될 수도 있다. 어른으로서 우리는 자신이 더 이상 또래의 행동에 그만큼 쉽사리 (c) 흔들리지 않는다고 생각하고 싶겠지만, 우리는 여전히 의심할 여지 없이 우리를 둘러싼 사람들에 의해 이런저런 방식으로 영향을 받는다. 사회적 압력은 스포츠 팀과 군대 같은 조직에 의해 흔히 활용된다. 사람들은 자신의 팀 동료들에 충성심을 느끼며 그들을 저지하고 싶어 하지 않으므로 (d) 최소한의(→ 최대한의) 노력을 제공한다. 마음 깊이 느끼는 충성심은 자기 훈련의 강력한 원천이 될 수 있다. 이러한 통찰력을 갖추었을 때, 우리의 삶을 향상시키기 위해 우리는 무엇을 할 수 있을까? 주제문 우리는 우리의 네트워크를 우리가 존경하고 우러러보는 사람들로 채울 필요가 있다. 이것이 우리에게 제공할 혜택은 우리 자신의 자기 훈련을 향상시키는 수준을 넘어선다. 그것은 궁극적으로 우리의 정서적 건강과 삶의 질을 (e) 높여줄 것이다.

구문 [1]Our brains, (it seems), see others *the same way* [(that[in which])] they see ourselves].
• [ ]는 '방법'을 나타내는 관계부사절로서 앞에 that[in which]이 생략된 것으로 볼 수 있으며, the same way를 수식한다.

[2]We need to **fill** our networks **with** *people* [that we admire] and [whom we look up to].
• 「fill A with B」는 'A를 B로 채우다'의 뜻이다. 두 [ ] 부분은 모두 목적격 관계대명사가 이끄는 관계사절로서 선행사 people을 수식한다.

07 | 3142 모의고사

p.92

31 ⑤ + ③	32 ③ + ②	33 ① + ③	34 ② + ④	35 ④ + ②	36 ⑤ + ③
37 ③ + ⑤	38 ③ + ④	39 ⑤ + ④	40 ④	41 ③	42 ⑤

31 ⑤ PLUS + ③

Traditional logic and metaphysics are themselves / in no better position / to understand and solve the riddle of man. ¹Rational, logical and metaphysical thought can comprehend only those objects [which have a consistent nature and truth]. ²It is, however, just this homogeneity / which we never find in man. The philosopher is not permitted to construct an artificial man; he must describe a real one. All the so-called definitions of man / are nothing but airy speculation // so long as they are not based upon and confirmed / by our experience of man. ³There is no other way (to know man) / than to understand his life and conduct. But what we find here / defies every attempt at inclusion within a single and simple formula. <u>Inconsistency is the very element of human existence.</u> Man has no "nature" — no simple or homogeneous being. He is a strange mixture (of being and nonbeing). His place is between these two opposite poles.

해석 전통적인 논리학과 형이상학은 그 자체가 인간의 수수께끼를 이해하고 해결하는 데 더 나은 입장에 있지 않다. 합리적이고, 논리적이고 형이상학적인 사고는 단지 일관된 성질과 진실을 지닌 그런 대상들만을 파악할 수 있다. 추론 근거 그러나 우리가 인간에게서 결코 발견하지 못하는 것은 바로 이러한 동질성이다. 철학자란 인위적인 인간(에 대한 이론)을 세우도록 허용되지 않는다. 그는 실제 인간을 서술해야 한다. 이른바 인간에 대한 모든 정의는 인간에 관한 우리의 경험에 바탕을 두지 않거나 그것으로 확인되지 않는다면 단지 비현실적인 추측에 불과하다. 인간의 삶과 행위를 이해하는 것 말고는 인간을 알 다른 방법이 없다. 그러나 우리가 여기에서 발견하는 것은 하나의 단순한 공식에 포함하려는 모든 시도를 허용하지 않는다. 주제문 모순이 바로 인간 존재의 본질이다. 추론 근거 인간은 어떤 '본질', 즉 단순하거나 동질의 것을 갖고 있지 않다. 인간은 존재와 비존재의 기이한 혼합물이다. 인간의 위치는 이런 상반되는 양극단 사이에 있다.

어휘 metaphysics 형이상학 cf. metaphysical 형이상학적인 riddle 수수께끼 consistent 일관된 airy 비현실적인; 공상적인 speculation 추측; 결론 conduct 행위, 행실 defy 허용하지 않다, 거부하다 formula 공식; 원칙 inconsistency 모순; 불일치 homogeneous 동질의 pole (서로 대조되는) 극; 막대기 [선택지 어휘] unity 통일성 fragility 연약함; 부서지기 쉬움

해설 빈칸이 후반부에 있는 경우 마지막 문장이 빈칸 문장에 대한 부연 설명으로 명백한 추론 근거가 되는 경우가 많다. 빈칸이 포함된 문장으로 보아 '무엇'이 인간 존재의 본질인지 파악해야 한다. 인간의 특성에는 동질성이 발견되지 않고, 인간의 생활과 행위는 하나의 단순한 공식에 포함될 수 없다. 또한, 마지막 부분이 보다 명확한 추론 근거가 되는데 '인간은 존재와 비존재의 기이한 혼합물', '인간은 상반되는 양극단 사이에 있다'는 내용으로 보아 빈칸에는 ⑤ '모순'이 가장 적절하다.

오답 Check
① 통일성 ② 연약함 ③ 연속성 ④ 적응성
→ ① ~ ④ 모두 지문의 내용과 관련 없는 오답임.

PLUS + 변형문제

어휘 inevitable 피할 수 없는
해설 인간의 본질은 모순성이라는 것이 주제이므로 이를 가장 잘 나타낸 제목은 ③ '인간 본성을 이해하는 열쇠'이다.
① 인간을 설명하기 위해 철학자들이 추구하는 것
→ 철학자가 인간의 본질인 모순성을 추구한다는 내용은 없음.
② 인간은 삶과 행위 사이에 서 있다
→ 인간을 알기 위해 삶과 행위를 이해해야 한다는 언급을 활용한 오답.
④ 진정한 인간의 피할 수 없는 운명: 일관성
→ 주제문과 반대됨.
⑤ 철학을 통해 인위적인 인간(의 이론)을 만드는 것
→ 철학자는 인위적인 인간(의 이론)을 만들도록 허용되지 않는다고 언급함.

구문 ¹Rational, logical |and| metaphysical *thought* can comprehend only *those objects* [**which** have a consistent nature and truth].
• 세 개의 밑줄 친 형용사는 콤마(,)와 and로 병렬 연결되어 명사 thought를 수식한다.
• [ ]는 관계대명사 which가 이끄는 관계사절로 앞에 있는 명사 those objects를 수식한다.

²**It is**, however, just *this homogeneity* / **which** we never find in man.
• 「it is ~ which ...」 강조 구문이 사용되어 this homogeneity를 강조하는데, which 대신에 that을 쓸 수도 있다.

³There is *no other way* (to know man) / **than** to understand his life and conduct.
• ( )는 형용사적 용법으로 쓰인 to부정사구로 no other way를 수식하며, than은 '~이외에'라는 의미의 접속사로 쓰였다.

Draw a circle on a piece of paper, // but leave a small gap / such that the circle is not all the way closed. Now stare at it for a couple minutes / and notice what happens. _{추론 근거} ¹For some people / the urge (to close it) is so strong // that they'll eventually pick up the pencil and draw it closed. The same dynamic can be applied / to stop procrastination from ruining your life. The trick is simply to start whatever project is front of you — just start anywhere. ²Psychologists call this the Zeigarnik effect, / named for the Russian psychologist [who first documented the finding // that when someone is faced with an overwhelming goal and is procrastinating as a result, // getting started anywhere will launch motivation (to finish // what was started)]. When you start a project — even if you begin with the smallest, simplest part — you begin drawing the circle. Then you'll move on to another part (draw more of the circle), and another (more circle), and so forth. _{주제문} The Zeigarnik effect reveals // that incompleteness represents instability to our brain.

【해석】 종이 한 장에 원을 그리되 원이 완전히 닫히지 않도록 작은 틈을 남겨 두어라. 이제 그것을 몇 분 동안 응시하고 무슨 일이 생기는지 주목하라. 추론 근거 어떤 사람들에게는 그것(틈)을 메우고 싶은 충동이 너무 강해서 결국 연필을 집어서 그것이 메꿔지도록 그릴 것이다. 동일한 역학이 미루는 버릇이 여러분의 삶을 망치지 못하게 하는 데 적용될 수 있다. 비결은 단지 여러분의 앞에 있는 어떤 프로젝트라도 시작하는 것이므로 그냥 아무 데서나 시작하라. 심리학자들은 이것을 자이가르닉 효과라고 부르는데, 누군가가 압도적인 목표에 직면해서 그 결과로 미적거리고 있을 때 어디서든 시작하는 것이 시작된 것을 끝내려는 동기 부여를 일으킬 것이라는 연구 결과를 처음 증명해 기록한 러시아 심리학자의 이름을 따서 붙인 것이다. 여러분이 프로젝트를 시작할 때 비록 가장 작고 가장 단순한 부분에서 시작한다고 하더라도, 여러분은 원을 그리기 시작하는 것이다. 그러면 여러분은 다른 부분(원의 더 많은 부분)으로 또 다른 것(더 많은 원) 등으로 넘어갈 것이다. 주제문 자이가르닉 효과는 불완전함이 우리 뇌에 불안정을 나타냄을 드러낸다.

【어휘】 gap 틈; 차이   urge 충동, 욕구; 충고하다; 재촉하다   dynamic 역학; 역동적인   procrastination 미루는 버릇; 지연   *cf.* procrastinate 미적거리다; 지연시키다   ◎Zeigarnik Effect 《심리학》 자이가르닉 효과   name for ~의 이름을 따서 붙이다   launch 시작하다, 일으키다; 출시하다   instability 불안정
[선택지 어휘] urgent 급한   inspiration 영감   heighten 고조시키다   intensify 강화하다
어휘◎ 자이가르닉 효과: 마치지 못한 일을 쉽게 마음속에서 지우지 못하는 현상으로 '미완성 효과'라고도 한다.

【해설】 원을 완전히 그리지 않으면 그것을 메우고 싶은 충동이 너무 강해 결국엔 메꾸게 되는 예를 통해, 자이가르닉 효과는 우리가 무언가를 우선 시작하는 것이 ③ '시작된 것을 끝내려는 동기 부여를 일으킬' 것을 말함을 알 수 있다.

【오답 Check】
① 급한 업무를 끝내려는 욕구를 제한할
→ 업무의 긴급성은 글에 언급되지 않음.
② 영감을 유발하는 새로운 목표를 가져올
→ 영감을 유발하는 새로운 목표는 언급되지 않음.
④ 미루는 버릇의 고조된 인식으로 이어질
→ 지문에 등장하는 어휘(procrastination)를 활용한 오답.
⑤ 처음부터 시작할 필요를 강화할
→ 시작이 아니라 끝맺고자 하는 충동을 이용함.

PLUS + 변형문제

【어휘】 tedious 지루한, 싫증나는   defeat 물리치다, 패배시키다   cope with 대처하다   put off 미루다, 연기하다   duty 임무, 직무; 의무

【해설】 자이가르닉 효과에 관한 글로, 일단 시작하는 것이 미루는 버릇을 없애는 비결이라고 했으므로, 주제로는 ② '과업을 시작함으로써 미루는 버릇을 타파하기'가 가장 적절하다.
① 여러분 자신을 지루한 프로젝트로부터 분리하기
→ 글의 내용과 관계없음.
③ 미룸으로써 어려운 프로젝트에 대처하기
→ 글의 내용과 반대되는 내용임.
④ 여러분의 일을 완수하는 데 있어 미루는 버릇의 역할
→ 미루는 버릇이 일을 완수하는 데 영향을 끼치는 것은 아님.
⑤ 가장 쉬운 임무를 선택함으로써 동기부여 높이기
→ 가장 단순한 부분에서 시작한다는 가정은 있으나 주된 내용은 아님.

【구문】 ¹For some people / *the urge* (to close it) **is so** strong // **that** they'll eventually pick up the pencil and draw it closed.
• ( )는 to부정사의 형용사적 용법으로 앞에 있는 the urge를 수식한다.
• '너무 …해서 ~하다'의 의미로 「so ... that ~」 구문이 사용되었다.

²Psychologists **call** *this* **the Zeigarnik effect**, / **named** for *the Russian psychologist* [**who** first documented the finding // that when someone is faced with an overwhelming goal and is procrastinating as a result, // getting started anywhere will launch *motivation* (to finish // what was started)].
• 주절은 「call+목적어(this)+목적격보어(the Zeigarnik effect)」의 구조이다.
• named 이하(named ~ was started)는 분사구로, the Zeigarnik effect를 보충 설명한다.
• [ ]는 관계사절로, 주격 관계대명사 who가 the Russian psychologist를 선행사로 한다.
• 밑줄 친 the finding과 that절은 동격 관계이다.
• ( )는 형용사적 용법으로 쓰인 to부정사구로 motivation을 수식한다.

In the old days, / when aircraft routinely fell out of the sky / because large and obvious components failed — the fuel pumps gave out or the engines exploded — // it felt sensible to cast aside the claims of organized religions / in favor of a trust in science. Rather than praying, / the urgent task was to study the root causes of malfunctions / and root out error through reason. <u>¹But as aviation has become ever more subject to scrutiny, // as every part has been equipped with backup systems, // so, too, have the reasons for becoming superstitious paradoxically increased.</u> The sheer remoteness of a catastrophic event occurring / invites us to forgo scientific assurances / in favor of a more humble stance (towards the dangers [which our feeble minds struggle to contain]). While never going so far / as to ignore maintenance schedules, / ²we may nevertheless <u>judge it far from unreasonable</u> / to take a few moments before a journey / to fall to our knees / and pray to the mysterious forces of fate [[to which all aircraft remain subject] and [which we might as well call God]].

어휘 component 구성요소 give out 작동을 멈추다, 정지하다; 바닥이 나다 sensible 현명한; 합리적인 cast aside ~을 버리다[없애다] malfunction 오작동, 기능 부전 root out ~을 근절시키다[뿌리 뽑다] aviation 비행 subject to ~을 받는[받아야 하는]; ~의 지배를 받는 scrutiny 정밀 조사 be equipped with ~을 갖추고 있다 backup 대안; 지원 superstitious 미신을 믿는, 미신적인 sheer 순전한; 순수한 remoteness 고립, 멀리 떨어짐 catastrophic 비극적인; 큰 재앙의 forgo 버리다 assurance 확신 humble 겸손한 stance 자세, 입장 feeble 연약한 contain 방지하다; 억누르다; 내포하다 maintenance 정비; 유지[지속] may as well ~해도 좋다; ~하는 편이 낫다
[선택지 어휘] inevitable 필연적인

해석 과거에 비행기가 크고 분명한 구성요소의 오동작으로, 예를 들면 연료 펌프가 작동을 멈추거나 엔진이 폭발하여 하늘에서 떨어지곤 하던 때에는 조직화된 종교의 주장들을 버리고 과학에 대한 신뢰를 택하는 것이 현명하게 느껴졌다. 다급한 과제는 기도하기보다는 오작동의 근본 원인을 연구하고 이성을 통하여 오류를 근절시키는 것이었다. 주제문/추론 근거 그러나 비행이 점점 더 정밀 조사를 받게 되고 모든 부품이 (위기에 대처할) 대안 시스템을 갖추게 되자, 역설적으로 미신을 믿어야 할 이유도 늘어났다. 추론 근거 비극적인 사건이 일어나는 것으로부터의 순전한 고립은(의역: 비극적인 사건이 일어날 가능성이 낮아진 것은) 우리가 과학적인 확신을 버리고 우리의 연약한 정신이 방지하려 애쓰는 위험을 향하여 더 겸손한 자세를 취하도록 이끈다. 그렇다고 절대 정비 스케줄을 무시하는 선까지 가지는 않지만, 그럼에도 우리는 여행 전에 몇 분 동안 무릎을 꿇고 여전히 모든 비행기를 지배하고 우리가 신이라고 불러도 좋을 신비한 운명의 힘에 기도를 드리는 것을 <u>결코 비합리적인 것이 아니라고 생각할</u> 수도 있다.

해설 우리가 비행 전 운명의 힘에 기도하는 것을 '어떻게' 여기는지 찾아야 한다. 비극적인 사건이 일어날 확률이 줄어들면서 역설적으로 우리가 미신에 의존해야 할 이유가 늘어나고 따라서 위험을 향해 더 겸손한 자세를 취한다고 했으므로, 빈칸에는 운명의 힘에 기도하는 것을 긍정적으로 바라보는 내용이 와야 한다. 따라서 빈칸에는 ① '결코 비합리적인 것이 아니라고 생각할'이 가장 적절하다. 빈칸 문장의 부정을 나타내는 어구인 far from의 의미를 파악하는 데 유의한다.

오답 Check
② 완전히 받아들일 수 없는 것이라고 여길
③ 우리 신자들에게 필수적이라고 생각하지 않을
→ ②, ③ 글의 내용과 반대되는 오답.
④ 운명의 힘의 결과로 여길
⑤ 신의 필연적인 힘에서 온 것으로 여길
→ ④, ⑤ 여기서 it은 가목적어로 to부정사구의 기도하는 행위를 의미하므로 기도가 신의 힘에서 온 것이라거나, 운명의 힘의 결과라는 것을 유추할 근거는 없음.

PLUS+ 변형응용문제

어휘 faith 신앙(심); 신념 set A at ease A를 안심시키다
해설 과학의 발전으로 비극적인 사건이 일어날 가능성이 낮아졌지만 역설적으로 우리는 여전히 위험을 향해 더 겸손한 자세를 취하며 미신을 믿는다는 내용으로, 제목으로는 ③ '과학은 우리를 완전히 안심시키기에는 충분하지 않다'가 가장 적절하다.
① 과학의 실패가 신앙심을 가져온다 → 정밀 조사를 받고, 보완 시스템을 갖추는 것은 오히려 과학의 발전으로 볼 수 있음.
② 신은 정말로 존재하는 신비한 힘인가?
④ 과학적 확신: 가야 할 길이 먼 곳
⑤ 사람들이 어떻게 재앙 후에 신앙심을 갖는가
→ ②, ④, ⑤ 글의 일부 내용을 활용한 오답.

구문 ¹But as aviation has become ever more subject to scrutiny, // as every part has been equipped with backup systems, // **so, too, have the reasons for becoming superstitious** *paradoxically increased*.
• so가 앞으로 나와 「so+조동사+주어+p.p.」의 구조로 도치가 일어났다.

²we may nevertheless judge **it** far from unreasonable / **to take** a few moments before a journey / to fall to our knees / and (to) pray to *the mysterious forces of fate* [[**to which** all aircraft remain subject] and [**which** we might as well call God]].
• judge 다음의 it은 가목적어이고, to take 이하가 진목적어이다.
• 첫 번째 [ ]는 '전치사+관계대명사' 형태의 to which가 이끄는 관계사절이고, 두 번째 [ ]는 목적격 관계대명사 which가 이끄는 관계사절로 선행사인 the mysterious forces of fate를 공통으로 수식한다.

07

A good way (to understand the story invention process) is to observe it firsthand. ¹Unfortunately, when people create a new story, // we have difficulty knowing exactly how they found the various pieces of the story [they are telling]. We cannot easily know // what has been invented out of thin air // and what has been adapted from prior experiences or other stories. 주제문 We can reasonably assume, however, // that true creation can hardly exist with respect to stories. Every story [we tell] has to have its basis / in something [that we have already experienced]. ²Of course, the better we are at telling stories, // the better we are at giving them the appearance of being complete fiction. ³This can mean // that even we (as tellers) see the story as fictional, / not realizing the adaptation process 추론 근거 [that we ourselves have used]. Even stories [that are pure fantasy] are adaptations of more realistic stories [where certain constraints of the real world are relaxed].

해석 이야기 창작 과정을 이해하는 한 가지 좋은 방법은 그것을 직접 관찰하는 것이다. 안타깝게도 사람들이 새로운 이야기를 만들 때, 우리는 그들이 들려주는 이야기의 다양한 부분들을 그들이 정확히 어떻게 발견했는지를 아는 데 어려움을 겪는다. 우리는 무엇이 난데없이 만들어졌고 무엇이 이전의 경험이나 다른 이야기로부터 각색되었는지를 쉽사리 알 수 없다. 주제문 그러나 우리는 이야기에 관해서는 진정한 창작은 거의 존재할 수 없다고 합리적으로 가정할 수 있다. 우리가 들려주는 모든 이야기는 우리가 이미 경험한 것에 그것의 근거를 가지고 있을 것이다. 물론 이야기를 하는 데 더 능숙하면 능숙할수록 우리는 그것에게 완전한 허구라는 외양을 갖춰주는 일을 더 잘하게 된다. 이것은 심지어 이야기꾼으로서 우리조차도 우리 자신이 사용했던 각색 과정을 깨닫지 못하고서 이야기를 허구로 본다는 것을 의미할 수 있다. 추론 근거 순수한 공상인 이야기들조차도 실제 세계의 특정 제약이 완화된 좀 더 현실적인 이야기의 각색이다.

어휘 firsthand 직접 out of thin air 난데없이 adapt 각색하다; 조정하다; 적응하다 cf. adaptation 각색; 적응 reasonably 합리적으로 assume 가정[추정]하다; (직책을) 맡다 with respect to ~에 관해서 constraint 제약, 제한
[선택지 어휘] sequence 연속적인 사건들; 순서, 차례 cluster 무리, 모음 echo (소리가) 울리다; 울림, 메아리 facilitate 촉진하다, 가능하게 하다

해설 이야기의 창작 과정을 살펴보면 순수한 창작은 거의 찾아볼 수 없고 대부분은 이전의 경험이나 다른 이야기를 각색한 것이며, 공상의 이야기도 잘 살펴보면 실제 세계의 규칙이 약간 완화되었을 뿐인 현실적인 이야기의 변주임을 알 수 있다고 했으므로 모든 이야기는 ② '우리가 이미 경험한 것에 그것의 근거'를 두고 있다고 할 수 있다.

오답 Check
① 사람들이 우리가 하고 있는 말을 믿게 만들려는 목적
③ 우리가 따라가기에 어렵지 않은 연속적인 사건들
④ 다른 이야기들의 모음, 이것은 다른 맥락들 전반에 울려 퍼진다
⑤ 청자의 흥미와 상상력을 촉진할 수 있는 어떤 소설들
→ 모두 글에서 근거를 찾을 수 없는 오답.

PLUS⁺ 변형문제

어휘 refuel 연료를 보급하다 tell apart 구별하다, 분간하다
해설 창작된 이야기가 현실 경험에 기반을 두고 있다는 내용이므로 글의 제목으로 가장 적절한 것은 ④ '경험: 이야기 창작의 기원'이다.
① 공상 과학 소설이 현실이 될 수 있을까?
→ 공상 과학 소설이 현실로 이루어진 사례에 관한 내용은 없음.
② 당신의 글쓰기 영감을 되살릴 비결
→ 글쓰기를 위한 영감을 얻는 내용은 언급되지 않음.
③ 현실과 허구를 구별하는 방법
→ 글에 언급되지 않은 내용.
⑤ 각색: 실화를 더 사실적으로 만들기
→ 각색은 현실 경험을 이야기로 바꾸는 것으로 언급됨.

구문 ¹Unfortunately, when people create a new story, // we **have difficulty knowing** exactly how they found the various pieces of *the story* [(which[that]) they are telling].
• 「have difficulty (in) v-ing」는 'v하는 데 어려움이 있다'의 뜻이다.
• 밑줄 친 how 이하는 knowing의 목적어 역할을 하는 명사절이다.
• [ ]는 앞에 목적격 관계대명사 which[that]가 생략되어 the story를 수식한다.

²Of course, **the better** we are **at** telling stories, // **the better** we are **at** giving them the appearance of being complete fiction.
• 「The 비교급 …, the 비교급 ~」구문은 '…하면 할수록 더 ~하다'의 뜻이다.
• 「be better at」은 '~을 더 잘하다, ~에 더 능숙하다'의 뜻이다.

³This can mean // **that** even we (as tellers) see the story as fictional, / **not realizing** *the adaptation process* [that we ourselves have used].
• 첫 번째 that은 접속사로 동사 mean의 목적어 역할을 하는 명사절(that ~ as fictional)을 이끈다.
• not realizing 이하는 부대상황을 나타내는 분사구문으로 '~하면서 ~하여'로 해석한다.
• [ ]는 선행사 the adaptation process를 수식하는 관계사절이다.

[1]In a popular sense, "insect" usually refers to familiar pests or disease carriers, (such as bedbugs, houseflies, clothes moths, Japanese beetles, mosquitoes and fleas), or to conspicuous groups, (such as butterflies, moths, and beetles). ① Many insects, however, are beneficial from a human viewpoint; // [2]they pollinate plants, produce useful substances, control pest insects, act as scavengers, / and serve as food for other animals. ② Furthermore, insects are valuable objects of study / in elucidating many aspects of biology and ecology. ③ [3]Much of the scientific knowledge of genetics has been gained from fruit fly experiments / and of population biology from flour beetle studies. ④ Scientists (familiar with insects) realize the difficulty / in attempting to estimate individual numbers of insects / beyond areas of a few acres or a few square miles in extent. ⑤ Insects are also used as environmental quality indicators (to assess water quality and soil contamination) / and are the basis of many studies of biodiversity.

[해석] 통속적으로 '곤충'은 빈대, 집파리, 옷좀나방, 알풍뎅이, 모기와 벼룩 같은 익숙한 해충이나 병균 매개체를 가리키거나 나비, 나방, 딱정벌레같이 눈에 잘 띄는 무리를 가리킨다. 주제문 ① 그러나 많은 곤충들이 인간의 관점에서 볼 때 유익한데, 그들은 식물을 수분하고 유용한 물질을 생산하고 해충의 만연을 막고 썩은 고기를 먹어 치우는 역할을 하고 다른 동물의 먹이로서 역할을 한다. ② 그뿐만 아니라, 곤충들은 생물학과 생태학의 많은 측면을 밝히는 데 있어서 귀중한 연구 대상이다. ③ 유전학의 많은 과학적 지식은 초파리 실험에서 얻어졌고 집단 생물학의 많은 과학적 지식은 밀가루에 꾀는 작은 갑충 연구에서 얻어졌다. ④ 곤충에 정통한 과학자들은 면적이 몇 에이커나 몇 제곱 마일을 넘어서는 지역에서 곤충의 개체수를 추정하려는 시도가 어려움을 깨달았다. ⑤ 곤충들은 또한 수질과 토양 오염을 평가하기 위한 환경 품질 지표로 사용되고 생물 다양성에 관한 많은 연구의 기초가 된다.

[어휘] pest 해충 conspicuous 눈에 잘 띄는 pollinate 수분하다 substance 물질, 본질 elucidate (사실 등을) 밝히다, 설명하다 aspect 측면, 양상 ecology 생태(학) genetics 유전학 estimate 추정[추산]하다 quality indicator 품질 지표 contamination 오염 biodiversity 생물의 다양성

[해설] 글의 처음 부분을 읽고 주제를 파악하면서 주제문과 다른 내용을 골라낸다. 무관한 문장은 주제와 관련 있는 어구를 넣어 만든다는 것에 유의한다. 전반적으로 글에서 곤충이 인간에게 유익한 점을 나열하고 있는데 ④는 곤충의 개체수를 추정하는 어려움에 대해 언급하고 있으므로 글의 전체 흐름과 무관하다.

[오답 Check]
③의 scientific knowledge가 ④의 Scientists와 자연스레 연결된다고 착각하지 않도록 유의한다. ③에서 언급된 어구가 ⑤에는 등장하지 않지만, 두 문장의 흐름은 자연스럽다.

PLUS+ 변형문제

[어휘] utilize 활용[이용]하다 cope with 해결하다, 대처하다 analyze 분석하다 trait 특성, 특징 categorization 범주화, 분류

[해설] 이 글은 인간에게 곤충이 유익하다고 말하며 그 예를 나열하고 있으므로, 주제로는 ② '환경뿐만 아니라 인간에 미치는 곤충의 역할'이 가장 적절하다.
① 우리 일상생활에 해충을 활용하는 것의 가능성
→ 해충과 일상생활에 국한된 것은 아님.
③ 감소하는 곤충 개체수에 대한 인식 높이기
→ 곤충 개체수는 무관한 문장에서 언급된 내용임.
④ 곤충의 특성을 분석함으로써 과학적 수수께끼 해결하기
→ 곤충이 과학적 수수께끼를 해결해 준다는 내용은 없음.
⑤ 특정한 곤충들의 복잡한 범주화의 이유
→ 도입을 활용해 만든 오답임.

[구문] [1]In a popular sense, "insect" usually **refers** to familiar pests or disease carriers, (such as bedbugs, houseflies, clothes moths, Japanese beetles, mosquitoes and fleas), or to conspicuous groups, (such as butterflies, moths, and beetles).
• 동사 refers에 밑줄 친 두 전치사구가 or로 병렬 연결되었다.

[2]they pollinate plants, produce useful substances, control pest insects, act as scavengers, / and serve as food for other animals.
• 밑줄 친 다섯 개의 동사구가 콤마(,)와 접속사 and로 연결되어 병렬 구조를 이룬다.

[3]*Much of the scientific knowledge* of genetics *has been gained* from fruit fly experiments / and (**much of the scientific knowledge**) of population biology (**has been gained**) from flour beetle studies.
• 접속사 and 뒤에는 반복되는 어구인 much of the scientific knowledge와 has been gained가 각각 생략되었다.

Climate change is throwing up some tricky dilemmas / for liberal-minded-people. The big problem is // that climate change is a global problem [that individuals don't seem to be able to solve].

(C) Economists would say // this inability is caused // because people act in their own self-interest. [1]Scientists are in no doubt about the vital and urgent need (to cut emissions of greenhouse gases), // which implies the necessity of institutional law enforcement.

(B) Since individuals and a free market have singularly failed, // it's very clear that consensus and concerted official action are needed / to make any headway. [2]In other words, if we are to avoid potential disaster on a global scale, // we have to accept that governments need to take control of measures (to limit carbon emissions).

(A) And yet, if they are taking such action to control it, // then they are, inevitably, restricting someone's freedom (to use it). 주제문 This is why climate control measures are proving so slow to make progress / and are so stuck in controversy.

해석 기후 변화는 자유주의 생각을 가진 사람들에게 어떤 까다로운 딜레마를 낳고 있다. 큰 문제는 기후 변화가 개인들이 해결할 수 있을 것 같지 않은 세계적 문제라는 것이다.
(C) 경제학자들은 사람들이 자기 자신의 사리사욕에 따라 행동하기 때문에 이 불능이 야기된다고 말할 것이다. 과학자들은 온실가스의 배출을 차단할 중대하고도 시급한 필요성에 대해 의심의 여지가 없는데, 이는 제도적 법률 시행의 필요성을 암시한다.
(B) 개인들과 자유 시장이 개별적으로는 실패했으므로, 어떠한 진전을 이루어내기 위해 합의와 협정된 공식적 행동이 필요하다는 점은 매우 분명하다. 다시 말해서, 세계적 규모로 일어나는 잠재적 재난을 피하고자 한다면, 우리는 정부가 탄소 배출을 제한하는 조치를 제어할 필요가 있음을 인정해야 한다.
(A) 그러나 그들이 그것을 제어하는 그러한 행동을 하고 있다면, 그렇다면 그들은 불가피하게 그것을 사용할 누군가의 자유를 제한하고 있는 것이다. 주제문 이것이 기후 통제 조치들이 진전을 이루기에 그토록 느린 것으로 판명되고 그토록 논쟁에 빠져 있는 이유이다.

어휘 throw up ~을 낳다; 지적하다; 포기하다 liberal 자유주의의; 진보적인 inability 불능, 무능(력) in one's own self-interest 사리사욕에서, 이기심에서 vital 중대한, 필수적인; 생명의 emission 배출(물) imply 암시[시사]하다 institutional 제도적인; (공공) 시설의; 규격화된 enforcement (법률의) 시행, 집행 singularly 개별적으로; 대단히; 특이하게 consensus 합의, 의견 일치 concerted 협정된; 협동의 make headway 진전하다, 나아가다 cf. headway 전진, 진보 measure 조치, 대책; 재다, 측정하다 inevitably 불가피하게 make progress 진전을 이루다, 전진하다 controversy 논쟁

해설 기후 변화가 개인의 행동으로 해결될 수 없는 문제라는 주어진 글 다음에는 그 이유에 대한 경제학자의 답변이 제시된 (C)가 나온다. (C) 뒷부분에는 과학자들의 기후 변화 문제 인식과 법률 시행의 필요성을 제시하며, 문제 해결책의 일환으로 (B)에서 개인적 차원이 아닌 정부 차원의 조치가 필요함을 역설한다. 마지막으로 And yet으로 시작하는 (A)에서는 정부의 개입이 필요함에도 불구하고 이것이 개인의 자유를 침해할 수 있기 때문에 논쟁적 이슈가 됨을 서술한다.

오답 Check
(A) 첫 부분에서 they는 governments를, such action은 정부의 탄소 배출 제한 조치를 지칭한다.

PLUS+ 변형문제
해설 기후 변화는 세계적인 문제이므로 정부가 탄소 배출을 통제하기 위해 조치를 취해야 하는데, 이는 또한 개인의 자유를 제한하는 것이므로 기후 변화의 해결은 여전히 논쟁에 빠져있다는 내용이므로 글의 주제로는 ③ '기후를 통제하는 것이 세계적으로 까다로운 문제인 이유'가 가장 적절하다.
① 세계적 탄소 생산을 제한하는 데 있어서 시장의 역할
② 탄소 배출을 규제하는 데 과학자들이 이뤄 온 성공
④ 사람들과 시장이 기후에 부정적으로 영향을 미친 방식들
⑤ 탄소 배출의 생산을 제한하는 가능성 있는 방법들
→ ①, ②, ④, ⑤ 모두 글에 언급된 어구를 활용했지만, 주제와는 거리가 먼 오답.

구문 [1]Scientists are in no doubt about *the vital and urgent need* (to cut emissions of greenhouse gases), // **which** implies the necessity of institutional law enforcement.
• ( )는 형용사적 용법으로 사용된 to부정사구로 앞에 나온 the vital and urgent need를 수식한다.
• which는 계속적 용법의 관계대명사로, 앞 문장 전체를 보충 설명한다.

[2]In other words, if we **are to** avoid potential disaster on a global scale, // we have to accept that governments need to take control of *measures* (to limit carbon emissions).
• are to는 be to-v 용법 중 '의도'를 나타낸다.
• ( )는 measures를 수식하는 형용사적 용법으로 쓰인 to부정사구이다.

The flu can kill tens of millions of people, // and unrelenting strains (of tuberculosis and cholera) continue to cause premature death / among populations throughout the world. [1]This means // humans have little or no immunity (to it), and everyone is at risk.

(B) In spite of our best efforts (to eradicate them), / these health problems are a continuing menace / to all of us. Just like there are only a few things [which do not have both positives and negatives], // however, the news isn't all bad.

(C) Even though we are bombarded / by potentially disease-causing threats, // our immune systems are remarkably adept at protecting us. However, this is not always the case. [2]Microorganisms (originating in the body) live in peaceful coexistence / with their human host / most of the time.

(A) [3]Specifically, for people (in good health) and [whose immune systems are functioning properly], / the organisms are usually harmless. But in sick people or people (with weakened immune systems), / these normally harmless potentially disease-causing organisms / can cause serious health problems.

어휘 unrelenting 끊임없는, 꾸준한; 가차 없는, 무자비한 strain 변종; 계통 premature 조기의; 너무 이른 immunity 면역력; 면제 eradicate 근절하다; 지우다 menace 위협, 협박; 골칫거리 bombard 공격하다; 폭격하다 remarkably 놀랍게도; 눈에 띄게, 뚜렷하게 adept 능숙한; 숙달된 microorganism 미생물 coexistence 공존 host 숙주, 주인 properly 제대로, 적절히

해설 주어진 글을 먼저 읽고, 각 단락에서 글의 흐름을 알려주는 단서가 되는 표현을 찾는다. 연결어나 지시어가 중요한 단서가 된다. 몇몇 질병으로 인해 모두가 위험에 처했다는 주어진 글 다음에는 질병을 없애려는 노력에도 여전히 위협을 받지만 그것이 완전히 나쁜 것이 아니라는 (B)가 와야 한다. 그 뒤로는 질병의 위협이 왜 나쁘지만은 않은지에 대한 설명인 (C)가 이어지고, 마지막으로 면역체계에 따라 보통은 무해하나 병든 사람에게는 문제가 될 수 있다는 보충 설명인 (A)가 오는 것이 적절하다.

오답 Check
(A)의 the organisms는 (C)의 Microorganisms ~ the body를 가리키므로 (C) 다음에 (A)가 이어지는 것이 적절하다.

PLUS + 변형문제

어휘 symbiotic 공생의; 공생하는 unremarkable 평범한
해설 이 글은 인간에게 대체로 무해한 미생물이 면역체계에 따라 건강 문제를 일으킬 수 있다는 내용이므로 주제로는 ⑤ '건강 문제를 예방하는 데 있어서 건강한 면역체계의 역할'이 적절하다.
① 많은 질병과 미생물의 공생하는 관계
→ 미생물은 면역체계에 따라 질병을 일으킬 가능성이 있는 것이지, 질병과 공생하는 관계는 아님.
② 사람에게 영향을 미치는 데 있어서 체내에 있는 미생물의 이점
→ 체내에서 생겨나는 미생물이 대체로 무해하다는 언급은 있지만 이점은 언급하지 않음.
③ 질병을 직면한 우리 면역체계의 평범한 능력
→ 면역체계가 놀랄 만큼 능숙하다고 설명하므로 평범한 능력이라 볼 수 없음.
④ 우리 스스로를 약화하지 않고 유해한 유기체를 제거하는 방법
→ 스스로를 약화하지 않는 방법은 언급되지 않음.

해석 독감은 수천만 명의 사람들을 죽일 수 있으며, 결핵과 콜레라의 끊임없는 변종은 전 세계의 인구 사이에서 조기 사망을 계속해서 야기한다. 이것은 인간이 그것에 대한 면역력이 거의 없거나 전혀 없으며, 모든 사람들이 위험에 처했음을 의미한다.
(B) 그것들을 근절하기 위한 우리의 최선을 다한 노력에도 불구하고, 이러한 건강 문제들은 우리 모두에게 지속적인 위협이다. 하지만, 긍정적인 면과 부정적인 면 둘 다를 가지고 있지 않은 것이 몇 안 되는 것처럼, 그 소식이 완전히 나쁜 것은 아니다.
(C) 비록 우리가 잠재적으로 질병을 유발하는 위협으로부터 공격받지만, 우리의 면역체계는 우리를 보호하는 데 놀랄 만큼 능숙하다. 하지만 항상 그런 것은 아니다. 체내에서 생겨나는 미생물은 대체로 인간 숙주와 평화롭게 공존하며 산다.
(A) 구체적으로 말하면 건강하며 면역체계가 제대로 기능하고 있는 사람들에게, 그 유기체들은 보통은 무해하다. 그러나 병든 사람이나 면역체계가 약한 사람들에게는, 이런 평상시에 무해한 잠재적으로 질병을 유발하는 유기체가 심각한 건강 문제를 일으킬 수 있다.

구문 [1]This **means** // (that) humans have little or no immunity to it, [and] (that) everyone is at risk.
• 동사 means 뒤에는 접속사 that이 생략된 명사절이 목적어로 왔다.
• 밑줄 친 두 개의 절이 콤마(,)와 and로 연결되었다.

[2]Microorganisms (originating in the body) live in peaceful coexistence / with their human host / most of the time.
• ( )는 Microorganisms를 수식하는 분사구이다.

[3]Specifically, for *people* (in good health) and [**whose** immune systems are functioning properly], / the organisms are usually harmless.
• [ ]는 소유격 관계대명사 whose가 이끄는 관계사절로 앞에 있는 명사 people을 수식한다.

The shape (of a protein) is important. Many proteins do their jobs / by binding to other proteins — sticking to them, usually temporarily, but in a controllable way. When the protein haemoglobin picks up or releases a molecule of oxygen, // it changes shape. (①) A protein is a long chain of amino acids, // and it gets its shape / by folding up into a compact tangle. (②) The shape of this is principally determined / by the sequence of amino acids. (③ ^{주제문} And yet, in practice, it's virtually impossible / to calculate the shape / from the sequence.) ¹The same sequence can fold up / in a gigantic number of ways, // and it is generally thought // that the actual shape [it chooses] is the one (with the least energy). (④) ²Finding this minimal energy shape, / among the truly gigantic list of possibilities, / is a bit like trying to rearrange some list (of thousands of letters of the alphabet) / in the hope of getting a paragraph (from Shakespeare). (⑤) Running through all the possibilities in turn is totally impractical: the lifetime of the universe is too short.

해석 단백질의 모양은 중요하다. 많은 단백질은 다른 단백질에 묶여서, 예를 들어 주로 일시적이지만 통제할 수 있는 방식으로 그것들에 들러붙어서, 자신의 일을 한다. 헤모글로빈 단백질은 산소의 분자를 얻거나 방출할 때 모양을 바꾼다. 단백질은 아미노산으로 된 긴 사슬인데, 그것은 접혀 조밀하게 얽힌 것에 넣어지면서 모양을 갖게 된다. 이것의 모양은 주로 아미노산의 순서로 결정된다. ^{주제문} 그러나 실제로는 그 순서로부터 모양을 추정하는 것이 사실상 불가능하다. 똑같은 순서가 방대하게 많은 방식으로 접힐 수 있고, 그것이 선택하는 실제 모양은 가장 적은 에너지를 가진 모양이라고 일반적으로 생각한다. 정말 방대한 가능성의 목록 사이에서 이 최소의 에너지 형태를 찾는 것은 셰익스피어의 한 문단을 얻으려는 희망으로 수천 개의 알파벳의 일부 목록을 재배열하려고 노력하는 것과 다소 같다. 우주의 생애는 너무나도 짧기 때문에 결국 모든 가능성을 빨리 살펴보는 것은 완전히 비현실적이다.

어휘 protein 단백질 bind to 묶다; 굳히다 temporarily 일시적으로; 임시로 haemoglobin 헤모글로빈; 혈색소 pick up 얻다, 획득하다; 듣게 되다 molecule 분자 amino acid 아미노산 compact 조밀한; 소형의 tangle 얽힌 것; 엉망인 상태 principally 주로 sequence 순서, 차례; 연속적인 사건들 virtually 사실상 gigantic 방대한; 막대한 rearrange 재배열하다 run through 빨리[급히] 살펴보다; ~속으로 퍼지다 impractical 비현실적인; 비실용적인 lifetime 생애; 일생

해설 주어진 문장을 읽은 후, 연결어나 지시어 등을 활용해야 한다. 주어진 문장은 And yet으로 시작하여 '그 순서(the sequence)'로부터 모양을 추정하는 것이 사실상 불가능하다는 내용이다. 따라서 그 앞 문장에는 '순서'에 관한 내용이 나와야 하는데 ③의 앞 문장은 단백질의 모양이 아미노산의 순서로 주로 결정된다는 내용이고, ③의 뒤 문장은 같은 순서가 여러 방식으로 접혀서 ④ 뒤에서 모양을 찾는 것이 어렵다는 이유로 이어지므로 주어진 문장은 글의 흐름이 바뀌는 부분인 ③에 들어가는 것이 적절하다.

오답 Check
③ 뒤의 문장은 주어진 문장의 원인을 나타내는데, 주어진 문장이 'And yet'의 역접의 접속부사로 시작되므로 ④에 위치할 수 없음에 유의한다.

PLUS+ ^{변형문제}

해설 이 글은 단백질은 아미노산의 순서에 의해 모양이 주로 결정되지만, 똑같은 아미노산의 순서가 방대하게 많은 방식으로 접힐 수 있으므로 아미노산의 순서로부터 단백질의 모양을 추정하는 것은 불가능하다는 내용이다. 따라서 글의 제목으로는 ④ '아미노산 순서가 단백질 모양을 나타낼 수 있는가?'가 적절하다.
① 단백질이 조밀한 형태를 얻는 방법
② 산소 분자가 단백질에 미치는 영향
→ ①, ② 글의 일부 내용을 활용한 오답임.
③ 세기의 발견: 단백질의 모양
→ 단백질의 모양을 발견한 것에 관한 내용은 아님.
⑤ 너무 늦기 전에 단백질의 수를 계산하라!
→ 단백질의 수와는 무관함.

구문 ¹The same sequence can fold up / in a gigantic number of ways, // [and] it is generally thought // that *the actual shape* [(which[that]) it chooses] is *the one* (with the least energy).
• 두 번째 절에서 it은 가주어, that이 이끄는 절이 진주어이다.
• [ ]는 목적격 관계대명사 which 또는 that이 생략된 관계사절로 앞에 있는 the actual shape를 수식하며 관계사절 내의 it은 a protein을 나타낸다.
• ( )는 전명구로 앞에 있는 the one을 수식하며 이때 one은 shape를 의미한다.

²**Finding** this minimal energy shape, / among the truly gigantic list of possibilities, / is a bit **like** trying to rearrange *some list* (of thousands of letters of the alphabet) / in the hope **of** getting *a paragraph* (from Shakespeare).
S   V   C
• 동명사 Finding이 이끄는 명사구(Finding ~ possibilities)는 주어 역할을 하며 like 이하 부분은 전명구로 보어 역할을 한다.
• 두 개의 ( )는 전명구로 각각 앞에 있는 명사 some list와 a paragraph를 수식한다.
• the hope와 getting a paragraph from Shakespeare는 동격을 이끄는 전치사 of로 연결된 동격 관계이다.

주제문
Labour migration is an important facet (of the development of markets).
[1]When countries industrialize, // workers move from rural to urban areas, / attracted by the higher wages (offered by industrial enterprises). (①) A similar phenomenon happens internationally: // huge numbers of migrants flowed to the New World during the 19th century // and international migration has remained important ever since. (②) As with internal migration, / economists stress the role of wage gaps (between different countries) in generating international migration: // migrants flow from low-wage to high-wage countries. (③) Eventually one might see a levelling off, // if wages begin to equalize across countries. (④) In practice, what is suggested by simple economic models implies // that migration is an intricate phenomenon. (⑤ [2]All sorts of cultural and social factors are involved, // and the issue has become so highly politicized, / for both the left and right, // that voters will embrace the positions of politicians [with whom they are ideologically aligned].) [3]Nevertheless, basic knowledge (of economics) helps to remind us // that labour migration is as much a part of the logic of globalization / as the expansion of international markets for goods and finance.

해석 주제문 노동력 이동은 시장 발달의 중요한 측면이다. 국가들이 산업화될 때, 노동자들은 산업 기업들이 제공하는 더 높은 임금에 끌리게 되어 시골에서 도시 지역으로 이주한다. 비슷한 현상이 국제적으로도 발생한다. 매우 많은 이주자들이 19세기 동안 신세계로 흘러들어 왔으며 국제적 이주는 그 이후로 계속 중요하게 남아 있다. 국내 이주와 마찬가지로, 경제학자들은 국제 이주를 발생시키는 데 있어서 다른 나라들 간의 임금 격차의 역할을 강조한다. 이주자들이 저임금 국가에서 고임금 국가로 흘러간다는 것이다. 결국 임금이 국가들 전역에서 대등해지기 시작한다면 변동의 안정화를 볼 수 있을지도 모른다. 실제로 단순한 경제학 모형에서 암시되는 것은 이주가 복잡한 현상임을 함축한다. 온갖 종류의 문화적 그리고 사회적 요소들이 관련되어 있으며, 그 문제는 진보와 보수 양측에게 너무나 정치적 논쟁거리가 되어서, 투표자들은 그들이 이념적으로 같은 태도를 가지는 정치인의 입장을 포용할 것이다. 그럼에도 불구하고, 경제학의 기초 지식이 노동력 이주가 상품과 금융에 대한 국제 시장의 확장만큼이나 세계화의 논리의 일부임을 우리에게 상기시켜주는 것에 도움을 준다.

어휘 labo(u)r 노동(력); 일하다; 애를 쓰다 migration 이동; 이주 cf. migrant 이주자; 이주하는 facet (측면; 양상 industrialize 산업화하다[되다] industrial 산업[공업]의 enterprise 기업 level off 안정되다; 수평을 유지하다 equalize 대등[동등]하게 되다[하다] in practice 실제로 intricate 복잡한; 뒤얽힌 politicize 정치적 논쟁거리로 삼다 embrace 포용[수용]하다 ideologically 이념적으로 align ~에게 같은 태도를 취하게 하다; 정렬시키다 remind 상기시키다

해설 ④ 전후로 글의 흐름이 바뀐다. ④ 이전에서는 노동자의 이주 이유를 이론적(경제학적) 측면에서 보아 임금 격차가 주된 원인임을 하나의 논조로 서술한다면, ④ 뒤의 문장은 '실제로(In practice)'라는 표현으로 시작하여 현실에서는 노동자 이주가 단순히 경제적으로만 설명될 수 없는 복잡한 현상일 수 있음을 말한다. 주어진 문장은 '온갖 종류의 문화적 사회적 요소들이 관련되어 있다'는 말로 시작되는데 이는 ⑤ 바로 앞부분의 an intricate phenomenon을 구체적으로 진술하고 ⑤의 앞 문장과 논리적인 반박 없이 연결되므로 주어진 문장은 ⑤에 위치해야 한다.

PLUS + 변형문제

어휘 immigration 이민(자), 이주; 입국 심사
해설 첫 문장과 마지막 문장을 통해, 노동력 이동이 복잡하더라도 그것은 시장의 확장과 더 나아가 세계화의 중요한 측면이라는 것이 글의 주제임을 알 수 있다. 따라서 주제로는 ④ '세계적인 규모에서 노동력 이동의 경제적 중요성'이 가장 적절하다.
① 세계화를 야기하는 주요 노동력 시장의 힘
② 세계적 환경에서 효율적인 노동력 이동 관리
③ 해외로의 이동으로부터 야기된 세계적 임금 균형
→ 글에 언급된 내용이지만, 일부 내용일 뿐임.
⑤ 한 나라의 경제에 있어서 해외 이민의 이점
→ ①, ②, ⑤ 글에 언급되지 않은 내용.

구문 [1]When countries industrialize, // workers move from rural to urban areas, / **attracted** by *the higher wages* (offered by industrial enterprises).
• attracted 이하는 '이유'를 나타내는 분사구문이다.
• ( )는 과거분사구로 앞에 있는 명사 the higher wages를 수식한다.

[2]All sorts of cultural and social factors are involved, // and the issue has become **so** highly politicized, / for both the left and right, // **that** voters will embrace the positions of *politicians* [**with whom** they are ideologically aligned].
• '너무 ~해서 …하다'의 뜻인 「so ~ that …」 구문이 사용되었다.
• [ ]는 '전치사+관계대명사' 형태의 with whom이 이끄는 관계사절로 선행사 politicians를 수식한다.

[3]Nevertheless, basic knowledge (of economics) helps to remind us // that labour migration is **as** much a part of the logic of globalization / **as** the expansion of international markets for goods and finance.
• 원급 비교 형태인 「as … as ~ (~만큼 …하다)」 구문으로 비교 대상은 labour migration과 the expansion of international markets for goods and finance이다.

40 ④

Apparently, the restricted linguistic environment of one's native language / does not inactivate unused perceptual mechanisms completely. Of course, we learn to listen primarily for the acoustic distinctions [that correspond to phonemic contrasts (in our own language)]. Given the right task or instructions, however, / we can detect unfamiliar acoustic distinctions // even though we do not perceive them as marking phonemic contrasts. Furthermore, with enough experience, / the perception of non-native distinctions / begins to operate at the phonemic level: // ^{추론 근거} ¹after considerable experience with spoken English, / native speakers of Japanese / can distinguish the phonemes /r/ and /l/ ^{추론 근거} categorically and almost as accurately as native English speakers. ²The fact // that perceptual mechanisms (available to us / as infants) can still operate after long disuse / causes trouble for hypotheses // that early experience with language / permanently alters some of the mechanisms (of speech perception).

↓

Although lack of (A) <u>contact</u> to certain phonemes at an early age / makes their recognition more difficult later, // the ability (to learn to identify them) (B) <u>endures</u> with age.

해석 보아하니 한 사람의 모국어의 제한된(모국어만 쓰는) 언어 환경이 사용되지 않은 지각 메커니즘을 완전히 비활성화하지는 않는 듯하다. 물론 우리는 주로 자국어 음소의 차이들에 상응하는 음향 차이들에 귀를 기울여 듣는 법을 배운다. 그러나 적절한 과제나 지시를 받는다면 우리가 그것(음향 차이)들을 눈에 띄는 음소의 차이들로 지각하지 않더라도 우리는 생소한 음향 차이들을 감지할 수 있다. 더욱이 충분한 경험이 있으면 비모국어의 차이들에 대한 지각이 음소 수준에서 작동하기 시작한다. ^{추론 근거} 회화체 영어에 상당한 경험을 쌓은 후에 일본어 원어민들은 /r/과 /l/ 음소들을 명확히 그리고 거의 영어 원어민들만큼 정확하게 구별할 수 있다. ^{추론 근거} 우리가 유아일 때 이용 가능한 지각 메커니즘이 오랜 미사용 후에도 여전히 작동할 수 있다는 사실은 어린 시절의 언어 경험이 일부의 음성 지각 메커니즘을 영구적으로 바꾸어 놓는다는 가설에 문제를 일으킨다.

↓

어렸을 때의 특정한 음소들에 대한 (A) 접촉의 결핍이 나중에 그것들을 인식하는 것을 더 어렵게 만들기는 하지만, 그것들을 식별하는 법을 배우는 능력은 나이가 들어도 (B) 지속된다.

어휘 apparently 보아[듣자]하니, 보기에; 분명히 inactivate 비활성화하다 perceptual 지각의 mechanism 메커니즘; 방법 primarily 주로; 처음에 acoustic 음향의; 청각의 correspond 상응[해당]하다; 일치하다 phonemic 음소의 cf. phoneme 음소 detect 감지하다, 발견하다 marking 눈에 띄게 하는, 특징 있는 considerable 상당한; 중요한 categorically 명확히 disuse 미사용; 폐지, 폐기 permanently 영구적으로 endure 지속 [계속]하다; 참다

해설 요약문을 통해 어렸을 때 특정 음소에 대해 '무엇'이 부족하면 나중에 그것들을 인식하는 것이 조금 더 어려워지지만, 그것을 확인하는 능력은 나이가 들어도 '어떻게' 되는지를 중점적으로 읽어야 한다. 우리가 처음 모국어를 배울 때 음소의 차이를 감지하기 위해 지각 메커니즘을 사용하는데, 이를 오랫동안 사용하지 않은 후에도 비모국어에서의 음소의 차이를 구별할 수 있게 되는 것으로 보아, 지각 메커니즘은 오랜 미사용 후에도 작동할 수 있다고 추론할 수 있다. 또한 어린 시절의 모국어만 접하는 제한된 언어 경험이 음성 지각 메커니즘을 영구적으로 바꾸어 놓는 건 아니므로 빈칸에는 ④ '(A) 접촉 – (B) 지속된다'가 적절하다.

오답 Check
(A) (B)
① 정확성 – 지속된다
→ 특정 음소를 충분히 경험하지 못하면 인지가 더 어려우므로 특정 음소의 정확성이 부족하다는 내용의 (A)는 틀렸고, (B)는 적절함.
② 접근 – 증가한다
→ (A)는 맞지만, 지각 메커니즘의 오랜 미사용 후에도 그것이 여전히 작동한다고만 언급하므로 그 능력이 증가한다는 (B)는 틀림.
③ 관련성 – 상실된다
→ 특정한 음소와의 관련성에 대한 부족은 언급되지 않았고, 오랜 미사용 후에도 차이를 인지하는 능력은 지속되므로 (A), (B) 둘 다 틀림.
⑤ 통찰력 – 변화한다
→ (A)와 (B) 모두 틀림.

구문 ¹after considerable experience with spoken English, // native speakers of Japanese / can distinguish the phonemes /r/ and /l/ categorically [and] almost **as** accurately **as** native English speakers.
- 접속사 and가 두 개의 밑줄 친 부사(구)를 병렬 연결한다.
- 두 번째 밑줄 친 부분은 「as ... as ~」의 원급 비교 구조로 '~만큼 …하게'를 의미한다.

²**The fact** // that *perceptual mechanisms* (available to us / as infants) can still operate after long disuse / **causes** trouble for hypotheses // that early experience with language / permanently alters some of *the mechanisms* (of speech perception).
- 밑줄 친 The fact와 바로 뒤의 that이 이끄는 명사절(that perceptual mechanisms ~ long disuse)은 동격 관계이며, 또한 밑줄 친 hypotheses와 바로 뒤의 that이 이끄는 명사절(that early experience ~ speech perception)도 동격 관계이다.
- 문장의 주어는 the fact, 동사는 causes이다.

For some people, there's so much sensory cross talk (in the brain) // that using one sense can (a) <u>simultaneously</u> activate another. This is best seen in the phenomenon (of synesthesia), / a syndrome of overly connected sensory pathways. For example, some people have an auditory-visual connection [in which hearing certain pitches causes them to see colors]. And those associations are (b) <u>consistent</u>: one color associated with one sound. Others have reported having an olfactory-visual connection [in which the scent of fresh lemons makes them picture angular shapes, // while the smell of raspberry or vanilla brings to mind rounded shapes]. There are many varieties of synesthesia, // because there are many combinations of senses, // but they all demonstrate the same insight: our sensory pathways are linked.

Our sensory systems are designed for (c) <u>survival</u>. ¹Initially processed through parallel pathways, / sensory signals are eventually integrated with each other, interpreted, and organized into a conceptual network. Our senses merge to create a singular, streamlined perception of the world. ²This (d) <u>collaboration</u> doesn't just enhance our conscious experience; it also creates a backup system // in case one of our senses fails. When a person goes blind, // the other sensory systems kick into gear, / attempting to (e) <u>widen</u> the gap in perception. The brain does its utmost / to rebuild our picture of the world, / even by recreating one sense by combining others.

[해석] 어떤 사람들에게는, 하나의 감각을 사용하는 것이 (a) 동시에 다른 감각을 활성화시킬 수 있다는 두뇌 속에서의 감각의 교차 대화가 많이 발생한다. 이것은 과도하게 연결된 감각 통로 증후군인 공감각 현상에서 가장 잘 볼 수 있다. 예를 들어, 어떤 사람들은 특정 높이의 음을 듣는 것으로 인해 색채를 보게 되는 청각–시각 연결을 가지고 있다. 그리고 그러한 연관은 (b) 일관적이다. 하나의 색채가 하나의 소리와 연관된다. 다른 사람들은 신선한 레몬 향이 각진 도형을 상상하게 하는 반면, 라즈베리나 바닐라 향은 둥근 도형을 떠올리게 하는 후각–시각 연결을 가지고 있다고 보고했다. 감각의 많은 조합이 있기 때문에 많은 종류의 공감각이 있지만, 그것들은 전부 동일한 통찰을 보여주는데, 우리의 감각 통로가 연결되어 있다는 점이다.
우리의 감각 체계는 (c) 생존을 위해 설계되어 있다. 처음에는 평행한 통로를 통해 처리되다가, 마침내 감각 신호들은 서로와 통합되고, 해석되며, 개념망으로 조직된다. 우리의 감각은 세계에 대한 단일하고 간결한 지각을 만들기 위해 병합된다. 이러한 (d) 협업은 우리의 의식적 경험을 고양해줄 뿐만 아니라, 우리의 감각 중 하나가 실패할 경우에 대비하여 보완 체계도 만들어준다. 어떤 사람이 장님이 될 때, 다른 감각 체계들이 활동을 시작해서, 지각에서의 공백을 (e) 넓히려(→ 채우려) 시도한다. 두뇌는 심지어 다른 감각들을 조합하여 하나의 감각을 재구성함으로써 우리의 세계상을 재구축하려고 전력을 다한다.

[어휘] sensory 감각의 simultaneously 동시에 activate 활성화시키다 phenomenon 현상 syndrome 증후군 auditory 청각의 pitch (음의) 높낮이, 고저 consistent 일관된 scent 향기; 냄새 angular 각이 진 parallel 평행의 integrate 통합하다 merge 합치다; 합병하다 streamlined 간결한, 유선형의 enhance 높이다. 향상시키다 backup 지원 kick into gear 활성화하다. 속도를 내기 시작하다 do one's utmost 전력을 다하다 [선택지 어휘] junction 교차로, 합류점

[해설] **41** 첫 번째 단락에서는 공감각을 근거로 우리의 감각 통로가 서로 연결되어 있음을 제시하며 두 번째 단락에서는 이러한 연결성이 생존에 유리하게 작용한다는 내용이 나오므로, 글의 제목으로 가장 적절한 것은 ③ '감각은 장벽을 극복하기 위해 서로 연결되어 있다'이다.
42 하나의 감각이 실패하면 다른 감각이 보완해준다고 했으므로 장님의 지각에서의 공백을 메우려고 다른 감각들이 작동할 것임을 알 수 있다. 따라서 (e) widen을 fill 등으로 바꿔 써야 한다.

[오답 Check]
41 ① 우리는 인지할 수 있는 것보다 더 많이 감지한다
→ 감각의 양이 아니라 감각 간의 연결에 대한 글임.
② 오감의 잠재력을 완전히 개방하라 → 잠재력에 대해 언급하지 않음.
④ 감각의 통로에 교차로는 없다 → 글의 주제와 반대됨.
⑤ 후각은 정서적 추억을 촉발한다
→ 후각–시각 연결을 예시로 들었으나 정서적 추억을 촉발한다는 내용은 없음.
42 감각 체계는 우리의 감각 중 하나가 실패할 경우에 대비하여 보완 체계를 만든다고 했고 그 예로 장님이 되었을 경우 다른 감각 체계들이 지각의 공백을 채운다고 했으므로 우리의 감각 체계는 우리의 생존을 위해 설계되어있음을 추론할 수 있다. 따라서 (c)의 survival은 적절하다.

[구문] ¹**Initially processed** through parallel pathways, / sensory signals *are* eventually <u>integrated</u> with each other, interpreted, and organized into a conceptual network.
• Initially processed ~ pathways는 수동 분사구문(= While they are initially processed through parallel pathways,)을 이끈다.
• 동사 are 다음에 과거분사 integrated, interpreted, organized가 콤마(,)와 and로 연결되어 병렬 구조를 이룬다.

²This collaboration does**n't just** enhance our conscious experience; it **also** creates a backup system // **in case** one of our senses fails.
• 「not just A but also B (A뿐만 아니라 B도)」 구문으로 but 대신에 세미콜론(;)을 쓴 것으로 볼 수 있다.
• in case는 '~할 경우에 대비해서'라는 뜻의 접속사이다.

31 ④ + ④	32 ① + ③	33 ③ + ③	34 ⑤ + ⑤	35 ③ + ②	36 ④ + ⑤
37 ② + ⑤	38 ③ + ④	39 ② + ④	40 ③	41 ①	42 ④

31 ④ PLUS + ④

An American naturalist suggested // that the pink color (of the flamingo) was an adaptation / so they would be less visible to predators against the setting sun. But in fact the pink color depends on their diet. If they eat a lot of shrimp / they go brighter pink, // if they don't eat a shrimp diet / they go a paler pink. ¹It would be very hard to argue // that the pink color was a Darwinian adaptation (to protect against predators) / rather than a consequence of the diet. That's one of the things [that is actually an extremely important issue within biology]: what's adaptive, what's not adaptive, what's accidental in some sort of ways. Some scientists would probably answer // there has to be an evolutionarily adaptive explanation for it — something arose during evolution / for other reasons or by accident / and then got converted for current purposes. ²The point is // that we need to be much more receptive / to there being multiple explanations (of what happens in nature). They cannot simply be reduced / to the working out of the imperative of the selfish genes.

어휘 naturalist 동식물학자; 자연주의자 adaptation 적응 (형태) *cf.* adaptive 적응성의; 적응할 수 있는 predator 포식자, 포식 동물 pale (색이) 연한; 창백한 accidental 우연한, 뜻하지 않은 evolutionarily 진화론적으로, 진화로 convert 개조하다; 바꾸다 receptive 수용적인, 잘 받아들이는 imperative 명령(적인) **[선택지 어휘]** discerning 안목이 있는 authentic 믿을 만한; 진짜인 defiant 저항[반항]하는 aggressive 공격적인

해설 홍학의 분홍색의 예시를 통해 자연에서 일어나는 일이 모두 진화론적으로 설명되는 것은 아님을 설명하고 빈칸 문장 뒤 문장에서도 자연의 다양한 설명들이 단지 하나의 입장으로 축소될 수 없다고 했으므로, 빈칸에는 ④ '수용적일'이 들어가야 알맞다.

오답 Check
① 저항하는 ② 안목이 있는
③ 믿을 만한 ⑤ 공격적인
→ 모두 글에서 근거를 찾을 수 없는 오답.

PLUS + 변형문제

어휘 reliability 신빙[신뢰]성, 확실성
해설 자연에서 일어나는 일이 모두 진화론적으로 설명 가능한 것은 아니므로 여러 가지 설명이 있다는 것에 수용적일 필요가 있다고 했으므로, 제목으로는 ④ '자연에서 모든 설명에 마음을 열어라'가 가장 적절하다.
① 어떤 특성이 적응인지 구별하는 방법들
② 왜 자연은 이기적인 유전자를 가지도록 진화했는가
③ 다윈 적응의 높은 신빙성
⑤ 자연에서 무엇이 우연한 일과 적응을 결정하는가
→ ①, ②, ③, ⑤ 모두 글에 언급된 어구를 활용한 오답으로, 주제와는 관련이 없음.

해석 한 미국 동식물학자는 홍학의 분홍색이 저녁놀이 질 때 포식자의 눈에 덜 띄기 위한 하나의 적응 형질이라고 주장했다. 하지만 사실 분홍색은 그것들의 먹이에 달려있다. 홍학이 새우를 많이 먹으면 더 선명한 분홍색을 띠고, 새우를 먹지 않으면 더 연한 분홍색을 띠게 된다. 추론 근거 분홍색이 먹이에 따른 결과가 아니라 포식자로부터 자신을 지키기 위한 다윈 적응이라고 주장하기는 아주 어려울 것이다. 그것이 실제로 생물학에서 굉장히 중요한 현안 중 하나이다. 어떤 면에서 무엇이 적응이고 무엇이 적응이 아닌 우연한 일일까? 몇몇 과학자들은 그것에 관한 진화론적으로 적응성의 설명이 있어야 한다고 대답할지도 모른다. 즉, 진화 동안 어떤 일이 다른 이유로 혹은 우연히 발생하였고, 그런 다음 현재의 목적에 맞춰 개조되었다는 것이다. 주제문 요점은 자연에서 일어나는 일에 여러 설명이 있다는 것에 훨씬 더 수용적일 필요가 있다는 것이다. 추론 근거 그것들은 단순히 이기적 유전자의 명령에서 나온 것이라고 축소될 수는 없다.

구문 ¹**It** would be very hard **to argue** // that the pink color was *a Darwinian adaptation* (to protect against predators) / rather than a consequence of the diet.
• It은 가주어, to argue 이하가 진주어이다.
• ( )는 형용사적 용법의 to부정사구로 a Darwinian adaptation을 수식한다.

²The point is // **that** we need to be much more receptive / to there being *multiple explanations* (of **what happens in nature**).
• 동사 is의 보어로 that이 이끄는 명사절(that ~ in nature)이 쓰였다.
• ( )는 형용사적 역할을 하는 전명구로 multiple explanations를 수식하고, ( ) 내에서 전치사 of의 목적어로 what이 이끄는 간접의문문이 사용되었다.

¹In 2013, Forbes magazine explored // exactly how Warren Buffett attempts to avoid succumbing to confirmation bias, // which causes people to interpret and recall information / in a way [that confirms their preexisting beliefs], // and what this means to financial investors. It warned: "For investors, confirmation bias is particularly dangerous. Once an investor starts to like a company, for example, // he may dismiss negative information / as irrelevant or inaccurate." The same can be said / for entrepreneurs or any businessperson. ²Explaining what it labeled the 'Buffett Approach,' // Forbes described the 2013 annual general meeting / for Berkshire Hathaway, a multinational conglomerate [for which Buffett is the chief executive officer]. Instead of inviting professional applauders, // who would applaud at whatever Buffett said, // he invited Doug Kass, a fund manager and constant critic (of Buffett and Berkshire Hathaway), as a guest speaker. Forbes described this as "largely unprecedented" / and applauded Buffett's simple act. Indeed, creating a culture of challenge / was one of the suggestions (for fighting confirmation bias).

해석 2013년에 포브스지는 워런 버핏이 사람들로 하여금 이전부터 존재하는 믿음을 확증하는 방식으로 정보를 해석하고 상기하도록 하는 확증 편향에 굴복하는 것을 피하려고 정확히 어떻게 시도하는지와 이것이 금융 투자자들에게 무엇을 의미하는지를 분석했다. 그것은 경고했다. "투자자들에게 확증 편향은 특히 위험합니다. 예컨대 일단 투자자가 어떤 회사를 좋아하기 시작하면, 그는 부정적인 정보를 관련 없거나 부정확한 것으로 일축할지도 모릅니다." 기업인이나 어떤 사업가에게도 마찬가지 말을 할 수 있다. '버핏 접근법'이라 칭하는 것을 설명하면서, 포브스지는 버핏이 최고 경영자로 있는 다국적 복합 기업인 Berkshire Hathaway의 2013년 연례 총회를 서술했다. 추론 근거 버핏이 하는 말이면 무엇이든지 박수를 쳐줄 전문 박수 부대를 초청하는 대신에, 그는 초청 연사로 펀드 매니저이자 버핏과 Berkshire Hathaway의 불변의 비평가인 더그 카스를 초대했다. 포브스지는 이를 '대체로 전례 없는' 것으로 서술했고 버핏의 단순한 행동에 갈채를 보냈다. 주제문 확실히 도전의 문화를 창조하는 것은 확증 편향과 맞서 싸우기 위한 제안들 중 하나였다.

어휘 succumb to ~에 굴복하다 ○confirmation bias 확증 편향 preexisting 이전부터 존재하는 dismiss 처리해 버리다; 퇴짜를 놓다 irrelevant 무관한 entrepreneur 기업인 label 부르다; 라벨을 붙이다 general meeting 총회 conglomerate 복합 기업; 집합 chief executive officer (= CEO) 최고 경영자 applauder 박수 치는 사람, 칭찬하는 사람 *cf.* applaud 박수를 치다; 갈채를 보내다 unprecedented 전례 없는; 새로운 **[선택지 어휘]** refutation 논박, 반박 admit 인정하다 flaw 결함, 결점 fellow 동료(의)

어휘⊕ 확증 편향: 선입관을 뒷받침하는 근거만 수용하고, 자신에게 유리한 정보만 선택적으로 수집하는 것이다. 자기가 보고 싶은 것만 보고 믿고 싶은 것만 믿는 현상인데, 정보의 객관성과는 상관없다.

해설 확증 편향에 맞서기 위해 무엇이 제안될 수 있는지 파악해야 한다. 확증 편향의 문제점을 언급하며 버핏이 확증 편향을 물리치기 위해 사용한 전략은 자신에 대한 무조건적인 찬성자가 아닌 비평가를 총회에 초청한 것이었으며, 이러한 전략을 ① '도전의 문화를 창조하는 것'으로 표현할 수 있다.

오답 Check
② 세세한 논박을 요청하는 것
③ 자신에게 문제가 있음을 인정하는 것
→ 자신에게 문제가 있다는 것과 그것을 인정하라는 언급은 없음.
④ 전략에서 결함을 확인하는 것
→ ②, ④ 버핏이 비평가를 초대하긴 했지만 논박을 요청하거나 전략의 결함을 확인했다는 언급은 없음.
⑤ 동료 임원의 전략을 비판하는 것
→ 다른 사람을 비판하는 것에 대한 언급은 없음.

PLUS⁺ 변형문제
어휘 stink 악취를 풍기다; 수상쩍다 hatch 부화시키다
해설 확증 편향의 문제점과 이를 피하기 위한 대책으로 도전의 문화를 창조하는 것을 워런 버핏의 일화를 예로 들어 언급하므로 요지로는 ③ '친구를 가까이하라, 하지만 적들은 더 가까이하라.'가 가장 적절하다.
① 공동 책임은 무책임이다.
② 윗물이 맑아야 아랫물이 맑다.
④ 남의 떡이 커 보인다.
⑤ 김칫국부터 마시지 마라.
→ ①, ②, ④, ⑤ 글의 주제와 무관한 내용임.

구문 ¹In 2013, Forbes magazine explored // exactly **how** Warren Buffett attempts to avoid succumbing to *confirmation bias*, // **which causes** people **to interpret** and **recall** information / in *a way* [that confirms their preexisting beliefs], // **and what** this means to financial investors.
• 동사 explored의 목적어로 밑줄 친 의문사 how가 이끄는 절과 what이 이끄는 절이 and로 연결되어 병렬 구조를 이룬다.
• which가 이끄는 관계대명사절은 계속적 용법으로 앞에 있는 confirmation bias를 보충 설명한다.
• which가 이끄는 절에서 동사 cause의 목적격보어로 to interpret과 (to) recall이 and로 병렬 연결된다.

²**Explaining what it labeled the 'Buffett Approach,'** // Forbes described the 2013 annual general meeting / for Berkshire Hathaway, *a multinational conglomerate* [**for which** Buffett is the chief executive officer].
• Explaining ~ 'Buffet Approach'는 부대상황을 나타내는 분사구문이고, 분사구문 내에서 선행사를 포함한 관계대명사 what이 Explaining의 목적어절을 이끈다.
• 밑줄 친 Berkshire Hathaway와 a multinational conglomerate 이하는 동격 관계이다.
• '전치사+관계대명사'의 형태인 for which가 이끄는 관계사절 [ ]가 앞에 있는 a multinational conglomerate를 수식한다.

The term 'straw man' refers to a form of informal fallacy (used in arguments and debates). A type of rhetorical device, straw man is based on exaggerating some portion of an opponent's stance. [1]The straw man argument is usually more absurd than the actual argument, / making it an easier target (to attack). For example, maybe you're arguing with a friend about global warming. You think // the government should raise fuel efficiency standards / to cut down the amount of CO_2 [we release over the next 20 years]. Your friend thinks cars have nothing to do with it, // and as you argue, he says something like, // "Our cities are built / so that we have to drive cars. Your solution will kill the economy. How would people get to work / without cars? It'll never work." [2]He's responding to an extreme version (of your proposal) [that's easier to shoot down than your real proposal]. He's arguing against the extreme idea // that we need to get rid of all cars // because it's easier than arguing against the moderate idea // that we need to raise fuel efficiency.

해석 '허수아비'라는 용어는 논쟁과 토론에서 사용되는 비형식적 오류의 한 형태를 가리킨다. 주제문 수사학적인 장치의 일종인 허수아비는 상대방의 입장의 일부분을 과장하는 것에 기반을 두고 있다. 허수아비 논법은 대체로 실제 논법보다 더 불합리해서 공격하기에 더 쉬운 표적이 되게 한다. 추론 근거 예를 들어, 어쩌면 당신은 친구와 지구 온난화에 관해 언쟁을 벌이고 있을지도 모른다. 당신은 정부가 향후 20년에 걸쳐 우리가 내뿜는 이산화탄소의 양을 줄이기 위해, 연료 효율 기준을 올려야 한다고 생각한다. 당신의 친구는 차가 그것과 아무런 관련이 없다고 생각하고, 당신이 주장하듯이 그도 다음과 같은 말을 한다. "우리 도시는 우리가 차를 운전해야만 하도록 지어져 있어. 네 해결책은 경제를 죽일 거야. 어떻게 사람들이 차 없이 출근하겠어? 그것은 전혀 효과가 없을 거야." 그는 당신의 실제 제안보다 맹비난하기 더 쉬운 당신의 제안의 극단적인 해석에 반응하고 있는 것이다. 그는 우리가 모든 차를 제거해야 한다는 극단적인 견해에 반박하고 있는데, 그것이 우리가 연료 효율을 올려야 한다는 온건한 견해에 맞서서 반박하는 것보다 더 쉽기 때문이다.

어휘 informal fallacy 비형식적 오류 rhetorical 수사학적인; 웅변술의 exaggerate 과장하다 *cf.* exaggeration 과장 stance 입장, 태도 absurd 불합리한; 어리석은 efficiency 효율(성); 능률 standard 기준, 규범 have nothing to do with ~와 아무 관련이 없다 extreme 극단적인, 지나친, 심각한 shoot down 맹비난하다; 격추하다 get rid of ~을 제거하다 moderate 온건한, 중도의; 적당한 [선택지 어휘] appeal to ~에 호소하다 authoritative 권위 있는; 권위적인 figure 인물; 모습, 몸매; 수치, 숫자 refute 반박하다 point out 지적하다 illogical 비논리적인

해설 빈칸 문장이 첫 한두 문장에 나오는 경우 주제문일 가능성이 크며, 이어지는 내용은 구체적인 보충 설명, 예시이므로 추론 근거가 나올 때까지만 읽어 내려간다. '연료 효율 기준을 높이자'는 당신의 제안을 '자동차를 모두 없애자는 제안'으로 극단적으로 해석하여 반박하는 친구의 예시를 통해 허수아비 논법은 ③ '상대방의 입장의 일부를 과장하는 것'에 기반을 두고 있음을 추론할 수 있다.

오답 Check
① 그 분야의 권위 있는 인물에 호소하는 것
② 상대방의 주장에 증거를 들어 반박하는 것
→ ①, ② 상식에 의존한 오답.
④ 논쟁 자체보다 상대방을 공격하는 것 → 언급되지 않음.
⑤ 상대방의 논법에 대한 비논리적인 면을 지적하는 것
→ 허수아비 논법과 반대되는 내용임.

PLUS⁺ 변형문제
어휘 convince 설득하다
해설 이 글은 허수아비 논법이 무엇인지 설명하는 글로 상대방의 견해의 일부분을 과장하는 비형식적인 오류의 형태를 잘 드러내는 제목은 ③ '조심하라. 당신의 상대방이 오류를 말하고 있다!'가 적절하다.
① 논쟁에서 과장을 예방하는 방법
→ 허수아비 논법이 상대방의 의견을 과장하는 것은 맞지만 그 예방법이 제시되지는 않음.
② 상대방을 설득하는 성공적인 안내서
→ 허수아비 논법과 반대되는 내용임.
④ 논쟁에서 허수아비가 되지 않는 방법들
→ 허수아비가 되지 않는 법에 대한 설명은 없음.
⑤ 허수아비 논법: 논쟁에서 최고의 방법
→ 논쟁에서 최고의 방법이라는 언급은 없음.

구문 [1]The straw man argument is usually more absurd than the actual argument, / **making it *an easier target* (to attack)**.
• making ~ to attack은 동시상황을 나타내는 분사구문이다.
• 「make+O+C」의 구조로 목적격보어 an easier target이 to attack의 수식을 받고, 여기서 목적어 it은 The straw man argument를 가리킨다.

[2]He's responding to *an extreme version* (of your proposal) [**that**'s easier to shoot down than your real proposal].
• ( )는 형용사 역할을 하는 전명구로 an extreme version을 수식한다.
• [ ]는 주격 관계대명사 that이 이끄는 관계사절로 선행사는 an extreme version of your proposal이다.

¹In one study, / six-month-olds watched // as a "climber," / which was nothing more than a disk of wood / with large eyes glued onto its circular "face," / started at the bottom of a hill / and repeatedly tried but failed to make its way to the top. After a while, a "helper," a triangle with similar eyes glued on, / would sometimes approach from farther downhill / and help the climber with an upward push. On other attempts, / a square "hinderer" would approach from uphill / and shove the circular disk back down. The experimenters wanted to know // if the infants, / uninvolved bystanders, / would cop an attitude toward the hinderer square. 추론 근거 When the experimenters gave the infants a chance (to reach out and touch the figures), // the infants showed a definite reluctance (to reach for the hinderer square), / as compared to the helper triangle. ²Moreover, when the experiment was repeated / with either a helper and a neutral bystander block or a hinderer and a neutral block, // the infants preferred the friendly triangle to the neutral block, / and the neutral block to the nasty square. 주제문 This study showed // that infants as young as 6 months of age / evaluate others / based on their social behavior toward third parties.

해석 한 연구에서 6개월 된 아이들이 둥근 '얼굴' 위에 큰 눈이 붙여진 나무 원반에 지나지 않는 '오름이'가 언덕 아래에서 출발하여 계속하여 노력하지만 정상으로 가는 데 실패하는 것을 보았다. 잠시 후에 비슷한 눈이 붙여진 삼각형인 '도우미'가 이따금 더 먼 언덕 아래에서 접근하여 오름이를 위로 밀어붙여서 도와주곤 했다. 다른 시도에서는 네모난 '훼방꾼'이 언덕 위에서 접근하여 둥근 원반을 다시 아래로 밀치곤 했다. 실험자들은 관여하지 않는 구경꾼인 유아들이 훼방꾼 네모에게 부정적 태도를 보일 것인지 알고 싶었다. 추론 근거 실험자들이 유아들에게 손을 뻗어 도형들을 만질 기회를 주었을 때, 유아들은 도우미 삼각형에 비하여 훼방꾼 사각형에게 손을 뻗는 데 명백히 주저하는 모습을 보였다. 게다가 도우미와 중립적 구경꾼 블록 혹은 훼방꾼과 중립적 블록 둘 중 하나로 실험이 반복되었을 때, 유아들은 중립적 블록보다 친밀한 삼각형을, 그리고 못된 사각형보다 중립적 블록을 더 좋아했다. 주제문 이 연구는 6달 연령의 어린 유아들이 제삼자에 대한 사회적 행동에 근거하여 다른 이들을 평가한다는 것을 보여준다.

어휘 nothing more than ~에 불과한 glue 붙이다 hinderer 훼방꾼 *cf.* hinder 저해[방해]하다 shove 밀치다 uninvolved 관여하지 않는 bystander 구경꾼 figure 도형; 수치; 숫자; 계산; 인물 definite 명백한 reluctance 꺼림 neutral 중립적인 nasty 못된 third party 제삼자
[선택지 어휘] aversion 혐오, 싫음 impede 방해하다, 지연시키다 distinguish 구별하다

해설 실험의 유아들은 남을 돕는 것처럼 보이는 도형을 좋아하고 남을 방해하는 것처럼 보이는 도형을 꺼리는 모습을 보이는데, 이를 종합하여 주제문인 빈칸으로 완성하면 유아들은 ⑤ '제삼자에 대한 사회적 행동에 근거하여 다른 이들을 평가한다'가 된다.

오답 Check
① 특정한 형태에 혐오 혹은 끌림을 드러낸다
→ 형태 자체에 대한 단순한 호불호를 알아보는 실험이 아님.
② 다른 사람들의 목표를 방해하는 중립적 태도를 인식한다
→ 목표를 방해하는 것이 중립적 태도라는 내용은 없음.
③ 긍정적 얼굴 표정과 부정적 표정을 구별한다
④ 다른 사람들의 감정을 그들의 표정으로 알아차릴 수 있다
→ ③, ④ 얼굴 표정에 대한 내용은 없음.

PLUS⁺ 변형문제

어휘 acquired 습득한, 후천적인(↔ innate 타고난) treat 대하다, 다루다

해설 실험에서 유아들이 남에게 호의적인 태도를 보이는 도형을 더 좋아하고 적대적인 태도를 보이는 도형을 꺼림을 알 수 있다. 따라서 글의 제목으로는 ⑤ '어떤 사람이 타인을 어떻게 대하는지가 그 사람에 대한 태도에 영향을 미친다'가 가장 적절하다.
① 둥근 모양에 대한 유아들의 후천적 선호
② 도형이 아이들의 사고력에 미치는 영향
③ 중립: 유아들이 이해하기 어려운 이유
④ 유아들은 특정한 행동들을 볼 때 부정적이게 된다
→ ① ~ ④ 모두 지문에 언급된 단어를 활용하여 만든 오답

구문 ¹In one study, / six-month-olds watched // **as** a *"climber,"* / **which** was nothing more than a disk of wood / **with** *large eyes* **glued** onto its circular *"face,"* / started at the bottom of a hill / and repeatedly tried but failed to make its way to the top.
• as가 이끄는 부사절에서 주어는 a "climber"이고 동사 started, tried, failed가 and와 but으로 병렬 연결되었다.
• 콤마(,) 뒤의 which는 계속적 용법의 관계대명사로 which가 이끄는 절이 a "climber"를 부연 설명한다.
• 관계대명사절 내의 「with+O+p.p.」는 'O가 ~되어[된 채로]'라는 의미로 분사 앞의 O가 분사의 의미상의 주어이다.

²Moreover, when the experiment was repeated / with either a helper and a neutral bystander block or a hinderer and a neutral block, // the infants **preferred** the friendly triangle **to** the neutral block, / and the neutral block **to** the nasty square.
• 「either A or B」는 'A 혹은 B 둘 중 하나'의 뜻이다.
• 「prefer A to B」는 'A를 B보다 더 좋아하다'의 뜻이다. and 뒤에는 반복되는 preferred가 생략되었다.

주제문
In ancient Egypt / a woman enjoyed the same rights as a man. What her rightful entitlement rights depended upon / was her social class, not her sex. ① All property descended in the female line, / on the assumption // that maternity is a matter of fact; / paternity a matter of opinion. ② When a man married an heiress, // he enjoyed her property // only so long as she lived, // but on her death / it passed to her daughter and daughter's husband. ③ ¹Marriage (in ancient Egypt) was a totally private affair [[in which the state took no interest] and [of which the state kept no record]]. ④ ²A woman was entitled / to administer her own property / and dispose of it // as she wished: She could buy, sell, / be executor (in wills) and witness (to legal documents), / bring an action (at court), / and adopt children. ⑤ ³In comparison, / an ancient Greek woman was supervised by a male guardian, // and many Greek women (living in Egypt / during the Ptolemaic Period), / observing Egyptian women (acting without a male guardian), / were encouraged to do so themselves.

어휘 entitlement 자격; 권리 *cf.* be entitled to-v ~할 자격이[권리가] 있다 property 재산; 소유(권) maternity 어머니임, 모성(↔ paternity 아버지임, 부성) heiress 여자 상속인 affair 일, 문제 dispose of ~을 처분하다[없애다] executor 유언 집행자; 수행자 will 유언(장); 의지 bring an action 기소하다 adopt 입양하다; 채택하다 guardian 보호자; 관리자 Ptolemaic (이집트의) 프톨레마이오스의

해설 글의 처음 부분을 읽고 주제를 파악하면서 주제문과 다른 내용을 골라낸다. 고대 이집트에서 여성은 사회적 계급에 따라 남성과 같은 권리를 누렸다는 내용의 글이므로 고대 이집트의 결혼이 사적인 영역이었다는 내용인 ③은 글의 흐름과 관계가 없다.

오답 Check
⑤는 고대 이집트 여성의 권리와 대조되는 고대 그리스 여성에 관한 내용이다.

PLUS+ 변형문제
어휘 discrimination 차별; 구별
해설 이 글은 고대 이집트의 여성들이 가진 권리와 높은 사회적 지위를 설명하고 있으므로 주제로는 ② '고대 이집트 여성이 가진 권한의 측면들'이다.
① 고대 이집트 사회에서의 성차별
→ 남성과 여성의 차별에 대한 내용은 아님.
③ 고대 그리스에서 재산 소유자로서 여성의 역할
→ 고대 그리스 여성들은 남성 보호자의 관리를 받음.
④ 사회에서 주요 역할을 하는 여성들의 이로운 영향
→ 이로운 영향에 대해 언급되지 않음.
⑤ 고대와 현대 사회에서 여성의 역할 차이
→ 고대와 현대 사회의 여성의 역할을 비교하는 내용은 없음.

해석 주제문 고대 이집트에서는 여성이 남성과 같은 권리를 누렸다. 그녀의 정당한 자격 권리가 달린 것은 그녀의 성별이 아니라 그녀의 사회적 계급이었다. ① 어머니임은 사실이고 아버지임은 견해상의 문제임을 전제로 하여, 모든 재산은 여계로 전해졌다. ② 한 남성이 여자 상속인과 결혼했을 때 그는 그녀가 살아 있는 동안에만 그녀의 재산을 누렸고 그녀가 죽으면 그것은 그녀의 딸과 사위에게 전해졌다. ③ 고대 이집트에서의 결혼은 국가가 관심을 갖지 않고 국가에서 어떠한 기록도 남기지 않는 전적으로 사적인 일이었다. ④ 여성은 자신의 재산을 관리하고 원하는 대로 그것을 처분할 자격이 있었다. 즉, 그녀는 사고 팔고 유언장의 집행자가 되고 법률 문서의 증인이 되고 법정에서 소송을 제기하고 자녀를 입양할 수 있었다. ⑤ 비교해보면, 고대 그리스 여성들은 남성 보호자의 관리를 받는데, 프톨레마이오스 시대에 이집트에 살던 많은 그리스 여성들은 남성 보호자 없이 행동하는 이집트 여성들을 지켜보고 그들 스스로 그렇게 하도록 용기를 얻었다.

구문 ¹Marriage (in ancient Egypt) was *a totally private affair* [[**in which** the state took no interest] and [**of which** the state kept no record]].
• 두 개의 '전치사+관계대명사'가 이끄는 절인 in which ~ no interest와 of which ~ no record가 and로 병렬 연결되어 동시에 a totally private affair를 수식한다.

²A woman was entitled / **to administer** her own property / and (to) **dispose** of it // as she wished: She *could* buy, sell, / be executor (in wills) and witness (to legal documents), / bring an action (at court), / and adopt children.
• to administer와 dispose는 and로 연결되며, dispose 앞의 to는 반복되어 생략되었다.
• 조동사 could 뒤에 동사원형 buy, sell, be, bring, adopt가 콤마(,)와 and로 병렬 연결되었다.

²In comparison, / an ancient Greek woman was supervised by a male guardian, // and *many Greek women* (living in Egypt / during the Ptolemaic Period), / observing *Egyptian women* (acting without a male guardian), / were encouraged to do so themselves.
• 첫 번째 ( ) 안의 현재분사구는 앞에 있는 명사 many Greek women을 수식한다.
• observing ~ a male guardian은 분사구문으로 동시상황을 나타내며, 두 번째 ( ) 안의 현재분사구는 앞에 있는 명사 Egyptian women을 수식한다.

36 ④ PLUS+ ⑤

Mathematics has been, is, and ever will be a current (running almost unseen beneath the surface of our affairs). We should, however, be careful / not to get carried away with the flow / by attempting to extend its application beyond its remit.

(C) There are places [where mathematics is completely the wrong tool for the job]: activities [in which human supervision is unquestionably necessary]. Even if some of the most complex mental tasks can be farmed out to an algorithm, // matters (of the heart) can never be broken down into a simple set of rules.

(A) No code or equation will ever imitate the true complexities (of the human condition). Nevertheless, a little mathematical knowledge in our increasingly quantitative society / can help us to harness the power (of numbers) for ourselves.

(B) ¹Simple rules allow us to make the best choices / and avoid the worst mistakes. ²Small alterations in the way [we think about our rapidly evolving environments] help us to 'keep calm' in the face of rapidly accelerating change, / or adapt to our increasingly automated realities.

해석 수학은 우리 일의 표면 아래에서 거의 보이지 않는 상태로 흐르는 물결이었고, 지금도 그러하며, 언제까지나 그러할 것이다. **주제문** 그러나 우리는 수학의 적용을 그 소관 너머로 연장시키려 시도함으로써 그 흐름에 휩쓸려가지 않도록 주의해야 한다.
(C) 수학이 일에 있어서 완전히 잘못된 도구인 곳들이 있다. 인간의 감독이 의심할 나위 없이 필요한 활동과 같이 말이다. 설령 가장 복잡한 정신적 과업이 알고리즘에 맡겨질 수 있을지라도, 마음의 문제는 결코 간단한 일련의 규칙들로 분해될 수 없다.
(A) 어떠한 코드나 방정식도 결코 인간 상태의 진정한 복잡성을 모방하지 못할 것이다. 그럼에도 불구하고 점점 더 양적인 우리 사회에서 약간의 수학적 지식은 우리가 스스로 숫자의 힘을 이용하도록 도울 수 있다.
(B) 간단한 규칙은 우리가 최고의 선택을 하고 최악의 실수는 피하도록 해준다. 빠르게 진화하는 환경에 대해 우리가 생각하는 방식에서의 작은 변화는 빠르게 가속되는 변화에 직면할 때 우리가 '침착함을 유지'하거나 점점 더 자동화되는 우리 현실에 적응하는 데 도움을 준다.

어휘 current (물·공기의) 흐름; 현재의; 전류 affair 일, 문제 extend 연장하다, 확대하다 application 적용, 응용; 지원(서) supervision 감독 unquestionably 의심할 나위 없이 farm out ~을 맡기다 ○algorithm 알고리즘 equation 방정식 quantitative 양적인 harness 이용[활용]하다 alteration 변화, 변경 accelerate 가속화하다 automate 자동화하다
어휘○ 알고리즘: 주어진 문제를 논리적으로 해결하기 위한 절차, 방법, 명령어들의 집합.

해설 수학을 그 소관 너머에 적용하는 것은 조심해야 하는 일이라고 한 주어진 글 다음에는 인간의 감독이 필요한 영역이나 마음의 문제에 수학을 적용하는 잘못을 언급하는 (C)가 이어져야 한다. 인간의 복잡한 정신에 적용되는 알고리즘의 한계에 대해 논한 (A)가 그다음에 연결된다. (A)의 중간 부분은 Nevertheless로 시작되며 '그럼에도 불구하고 수학을 아는 것은 도움이 된다'로 논지가 전환되는데, 이를 이어받은 (B)에서는 수학적 지식이 현명한 판단과 빠른 현대 사회에의 적용에 도움을 줄 수 있다는 내용으로 글이 마무리된다.

PLUS+ 변형문제

해설 수학은 보이지는 않아도 항상 우리 생활의 기저에 존재하는데, 적용 가능한 범위를 넘어 사용하는 것은 적절하지 않지만 수학적 지식은 우리 현실에 도움이 된다고 했으므로 이를 모두 포괄할 수 있는 글의 요지로는 ⑤가 가장 적절하다.
① → 일상 속에 적용된 수학적 원리에 관한 내용은 없음.
② → 수량화가 방해된다는 언급은 없음.
③ → 수학이 삶의 문제들을 해결해준다는 언급은 없음.
④ → 정신적 과업이 알고리즘에 맡겨질 수 있을지라도, 마음의 문제는 결코 간단한 일련의 규칙들로 분해될 수 없다고 했음.

구문 ¹Simple rules **allow** *us* **to make** the best choices / and **avoid** the worst mistakes.
• 「allow+O+C」의 구조로 allow는 목적격보어로 to부정사를 취한다. 이 문장에서는 목적격보어인 to make와 (to) avoid가 and로 연결되었다.

²**Small alterations** in *the way* [(that [in which]) we think about our rapidly evolving environments] **help** *us* **to 'keep'** calm' in the face of rapidly accelerating change, / or **adapt** to our increasingly automated realities.
(S 아래: Small alterations, V 아래: help)
• Small alterations가 주어이고 help가 동사이다.
• [ ]에는 관계사 that[in which]이 생략되어 the way를 수식한다.
• 「help+O+C」 구문은 목적격보어로 to부정사 또는 원형부정사를 취할 수 있다. 여기에서는 to부정사가 쓰였으며, to keep과 (to) adapt가 콤마(,)와 or로 연결되어 병렬 구조를 이룬다.

37 ② PLUS+ ⑤

Bad deflation occurs // when spending collapses and companies have to cut their prices to prop up sales, // just as hotels cut their rates when tourist traffic dries up. If people expect falling prices, // they may delay purchases // since their money will buy more later.

(B) Employers must lay some workers off to cope with falling prices. ¹Workers initially resist pay cuts, // but eventually, fear of unemployment persuades them to accept lower pay.

(A) If prices and wages are falling at the same rate, then, // is anyone the worse for it? Paychecks have shrunk // but because prices have as well, / purchasing power remains the same.

(C) ²The problem is that debt is fixed // as incomes and prices fall, // so the burden of debt rises. Homeowners slash spending / to keep up with their mortgage payments. Or worse, the home can't be sold for enough to repay the loan.

해석 나쁜 디플레이션은 관광객의 왕래가 줄어들 때 호텔이 요금을 인하하듯이 소비가 붕괴되고 회사들이 판매를 지원하기 위해 가격을 인하해야 할 때 일어난다. 사람들이 가격 하락을 기대한다면, 그들의 돈이 나중에 더 많이 살 수 있기 때문에 구매를 미룰 수도 있다.
(B) 고용주들은 가격 하락에 대처하기 위해 일부 노동자들을 정리 해고해야 한다. 노동자들은 처음에는 임금 삭감에 저항하지만, 결국 실업에 대한 두려움이 그들에게 더 낮은 임금을 받아들이도록 설득한다.
(A) 만약 물가와 임금이 같은 비율로 떨어지고 있다면, 그것 때문에 누가 더 나빠지겠는가? 임금이 줄어들지만 물가도 마찬가지이기 때문에 구매력은 그대로 유지된다.
(C) 문제는 소득과 물가가 하락하면서 부채는 고정되어 있기 때문에 부채 부담이 늘어난다는 것이다. 주택 소유자들은 그들의 담보 대출금을 계속 내기 위해 지출을 대폭 줄인다. 더 나쁘게도, 대출금을 상환할 만큼(의 가격으로) 주택을 팔 수 없다.

어휘 deflation 디플레이션; 물가 하락 collapse 붕괴하다 prop up 지원하다; ~을 받쳐 넘어지지 않게 하다 traffic (사람·차 등의) 왕래 dry up 줄어들다, 고갈되다 lay off 해고하다 be the worse for ~ 때문에 더 나빠지다 shrink 줄어들다; 움츠러들다 slash 대폭 줄이다; 긋다 keep up with (할부금 등을) 계속 내다; 알게 되다 mortgage (담보) 대출(금) loan 대출(금); (특히 돈을) 빌려주다

해설 나쁜 디플레이션에 대한 설명으로 가격 하락을 기대해 소비자가 구매를 미룬다는 내용의 주어진 글 다음에는 그로 인한 정리 해고와 임금 삭감이 이어진다는 (B)가 와야 한다. 그리고 앞의 내용을 포함하는 물가와 임금이 같은 비율로 떨어질 때의 상황을 언급하며 구매력은 유지된다는 (A)가 오고 마지막으로 구매력이 유지되더라도 부채 부담으로 인한 문제가 발생한다는 (C)가 오는 것이 적절하다.

오답 Check
(A)는 디플레이션 이후의 상황으로, 주어진 글 다음에 바로 연결할 가능성도 있지만 주어진 글에서 언급된 물가 하락과 (B)에서 언급된 임금 삭감을 함께 설명하므로 (B) 뒤에 나오는 것이 적절하다.

PLUS+ 변형문제
어휘 fluctuate 오르내리다, 수시로 변하다 inflation 인플레이션; 물가의 폭등 drive (어떤 방향으로) 몰다
해설 전반적으로 디플레이션이 발생하는 원인과 그 결과에 대해 나열하고 있으므로, 제목으로 가장 적절한 것은 ⑤ '일반 물가 수준 하락의 원인과 결과들'이다.
① 왜 디플레이션이 발생하고 물가 수준은 오르내리는가
→ 디플레이션의 원인은 언급되었지만, 물가 수준이 오르내리는 원인은 언급되지 않음.
② 디플레이션 동안 가계 부채를 해결하는 방법들
→ 부채는 언급되었지만, 해결 방법은 언급되지 않음.
③ 디플레이션 대 인플레이션, 고용주들에게 어떤 것이 더 나쁜가?
→ 둘을 비교하는 내용은 없음.
④ 소비자의 어떤 구매 행동이 가격을 결정하는가
→ 소비자들이 구매를 미루면 가격이 하락한다는 언급은 있지만 글 전체를 포괄하는 제목이 될 수는 없음.

구문 ¹Workers initially resist pay cuts, // but eventually, fear of unemployment **persuades** *them* **to accept** lower pay.
• 「persuade+O+C」의 구조로 'O가 ~하도록 설득하다'를 의미하며 목적격보어 자리에 to부정사가 온다.

²The problem is **that** debt is fixed // **as** incomes and prices fall, // so the burden of debt rises.
• 밑줄 친 that절은 be동사의 보어 역할을 하는 절이며, 주어와 동격을 이룬다.
• that절 안의 as는 '~하면서'라는 의미의 부사절을 이끄는 접속사이다.

38 ③ PLUS+ ④

A coral reef is one of the most biologically diverse ecosystems on earth, / rivaled only by tropical rain forests. (①) The environment of the coral reef is formed over thousands of years / by the life cycle (of vast numbers of coral animals). (②) The main architect of the reef is the stony coral, a relative of the sea anemone [that lives in tropical climates / and secretes a skeleton of almost pure calcium carbonate]. (③ Its companion is the green alga, a tiny unicellular plant, // which lives within its tissues.) ¹The organisms coexist in a mutually beneficial relationship, / with the algae consuming carbon dioxide (given off by the corals) and the corals thriving in the abundant oxygen (produced photosynthetically by the algae). (④) When the coral dies, // its skeleton is left, // and other organisms grow on top of it. (⑤) ²Over the years, the sheer mass of coral skeletons, / together with those of associated organisms, / combine to form the underwater forest [that divers find so fascinating].

해석 산호초는 지구상에서 가장 생물학적으로 다양한 생태계 중 하나로, 오직 열대 우림에 의해서만 견주어진다(의역: 열대 우림만이 산호초만큼 생물학적으로 다양한 생태계를 가질 수 있다). 주제문 산호초의 환경은 수천 년에 걸쳐 방대한 수의 산호 동물의 생활사에 의해 형성된다. 그 암초의 주요 건축가는 열대 기후에 살면서 거의 완전한 탄산칼슘 뼈대를 분비하는 말미잘의 친척인, 돌산호이다. 그것(돌산호)의 동반자는 작은 단세포 식물인 녹조인데, 그것(녹조)은 그것(돌산호)의 조직 안에서 산다. 조류는 산호가 발산하는 이산화탄소를 섭취하고 산호는 조류가 광합성에 의해서 생산하는 풍부한 산소 안에서 무성해지면서, 그 유기체들은 상호 간에 유익한 관계로 공존한다. 산호가 죽으면 그 뼈대가 남고, 그 위에서 다른 유기체가 자란다. 수년에 걸쳐, 산호 뼈대의 완전한 덩어리는, 관련 유기체의 그것(뼈대)들과 함께, 결합하여 잠수부들이 매우 매력적이라고 느끼는 수중 숲을 형성한다.

어휘 rival ~에 필적하다[비할 만하다]; ~와 경쟁하다; 경쟁자; 경쟁하는 tropical 열대(지방)의, 열대성의 architect 건축사, 설계자 relative 친척; 비교상의, 상대적인 secrete 분비하다; 비밀로 하다 calcium carbonate 탄산칼슘 companion 동반자; 동료 alga (pl. algae) 조류(藻類)《물속에 사는 하등 식물의 한 무리》 unicellular 단세포의 tissue 조직 coexist 공존하다 mutually 서로, 상호 간에 give off 발산하다 thrive in 무성해지다; 번성하다 abundant 풍부한 photosynthetically 광합성에 의해서 sheer 완전한, 순전한; 얇은 mass 덩어리; (양이) 많은; (일반) 대중; 질량 associate 결합시키다; 연상하다, 연관 짓다 fascinating 매력적인, 대단히 흥미로운

해설 주어진 문장을 읽은 후, 연결어나 지시어 등을 활용해야 한다. 또는, 글의 흐름이 끊기는 곳을 찾는다. 녹조의 특징을 언급하는 주어진 문장에서 Its companion은 문맥상 돌산호의 동반자가 되는 것을 의미하므로 돌산호가 산호초의 주요 건축가라는 내용과 녹조와 돌산호가 상호 유익한 관계로 공존한다는 내용 사이, 즉 ③에 들어가야 적절하다.

오답 Check
이 지문에서는 대명사가 특히 여러 번 등장하므로 각각이 무엇을 지칭하는지 유의하며 읽어야 한다. ③ 뒤 문장의 The organisms는 돌산호와 녹조를 의미한다.

PLUS+ 변형문제

해설 이 글은 산호초 내의 생태계가 생물학적으로 다양하다고 말하며, 산호초가 수천 년에 걸쳐 형성되는 과정을 설명하므로, 제목으로는 ④ '해양 왕국에서 다양한 생태계의 설립'이 가장 적절하다.
① 어떻게 열대 기후가 산호초가 형성되도록 돕는가
→ 열대 우림은 언급했지만, 열대 기후가 산호초 형성을 돕는다는 내용은 없음.
② 바다에서 유기체들의 공존의 어려움
→ 돌산호와 녹조의 공존에 관한 설명으로 만든 오답.
③ 지구 온난화 감소에 있어서 산호의 효과적인 역할
→ 상식적인 내용으로 만든 오답.
⑤ 해양의 복잡한 먹이 사슬: 작은 단세포 식물에서부터
→ 작은 단세포 식물인 녹조가 지문에 언급되었지만, 먹이 사슬은 언급되지 않음.

구문 ¹The organisms coexist in a mutually beneficial relationship, / **with** *the algae* **consuming** *carbon dioxide* (given off by the corals) **and** *the corals* **thriving** in *the abundant oxygen* (produced photosynthetically by the algae).
• 「with+O+v-ing」는 부대상황을 나타내는 분사구문으로 '~하면서, ~하여'로 해석한다. 여기서는 with의 목적어로 the algae와 the corals가 and로 병렬 연결되었다.
• 두 개의 ( )는 모두 과거분사구로 각각 앞의 명사 carbon dioxide와 the abundant oxygen을 수식한다.

²Over the years, the sheer mass of coral skeletons, / **together with** *those* **of associated organisms**, / combine to form *the underwater forest* [**that** divers find so fascinating].
• together with ~ organisms가 문장의 주어와 동사 사이에 삽입되었고, those는 skeletons를 의미한다.
• [ ]는 목적격 관계대명사 that이 이끄는 관계사절로 선행사는 the underwater forest이다.

According to the Greek philosopher Diogenes, / mastery of the self, or "self-sufficiency," leads to both happiness and freedom / but requires constant practice and training / in the face of adversity. (①) [1]His uncompromising philosophy requires // that one should abandon all property, possessions, family ties, and social values / in order to minimize the distraction of "illusory" emotional and psychological attachments. (② <u>Furthermore</u>, one must aggressively attack society / to help liberate others, / and purposefully lay oneself open to ridicule and abuse / in order to retain <u>this emotional detachment</u>.) Though more radical and uncompromising, // Diogenes' philosophy has its counterpart / in the teachings of the oriental schools of Buddhism and Taoism. (③)

주제문
However, critics complain // that Diogenes' lifestyle is self-indulgent, / relying on the generosity and productivity of others / to support his drifting lifestyle. (④) There is a philosophical point here, not just a pragmatic one, (concerning the universalizability of ethical rules for life). (⑤) [2]If everyone were to follow Diogenes' example, // society would collapse, / making it economically impossible / for anyone — including Diogenes — to concentrate on the mastery of the self.

해석 그리스 철학자 디오게네스에 의하면 극기(克己), 즉 '자족'은 행복과 자유 모두로 인도하지만 역경 앞에서 끊임없는 연습과 훈련을 요구한다. 그의 단호한 철학은 사람이 '환상에 불과한' 감정적이고 심리적인 애착의 주의 분산을 최소화하기 위해 모든 재산, 소유물, 가족 간의 유대, 사회적 가치를 포기해야 한다고 요구한다. 더욱이 사람은 다른 사람들을 자유롭게 하는 것을 돕기 위해 대단히 적극적으로 사회를 공격하고 이러한 감정적 분리를 유지하기 위해 의도적으로 자신이 조롱과 모욕의 대상이 되어야만 한다. 더 급진적이고 단호하기는 하지만, 디오게네스의 철학은 동양의 불교와 도교 학파들의 가르침에 상응하는 것이 있다. 주제문 그러나 비평가들은 디오게네스의 생활 양식이 제멋대로 하는 것이며 그의 방랑하는 생활 양식을 유지하기 위해 다른 사람들의 관대함과 생산성에 의존한다고 불평한다. 여기에 삶에 대한 윤리적 규율의 보편화 가능성에 관련한, 단지 실용적인 요점만이 아닌 철학적인 요점이 있다. 모든 사람이 디오게네스의 본을 따른다면 사회는 붕괴되어 디오게네스를 포함해 누구든 극기에 전념하는 것이 경제적으로 불가능해질 것이다.

어휘 mastery 지배[장악]력; 숙달, 통달 self-sufficiency (자급) 자족 adversity 역경; 불운 uncompromising 단호한; 타협하지 않는 tie 유대, 관계; 묶다 illusory 환상에 불과한 attachment 애착, 집착; 결부 aggressively 적극적으로; 공격적으로 liberate 자유롭게 해주다 lay oneself open to (공격·비판 따위의) 목표가 되다 ridicule 조롱; 비웃다 abuse 모욕; 학대; 오용 retain 유지[보유]하다 detachment 분리; 이탈 radical 급진적인; 과격한 counterpart 상응하는 것; 한 쌍의 한쪽 oriental 동양의 self-indulgent 제멋대로 하는; 방종한 drift 방랑하다; 표류하다 pragmatic 실용[현실]적인 universalizability 보편화 가능성

해설 주어진 문장을 읽은 후, 연결어나 지시어 등을 활용해야 한다. 더욱이(Furthermore)로 시작하는 주어진 문장에서 this emotional detachment가 무엇인지 찾아야 한다. 디오게네스의 철학을 설명하는 ② 앞 문장에서 언급된 '환상에 불과한' 감정적이고 심리적인 애착의 주의 분산을 최소화하는 것을 주어진 문장의 '감정적 분리'로 볼 수 있으므로 디오게네스 철학의 설명을 덧붙이는 주어진 문장은 ②에 이어지는 것이 적절하다.

오답 Check
③ 이후 문장들에서 디오게네스 철학을 비판하고 철학적 요점에서 디오게네스의 본을 따른다면 사회가 붕괴할 것이라고 결론지으므로 주어진 문장은 ③ 이후에 나올 수 없다.

PLUS+ 변형문제
어휘 bring about ~을 유발하다 embrace 수용하다, 받아들이다; (껴)안다 self-indulgence 방종, 제멋대로 함
해설 이 글은 디오게네스 철학의 개념과 비판적 견해를 다루므로 제목은 ④ '디오게네스의 철학은 사회의 파괴를 야기한다'이다.
① 급진적인 철학이 동양의 종교에 영향을 미치는 방식
→ 불교와 도교의 가르침과 상응한다고 언급하지만 영향을 미치는 방식은 언급하지 않음.
② 사회를 버리는 것은 사회적 관계를 줄인다
→ 상식과 관련된 내용으로 주제와 관련 없음.
③ 디오게네스 철학에서 자족의 비결
→ 글의 일부 내용으로 전체를 나타내지 못함.
⑤ 모든 사람이 디오게네스의 방종을 수용해야 하는 이유
→ 글에서 방종을 비판하므로 주제와 반대됨.

구문 [1]His uncompromising philosophy **requires** // **that** one should <u>abandon</u> all property, possessions, family ties, and social values / in order to minimize the distraction of "illusory" emotional and psychological attachments.
- 주절의 동사가 주장, 명령, 요구, 제안 등을 의미할 때 목적어로 나오는 that절의 동사로는 「(should +)동사원형」이 나와야 한다. 이때 종종 should가 생략되는 경우도 있다.

[2]If everyone were to follow Diogenes' example, // society would collapse, / **making it economically impossible** / *for anyone* — *including Diogenes* — **to concentrate on the mastery of the self**.
- making 이하는 분사구문으로 부대상황을 나타낸다.
- 분사구문 내에 「make+O+C」의 구조가 쓰였는데, 밑줄 친 it은 가목적어, to concentrate ~ the self가 진목적어이고, economically impossible이 목적격보어이다.
- for anyone ~ Diogenes는 to부정사의 의미상 주어이다.

A few years ago, / three Harvard researchers gave / dozens of Asian American women (at Harvard) a difficult math test. But before getting them started, / the researchers asked them to fill out a questionnaire (about themselves). ¹These Asian American women were members of two in-groups with conflicting norms: they were Asians, a group (recognized as being good at math), and they were women, a group (recognized as being poor at it). ²One set of participants received a questionnaire (asking about what languages they, their parents, and grandparents spoke // and how many generations of their family had lived in America). These questions were designed / to trigger the women's connection to Asian Americans. Other subjects answered inquiries (about coed dormitory policy), designed to trigger their connection to women. A third group, the control group, was quizzed about their phone and cable TV service. ³After the test, the researchers found // that the women [who had been manipulated / to think of themselves / as Asian Americans] had done better on the test / than did the control group, // who, in turn, had done better than the women (reminded of their female in-group).

↓

According to the experiment, / cueing an (A) identity [that is stereotyped] actually influenced the (B) performance of members of the group / to follow the stereotype.

해석 몇 년 전에 세 명의 하버드대 연구자들이 하버드의 수십 명의 아시아계 미국인 여성들에게 어려운 수학 시험을 냈다. 그러나 그들이 시작하게 하기 전에, 연구자들은 그들이 자신에 대한 설문지에 기입하도록 요청했다. 이 아시아계 미국인 여성들은 충돌하는 규범을 가진 두 개의 내집단의 구성원들이었다. 그들은 수학을 잘하는 것으로 인식되는 집단인 아시아계이자, 그것을 못하는 것으로 인식되는 집단인 여성이었다. 한 집단의 참가자들은 그들과 그들의 부모와 조부모가 무슨 언어를 말하는지 그리고 그들의 가족의 몇 세대가 미국에서 살았는지를 묻는 설문지를 받았다. 이 질문들은 아시아계 미국인과 이 여성들의 관련성을 촉발시키도록 고안되었다. 다른 피실험자들은 여성과 그들의 관련성을 촉발시키도록 고안된 남녀 공용 기숙사 정책에 대한 질문에 답했다. 세 번째 집단은 대조군으로, 그들의 전화와 케이블 TV 서비스에 대한 질문을 받았다. 추론 근거 실험 후에 연구자들은 자신을 아시아계 미국인으로 생각하도록 조종된 여성들이 대조군보다 시험에서 더 잘했고, 대조군은 차례로 자신의 여성 내집단을 상기하게 된 여성들보다 더 잘했음을 알아냈다.

↓

실험에 따르면, 고정관념이 형성된 (A) 정체성의 신호를 주는 것이 집단 구성원의 (B) 수행에 실제로 영향을 주어 고정관념을 따랐다.

어휘 dozens of 수십의, 많은 questionnaire 설문지 ⊙in-group 내집단 conflicting 충돌[상충]하는 norm 규범; 표준; 기준 trigger 촉발시키다; 계기 inquiry 질문; 조사 control group 대조군 ((실험에서 어떤 조작이나 조건도 가하지 않은 집단)) manipulate 조종하다 think of A as B A를 B로 생각하다[여기다] remind A of B A에게 B를 상기시키다 cue 신호(를 주다) stereotyped 고정관념이 형성된; 진부한
어휘⊙ 내집단: 가치관과 행동 방식이 비슷하여 구성원이 애착과 일체감을 느끼는 집단.

해설 요약문으로 보아 고정관념이 형성된 '무엇'에 대한 신호를 주는 것이 구성원의 '무엇'에 영향을 주었는지 찾아야 한다. 실험에서 피실험자들이 설문지를 통해 자신을 아시아계 미국인으로 혹은 여성으로 규정하도록 유도되었는데 이는 '정체성(identity)'에 대한 고정관념의 촉발 신호로 볼 수 있으며, 피실험자들은 자신이 어떠한 고정관념에 주목하도록 유도되었는지에 따라 그들의 수학 시험의 '수행(performance)' 결과가 달리 나타났다.

오답 Check
　　(A)　　(B)
① 집단 – 행동
→ (A)는 맞지만, (B)는 수학 시험을 수행하는 데 영향을 미친 것이므로 행동이라 볼 수 없음.
② 성격 – 평가
→ 아시아계 미국인 또는 여성으로 규정하게 된 것은 성격과 관련이 없으므로 (A)는 틀리고, 수학 시험을 수행하는 데 영향을 미친 것이므로 평가라 볼 수 없으므로 (B)도 틀림.
④ 심리 – 선호
→ (A)에 대한 근거는 부족하며, (B)는 틀림.
⑤ 지위 – 자아상
→ 아시아계 미국인 또는 여성으로 규정하게 된 것은 지위와 관련이 없으므로 (A)는 틀리고, 수학 시험을 수행하는 데 영향을 미치므로 (B)도 틀림.

구문 ¹These Asian American women were members of two in-groups with conflicting norms: they were Asians, *a group* (recognized as being good at math), and they were women, *a group* (recognized as being poor at it).

• 밑줄 친 Asians와 a group ~ at math 그리고 women과 a group ~ at it이 각각 동격 관계이다.
• 두 개의 ( )는 바로 앞에 나온 a group을 각각 수식하는 분사구이다.

[2]One set of participants received *a questionnaire* (asking about <u>what languages they, their parents, and grandparents spoke</u> // <u>and</u> <u>how many generations of their family had lived in America</u>).
- ( )는 a questionnaire를 수식하는 현재분사구이다.
- ( ) 내에서 전치사 about의 목적어로 밑줄 친 두 개의 의문사절이 and로 연결되어 병렬 구조를 이룬다.

[3]After the test, the researchers found // that *the women* [**who** had been manipulated / to think of themselves / as Asian Americans] had done better on the test / **than** did *the control group*, // who, in turn, had done better than *the women* (reminded of their

<u>V</u>　<u>S</u>

female in-group).
- [ ]는 주격 관계대명사 who가 이끄는 관계사절로 바로 앞에 나온 the women을 수식한다.
- 굵게 표시된 than 다음에 주어(the control group)와 동사(did)가 도치되었다.
- 콤마 뒤의 who는 계속적 용법의 관계대명사로 who가 이끄는 절이 앞에 나온 the control group을 보충 설명한다.
- ( )는 바로 앞의 the women을 수식하는 분사구이다.

41 ① 　 42 ④

[1]The reason [travels are mentally useful] involves a unique characteristic of cognition, // in which problems [that feel 'close' — and the closeness can be physical, temporal or even emotional —] get contemplated in a more concrete manner. As a result, when we think about things [that are nearby], our thoughts are constricted, / bound by a more (a) <u>limited</u> set of ideas. While this habit can be helpful — it allows us to focus on the facts at hand — // it also (b) <u>inhibits</u> our imagination. Consider a field of corn. [2]When you're standing in the middle of a farm, / the air smelling faintly of fertilizer and popcorn, // your mind is automatically drawn to thoughts (related to the primary definition of corn, // which is that it's a plant, a cereal, a staple of Midwestern farming). But imagine that same field of corn / from a different perspective. Instead of standing on a farm, you're now in a crowded city street (dense with taxis and pedestrians). The plant will no longer be just a plant; instead, your vast neural network will pump out / all sorts of (c) <u>associations</u>. You'll think about unhealthy corn syrup, obesity, and the Farm Bill: // you'll contemplate those corn mazes for kids at state fairs and the deliciousness of succotash (made with bacon and beans). The noun is now a vast web of connections. And this is why travel is so open to (d) <u>clarity</u>: When you escape from the place [you spend most of your time], // the mind is suddenly made aware of / all those unusual ideas (previously suppressed). You start thinking about obscure possibilities — corn can fuel cars! — [that never would have occurred to you // if you'd stayed back on the farm]. Furthermore, this (e) <u>expansive</u> kind of cognition comes with practical advantages, // since you can suddenly draw on a whole new set of possible solutions.

해석 여행이 정신적으로 유용한 이유는 인식의 독특한 특성과 관련되는데, 그(인식의 독특한 특성) 안에서 '가깝게' 느껴지는 문제들(가까움은 물리적, 시간적 혹은 심지어 정서적일 수도 있다)은 더 구체적인 방식으로 심사숙고된다. 그 결과 우리가 가까이 있는 것들에 대해 생각할 때, 우리의 생각은 수축하며, 더욱 (a) 제한된 일련의 생각에 얽매인다. 이러한 습관이 도움이 될 수도 있지만(이는 우리가 당면한 사실에 집중하는 것을 허용한다) 그것은 또한 우리의 상상력을 (b) 억제한다. 옥수수밭을 생각해보라. 공기 중에 희미하게 비료와 팝콘 냄새가 나며 당신이 농장 한가운데 서 있을 때, 당신의 정신은 옥수수의 주요한 정의(즉 식물, 곡물, 중서부 농업의 주요 산물)와 관련된 생각으로 자동으로 이끌리게 된다. 그러나 그 동일한 옥수수밭을 다른 관

어휘 cognition 인식, 인지　temporal 시간의; 일시적인　contemplate 심사숙고하다; 고려[생각]하다　concrete 구체적인; 실제[현실]의　constrict 수축하다; 위축시키다　bound 얽매인; 꼭 ~할 것 같은　association 연상; 연계; 협회　inhibit 억제하다　faintly 희미하게, 어렴풋이　staple 주요 산물; 주식(主食); 주요한　dense 밀집한; 짙은　pedestrian 보행자(의)　maze 미로　expansive 광범위한; 광활한　draw on 활용[이용]하다; 끝나 가다　**[선택지 어휘]** juice 정수, 본질; 즙, 주스　migratory 이동하는; 방랑하는　take control of ~을 통제[제어]하다

해설 **41** 제목 유형은 글의 핵심을 나타내면서도 압축적이고 상징적인 다양한 형태로 표현될 수 있음에 유의한다. 여행을 통해 문제를 평소와 다른 풍경에서 바라보게 되면 새로운 연상이 활성화되어 평소 억압되어 있던 색다른 인식이 가능해지므로 해결책도 도출해 낼 수 있다는 내용의 글이므로, 제목으로 가장 적절한 것은 ① '여행은 당신의 창의적 정수를 짜내는 것을 도울 수 있다'이다.
42 여행은 평소 제한돼 있던 우리의 인식을 명료함을 넘어선 불확실성의 지평으로 열어주는 기능을 하므로 (d) clarity를 uncertainty와 같은 표현으로 바꿔 써야 한다.

오답 Check
41 ② 왜 우리는 여행하는가? 우리는 이동하는 종이다
→ 우리가 여행을 하는 이유에 관한 글은 아님.
③ 혼자 하는 여행은 더 창의적인 문제 해결로 이끈다
→ 여행을 혼자 하는 것이 더 창의적인 해결을 이끈다는 내용은 없음.
④ 여행은 여러분의 관점을 변화시키고 여러분이 자기 자신이 되도록 돕는다 → 관점을 변화시키는 것은 어느 정도 맞지만, 자기 자신이 되도록 돕는다는 내용은 없음.
⑤ 여행하고 싶은가? 그것은 여러분의 삶을 통제하는 것에 관한 것이다 → 여행이 삶을 통제한다는 언급은 없음.
42 (a)가 포함된 문장에서 우리가 가까이 있는 것들에 대해 생각할 때, 우리의 생각은 수축하여 제한된 연상에 얽매인다고 했으므로 상상력을 (b) '억제한다'는 올바르다.

점에서 상상해보라. 농장에 서 있는 대신 당신은 지금 택시와 보행자들이 밀집한 붐비는 도시 거리에 있다. 그 식물은 더 이상 그냥 식물이 아닐 것이다. 대신에 당신의 광대한 신경망은 온갖 종류의 (c) 연상을 퍼 올릴 것이다. 당신은 건강에 좋지 않은 옥수수 시럽, 비만, 그리고 농업 법안에 대해 생각할 것이다. 당신은 주 박람회의 어린이를 위한 옥수수 미로, 그리고 베이컨과 콩으로 만들어진 옥수수 콩 요리의 맛 좋음을 생각할 것이다. 그 명사는 이제 연상의 거대한 망이다. 주제문 그리고 이것이 여행이 그토록 (d) 명료함(→ 불확실성)에 열려 있는 이유이다. 당신이 당신의 대부분의 시간을 쓰는 장소로부터 벗어날 때, 정신은 갑자기 이전에 억눌려 있던 그 모든 색다른 생각들을 인식하게 된다. 당신은 농장에 머물렀다면 결코 떠오르지 않았을 모호한 가능성들(옥수수가 자동차에 연료를 공급할 수 있어!)에 대해 생각하기 시작한다. 게다가 이러한 (e) 광범위한 종류의 인식은 당신이 갑자기 전적으로 새로운 일련의 가능한 해결책들을 활용할 수 있으므로 실용적인 이점과 함께 온다.

구문 [1]*The reason* [(why) travels are mentally useful] involves *a unique characteristic of cognition*, // in **which** *problems* [that feel 'close'— and the closeness can be physical, temporal or even emotional—] get contemplated in a more concrete manner.

- 첫 번째 [ ]는 관계부사 why가 생략된 관계사절로 주어인 The reason을 수식한다.
- 계속적 용법으로 쓰인 관계대명사 which의 선행사는 a unique characteristic of cognition이고, in which가 이끄는 절 내에서 [ ]는 problems를 수식한다.

[2]When you're standing in the middle of *a farm*, / *the air* **smelling** faintly of fertilizer and popcorn, // your mind is automatically drawn to *thoughts* (related to *the primary definition of corn*, // **which** is that it's a plant, a cereal, a staple of Midwestern farming).

- 밑줄 친 부분은 주어가 명시된 분사구문으로, the air가 분사구문의 의미상 주어이다.
- ( )는 과거분사 related가 이끄는 분사구로 thoughts를 수식한다.
- which는 계속적 용법으로 쓰인 관계대명사로 선행사 the primary definition of corn을 보충 설명한다.

| 31 ① + ② | 32 ④ + ④ | 33 ① + ① | 34 ④ + ③ | 35 ④ + ① | 36 ② + ③ |
| 37 ③ + ③ | 38 ⑤ + ⑤ | 39 ② + ② | 40 ③ | 41 ② | 42 ⑤ |

31 ① PLUS+ ②

Although resources and houses are both built over time, // resource construction isn't like building construction — / starting with one brick, putting another one on top of that one, and another one on top of that one. Building resources is more like being a currency broker, / trading one resource for another / depending on what you need and what the market demands, / striving to come out ahead / at the end of the day. 주제문 Resources are, in large part, very <u>fluid</u>. Much of what we do every day / is to convert some resource — especially time or energy — into some other resource. Money can buy a bigger house, // knowledge can translate into a better job, // and time (spent with friends) builds "capital" in those friendships. Even social roles, such as that of child, can be converted into resources, such as money. [1]Depending on what our needs and goals are, / we organize our resources toward meeting those needs and reaching those goals, / using resources (in one area) to build resources (in another) / or using momentum (in one area) to overcome a roadblock (in another).

[해석] 자원과 집은 모두 시간이 흐르면서 형성되지만 자원 구축은 벽돌 한 개로 시작해 그것 위에 또 하나를 놓고, 그것 위에 또 하나를 놓는 건물 건축과는 같지 않다. 자원을 쌓는 것은 자신이 필요한 것과 시장이 요구하는 것에 따라 한 자원을 다른 것으로 교환하며 하루가 끝날 때 수익을 내려고 애쓰는 통화 중개인이 되는 것에 더 가깝다. 주제문 자원은 대부분 매우 유동적이다. 추론 근거 우리가 매일 하는 일의 대부분이 어떤 자원, 특히 시간이나 에너지를 다른 어떤 자원으로 변환하는 것이다. 돈은 더 큰 집을 살 수 있고 지식은 더 좋은 직장으로 바뀔 수 있고 친구들과 보낸 시간은 그 우정에 '자본'을 쌓아 준다. 심지어 자식의 역할과 같은 사회적 역할조차도 돈과 같은 자원으로 변환될 수 있다. 우리의 욕구와 목표가 무엇인지에 따라 우리는 그 욕구를 충족하고 그 목표를 달성하는 방향으로 자원을 조직한다. 한 영역의 자원을 이용해 다른 영역에 자원을 쌓거나 한 영역의 추진력을 이용해 다른 영역의 장애를 극복함으로써 말이다.

[어휘] resource 자원; 수단 broker 중개인 strive to ~하려 애쓰다 come out ahead 수익[이익]을 올리고 끝나다; 최후에는 이득을 보다 convert 변환[전환]하다, 바꾸다 momentum 추진력; 탄력; 가속도 overcome 극복하다 roadblock 장애[방해](물); 바리케이드 [선택지 어휘] minute 사소한; 미세[상세]한; (시간의 단위) 분 feasible 실현 가능한; 적합한 cumulative 누적적인, 누적되는

[해설] 빈칸 문장 뒤 문장을 보면, 어떤 자원을 다른 자원으로 변환이 가능하고, 우리는 한 영역의 자원을 이용해 다른 영역에 자원을 쌓거나 장애를 극복함으로써 우리의 욕구를 충족하고 목표를 달성한다고 했으므로, 이러한 자원의 특징을 나타내는 것은 ① '유동적'이 가장 적절하다.

[오답 Check]
② 제한된 ③ 사소한 ④ 실현 가능한 ⑤ 누적적인
→ ② ~ ⑤ 모두 글에서 근거를 찾을 수 없는 자원의 특성이므로 오답.

PLUS+ 변형문제

[어휘] ultimate 궁극적인; 최종의 ease 용이함; 편의성
[해설] 자원은 유동적으로 활용이 가능하므로 이를 이용해 우리의 욕구를 충족하고 목표를 달성할 수 있다는 내용이므로 글의 제목으로는 ② '목표를 달성하기 위해 자원을 유연하게 활용하라'가 가장 적절하다.
① 통화 중개인의 궁극적인 목표
③ 시간을 절약하라, 그러면 여러분의 자원이 늘어날 것이다
→ ①, ③ 글의 일부 내용을 활용한 오답.
④ 자원의 합이 그것의 부분들보다 더 큰가?
⑤ 자원의 특성: 조직화의 용이함
→ ④, ⑤ 글에 언급되지 않음.

[구문] [1]Depending on what our needs and goals are, / we organize our resources **toward** meeting those needs and reaching those goals, / **using** resources (in one area) to build resources (in another) / or using momentum (in one area) to overcome a roadblock (in another).
• 전치사 toward의 목적어로 밑줄 친 두 개의 동명사구가 and로 연결되어 병렬 구조를 이룬다.
• using 이하는 모두 부대상황을 나타내는 분사구문으로 밑줄 친 두 부분이 or로 병렬 연결되었다.

32 ④ PLUS+ ④

주제문
Although convenient, // hasty generalization can lead to costly and catastrophic results. ^{추론 근거} ¹There is an example in *Alice's Adventures in Wonderland*, // where Alice infers that, // since she is floating in a body of water, // a railway station, and thus help, must be close by: ²"Alice had been to the seaside once in her life, / and had come to the conclusion, // that wherever you go to on the English coast // you find a number of bathing machines in the sea, some children (digging in the sand with wooden spades), then a row of lodging houses, and behind them a railway station." ^{추론 근거} In another example, it may be argued // that an engineering assumption led to the explosion of the Ariane 5 rocket / during its first test flight: The control software had been extensively tested / with the previous model, Ariane 4 — // but unfortunately these tests did not cover / all the possible scenarios of the Ariane 5, // so it was wrong / to assume that the data would carry over. Signing off on such decisions / typically comes down to engineers' and managers' ability (to argue).

해석 주제문 편리하긴 하지만, 성급한 일반화는 희생이 큰 파멸적인 결과를 초래할 수 있다. 추론 근거 〈이상한 나라의 앨리스〉에 한 예가 있는데, 거기서 앨리스는 자신이 물에 떠 있기 때문에 기차역이, 따라서 도움도, 가까이에 분명히 있을 것이라고 추측한다. '앨리스는 살면서 딱 한 번 바닷가에 간 적 있었기에 영국 해안 어디를 가든 바다에 많은 이동식 탈의실과 나무 삽으로 모래를 파는 몇 명의 아이들, 그리고 일렬로 늘어선 하숙집들과 그것들 뒤의 철도역을 보게 될 것이라는 결론에 도달했다.' 추론 근거 또 다른 예로, 한 공학 가설로 첫 번째 시험 비행 도중에 Ariane 5 로켓이 폭발할 것이라고 주장할 수도 있다. 제어 소프트웨어는 이전 모델인 Ariane 4를 가지고 광범위하게 테스트 되었지만 불행히도 이 테스트들은 Ariane 5의 모든 가능한 시나리오를 포함하지 못했기에 데이터가 이어질 것이라고 추정하는 것은 잘못된 것이었다. 그러한 결정에 대해 승인하는 것은 일반적으로 공학자들과 관리자들의 논쟁하는 능력으로 요약된다.

어휘 catastrophic 파멸적인; 대재해의 infer 추론[추측]하다 bathing machine 이동식 탈의실 spade 삽 lodging house 하숙집; 간이 숙박소 cover 포함하다; 다루다; 씌우다 carry over 이어지다; 계속 추진되다 sign off ~에 대해 승인[허가]하다 come down to ~로 요약[설명]되다 **[선택지 어휘]** premise 전제; 근거 hasty 성급한; 허둥대는 generalization 일반화 ambiguous 모호한

해설 빈칸이 첫 한두 문장에 있는 경우 주제문일 가능성이 크고, 이어지는 내용은 구체적인 예시, 상술이므로 추론 근거가 포착될 때까지만 읽어 내려간다. 앨리스가 단지 한 번 바닷가를 가보고 나서 모든 영국 해안이 그와 동일하게 근처에 기차역이 있을 것이라고 추측하고 또 다른 예에서 이전 모델의 테스트 데이터를 신형 모델에 그대로 적용하는 건 잘못되었다고 했으므로 빈칸에는 ④ '성급한 일반화'가 적절하다.

오답 Check
① 선택적 관심
② 무관한 전제 → 매력적인 오답으로 이전 모델의 테스트 결과를 다른 모델에 적용한 것은 전제 때문이 아니라 일반화를 나타내는 것임.
③ 우연한 사례
⑤ 모호한 정의
→ ①, ③, ⑤는 지문의 주제와는 관계가 없는 오답임.

PLUS+ 변형문제
어휘 intuition 직관; 직감 equivocal 애매한; 불분명한
해설 주제문으로 보아 제목으로 가장 적절한 것은 ④ '성급한 논리적 추론이 희망하는 결과를 망칠 수 있다'이다.
① 첫 번째 시도는 일련의 결과를 초래한다
→ 지문에 언급되지 않은 내용임.
② 한 사건과 다른 사건을 직관으로 연결하라
→ 연결하는 것은 주제문과 반대되는 내용임.
③ 우연한 발견이 현명한 해결책으로 이끈다
→ 지문에 언급되지 않은 내용임.
⑤ 공학 기술에서 성능 테스트의 애매한 기준
→ 두 번째 추론 근거를 활용한 것으로 애매한 기준은 언급하지 않음.

구문 ¹There is an example in *Alice's Adventures in Wonderland,* // **where** Alice infers **that**, // since she is floating in a body of water, // a railway station, and thus help, must be close by: ~.
• where 이하는 관계부사 where가 이끄는 관계부사절로 Alice's Adventures in Wonderland를 보충 설명한다.
• 관계부사절 내에서 동사 infers의 목적어로 that이 이끄는 명사절이 나오는데, that과 주어(a railway station, ~ help) 사이에 since가 이끄는 이유의 부사절이 삽입되었다.

²"Alice had been to the seaside once in her life, / and had come to <u>the conclusion</u>, // **that** wherever you go to on the English coast // you **find** <u>a number of bathing machines in the sea</u>, *some children* (digging in the sand with wooden spades), then <u>a row of lodging houses</u>, and <u>behind them a railway station</u>."
• 접속사 that은 앞에 있는 명사 the conclusion을 부연 설명하는 동격절을 이끈다.
• 동사 find의 목적어로 쓰인 밑줄 친 네 개의 명사구가 콤마(,)와 접속사 and로 연결되어 병렬 구조를 이룬다.

09

주제문

Research psychologists have rejected / much of Freudian theory, // but one idea [Freudian therapists and experimental psychologists agree on today] is // that our ego fights fiercely / to defend its honor. This agreement is a relatively recent development. <u>추론 근거</u> ¹For many decades, research psychologists thought of people / as detached observers [who assess events and then apply reason / to discover truth and decipher the nature of the social world]. We were said to gather data on ourselves / and to build our self-images / based on generally good and accurate inferences. ²In that traditional view, a well-adjusted person / was thought to be like a scientist of the self, // whereas an individual [whose self-image was clouded by illusion] was regarded as vulnerable to, / if not already a victim of, / mental illness. Today, we know // that <u>the opposite is closer to the truth</u>. <u>추론 근거</u> Normal and healthy individuals — students, professors, engineers, doctors, business executives — tend to think of themselves / as not just competent but proficient, even if they aren't.

어휘 Freudian 프로이트의   detached 초연한; 분리된   decipher 해독하다; 판독하다   inference 추론; 추정   well-adjusted 정서적으로 안정된; 잘 적응한   cloud 흐리게 하다; 더럽히다   illusion 착각; 환각   be regarded as ~로 여겨지다   vulnerable 피해를 입기 쉬운; 취약한   executive 간부, 임원   competent 유능한   proficient 능숙한, 숙련된
[선택지 어휘] deny 부정[부인]하다

해설 빈칸이 후반부에 있는 경우 빈칸 문장 뒤 이어지는 마지막 문장이 부연 설명으로 명백한 추론 근거가 되는 경우가 많다. 과거의 의견처럼, 우리가 자신에 대한 데이터를 수집한 후에 논리적 추론에 근거해서 자아상을 구축하는 것이 아니라, 오늘날 우리는 자신의 능력이 뛰어나지 않더라도 훨씬 더 뛰어난 자아상을 갖는다는 것이 글의 내용이므로 빈칸에는 ① '그 반대가 진실에 더 가깝다'라는 말이 들어가야 가장 적절하다.

오답 Check

② 그것은 오직 그 반대로만 작용한다
→ 전통적인 견해와 반대로 작용하는 상황이 제시되긴 하지만, 그러한 '경향이 있다'고 했으므로 항상 반대로만 작용하는 것은 아님.

③ 아무도 전통적인 견해를 부정할 수 없다
→ 전통적인 견해와 반대되는 내용이 빈칸 뒤 문장에 이어짐.

④ 관점은 매우 애매하다
→ 오늘날의 전문가들이 동의하는 관점이므로 반대되는 설명임.

⑤ 그 개인들은 고려되지 않아야 한다
→ 글의 요지와 전혀 관련이 없음.

PLUS + 변형문제

어휘 prejudice 편견   objective 객관적인   vulnerability 취약성, 상처받기 쉬움   victim 희생자, 피해자

해설 오늘날의 심리학자들과 프로이트주의 치료 전문가들이 동의하는 생각을 가장 잘 나타낸 제목은 ① '우리의 자아상을 과장하는 우리의 추구'이다.
② 객관적인 관찰자로서 모든 편견에서 벗어나라
→ 오늘날의 상황과 반대됨.
③ 개인의 긍정적인 상상에 영향을 받지 않는 방법
→ 긍정적 상상에 영향을 받지 않는 방법은 언급되지 않음.
④ 정신질환의 희생자가 되는 것에 대한 사람들의 취약성
→ 글의 일부 단어를 활용한 오답으로 주제문과 관련 없음.
⑤ 자아상을 형성함에 있어서 객관적 분석으로 향하는 우리의 자아
→ 전통적인 의견에 대한 내용임.

해석 주제문 연구 심리학자들은 프로이트 이론의 많은 부분을 거부했지만, 오늘날의 프로이트주의 치료 전문가들과 실험 심리학자들이 동의하는 하나의 생각은 우리의 자아는 자신의 명예를 지키기 위해 맹렬하게 싸운다는 것이다. 이 의견의 일치는 비교적 최근의 진전된 일이다. 추론 근거 수십 년 동안, 연구 심리학자들은 인간이 진실을 발견하고 사회적 세계의 속성을 해독하기 위해 사건을 평가하고 나서 이성을 쓰는 초연한 관찰자라고 간주했다. 우리는 자신에 대한 데이터를 수집한 후에 대체로 훌륭하고 정확한 추론에 근거하여 자아상을 구축한다고 했다. 그런 전통적인 견해에 따르면, 정서적으로 안정된 사람은 자신에 대한 과학자나 마찬가지로 여겨졌고, 반면에 착각으로 자아상이 흐려진 개인은 이미 정신질환의 피해자가 된 것이 아니라면 그것의 피해를 입기 쉬울 것이라고 여겨졌다. 오늘날, 우리는 그 반대가 진실에 더 가깝다는 것을 알고 있다. 추론 근거 정상적이고 건강한 개인— 학생, 교수, 공학자, 의사, 회사 간부 —은 자신이 실제로 그렇지 않더라도 자신을 유능할 뿐만 아니라 몹시 뛰어난 사람으로 생각하는 경향이 있다.

구문 ¹For many decades, research psychologists **thought of** people / **as** *detached observers* [**who** assess events and then apply reason / to discover truth and decipher the nature of the social world].
• 「think of A as B」의 구조로 'A를 B로 생각하다'라는 의미이다.
• [ ]는 주격 관계대명사 who가 이끄는 관계사절로 선행사인 detached observers를 수식한다.

²In that traditional view, a well-adjusted person / was thought to be like a scientist of the self, // whereas *an individual* [**whose** self-image was clouded by illusion] was regarded as vulnerable <u>to</u>, / <u>if not already a victim of</u>, / **mental illness**.
• [ ]는 소유격 관계대명사 whose가 이끄는 관계사절로 앞에 있는 명사 an individual을 수식한다.
• 밑줄 친 부분은 앞에 있는 전치사 to와 뒤에 있는 목적어 mental illness 사이에 삽입된 부사절로, 반복되는 주어(an individual ~ by illusion)와 be동사(was)가 생략되었다. 밑줄 친 부분에 있는 전치사 of의 목적어는 mental illness이다.

¹Imagine // that a large number of observers are shown a glass jar (containing coins) / and are challenged to estimate the number of coins in the jar. This is the kind of task [in which individuals do very poorly], // but pools of individual judgments hit the mark. The mechanism is straightforward: the average of many individual errors tends toward zero. However, this works well // only when the observers are completely independent from one another. If the observers lean in the same direction, // the collection of judgments will not help. For this reason, when there are multiple witnesses to an event, // they are not allowed to discuss their testimony beforehand. The goal is not only to prevent the cheating (of hostile witnesses), // it is also to prevent unbiased witnesses from affecting each other. ²When this practice is not enforced, // witnesses will tend to make similar errors in their testimony, // which reduces the total value of the information [they provide].

해석 수많은 관찰자가 동전이 들어 있는 유리병을 보고 병 안에 있는 동전의 숫자를 추정할 것을 요구받는다고 상상해 보아라. 이것은 개개인은 매우 형편없이 추측하지만, 개별적 판단들이 모이면 예상이 적중하는 종류의 과업이다. 기제는 간단하다. 주제문 **많은 개개인이 범하는 오류의 평균은 0을 향하는 경향이 있다.** 하지만 이는 관찰자들이 서로 전적으로 독립적일 때에만 효과가 있다. 관찰자들이 같은 방향으로 기운다면, 판단의 모음은 도움이 되지 않을 것이다. 추론 근거 이러한 이유로, 한 사건에 다수의 목격자가 있을 때, 그들은 사전에 자신의 증언을 의논하는 것이 허락되지 않는다. 이것의 목표는 적의를 가진 목격자의 속임수를 방지하기 위해서뿐만 아니라, 선입견 없는 목격자들이 서로 영향을 끼치지 못하게 하기 위함이다. 이 관행을 시행하지 않으면, 목격자들은 증언에서 유사한 오류를 범하는 경향을 보일 것이며, 이는 그들이 제공하는 정보의 총체적인 가치를 떨어뜨린다.

어휘 estimate 추정하다 hit the mark 예상이 들어맞다; 목표를 달성하다(↔ miss the mark 예상이 빗나가다; 목표 달성에 실패하다) mechanism (특정한 기능을 수행하는) 구조, 기제; 기계 장치 straightforward 간단한, 쉬운; 솔직한 multiple 많은, 다수의; ((수학)) 배수 testimony 증언; 증거 beforehand 사전에, ~전에 미리 hostile 적대적인; 강력히 반대하는 unbiased 선입견[편견] 없는, 편파적이지 않은 enforce (법을) 집행[시행]하다; 강요하다
[선택지 어휘] diversity 다양성 reliable 신뢰할 수 있는, 믿을 만한 assumption 가정, 추정

해설 지문 전반부의 내용은 유리병에 들어있는 동전 개수를 추정할 때 개개인의 의견을 따로 보면 오류가 많지만 합치면 오류의 평균은 0에 가까워진다는 것이다. 다음에 이어지는 빈칸 문장은 '어떤' 경우에만 이 방법이 효과가 있는지를 제시하는데, 빈칸 뒷부분에서 목격자들이 사전에 증언을 의논하는 것을 금지한다는 내용이 나오므로 빈칸에 들어갈 조건은 ④ '관찰자들이 서로 전적으로 독립적인' 것이 된다.

오답 Check
① 참가자들이 신뢰할 수 있는 의견을 다양하게 가지고 있을
→ 다양한 의견에 대한 언급은 없음.
② 관찰자들이 상황에 대해 과학적으로 생각할
→ 과학적인 사고에 대한 언급은 없음.
③ 결론을 많은 사람의 가정에 근거를 둘
→ 다른 사람의 영향을 차단해야 한다는 글의 내용과 반대됨.
⑤ 참가자들이 양측의 사안을 존중할
→ 글에 언급되지 않은 내용임.

PLUS + 변형문제

어휘 pitfall 함정; 위험 degrade 저하시키다; 비하하다
해설 관찰자들이 서로 전적으로 독립적일 때 개개인이 범하는 오류의 평균은 0을 향하는 경향이 있다고 했으므로 글의 제목으로 가장 적절한 것은 ③ '사회적 영향을 막는 것이 어떻게 정확성을 향상하는가'이다.
① 독립적 사고와 책임 → 독립적 사고에 대한 책임은 언급되지 않음.
② 목격자 증언과 기억 편향 → 글에 언급된 어구를 활용한 오답.
④ 집단사고의 함정: 비판적 사고를 저하시키는 것
→ 비판적 사고에 대한 내용이 아님.
⑤ 집단의 지혜: 왜 다수가 소수보다 더 똑똑한가
→ 글의 앞부분을 활용한 오답.

구문 ¹Imagine // that **a large number of observers** are shown *a glass jar* (containing coins) / and are challenged to estimate **the number of coins** in the jar.
• 「a large number of+복수명사」는 '다수의, 많은'이란 뜻으로 복수동사와 함께 쓰인다. 밑줄 친 두 동사구가 and로 병렬 연결되었다.
• ( )는 a glass jar를 수식하는 분사구이다.
• 「the number of+복수명사(+단수동사)」는 '~의 수'란 뜻이다.

²When this practice is not enforced, // witnesses will tend to make similar errors in their testimony, // **which** reduces the total value of *the information* [(which[that]) they provide].
• which 이하 관계대명사절은 앞의 witnesses ~ testimony를 보충 설명한다.
• [ ]는 목적격 관계대명사 which 또는 that이 생략된 관계사절로 선행사 the information을 수식한다.

35 ④ PLUS⁺ ①

주제문
¹The growth characteristics (of weeds) / and the colour (of their leaves and flowers) / may be as important as their presence / in revealing information (about the soil). ① The observant farmer and gardener / will notice subtle changes (in the weed populations on his land) in response to his agricultural practices. ② As his soil improves // he may find // that chickweed, chicory, common groundsel, common horehound, and lambsquarter / become the dominant weeds. ③ However, if he finds // that the daisy, wild carrot, and wild radish / become dominant, / he should review his practices // as these weeds thrive on soils (of low fertility). ④ ²As all weeds are considered bad for crop growth, // removing them all is thought the best way (to deal with them), // although this method can be both time-consuming and tough work. ⑤ The addition of well-balanced compost, organic manures, and other fertilizers / together with certain cultivation and drainage practices / may be required to bring the soil back / into production.

해석 주제문 토양에 대한 정보를 밝힘에 있어서 잡초의 생장 특징과 그것들의 잎과 꽃의 색깔은 잡초의 존재만큼이나 중요할지도 모른다. ① 관찰력 있는 농부와 정원사는 자신의 농업 실행에 대한 반응으로 자신의 땅에 있는 잡초 개체수의 미묘한 변화를 알아차릴 것이다. ② 그의 토양이 향상될 때 그는 별꽃, 치커리, 보통 개쑥갓, 보통 쓴 박하, 그리고 명아주가 지배적인 잡초가 되는 것을 알게 될지도 모른다. ③ 그러나 그가 데이지, 야생 당근, 그리고 야생 무가 지배적이게 됨을 알게 된다면, 이러한 잡초들이 생산력이 낮은 토양에서 번성하기 때문에 그는 자신의 실행을 검토해야 한다. ④ 모든 잡초들은 농작물 성장에 나쁜 것으로 여겨지기 때문에 비록 이 방법(그것들을 모두 없애는 것)이 시간이 걸리고 고된 일일 수도 있지만 모두 없애는 것이 그것들을 해결하는 최고의 방법으로 여겨진다. ⑤ 토양의 생산성을 돌려놓기 위하여 일정한 경작과 배수 실행과 더불어 잘 균형 잡힌 퇴비, 유기농 거름과 다른 화학 비료들의 추가가 요구될지도 모른다.

어휘 observant 관찰력 있는; 준수하는 subtle 미묘한; 옅은 agricultural 농업의 chickweed 별꽃 groundsel 개쑥갓 horehound 쓴 박하 lambsquarter 명아주 dominant 지배적인; 우세한 radish 무 thrive 번성[번영]하다 fertility 생산력; 비옥도 deal with 해결하다; 다루다 time-consuming 시간이 걸리는 compost 퇴비; 혼합 비료; 혼합물 fertilizer 화학 비료 cultivation 경작, 재배 drainage 배수; 배출된 물

해설 무관 문장은 주제와 관련 있는 어구를 넣어 만든다는 것에 유의한다. 잡초를 살펴보아 토양의 상태에 대한 정보를 얻고, 잡초를 통해 토양의 상태가 나쁜 것을 알게 되었을 때 비료와 경작법, 배수 등에 변화를 꾀하여 토질을 향상할 수 있다는 내용의 글이다. ④는 잡초를 모두 제거하는 것이 최고의 방법이라고 설명하므로 이는 토양에 대한 정보를 밝히는 데 잡초를 활용할 수 있다는 글의 전체적인 흐름과 관계가 없다.

오답 Check
⑤는 생산력이 낮은 토양을 발견할 때의 대처법에 대한 내용으로 글의 소재인 잡초는 언급되지 않으나 ③과 밀접한 관련이 있다.

PLUS⁺ 변형문제
어휘 profitable 수익성이 좋은 produce 농작물; 수확물
해설 이 글은 잡초의 종류에 따라 토양의 생산력을 파악할 수 있으므로 잡초가 농업에 중요하다는 내용이므로, 주제로는 ① '토양의 생산력을 보여주는 데 있어서 잡초의 역할'이 가장 적절하다.
② 잡초 피해를 예방하기 위한 밭 형성하기
③ 더 수익성이 있는 농산물을 위한 다양한 토양의 종류
④ 토양을 영양분이 풍부하도록 유지시키는 화학 비료의 중요성
→ 화학 비료로 토양의 생산력을 회복할 수 있다고 언급했지만, 글 전체를 나타내지 못함.
⑤ 기술을 통해 식물 건강을 알아내는 방법
→ 식물의 건강이 아닌 토양의 생산력에 관한 내용이고, 기술도 언급되지 않음.

구문 ¹The growth characteristics (of weeds) / and the colour (of their leaves and flowers) / may be **as** *important* **as** their presence / in revealing information (about the soil).
• 밑줄 친 부분은 「as ... as ~(~만큼 …하다)」의 원급 비교 구문으로 동사 be의 보어 역할을 한다.

²**As** all weeds are considered bad for crop growth, // removing them all is thought *the best way* (to deal with them), // **although** this method can be both time-consuming and tough work.
• As는 이유를 나타내는 부사절 접속사이고, 주절의 주어는 removing them all이고 동사는 is thought이다.
• ( )는 앞에 있는 the best way를 수식한다.
• although가 이끄는 부사절 내에서 상관 접속사 「both A and B」가 밑줄 친 두 개의 형용사를 병렬 연결한다.

Most people think of sneezes as symptoms — but that's really only half the story. ¹A normal sneeze occurs // when the body's self-defense system senses a foreign invader (trying to get in through your nasal passages) / and acts to repel the invasion / by expelling it with a sneeze. But sneezing when you've got a cold?

(B) There's obviously no way (to expel the cold virus) // when it's already lodged in your upper respiratory tract. 주제문 That sneeze is a whole different animal — the cold virus has learned to trigger the sneezing // so it can find new places (to live) / by infecting your family, your colleagues, and your friends.

(A) 주제문 So yeah, sneezes are symptoms, // but they've evolved a simple and efficient method of host manipulation. When they're caused by a cold, // they're symptoms (with a purpose), // and the purpose isn't yours.

(C) That's true for many of the things [we think of as symptoms of infectious disease]. ²They're actually the product (of host manipulation) // as whatever bacteria or virus has infected us works to engage our unconscious assistance / in making the jump to its next host.

해석 대부분의 사람들은 재채기를 증상으로 생각하지만, 그것은 정말로 단지 이야기의 절반(사실의 한 부분)일 뿐이다. 보통의 재채기는 신체의 자기방어 시스템이 콧구멍을 통해 들어오려고 시도하는 이질적인 침입자를 감지하고, 재채기로 그것을 쫓아내서 침입을 격퇴하기 위한 행동을 할 때 생긴다. 하지만 감기에 걸렸을 때의 재채기하는 것은?
(B) 감기 바이러스가 이미 상부 기도에 머무를 때 쫓아낼 방법은 분명히 없다. 주제문 그 재채기는 완전히 다른 녀석이다. 감기 바이러스는 여러분의 가족과 동료와 그리고 친구들을 감염시킴으로써 새로운 살 곳을 찾기 위해 재채기를 유발하는 것을 배웠다.
(A) 주제문 그러니까, 재채기는 증상이지만, 그것들은 숙주 조종의 간단하고 효과적인 방법을 발전시켰다. 재채기가 감기로 인한 것이면, 그것은 목적이 있는 증상이며, 그 목적은 여러분의 것이 아니다.
(C) 그것은 우리가 전염병 증상이라고 생각하는 많은 것들에도 해당한다. 그것들은 우리를 감염시키는 어떤 박테리아나 바이러스든 다음 숙주로 뛰어오르는 데 우리가 무의식적으로 도움을 주도록 작용하기 때문에 실제로 숙주 조종의 산물이다.

어휘 symptom 증상   foreign 이질의, 바깥에서 침입한   invader 침입자 cf. invasion 침입   nasal passages 콧구멍, 비강   repel 격퇴하다; 반박하다; 저항하다   expel 쫓아내다, 물리치다   lodge 머무르게 해 주다   respiratory tract ((해부)) 기도   infect 감염시키다 cf. infectious disease 전염병   host (기생생물의) 숙주   manipulation 조종, 조작   unconscious 무의식적인

해설 주어진 글에서 보통의 재채기를 설명한 후 감기에 걸렸을 때의 재채기에 대한 질문으로 끝났으므로 이어지는 내용은 감기로 인한 재채기에 대한 설명이어야 자연스럽다. 그러므로 (B)가 와야 하고 앞의 내용을 요약하고 (B)에 대한 부연 설명을 하는 (A)가 그 뒤에 이어진다. 감기에 의한 재채기는 목적이 있는 것이라는 (A)에 이어서 그런 목적이 있는 증상이 다른 전염병 증상에도 해당한다고 설명한 (C)가 마지막으로 와야 적절하다.

오답 Check
(A)의 'So yeah'를 통해, (A)의 내용이 앞에서 이미 나왔던 것을 다시 한번 정리하는 것임을 파악해야 한다. 따라서 (B)가 (A)보다 먼저 나와야 하는 것에 유의한다.

PLUS + 변형문제
어휘 reflex 반사 (작용); 반사성의
해설 이 글은 감기에 걸렸을 때의 재채기는 보통의 재채기와 다르게 바이러스가 퍼지기 위해 숙주를 조종하여 나타나는 증상임을 설명하는 글이다. 따라서 제목으로 가장 적절한 것은 ③ '감기 바이러스에 의한 재채기에 관한 사실들'이다.
① 감기 바이러스에 걸리는 과정
→ 감기에 걸리는 과정은 설명되지 않음.
② 감기 바이러스를 효과적으로 쫓아내는 방법들
→ 감기 바이러스가 상부 기도에 있을 때 쫓아낼 방법은 없다고 언급함.
④ 조종: 우리 신체의 자기방어 시스템
→ 오히려 조종은 바이러스의 확산 시스템임.
⑤ 재채기 반사: 이질적인 침입자와 싸우기
→ 이질적인 침입자를 쫓아내기 위한 재채기는 보통의 재채기에 관한 내용임.

09

구문 ¹A normal sneeze occurs // **when** the body's self-defense system senses a foreign invader (trying to get in through your nasal passages) / and acts to repel the invasion / by expelling it with a sneeze.
• when이 이끄는 부사절(when ~ a sneeze) 내에서 동사 senses와 acts가 and로 연결되어 병렬 구조를 이룬다.
• ( )는 현재분사구로 앞에 있는 a foreign invader를 수식한다.

²They're actually the product (of host manipulation) // **as** whatever bacteria or virus has infected us works to engage our
　　　　　　　　　　　　　　　　　　　　　　　　　　　　　S'　　　　　　　　　　　　　V'
unconscious assistance / in making the jump to its next host.
• as는 '~때문에'라는 의미의 이유를 나타내는 접속사로 부사절을 이끈다.
• as절의 주어는 밑줄 친 부분, 즉 복합관계대명사 whatever가 이끄는 명사절로, '~하는 것은 무엇이든'의 뜻이며 동사는 works이다.

Historically, ethics is not concerned with the natural environment. Instead, it is an attempt (to answer either of two questions): // "How ought I to treat others?" and "What actions that affect others are morally right?"

(B) Nature is not included in these, / except as some part of nature [that "belongs" to some human being]. That is, polluting a stream is morally wrong // only if this action diminishes someone's enjoyment (of the stream) or its utility. The stream has no value / and no ethical standing.

(C) However, we realize // that we owe responsibility to nature / for its own sake. But how? ¹Scientists and engineers look at the world objectively with technical tools, // which are often inappropriate for solving value problems. ²We are ill-equipped to make decisions // where the value of nature is concerned.

주제문
(A) In response to these value-laden questions, / a new form of applied ethics, environmental ethics, has evolved / to address issues (on human interactions with nonhuman nature). It helps people develop an ethical attitude towards nature.

어휘 ethics 윤리학 cf. ethical 윤리적인 be concerned with ~와 관계[관련]가 있다; ~에 관심이 있다 attempt 시도(하다) morally 도덕적으로 diminish 감소시키다; 줄이다 enjoyment 향유, 향락; 즐거움 utility 효용; 유용 standing 지위; 서 있는 owe A to B B에게 A를 느끼고[품고] 있다; B에게 A를 빚지다 for one's sake ~을 위해서 ill-equipped 준비가 안 된; 장비[기술]를 제대로 갖추지 않은 value-laden 가치 판단적인 applied 응용의; 적용된 address 다루다; 연설하다

해설 윤리학은 자연과 관계가 없는, 인간의 행동과 영향에 관한 질문을 던지는 분야라는 주어진 글 다음에 이 문제를 자연의 측면에서 논한 (B)가 나온다. '자연은 인간과 관계를 맺는 부분을 제외하고는 이것들에 포함되지 않는다'는 (B)의 내용에서 '이것들'은 주어진 문장에 나온 윤리학이 던지는 인간과 관련된 질문을 가리킨다. However로 이어지는 (C)에서는 그럼에도 불구하고 인간은 자연에 책임감을 느끼지만, 현대의 과학 기술로 이 질문에 답을 하는 것은 부적절하다는 내용 다음에 그러한 한계에 대응하고자 환경 윤리학이 발달하게 되었다는 (A)가 (C)의 해결책으로서 이어지는 것이 적절하다.

해석 역사적으로 윤리학은 자연환경과 관계없다. 대신에 그것은 "나는 다른 사람들을 어떻게 대해야 하는가?" 그리고 "다른 사람에게 영향을 미치는 어떤 행동이 도덕적으로 올바른가?"라는 두 질문 중 하나를 대답하려는 시도이다.
(B) 자연은 어떤 인간에게 '속하는' 자연의 일부분을 제외하고는 이것들(두 질문)에 포함되지 않는다. 다시 말해서, 시냇물을 오염시키는 것은 이 행동이 시냇물에 대한 누군가의 향유 혹은 그것의 효용성을 감소시키는 경우에만 도덕적으로 그릇된 것이다. 시냇물은 어떠한 가치와 도덕적 지위도 갖지 않는다.
(C) 그러나 우리는 우리가 자연을 위하여 자연에 책임감을 느끼고 있음을 깨닫는다. 하지만 어떻게(자연에 책임을 져야 하는가)? 과학자들과 기술자들은 기술적 도구를 가지고 세상을 객관적으로 바라보는데, 그것들은 종종 가치문제를 해결하기에는 부적절하다. 우리는 자연의 가치가 관련된 곳에서 결정을 내릴만한 준비가 되지 않았다.
(A) 주제문 그러한 가치 판단적인 질문들에 응하여, 응용 윤리학의 새로운 형태인 환경 윤리학이 인간 이외의 자연과 인간의 상호작용 문제를 다루기 위해 발전해왔다. 그것은 사람들이 자연을 향하여 윤리적인 태도를 발달시키는 데 도움을 준다.

오답 Check
(B)와 (A)의 초반부에 등장하는 these는 모두 주어진 문장의 두 질문을 가리키는데, (B)는 그 질문에 자연이 포함되지 않는다는 설명을 더하지만 (A)의 경우 질문에 대한 해결책이 제시되므로 주어진 문장 바로 뒤에는 (B)가 이어지는 것이 적절하다.

PLUS⁺ 변형문제
어휘 emergence 출현, 발생
해설 이 글은 자연이 관련된 가치문제를 해결하기 위해 환경 윤리학이 발전해왔다는 내용이므로 주제로는 ③ '환경 윤리학의 출현'이 가장 적절하다.
① 가치문제의 한계점
→ 언급된 사실이나, 글 전체의 주제는 아님.
② 윤리에 답하는 것의 어려움
→ (C)에서 언급되었지만 환경 윤리학 출현의 이유에 해당함.
④ 의사 결정에 있어서 적절한 도구
→ 도구를 사용함에도 가치문제를 해결하기에는 부적절하다고 언급함.
⑤ 자연의 가치에 대한 결정을 내리는 것 → 자연 가치와 관련된 결정을 내리기 위해 탄생한 '환경 윤리학'을 포함하지 않음.

구문 ¹Scientists and engineers look at the world objectively with *technical tools*, // **which** are often inappropriate for solving value problems.
• which는 계속적 용법으로 쓰인 관계대명사로 which가 이끄는 절이 선행사 technical tools를 부연 설명한다.

²We are ill-equipped to make decisions // **where** the value of nature is concerned.
• 의문부사 where는 장소 부사절을 이끌어 주절의 내용을 보충해 준다.

Anthropologists have found // that cultures vary enormously in their liking (for bitter, sour, and salty flavors), // but a taste (for sweetness) appears to be universal. (①) ¹This goes for many animals, too, // which shouldn't be surprising, // since sugar is the form [in which nature stores food energy]. (②) By encasing their seeds / in sugary and nutritious flesh, / fruiting plants (such as the apple) hit on an ingenious way (of exploiting the mammalian sweet tooth). (③) In exchange for fructose, / the animals provide the seeds with transportation, / allowing the plant to expand its range. (④) ²As parties to this grand coevolutionary bargain, / animals (with the strongest preference for sweetness) and plants (offering the biggest, sweetest fruits) have prospered together and multiplied. (⑤ As a precaution, / the plants took certain steps / to protect their seeds from the eagerness of their partners.) ³They had held off on developing sweetness and color // until the seeds matured completely — before then fruits tend to be inconspicuously green — // and in some cases, the plants developed poisons in their seeds / to ensure that only the sweet flesh is consumed.

해석 인류학자들은 쓴맛, 신맛과 짠맛에 대한 선호에 있어서는 문화가 대단히 서로 다르지만, 단 맛에 대한 취향은 보편적인 것처럼 보인다는 점을 발견했다. 이것은 많은 동물에게도 적용되는데, 당은 자연이 식량 에너지를 저장하는 형태이므로 이는 놀라운 일이 아닐 것이다. 씨앗을 달콤하고 영양분이 풍부한 과육 속에 집어넣음으로써, 사과 같은 과실 식물은 포유류가 단 것을 좋아하는 것을 이용하는 독창적인 방법을 생각해냈다. 과당과 교환하여 동물들은 씨앗에게 수송을 제공하여, 식물이 자신의 범위를 확장하는 것을 허용한다. **주제문 이 웅장한 공동 진화의 거래에 참여하는 당사자로서, 달콤함에 대한 가장 강력한 선호를 가지는 동물과 가장 크고 가장 달콤한 과일들을 제공하는 식물은 함께 번성하여 증식해왔다.** 예방책으로 식물들은 자신의 파트너의 열망에서 자신의 씨앗을 보호하기 위해 특정한 조치를 취했다. 그것들은 씨앗이 완전히 성숙할 때까지 당도와 색깔을 발달시키는 일을 미뤘고(그 전에 과일은 주의를 끌지 않게 녹색인 경향이 있다), 어떤 경우에 식물들은 오직 달콤한 과육만이 섭취되는 것을 확실히 하기 위하여 자신의 씨앗 속에 독을 발달시켰다.

어휘 anthropologist 인류학자   vary 서로 다르다, 달라지다   enormously 대단히, 엄청나게   universal 보편적인   go for ~에 해당되다; ~을 좋아하다   encase 집어넣다   flesh 과육; 살   hit on 불현듯 ~을 생각해 내다[떠올리다]   ingenious 독창적인; 정교한   exploit 이용하다; 착취하다   mammalian 포유류의   sweet tooth 단 것을 좋아함   party 당사자; 출석자; 사교모임   coevolutionary 공동 진화의   bargain 거래; 계약   prosper 번성[번영]하다   precaution 예방; 조심   eagerness 열망; 갈망   hold off 미루다; 시작하지 않다   mature 익히다, 성숙시키다; 익은, 성숙한   inconspicuously 주의를 끌지 않게

해설 주어진 문장은 예방책으로 식물들이 씨앗을 보호하기 위해 조치를 취했다는 내용인데 그 조치들은 ⑤ 다음의 문장에서 색깔과 당도 발달의 지연, 씨앗이 독성을 갖게 하는 것으로 제시된다. ⑤ 이전 문장은 당도 높은 과실 섭취가 동물에게도 식물에도 이로운 협력적 관계를 만들어 낸다는 내용으로 주어진 문장에 드러난 동물로부터 씨앗을 보호한다는 내용과 반대이므로 글의 흐름이 ⑤에서 전환되는 것을 볼 수 있다.

오답 Check
주어진 문장의 their partners는 문맥상 ④ 다음에 나오는 문장의 animals를 나타낸다.

PLUS+ 변형문제
어휘 precondition 필수 조건; 조건을 갖추다   reciprocal 상호 간의; 호혜적인
해설 이 글은 당도 높은 과일을 활용한 동물과 식물의 협력 관계를 다룬 글이므로 주제로는 ⑤ '과일과 관련된 식물과 동물 사이의 상호 간의 거래'가 적절하다.
① 식물이 수송을 위해 동물을 사용한 방법
→ 지문의 일부 내용을 활용한 오답임.
② 식물이 가장 달콤한 과일을 생산하기 위한 필수 조건
→ 필수 조건이 아닌 달콤한 과일을 생산하게 된 원인이 언급됨.
③ 짧은 시간에 덜 익은 과일을 익게 하는 방법
→ 상식과 관련된 내용으로 지문과는 무관함.
④ 성숙에 있어서 동물과 씨앗 사이의 관계
→ 성숙에 관해 동물과 씨앗의 관련성에 대한 언급은 없음.

구문 ¹*This goes for many animals, too,* // **which** shouldn't be surprising, // since sugar is *the form* [**in which** nature stores food energy].
• 계속적 용법의 관계대명사 which가 이끄는 절은 앞 문장 전체를 선행사로 하여 보충 설명한다.
• [ ]는 '전치사+관계대명사' 형태의 in which가 이끄는 절로 앞에 있는 the form을 수식한다.

²As parties to this grand coevolutionary bargain, / *animals* (with the strongest preference for sweetness) `and` *plants* (offering the biggest, sweetest fruits) have prospered together and multiplied.
• 두 개의 ( )는 차례대로 전명구와 현재분사구로 각각 앞에 있는 명사 animals와 plants를 수식한다.
• 밑줄 친 두 개의 명사구 animals ~ sweetness와 plants ~ fruits는 and로 병렬 연결되어 문장의 주어 역할을 한다.

³They **had held off** on developing sweetness and color // **until** the seeds **matured** completely ~.
• until이 이끄는 부사절의 기준 시점(과거)까지 계속된 행동을 나타내므로 주절의 동사는 과거완료시제(had p.p.)가 사용되었다.

One of the most common types of entertainment programming on television / involves high levels of violence. Violence also finds its way into advertising. (①) ¹It may surprise you, however, // that violent TV programming actually reduces memory for the commercials in those shows / and reduces the chance / that people will intend to buy those products. (② ²In attempting to explain this finding, / researchers suggest // one reason may be / that watching violence raises one's physiological arousal / by making people angry and putting them in a bad mood.) An angry mood can prime aggressive thoughts, // which in turn may interfere with recall of the ad content. (③) Negative moods are known to interfere with the brain's encoding of information. (④) ³Also, the effort (taken to try to repair the bad mood) may distract one from attending to and processing the ad. (⑤) Thus, it may be // that advertisers are not getting as much "bang for their buck" with violent content / as with nonviolent content.

해석 가장 흔한 형태의 TV 오락 프로 편성 중 하나는 높은 수준의 폭력을 수반한다. 폭력은 또한 광고 속으로 스며든다. 주제문 하지만 폭력적인 TV 프로 편성이 실제로 그런 프로에 들어가는 광고에 대한 기억을 감소시키고 사람들이 그 상품을 사려는 의향을 가질 가능성을 감소시킨다는 것은 여러분을 놀라게 할지도 모른다. 이런 연구 결과를 설명하고자 시도하면서 연구자들은 폭력을 시청하는 것이 사람들을 화나게 만들고 그들을 기분 나쁘게 함으로써 생리적 흥분을 일으키는 것이 한 가지 이유일 수도 있음을 시사한다. 분노의 기분은 공격적인 생각을 조성할 수 있고, 그것이 결과적으로 광고 내용의 회상을 방해할 수 있다. 부정적인 기분은 뇌가 정보를 부호화하는 것을 방해한다고 알려져 있다. 또한 나쁜 기분을 원상으로 회복하는 데 드는 노력은 그 광고에 주의를 기울이고 그것의 내용을 처리하는 것에 집중하지 못하게 한다. 따라서 광고주들은 폭력적인 내용으로는 비폭력적인 내용으로 얻을 수 있는 만큼의 '본전을 뽑을 수 있을 만한 가치'를 얻지 못하게 될 것이다.

어휘 commercial 광고 (방송); 상업의   finding 연구 결과, 발견   physiological 생리적인   arousal 자극   put A in a bad mood A를 기분 나쁘게 하다   prime 준비시키다, 자극하다; 주된; 최고의   aggressive 공격적인   interfere 방해하다, 간섭하다   recall 회상   content 내용   ⊙encoding 부호화, 코드화   distract (마음·주의 등이) 집중이 안 되게 하다
어휘⊙ 부호화: 정보 처리 과정의 한 형태로 감각을 통해 들어온 정보를 뇌에서 처리하고 저장할 수 있도록 유의미한 형태로 바꾸는 것.

해설 주어진 문장에서 this finding에 대한 설명으로서 폭력의 시청이 생리적 흥분을 일으키는 것이 한 가지 이유일 수 있다고 했으므로 주어진 문장은 this finding에 대한 구체적인 내용 다음에 오는 게 적절하다. ② 앞에 나오는 내용, 즉 폭력적 TV 프로 편성이 광고의 상품을 사려는 의향을 줄어들게 한다는 것이 finding에 어울리는 내용이고 ② 뒤는 생리적 자극, 즉 분노의 기분이 광고 내용 회상을 방해한다는 내용으로서 주어진 문장을 자세하게 설명해 주고 있으므로 주어진 문장은 ②에 와야 한다.

PLUS + 변형문제

어휘 be drawn to ~에 끌리다
해설 폭력적인 TV 프로가 부정적인 감정을 불러일으켜서 사람들이 광고를 기억하고 상품을 구입할 의향을 감소시킨다는 내용이므로 글의 주제로 가장 적절한 것은 ② '폭력적인 프로그램들이 광고 효과에 미치는 악영향'이다.
① 시청자들이 폭력적인 프로그램에 이끌리는 이유들
→ 시청자가 폭력적인 프로그램에 이끌리는 이유는 언급되지 않음.
③ 광고 시청자들에게 부정적인 감정을 유발하지 않기 위한 노력들
→ 부정적인 감정을 유발하지 않기 위해 어떤 노력을 하는지는 언급된 바 없음.
④ 나쁜 광고로 인한 부정적인 감정들을 극복하는 방법들
→ 부정적인 감정을 극복하는 방법은 언급되지 않음.
⑤ 폭력적인 내용과 비폭력적인 내용을 구별하는 것의 필요성
→ 폭력적인 내용과 비폭력적인 내용을 구별하는 것에 대한 내용은 없음.

구문 ¹**It** may surprise you, however, // **that** violent TV programming actually reduces memory for the commercials in those shows / and reduces the chance / **that** people will intend to buy those products.
• It은 가주어 that 이하가 진주어이다.
• 밑줄 친 the chance와 that people ~ those products는 동격 관계이다.

²In attempting to explain this finding, / researchers suggest // (that) one reason may be / **that** watching violence raises one's physiological arousal / by **making** people angry and **putting** them in a bad mood.
• 동사 suggest의 목적어로 that이 이끄는 명사절이 쓰였으며, 여기서 접속사 that은 생략되었다.
• 밑줄 친 명사절에서 may be 뒤의 that은 보어로 쓰인 명사절을 이끄는 접속사이다.
• 전치사 by의 목적어로 동명사구 making ~ angry와 putting ~ mood가 and로 연결되었다. 「by v-ing」는 '~함으로써'의 의미이다.

³Also, the effort (taken to try to repair the bad mood) may distract one *from* attending to and processing **the ad**.
• ( )는 the effort를 수식하는 과거분사구이다.
• 전치사 from의 목적어로 attending to와 processing이 and로 연결되었고 the ad는 두 동명사(구)의 공통 목적어이다.

The psychologists (at the University of British Columbia) were interested in looking at // how the color of interior walls influence the imagination. [1]Six hundred subjects, most of them undergraduates, were recruited, // and they were made / to perform a variety of basic cognitive tests (displayed against red-, blue- or neutral-colored backgrounds). The differences were striking. People [who took tests in the red condition] — surrounded by walls the color of a stop sign — were much better at / such skills as catching spelling mistakes / or keeping random numbers in short-term memory. According to the scientists, / this is // because people automatically associate red with danger. However, a completely different set of psychological benefits / were indicated by the color blue. While people (belonging to the blue group) performed worse on short-term memory tasks, // they did far better on those (requiring some imagination, / such as designing a children's toy / out of simple geometric shapes). [2]In fact, subjects (in the blue condition) generated twice as many outputs as subjects (in the red condition).

↓

> Red-colored backgrounds are advantageous in the performance of measuring (A) alertness, while the blue-colored ones are advantageous in increasing (B) originality.

해석 British Columbia 대학의 심리학자들은 내벽의 색이 어떻게 상상력에 영향을 미치는지를 보는 데 관심을 가졌다. 대부분이 학부생인 600명의 피실험자가 모집되었고, 그들에게 붉은색이나 푸른색이나 아니면 중간색의 배경에 붙여 전시된 다양한 기초 인지 테스트를 수행하도록 했다. 그 차이는 현저했다. 추론 근거 정지 신호의 색인 벽으로 둘러싸인 붉은색 조건에서 테스트를 치른 사람들은 철자 실수를 잡아내거나 무작위 숫자를 단기 기억으로 유지하는 것과 같은 기술을 훨씬 더 잘했다. 과학자들에 따르면 이것은 사람들이 붉은색을 자동적으로 위험과 연관 지어 생각하기 때문이라고 한다. 그러나 전적으로 다른 추세의 심리적 이점이 푸른색에서 나타났다. 추론 근거 푸른색 집단에 속한 사람들은 단기 기억 과업은 더 서투르게 했지만, 그들은 단순한 기하학적 모양에서 어린이 장난감을 설계하는 것과 같은 어떤 상상력을 필요로 하는 과업에서 훨씬 더 잘했다. 실제로 푸른색 조건에 있던 피실험자들은 붉은색 조건에 있던 피실험자들보다 두 배 많은 생산물을 만들어 냈다.

↓

> 붉은색 배경은 (A) 각성도를 측정하는 수행에 유리한 반면 푸른색 배경은 (B) 독창성을 증가하는 데 유리하다.

어휘 undergraduate 대학[학부] 재학생   recruit 모집하다; 조달하다   neutral 중간색의; 중립의   striking 현저한; 이목을 끄는   associate A with B A와 B를 연관 지어 생각하다   geometric 기하학적인   output 생산물; 산출량   alertness 각성도; 기민   originality 독창성   **[선택지 어휘]** solidarity 결속, 연대

해설 요약문을 통해 붉은색과 푸른색 배경이 각각 무엇에 유리한지를 파악한다. 실험 결과로 붉은색 배경의 피실험자들이 실수를 잡아내거나 단기 기억으로 숫자를 기억하는 것을 더 잘했고, 푸른색 배경의 피실험자들은 상상력을 발휘하여 만들어 내는 것을 훨씬 더 잘했다고 했으므로 빈칸에는 ③ '(A) 각성도 – (B) 독창성'이 적절하다.

오답 Check

	(A)	(B)

① 유연성 – 영감
→ (B)는 맞지만, 유연성과 관련된 결과는 언급하지 않음.

② 신속함 – 결속
→ (A), (B) 모두 오답.

④ 주의 집중 – 인식
→ (A)는 맞지만, (B)는 언급 없음.

⑤ 정확성 – 적응성
→ (A)는 맞지만, (B)는 상상력이 풍부한 것과 관련 없음.

구문 [1]Six hundred subjects, most of them undergraduates, were recruited, // [and] they **were made** / **to perform** a variety of basic cognitive tests (displayed against red-, blue- or neutral-colored backgrounds).
- and 뒤의 절은 동사 make가 쓰인 SVOC 문형을 수동태로 쓴 것으로, 본래 능동태 문장에서 원형부정사였던 목적격보어가 수동태가 되면서 to perform이 되었다.
- ( )는 과거분사구로 앞에 나온 명사구 a variety of basic cognitive tests를 수식한다.

[2]In fact, *subjects* (in the blue condition) generated **twice as** *many outputs* **as** *subjects* (in the red condition).
- 두 개의 ( )는 전명구로 각각 앞에 있는 명사 subjects를 수식한다.
- twice as ~ subjects는 「배수사+as 원급 as ~」의 구조로 '~보다 두 배 …한'의 의미이다.

Ideas can be patented, or copyrighted. Patents and copyrights can affect / the spread of ideas and society. ¹A lot (a) <u>fewer</u> books would have been written // if the estate of Johannes Gutenberg, // which included typography, had collected a fee on every one. It's not just companies / that thrive by imitating their competitors. Entire countries can (b) <u>accelerate</u> their development / by strategically copying the ideas and technologies [that other countries already use]. ²Eckhard Höffner, an economic historian, attributes Germany's rapid industrial development (in the nineteenth century) to weak copyright laws, // which encouraged publishers to flood the country / with cheap and often plagiarized copies (of essential technical manuals). Japan's computer makers benefited from a government order // that IBM make its patents (c) <u>available</u> / as a condition of doing business there. More recently, China's adaptation of existing ideas (from other countries) / has resulted in significant economic growth. ³Since 1978, / it has moved workers / from unproductive farms and state-owned companies / to more productive privately-owned factories [that used machinery and technology (bought, borrowed, and sometimes stolen — which means it is obtained unethically — from foreigners)]. Foreign companies are routinely required to (d) <u>share</u> their expertise with local partners / as a condition of doing business in China. Still, once a country has copied all the ideas it can, // future growth depends on / waiting for new ideas or developing its own. 주제문 Inevitably, a country (at the technological frontier) grows more (e) <u>sharply</u> than one (catching up to the frontier). That's just // what happened to Japan, and it could also happen to China.

해석 아이디어는 특허권을 얻거나 저작권의 보호를 받을 수 있다. 특허권과 저작권은 아이디어의 확산과 사회에 영향을 줄 수 있다. 만약 요하네스 구텐베르크의 재산권이, 그것은 활판 인쇄술을 포함하는데, 모든 책에 비용을 징수했다면, 훨씬 (a) 더 적은 책들이 쓰였을 것이다. 경쟁자들을 모방해서 번영하는 것은 단지 회사들뿐이 아니다. 모든 나라가 다른 나라에서 이미 사용하는 아이디어와 기술을 전략적으로 베껴서 자국의 발전을 (b) 가속화할 수 있다. 경제사학자인 Eckhard Höffner는 19세기의 독일의 급격한 산업 발전을 약화된 저작권법의 결과로 보는데, 그것은 중요한 기술 매뉴얼의 값싸고 종종 표절된 책자들이 전국에 넘쳐나도록 출판업자들을 장려했다. 일본의 컴퓨터 제작자들은 IBM 사가 일본에서 사업을 한다는 조건으로 회사의 특허권을 (c) 이용 가능하게 한 정부의 명령에서 이익을 얻었다. 더 최근에, 다른 나라의 기존 아이디어를 중국이 응용한 것은 엄청난 경제적 성장을 초래했다. 1978년 이래로 중국은 노동자들을 비생산적인 농장과 국가 소유의 회사에서 외국인들로부터 사 오고 빌려오고 때때로 훔쳐 온(이것은 비윤리적으로 얻었다는 것을 뜻한다) 기계와 기술을 사용하는 더 생산적이고 사적 소유의 공장으로 이주시켰다. 외국 회사들은 관례대로 중국에서 사업을 한다는 조건으로 지역 협력체와 그들의 전문 기술을 (d) 공유하기를 요구받는다. 그러나 일단 한 나라가 할 수 있는 모든 아이디어를 베껴 왔다면, (그 나라의) 미래의 성장은 새로운 아이디어를 기다리거나 그 자국의 아이디어를 개발하는 것에 달렸다. 주제문 불가피하게, 기술적으로 최첨단에 있는 나라는 그 최첨단을 따라잡고 있는 나라보다 더 (e) 급격하게(→ 느리게) 성장한다. 그것이 바로 일본에서 일어났던 일이고, 그것은 중국에서도 일어날 수 있다.

어휘 **patent** 특허(권을 주다); 특허의   **copyright** 저작권[판권] (으로 보호하다)   **estate** ((법)) 재산(권), 부동산(권)   ⊕**typography** 활판 인쇄술   **thrive** 번영[번성]하다   **strategically** 전략적으로   **flood** ∼에 넘쳐나게 하다; 침수시키다   **plagiarize** 표절하다   **adaptation** 응용; 각색; 적응   **unethically** 비윤리적으로   **routinely** 관례대로; 일상적으로   **expertise** 전문 기술[지식]   **inevitably** 불가피하게; 확실히   **frontier** 최첨단 (분야); 국경; 한계   **catch up to** ∼을 따라잡다   **[선택지 어휘]** **double-edged** 양날의; 두 가지로 해석될 수 있는, 애매한

어휘⊙ 활판 인쇄술과 구텐베르크: 1440년대 요하네스 구텐베르크가 발명한 것으로, 활판 인쇄술이 서양에 등장하며 책의 대량 생산이 가능해졌다.

해설 **41** 새로운 아이디어나 기술은 특허권이나 저작권으로 보호를 받아야 하지만 그 규제를 풀어 놓으면 오히려 그것을 모방하는 국가의 경제가 더 급격히 발전하는 이중적인 특성이 있다는 것이 글의 요지이다. 그러므로 제목으로는 ② '특허권 및 저작권: 양날의 검'이 적절하다.
42 예시로 나온 일본이나 중국의 경우 아이디어나 기술을 모방해서 급격한 경제 성장을 이루었지만, 이미 할 수 있는 모든 것을 모방한 이후, 즉 기술적으로 최첨단에 있는 나라가 된 후에는 새로운 아이디어를 기다리거나, 자국의 아이디어를 개발해야 한다. 따라서 그들 국가를 모방하는 나라보다 성장이 더 느릴 수밖에 없으므로 (e)의 sharply는 slowly 등으로 고치는 것이 적절하다.

오답 Check
41 ① 저작권법 강화의 필요성
→ 저작권법을 강화해야 한다는 언급은 없음
③ 아이디어와 기술을 베끼는 것의 비윤리적인 측면
→ 아이디어와 기술을 비윤리적으로 베끼는 사례는 언급되었지만, 전반적으로 그 측면을 설명하는 글은 아님.
④ 특허권 및 저작권: 차이점과 유사성
→ 특허권과 저작권을 비교·대조하는 내용은 아님.
⑤ 아이디어 및 기술: 경제 성장의 주요 요인
→ 아이디어와 기술이 경제 성장의 큰 요인이 되는 것은 맞지만, 주된 내용은 아님.
42 일본 정부가 IBM 사에게 특허권을 '이용 가능하게' 하도록 명령해야 일본의 컴퓨터 제작자들이 그 특허권을 이용해 이익을 얻게 되므로 (c)의 available은 적절하다.

¹A lot fewer books **would have been** written // **if** *the estate of Johannes Gutenberg,* // **which** included typography, **had collected** a fee on every one.

• 「If+S'+had p.p., S+would have p.p.」는 가정법 과거완료 구문으로 과거 사실에 대한 반대 상황의 가정이다.

• which는 계속적 용법으로 쓰인 관계대명사로 the estate of Johannes Gutenberg를 보충 설명한다.

²Eckhard Höffner, an economic historian, **attributes** Germany's rapid industrial development (in the nineteenth century) **to** *weak copyright laws*, // **which** encouraged publishers to flood the country / with cheap and often plagiarized copies (of essential technical manuals).

• 여기에서 「attribute A to B」는 'A를 B의 결과로 보다'의 의미이다.

• which는 계속적 용법의 관계대명사로 선행사 weak copyright laws를 보충 설명한다.

³Since 1978, / it has moved workers / from unproductive farms and state-owned companies / to *more productive privately-owned factories* [**that** used *machinery and technology* (bought, borrowed, and sometimes stolen — which means it is obtained unethically — from foreigners)].

• 밑줄 친 it은 앞 문장의 China를 의미한다.

• 「from A to B(A에서 B로)」 형태의 전명구가 사용되었으며, 주격 관계대명사 that이 이끄는 [ ]는 B에 해당하는 more productive privately owned factories를 수식한다.

• [ ] 내에서 ( )는 과거분사구로 machinery and technology를 수식한다.

09

| 31 ④ + ⑤ | 32 ② + ④ | 33 ① + ② | 34 ③ + ③ | 35 ④ + ⑤ | 36 ② + ① |
| 37 ⑤ + ④ | 38 ④ + ③ | 39 ④ + ④ | 40 ② | 41 ⑤ | 42 ④ |

31 ④ PLUS+ ⑤

주제문
For scientific problems [where the solution is likely buried in our creativity], / the answer arrives // only if we collaborate. Ben Jones, a professor at the Kellogg Business School of Management, / has demonstrated this / by analyzing trends (in "scientific production.")
추론 근거
By analyzing 19.9 million peer-reviewed papers and 2.1 million patents (from the last fifty years), / [1]he was able to show // that more than 99 percent of scientific subfields have experienced increased levels of alliance, / with the size of the average team increasing by about 20 percent per decade. While the most cited studies (in a field) used to be the product of lone geniuses, // he has demonstrated that the best research now emerges from groups. [2]It doesn't matter what the researchers are studying: // science papers (produced by multiple authors) are cited / more than twice as often as those (authored by individuals). This trend was even more apparent when it came to highly successful papers, // which were more than six times as likely to come from a team of scientists.

해석 주제문 해결책이 우리의 창의성 안에 숨겨져 있는 것 같은 과학적 문제에서 해답은 우리가 협력해야만 찾아온다. Kellogg 경영대학원의 교수인 Ben Jones는 '과학적 저작물'의 동향을 분석함으로써 이것을 증명했다. 추론 근거 지난 50년 동안의 1,990만 건의 동료 심사를 받은 논문과 210만 건의 특허를 분석함으로써, 그는 평균 팀의 규모가 10년마다 약 20퍼센트씩 증가하면서 99퍼센트가 넘는 과학 하위 분야에서 협력의 정도가 증가했다는 것을 보여줄 수 있었다. 한 분야에서 가장 많이 인용된 연구들이 과거에는 천재들 단독의 저작물이었지만 최고의 연구는 이제 집단에서 나온다는 것을 그는 증명해 왔다. 연구자들이 무엇을 연구하고 있는지는 중요하지 않으며, 다수의 저자가 만들어낸 과학 논문들이 개인들이 저술한 것들보다 두 배 넘게 더 자주 인용된다. 이런 경향은 매우 성공적인 논문들에 관한 한 훨씬 더 뚜렷했는데, 그 논문들은 과학자 팀에서 나올 가능성이 여섯 배가 넘었다.

어휘 peer-reviewed 동료 심사를 받은   patent 특허(권)   subfield (학문의) 하위 분야   alliance 협력, 협조; 동맹   cite 인용하다   lone 혼자인, 단독의   author 작가, 저자; 쓰다, 저술하다   apparent 뚜렷한; 명백한   when it comes to ~에 관한 한   [선택지 어휘] persevere 견디다, 참다   contradict 반박하다, 부정하다; 모순되다   contemplate 심사숙고하다

해설 빈칸이 첫 한두 문장에 있는 경우, 그 문장이 주제문일 가능성이 크다. 빈칸에 뒤이어 나오는 연구의 결과로 99퍼센트가 넘는 과학 하위 분야에서 협력의 정도가 증가했다는 것을 보여주었고 최고의 연구가 이제 과거와는 달리 집단에서 나온다고 했으므로 빈칸에는 ④ '협력해야'가 적절하다.

오답 Check
① 견뎌야 → 지문에 언급되지 않음.
② 연구해야 → '함께' 연구하는 것이 중요함.
③ 반박해야
⑤ 심사숙고해야
→ ③, ⑤ 모두 지문과는 거리가 먼 내용임.

PLUS + 변형문제
어휘 credibility 신뢰성; 진실성   collective 집단(적인); 공동의
해설 과학적 문제에서 해답은 우리가 다수와 협력해야만 찾아온다는 내용의 글로, 협력의 중요성을 강조하므로 제목으로는 ⑤ '집단이 최고의 결과를 달성한다'가 적절하다.
① 요리사가 너무 많으면 수프를 망친다(사공이 많으면 배가 산으로 올라간다) → 지문과 반대되는 내용.
② 과학적 분석이 정말로 정확한가?
③ 과학적 저작물: 외로운 여정
④ 동료 심사를 받은 논문의 신뢰성
→ ②, ③, ④ 모두 지문에 나온 어구를 활용하여 만든 오답임.

구문 [1]he was able to show // that more than 99 percent of scientific subfields have experienced increased levels of alliance, / **with** the size of the average team **increasing** by about 20 percent per decade.
• 「with+O(the size of the average team)+v-ing(increasing ~ per decade)」는 부대상황을 나타내는 분사구문이며, 'O가 v하면서'로 해석한다.

[2]**It** doesn't matter **what the researchers are studying**: // science papers (produced by multiple authors) are cited / more than twice as often as **those** (authored by individuals).
• It은 가주어, what이 이끄는 명사절이 진주어이다.
• 두 개의 ( )는 모두 과거분사구로 각각 앞의 명사 science papers, those를 수식한다. 이때, those는 앞에 나온 science papers를 대신 받는 대명사이다.

Most people think of redundancy as repetition, // and, usually, redundancy in this sense has a negative connotation. In the psycholinguistic sense, / redundancy is quite different: // it is a necessary and naturally occurring characteristic of language [that makes sure of accurate information transmission]. ¹An example (of this type of redundancy) / is found in a sentence / such as "The teachers were grading their papers," // in which the plurality (of the subject) is conveyed / by the -s ending, by the plural verb form *were*, and by the plural pronoun *their*. In case the reader or listener misses the plural marker on the subject, // either the verb or the pronoun will convey the same information (about the subject's plurality). In acquiring language, / whether spoken or written, / learners must grasp the redundancy (of the language) // if they wish to guarantee an information exchange. In this sense, redundancy is a positive and necessary feature of the communication capacity of language.

해석 사람들은 대부분 불필요한 중복을 반복이라고 생각하며, 대개 이러한 의미에서 불필요한 중복은 부정적인 함축 의미를 지닌다. 주제문 심리 언어학적 의미에서, 중복은 상당히 다르다. 그것은 정확한 정보 전달을 보장해 주는 필수적이면서 자연적으로 발생하는 언어의 특징이다. 이런 종류의 중복의 한 가지 예가 "The teachers were grading their papers.(교사들이 자신들의 시험지를 채점하고 있었다.)"와 같은 문장에서 발견되는데, 이 문장에서는 -s라는 어미, 동사의 복수 형태인 were, 그리고 복수 대명사인 their에 의해 주어의 복수성이 전달된다. 추론 근거 독자나 청자가 주어에 있는 복수 표지를 놓치는 경우에 대비하여, 동사나 대명사가 주어의 복수성에 관한 같은 정보를 전달해 줄 것이다. 음성 언어이건 문자 언어이건 간에, 언어를 습득하는 과정에서, 정보의 교환을 보장하고 싶다면 학습자는 언어의 중복을 완전하게 익혀야 한다. 주제문 이러한 의미에서, 중복은 언어의 의사소통 능력의 긍정적이고 없어서는 안 될 특징이다.

어휘 redundancy 불필요한 중복; 여분, 과잉 connotation 함축 의미 psycholinguistic 심리 언어학의 transmission 전달, 전송; 전염 plurality 복수(인 상태), 다수 cf. plural 복수형(의) convey 전하다, 전달하다 marker 표시[표지](물) subject 주어; 주제; 과목; 연구 대상 grasp 습득하다, 이해하다; 붙잡다 guarantee 보장하다 [선택지 어휘] consistent 일관된, 변함없는 (↔ inconsistent 일관성이 없는, 일치하지 않는) phrasing 말, 표현 interpretation 해석, 설명

해설 중복이 언어에서 '무엇'을 보장해주는지 찾아야 한다. 빈칸 문장 바로 뒤에 예시가 이어지므로 이를 종합하여 추론한다. 문장의 모든 요소에 걸쳐 주어의 복수성이 반복적으로 나타나기 때문에 주어에서 이 표지를 놓친다고 하더라도 다른 부분에서 그 정보를 얻을 수 있다고 했다. 즉 반복을 통해 정확한 정보를 얻을 수 있다는 뜻이며, 후반부에서도 중복은 정보의 교환을 보장하기 위해서 필요한 것이라고 했으므로 빈칸에 가장 적절한 것은 ② '정확한 정보 전달'이다.

오답 Check
① 모순이 없고 올바른 표현
→ 모순의 유무에 대한 언급은 없음.
③ 복잡한 개념에 대한 효과적인 표현
→ 복잡한 개념은 언급되지 않음.
④ 음성 언어의 충분한 (표현) 능력
→ 언어의 중복은 음성 언어에 한정된 것이 아님.
⑤ 화자의 심리 상태에 대한 해석
→ 화자의 심리 상태는 언급되지 않음.

PLUS + 변형문제

어휘 transition 변천 side effect 부작용 eliminate 제거하다, 없애다 efficiency 효율성

해설 언어에서 중복은 정확한 정보 전달에 필수 요소이므로 이를 이해하는 것의 중요함을 설명하는 글이므로 주제로 가장 적절한 것은 ④ '의사소통을 위해 중복을 이해하는 것의 중요성'이다.
① 인간 언어에서 언어학 표지의 변천
→ 언어학적 표지의 변천사에 관한 내용이 아님.
② 중복을 추가함으로써 정보를 전달하려는 시도
→ 중복을 추가해 정보를 전달하려는 시도는 언급되지 않았음.
③ 의사소통에서 중복을 제거하는 것의 부작용
→ 중복을 제거해서 일어나는 부작용에 관한 내용이 아님.
⑤ 중복을 피함으로써 의사소통 효율성을 증가시키는 방법들
→ 중복을 피한다는 것은 글의 내용과 반대됨.

구문 ¹*An example* (of this type of redundancy) / is found in a sentence / such as *"The teachers were grading their papers,"* // **in which** the plurality (of the subject) is conveyed / by the -s ending, by the plural verb form *were*, and by the plural pronoun *their*.
• in which는 '전치사+관계대명사'로, 관계부사 where로 바꿔 쓸 수 있다.

Could it be // that we are drawn instinctively to flowers? Some evolutionary psychologists have proposed an interesting answer. Their hypothesis goes like this: // ¹our brains developed / under the pressure of natural selection / to make us good at searching for provisions, // which is how humans have spent 99 percent of their time on earth. The presence of flowers / is a reliable predictor of future food. People [who were drawn to flowers, and who further could distinguish among them / and then remember where in the landscape they'd seen them], would be much more successful at seeking provisions / than people [who were blind to their significance]. ²According to the neuroscientist Steven Pinker, // who outlines this theory in *How the Mind Works*, / natural selection was bound to favor / those among our ancestors [who noticed flowers / and had a gift for botanizing — for recognizing plants, classifying them, and then remembering // where they grow]. In time the moment of recognition would become pleasurable, // and the signifying thing a thing of beauty.

해석 우리는 본능적으로 꽃에 이끌릴 수 있을까? 일부 진화 심리학자들은 흥미로운 답을 제시했다. 그들의 가설은 다음과 같다. 우리의 두뇌는 자연선택의 압박 아래 우리가 식량을 찾는 것에 능하게 만들기 위해 발달했고, 그렇게 되어 인간은 그들의 시간 중 99퍼센트를 지상에서 보냈다. 꽃의 존재는 머지않아 식량이 있다는 믿을 만한 전조가 되는 것이다. 주제문/추론 근거 꽃에 이끌렸던 사람, 나아가 꽃을 구별할 수 있었고, 그 풍경에서 그 꽃을 봤던 곳을 기억할 수 있는 사람들은 그것들(꽃)의 중요성을 깨닫지 못한 사람들보다 식량을 찾는 데 훨씬 더 성공적이었을 것이다. 신경 과학자 Steven Pinker에 따르면, 그는 이 이론을 〈마음은 어떻게 작동하는가〉에서 간략하게 설명하는데, 자연선택은 우리 조상 가운데서 꽃을 알아보고 식물을 연구하는 재능을 가진 사람, 즉 식물을 알아보고, 그것을 분류하고 나서 그것들이 어디에서 자라는지 기억하는 사람들을 선호했음에 틀림이 없다. 곧 (꽃을) 인지하는 순간은 즐거움이 되고, 전조가 되는 대상은 아름다운 것이 되었을 것이다.

어휘 natural selection 자연선택 provision 식량; 공급; 대비 reliable 믿을 만한 predictor 전조가 되는 것; 예언자 blind ~을 깨닫지 못하는; 눈먼 outline 약술하다; ~의 요점을 말하다 be bound to-v 틀림없이[반드시] v하다 botanize 식물을 연구[채집]하다 recognition 인지, 인식 signify ~의 전조가 되다; 의미하다 [선택지 어휘] notable 주목할 만한 reproduce 번식하다; 재생[재현]하다 imprecise 부정확한, 애매한

해설 빈칸 문장으로 보아 꽃의 존재가 '무엇'인지 찾아야 한다. 빈칸이 중반부에 있으므로 단서가 있을 확률이 높은 뒤 문장을 본다. 꽃의 중요성을 깨닫고 그것에 이끌렸던 사람들은 그렇지 못한 사람들보다 식량을 찾는 데 더 성공적이었다고 설명하므로, 꽃의 존재로는 ① '머지않아 식량이 있다는 믿을만한 전조가 되는 것'이 가장 적절하다.

오답 Check
② 독을 피하기 위한 정확한 수단
→ 꽃의 독에 관한 내용은 없음.
③ 자연에서의 진화의 주목할 만한 모습
→ 본문의 evolutionary를 활용한 오답.
④ 번식하려는 자연의 욕망의 모습
→ 자연의 번식에 관한 내용은 없음.
⑤ 자원을 찾는 부정확한 방법
→ 꽃의 존재는 곧 식량의 존재를 나타내므로 오히려 정확한 방법으로 봐야 함.

PLUS+ 변형문제

어휘 prosper 번성[번영]하다 evoke 불러일으키다
해설 꽃은 곧 식량의 전조가 되는 것이고, 자연선택은 꽃을 알아보는 사람들을 선호했다는 내용으로 글의 제목으로는 ② '꽃이 없었다면, 우리는 존재하지 않았을 것이다'가 가장 적절하다.
① 무엇이 우리를 성공적인 사냥꾼으로 만들었는가?
→ 글 내용의 일부로 언급되었지만 전체를 나타낼 수 없음.
③ 자연선택은 우리가 번성하도록 이끌었다
→ 꽃을 알아보는 조상들이 자연선택으로 생존한 것이므로 자연선택 자체가 우리의 번성을 이끈 것은 아님.
④ 꽃은 우리의 정신에 무엇을 불러일으키는가?
→ 인간의 정신에 영향을 미치는 것은 아님.
⑤ 자연선택의 생물학적 이점
→ 자연선택의 생물학적 이점에 대해 언급하지 않음.

구문 ¹our brains developed / under the pressure of natural selection / to **make** us *good at searching for provision*, // **which** is **how** humans have spent 99 percent of their time on earth.
• 밑줄 친 to부정사구는 「make+O+C」의 구조로 us는 to make의 목적어, good at searching for provision은 목적격보어이다.
• 계속적 용법의 관계사절을 이끄는 which는 밑줄 친 to부정사구를 가리키며 이를 보충 설명한다.
• how는 관계부사로 the way를 선행사로 하지만 how와 the way는 함께 쓰일 수 없으므로 the way가 생략되었다.

²According to *the neuroscientist Steven Pinker*, // **who** outlines this theory in *How the Mind Works*, / natural selection was bound to favor / *those among our ancestors* [**who** noticed flowers / and had a gift for botanizing — *for* recognizing plants, classifying them, and then remembering // where they grow].
• who는 계속적 용법의 관계대명사로 앞에 있는 명사 the neuroscientist Steven Pinker를 보충 설명한다.
• [ ]는 관계대명사 who가 이끄는 관계사절로 선행사 those ~ ancestors를 수식한다.
• 전치사 for의 목적어로 밑줄 친 recognizing, classifying, remembering이 콤마(,)와 and로 병렬 연결되었다.

34 ③ PLUS + ③

To look at a novel or a sculpture or to listen to a piece of music / as if it were simply an object — a "what" to be analyzed — / is to perceive only the illusion. Reality can be experienced // only when we understand how the art emerges from and relates to life itself. More than sixty years ago / the educational philosopher John Dewey argued (in his classic *Art as Experience*) // that conventional art education fails in exactly the same way science education fails — by concealing rather than revealing the links between theory and practice. ¹For Dewey, / the more we consider artistic objects distinct from the original experience [that formed them], // the more we cut art off into a separate realm and remove its significance. ²The "refined and intensified forms of experience [that are works of art]" are thus disconnected from "the everyday events, doings, and sufferings [that are universally recognized to constitute experience]."

어휘 object (연구) 대상; 물체; 목적, 목표   analyze 분석하다   illusion 환상   emerge 생겨나다; 나타나다   relate 관련시키다   conventional 전통적인; 형식적인   A rather than B B라기보다는 A   distinct 별개의; 뚜렷한   realm 영역, 범위   significance 의미; 중요성, 중대성   refined 정제된   intensified 심화된   constitute 구성하다   **[선택지 어휘]** exclusive 유일한; 독점적인   aesthetic 미적인; 미학(적)

해석 마치 그것이 단지 하나의 대상 — 분석되어야 할 '것'— 인 것처럼 소설이나 조각품을 보거나 음악 작품을 듣는 것은 단지 환상만을 감지하는 것이다. 추론 근거 실재는 우리가 어떻게 예술이 삶 자체에서 생겨나고 삶에 연관되는지를 이해할 때만 경험될 수 있다. 60년도 더 전에 교육 철학자인 John Dewey는 그의 고전인 〈경험으로서의 예술〉에서 전통적인 예술 교육이 과학 교육이 실패한 것과 정확히 똑같은 방식으로, 즉 이론과 실재 사이의 연관성을 밝히기보다는 숨김으로써 실패했다고 주장했다. 주제문 Dewey에게 있어서 우리가 예술적 대상을 그것들을 만든 원래 경험과 별개의 것으로 여기면 여길수록, 우리는 점점 더 예술을 잘라내어 별개의 영역으로 집어넣고 예술의 의미를 없앤다. '예술 작품인 경험의 정제되고 심화된 형태'는 따라서 '경험을 구성한다고 보편적으로 인정되는 일상의 사건, 행동, 고통'과 단절된다.

해설 빈칸 문장을 통해 예술적 대상을 '어떻게' 할수록 예술의 의미를 없애는지 찾아야 함을 알 수 있다. 앞의 내용에서 실재는 예술과 삶을 연관시켜야 한다고 했으므로 빈칸은 예술적 대상을 삶과 분리하는 것, 즉 경험과 분리하는 것을 의미하는 내용이 들어가야 한다. 이에 해당하는 것은 ③ '그것(예술 작품)들을 만든 원래의 경험과 별개의'이다.

오답 Check
① 그것들의 제작 과정 때문에 유일한
② 관객의 관점에서 그것들의 복잡성으로 인해 제한되는
④ 그것들의 창조를 둘러싼 상황에 직접적으로 연관되는
→ 정답과 반대되는 내용.
⑤ 그것들의 위치에서 영원한 미적 대상으로서 의미 있는
→ ①, ②, ⑤ 예술과 관련하여 연상되는 내용이지만 글에 언급되지 않음.

PLUS + 변형문제

어휘 appreciate 감상하다; 진가를 알아보다[인정하다]; 고마워하다   independently 자유로이, ~와 관계없이; 독립하여

해설 이 글은 예술을 이해하는 데 있어서 경험과의 연관성이 중요하다는 것을 말하고 있으므로 제목으로 가장 적절한 것은 ③ '경험과 연결: 예술의 실재로 가는 길'이다.
① 예술을 더 잘 이해하라: 교육으로부터의 분리
→ 예술 교육이 실패했다는 내용이지만 교육에서 분리해야 한다는 것은 아님.
② 예술적 대상을 자유롭게 감상하는 방법
→ 예술 작품 감상법에 대한 내용은 없음.
④ 분리에서 결합에 이르는 예술의 창조
→ 예술의 창조 방식에 관한 내용은 아님.
⑤ 독창적인 작품은 어디에서 나오는가: 대상의 밖에서
→ 독창적인 작품이 대상 밖에서 나온다는 내용은 언급되지 않음.

구문 ¹For Dewey, / **the more** we consider artistic objects distinct from *the original experience* [**that** formed them], // **the more** we cut art off into a separate realm and remove its significance.
• 「the 비교급 ~, the 비교급 ...」 구문으로 '~하면 할수록, 더 ...하다'의 의미이다.
• [ ]는 주격 관계대명사 that이 이끄는 관계사절로 선행사 the original experience를 수식한다.
• 밑줄 친 동사 cut과 remove가 접속사 and로 연결되어 병렬 구조를 이룬다.

²The "*refined and intensified forms of experience* [**that** are works of art]" are thus disconnected from "*the everyday events, doings, and sufferings* [**that** are universally recognized to constitute experience]."
• 첫 번째 [ ]는 주격 관계대명사 that이 이끄는 관계사절로, 선행사 refined and intensified forms of experience를 수식한다.
• 두 번째 [ ]도 또한 주격 관계대명사 that이 이끄는 관계사절로, 선행사 the everyday events, doings, and sufferings를 수식한다.

Edward Muybridge was very influential in the late 1800s, // after he began taking multiple photographs of running horses. ① ¹Cinematography, the rapid viewing of a succession of images, / was a direct development of his photographic invention, // which takes advantage of our mind's inability (to process separate images [that appear in rapid succession]). ② ²Cinematography has led to time-lapse photography, // in which very slow events, (such as a flower opening / or the rise and fall of the tides), are photographed / not thirty times per minute like most movies, / but once an hour or once a week. ③ They are then viewed / at a fast enough speed // that we cannot separate the individual movements. ④ Similarly, the first attempts (in film processing) were possible / due to research [which brought about continuous progress / in many aspects of still photography]. ⑤ The result is a representation of long periods of time / onto short ones — a sort of time distortion (similar to physically viewing the letters / in "SHORT" at an angle).

해석 Edward Muybridge는 달리는 말의 여러 장의 사진을 찍기 시작한 이후 1800년대 후반에 매우 영향력이 컸다. ① 일련의 이미지를 빠르게 보는 영화 촬영 기법은 그의 사진술의 발명의 직접적인 발전이었는데, 그것은 우리 정신이 빠르게 잇달아 나타나는 별개의 이미지들을 처리할 능력이 없는 것을 이용한다. ② 영화 촬영 기법은 저속 촬영 기법으로 이어졌는데, 그 기법에서는 꽃이 피거나 조수의 밀물과 썰물 같은 아주 느린 사건이 대부분의 영화처럼 분당 30회가 아니라 시간당 한 번 혹은 주당 한 번 촬영된다. ③ 그런 다음 그것들을 우리가 각각의 움직임을 분리할 수 없을 정도로 빠르게 보여준다. ④ 마찬가지로, 필름 처리에서의 첫 번째 시도는 스틸 사진(일반적인 사진) 기법의 많은 측면에 지속적인 발전을 가져 온 연구 덕분에 가능했다. ⑤ 그 결과는 장기간의 시간을 단기간으로 나타내는 것인데, 이는 실제로 글자를 비스듬히 '짧게' 보는 것과 비슷한 일종의 시간 왜곡이다.

어휘 influential 영향력이 큰; 영향을 미치는 a succession of 일련의 take advantage of ~을 이용하다[기회로 활용하다] inability 할 수 없음, 무능 in succession 잇달아, 계속하여 time-lapse 저속 촬영의 attempt 시도(하다) bring about ~을 유발하다 aspect 측면, 양상 still photography 스틸 사진(움직이는 사진인 영화와 대조되는 얕반적인 사진) representation 나타낸[묘사한] 것; 대표, 대리 a sort of 일종의 distortion 왜곡 physically 실제로; 물리적으로 at an angle 비스듬히

해설 영화 촬영 기법이 생겨난 배경과 그에 이어진 저속 촬영 기법을 소개하는 글에서, 필름 처리의 첫 시도에 일반 사진 기법에 발전을 가져온 연구가 영향을 주었다는 내용인 ④는 전체적인 글의 흐름과 무관하다.

오답 Check
③, ⑤ 문장은 모두 ②에서 소개된 저속 촬영 기법에 대한 보충 설명에 해당한다.

PLUS+ 변형문제

해설 이 글은 영화 촬영 기법이 탄생하게 된 배경에 이어 저속 촬영 기법을 소개하는 글이므로 제목으로는 ⑤ '움직임을 포착함에 있어서 촬영 기술의 발달'이 가장 적절하다.
① Muybridge의 사진술의 탄생
→ Muybridge의 사진술이 영화 촬영 기법으로 발전했다는 내용이지, 그의 사진술의 탄생을 다루지는 않음.
② 영화 촬영 기법: 시지각의 왜곡
→ 일부 촬영 기법에 해당하는 내용임.
③ 더 느리게 사진 찍힐수록, 이미지는 더 선명하다
→ 사진을 찍는 속도와 이미지의 선명함의 관계는 언급되지 않음.
④ 저속 촬영 기법이 영화 산업을 격상시켰다
→ 저속 촬영 기법은 여러 촬영 기법 중 하나에 불과하고 그것이 영화 산업을 격상시켰다는 내용은 없음.

구문 ¹Cinematography, the rapid viewing of a succession of images, / was a direct development of his photographic invention, // which takes advantage of our mind's inability (to process separate images [that appear in rapid succession]).
• 밑줄 친 두 부분은 동격 관계이다.
• which는 계속적 용법의 관계대명사로 which 이하가 Cinematography를 보충 설명한다.
• ( )는 형용사 역할을 하는 to부정사구로 our mind's inability를 수식하고, to부정사구 내에서 주격 관계대명사 that이 이끄는 [ ]가 separate images를 수식한다.

²Cinematography has led to time-lapse photography, // in which very slow events, (such as a flower opening / or the rise and fall of the tides), are photographed / not thirty times per minute like most movies, / but once an hour or once a week.
• '전치사+관계대명사' 형태인 in which가 이끄는 절이 앞에 있는 명사 time-lapse photography를 보충 설명한다.
• ( ) 안의 전명구는 앞에 있는 very slow events를 수식한다.
• 밑줄 친 두 부분을 상관접속사 「not A but B(A가 아니라 B)」가 병렬 연결한다.

주제문
Engagement and exploration are enhanced // when the process includes some uncertainty and surprise. ¹Scientists [who study animal behavior] have known this / for many years.

(B) The famous psychologist B. F. Skinner found // that intermittent, or random, rewards lead to more robust behavior. For example, if a monkey discovers / that sometimes pressing a bar produces a piece of fruit / and other times it doesn't, // the monkey will press the bar more consistently, / knowing that sometimes the effort will pay off.

(A) ²This psychological principle is used all over Las Vegas, // where gamblers play on the slot machines for hours, / waiting for random payouts. This principle can be used to enhance creativity / by giving intermittent recognition for creative work.

(C) Consider using surprise rewards for creative contributions, / or randomly giving special bonuses for particularly innovative ideas. Knowing that at any time there could be a wonderful surprise as a reward / leads to enhanced creative work.

해석 주제문 **참여와 탐구는 그 과정이 어느 정도의 불확실성과 놀라움을 포함할 때 향상된다.** 동물 행동을 연구하는 과학자들은 이것을 오랫동안 알고 있어왔다.
(B) 저명한 심리학자 B. F. Skinner는 간헐적이거나 무작위적인 보상이 더욱 강한 행동으로 이어진다는 것을 발견했다. 예를 들어, 어떤 원숭이가 때때로 막대기를 누르는 것이 열매 한 조각을 가져다주고 다른 때는 그렇지 않다는 것을 발견한다면, 그 원숭이는 때때로 그 노력이 성공할 것을 알고 그 막대기를 더 지속적으로 누를 것이다.
(A) 이러한 심리학적 원리는 라스베이거스 전역에서 사용되는데, 그곳에서 도박꾼들은 무작위적인 보상을 기다리며 몇 시간씩 슬롯머신 게임을 한다. 이런 원리는 창의적 작업에 대해 간헐적인 인정을 해줌으로써 창의력을 향상시키는 데 이용될 수 있다.
(C) 창의적인 기여에 깜짝 보상을 해주거나, 특히 혁신적인 아이디어에 무작위로 특별 보너스를 주는 것을 고려해 보라. 언제든 보상으로 멋진 깜짝 선물이 있을 수 있다는 것을 아는 것은 향상된 창의적 작업으로 이어진다.

어휘 engagement 참여; 약속; 약혼 exploration 탐구; 탐험, 답사 enhance 향상시키다, 높이다 uncertainty 불확실성; 반신반의 intermittent 간헐적인, 간간이 일어나는 random 무작위의; 임의적인 cf. randomly 무작위로 reward 보상; 현상금, 사례금 robust 강한, 튼튼한; 원기 왕성한 consistently 지속적으로, 일관하여 pay off 성공하다, 성과를 올리다 principle 원리, 원칙 gambler 도박꾼, 노름꾼 recognition 인정; 인식, 알아봄 contribution 기여, 공헌; 기부, 기증 innovative 혁신적인, 쇄신적인

해설 참여와 탐구가 그 과정이 어느 정도의 불확실성과 놀라움을 포함할 때 향상된다는 것을 동물의 행동을 연구하는 과학자들은 오랫동안 알고 있었다는 주어진 글 다음으로 B. F. Skinner라는 심리학자가 원숭이 연구에서 발견한 것을 예로 들어 설명하는 (B)가 이어지고, 이러한 심리학적 원리(This psychological principle)가 도박꾼들에게, 그리고 창의적 작업을 하는 사람들에게도 이용될 수 있다는 내용의 (A)가 연결된다. 그다음 창의적 작업을 하는 사람들에게 주어지는 간헐적인 인정의 구체적인 예에 해당하는 (C)가 오는 것이 적절하다.

오답 Check
(A)에서 '이러한 심리학적 원리'는 (B)의 원숭이 연구를 통해 발견한 무작위적인 보상을 위해 특정 행위를 지속적으로 반복하는 원리를 말한다는 것에 유의한다.

PLUS⁺ 변형문제
어휘 detrimental 해로운
해설 어느 정도의 불확실성과 놀라움을 포함할 때 참여와 탐구가 향상되는데, 이러한 무작위적인 보상이 창의력 향상을 이끄는 유인책이 될 수 있다고 했으므로, 글의 제목으로는 ① '예측할 수 없는 보상으로 혁신 촉진하기'가 가장 적절하다.
② 무작위적인 보너스가 혁신에 해로운 이유 → 무작위적인 보상이 창의적 작업에 도움이 된다고 했으므로 글의 내용과 반대됨.
③ 칭찬은 동물도 올바로 행동하게 만든다는 말은 사실인가? → 원숭이 연구가 나오긴 하지만 단순히 칭찬으로 올바른 행동을 유발시킨 것이 아님.
④ 보장된 보너스가 없다면 창의적인 작업도 없다 → 보너스가 보장되지 않고 간헐적이거나 무작위적이라도 창의력을 향상시킬 수 있음.
⑤ 불변의 진리: 인내는 쓰고 열매는 달다 → 인내를 통해 얻어낸 보상에 대한 내용은 없음.

구문 ¹*Scientists* [**who** study animal behavior] have known this / for many years.
- [ ]는 주격 관계대명사 who가 이끄는 관계사절로 Scientists를 수식한다.

²This psychological principle is used *all over Las Vegas,* // **where** *gamblers* play on the slot machines for hours, / **waiting for random payouts**.
- where ~ payouts는 관계부사절로 앞의 선행사 all over Las Vegas 혹은 Las Vegas를 보충 설명한다.
- waiting for random payouts는 gamblers를 의미상 주어로 하며 동시 상황을 나타내는 분사구문으로 '~하면서'의 뜻으로 해석된다.

[1]At the center of Niccolò Machiavelli's political philosophy / is the Renaissance idea of viewing human society in human terms. To achieve this, / he analyzed human nature / based on his observations of human behavior, // which leads to the conclusion // that the majority of people are by nature selfish, short-sighted, and easily deceived.

(C) While they might appear to be an obstacle (to creating an efficient, stable society), // Machiavelli argues // that some of these human failings can in fact be useful / in establishing a successful society, // though this requires the correct leadership.

(B) Man's innate self-centeredness, for example, / is shown in his instinct for self-preservation. [2]However, when threatened by aggression or a hostile environment, // he reacts with acts of courage, hard work, and cooperation.

(A) Other negative human traits can also be turned to the common good, / such as the tendency (to imitate) / rather than think as individuals. [3]This, (Machiavelli notes), leads people / to follow a leader's example / and act cooperatively.

해석 니콜로 마키아벨리 정치철학의 중심에는 인간적 측면에서 인간사회를 보는 르네상스 사상이 있다. 그런 관점을 취하기 위해 그는 우선 그가 관찰한 인간 행동에 기초해 인간 본성을 분석하는데, 이것은 대다수의 사람들은 본래 이기적이고 근시안적이고 속임수에 쉽게 넘어간다고 결론짓게 한다.
(C) 그것들이 효율적이고 안정적인 사회를 세우는 데 걸림돌이 될 것처럼 보일 수도 있지만, 마키아벨리는 그러한 인간의 결점들이 비록 적절한 지도자를 필요로 하지만(의역: 적절한 지도자가 있으면) 인간의 결점들 중 일부는 성공적인 사회를 건설하는 데 사실상 유용할 수도 있다고 주장한다.
(B) 예를 들어 인간의 선천적인 자기중심성은 자기 보호 본능에서 드러난다. 하지만 공격이나 적대적 환경의 위협을 받으면 인간은 용기 있는 행동, 노력, 협동으로 반응한다.
(A) 인간의 다른 부정적 특성들도 공익에 이바지할 수 있는데, 개인으로 생각하기보다 다른 사람을 모방하려는 성향도 그런 예다. 마키아벨리는 이것이 사람들이 지도자를 본받고 서로 협동하도록 이끈다고 말한다.

어휘 short-sighted 근시안적인 deceive 속이다 obstacle 걸림돌, 장애물 efficient 효율적인 stable 안정적인 failing 결점; 실패 innate 선천적인; 타고난 self-centeredness 자기중심성 instinct 본능; 직관 self-preservation 자기 보호 aggression 공격(성) hostile 적대적인 common good 공익 example 본보기, 모범; 예, 사례

해설 인간의 본성이 부정적이라는 마키아벨리의 견해를 설명하는 주어진 글에 이어, 대조를 나타내는 접속사 While로 시작하여 그러한 특성이 성공적인 사회를 건설하는 데 유용할 수도 있다고 주장하는 (C)가 나온다. 그 예로 자기중심성이 유용할 수 있음을 설명하는 (B)가 이어지고 마지막으로 다른 부정적 특징인 모방하려는 성향의 긍정적 영향을 나타내는 내용인 (A)가 오는 것이 가장 적절하다.

오답 Check
(B)에서 '인간의 자기중심성이 용기 있는 행동, 노력, 협동으로 반응하는 것'은 (C)에서 말하는 '인간의 결점들 중 일부는 사회를 건설하는 데 유용할 수도 있는' 것의 예시임에 유의한다.

PLUS+ 변형문제

해설 인간의 본성에 있는 부정적인 특성들이 성공적인 사회를 건설하는 데 유용할 수 있고, 공익에 이바지할 수 있다는 마키아벨리의 견해를 나타낸 요지로는 ④가 가장 적절하다.
→ ①, ②, ③, ⑤ 모두 글의 일부 내용을 활용한 것으로 글 전체의 요지가 될 수는 없음.

구문 [1]At the center of Niccolò Machiavelli's political philosophy / is the Renaissance idea **of** viewing human society in human terms.
• 전명구(At ~ philosophy)가 문두에 나와 주어(the Renaissance idea ~ human terms)와 동사(is)가 도치되었다.
• 밑줄 친 두 부분은 동격으로, of가 동격을 나타내는 어구(viewing ~ terms)를 이끈다.

[2]However, **when threatened by aggression or a hostile environment**, // he reacts with acts of courage, hard work, and cooperation.
• when threatened ~ a hostile environment는 의미를 분명히 하기 위해 접속사를 생략하지 않은 분사구문이다.

[3]This, (Machiavelli notes), **leads** *people* **to follow** a leader's example and **act** cooperatively.
• ( )는 주어와 동사 사이에 삽입된 절이다.
• 「lead+O+C」 구문은 'O가 ~하도록 이끌다'를 의미하며, 목적격보어로 쓰인 to부정사 to follow와 (to) act가 and로 연결되었다.

Social neuroscientist John Cacioppo conducted a 2009 brain imaging study / to identify differences (in the neural mechanism of lonely and nonlonely people). (①) ¹In this study, a key ingredient (in loneliness) has nothing to do with being physically alone, / and everything to do with feeling alone. (②) While in an MRI machine, / subjects viewed a series of images, some with positive connotations, (such as happy people doing fun things), and others with negative associations, (such as quarrels in the workplace). (③) As the two groups watched pleasant imagery, the area of the brain [that recognizes rewards] showed a significantly greater response in nonlonely people / than in lonely people. (④ Similarly, solitary subjects / responded much more strongly to unpleasant images of people / than to pleasant images of objects.) Their counterparts showed no such difference. (⑤) ²In short, people (with an acute sense of loneliness) appear to have a reduced response to things [that make most people happy], and a heightened response to the bad emotions of others.

해석 사회 신경 과학자인 John Cacioppo는 외로운 사람들과 외롭지 않은 사람들의 신경 기제의 차이를 확인하고자 2009년 뇌 영상 연구를 수행했다. 이 연구에서, 외로움의 핵심 요인은 물리적으로 홀로 있음과 아무런 관계가 없고, 외롭다고 느끼는 것과 모든 관계가 있다. MRI 기계 속에 있는 동안 피실험자들은 일련의 이미지들을 보았는데, 어떤 것들은 재미있는 일을 하는 행복한 사람들 같은 긍정적인 함의를 가졌고 다른 것들은 직장에서의 불화와 같은 부정적인 연상을 가졌다. 두 집단이 즐거운 이미지를 봤을 때, 보상을 인식하는 두뇌 영역이 외로운 사람들에게서보다 외롭지 않은 사람들에게서 상당히 더 큰 반응을 보였다. 마찬가지로 외로운 피실험자들은 대상들의 즐거운 이미지들보다 사람들의 불쾌한 이미지들에 훨씬 더 강하게 반응했다. 그들의 상대 피실험자들은 그러한 차이를 보이지 않았다. 주제문 요컨대 외로움에 대한 예민한 감각을 가진 사람들이 대부분의 사람들을 행복하게 만드는 사물에 대한 감소된 반응과, 다른 사람들의 나쁜 감정에 대해 고조된 반응을 가지는 것처럼 보인다.

어휘 neuroscientist 신경 과학자 conduct 수행(하다); 행동(하다); 지휘하다 neural 신경의 ingredient 요인, 구성 요소; 재료 have nothing to do with ~와 아무 관계가 없다 subject 실험 대상, 피험자; 주제; 학과, 과목 connotation 함의, 암시, 연상 association 연상; 협회 quarrel 불화, 싸움; 불만 solitary 외로운, 고독한 counterpart 상대, 대응 관계에 있는 사람 acute 예민한; 날카로운 heighten (감정 등을) 고조시키다; 강조[과장]하다

해설 주어진 문장을 읽은 후, 연결어나 지시어 등을 활용해야 한다. ④ 다음 문장에 '그들의 상대(Their counterparts)'가 나오는데, ④ 이전의 문장에서는 외로운 피실험자들과 외롭지 않은 피실험자들 두 집단을 비교하여 그들의 실험 결과가 모두 제시되므로 '상대'라고 지칭할 대상이 없다. 반면에 주어진 문장에서는 외로운 피실험자들에 대한 실험 결과만 제시되어 있으므로, 주어진 문장이 ④에 위치하면 ④ 다음 문장의 '상대'는 '외롭지 않은 피실험자들'임을 유추할 수 있다.

오답 Check
③ 다음의 문장은 즐거운 이미지에 대한 결과이고, 주어진 문장은 불쾌한 이미지에 대한 결과이고, ⑤ 뒤의 문장은 실험의 전반적인 시사점이다.

PLUS+ 변형문제

어휘 sympathy 공감, 동정, 연민 association 연상, 연관 arouse 불러일으키다; 깨우다

해설 이 글은 외로움의 여부에 따른 사람들의 신경 기제의 차이를 확인하기 위한 연구 내용으로 외로움의 여부에 따라 이미지에 대해 다른 정도의 반응을 보인다는 연구 결과로 보아 제목으로는 ③ '외로움은 다른 수준의 반응을 불러일으킨다'가 가장 적절하다.
① 부정적인 연상이 일으키는 공감
② 직장에서 긍정적인 태도의 효과
④ 물리적으로 홀로 있음이 사람들을 외롭게 하는가?
⑤ 보상 인식하기: 행복해지기 위한 뇌의 전략
→ ①, ②, ④, ⑤ 모두 지문에 나온 어구를 활용하였지만, 주제와는 관련 없는 오답.

구문 ¹In this study, *a key ingredient* (in loneliness) **has** nothing to do with being physically alone, [and] everything to do with feeling alone.
• 문장의 동사 has의 목적어로서 밑줄 친 두 부분이 and로 병렬 연결되었다.

²In short, *people* (with an acute sense of loneliness) appear to have a reduced response to *things* [**that** make most people happy], / [and] a heightened response to the bad emotions of others.
• ( )는 형용사적 용법으로 쓰인 전명구로 문장의 주어 people을 수식한다.
• [ ]는 주격 관계대명사 that이 이끄는 관계사절로 선행사 things를 수식한다.
• to have의 목적어로 쓰인 밑줄 친 부분이 and로 연결되었다.

A rudimentary variety of determinism is the view // that events occurred in the past / simply for the purpose of creating the present situation. (①) ¹This is the belief // that it is the ultimate end that brings about the chain of events, / rather than the causes (operating beforehand). (②) This underlies the popular notion of so-called progress, / with the suggestion // that events (in the past) worked together towards success. (③) However, deterministic theories actually go / beyond the scope of a scientific law. (④ Gravity doesn't say // I will fall to the ground tomorrow, / but that I shall fall downward // if for some reason I fall at all; // biology doesn't predict // that I will die at 74, my life expectancy, / but only that I am likely to, and more likely // if I smoke too much in the meantime.) ²In the same way, most scientific laws only state probabilities, / with plenty of scope allowed for human choices. (⑤) ³It is more fruitful to look at history this way, / to seek lesser but more meaningful laws, "if ... then" conditions.

어휘 rudimentary 미숙한; 기본의; 초보의 ultimate 궁극적인 underlie 기저를 이루다 scope 영역, 범위; 여지, 기회 life expectancy 기대 수명 in the meantime 그동안에 state 진술하다, 명시하다; 상태; 국가, 나라 probability 개연성 allow for ~을 감안[참작]하다 fruitful 유익한, 생산적인

해설 주어진 문장을 읽은 후, 연결어나 지시어 등을 활용해야 한다. 또는, 글의 흐름이 끊기는 곳을 찾는다. 주어진 문장의 내용은 중력과 기대 수명에 대한 과학 법칙을 언급하고 있으므로 결정론에 대한 설명을 하는 글에서 과학 법칙을 언급하기 시작한 문장 다음에, 그리고 다른 과학 법칙들도 마찬가지로 개연성을 언급할 뿐이라는 문장 앞에 들어가야 가장 적절하므로 주어진 문장의 위치는 ④이다.

오답 Check
④ 뒤의 문장은 과학 법칙의 성격에 관한 설명으로, 주어진 글이 ⑤에 들어가는 것으로 착각하지 않도록 유의한다. ④ 뒤의 문장에서 In the same way(이와 마찬가지로)가 나오는 것으로 보아, 과학 법칙의 개연성을 보여주는 예시인 주어진 글이 먼저 나와야 한다.

PLUS+ 변형문제

해설 필자는 역사를 볼 때에는 결정론적 관점보다는 인간의 선택을 감안한 수많은 여지가 있는 과학 법칙의 관점에서 보는 것이 더 유익하다고 말하고 있으므로, 필자의 주장으로는 ④가 가장 적절하다.
① → 지문과 반대되는 내용.
② → 지문과 반대되는 내용.
③ → 어떤 교육이 선행되어야 한다는 내용은 아님.
⑤ → 지문에 나온 어구를 활용한 오답.

해석 한 미숙한 종류의 결정론은 사건들이 단순히 현재의 상황을 만들어낼 목적으로 과거에 일어났다는 견해이다. 이것은 일련의 사건을 초래하는 것은 앞서 작용하는 원인이라기보다는 궁극적 목적이라는 믿음이다. 이것은 과거의 사건들이 성공을 향해 협력하고 있다는 암시와 함께 흔히 '진보'라는 대중적인 개념의 기저를 이룬다. 그러나 결정 이론은 실제로는 과학 법칙의 영역을 넘어선다. 중력은 내가 내일 땅에 넘어질 것이라고 말해주지는 않지만, 어떤 이유로든 내가 넘어진다면 아래쪽으로 넘어질 것이라는 것은 말해줄 따름이다. 또한 생물학은 내가 내 기대 수명인 74세에 죽을지를 예측하지 못하지만, 단지 내가 그럴 것 같다고, 그리고 내가 그동안 너무 많이 담배를 피운다면 그럴 가능성이 더 크다는 것을 예측할 뿐이다. 이와 마찬가지로, 대부분의 과학 법칙들은 인간의 선택에 수많은 여지를 감안한 채로 단지 개연성을 언급할 뿐이다. 주제문 이런 식으로 역사를 보는 것, 즉 수는 더 적지만 더 의미 있는 법칙들, '만일 ~라면 그때에는 …일 것이다' 식의 조건을 찾는 것이 더 유익하다.

구문 ¹This is the belief // **that it is** *the ultimate end* **that** brings about the chain of events, / rather than *the causes* (operating beforehand).

• that it is ~ operating beforehand는 동격의 명사절로 the belief를 부연 설명한다.
• 동격의 that이 이끄는 절 내에서 「it is ... that ~ (~한 것은 바로 …이다)」의 강조 구문이 사용되어 the ultimate end를 강조하고 있다.
• ( )는 분사구로서 앞에 있는 the causes를 수식한다.

²In the same way, most scientific laws only state probabilities, / **with** *plenty of scope* **allowed for human choices**.
• 「with+O+p.p.」의 구조로 쓰인 분사구문으로 '((부대상황)) O를 ~한 채로'의 의미이다.

³**It** is more fruitful **to look at** history this way, / to seek lesser but more meaningful laws, "if ... then" conditions.
• it은 가주어이고, to look at 이하가 진주어이다.
• 콤마(,)는 밑줄 친 두 부분, 즉 this way와 to seek ~ conditions가 동격 관계임을 나타낸다.

Suppose you drop lumps of sugar / in two adjacent areas. If you are a student of statistics, // you may expect the ants to divide themselves / between the two food areas. This is because there is no reason [why ants should prefer one food area to the other]. But you may be surprised to find // that the train of ants moves toward only one food area. Why?
추론 근거
The behavior (of individual ants) influences the group. The first ant may randomly choose one location. ¹The choice (of the first ant) resulted in a train of ants (following suit), // which magnifies the primary action. Economists study such behavior / as part of the interacting agent models.
주제문
A businessman may have randomly selected a street to establish his shop, // but other businessmen (wanting to do the same business) follow his or her action. ²That's why Bangalore first housed all software companies in India, // as did the Silicon Valley in the US. Or why a particular street has all shops (selling paper products).

↓

As ants do, // humans tend to follow an (A) initial action as an agent model, // and this tendency is applied to the business field [in which the same business competitors (B) cluster together].

해석 여러분이 설탕 덩어리를 두 곳의 인접한 지역에 떨어뜨린다고 가정해보자. 만약 여러분이 통계학 연구자라면 개미들이 두 개의 먹이 구역 사이에서 갈라질 것을 기대할지도 모른다. 왜냐하면 개미들이 한 먹이 구역을 다른 곳보다 더 선호해야 할 이유가 없기 때문이다. 그러나 여러분은 개미들의 긴 열이 한 먹이 구역으로만 이동하는 것을 알면 놀랄지도 모른다. 왜 그러는가? 추론 근거 개개의 개미의 행동은 집단에 영향을 준다. 첫 번째 개미는 무작위로 한 위치를 선택할지 모른다. 첫 번째 개미의 선택은 남이 하는 대로 따르는 개미들의 긴 열의 결과를 낳았고, 그것은 처음의 행동을 확대시킨다. 경제학자들은 그런 행동을 상호 작용하는 행위자 모델의 일부로서 연구한다. 주제문 한 사업가는 자기 상점을 설립하기 위해 임의적으로 거리를 선택했을지도 모르지만, 같은 사업을 하려고 하는 다른 사업가들은 그의 행동을 따른다. 그것이 벵갈루루가 미국에서 실리콘밸리가 그러했듯이 인도의 모든 소프트웨어 회사를 처음 수용했던 이유이다. 아니면 왜 특정 거리에 종이 제품을 파는 모든 상점이 있겠는가.

↓

개미들이 그렇듯, 인간도 행위자 모델로서 (A) 처음의 행동을 따르는 경향이 있고, 이런 경향은 같은 사업 경쟁자들이 함께 (B) 모이는 사업 분야에 적용된다.

어휘 lump 덩어리; 혹 adjacent 인접한; 근방의 statistics 통계학; 통계 자료 follow suit 남이 하는 대로 따라 하다 magnify 확대하다; 과장하다 primary 최초[초기]의; 주요한, 주된 agent 행위자; 대리인 house 수용하다; 묵게 하다 cluster 모이다; 무리

해설 요약문을 통해 사람들이 어떤 행동을 따르는 경향이 있고, 같은 사업 경쟁자들이 함께 무엇을 하는지를 파악한다. 이 글은 개미들이 처음의 행동을 한 개미를 따라 한 비유적 이야기를 통해 사업도 첫 사업체가 자리 잡은 곳에 따라 모인다는 것을 설명한다. 그러므로 빈칸에는 ② '(A) 처음의 – (B) 모이다'가 적절하다.

오답 Check

(A)	(B)
① 집단 – 분석하다
→ (A)는 맞지만, '분석'에 관한 언급은 없음.
③ 어리석은 – 합병하다
→ (A), (B) 모두 틀림.
④ 모험적인 – 성장하다
→ (A), (B) 모두 언급되지 않음.
⑤ 무작위의 – 협동하다
→ (A)는 언급된 단어이지만 처음 선택을 하는 방식일 뿐이고, (B)는 언급되지 않음.

구문 ¹The choice (of the first ant) resulted in a train of ants (following suit), // which magnifies the primary action.
• ( )는 각각 앞에 있는 명사 The choice, a train of ants를 수식한다.
• 계속적 용법의 관계대명사 which가 이끄는 절(which ~ action)이 a train ~ following suit를 보충 설명한다.

²That's why Bangalore first housed all software companies in India, // as did the Silicon Valley in the US.
• as는 양태의 부사절 접속사로 '~듯이'라는 의미이며, as가 이끄는 부사절 내에서 주어 the Silicon Valley와 대동사 did가 도치되었다.

Salicylic acid is found / in copious amounts in the bark of willow trees. In fact, the ancient Greek physician Hippocrates described a bitter substance — salicylic acid — (drawn from willow bark) [that could (a) ease aches and reduce fevers]. Other cultures (in ancient times) also used willow bark as a medicine, // and salicylic acid itself is a key ingredient / in many modern anti-acne face washes. Although willow is a well-known producer (of salicylic acid), this chemical is (b) manufactured / in various amounts by all plants. But why would a plant produce a pain reliever and fever reducer? Salicylic acid is not made / for our benefit. ¹For plants, it is salicylic acid // that is a defence hormone [that (c) increases the plant's immune system]. Plants produce it // when they've been attacked / by bacteria or viruses. ²Salicylic acid is soluble and released / at the exact spot of infection / to signal through the veins / to the rest of the plant [that bacteria are on the loose]. The healthy parts of the plant respond / by initiating a number of steps [that either kill the bacteria / or stop the plague's spread]. One includes blocking the movement of the bacteria / to other parts of the plant. Areas of white spots (appearing on leaves) are proof of these barriers. ³These are // where cells have killed themselves // so that the bacteria can't (d) block farther.

주제문
At a broad level, salicylic acid serves (e) similar functions / in both plants and people. Salicylic acid is // what plants use / to help ward off infection. We've used salicylic acid / since ancient days, // and we use the modern derivative of aspirin // when we have an infection [that causes aches and pains].

어휘 copious 다량의; 풍부한 bark 나무껍질 willow tree 버드나무 substance 물질 physician 의사 ease 덜어주다; 완화하다; 편함 ache 아픔, 통증 acne 여드름 immune system 면역 체계 soluble 녹기 쉬운 infection 감염; 오염 vein 잎맥; 혈관 on the loose 잡히지 않은[자유로운] initiate 시작하다; 착수하다 plague 전염병 ward off 막다, 피하다 derivative 파생물; 유도된 **[선택지 어휘]** intrinsic 본질적인; 내재한

해설 **41** 이 글은 살리실산의 기능과 식물들이 그것을 이용하는 방식을 설명하고 마지막으로 인간이 그것을 활용한 예를 언급하므로 제목으로는 ⑤ '식물과 인간을 위한 살리실산의 이점'이 적절하다.

42 (d)가 있는 문장의 주어 These는 앞 문장의 Areas of white spots를 나타내는데, 이는 박테리아가 식물의 다른 부위로 이동하는 것을 막는 장벽의 증거라고 설명한다. 그러므로 (d)의 block은 spread로 고치는 것이 적절하다.

오답 Check
41 ① 살리실산의 과학적 기능
② 살리실산: 아스피린의 원형
→ ①, ② 글의 일부 내용을 활용한 오답.
③ 나무의 본질적 가치: 고통 감소 → 살리실산을 생성하여 고통을 감소시킨다고 언급했으나, 이를 나무의 본질적 가치로 볼 수는 없음.
④ 잘 알려진 고대 의학사 → 글의 일부 내용을 활용한 오답.
42 (e) 다음에 나오는 문장에서 인간이 살리실산을 활용한 예를 보면 살리실산이 식물에 끼치는 영향이 인간에게 끼치는 기능과 유사하다는 것을 알 수 있다.

해석 버드나무 껍질에서는 다량의 살리실산이 발견된다. 실제로 고대 그리스의 의사였던 히포크라테스는 버드나무에서 나와 통증을 (a) 줄이고 열을 낮출 수 있는 쓴 물질, 즉 살리실산을 설명했다. 고대 다른 문화권에서도 버드나무 껍질을 약으로 썼고, 살리실산 자체는 현대의 많은 여드름 치료용 세안제의 주요 재료이다. 버드나무는 살리실산의 잘 알려진 생성원이지만, 사실 모든 식물들에서 이 화학물질이 다양한 양으로 (b) 생성된다. 하지만 왜 식물이 진통제와 해열제를 생산할까? 살리실산은 인간의 이익을 위해 만들어지지 않는다. 식물에 있어 식물의 면역 체계를 (c) 증대시키는 '방어 호르몬'이 바로 살리실산이다. 식물은 박테리아나 바이러스의 공격을 받았을 때 그것(살리실산)을 생성한다. 살리실산은 쉽게 녹고 감염된 정확한 부위에 퍼져서 잎맥을 통해 박테리아가 잡히지 않은 나머지 부분에 신호를 보낸다. 식물의 건강한 부위는 박테리아를 죽이거나 전염병이 퍼지는 것을 막는 몇 가지 조치들을 시작함으로써 반응한다. 하나는 박테리아가 식물의 다른 부위로 이동하는 것을 막는 것을 포함한다. 잎 위에 나타나는 흰색 점의 영역은 이러한 장벽의 증거이다. 이 점들은 잎의 세포들이 스스로를 죽여서 박테리아들이 더 멀리 (d) 막지(→ 퍼지지) 못하게 하는 영역이다.
주제문 넓은 범위에서 보면 살리실산은 식물과 인간 모두에게 (e) 유사하게 기능한다. 살리실산은 감염을 막기 위해 식물이 활용하는 것이다. 우리 역시 고대부터 살리실산을 사용해 왔고, 아픔이나 고통을 야기하는 전염병에 걸릴 때 아스피린이라는 현대적 파생 물질을 이용한다.

구문 ¹For plants, **it is** *salicylic acid* // **that** is *a defence hormone* [**that** increases the plant's immune system].
• 「it is ~ that ...」 강조 구문이 쓰여 salicylic acid를 강조하고 있다.
• [ ] 내의 that은 주격 관계대명사로 관계사절을 이끌어 선행사 a defence hormone을 수식한다.

²Salicylic acid is soluble and released / at the exact spot of infection / **to signal** through the veins / to *the rest of the plant* [**that** bacteria are on the loose].

• to signal은 부사적 용법으로 '~하기 위해서'의 의미이며 [ ]는 관계부사 that이 이끄는 관계사절로 the rest of the plant를 선행사로 한다.

³These are // **(the places) where** cells have killed themselves // **so that** the bacteria can't spread farther.

• where는 일반적인 선행사 the place가 생략된 관계부사이다.

• so that은 목적을 나타내는 부사절 접속사로 '~하기 위해서'의 의미이다.

31 ④ + ①	32 ① + ⑤	33 ④ + ④	34 ③ + ④	35 ④ + ①	36 ④ + ⑤
37 ⑤ + ⑤	38 ④ + ④	39 ③ + ⑤	40 ③	41 ③	42 ⑤

31 ④ PLUS+ ①

주제문
Early experiences in the arts are important // because they produce intellectual as well as aesthetic gains. In the best-researched example, / participation in music seems to do mysterious / but wonderful things. [1]Music educators have recently become so concerned about parents (sending kids off to computer camps instead of music lessons) // that they have begun funding some expert studies. Researchers at the University of California, Irvine, studied // how regular piano practice and computer training affect children's spatial-temporal skills. Such skills are key to understanding proportion, geometry, and other mathematical and scientific concepts. After six months, the piano-taught children in the study had dramatically improved their scores on a spatial-temporal task, // whereas the computer training had shown little effect. "If I were a parent, // I'd want to take these findings into consideration," reported one of the experiment's designers.

해석 **주제문** 예술을 일찍 경험하는 것은 중요한데, 그것이 심미적 이득뿐 아니라 지적인 이득도 만들어내기 때문이다. 가장 잘 연구된 예에서, 음악(활동)에 참여하는 것은 불가사의하지만 놀라운 일을 하는 것처럼 보인다. 최근 음악 교육가들은 아이들을 음악 레슨 대신 컴퓨터 캠프에 보내는 부모들에 대해 매우 염려하여 어떤 전문적인 연구에 자금을 지원하기 시작했다. 어바인에 있는 캘리포니아 대학의 연구자들은 정기적인 피아노 연습과 컴퓨터 훈련이 아이들의 공간적·시간적 기능에 어떻게 영향을 미치는지 연구했다. 그러한 기능은 비율, 기하학, 그 외 수학적, 과학적 개념을 이해하는 데 핵심적이다. **추론 근거** 6개월 후, 연구에서 피아노를 배운 아이들은 공간적·시간적 과제에서 점수가 극적으로 향상된 데 반해, 컴퓨터 훈련은 거의 효과를 보이지 않았다. 실험 설계자 중 한 명은 "내가 부모라면, 이런 결과를 고려해보고 싶을 것이다."라고 전했다.

어휘 **intellectual** 지적인 **A as well as B** B뿐만 아니라 A도 **aesthetic** 미(美)의, 심미적인; 미학의 **spatial-temporal skill** 공간적·시간적 기능 **proportion** 비율; 부분; 균형 **geometry** 기하학 **dramatically** 극적으로; 희극[연극]적으로 **take A into consideration** A를 고려하다 **[선택지 어휘] functional** 기능적인; 실용적인

해설 예술의 조기 경험으로 얻을 수 있는 또 다른 이득이 무엇인지 찾아야 한다. 글 중반부에 등장하는 음악가들이 자금을 지원한 실험의 결과를 단서로 컴퓨터 훈련 대신 피아노 연습을 꾸준히 한 아이들이 공간적·시간적 기능에서 극적인 발전을 보였고, 이 기능은 지적인 활동과 관련된 분야를 이해하는 데 중요한 기능이라고 했다. 따라서 심미적 이득 외에 얻을 수 있는 것은 ④ '지적인' 이득임을 알 수 있다.

오답 Check
① 직관적인   ② 정서적인
→ ①, ② 모두 본문에 언급된 바 없음.
③ 실용적인   ⑤ 기능적인
→ ③, ⑤ 공간적·시간적 기능 발달이 지적 이해에 도움이 된 것은 실질적이고 실용적인 이득과 거리가 있음.

PLUS+ 변형문제

해설 첫 문장에서 지적인 이득을 만들어내는 예술을 일찍 경험하는 것이 중요하다고 했고 이후에 나오는 연구에서도 음악에 참여하는 것이 공간적·시간적 과제 점수를 높였다고 했다. 따라서 글의 제목으로는 ① '예술 교육이 아이의 두뇌를 신장시키는가?'가 가장 적절하다.
② 수학을 잘한다는 것은 피아노를 잘 친다는 것을 의미한다
→ 수학 실력과 피아노 실력 간의 상관관계에 대한 글이 아님.
③ 피아노와 컴퓨터를 가르치는 것의 이점들
→ 컴퓨터 교육의 이점은 언급되지 않음.
④ 오늘날 음악 교육가들의 가장 큰 걱정
→ 부모들로 인해 음악 교육가들이 염려한다는 이야기는 연구가 실행된 배경에 대한 내용으로 글을 아우르는 내용은 아님.
⑤ 어떻게 주기적인 연습이 공간적·시간적 기능에 영향을 미치는가 → 단순히 주기적인 연습이 공간적·시간적 기능에 영향을 미친다는 언급은 없음.

구문 [1]Music educators have recently become **so** concerned about *parents* (sending kids off to computer camps instead of music lessons) // **that** *they* have begun funding some expert studies.
• 결과를 나타내는 「so ~ that ... (너무 ~해서 …하다)」 구문이 쓰였으며, that 뒤에 이어지는 they는 music educators를 가리킨다.
• ( )는 parents를 수식하는 현재분사구이다.

People often think that a proposition is true / because it has not yet been proven false // or a proposition is false / because it has not yet been proven true. Carl Sagan gives this example: "There is no compelling evidence // that UFOs are not visiting the Earth; therefore UFOs exist, // and there is intelligent life elsewhere in the universe." [1]Similarly, before we knew how the pyramids were built, // some concluded that, / unless proven otherwise, / they must have been built by a supernatural power.
주제문
But in fact, the "burden of proof" always lies / with the person (making a claim). [2]More logically, // and as several others have put it, // one should ask what is likely based on evidence (from past observation).
추론 근거
[3]Which is more likely: That an object (flying through space) is a man-made artifact or natural phenomenon, / or that it is aliens (visiting from another planet)? Since we have frequently observed the former and never the latter, // it is more reasonable to conclude // that UFOs are probably not aliens (visiting from outer space).

해석 사람들은 종종 아직 잘못된 것으로 입증되지 않았기에 명제가 사실이라고, 또는 아직은 진실이라 입증되지 않았기에 명제가 거짓이라고 생각한다. Carl Sagan은 이런 예를 든다. "UFO가 지구를 방문하지 않고 있다는 설득력 있는 증거는 없다. 따라서 UFO는 존재하며 우주 다른 곳에는 지적 생명체가 있다." 마찬가지로 피라미드가 어떻게 건설되었는지 우리가 알게 되기 이전에, 일부 사람들은 달리 증명되지 않는 한, 피라미드는 분명히 초자연적인 힘에 의해 건설되었을 것이라고 결론지었다. 주제문 그러나 사실 '입증의 부담감'은 항상 주장을 하는 사람에게 있다. 좀 더 논리적으로, 그리고 몇몇 다른 사람들이 말했듯이, 과거의 관찰에서 나온 증거에 근거하여 무엇이 가능성이 있는지 물어봐야 한다. 추론 근거 어느 쪽이 더 가능성이 높은가: 우주를 날아다니는 물체가 인간이 만든 인공물이나 자연 현상인가, 아니면 다른 행성에서 찾아온 외계인들인가? 우리는 빈번하게 전자를 관찰해왔고 후자는 전혀 관찰하지 않았으므로, UFO는 십중팔구 우주 공간에서 찾아온 외계인은 아닐 거라고 결론 내리는 게 더 타당하다.

어휘 proposition 명제; 제안 compelling 설득력 있는; 강제적인 otherwise 달리; 그렇지 않으면 burden 부담[짐](을 지우다) claim 주장(하다); 청구(하다) artifact 인공물
[선택지 어휘] inference 추론 assumption 가정; 가설

해설 빈칸 문장으로 보아 '무엇'에 근거하여 어떤 것의 가능성 여부를 물어봐야 하는지 판단해야 한다. 빈칸이 중반부에 있을 경우, 단서는 빈칸 뒷부분에 있을 가능성이 높다. 우주를 날아다니는 물체가 인공물이나 자연현상인지, 아니면 외계인인지 묻는 질문에 과거로부터 현재까지 관찰된 적이 있는지 여부에 따라 외계인이 아닐 거라 결론 내리는 게 타당하다고 했으므로, 빈칸에 들어갈 말로는 ① '과거의 관찰에서 나온 증거'가 적절하다.

오답 Check
② 증거가 필요하지 않은 진실 → 외계인의 존재 유무를 판단하는 데 관찰 경험의 여부에 따르므로 증거가 필요하지 않다고 볼 수 없음.
③ 다양한 자료로부터의 추론
→ 과거의 관찰 경험의 여부에 따르므로 다양한 자료는 아님.
④ 현재의 기대와 추정
→ 기대와 추정이 아닌 과거의 관찰 경험에 의한 것이어야 함.
⑤ 아직 틀렸음이 입증되지 않은 명제
→ 첫 문장의 내용을 활용한 오답.

PLUS + 변형문제

어휘 faith 믿음, 신뢰; 신앙(심)
해설 어떤 명제를 입증하기 위해서는 과거의 관찰에서 나온 증거에 근거하여 무엇이 더 가능성이 있는지 물어봐야 한다고 했으므로, 글의 제목으로는 ⑤ '정보 없이는 믿음을 정당화할 수 없다'가 가장 적절하다.
① 역사적인 미스터리를 다루는 방법
→ Carl Sagan의 예시에서 연상되는 내용의 오답.
② 증거가 있는 곳에, 믿음이 있다
③ 우리는 새로운 증거의 바다에서 살고 있다
→ ②, ③ 증거를 활용한 오답으로 주제와 거리가 멈.
④ UFO: 인간이 만든 인공물 대 외계인의 증거
→ 글에 자주 언급된 단어를 활용한 오답.

구문 [1]Similarly, before we **knew** how the pyramids were built, // some concluded that, / **unless proven otherwise**, / they must have been built / by a supernatural power.
• 간접의문문 「의문사(how)+주어(the pyramids)+동사(were built)」가 부사절의 동사 knew의 목적어로 쓰였다.
• unless proven otherwise는 주절의 동사 concluded의 목적어로 사용된 명사절(that ~ power)에서 접속사 that과 주어(they) 사이에 삽입된 접속사를 포함한 분사구문이다.

[2]More logically, // and as several others have put it, // one **should ask** what is likely based on *evidence* (from past observation).
• 동사 should ask의 목적어로 의문사 what이 이끄는 간접의문문(what ~ past observation)이 쓰였다.
• ( )는 전명구로 앞에 있는 명사 evidence를 수식한다.

[3]Which is more likely: That *an object* (flying through space) is a man-made artifact or natural phenomenon, // or that it is *aliens* (visiting from another planet)?
• 두 개의 ( )는 현재분사 flying과 visiting이 이끄는 분사구로 각각 앞에 있는 명사 an object와 aliens를 수식한다.
• 두 개의 that절이 콤마(,)와 or로 병렬 연결되었다.

[1]Most recent works (of Western theatre dance) have been created by choreographers, // who have been regarded / as the authors and owners of their works / in a way (comparable to writers, composers, and painters). New York choreographer Merce Cunningham has crossed artistic barriers // and stretched the parameters of dance. <u>He always</u> <u>looks for pattern-forming inspiration, randomly mixing dance elements.</u> He begins by outlining the movement, timing, spacing, number of dancers. He then assigns each a different variable / and generates their combinations, / such as the flip of a coin. As Carolyn Brown, one of Cunningham's dancers, has said, // "The dances are treated more as puzzles than works of art; // the pieces are space and time, shape and rhythm." [2]Cunningham's choreography is considered / to avoid traditional preconceptions / and explore all possible arrangements (inherent in the art of dance), // in the same way new gene combinations are generated / with every throw of the reproductive dice. As Cunningham says, // "You can see what it is like / to break these actions up in different ways" / and then see what surprises new combinations may hold.

해석 서구 극장 무용의 최근 작품들 대부분은 안무가들에 의해 창작되었는데, 이들은 작가, 작곡가, 화가와 필적하는 방식으로 자신의 작품의 저자이자 주인으로 간주되어 왔다. 뉴욕의 안무가 Merce Cunningham은 예술의 장벽을 넘어서 춤의 한계를 뻗어 나가게 했다. 그는 항상 춤의 요소들을 무작위로 혼합하여 패턴을 형성하는 영감을 찾는다. 그는 동작, 타이밍, 간격, 댄서들의 수에 대한 윤곽을 그림으로써 시작한다. 그는 그러고 나서 동전 던지기와 같이(의역: 무작위로) 각각에게 다른 변수를 배정하고 그것들의 조합을 생성한다. Cunningham의 댄서 중 한 명인 Carolyn Brown이 말한 것처럼 "춤은 예술 작품이라기보다는 퍼즐로 더 많이 취급된다. (퍼즐의) 조각은 공간과 시간, 형태와 리듬이다." Cunningham의 안무법은 번식의 주사위를 던질 때마다 새로운 유전자 조합이 생성되는 것과 같은 방식으로 전통적인 선입견을 피하고 춤의 예술에 내재한 모든 가능한 방식을 탐구한다고 여겨진다. Cunningham이 말하는 것처럼 "여러분은 이러한 행동들을 다양한 방식으로 쪼개는 것이 어떠할지 알 수 있고" 그러고 나서 새로운 조합들이 어떠한 놀라움을 갖게 될지 볼 수 있다.

어휘 comparable to ~에 필적하는[맞먹는] parameter 한계; 지침 inspiration 영감 outline 윤곽을 그리다; 약술하다 assign 배정[배치]하다; 임명[부여]하다 variable 변수; 변동이 심한 generate 생성하다, 만들어내다 combination 조합, 결합 preconception 선입견; 편견; 예상 arrangement (처리) 방식; 준비; 배열 inherent 내재하는, 타고난 reproductive 번식의; 재생[재현]시키는 dice 주사위 **[선택지 어휘]** conventional 전통[관습]적인 disorderly 무질서한 systematic 체계[조직]적인

해설 Cunningham은 춤의 각 요소들에 무작위로 다른 변수를 배정하고 그 조합을 생성하고, 춤을 공간과 시간, 형태와 리듬이라는 조각으로 만드는 퍼즐로 취급하여 예측치 못한 결과물을 얻어낸다. 이러한 창작 기법을 가장 잘 나타낸 빈칸에 들어갈 말은 ④ '춤의 요소들을 무작위로 혼합하여 패턴을 형성하는 영감'이다.

오답 Check
① 자연스러운 춤 동작의 특성의 이점들
→ 자연스러운 춤 동작은 언급되지 않음.
② 춤의 모든 영역에 걸쳐 확장되는 강력한 기술
→ 춤의 모든 영역에 걸친 기술은 언급되지 않음.
③ 서로 다른 춤 형식들에 내재된 전통적 패턴들
→ 오히려 전통적인 선입견을 피한다고 했으므로 지문 내용과 반대됨.
⑤ 무질서한 동작의 체계적인 동작으로의 변형
→ Cunningham의 안무법을 무질서한 동작을 체계적인 동작으로 변형한 것으로 볼 수 없음.

PLUS+ 변형문제
어휘 abstraction 추상 (작용); 방심
해설 춤의 요소를 무작위로 혼합하여 패턴을 형성한 안무가 Merce Cunningham의 방식을 설명한 글로 그는 전통적인 선입견을 피하고, 춤의 모든 방식을 탐구하여 새로운 조합을 만들어 낸다고 했으므로 글의 주제로는 ④ '한 안무가의 춤을 발전시키는 독특한 방법'이 적절하다.
① 서구 극장에서 새로운 안무법의 필요성
② 춤에서 전통적인 선입견을 피하는 방법
③ 춤의 조합을 만드는 데 기여하는 요소들
⑤ 추상 작용으로 움직임을 만들어내는 것에 대한 비평가들의 부정적 견해
→ 모두 지문에 언급된 단어를 활용하여 만든 오답.

구문 [1]*Most recent works* (of Western theatre dance) have been created by *choreographers*, // **who** have been regarded / as the authors and owners of their works / in *a way* (comparable to writers, composers, and painters).
• who는 계속적 용법의 관계대명사로 who가 이끄는 절이 choreographers를 보충 설명한다.
• 첫 번째 ( )는 전명구, 두 번째 ( )는 형용사구로 각각 앞에 있는 명사 Most recent works와 a way를 수식한다.

[2]Cunningham's choreography is considered / to avoid traditional preconceptions / 〔and〕 (to) explore *all possible arrangements* (inherent in the art of dance), // **in the same way** new gene combinations are generated / with every throw of the reproductive dice.
• 원래 SVOC 문형이던 것을 수동태로 표현한 것으로, 문장의 보어로 밑줄 친 두 부분이 and로 병렬 연결되었다.
• ( )는 형용사구로 all possible arrangements를 수식한다.
• in the same way는 종속접속사로 주절과 비슷한 내용을 설명하는 절을 이끈다.

Grasshoppers behave as solitary insects / immediately after hatching or when isolated, // but if they are forcibly crowded for as little as 6 hours // they subsequently tend to group together, / or exhibit gregarious behavior. ¹For a long time / scientists thought // the grasshopper "migrants" [that appeared so suddenly] were a unique species (arriving from and departing for unknown locations). 주제문/추론 근거 Now we know // that the migrants are a "phase" (of a common grasshopper species [that changes its color, form, and behavior / in response to crowding]). 추론 근거 Proof comes from experiments: to create these "migrants" from isolated individuals, / one takes a nymph, // which is the immature stage of a grasshopper, / puts it in a jar, / and has a motor-driven brush tickle it continuously. ²The constant tickling mimics the crowding, // which triggers the nervous system to alter the hormones [that result in development (into the restless migratory phase / with a different color, wing length, and behavior)]. It is a good example [that shows // "changes (in gene expression) can be triggered / by the environment]."

해석 메뚜기들은 부화를 한 직후나 고립될 때 군거하지 않는 곤충으로 행동하지만, 그들이 최소한 6시간 동안 강제적으로 모이게 되면, 그들은 그 다음에 함께 집단을 형성하거나 군거하는 행동을 보여주는 경향이 있다. 오랫동안 과학자들은 아주 갑자기 나타난 메뚜기 '이주자들'은 (미지의 장소에서) 와서 미지의 장소를 향해 떠나가는 하나의 독특한 종이라고 생각했다. 주제문/추론 근거 오늘날 우리는 이주 메뚜기들이 개체수 과밀에 반응하여 자신의 색깔, 형태, 행동을 변화시키는 일반적인 메뚜기 종의 한 '단계'라는 것을 안다. 추론 근거 실험을 통해 증명이 가능하다. 별개의 개체들로부터 이들 '이주 메뚜기들'을 만들어 내기 위해 메뚜기의 미성숙한 단계인 유충을 한 마리 잡아 병에 넣고, 모터로 움직이는 브러시를 이용해 계속 간지럼을 태우도록 한다. 계속되는 간지럼은 개체수 과밀 상태와 흡사한 상황을 연출하고, 이것은 다른 색깔, 다른 날개 길이, 다른 행동과 더불어 끊임없이 이주하는 단계로 발전시키는 것을 초래하는 호르몬을 변경하도록 신경계를 자극한다. 이는 '유전자 발현의 변화가 환경에 의해 촉발될 수 있다'는 것을 보여주는 좋은 사례이다.

어휘 solitary 군거하지 않는; 혼자의 hatch 부화하다; 꾀하다 subsequently 그다음에, 나중에, 이어서 migrant 이주자; 이동하는 *cf.* migratory 이주하는; 이동하는 phase 단계; 양상 nymph 유충 tickle 간질이다 mimic 흡사하다; 흉내 내다 alter 변경하다 restless 끊임없는 **[선택지 어휘]** mutual 상호 간의; 공통의 gene expression 유전자 발현 inherent 타고난; 내재하는 instinct 본능; 직관

해설 빈칸 문장으로 보아 앞의 사례가 무엇을 나타내는지 파악해야 함을 알 수 있다. 과거에는 이주하는 독특한 메뚜기종이 있다고 생각했지만, 개체수가 밀집하는 환경으로 인해 일반적인 종도 색깔, 형태, 행동을 변화와 더불어 끊임없이 이주하는 단계로 발전했다는 것을 실험으로 증명하는 내용으로 보아, 빈칸에는 ③ '유전자 발현의 변화가 환경에 의해 촉발될 수 있다'가 적절하다.

오답 Check
① 상호 간의 협력이 종의 생존을 위한 핵심이다
→ 협력과 생존에 대한 언급은 없음.
② 종의 가장 튼튼한 구성원이 항상 가까스로 살아남는다
→ 가장 튼튼한 구성원에 대한 언급은 없음.
④ 이주하는 능력은 동물의 일부 종에서 타고난 본능이다
→ 타고난 본능이 아닌, 환경에 의해 촉발된 것으로 글의 내용과 반대되는 오답.
⑤ 이주는 한 방향의 과정이 아니라 다방면의 과정이다
→ 이주의 방향성에 관한 언급은 없음.

PLUS+ 변형문제

해설 개체수가 과밀한 환경으로 인해 일반적인 종도 색깔, 형태, 행동과 함께 끊임없이 이주하는 단계로 발전하게 되었다는 내용이므로 글의 주제로는 ④ '메뚜기가 자신의 행동을 바꾸고 군거하게 되는 방식'이 적절하다.
① 메뚜기가 군거하지 않는 생물인 경향이 있는 이유
→ 일부 상황에서 군거하지 않는 것이지 그런 경향이 있다는 언급은 없음.
② '이주자' 메뚜기가 새로운 종이라는 발견
→ 과거의 의견으로 오늘날의 의견이 주제와 맞지 않음.
③ 유전학이 메뚜기가 이주하는 단계로 들어서게 하는 이유
→ 유전학이 아닌 개체수가 과밀한 환경이 그 단계로 들어서게 함.
⑤ 메뚜기가 다른 것들로부터 고립을 추구하도록 이끄는 호르몬의 변화 → 고립을 추구하게 만드는 호르몬에 대한 언급은 없음.

구문 ¹For a long time / scientists thought // *the grasshopper "migrants"* [**that** appeared so suddenly] were *a unique species* (arriving from and departing for unknown locations).
• [ ]는 주격 관계대명사 that이 이끄는 관계사절로 앞에 있는 the grasshopper "migrants"를 수식한다.
• arriving from 이하는 분사구로 a unique species를 수식한다.

²*The constant tickling mimics the crowding*, // **which** triggers the nervous system to alter *the hormones* [**that** result in development (into the restless migratory phase / with a different color, wing length, and behavior)].
• which는 계속적 용법의 관계대명사로 which가 이끄는 절이 앞에 있는 절 전체에 대한 보충 설명을 한다.
• [ ]는 주격 관계대명사 that이 이끄는 관계사절로 앞에 있는 the hormones를 수식한다.

주제문

Closely observing the color (of the ocean surface) / provides a powerful means (of determining ocean productivity). ① The ocean reflects the color of the sky, // but even on cloudless days / the color of the ocean is not a consistent blue. ② ¹Variations (in ocean color) are determined / primarily by variations (in the concentrations of algae and phytoplankton), // which are the basis of the marine food chain. ③ ²Because these microscopic plants absorb blue and red light more readily / than green light, // regions (of high phytoplankton concentrations) appear greener / than those (with low concentration). ④ <u>Sunlight, water, and nutrients are essential / for phytoplankton to survive, so any of these ingredients / over time for a given region / will affect the phytoplankton variations.</u> ⑤ Because fish feed on the phytoplankton, // regions (of greener sea) indicate the possibility (of greater fish population).

해석 주제문 해양 표면의 색깔을 면밀히 관찰하는 것은 해양 생산성을 밝혀내는 강력한 수단을 제공한다. ① 바다는 하늘의 색을 반영하지만, 구름 한 점 없는 날에도 바다의 색깔은 일관된 푸른색이 아니다. ② 해양 색깔의 변화는 주로 해조류와 식물성 플랑크톤의 농도 변화에 의해 결정되는데, 그것들은 주로 해양 먹이 사슬의 기저이다. ③ 이 미세한 식물들은 푸른빛과 붉은빛을 녹색 빛보다 더 쉽사리 흡수하기 때문에 식물성 플랑크톤 농도가 높은 지역은 낮은 농도의 지역보다 더 녹색 빛으로 보인다. ④ 햇빛, 물 그리고 영양분은 식물성 플랑크톤이 살아가는 데 필수적이어서 이 요소들 중 어느 것이든 정해진 지역에서 시간이 지남에 따라 식물성 플랑크톤의 변화에 영향을 줄 것이다. ⑤ 물고기들은 식물성 플랑크톤을 먹고살기 때문에 더 녹색 빛의 바다 지역은 더 많은 어류 개체수의 가능성을 나타낸다.

어휘 determine 알아내다, 밝히다; 결정하다 productivity 생산성 reflect 나타내다, 반영하다; 반사하다, 비추다 consistent 일관된; 일치하는 primarily 주로 variation 변화; 변이 concentration 농도; (정신) 집중 alga (pl. algae) 해조(류) phytoplankton 식물성 플랑크톤 microscopic 미세한; 현미경을 이용한 absorb 흡수하다; (주의를) 빼앗다 readily 쉽사리; 기꺼이 ingredient 요소; 재료 given 정해진; 주어진 feed on ~을 먹고살다[먹다]

해설 해양 표면의 색깔은 해조류와 식물성 플랑크톤 농도 변화에 의해 결정되는데, 물고기는 식물성 플랑크톤을 먹고 살아가므로, 해양 표면의 색깔에 따라 해양 생산성을 알 수 있다는 글이다. 그러나 ④는 플랑크톤이 살아가는 데 영향을 주는 요소들에 대해 말하고 있으므로 글의 흐름을 벗어난다.

오답 Check
①은 바다의 색에 영향을 주는 것은 하늘뿐만이 아님을 의미한다.

PLUS+ 변형문제

어휘 signify 의미하다; 중요하다, 문제가 되다 yield 수확량; 생산하다; 항복하다; 양보하다

해설 글의 주제문인 첫 번째 문장을 제목으로 잘 표현한 것은 ① '해양 표면의 색깔이 의미하는 것'이 적절하다.
② 어업 수확량을 늘리기 위해 시도하는 방법
③ 푸른색과 붉은색에 대한 미세한 식물들의 선호
④ 미세한 식물들의 낮은 농도 비율
⑤ 많은 변화들이 어떻게 어류 개체수를 결정하는가
→ ②, ③, ④, ⑤ 모두 지문에 언급된 일부 어구를 사용해 만든 제목이지만, 글의 주제와는 거리가 멀기 때문에 적절한 제목으로 볼 수 없음.

구문 ¹Variations (in ocean color) are determined / primarily by variations (in the concentrations of *algae and phytoplankton*), // **which** are the basis of the marine food chain.
• which는 선행사인 algae and phytoplankton을 보충 설명하는 절을 이끄는 계속적 용법의 관계대명사이다.

²Because these microscopic plants absorb blue and red light more readily / than green light, // *regions* (of high phytoplankton concentrations) appear **greener** / than *those* (with low concentration).
• 두 개의 ( )는 각각 앞에 있는 명사 regions와 those를 수식하는 전치사구이다.
• 「비교급+than」 구문이 쓰여 밑줄 친 regions of ~ concentrations와 those with low concentration을 비교한다. 이때 those는 regions를 나타낸다.

주제문
Evolutionary psychologists hypothesize // that the human mind is equipped / with many (some say very many) different evolved psychological mechanisms.

(C) ¹Instead of viewing the mind as a single all-purpose "problem-solver," / evolutionary psychologists consider it in roughly the way [we consider the body]. We understand // that the body does not contain a *single* physical mechanism.

(A) Rather, it possesses different mechanisms (to confront different problems): a liver (to filter out toxins), / lungs (to take in oxygen), / antibodies (to fight off bacteria and viruses), / and so on. ²It's true // that each mechanism is profoundly limited in what it can do.

(B) However, / this cost is made up for by the benefits. ³With only one task (to complete), / each system should be efficient. And even if some systems break down (you lose your eyesight, for example), // most other systems should remain operational. Evolutionary psychologists contend // that this is the way [we should understand the human mind].

해석 주제문 진화심리학자들은 인간 정신이 여러 가지 (어떤 이들의 말로는 매우 많은) 다른 진화된 심리적 기제를 갖추고 있다는 가설을 세운다.
(B) 정신을 단 하나의 만능 '문제 해결사'로 보는 대신 진화심리학자들은 정신을 대략 우리가 신체를 보는 방식으로 바라본다. 우리는 신체가 '단 하나의' 신체적 기제만 가지고 있지 않다는 것을 안다.
(A) 오히려, 그것(신체)은 각각 다른 문제들과 맞설 다른 기제들을 가지고 있는데, 즉 독소를 걸러 내는 간, 산소를 흡수하는 폐, 박테리아와 바이러스와 싸워 물리치는 항체 등이다. 각각의 기제가 할 수 있는 일이 아주 제한적인 것은 사실이다.
(C) 하지만, 이러한 손실은 (얻어지는) 이득으로 만회된다. 겨우 하나의 완수할 과업만 있기 때문에 각 체계는 효율적일 것이다. 그리고 일부 체계들이 고장이 난다 하더라도 (예를 들어 시력을 잃는다 하더라도), 대부분의 다른 체계들은 여전히 기능을 다하고 있을 것이다. 진화심리학자들은 이것이 우리가 인간 정신을 이해해야 하는 방식이라고 주장한다.

어휘 evolutionary 진화의; 점진적인 *cf.* evolve 진화[발달]시키다 hypothesize 가설을 세우다 be equipped with ~을 갖추고 있다 mechanism (특정한 기능을 수행하는) 구조, 기제; 기계 장치 all-purpose 다목적의, 만능의 roughly 대략, 거의; 거칠게 confront 맞서다, 직면하다 filter out ~을 걸러내다 antibody 항체 fight off ~와 싸워 물리치다, 제거하다 profoundly 완전히; (영향 등을) 깊이 make up for ~을 만회하다, 보충하다 operational 기능을 다하는; 사용할 수 있는; 조작상의 contend (that) (~을 사실이라고) 주장하다; (~을 얻으려고) 다투다

해설 주어진 글은 진화심리학자들이 인간 정신이 여러 가지 다른 심리적 기제를 갖추었다는 가설을 세웠다는 내용이다. 그 뒤에는 그 가설 내용을 신체에 비유해 설명하는 (C)가 오는 것이 적절하다. (C)의 마지막에서 신체가 단 하나의 기제만 가지고 있지 않다고 언급했으므로, 신체는 각각 다른 기제들을 가지고 있다는 내용의 (A)가 이어져야 자연스럽다. 또한 (A)에서 각 기제의 제한적인 면에 대해서 말하고 있으므로, 이로 인한 손실(this cost)은 다른 이득들로 상쇄될 수 있으며 인간 정신도 이와 같이 이해해야 한다고 끝맺는 내용의 (B)가 마지막에 와야 한다.

오답 Check
인간 정신이 여러 심리적 기제를 갖추었다는 가설을 신체에 비유해 설명하는 흐름이 자연스러우므로 (C)는 주어진 문장 뒤에 오는 것이 적절하다.

PLUS + 변형문제
어휘 be comprised of ~로 구성되다
해설 인간 정신이 여러 다른 심리적 기제로 이루어져 있다는 진화심리학자들의 가설을 신체에 빗대어 설명하는 글이므로 글의 주제로 가장 적절한 것은 ⑤ '다양한 기제로 이루어진 인간의 정신'이다.
① 문제 해결에 있어 인간 사고의 역할
→ 지문에 언급된 내용을 활용한 오답.
② 인간의 정신 기제의 진화
→ 인간 정신이 어떻게 진화해왔는지에 관한 내용이 아님.
③ 인간 신체에 미치는 정신적 기능의 영향
→ 정신이 신체에 영향을 미친다는 내용은 없음.
④ 인간 정신과 신체에 관한 실험적 대조
→ 신체는 여러 기제들로 이루어진 정신을 빗대어 설명하는 비유로 나온 내용임. 정신과 신체를 실험적으로 대조하는 내용은 없음.

구문 ¹Instead of **viewing** the mind **as** a single all-purpose "problem-solver," / evolutionary psychologists **consider** it in roughly *the way* [we consider the body].
• 「view A as B」는 'A를 B로 보다[여기다]'의 의미이다.
• 「consider+O+C」의 구조로 목적어 it은 the mind를 지칭한다.
• [ ]는 관계부사 how가 이끄는 관계사절로 선행사 the way를 수식하는데, how와 the way는 함께 쓸 수 없으므로 관계사가 생략되었다.

²**It's** true // **that** each mechanism is profoundly limited in what it can do.
• It은 가주어이고, that 이하가 진주어이다.
• what it can do는 전치사 in의 목적어로 쓰인 관계대명사 what이 이끄는 명사절이다.

³**With** *only one task* (to complete), / each system **should** be efficient.
• With은 '이유'를 나타내는 부사구를 이끄는 전치사이다.
• should는 '~해야 한다'의 '의무'가 아닌 '~일 것이다'의 '추측'의 의미로도 쓰인다.

The instruments (used in a modern orchestra) have changed tremendously / since even the late-nineteenth century. Yet Beethoven, Mozart, and Haydn seemed able to come up with awfully good pieces / in spite of the technical deficiencies of their technology (poorly tuned woodwinds, brass with limited agility, etc.).

(C) A major trend (of the last couple of decades) / has even been to use these less-developed instruments / to play more "historically accurate" versions of the pieces. These recordings are often more popular and more critically admired / than recordings [that are more technically perfect (more in tune, better balanced, greater range of instrumental timbre, etc.)].

(B) This is not different from other domains, / even technological ones. A major movement in video games in the last few years / has been retro.

(A) ¹There is no question / that new games offer a greater palette of graphical and interface possibilities, // but that doesn't mean / that they will be more fun or engaging. ²The success (of a work) depends on how it uses its medium, / not on the absolute sophistication (of that medium).

해석 현대 오케스트라가 사용하는 악기는 심지어 19세기 후반 이후에도 많이 변했다. 하지만, 베토벤, 모차르트, 그리고 하이든은 (제대로 조율되지 않은 목관 악기, 경쾌함에 한계가 있는 금관 악기 등과 같은) 장비의 기술적 부족이 있었음에도 매우 훌륭한 작품을 만들어 내었다.
(C) 지난 수십 년간의 주요 흐름은 심지어 이런 발전이 덜 되어진 악기를 사용하여 그 작품을 더 '역사적으로 정밀한' 형식으로 연주하는 것이었다. 이런 녹음은 (조율이 더 잘되고, 균형이 더 잘 잡혀 있고, 더 큰 범위의 악기 음색 등과 같은) 기술적으로 더욱 완벽한 녹음보다 자주 더 인기를 끌고 비평가들에게 더욱 존중받는다.
(B) 이것은 다른 분야에서도 다르지 않고, 심지어 기술 영역에서도 그러하다. 지난 몇 년간의 비디오 게임에서의 주된 변화는 복고풍이었다.
(A) 새 게임이 더 많은 색깔의 그래픽 및 인터페이스 가능성을 제공하는 것에는 의문이 없지만, 그것이 그것들이 더 재미있거나 관심을 사로잡는다는 것을 의미하지는 않는다. 주제문 작품의 성공은 수단을 어떻게 사용하는가에 달려 있지, 그 표현 수단의 절대적 정교함에 달려있지 않다.

어휘 instrument 악기, 도구 tremendously 매우, 엄청나게 come up with ~을 생산하다; 제시[제안]하다 awfully 매우, 몹시 deficiency 부족, 결핍 woodwind 목관 악기 brass 금관 악기, 놋쇠 accurate 정확한 recording 레코드, 녹음 admired 존경 받는 range 범위, 폭; 다양성 domain 분야, 영역 retro 복고(풍)의 palette 색깔들; 팔레트 engaging 흥미를 끄는, 매력적인 medium 도구, 수단; 매체; 중간의 sophistication 정교; 세련, 교양

해설 주어진 글은 기술적 제약이 있는 악기로 거장들이 훌륭한 음악을 만들었다는 내용이다. 그 다음에는 (C)의 이런 덜 발전된 악기(these less-developed instruments)가 주어진 글의 장비의 기술적 부족과 상응하는 말이므로 (C)가 맨 먼저 오는 것이 적절하다. 이러한 경향이 다른 영역에서도 마찬가지라고 언급하고 비디오 게임을 예로 든 (B)가 그 다음에 이어지고, 비디오 게임에서의 복고적인 성격을 설명하는 (A)가 마지막에 오는 것이 적절하다.

PLUS+ 변형문제

어휘 craftsman 장인, 숙련공 blame 탓하다
해설 성공은 수단을 어떻게 사용하는가에 달려 있지, 그 표현 수단의 절대적 정교함에 달려있지 않다고 했으므로 글의 요지로 가장 적절한 것은 ⑤ '훌륭한 장인은 결코 도구를 탓하지 않는다.'이다.
① 모든 구름에는 은빛 줄기가 있다(모든 안 좋은 일에는 좋은 면이 있다).
② 일찍 일어나는 새가 벌레를 잡는다.
③ 말보다 행동이 중요하다.
④ 필요는 발명의 어머니이다.
→ 모두 글의 내용과 관계없는 속담.

구문 ¹There is no question / that new games offer a greater palette of graphical and interface possibilities, // but that doesn't mean /

that they will be more fun or engaging.
• that ~ possibilities 부분은 명사 question의 내용을 담고 있는 동격절이다
• 동사 mean 뒤의 that은 목적어 역할을 하는 명사절(that ~ engaging)을 이끄는 접속사이다.

²The success (of a work) depends on how it uses its medium, / not on the absolute sophistication (of that medium).
• depends on의 목적어로 how가 이끄는 간접의문문(how ~ its medium)이 쓰였다.

¹The placebo effect is an apparent cure or improved state of health (brought about / by a substance, product, or procedure) [that has no generally recognized therapeutic value]. (①) ²It is not uncommon for patients to report // improvements (based on what they expect, desire, or were told) would happen / after taking simple sugar pills [that they believed were powerful drugs]. (②) The placebo effect / is related to the brain's reward system, // and it's not a big leap / to say // that much of marketing is trying to achieve a non-medical placebo effect in the minds of customers. (③) About 10 percent of the population / is believed to be exceptionally susceptible to the power of suggestion / and may be easy targets for aggressive marketing. (④ Although the placebo effect is generally harmless, // it does account for the expenditure of millions of dollars (on health products and services every year), // and they are responsible for the figure.) For instance, megadoses of vitamin C / have never been proven to treat cancer // but expenditures (on them) add up to over 30 billion dollars a year. (⑤) People [who mistakenly use placebos // when medical treatment is urgently needed] increase their risk for health problems.

해석 위약 효과는 일반적으로 공인된 치료 가치를 갖지 못하는 물질이나 제품 또는 방법이 유발하는 표면상의 치료나 호전된 건강 상태이다. 환자들이 효능 있는 약이라고 믿었던 단순한 설탕 알약을 복용한 후, 그들이 기대하거나, 소망하거나 또는 듣는 것에 근거하여 호전이 일어날 거라고 이야기하는 것은 드문 일이 아니다. 위약 효과는 뇌의 보상 체계와 관련이 있고, 그래서 수많은 마케팅이 소비자들의 마음속에 비의료적인 위약 효과를 이루기 위해 노력하고 있다는 것은 지나친 비약이 아니다. 인구의 약 10%는 제안의 힘에 유난히 영향을 받기 쉬운 것으로 여겨지고 공격적 마케팅의 쉬운 표적이 될 수도 있다. 비록 위약 효과가 일반적으로는 무해하지만 그것은 매년 건강 제품과 서비스에 수백만 달러의 지출을 정말로 차지하고, 그들은 그 수치에 책임이 있다. 예를 들어 비타민 C의 대량 투여는 암을 치료한다고 입증된 적이 전혀 없지만 그것에 쓰인 지출은 한 해 총 300억 달러가 넘는다. 의료적 치료가 시급하게 필요할 때 위약을 잘못 사용하는 사람들은 자신들의 건강 문제에 대한 위험을 증가시킨다.

어휘 ○placebo effect 위약 효과   apparent 표면상의, 겉보기에는; 명백한, 분명한   bring about ~을 유발[야기]하다   procedure 방법; 절차   therapeutic 치료의   leap (상상·논리의) 비약; 발전   exceptionally 유난히, 특별히   be susceptible to ~에 영향을 받기 쉽다   aggressive 공격적인; 적극적인   account for 차지하다; 설명하다   expenditure 지출; 비용   megadose(s) 대량 투여   urgently 긴급하게; 절박하게
어휘○위약 효과: 의사가 효과 없는 가짜 약 혹은 꾸며낸 치료법을 환자에게 제안했는데, 환자의 긍정적인 믿음으로 병세가 호전되는 현상.

해설 주어진 글은 위약 효과가 무해하지만 건강 제품과 서비스에 많은 지출을 차지하고, 그들(they)에게 그 책임이 있다는 내용이다. 문맥상 주어진 문장의 그들(they)은 ③ 이후 문장에 있는 공격적인 마케팅에 유난히 취약한 사람들을 의미하고, 마케팅의 쉬운 표적이 되어 건강 제품에 많은 돈을 지불하는 것이므로 주어진 문장은 ④에 자리하는 것이 적절하다. ④ 뒤에는 위약 효과를 활용한 건강 제품의 예인 비타민 C에 지출하는 사례가 이어진다.

오답 Check
주어진 문장의 the figure가 ④ 뒤의 문장의 30 billion dollars를 가리킨다고 착각하지 않도록 한다.

PLUS+ 변형문제

어휘 application 활용; 적용
해설 이 글은 위약 효과를 활용한 마케팅으로 인해 건강 제품에 많은 돈을 지출하고 또한 건강 문제의 위험을 증가시키는 것으로 이어지는 결과에 대한 것으로 이를 잘 나타낸 제목은 ④ '위약 효과가 여러분의 지갑과 건강을 표적으로 삼고 있다'가 적절하다.
① 상품에 더 많은 소비를 유인하는 방법들
→ 위약 효과를 활용한 소비에 관한 언급은 있지만, 그 방법들을 나열하지 않음.
② 공격적인 마케팅을 피하고 현명하게 쇼핑하는 방법
→ 위약 효과가 가져오는 문제점의 결과를 설명할 뿐 그 마케팅을 피하는 방법은 언급하지 않음.
③ 의학적 치료에 영향을 미치는 제안의 힘
→ 위약 효과가 의학적 치료에 영향을 미친다는 언급은 없음.
⑤ 왜 위약 효과의 활용이 이렇게 인기가 있는가?
→ 위약 효과의 인기 이유는 언급되지 않음.

구문 ¹The placebo effect is *an apparent cure or improved state of health* (brought about / by *a substance*, *product*, or *procedure* [that has no generally recognized therapeutic value]).
• ( )는 brought about이 이끄는 분사구로 앞에 있는 명사 an apparent ~ of health를 수식한다.
• 밑줄 친 세 개의 명사는 콤마(,)와 or로 연결되어 병렬 구조를 이루며, 관계대명사 that이 이끄는 절이 그 명사들을 수식한다.

²**It** is not uncommon / *for patients* **to report** // (that) *improvements* (based *on* what they expect, desire, or were told) would happen / after taking *simple sugar pills* [**that** (they believed) were powerful drugs].
• It은 가주어, for patients가 의미상의 주어, to report 이하가 진주어이며, to부정사의 목적어로 접속사 that이 이끄는 명사절이 나오는데, 이때 that은 종종 생략된다.
• 두 번째 ( )는 improvements를 수식하며, 전치사 on의 목적어로 선행사를 포함한 관계대명사 what이 이끄는 명사절이 쓰였다.
• [ ]는 선행사 simple sugar pills를 수식하는 관계사절로 주격 관계대명사 that과 동사(were) 사이에 they believed가 삽입되었다.

¹Approximately 250,000 years ago, / a few thousand Homo sapiens migrated out of Africa / aided by a brain [that was not only sophisticated enough to adapt to new environments, / but also one [that had evolved the capacity (for the transmission of knowledge from one generation to the next)]]. (①) Humans were born to learn: Long before writing and the Internet were invented, // humans had the capacity (to communicate with each other in ways [that no other animal could]). (②) ²With communication / came an explosion in technology and skills, // which led to our overall growth as a species. (③) These were not information (in our genes) / but rather knowledge (obtained from others): // Our ancestors had thousands of years of knowledge (passed down from each generation).) That's why every newborn baby does not have to start from scratch. (④) This is such an obvious fact about human civilization // that we often forget that we are the only animals on this planet [that retain skills and knowledge [that we pass on to our offspring]]. (⑤) Other animals can learn about their environments // but no other animal has the human capacity (for acquiring thousands of years of experience within a lifetime).

해석 약 25만 년 전, 새로운 환경에 적응할 만큼 정교했을 뿐만 아니라, 한 세대에서 다음 세대로 지식을 전달하는 능력을 발전시켜 온 두뇌의 도움을 받아 수천 명의 호모 사피엔스가 아프리카에서 이주했다. 인간은 배우기 위해 태어났다. 글과 인터넷이 발명되기 훨씬 전에, 인간은 다른 어떤 동물들도 할 수 없는 방식으로 서로 의사소통하는 능력을 갖추고 있었다. 의사소통과 함께 과학기술과 기술이 폭발적으로 증가했고, 그것은 한 종으로서 우리의 전반적인 성장으로 이어졌다. **주제문** 이것들은 우리의 유전자에 있는 정보가 아니라 다른 사람들로부터 획득한 지식이었는데, 우리 조상들은 각 세대로부터 물려받은 수천 년의 지식이 있었다. 그래서 모든 신생아는 맨 처음부터 시작할 필요가 없는 것이다. 이것은 인간 문명에 관한 너무나 명백한 사실이기에 우리는 우리가 자손에게 물려주는 기술과 지식을 보유하고 있는 이 지구상에서 유일한 동물이라는 사실을 종종 잊어버린다. 다른 동물들은 그들의 환경에 대해 배울 수 있지만, 다른 어떤 동물도 일생 수천 년의 경험을 얻을 수 있는 인간의 능력을 갖추고 있지 않다.

어휘 migrate 이주[이동]하다 aid 돕다, 거들다; 원조, 지원 sophisticated 정교한 transmission 전달, 전송 explosion 폭발적 증가 from scratch 맨 처음부터; 아무런 사전 지식[정보] 없이 obvious 분명한, 명백한 civilization 문명 retain 보유하다 pass on to ~로 전하다[옮기다] offspring 자손

해설 주어진 문장을 읽은 후, 연결어나 지시어 등을 활용해야 한다. 주어진 문장에서 '이것들(these)'은 조상으로부터 획득한 지식이라고 했는데, 글에서 '지식'이라 일컬을 수 있는 것은 ③ 앞의 '과학기술과 기술'이다. 따라서 주어진 문장은 의사소통 능력으로 과학기술과 기술이 폭발적으로 증가했고 이는 인류의 성장으로 이어졌다는 내용 다음에, 또한 그로 인해 신생아가 처음부터 시작할 필요가 없다는 내용 앞에 와야 하므로 ③에 들어가는 것이 적절하다.

오답 Check 조상으로부터 획득한 지식이 쌓여서 오늘날의 과학기술과 기술이 폭발적으로 증가한 것이므로 ③ 앞에 오는 문장을 결과, 주어진 문장을 원인으로 볼 수 있다. ③ 다음에 나오는 That's why는 앞 문장에 대한 또 다른 결과를 나타낸다.

PLUS + 변형문제

해설 이 글은 인류는 조상으로부터 물려받은 의사소통 능력과 지식으로 발전했고, 인간은 기술과 지식을 자손에게 물려주는 유일한 동물임을 설명하고 있다. 따라서 요지로 가장 적절한 것은 ⑤ 이다.
① → 인간이 다른 어떤 동물들도 할 수 없는 방식으로 의사소통했다는 언급은 있으나 이를 더 뛰어나다고 볼 수 없고 글 전체 내용을 포괄할 수도 없음.
② → 도입에서 정교한 두뇌가 언급되었지만, 두뇌 발달의 이유가 의사소통이라는 내용은 없음.
③ → 언급된 내용이긴 하지만, 글 전체의 요지가 될 수는 없음.
④ → 글에서 추론할 수 있는 사실이나 글 전체의 요지는 아님.

구문 ¹Approximately 250,000 years ago, / a few thousand Homo sapiens migrated out of Africa / **aided** by *a brain* [that was not only sophisticated enough to adapt to new environments, // but also *one* [that had evolved *the capacity* (for the transmission of knowledge from one generation to the next)]].
• aided 이하는 부대상황을 나타내는 분사구문이다.
• 밑줄 친 두 부분이 상관접속사 「not only A but (also) B」로 연결된다.
• 첫 번째 [ ]는 주격 관계대명사 that이 이끄는 관계사절로 선행사 a brain을 수식하고, 그 안의 that had ~ to the next는 one을, ( )는 the capacity를 각각 수식한다. 여기서 one은 a brain을 나타낸다.

²**With communication** / came an explosion in technology and skills, // **which** led to our overall growth as a species.
• 강조를 위해 전명구가 앞으로 나가 문장의 주어와 동사가 도치되었다.
• which는 앞에 나온 절 전체를 보충 설명하는 계속적 용법의 관계대명사이다.

An elite-level gymnast took a semester off from his university study / in order to dedicate maximum time and attention to his training / before the upcoming competitive season. The coach agreed to work with the gymnast / in his off time alone in an empty gym. It seemed like an ideal situation, / a coach's undivided attention, no distractions — perfect. However, in about a week, / the gymnast's interest (in the training process) declined, his emotional state worsened, / and the stability (of the learned skills) worsened as well. Workouts became mechanical actions / without emotional color. It was quite obvious // that the cause of the recession (in the gymnast's performance) was due to the absence of the social environment. After some discussion and reasoning, / the coach decided to resume the gymnast's training in his "old time." It was the right decision. ¹The next day, / the gymnast entered the gym smiling, / happy to see all his teammates and the usual working atmosphere. It could be said // that he was at his best at his training session / that day. ²The situation having changed dramatically, / within a week / he restored and improved his skills.

↓

If a talented individual is far removed from their (A) surroundings and asked to perform, // the results may prove (B) unsatisfactory.

해석 엘리트 수준의 한 체조 선수가 다가오는 경기 시즌 전에 자신의 훈련에 최대한의 시간과 관심을 바치기 위해 대학 공부를 한 학기 쉬었다. 코치는 빈 체육관에서 혼자 쉬는 시간에 체조 선수와 함께 운동하기로 동의했다. 그것은 코치의 전적인 관심을 받는, 집중을 방해하는 것이 없는 이상적인 상황처럼 보였다. 완벽했다. 그러나 약 일주일 만에 훈련 과정에 대한 체조 선수의 관심이 줄어들었고, 그의 정서 상태가 악화했으며, 학습된 기술의 안정성도 악화되었다. 연습은 감정적인 색채가 없이 기계적인 행동이 되었다. ^{추론 근거} 체조 선수의 연기의 후퇴가 사회적 환경의 부재로 인한 것임은 꽤 분명했다. 약간의 논의와 추론 후에 코치는 체조 선수의 훈련을 그의 '이전 시간'에 다시 시작하기로 결정했다. 그것은 옳은 결정이었다. 다음날, 그 체조 선수는 자신의 모든 동료들과 평소의 운동 환경을 보게 되어 기뻤기에 웃으면서 체육관에 들어왔다. 그날 그의 훈련 시간에서 그는 그의 가장 좋은 상태에 있었다고 말할 수 있다. 상황은 극적으로 변해서, 일주일 만에 그는 자신의 기술을 회복하고 향상시켰다.

↓

만약 재능 있는 개인이 그들의 (A) 주위 환경에서 멀리 떨어져 수행하도록 요청받는다면, 그 결과는 (B) 만족스럽지 못한 것으로 밝혀질지도 모른다.

어휘 gymnast 체조 선수; 체육 교사   dedicate 바치다; 전념[헌신]하다; 헌정하다   undivided 전적인; 분리되지 않은   distraction 집중을 방해하는 것   stability 안정성   mechanical 기계적인; 기계(상)의   recession 후퇴; 불황, 불경기   resume 다시 시작하다; 되찾다, 회복하다   atmosphere 환경; 분위기; 대기   restore 회복하다; 복원[복구]하다

해설 요약문을 통해, 재능 있는 개인이 그들의 '무엇'으로부터 멀리 떨어져 수행할 때, 결과가 '어떤지'를 찾아야 한다. 지문의 내용은 한 체조 선수가 훈련에 집중하기 위해 대학 공부를 한 학기 쉬었을 때, 그 결과가 악화되었다는 예시 후에, 그 후퇴는 사회적 환경의 부재로 인한 것임을 말하고 있다. 그러므로 빈칸에는 ③ '(A) 주위 환경 – (B) 만족스럽지 못한'이 적절하다.

오답 Check

    (A)   (B)

① 공동체 – 고무적인
→ (A)는 맞지만, 결과가 고무적이지는 않음.

② 임무 – 가치 있는
→ (A), (B) 모두 틀림.

④ 학업 – 역효과를 낳는
→ (B)는 맞지만, (A)가 틀림.

⑤ 가족 – 안정적인
→ (A), (B) 모두 틀림.

구문 ¹The next day, / *the gymnast* entered the gym **smiling**, / (being) happy to see all his teammates and the usual working atmosphere.
• smiling은 the gymnast를 수식하는 현재분사이다.
• happy 이하는 being이 생략되어 형용사로 시작하는 분사구문으로 이유를 나타낸다.

²*The situation* having changed dramatically, / within a week / he restored and improved his skills.
• The situation ~ dramatically는 주어가 명시된 분사구문으로, The situation이 분사구문의 의미상 주어이다. 문장의 주어와 분사구문의 의미상 주어가 다를 경우, 의미상 주어를 명시한다.

주제문
Today, many landscape architects like the word 'natural.' They talk about 'natural surveillance', for instance, 'natural access control.' The idea is // that instead of conventional methods of military-level surveillance, / you exploit thoughtful design // so that neighborhoods become naturally self-policing. Crime is much (a) less likely in settings [where people are more involved in each other's lives / and care about their shared spaces]. This means // housing must be 'human'-scale. In a large development, housing should be divided / into small enclaves with a (b) common space [where neighbours are likely to meet casually all the time] — something [which can be enhanced by landscaping gardens]. ¹But each enclave needs to be at least subtly different / to (c) personalize it, / and given features (such as signs and ornaments in styles) [that may have special meaning for the residences]. The mutual space needs to be attractive, too, (with places for sitting), // and the boundaries (between common and private space) need to be soft and appealing / to encourage a sense of pride and common ownership. This common space, and the arrangement of doors and windows (to face it), may help, too, to reduce social (d) isolation, another factor behind crime.

Natural access control means using architectural design / to discourage intruders. For instance, it's worth creating space (for planting and plant barriers) / rather than building a lot of walls, bars and concrete. Planting not only gives a place a more attractive, cared-for look; // ²burglars are actually more (e) encouraged by flower beds and bushes // than they are by walls. It's surprisingly hard / to climb over a bush! Architectural devices (like these) are being used more and more, // and police and social workers are now often brought in / as consultants on architectural schemes.

해석 주제문 오늘날 많은 경관 건축가들은 '자연적'이라는 단어를 좋아한다. 예를 들어 그들은 '자연적 감시'와 '자연적 접근 통제'에 대해 이야기한다. 그 생각은 전통적인 군사적 수준의 감시 방식 대신, 사려 깊은 설계를 활용해서 지역이 자연적으로 스스로 치안 유지를 하게 되도록 한다는 것이다. 범죄는 사람들이 서로의 삶에 더 많이 관여하고 자신들의 공유된 공간에 관심을 갖는 환경에서 훨씬 더 일어날 가능성이 (a) 적다. 이것은 주택이 '인간적' 척도여야 한다는 것을 의미한다. 대규모 개발에서, 주택은 이웃들이 항상 무심코 만날 수 있는 (b) 공통의 공간이 있는 작은 고립된 장소들로 나누어져야 하는데, 그것은 자연식 정원에 의해 강화될 수 있다. 그러나 각각의 고립된 장소는 그것을 (c) 개인화하기 위해 적어도 미묘하게 서로 달라야 하며, 주거지에 특별한 의미를 가질 수 있는 양식에서의 표식이나 장식 같은 특징을 부여받아야 한다. 공동 공간 역시 앉을 자리가 있어 매력적이어야 하며, 공통 공간과 사적 공간의 경계는 자부심과 공동의 주인의식을 고취하도록 유연하고 매력적이어야 한다. 이러한 공통적인 공간, 그리고 그것을 향하는 문과 창문들의 배치 역시 범죄 이면의 또 다른 요인인 사회적 (d) 고립을 줄이는 데 도움이 될 수도 있다.

자연적 접근 통제는 침입자를 단념시키기 위해 건축 설계를 사용하는 것을 의미한다. 예를 들어, 벽과 차단물과 콘크리트를 많이 쌓기보다는 (나무를) 심고 장벽 식물을 세울 수 있는 공간을 만드는 것이 가치가 있다. (나무) 심기는 한 장소에 더 매력적이고 돌봄을 받는 외관을 줄 뿐 아니라 도둑들은 실제로 벽에 의한 것보다는 화단과 덤불에 의해 더 (e) 고무된다(→ 단념하게 된다). 덤불을 오르는 것은 놀랍도록 어렵다! 이와 같은 건축적 장치는 점점 더 많이 사용되고 있으며, 이제 경찰관과 사회복지사는 건축 계획에 관한 자문역으로 종종 참여하고 있다.

어휘 ◦natural surveillance 자연적 감시 ◦natural access control 자연적 접근 통제 conventional 전통적인; 형식적인 surveillance 감시; 감독 exploit 활용하다; 개발하다 self-policing 스스로 치안 유지를 하는 casually 무심코; 우연히 landscaping garden 자연식 정원 subtly 미묘하게 personalize 개인화하다 ornament 장식(품) mutual 공동의; 상호의 boundary 경계; 한계 appealing 매력적인, 호소하는 ownership 주인의식; 소유(권) arrangement 배치, 배열 isolation 고립 intruder 침입자 burglar 도둑, 강도 scheme 계획 [선택지 어휘] visibility 가시성 victim 피해자, 희생(자)

어휘◦ 자연적 감시: 건물이나 시설을 가시성이 최대화되도록 배치하여 낯선 사람들의 활동을 보다 용이하게 인지할 수 있게 한다는 것. 범죄가 발생하기 전에 그 가능성을 감소시키는 것이 목적.

자연적 접근 통제: 일정한 지역에 접근하는 사람들을 정해진 공간으로 유도하거나 외부인의 출입을 통제하도록 설계함으로써 접근에 대한 심리적 부담을 증대시켜 범죄를 예방하는 원리.

해설 **41** 범죄를 예방하기 위해 전통적인 군사적 수준의 감시 방식 대신, 주택지의 환경을 계획적으로 디자인하여 지역이 자연적으로 스스로 치안 유지가 가능하여지도록 하는 것에 관한 글이므로, 제목으로는 ③ '자연을 디자인하는 것을 통한 범죄 예방'이 가장 적절하다.

42 (e)가 포함된 문장 앞에서 범죄 예방의 방법 중 하나로 나무를 심고 장벽 식물을 세우는 것이 가치가 있다고 했고, (e)문장의 not only 뒤에 Planting의 장점이 나오는 것으로 보아, 그 장점이 뒤에서도 이어져야 하므로, 도둑이 벽보다 화단과 덤불에 의해 고무되는 것이 아닌, 단념하게 된다는 뜻의 discouraged 등으로 바꿔 써야 한다.

오답 Check
41 ① 향상된 가시성은 향상된 보안을 뜻한다
→ 자연적 감시에 관한 설명이지만, 글의 일부 내용에 불과함.
② 기술이 범죄를 줄이는 데 어떻게 도움이 될 수 있을까?
→ 기술을 사용한 범죄 예방은 언급되지 않음.
④ 범죄와 환경: 유형 및 해결책
→ 범죄의 유형을 설명하는 글은 아님.
⑤ 환경 범죄와 그 피해자들: 현재와 과거
→ 환경 범죄의 피해자들은 글에 등장하지 않음.

구문
¹But each enclave needs **to be** at least subtly different to personalize it, / and given features (such as signs and ornaments in styles) [that may have special meaning for the residences].
• 밑줄 친 두 부분은 to be의 보어로 and로 연결되어 병렬 구조를 이룬다.
• ( )는 전명구로 features를 수식하고, [ ]는 주격 관계대명사 that이 이끄는 관계사절로 선행사는 styles이다.

²burglars are actually **more** discouraged by flower beds and bushes // **than** they are (discouraged) by walls.
• 「more ~ than ...」 형태의 비교급 구문으로 they are 뒤에 반복되는 discouraged가 생략되었다.

| 31 ② + ④ | 32 ② + ④ | 33 ② + ② | 34 ⑤ + ⑤ | 35 ③ + ⑤ | 36 ② + ③ |
| 37 ⑤ + ⑤ | 38 ④ + ③ | 39 ③ + ③ | 40 ④ | 41 ④ | 42 ④ |

31 ② PLUS + ④

주제문
Any tree's life is <u>uncertain</u>. A tree doesn't move; yet it must cast its pollen / as far from its own territory as possible / and then disperse its seeds into its own sphere of influence. It has evolved amazing mechanisms / to achieve this, / from exploiting animals as agents of dispersal / to attaching propellers. Anyone [who has seen the mist of pollen / above an evergreen forest] knows the extravagant profligacy of trees / to ensure survival of a very few. ^{추론 근거} ¹Wherever a seed lands, // its fate is sealed, // and for most that means / lying exposed to insects, birds, or mammals, withering on rocks, or drowning in water. ^{추론 근거} Even when a seed lands on soil, // its future is in doubt. ²That tiny seed contains its entire inheritance (from its parent), a store of food (to get it through its first growth), and a genetic blueprint (informing the growing plant / to send its root down and its stem up / and telling it how to capture the energy, water, and materials [it needs to live]). Its life is programmed; // yet it must also be flexible enough to handle unexpected storms, drought, fire, and predators.

해석 주제문 어떠한 나무의 생명도 불확실하다. 나무는 움직이지 않는다. 하지만 그것은 가능한 한 자신의 영역으로부터 멀리 꽃가루를 보내야 하고 그러고 나서 그 씨앗들을 자신의 세력권으로 퍼뜨려야 한다. 나무는 이것을 완수하기 위해, 확산의 매개체로 동물을 이용하는 것에서부터 프로펠러를 부착하는 것까지 놀라운 메커니즘을 진화시켰다. 상록수 숲 위의 꽃가루의 연무를 본 사람이라면 극소수의 생존을 보장하기 위해 나무가 하는 사치스러운 낭비를 안다. 추론 근거 씨앗이 어디에 착륙하든 그 운명은 정해져 있는데, 그것은 대부분의 경우 (씨앗이) 곤충이나 새나 포유류에 노출되어 있거나 바위 위에서 말라 죽거나 아니면 물에 빠지는 것을 의미한다. 추론 근거 씨앗이 토양에 착륙할 때도, 그 미래는 불확실하다. 그 작은 씨앗은 모체로부터 받은 유산 전체와 씨앗이 처음의 성장을 하기 위한 식량의 저장, 그리고 성장하는 나무가 그 뿌리를 내리고 줄기를 세우도록 알려주고 그것이 살아가는 데 필요한 에너지와 물과 물질을 획득하는 방법을 말해주는 게놈 지도를 포함한다. 나무의 생명은 계획되어 있지만 그것은 또한 예상치 못한 폭풍, 가뭄, 화재와 포식자들을 다루기에 충분할 만큼 유연해야 한다.

어휘 pollen 꽃가루, 화분   disperse 퍼뜨리다; 흩뜨리다 *cf.* dispersal 확산; 분산 exploit 이용하다; 활용하다 agent 대리인 extravagant 사치스러운 seal 확정 짓다; 밀폐하다 wither 말라 죽다; 시들다 drown 물에 빠지다 inheritance 유산; 상속 재산 get through ~을 하다; 다 써버리다 ◦genetic blueprint 게놈 지도 program 계획을 세우다
[선택지 어휘] elaborate 정교한; 자세히 설명하다 integrative 통합하는 irreversible 되돌릴 수 없는 paradoxical 역설적인
어휘◦ 게놈 지도: 특정 생물의 게놈 배열 상태를 나타낸 것으로, 게놈 지도를 통해 염색체의 어느 위치에 어떤 유전자가 있는지 알 수 있음.

해설 나무의 생명이 '어떠한지'를 파악해야 한다. 나무는 번식하기 위해 동물 매개체를 이용하거나 씨앗에 프로펠러를 달기도 하고 또 극소수의 생존을 위해 엄청난 양의 씨앗을 만들어낸다. 그런데도 그중 대부분은 죽고, 땅에 떨어진다 해도 미래가 불확실하다고 했으므로 빈칸에는 ② '불확실한'이 적절하다.

오답 Check
① 정교한 ③ 통합하는 ④ 되돌릴 수 없는 ⑤ 역설적인
→ ①, ③, ④, ⑤ 모두 나무의 생명에 관한 특징을 나타낼 수 없는 오답임.

PLUS + 변형문제
어휘 vulnerability 취약성 transmit (자손에게) 물려주다
해설 나무의 노력에도 불구하고 살아남기 어려운 것이 주제이므로 가장 적절한 제목은 ④ '나무의 취약성과 살아남으려는 노력'이다.
① 왜 몇몇 나무는 심각한 위험에 처하는가?
→ 일부 나무에 한정된 내용은 아님.
② 자연의 비밀을 발견하려는 노력
→ 자연의 비밀은 언급되지 않음.
③ 나무의 생존을 위해 필요한 필수 조건
→ 나무의 생존이 어려운 이유를 언급함.
⑤ 자손에게 특질을 물려주는 나무의 능력
→ 글에 언급된 어휘(inheritance)를 활용하여 만든 오답.

구문 ¹Wherever a seed lands, // its fate is sealed, // and for most that **means** / lying exposed to insects, birds, or mammals, withering on rocks, or drowning in water.
• 동사 mean은 동명사를 목적어로 취할 경우 '~하는 것을 의미한다'를 뜻하며, 밑줄 친 세 개의 목적어구가 콤마(,)와 or로 병렬 연결된다.

²That tiny seed **contains** *its entire inheritance* (from its parent), *a store of food* (to get it through its first growth), and *a genetic blueprint* (**informing** (that) the growing plant / to send its root down and its stem up / and **telling** it how to capture *the energy, water, and materials* [it needs to live]).
• 문장의 동사 contains의 목적어로 세 개의 밑줄 친 명사구가 콤마(,)와 and로 연결되어 병렬 구조를 이룬다.
• 세 개의 ( )는 각각 앞에 있는 명사 its entire inheritance, a store of food, a genetic blueprint를 수식한다.
• informing ~ to live에서 두 개의 분사구 informing ~ its stem up, telling ~ to live가 and로 병렬 연결되었다.

Humans generally act to avoid episodes of treacherous personal trouble, // and many of today's "hostile forces of nature" [that would have put our ancestors in jeopardy] have been harnessed or controlled. We have laws (to deter robbery, assault, and murder). We have police (to perform many of the functions (previously performed by one's friends)). We have medical knowledge [that has eliminated or reduced many sources of disease and illness]. We live in an environment [that is in many ways safer and more stable than that (inhabited by our ancestors)].
주제문/추론 근거
¹Paradoxically, therefore, we suffer from a relative scarcity of serious events [that would allow us to accurately assess those [who are deeply engaged in our welfare] and discriminate them from our fair-weather friends]. ²It is possible // that the loneliness and sense of alienation [that many feel in modern living] — a lack of a feeling of deep social connectedness / despite the presence of many warm and friendly interactions — might stem from the lack of critical assessment events [that tell us who is deeply engaged in our welfare].

해석 인간은 일반적으로 위험한 개인적 어려움이 있는 사건들을 피하려고 행동하고, 우리의 선조들을 위험에 빠뜨렸던 오늘날의 '자연의 적군들' 중 많은 것들은 지배되거나 통제되었다. 우리는 강도, 폭행, 그리고 살인을 막기 위한 법을 갖고 있다. 우리에게는 전에는 친구들에 의해 수행되었던 기능들 중 많은 것들을 수행하는 경찰이 있다. 우리는 질병과 아픔의 많은 근원들을 제거하거나 감소시킨 의학적 지식을 가지고 있다. 우리는 많은 면에서 우리 선조들이 살았던 것보다 더 안전하고 더 안정적인 환경에서 살고 있다. 주제문/추론 근거 그러므로 역설적이게도 우리는 우리의 행복에 깊게 관련이 있는 사람을 정확하게 평가하고 그들을 정작 필요할 때 도움이 되지 않는 친구와 구별하게 해 주는 중대한 사건들의 상대적 결핍을 겪고 있다. 현대의 삶에서 많은 이들이 느끼는 외로움과 소외감, 즉 많은 따뜻하고 친근한 상호 작용이 있음에도 불구하고 깊은 사회적 유대감의 결여는 아마 누가 우리의 행복에 깊이 관여하고 있는지를 우리에게 알려주는 평가의 기회가 되는 중대한 사건들의 결핍에서 나올 것이다.

어휘 hostile 적대적인 harness 지배하다, 억제하다 put A in jeopardy A를 위험에 빠뜨리다 ancestor 조상, 선조 deter (범죄 등을) 막다 assault 폭행 eliminate 제거하다 inhabit 살다 paradoxically 역설적으로 scarcity 부족, 결핍 assess 평가하다 *cf.* assessment 평가 discriminate 식별하다 fair-weather friend 정작 필요할 때 도움이 되지 않는 친구 alienation 소외 stem from ~생기다, ~에서 기인하다 **[선택지 어휘]** fragility 허약함, 깨지기[부서지기] 쉬움 tolerance 관용 humanity 인간성; 인류; 인간애

해설 현대인들은 선조들보다 더 안전하고 곤경에 처하는 횟수가 줄어들게 되었는데, 동시에 중대한 사건이 생겼을 때 진정한 친구가 누구인지 평가할 수 있는 기회도 줄어들게 되었다. 그러므로 빈칸에는 ② '평가의 기회가 되는 중대한 사건들의 결핍'이 들어가야 가장 적절하다.

오답 Check
① 인간관계의 허약함 → 현대 삶의 특징으로 언급된 내용.
③ 멈출 수 없는 생존 경쟁 → 생존 경쟁은 언급되지 않음.
④ 사회적 네트워크 다양성의 영향
→ 네트워크의 다양성은 언급되지 않음.
⑤ 사회의 관용과 인간성의 부족
→ 사회의 관용과 인간성 부족은 언급되지 않음.

PLUS+ 변형문제

어휘 superficial 가벼운; 깊이 없는; 피상적인
해설 과거에 비해 사회가 안전해짐에 따라 누가 우리의 행복[안전]에 관여하는지 알기가 어려워졌다는 것이 글의 요지이므로, 글의 제목으로는 ④ '더 안전해질수록 진정한 친구 구별하기는 더 어려워진다'가 적절하다.
① 현대의 도덕적 가치의 감소
→ 현대에 도덕적 가치가 줄어든다는 언급은 없음.
② 사회 구성원들과 안전하게 연결되는 방법들
→ 사회 구성원들이 서로 연결되는 방식에 대한 내용은 없음.
③ 현대 사회: 진짜 친구를 사귀기엔 너무 경쟁적
→ 현대 사회가 경쟁적이기 때문에 친구를 사귀기 어렵다는 내용은 없음.
⑤ 가벼운 관계에서 오는 부정적인 감정들
→ 부정적인 감정에 대한 언급은 없음.

구문 ¹Paradoxically, therefore, we suffer from a relative scarcity of *serious events* [that would **allow** *us* to accurately assess *those* [who are deeply engaged in our welfare] **and** (to) discriminate them from our fair-weather friends].
• 두 개의 [ ]는 각각 serious events와 those를 수식하는 관계사절이다.
• 첫 번째 [ ] 내에는 「allow+O+C」구조가 쓰여 두 개의 목적격보어 to assess와 (to) discriminate가 and로 병렬 연결된다. 이때 discriminate 앞의 to는 반복되어 생략되었다.

²**It** is possible // **that** *the loneliness and sense of alienation* [**that** many feel in modern living] — a lack of a feeling of deep social connectedness / despite the presence of many warm and friendly interactions — might stem from the lack of *critical assessment events* [**that** tell us who is deeply engaged in our welfare].
• It은 가주어이고 that 이하가 진주어이다.
• 두 개의 [ ]는 각각 the loneliness and sense of alienation과 critical assessment events를 수식하는 관계대명사절이다.

주제문

We often choose to use equivocal language // when we're in a situation [when none of our options is a good one]. ¹Suppose, for example, // that you're asked to provide a reference for your friend Dylan, // who is applying for a job on the police force (in your town). ²One of the questions [you're asked] is // how well Dylan handles pressure. Even though Dylan's your friend, // you can immediately think of several occasions [when he hasn't handled pressure well]. Now you're caught in a bind. On the one hand, you want Dylan to get the job // because he's your friend. On the other hand, you don't want to lie to the police lieutenant [who's phoning you for the reference]. Several studies have shown // that when we're faced with two unappealing choices (such as these), / we often use ambiguous language to get ourselves out of that bind. In response to the lieutenant's question (about how well Dylan handles pressure), for instance, / you might say something like this: "Well, that depends; there are lots of different kinds of pressure."

해석 주제문 우리는 종종 우리가 선택할 수 있는 것들 중 어떤 것도 좋은 것이 아닌 상황에 빠졌을 때 모호한 언어를 사용하는 것을 선택한다. 추론 근거 예를 들어, 여러분이 친구 Dylan을 위해서 신원 보증을 해달라는 요청을 받았는데, 그가 여러분 도시에 있는 경찰직에 지원하고 있다는 가정해보자. 여러분이 요청받은 질문 중 하나는 Dylan이 중압감을 얼마나 잘 처리하는가이다. Dylan이 여러분의 친구이긴 하지만, 여러분은 그가 중압감을 잘 다루지 못한 경우가 여러 번 있었음을 즉시 생각할 수 있다. 이제 여러분은 곤경에 처한다. 한편으로는, 여러분은 Dylan이 친구이기 때문에 그가 그 직업을 얻기를 원한다. 다른 한편으로는, 여러분은 신원 보증을 해달라고 여러분에게 전화하고 있는 경찰 부서장에게 거짓말을 하고 싶지 않다. 추론 근거 몇몇 연구는 우리가 이와 같이 두 개의 유쾌하지 못한 선택에 직면할 때 우리가 종종 그 곤경에서 스스로 벗어나기 위해 모호한 언어를 사용한다는 것을 보여주었다. 예를 들면, Dylan이 얼마나 잘 중압감을 처리하는지에 대한 부서장의 질문에 답하여 여러분은 이런 말을 할지도 모른다: "글쎄요, 그건 확실히 알 수 없죠. 수많은 다른 종류의 중압감이 있으니까요."

어휘 equivocal 모호한 reference 신원 보증(인); 참고, 참조 immediately 즉시, 즉각 occasion 경우, 때 bind 곤경; 묶다; 감다 lieutenant (경찰·소방서의) 부서장; 상관 대리; 중위 be faced with ~에 직면하다 unappealing 유쾌하지 못한, 매력 없는 ambiguous 모호한

해설 빈칸 문장 다음에 이어지는 예시를 통해 답을 찾을 수 있다. 친구의 신원 보증을 요청받은 중에 친구의 단점을 말하기도, 거짓말을 하기도 곤란한 질문에 답해야 할 때 우리는 스스로 벗어나기 위해 모호한 언어를 사용한다고 했으므로, 빈칸에는 그 상황을 나타내는 ② '선택할 수 있는 것들 중 어떤 것도 좋은 것이 아닌 상황'이 적절하다. 또한 두 번째 추론 근거에 있는 '두 개의 유쾌하지 못한 선택에 직면할 때'를 통해서도 추론이 가능하다.

오답 Check
① 하나의 긍정적인 결론으로 이어지는 사건
③ 우리에게 많은 합리적인 선택들을 제공하는 입장
④ 우리가 최선을 다함에도 불구하고 우리의 통제를 넘어서는 상황
⑤ 우리가 어떠한 것도 할 필요가 없는 무관심한 상태
→ ①, ③, ④, ⑤ 모두 지문에 나온 예시의 상황과 맞지 않음.

PLUS+ 변형문제

어휘 acquaintance 아는 사람 specific 특정한; 구체적인

해설 우리가 딜레마에 빠졌을 때, 모호한 언어를 사용한다는 내용이므로 제목으로는 ② '딜레마를 해결하는 방법: 모호한 말'이 알맞다.
① 왜 여러분의 친구들은 직설적으로 말하는 경향이 있는가?
③ 아는 사람이 진실하게 말하는지 판단하기
④ 어떻게 우리가 특정한 말을 사용하여 문제를 논하는가
→ 모호한 말을 사용한다는 글의 내용과 반대됨.
⑤ 여러분의 친구를 대변하여 그들이 일자리를 얻는 것을 돕기
→ ①, ③, ⑤ 모두 글에 나온 어구를 활용한 오답임.

구문 ¹Suppose, for example, // that you're asked to provide a reference for *your friend Dylan*, // **who** is applying for a job on the police force (in your town).
• 관계대명사 who가 계속적 용법으로 사용되어, 선행사 your friend Dylan에 대해 부연 설명한다.

²One of *the questions* [(which[that]) you're asked] is // how well Dylan handles pressure.
• [ ]는 목적격 관계대명사 which[that]가 생략된 관계사절로 선행사 the questions를 수식한다.
• 밑줄 친 부분은 문장의 보어로 쓰인 의문사 how가 이끄는 간접의문문(의문사+주어+동사)이다.

There is obviously a wide gap (between the promises of the 1948 Declaration and the real world of human-rights violations). In so far as we sympathize with the victims, // we may criticize the UN and its member governments / for failing to keep their promises. However, we cannot understand the gap (between human-rights ideals and the real world of human-rights violations) by sympathy or by legal analysis. Rather, it requires investigation / by the various social sciences (of the causes of social conflict and political oppression, / and of the interaction between national and international politics). The UN introduced the concept of human rights into international law and politics. ¹The field of international politics is, however, dominated by states and other powerful actors (such as multinational corporations) [that have priorities other than human rights]. ²It is a leading feature of the human-rights field // that the governments of the world proclaim human rights / but have a highly variable record of implementing them. We must understand why this is so.

해석 1948년 세계 인권 선언의 약속과 인권 침해의 현실 세계 사이에는 분명히 큰 차이가 있다. 우리가 희생자들을 동정하는 한, 우리는 UN과 그 회원국 정부가 약속을 지키지 않았다고 비판할 수도 있다. 추론 근거 그러나 우리는 인권의 이상과 인권 침해의 현실 세계의 괴리를 동정이나 법률 분석으로 이해할 수 없다. 오히려 그것은 사회적 갈등과 정치적 탄압의 원인, 그리고 국내 정치와 국제 정치 간의 상호 작용에 대한 다양한 사회과학의 조사를 필요로 한다. UN은 인권이라는 개념을 국제법과 국제 정치에 도입했다. 추론 근거 그러나 국제 정치 분야는 인권 이외의 다른 우선 사항들이 있는 국가 및 다른 영향력 있는 행위자(다국적 기업 등)가 장악하고 있다. 주제문 세계 각국 정부가 인권을 선언하고 있지만, 그것을 실행에 옮기는 데는 매우 가변적인 기록을 갖고 있다는 것이 인권 분야의 대표적인 특징이다. 우리는 이것이 왜 그런지 이해해야 한다.

어휘 obviously 분명히, 확실히 ◆1948 Declaration 1948년 (UN) 세계 인권 선언 violation 침해, 위반 in so far as ~하는 한 sympathize with ~을 동정하다; ~와 공감하다 victim 희생자, 피해자 criticize 비판[비난]하다 investigation 조사, 연구 oppression 탄압, 억압 multinational corporation 다국적 기업 priority 우선 사항, 우선적인 것, 우선순위 proclaim 선언[공표]하다 variable 가변적인 implement 실행에 옮기다
[선택지 어휘] substantive 실질적인; 중요한 ethnic identity 인종[민족] 정체성
어휘◆ 세계 인권 선언: 1948년 12월 10일 파리에서 개최된 제3회 UN 총회에서 채택된 인권에 대한 선언으로 제2차 세계 대전에서의 인권 침해에 대한 반성과 인간의 기본 권리 존중을 위해 채택되었다.

해설 세계 인권 선언의 약속과 인권 침해의 현실 세계 사이에는 분명히 큰 격차가 있다는 내용과 국제 정치 분야에서는 인권이 우선순위가 아닐 수 있다는 내용에서 인권의 특징으로 추론할 수 있는 것은 정부가 ⑤ '그것을 실행에 옮기는 데는 매우 가변적인 기록을 갖고 있다'는 것이 가장 적절하다.

오답 Check
① 자신들의 실질적인 권한을 강화하려 하다
→ 정부가 권한을 강화하려 한다는 내용은 언급되지 않음.
② 정치적인 상황에서 쉽게 갈등을 초래한다 → 정치적인 상황에서 갈등을 초래하기보다 인권의 우선순위를 뒤로 미룬다고 했음.
③ 인종 정체성에 근거해 문제를 다룬다
→ 인종에 대한 문제는 언급되지 않음.
④ 문제를 위해 싸우기 위해 책임감을 고수한다
→ 정부가 책임감을 고수한다는 내용은 언급되지 않음.

PLUS⁺ 변형문제
어휘 eradicate 뿌리 뽑다, 근절하다
해설 국가마다 다른 우선순위와 세력에 의해 세계 인권 선언의 실행에 현실과 이상의 괴리가 있다는 내용이므로 글의 제목으로 가장 적절한 것은 ⑤ '인권: 원칙과 실행 사이의 괴리'이다.
① 인권의 보편적 시행
→ 글은 인권 보장이 국가별 정세에 따라 보편적이지 않다는 내용이므로 오답.
② 인권: 국제 정치의 우선순위
→ 인권이 정세에 따라 다른 우선순위에 밀릴 수도 있다고 했으므로 오답.
③ 인권 침해를 뿌리 뽑기 위한 유엔의 노력
→ 글에 언급되지 않은 내용.
④ 분열 좁히기: 모두에게 인권을 보장하는 방법
→ 분열을 해소하기 위한 방법은 언급되지 않음.

구문 ¹The field of international politics is, however, dominated by *states and other powerful actors* (such as multinational corporations) [that have priorities other than human rights].
• [ ]는 주격 관계대명사 that이 이끄는 관계사절로 states ~ multinational corporations를 수식한다.

²**It** is a leading feature of the human-rights field // **that** the governments of the world proclaim human rights / but have a highly variable record of implementing *them*.
• It은 가주어, that 이하가 진주어이다.
• 밑줄 친 두 동사구가 but으로 병렬 연결되었다.
• 마지막의 them은 문맥상 human rights를 지칭한다.

주제문
Future land use and food security will be determined / largely by the dynamics and interactions (of agricultural markets), climatic suitability, and direct interventions (along the supply chain). ① ¹More than any other major economic sector, / agriculture is highly dependent on local climatic conditions / and is expected to be highly responsive to changes in climate [that are expected in coming decades]. ② This sensitivity (toward the climate) is compounded / by pressure (on the global agricultural system) / to meet food security objectives. ③ While climate change effects will be felt everywhere, // some regions will be more negatively affected than others — up to a point. ④ ²Additionally, rapid increases (in global demand for agricultural commodities for food, animal feed and fuel) are driving dramatic changes in the way [we think about crops and land use]. ⑤ Along with recent supply side shocks (driven by extreme weather events and other disasters), / these conditions have led to wild swings in agricultural commodity markets.

해석 주제문 미래의 토지 이용과 식량 안보는 농업 시장의 역학 및 상호 작용, 기후 적합성, 공급망을 따라 이뤄지는 직접 개입에 의해 주로 결정될 것이다. ① 농업은 다른 어떤 주요한 경제 분야보다도 지역 기후 조건에 크게 의지하고 있고, 향후 수십 년 동안 예상되는 기후 변화에 대해 매우 민감할 것으로 예상된다. ② 이런 기후에 대한 민감성은, 식량 안보 목표를 충족시키기 위해 세계 농업 체제에 가해지는 압력에 의해 악화된다. ③ 기후 변화의 영향은 어디에서나 느낄 수 있지만 일부 지역은 다른 지역보다 어느 정도 더 부정적인 영향을 받을 것이다. ④ 게다가, 식량, 동물 사료와 연료에 쓰려는 농산물에 대한 세계적 수요의 급격한 증가는 우리가 농작물과 토지 이용에 대해 생각하던 방식에 극적인 변화를 몰고 오고 있다. ⑤ 극단적인 기상 사태와 다른 재난에 의해 야기된 최근의 공급 측면 충격과 함께, 이러한 조건들은 농산물 시장에서 격렬한 변동을 야기했다.

어휘 ❶food security 식량 안보 dynamics 역학; (원)동력 agricultural 농업의 cf. agriculture 농업 suitability 적합성 intervention 개입; 간섭; 중재 sector 부문, 분야 dependent 의지[의존]하는 responsive 민감한; 즉각 반응하는; 호응하는 sensitivity 민감성 compound 악화시키다; 혼합하다; 혼합(체) agricultural commodities 농산물 drive 몰아가다, 만들다 dramatic 극적인 crop 농작물, 수확물 extreme 극단적인
어휘❶ 식량 안보: 인구의 증가, 천재적 재해·재난, 전쟁 등이 발생할 때를 대비하여 항상 얼마간의 식량을 확보하여 유지하는 것

해설 글의 처음 부분을 읽고 주제를 파악하면서 주제문과 다른 내용을 골라낸다. 무관 문장은 주제와 관련 있는 어구를 넣어 만든다는 것에 유의한다. 여러 요인으로 미래의 토지 이용과 식량 안보가 결정될 것이라는 주제문에 이어서, 농업의 기후 민감성이 식량 안보의 이유로 세계 농업 체제에 압력을 가하고, 또 곡물과 토지 이용에 극적인 변화를 가져와 결국 농산물 시장에서 격렬한 변동을 야기했다는 내용이므로 기후 변화의 부정적 영향이 지역에 따라 다를 수 있다는 ③은 글의 흐름과 관련이 없다.

PLUS+ 변형문제

어휘 catastrophe 재앙, 참사 produce 농산물; 생산하다
해설 글 전체적으로 우리의 미래 토지 이용과 식량 안보에 영향을 주는 요소들을 설명하므로 제목으로는 ⑤ '무엇이 우리의 잠재적인 토지 이용과 식량 안보에 영향을 주는가?'가 가장 적절하다.

① 기후 변화: 잠재적 재앙
→ 기후 변화가 언급되긴 했지만, 재앙으로 볼 수는 없음.

② 세계적인 농업 변화를 예방하는 방법
→ 농업 변화는 예상되지만, 그 예방법에 관해서는 언급되지 않음.

③ 농산물에 대한 급격히 증가하는 수요의 원인
→ 일부의 내용으로 글 전체를 아우를 수는 없음.

④ 세계 농업 체제에 가해지는 증가하는 압박
→ 식량 안보를 위해 압박이 가해진다는 내용은 있지만 글의 일부 내용임.

구문 ¹**More than any other** major economic sector, / agriculture is highly dependent on local climatic conditions / [and] is expected to be highly responsive to *changes in climate* [**that** are expected in coming decades].
• 「more than any other ~」는 '다른 어떤 ~보다도 더'의 의미로 비교급을 이용한 최상급 표현이다.
• 문장의 동사인 두 개의 is가 and로 연결되어 병렬 구조를 이룬다.
• [　]는 주격 관계대명사 that이 이끄는 관계사절로, changes in climate를 수식한다.

²Additionally, *rapid increases* (in global demand for agricultural commodities for food, animal feed and fuel) are driving dramatic changes in *the way* [we think about crops and land use].
• (　)는 형용사 역할을 하는 전명구로 주어인 rapid increases를 수식한다.
• [　]는 관계부사절로, 선행사 the way와 관계부사 how는 같이 쓰이지 않으므로 how가 생략되었다.

One evening in the late 1920s, Richard Hollingshead Jr. tested a creative idea: / watching a movie from the front seat of a car (parked in his driveway). He set up a movie screen in front of the car / and put the movie projector on top of his car.

(B) The arrangement worked fine. [1]Then Hollingshead began to wonder about the practicality (of building a large outdoor movie theater [where people could conveniently watch a movie from their cars]).

(A) But he realized // he needed some assurance // that light rain wouldn't interfere with viewing the movie, // so he set up a lawn sprinkler / to simulate rain on his car window. [2]He also tested the feasibility (of eating snacks in the car / while watching the movie).

(C) So it was wise that Hollingshead didn't immediately assume // that his idea would be feasible. He first tested his "automobile movie theater" idea on a small scale, // before he invested the large amounts of money, time, and effort (required to build a full-scale drive-in movie theater).

해석 1920년대 후반 어느 날 저녁, Richard Hollingshead Jr.는 자신의 차고 진입로에 세워둔 자동차 앞좌석에서 영화를 본다는 창의적인 아이디어를 시험했다. 그는 차 앞에 영화 스크린을 설치했고 자동차 위에 영화 영사기를 올려두었다.
(B) 그 배치는 잘 작동했다. 그다음에 Hollingshead는 사람들이 그들의 자동차에서 편하게 영화를 볼 수 있는 커다란 야외 영화관 건설의 실용성에 대해 궁금해하기 시작했다.
(A) 하지만 그는 약한 비가 영화 보는 것을 방해하지 않을 것이라는 어느 정도의 확신이 필요하다는 것을 깨닫고 자동차 창문 위에 비를 모의 실험하기 위해 잔디 스프링클러를 설치했다. 그는 또한 영화를 보면서 차 안에서 간식을 먹는 실현 가능성도 시험했다.
(C) 그렇게 Hollingshead가 자신의 아이디어가 실현 가능할 것이라고 즉시 생각하지 않은 것은 현명했다. 그는 우선 자신의 '자동차 극장' 아이디어를 소규모로 시험해 보고 나서, 본격적인 자동차 극장을 건설하는 데 필요한 엄청난 양의 돈과 시간과 노력을 투자했다.

어휘 arrangement 배치[배열]; 계획 practicality 실용성; 실현 가능한 일 assurance 확신; 보증 interfere with ~을 방해하다 simulate 모의 실험하다; ~을 흉내 내다; ~인 체하다 feasibility 실현 가능성 cf. feasible 실현 가능한, 실행할 수 있는 full-scale 본격적인; 실물 크기의

해설 주어진 글을 먼저 읽고, 각 단락에서 글의 흐름을 알려주는 근거가 되는 표현을 찾는다. 연결어나 지시어가 중요한 단서가 된다. 자기 아이디어를 실험한 주어진 글 다음에는 그 배치가 잘 작동했다는 (B)가 와야 하고, 야외 영화관의 실용성을 궁금해한다는 내용 다음에 확신을 위해 비와 간식을 먹는 실현 가능성도 실험해 보는 (A)가 나오는 것이 적절하다. 마지막으로 본격적인 건설 이전에 소규모 시험을 한 것은 현명했다고 평가하는 (C)가 오는 게 자연스럽다.

오답 Check
주어진 글 뒤에 (C)가 바로 이어진다면 (B)의 연결이 어색해지므로 주어진 글의 마지막 문장 He set up ~ his car.를 바로 나타내는 (B)의 The arrangement가 먼저 나와야 한다.

PLUS + 변형문제
어휘 implement 충족시키다; 실행[이행]하다 accidental 우연의
해설 이 글은 오래전 자동차 극장을 떠올리고, 실용성을 시험했던 한 남성의 일화를 나타내므로 ③ '첫 번째 자동차 극장이었을지도 모르는 것'이 적절하다.
① 야외 활동: 더 이상 그렇게 야외의 것이 아닌
→ 주제는 영화를 야외에서 즐기려는 시도이므로 반대됨.
② 자신의 호기심을 충족하는 데 있어서의 한 남자의 실패
→ 호기심 충족의 성공 여부는 언급되지 않음.
④ 야외극장의 실현 가능성을 높이는 방법
→ 실현 가능성을 시험한 내용은 있지만 그 가능성을 높이는 법은 언급되지 않음.
⑤ 우연한 발견이 오락의 인기 있는 형태가 되었다
→ 실험을 통한 것이므로 우연한 발견이 아니고, 인기 있는 오락이 되었다는 점도 언급되지 않음.

구문 [1]Then Hollingshead began to wonder about *the practicality* (of building *a large outdoor movie theater* [where people could conveniently watch a movie from their cars]).
• ( )는 전명구로 앞에 있는 명사 the practicality와 동격 관계이다.
• [ ]는 a large ~ theater를 수식하는 관계부사절이다.

[2]He also tested *the feasibility* (**of** eating snacks in the car / while watching the movie).
• ( )는 of가 이끄는 전명구로 the feasibility와 동격 관계이다.
• 밑줄 친 while ~ the movie는 접속사를 포함한 분사구문으로 동시 상황을 나타낸다.

Cold ocean currents are large masses of cold water [that move towards the equator, from a level of high altitude to lower levels]. ¹They absorb the heat [they receive in the tropics], thereby cooling the air (above them).

(C) The cold currents often form // when the air on the subtropical high blows over a cold mass of water, then the cold air is dragged to the equator. Warm currents, on the other hand, are large masses of warm water / moving further away from the equator, at higher temperatures.

(B) They form // when salty cold water becomes heavy and sinks, / (in the process) forcing warm and lighter water to move / in the opposite direction. The influence (of the flow of currents) usually depends on / the level of saltiness of the water, the rotation of the earth, the topography of the land and the orientation of the wind.

(A) ²It is these // that bring cold water to the surface of the earth from the depths, // and (in the process) they force away the original surface water. This happens / in a clockwise direction above the equator, / and counterclockwise below it. So the ocean is often cooler / to the eastern coastal side / than the western.

해석 한류는 높은 고도에서 낮은 고도로, 적도를 향해 이동하는 많은 양의 차가운 물이다. 그것들은 열대 지방에서 받는 열을 흡수하여 그것들 위의 공기를 식힌다.
(C) 한류는 종종 아열대 고기압의 공기가 대량의 차가운 물 위로 불 때 형성되는데, 그러고 나서 차가운 공기는 적도로 끌려간다. 반면에, 난류는 더 높은 온도로, 적도에서부터 더 멀리 이동하는 많은 양의 따뜻한 물이다.
(B) 그것들은 짠 차가운 물이 무거워지고 가라앉을 때 생기는데, 그 과정에서 따뜻하고 더 가벼운 물이 반대 방향으로 이동하도록 만든다. 해류의 흐름의 영향력은 보통 물의 염분 정도, 지구의 자전, 땅의 지형과 바람의 방향에 달려있다.
(A) 심연에서부터 지구 표면으로 차가운 물을 가져오는 것이 이것들로, 그 과정에서 그것들이 원래 있던 표층수를 다른 곳으로 가게 한다. 이것은 적도 위에서는 시계 방향으로, 적도 아래에서는 반시계 방향으로 일어난다. 그래서 바다는 종종 서쪽보다 동쪽 해안이 더 차가운 것이다.

어휘 current 해류, 기류; 현재의 equator 적도 altitude 고도 absorb 흡수하다 the tropics 열대 지방 subtropical high 아열대 고기압 saltiness 염분, 소금기가 있음 rotation 자전; 회전 topography 지형 orientation 방향; 성향; 예비 교육 clockwise 시계 방향으로(↔ counterclockwise 반시계 방향으로) coastal 해안의

해설 주어진 글을 먼저 읽고, 각 단락에서 글의 흐름을 알려주는 근거가 되는 표현을 찾는다. 연결어나 지시어가 중요한 단서가 된다. 이 글은 해류에 대한 설명으로 주어진 글이 차가운 해류의 개념에 대해 설명하므로 한류가 형성되는 내용인 (C)가 먼저 나와야 와야 하고 (C)의 두 번째 문장이 난류의 개념에 대한 내용이므로 난류의 형성 과정을 설명하는 (B)가 그다음에 와야 적절하다. (A)의 지시대명사 these는 (B)의 해류에 영향을 주는 네 요소를 가리키므로 마지막으로 (A)가 와야 적절하다.

오답 Check
(A)에 나오는 지시대명사 these를 주어진 글 마지막의 them이나 (C)의 마지막에 나오는 higher temperatures로 착각하지 않도록 유의한다.

PLUS+ 변형유형문제
해설 한류와 난류의 형성 방법과 그 흐름에 영향을 주는 요소들을 설명하는 글로, 제목으로는 ⑤ '바다의 한류와 난류는 어떻게 형성되는가'가 적절하다.
① 왜 바다에서 난류가 형성되는가
→ 글의 일부 내용으로 만든 오답임.
② 바다는 더 짤수록, 더 차갑다
→ 해수의 염도와 온도의 관계는 언급되지 않음.
③ 무엇이 해수 온도를 안정적으로 만드는가
→ 해류에 영향을 주는 요소들은 언급되었지만, 그것들이 해수 온도를 안정적으로 만든다는 언급은 없음.
④ 해수 온도의 풀리지 않은 비밀
→ 해수 온도가 형성되는 방법을 다룬 지문으로 글과 반대됨.

구문 ¹They absorb *the heat* [(which[that]) they receive in the tropics], / **thereby cooling** *the air* (above them).
• [ ]는 생략된 목적격 관계대명사 which[that]가 이끄는 관계사절로 선행사 the heat을 수식한다.
• thereby cooling 이하는 결과를 나타내는 분사구문으로 분사구 내에서 above them이 the air를 수식한다.

²**It is** *these* // **that** bring cold water to the surface of the earth from the depths, // and in the process they force away the original surface water.
• 「it is ~ that ...(…하는 것은 바로 ~이다)」 강조 구문이 쓰여 these를 강조한다. 이때 these는 (B) 마지막에 나온 네 요소(the level of saltiness of the water, the rotation of the earth, the topography of the land and the orientation of the wind)를 의미한다.

38 ④ PLUS+ ③

주제문
The education of a traditional navigator / was the work of a lifetime, // and learning the sidereal compass, a special compass used in Polynesia, / was but a small part of it. (①) ¹The star positions were usually taught / to junior sailors / by master seamen (using classroom techniques ashore / as well as on-the-job training at sea). (②) ²A typical classroom session might present the students with a model canoe (surrounded by a circle of thirty-two stones (representing the direction-finding star cycles)). (③) These cycles are // what they would be required to name / when pointed to at random. (④ They would further be expected to name all the stars of each cycle / in order of their appearance.) And as a more advanced exercise, / they had to name the reciprocal of each star — that is, the star [that lies on the exact opposite compass point]. (⑤) Those corresponding are important // because they represent the directions of return voyages.

해석 주제문 전통적인 항해자의 교육은 평생의 작업이었으며 폴리네시아에서 사용하는 특별한 나침반인 항성 나침반을 익히는 것은 교육의 작은 부분에 불과했다. 별자리들은 대개 바다에서의 실지로 배우는 훈련뿐만 아니라 육상에서의 교실 강의 기법도 사용해 우두머리 선원들에 의해 하급 선원들에게 가르쳐졌다. 전형적인 교실 수업에서는 학생들에게 방위를 찾아내는 별 주기들을 나타내는 32개의 돌로 만들어진 원으로 둘러싸인 모형 카누를 제공했을 것이다. 이러한 주기들은 무작위로 지목되었을 때 그들이 이름을 대도록 요구받았을 것이다. 그들은 더 나아가 각 주기의 모든 별들의 이름을 그것들의 출현 순서대로 말하도록 기대되었을 것이다. 그리고 더 심화된 수준의 훈련으로서 그들은 각 별의 '상대', 즉 정반대의 나침반 지점에 놓여 있는 별의 이름을 대야 했다. 그 상응하는 별들은 귀항의 방위를 나타내기 때문에 중요하다.

구문 ¹The star positions were usually taught to junior sailors / by *master seamen* (**using** classroom techniques ashore / as well as on-the-job training at sea).
• using 이하는 앞에 있는 master seamen을 수식하는 현재분사구이다.
• 상관접속사 as well as는 두 개의 밑줄 친 명사구를 병렬 연결한다.

²A typical classroom session might **present** the students **with** *a model canoe* (surrounded by *a circle of thirty-two stones* (representing the direction-finding star cycles)).
• 「present A with B」는 'A에게 B를 주다'라는 의미이고, 첫 번째 ( )는 과거분사구로 앞에 있는 a model canoe를 수식한다.
• 그 안의 두 번째 ( )는 현재분사구로 앞에 있는 a circle of thirty-two stones를 수식한다.

어휘 navigator 항해사 ashore 육상에(서); 해변에 on-the-job 실지[실습으로] 배우는 typical 전형적인, 일반적인 represent 나타내다; 대표[대신]하다 at random 무작위로 appearance 출현; (겉)모습 reciprocal 상대되는 것; 상호의 corresponding 상응하는, 대응하는 voyage 항해

해설 주어진 문장의 further로 보아 이와 비슷한 내용이 앞 문장에 나올 것이라고 추측할 수 있다. 이 글은 전통적인 항해자의 교육 방법에 대한 내용으로 ②의 뒤 문장에서부터 교실 수업에서의 교육 방법으로 star cycles(별 주기)를 나타내는 모형 카누를 이용한다고 언급한다. 이어서 ③의 뒤 문장에서는 학생들이 These cycles(이러한 주기들)를 이용해 무작위로 지목되었을 때 이름을 대도록 요구되었다고 나온다. 따라서 출현 순서대로 이름을 댄다는 주어진 문장은 ③ 다음에 나오는 문장보다 조금 더 심화된 내용이므로 그 이후인 ④에 나오는 것이 적절하다.

오답 Check
④ 다음에 나오는 문장은 정반대의 나침반 지점에 놓인 별의 이름을 대는 내용으로 주어진 문장보다 더 심화된 훈련(a more advanced exercise)으로 봐야 한다. ⑤ 다음의 Those corresponding은 앞 문장의 the reciprocal of each star를 받는 것으로 ⑤ 앞뒤 문장의 흐름은 자연스럽다.

PLUS+ 변형문제
어휘 navigational 항해의; 비행의
해설 이 글은 과거의 전통적인 항해자가 되기 위한 교육의 종류와 교실 수업에서 모형 카누를 이용해 어떤 식으로 교육이 이뤄졌는지 다룬 글이므로 주제로는 ③ '전통적인 항해자가 점진적으로 교육을 받았던 방식'이 적절하다.
① 별의 전통적인 이름을 학습하는 것의 어려움
② 폴리네시아에서 항해 교육의 중요성
④ 전통적인 항성 나침반을 설계하는 방법
→ 나침반을 활용한 학습 방법으로 설계하는 방법은 언급되지 않음.
⑤ 항해자들이 별의 위치를 기억할 필요성
→ ①, ②, ⑤ 모두 글의 일부 내용을 활용한 오답임.

People spend much of their waking lives / passively listening to music. [1]You might expect, as a very simple hypothesis, // that we tend to enjoy the music [we hear the most] — / the same version of the "mere exposure" effect regarding food. (①) The problem, though, is // that too familiar becomes unpleasant. (②) A rule of pleasure is // that it is an inverted U (a ∩) — // when you first experience something, it's hard to process and not enjoyable; // upon repeated exposure, it's easy to process and gives pleasure; // then it gets too easy, and therefore boring or even annoying. (③ We might be cautious about a food at first, then eat it frequently and with joy, // but few people would enjoy eating the same main course / for a thousand meals in a row.) For music, the middle peak of the inverted U / can last a little longer than that, // but any song will become unbearable // if you hear it often enough. (④) The shape of the curve is stretched and squeezed / by the complexity of the music. (⑤) [2]A complex piece might take a long while to like / and then a long time to get sick of; // usually a simple children's song will go through the curve / a lot quicker.

해석 사람들은 그들의 깨어 있는 생활의 많은 부분을 수동적으로 음악을 듣는 데 보낸다. 여러분은 아주 단순한 가정으로서 우리가 가장 많이 듣는 음악을 즐기는 경향이 있다고 예상할 수도 있을 것인데, 즉 음식에 관한 '단순 노출' 효과와 같은 버전이다. 그러나 문제는 너무 친숙하면 불쾌해진다는 것이다. **주제문** 즐거움의 법칙은 거꾸로 된 U(∩)라는 것으로 여러분이 처음 어떤 것을 경험할 때, 그것은 처리하기가 어렵고 즐겁지가 않다. 반복적으로 노출되면 그것은 처리하기 쉽고 기쁨을 준다. 그다음 그것은 너무 쉬워지고 따라서 지루하거나 심지어 짜증스럽게 된다. 우리는 처음에는 음식에 대해 조심하고, 그다음에는 자주, 그리고 기꺼이 그것을 먹기도 하지만, 연속해서 천 끼의 식사로 똑같은 주요리를 즐겨 먹는 사람은 거의 없을 것이다. 음악에 있어서, 거꾸로 된 U의 중간 봉우리는 그것보다는 조금 더 오래 갈 수 있지만 어떤 노래라도 여러분이 충분히 자주 들으면 견딜 수 없게 될 것이다. 곡선의 모양은 음악의 복잡성에 의해 늘려지거나 압착된다. 복잡한 작품은 좋아하려면 오랜 시간이 걸리고 그래서 싫증이 나는 데 오랜 시간이 걸릴지도 모른다. 보통 단순한 동요는 곡선을 훨씬 더 빨리 통과할 것이다.

어휘 passively 수동적으로 hypothesis 가설, 추정, 추측
ㅇmere exposure effect 단순 노출 효과 inverted 거꾸로 된, 반전된 cautious 조심스러운, 신중한 frequently 자주, 빈번히 in a row 연속해서 unbearable 견딜[참을] 수 없는 get sick of ~에 싫증이 나다 go through 통과하다; 승인되다; 경험하다
어휘ㅇ 단순 노출 효과: 1960년대 폴란드 출신의 미국 심리학자 로버트 자이언스(Robert Zajonc)에 의해 소개된 개념으로, 낯설거나 무관심한 자극이라도 단순히 자주 접하는 것만으로도 긍정적인 태도가 형성될 수 있다는 것을 뜻한다.

해설 주어진 문장을 읽은 후, 연결어나 지시어 등을 활용해야 한다. 또는, 글의 흐름이 끊기는 곳을 찾는다. 주어진 문장은 거꾸로 된 U의 곡선을 가진 즐거움의 법칙을 음식에 적용한 예이므로 즐거움의 법칙을 설명한 글(②) 다음에 나와야 한다. 또한, 같은 법칙을 음악에 적용한 예가 ③ 뒤에 나오는데, a little longer than that에서 that이 주어진 문장에 언급된 음식의 경우를 가리키므로 음악에 적용한 예시가 나오기 전인 ③에 들어가는 것이 가장 적절하다.

오답 Check
마지막 문장은 '곡선의 모양이 복잡성에 의해 늘려지거나 압착된다.'에 대한 예시이므로 ④ 뒤의 문장과 ⑤ 뒤의 문장의 연결은 자연스럽다.

PLUS + 변형문제

해설 즐거움의 법칙에 대한 글로, 처음 어떤 것을 경험할 때는 어렵고 즐겁지 않지만 반복적으로 경험하면 쉽고 기쁨을 주고, 그다음에는 너무 쉬워지고 지겨워진다고 했으므로, 글의 요지로 ③이 적절하다.
① → 음악의 단조로움과 청중이 쉽게 그것에 빠져드는 것의 관계는 언급하지 않음.
② → 환경에 따라 취향이 좌우된다는 언급은 없음.
④ → 거꾸로 된 U자를 음악에 적용한 예가 나오므로 반대된 설명임.
⑤ → 그럴듯하지만 글에 설명되지 않은 상식에 의거한 오답임.

구문 [1]You might **expect**, as a very simple hypothesis // **that** we tend to enjoy *the music* [(which[that]) we hear the most] — / the same version of the "mere exposure" effect regarding food.
• 첫 번째 접속사 that은 동사 expect의 목적어 역할을 하는 명사절을 이끈다.
• [ ]는 the music을 수식하는 관계사절로 목적격 관계대명사 which[that]가 생략되었다.

[2]A complex piece might take a long while *to like* / and then (take) a long time *to get sick of*; // usually a simple children's song will go through the curve / a lot quicker.
• 「take+시간+to-v」의 형태가 접속사 and로 연결되어 병렬 구조를 이루며, and 뒤에는 반복되는 동사 take가 생략되었다.

Researchers [who study all kinds of animals — from mammals to reptiles to insects —] / have long noted the ability of some organisms (to produce offspring (suited to their environment)). The vole is a furry little rodent [that looks something like a fat mouse]. [1]Depending upon the time of year [its mother is due to give birth], / baby voles are born with either a thick coat or a thin coat. The gene for a thick coat / is always there — it's just turned on or off / depending on the level of light [the mother senses in her environment / around the time of pregnancy]. The mother of the tiny freshwater flea *Daphnia* / will produce offspring (with a larger helmet and spines) // if it's going to give birth in an environment (crowded with predators). [2]One species of lizard is born / with a long tail and large body or a small tail and small body / depending on one thing only — whether their mother smelled a lizard-eating snake / while pregnant. When her babies are entering a snake-filled world, // they are born with a long tail and big body, / making them less likely to be snake food.

↓

Some animals have the ability (to (A) <u>determine</u> the characteristics of their offspring / on the basis of the mother's (B) <u>experiences</u> during pregnancy).

해석 포유류에서 파충류와 곤충에 이르기까지 모든 종류의 동물을 연구하는 연구원들은 일부 유기체의 환경에 적합한 자손을 생산하는 능력에 오랫동안 주목해 왔다. 들쥐는 살찐 생쥐처럼 생긴 털로 덮인 작은 설치류이다. 어미가 출산할 예정인 시기에 따라, 새끼 들쥐들은 두꺼운 털가죽이나 얇은 털가죽을 갖고 태어난다. 두꺼운 털가죽의 유전자는 항상 거기에 있는데 그것은 어미가 임신 기간쯤 그 환경에서 감지하는 빛의 수준에 따라 켜지거나 꺼진다. 작은 민물 벼룩의 어미는 포식자가 붐비는 환경에서 새끼를 낳는다면 더 큰 투구와 가시를 가진 자손을 낳을 것이다. 도마뱀의 한 종은 오직 한 가지에 의존해서 긴 꼬리에 긴 몸을 가지고 태어나거나 작은 꼬리에 작은 몸을 가지고 태어나는데, 그것은 어미가 임신 중에 도마뱀을 잡아먹는 뱀의 냄새를 맡았는지 아닌지의 여부이다. 새끼들이 뱀이 득실대는 세계로 들어갈 때 그것들이 긴 꼬리와 긴 몸을 가지고 태어나면 뱀의 먹이가 될 가능성이 낮아지게 된다.

↓

일부 동물들은 임신 중 어미의 (B) 경험에 근거하여 자손의 특징을 (A) 결정하는 능력을 가지고 있다.

어휘 mammals 포유류 reptiles 파충류 offspring 자손 suit 알맞다, 적합하다 vole 들쥐 furry 부드러운 털[모피]로 덮인; 모피의 rodent 설치류 동물 due ~하기로 되어 있는, 예정된; ~ 때문에 daphnia 《동물》 물벼룩류 spine 가시; 척추, 등뼈 predator 포식자 **[선택지 어휘]** migration 이동; 이주

해설 요약문을 먼저 보면 일부 동물들이 어미의 임신 중에 발생하는 '무엇'에 근거하여 자손의 특징을 '어떻게 하는' 능력을 갖는지 찾아야 한다. 지문에는 임신 기간 중 주변 환경에서 겪는 경험에 따라 환경에 적응하도록 새끼의 특징을 결정해서 낳는 여러 동물의 예가 나오므로 빈칸에는 ④ '(A) 결정하는 – (B) 경험'이 들어가야 적절하다.

오답 Check

본문에 주제문이 명시되어있지 않아 각각의 예시로 공통점을 도출해 주제 및 요약문을 추론해야 한다. 본문에 쓰인 단어가 나오지 않고 연상 가능한 단어로 선택지가 구성된 것에 유의한다.

　　　(A)　　　(B)
① 결합하는 – 영양
→ 새끼의 특징을 결합한다는 언급은 없고, 어미의 임신 중 영양에 관한 내용 또한 없으므로 (A), (B) 모두 오답.
② 변경하는 – 스트레스
→ (A)는 맞지만 (B)에 대한 언급은 없음.
③ 밝히는 　 – 이동
→ 어미가 새끼의 특징을 노출시킨다고 볼 수 없고, 어미가 임신 중 이동한다는 내용은 없으므로 (A), (B) 모두 오답.
⑤ 나누는 　 – 선호
→ 새끼의 특징을 결정하는 것이지 나눈다는 언급은 없고, 어미의 선호에 근거한 것은 아니므로 (A), (B) 모두 오답.

구문 [1]Depending upon *the time of year* [(when) its mother is due to give birth], / baby voles are born with either a thick coat or a thin coat.
- [ ]는 관계부사 when이 생략된 관계사절로 선행사 the time of year를 수식한다.
- 상관접속사 「either A or B」가 밑줄 친 두 개의 명사구를 병렬 연결한다.

[2]One species of lizard is born / with a long tail and large body or a small tail and small body / depending on *one thing* only — whether their mother smelled a lizard-eating snake / while (being) pregnant.
- 등위접속사 or가 밑줄 친 두 개의 명사구를 병렬 연결한다.
- 대시(—) 이후에 나오는 whether가 이끄는 명사절은 one thing과 동격 관계이고, while 이하는 접속사가 있는 분사구문으로 being이 생략되었다.

In recent years, / the word 'natural' has acquired a positive aura. Every GM food has been labelled 'unnatural' by its opponents, // as if that is enough to damn it forever, while advertisers can put a (a) positive spin on just about anything / by describing it as 'natural.' In one of those ironies, / an orange tart (labelled as full of 'natural orange flavor') has almost certainly never been near an orange, natural or unnatural. ¹Food retailers can legally label food as 'naturally flavored' // if the cocktail of chemicals [it contains] creates a taste [that just vaguely resembles the real thing]. Yet just why is natural so easily seen as good and unnatural bad? After all, diseases (such as malaria and cholera) are natural. In fact, death is quite natural, too. ²It is in part a hangover (from the ancient belief) // that things (in their proper, natural form) were, in their way, (b) perfect, / and, (in Christian times), reflections of God's creation. ³(c) Unnatural things were distortions of these flawless forms (created by the devil). When people talked about 'unnatural acts' // they were talking about something a lot nastier / than making 'natural strawberry flavor' drinks from chemicals. That ancient prejudice has been (d) removed in the modern world / by big manufacturing companies and agribusinesses, scientists and food technologists. 'Natural' seems to be wholesome, tried-and-tested / over millions of years. It's free from dangerous artifice. In this sense, nature is always (e) natural.

해석 최근 몇 년 동안 '자연 그대로의'라는 단어는 긍정적인 분위기를 얻었다. 모든 유전자 변형 식품은 반대자들에 의해 마치 그것이 그것(모든 유전자 변형 식품)을 영원히 비난하기에 충분하다는 듯이 '자연적이지 않다'는 꼬리표가 붙여졌고, 반면에 광고주들은 단지 어떤 것에 대해 '자연 그대로의'라고 묘사함으로써 그것에 대한 (a) 긍정적 해석을 부여할 수 있다. 그러한 아이러니들 중 하나로 '자연 그대로의 오렌지 맛'으로 가득 차 있다고 상표가 붙은 오렌지 타르트는 자연적이건 비자연적이건 거의 확실히 오렌지 근처에도 가지 않았다. 식품 소매업자들은 식품이 함유한 화학 물질의 혼합물이 진짜와 그저 약간 닮은 맛을 만들어낸다면 그 식품에 법적으로 '자연 그대로의 맛이 나는'이라고 상표를 붙일 수 있다. 그런데도 왜 자연적인 것은 그렇게 쉽사리 좋게 여겨지고 비자연적인 것은 나쁘게 여겨지는가? 어쨌든 말라리아와 콜레라 같은 질병들은 자연적이다. 사실 죽음 역시 꽤 자연적이다. 적절하고 자연적인 형태 안에서 사물들이 그 나름대로 (b) 완벽했으며, 기독교 시대에서는, 신의 창조의 반영이라는 것은 부분적으로는 아주 오래된 믿음에서 나온 여파이다. (c) 자연적이지 못한 것들은 악마가 만들어낸, 이런 흠잡을 데 없는 형태의 왜곡이었다. 사람들이 '자연스럽지 않은 행동'에 대해 이야기할 때 그들은 화학 물질로 '자연 그대로의 딸기 맛' 음료를 만드는 것보다 훨씬 더 불쾌한 어떤 것에 대해 이야기하고 있었다. 그 오래된 편견은 현대 세계에서 거대 제조업체와 기업식 농업, 과학자와 식품 기술자들에 의해 (d) 제거되었다(→ 강화되었다). 주제문 '자연 그대로의'는 수백 만년에 걸쳐 유익하고 믿을 수 있다고 증명된 것으로 보인다. 그것은 위험한 술책으로부터 자유롭다. 이런 의미에서 자연은 언제나 (e) 자연적이다.

어휘 ○GM food 유전자 변형 식품 label A (as) B A에게 B라는 꼬리표를 붙이다 opponent 반대자; 반대하는 damn 비난[저주]하다 put a spin on ~을 해석하다 retailer 소매업자 cocktail 혼합물; 칵테일 vaguely 약간; 막연히; 모호하게 resemble 닮다, 비슷하다 hangover 여파; 잔존물; 숙취 in one's way 그 나름대로 distortion 왜곡 nasty 불쾌한; 끔찍한; 못된 manufacturing 제조(업)의 agribusinesses 기업식 농업 wholesome 유익한; 건강에 좋은 tried-and-tested 믿을 수 있다고 증명된 artifice 술책; 기술 [선택지 어휘] foe 적 artifact 인공물 alter 바꾸다 turn away 거부[거절]하다; 물리치다
어휘○유전자 변형 식품(genetically modified food): 유전자 조작 또는 재조합 등의 기술을 통해 재배·생산된 농산물을 원료로 만든 식품

해설 41 주제문을 먼저 찾아 이를 가장 잘 반영한 선택지를 고른다. 제목 유형은 글의 핵심을 나타내면서도 압축적이고 상징적인 다양한 형태로 표현될 수 있음에 유의한다. 주제문을 보면, '자연 그대로의' 것을 좋은 것으로 '자연적이지 않은' 것은 나쁜 것으로 여기는 것은 오래된 믿음에서 비롯되었고 현대 세계에서 강화되어 '자연적인' 것은 오랜 기간에 걸쳐 믿을 수 있는 것으로 여겨지게 되었다는 내용이므로 글의 제목으로는 ④ '왜 사람들은 비자연적인 것을 거부하는가?'가 적절하다.
42 도입부에서 광고주들이 상품을 자연 그대로라고 묘사함으로써 긍정적 해석을 부여했다는 것으로 보아 '자연 그대로의'에 대한 오래된 편견이 현대 세계에서 제거된 것이 아니라 강화되었으므로 (d) removed는 reinforced 등으로 바뀌어야 적절하다.

오답 Check
41 ① 대자연: 인간의 친구이자 적
② 인공물은 인간의 본성이고 자연은 신의 예술이다
③ 인간 활동이 자연환경을 바꾼다
⑤ 얼마나 많은 환경이 실제로 자연적인가?
→ ①, ②, ③, ⑤ 모두 '자연, 자연 그대로의'라는 핵심어를 활용한 오답임.
42 (b)가 있는 문장은 자연적인 것들에 대한 설명으로 뒤 문장의 'these flawless forms'를 통해 적절한 쓰임임을 유추할 수 있다.

구문 ¹Food retailers can legally label food as 'naturally flavored' // if *the cocktail of chemicals* [(which[that]) it contains] creates *a taste* [that just vaguely resembles the real thing].
• 첫 번째 [ ]는 목적격 관계대명사 which[that]가 생략된 관계사절로 선행사 the cocktail of chemicals를 수식한다.
• 두 번째 [ ]는 주격 관계대명사 that이 이끄는 관계사절로 선행사는 a taste이다.

[2]**It** is in part a hangover (from the ancient belief) // **that** things (in their proper, natural form) were, in their way, <u>perfect</u>, / <u>and</u>, (in Christian times), <u>reflections of God's creation</u>.

• it은 가주어, that 이하가 진주어이다.

• that절 내의 and가 밑줄 친 두 개의 보어(perfect와 reflections of God's creation)를 병렬 연결한다.

[3]Unnatural things were *distortions of these flawless forms* (created by the devil).

• ( )는 과거분사 created가 이끄는 분사구로 distortions of these flawless forms를 수식한다.